D0578267

Anthropological Resources:
A Guide to Archival, Library and Museum Collections

Anthropological Resources:
A Guide to Archival, Library and Museum Collections

Compiled by Library-Anthropology Resource Group (LARG)

Lee S. Dutton, *Editor*

Garland Publishing
New York & London
1999

Published in 1999 by
Garland Publishing Inc.
A Member of the Taylor & Francis Group
19 Union Square West
New York, NY 10003

10   9   8   7   6   5   4   3   2   1

Library of Congress Cataloging-in-Publication-Data

Anthropolgical resources : a guide to archival, library, and museum collections /
    edited by Lee S. Dutton
        p.   cm. — (Garland reference library of social science ; v. 864)
        Includes bibliographical references and index.
        ISBN 0–8153–1188–5 (alk. paper)
        1. Anthropological archives — Directories.   2. Anthropological museums
    and collections — Directories.   3. Anthropology—Library resources —
    Directories.   I. Dutton, Lee S. II. Series.

GN14.A77 1998
026'.301'025—dc21   98-37660
                                                               CIP

Printed on acid-free, 250 year-old-life paper
Manufactured in the UnitedStates of America

Contents

Preface

This guide provides access to information on the rich and often little-known legacy of anthropological scholarship preserved in selected archives, libraries or museums in many parts of the world. The central focus of the guide is on primary, non-artifactual documentation of anthropological significance—such as original scholars' fieldnotes, site reports, papers, manuscripts, archives, oral history collections, sound recordings, photographs, films and videos. Attention has also been given to some selected library collections in anthropology, folklore or area studies.

Most of the entries have been authored by anthropologists, librarians, archivists or curators whose expertise in their respective areas of specialization and detailed knowledge of the collections enhance the value of the contributions. The names of the principal contributors follow their respective entries, and are also collectively acknowledged in the List of Contributors.

How the Guide Was Compiled

Planning for this Library-Anthropology Resource Group (LARG) project began in 1992. In the preparation of the guide, we have relied mainly on the willingness of many individual contributors to collect and organize information on particular repositories, and to write the respective entries. In the course of the project, many persons responded to our invitations to prepare contributions. The contributor texts have been edited for general consistency and, when possible, returned to the respective authors for a final reading. In an effort to fill in some of the many remaining omissions or gaps, brief personal visits were made to some selected repositories—in Canada (Ottawa, Hull and Toronto); the U.S. (Chicago, the District of Columbia, Philadelphia, New York City, Cambridge and elsewhere); and Western Europe (London, Paris, Leiden, Amsterdam and The Hague)—that had not otherwise been described by contributor entries. Many of these personal visits were useful and yielded additional entries. A few repositories (mainly in certain U.S. locations) have been briefly described by means of summary entries (these are not followed by either author or informant names). Only a few repositories that were contacted preferred not to be represented in this guide. Research access to documentation in the latter locations may be quite limited—or may be unavailable.

Scope of the Guide

The subject scope of *Anthropological Resources* is broad, encompassing social and cultural anthropology, ethnology, physical and biological anthropology, archaeology, folklore and some aspects of linguistics.

In the compilation of this volume, some emphasis has been given to the identification of collections and documentation concerning indigenous (and traditionally non-urban) peoples (such as the Ainu, Blackfoot, Fijians, Inuit, Māori, Mongo, Ona and many others) who were among the early subjects of anthropological inquiry. In many cases the archival material on these peoples is virtually the only surviving record of their traditional culture.

The guide does not, however, limit itself to peoples living in small-scale societies. There are also entries describing selected collections of material on partly urbanized peoples of North America, Europe, Asia or other regions. In general, the contributors were invited to focus on the collections that seemed most important to them.

Organization of the Entries

The ca. 246 entries in this guide are organized according to the geographic locations of repositories. An outline of repository locations (see Organization of the Entries) provides ready access to entries by geographic location. Entries for repositories in a particular city are sub-arranged by institutional or corporate names.

The individual entries typically consist of a concise directory section, followed by a narrative section that describes the content and research value of the repository or collection and also provides some information on its historical background. Due to the large size of many of the collections, entries typically cite only a small portion of the available documentary resources. Selected sources of additional information (guides, catalogs, finding aids, articles, indexes, etc.) have been cited when known. Website URLs have also been cited when available.

Two indexes have been provided to assist readers in the use of the guide. These are, respectively, the Index of Personal Names, and the Keyword Index of Selected Ethnic Group Names. The former index provides access to personal name references in the text, including references to locations of scholars' manuscripts, papers, etc., in museum, archival or library collections. The Index of Personal Names indicates, for example, that scholarly papers of the late Africanist anthropologist, Melville J. Herskovits, may be found at the Schomburg Center for Research in Black Culture, NYPL; also at the Melville J. Herskovits Library of African Studies, Northwestern University; and at the Library of the American Philosophical Society in Philadelphia. In addition, film footage recorded by Herskovits in Africa is preserved at the Human Studies Film Archives in Washington, D.C. The Keyword Index of Selected Ethnic Group Names provides keyword access to ethnic group name references throughout the text.

It should be added that this guide is intended to be used in conjunction with the many on-line catalogs, websites and other information sources now available. These research aids will often provide records of many additional items of documentation.

Coverage of Repositories

A majority (but not all) of the major U.S. and Canadian repositories in anthropology are represented in this volume. Repositories in Great Britain, France, the Netherlands and several other countries are more selectively represented. Due to limitations of editorial time and resources, only a rather limited number of repositories located outside North America or Western Europe could be included in this first edition of *Anthropological Resources*.

The guide is intended to make available, in concise form, information on non-artifactual collections in anthropology that are often exceptionally large and organizationally complex. Among the larger repositories represented here are the National Anthropological

National Museum of the American Indian (in Manhattan; the Bronx, New York City; and Suitland, Maryland), the American Philosophical Society (Philadelphia), the Archives of Traditional Music (Bloomington, Indiana), the Canadian Museum of Civilization (Hull, Québec), the British Library (London), the Bibliothèque nationale de France (Paris), the Musée de l'Homme (Paris), the Koninklijk Museum voor Midden-Afrika (Tervuren, Belgium), and many others.

Selected library collections of anthropological importance have also been included. Among these are the Alaska and Polar Regions Department, Elmer E. Rasmuson Library, University of Alaska, Fairbanks; the Asia Collections, Cornell University Libraries (Ithaca); the Melanesian Studies Resource Center, University of California, San Diego (La Jolla, Calif.); the Legatum Warnerianum (Oriental Department), University Library, Leiden University; the Library of the Van Vollenhoven Institute for Law and Administration in Non-Western Countries (Leiden); and others.

If a subsequent edition of this guide should be compiled, it is hoped that entries on archival and documentary resources in many additional museums, archives and libraries (in the Americas, Europe, the Middle-East, Africa, Asia and/or Oceania) may be included. Suggestions for additional entries to be included in a future edition of the guide (or other reader comments) may be faxed or mailed to the editor: Lee S. Dutton, Founders Memorial Library, Northern Illinois University, DeKalb, IL 60115 USA; fax no. (815) 753-2003. Please include your e-mail address, if available, with any communication.

Purposes of the Guide

It is hoped that this guide may serve as a useful addition to the list of available information sources in anthropology, and will facilitate use of the surviving archival documentation that constitutes the historical record of research in this field.

It is also hoped that the guide may be of assistance to diverse peoples in accessing the documentary materials, images and sound recordings that preserve, describe, or otherwise represent their own cultural heritages.

Issues regarding the preservation of anthropological fieldnotes, manuscripts and other documentation in archival settings have been mentioned in passing by several of the contributors of entries. We learn that, in a number of instances, neglect, organizational confusion, inadequate conservation efforts, or other causes have led to the loss of unique archival records of human culture. It is hoped that increased awareness of the value of such documentary resources may foster needed (but usually costly) conservation and preservation efforts.

For a useful survey on the role of fieldnotes in anthropological inquiry, readers may refer to Roger Sanjek (editor), *Fieldnotes: The Makings of Anthropology* (Ithaca: 1990).

Acknowledgments

Many individuals and institutions contributed to this project. Our greatest debt is to the many scholars, archivists, librarians and other specialists who prepared entries for inclusion in the guide or translated entries from various languages into English. The names of 146 principal authors of entries follow their respective entries, and are also acknowledged in the general List of Contributors. In addition to gathering needed information, organizing and writing the entries, many of the contributors also updated the edited versions of their entries, provided leads to other significant documentary resources, or offered other assistance. Many contributors went beyond the call of duty in bringing to light information on previously inaccessible or little-known documentation, or by helping in other ways to bring this project to a successful conclusion.

The Field Museum of Natural History, Loyola University of Chicago, Northeastern Illinois University, Northern Illinois University, Northwestern University and the University of Chicago all allowed the members of the editorial board time to work on the project. Our late colleague, Sol Tax (1907-1995), contributed his knowledge and experience during early phases of the project, as well as some funds that enabled us to make prints of, or to secure authorizations to publish, several of the photographs reproduced in this volume. Fr. Francis X. Grollig, S.J., also lent his insights and encouragement to the work of the editorial board, although his participation during the later phases of the project was unfortunately limited by health concerns. The Field Museum of Natural History provided LARG with convenient meeting space at the heart of Chicago's lively Museum Campus—a museum locale that combines striking natural history displays with panoramic views of Lake Michigan.

Special thanks are also due to many archivists, scholars, librarians, specialists or friends who assisted by providing information or other assistance in the course of the project. Some (but not all) of these persons are mentioned in notes following individual entries in the guide.

Grant A. Olson authored the text on the cremation volume (*nangsü anuson ngānsop*) collection at Wat Bovornives Vihara, in Bangkok, Thailand, which was made available to other authors of entries. John Leslie provided helpful information on the resources at the Canadian Department of Indian and Northern Affairs (in Hull, Québec) and also read and commented on a draft of the "Canada" section of the manuscript. Margaret R. Dittemore (Anthropology Branch Library, National Museum of Natural History), James R. Glenn (National Anthropological Archives, National Museum of Natural History [now retired]) and Robert Kvasnicka (National Archives, Washington, D.C.) shared their knowledge of the wealth of anthropological resources preserved in District of Columbia-area repositories. Diane Vogt O'Connor (U.S. National Park Service) provided information on the extensive and rather decentralized archival systems of the National Park Service. Kathryn Creely organized the entries for the many Yale University collections, suggested other repositories for inclusion and read certain portions of the text. Douglas M. Haller pointed out some additional repositories in the Greater Philadelphia area. Jacqueline Dubois and Dominique Morelon (Musée de l'Homme, in Paris) provided information on archival resources at that great repository, as well as advice on some other libraries and archives in the Paris region. In London, Jonathan Benthall (Royal Anthropological Institute of Great Britain and Ireland) and Ann Lum (Natural History Museum) were particularly helpful, while in the Netherlands, Rahadi S. Karni, Jan Just Witkam and Albert J. Dekker provided information on some Dutch archives, museums or libraries. Thanks are also due to colleagues Nestor Osario and David Shavit, who checked some name transcriptions, and to William Baker and Richard Huskey, M.D., who also provided some assistance. Members of the Council for the Preservation of Anthropological Records (CoPAR) provided information on the useful activities of that organization.

At Garland Publishing, editors Kristi Long, Phyllis Korper and Kennie Lyman assisted in many ways. Phyllis Korper read an early version of the manuscript and Kristi Long later read the full manuscript.

Linda Groat, Vicky Smith and Janet Engstrom all provided valuable help with word processing and other tasks. Megan Newton prepared much of the personal name index, and Steven Delchamps prepared a draft of the ethnic group name index. Jack Hendricks, Ed Tonry and Theresa Paulson converted files to PC format, helped to resolve hardware problems, or assisted in other ways.

The Library-Anthropology Resource Group (LARG)

LARG is a Chicago-based group of librarians and anthropologists who, since 1971, have met periodically to discuss bibliographic needs in the field of anthropology and to create useful reference publications. LARG was founded in 1971 by the late Sol Tax, Professor of Anthropology at the University of Chicago, with considerable help from Jan Wepsiec, Social Sciences Bibliographer at the University of Chicago Library, and Fr. Francis X. Grollig, Professor of Anthropology at Loyola University of Chicago. Throughout its history, LARG has worked to encourage cooperation between librarians and anthropologists and to fulfill some of the continuing reference needs in a field that has not been well endowed with reference publications.

LARG publications include *Serial Publications in Anthropology*, edited by Sol Tax and Francis X. Grollig (Chicago: University of Chicago Press, 1973); *Anthropological Bibliographies: A Selected Guide*, edited by Margo L. Smith and Yvonne Damien (South Salem, N.Y.: Redgrave Publishing Co., 1981); *Serial Publications in Anthropology*, revised ed., edited by Francis X. Grollig, S.J. and Sol Tax (South Salem, N.Y.: Redgrave Publishing Co., 1982); *Biographical Directory of Anthropologists Born Before 1920*, edited by Thomas L. Mann (New York: Garland Publishing, 1988); and *International Dictionary of Anthropologists*, edited by Christopher Winters (New York: Garland Publishing, 1991). The present publication, *Anthropological Resources: A Guide to Archival, Library and Museum Collections* (New York: Garland Publishing, 1999), edited by Lee S. Dutton, is the sixth reference title produced under LARG auspices.

The URL of the Library-Anthropology Resource Group is http://www.lib.uchicago.edu:80/LibInfo/SourcesBySubject/Anthropology/larg.html.

Lee S. Dutton

List of Contributors

Anne Alexander
Library
Department of Ethnography
British Museum
Museum of Mankind
6 Burlington Gardens
London W1X 2EX
United Kingdom

Nigel Allan
Wellcome Institute Library
Wellcome Institute for the History of
Medicine
183 Euston Road
London NW1 2BE
United Kingdom

Susan J. Allen
Department of Egyptian Art
The Metropolitan Museum of Art
1000 Fifth Avenue
New York, NY 10028-0198
USA

Belen B. Angeles
University Library
University of the Philippines
Diliman, Quezon City
Philippines

David Bade
Library
University of Chicago
1100 E. 57th St.
Chicago, IL 60637
USA

Joyce M. Banks
Reference and Information Services
Division
National Library of Canada
395 Wellington St.
Ottawa, ON, K1A 0N4
Canada

Edita R. Baradi
Economic Growth Center Collection
Yale University
140 Prospect St.
P.O. Box 208263
New Haven, CT 06520-8263
USA

Juliette Barbet
Musée national des Arts
asiatiques—Guimet
6, place d'Iéna
75116 Paris
France

Anna Lisa Bebi
Biblioteca di Antropologia
Instituto de Antropologia
Università degli Studi di Firenze
via del Proconsolo 12
50122 Firenze
Italy

Jan Bell
Arizona State Museum
University of Arizona
Tucson, AZ 85721
USA

Jane Bennett
Refugee Studies Center
University of Minnesota
104 Nicholson Hall
216 Pillsbury Dr., SE
Minneapolis, MN 55455
USA

Jonathan Benthall
Royal Anthropological Institute of Great
Britain and Ireland
50 Fitzroy St.
London W1P 5HS
United Kingdom

Pam Bjornson
Canadian Institute for Historical
Microproductions
P.O. Box 2428, Station D
Ottawa, ON, K1P 5W
Canada

Peter J. Blodgett
Henry E. Huntington Library
1151 Oxford Road
San Marino, CA 91108
USA

Michel Brisebois
Reference and Information Services
Division
National Library of Canada
395 Wellington St.
Ottawa, ON, K1A 0N4
Canada

Nancy Brown
Center for Southwest Research
General Library
University of New Mexico
Albuquerque, NM 87131-1466
USA

Bridget Burke
Beinecke Rare Book and Manuscript
Library
Yale University
P.O. Box 208240
New Haven, CT 06520-8240
USA

Kathleen Cann
Cambridge University Library
West Road
Cambridge CB3 9DR
United Kingdom

Beverly Carlson
American Baptist Historical Society
P.O. Box 851
Valley Forge, PA 19482-0851
USA

Jefferson Chapman
Frank H. McClung Museum
University of Tennessee
1327 Circle Park Drive
Knoxville, TN 37996-3200
USA

Madelyn Cook
Arizona State Museum
University of Arizona
Tucson, AZ 85721
USA

Kathryn Creely
Social Sciences and Humanities Library
University of California, San Diego
9500 Gilman Drive
La Jolla, CA 92093-0175
USA

Philip N. Cronenwett
Special Collections
Dartmouth College Library
Hanover, NH 03755
USA

Moore Crossey
African Collection
Yale University Library
130 Wall St.
P.O. Box 208240
New Haven, CT 06520-8240
USA

Mary B. Davis
Huntington Free Library and Reading
Room
9 Westchester Square
Bronx, NY 10461
USA

Deborah Day
Library
Scripps Institution of Oceanography
0175C, UCSD
9500 Gilman Drive
La Jolla, CA 92093-1075C
USA

Stella De Sa Rego
Center for Southwest Research
General Library
University of New Mexico
Albuquerque, NM 87131-1466
USA

Francisco R. Demetrio, S.J.
Museum and Archives
Xavier University
Cagayan de Oro City, 9000
Philippines

Hugh A. Dempsey
Glenbow Museum
130 9th Avenue S.E.
Calgary, AB, T2G 0P3
Canada

Donald L. DeWitt
Western History Collections
University of Oklahoma Libraries
Room 452, Monnet Hall
Norman, OK 73019
USA

Margaret R. Dittemore
Anthropology Branch Library
National Museum of Natural History
10th St. & Constitution Avenue, N.W.
Washington, DC 20560
USA

Samuel R. Dunlap
Library
Scripps Institution of Oceanography
0175C, UCSD
9500 Gilman Drive
La Jolla, CA 92093-0175C
USA

Thomas A. DuRant
National Park Service Historic
Photographic Collection
Harpers Ferry Center
National Park Service
Harpers Ferry, WV 25425
USA

Lee S. Dutton
Southeast Asia Collection
Founders Memorial Library
Northern Illinois University
DeKalb, IL 60115-2868
USA

Elizabeth Edwards
Pitt-Rivers Museum
University of Oxford
South Parks Road
Oxford OX1 3PP
United Kingdom

Clark A. Elliott
University Archives
Pusey Library
Harvard University
Cambridge, MA 02138
USA

Alan Ferg
Arizona State Museum
University of Arizona
Tucson, AZ 85721
USA

M.R. Fernando
Library
Department of Anthropology
Research School of Pacific and Asian
Studies
Australian National University
Canberra ACT 2100
Australia

Julia Finn
Departmental Library
Department of Indian Affairs and
Northern Development Canada
Ottawa, ON, K1A OH4
Canada

Christraud M. Geary
Eliot Elisofon Photographic Archives
National Museum of African Art
MRC 708
950 Independence Avenue, S.W.
Washington, DC 20560
USA

Jean Geil
School of Music
University of Illinois at Urbana-
Champaign
2136 Music Building
1114 W. Nevada
Urbana, IL 61801
USA

James R. Glenn
National Anthropological Archives
Room 60-A, MRC 152
National Museum of Natural History
10th St. and Constitution Ave., N.W.
Washington, DC 20560
USA

Fe Susan Go
Harlan Hatcher Graduate Library
University of Michigan
Ann Arbor, MI 48109-1612
USA

Mary Graham
Arizona State Museum
University of Arizona
Tucson, AZ 85721
USA

Polly S. Grimshaw
Folklore Collection
Indiana University Library
Tenth St. & Jordan Avenue
Bloomington, IN 47405
USA

Beth Grindell
Arizona State Museum
University of Arizona
Tucson, AZ 85721
USA

Kristine A. Haglund
Library/Archives
Denver Museum of Natural History
2001 Colorado Blvd.
Denver, CO 80205-5798
USA

Nora Hague
McCord Museum of Canadian History
690 Sherbrooke St. West
Montréal, PQ, H3A 1E9
Canada

Douglas M. Haller
Archives
Museum of Archaeology and
Anthropology
University of Pennsylvania
33rd and Spruce Streets
Philadelphia, PA 19104-6324
USA

Lewis Hill
Collection of South-East Asian Art and
Traditional Craftsmanship
Centre for South-East Asian Studies
University of Hull
Hull HU6 7RX
United Kingdom

Martha Hill
Peabody Museum of Natural History
Yale University
170 Whitney Avenue
P.O. Box 208118
New Haven, CT 06520-8118
USA

Laura Holt
Museum of Indian Arts and
Culture/Laboratory of Anthropology
Museum of New Mexico
P.O. Box 2087
Santa Fe, NM 87594-2087
USA

Marie S. Holmes
Santa Barbara Museum of Natural History
2559 Puesta del Sol Road
Santa Barbara, CA 93105
USA

John P. Homiak
Human Studies Film Archives
National Museum of Natural History
10th St. and Constitution Avenue
Washington, DC 20560
USA

Janet Horncy
Alexander Turnbull Library
58-78 Molesworth St.
P.O. Box 12-349, Wellington
New Zealand

Kathy Hubenschmidt
Arizona State Museum
University of Arizona
Tucson, AZ 85721
USA

Stephen Innes
New Zealand and Pacific Collection
Library
University of Auckland
Private Bag 92019
Auckland
New Zealand

Barbara Isaac
Peabody Museum of Archaeology and
Ethnology
Harvard University
11 Divinity Avenue
Cambridge, MA 02138
USA

Fritz Jandry
Arizona State Museum
University of Arizona
Tucson, AZ 85721
USA

David Jervis
British Library
96 Euston Road
St. Pancras, London
NW1 2DB
United Kingdom

Karl Kabelac
Department of Rare Books and Special
Collections
Rush Rhees Library
University of Rochester
Rochester, NY 14627-0055
USA

Libby Kahane
Jewish National and University Library
P.O.B. 34165
Givat Ram
Jerusalem
Israel

Seth Kasten
Burke Library
Union Theological Seminary
3041 Broadway
New York, NY 10027
USA

Belinda Kaye
American Museum of Natural History
79th St. and Central Park West
New York, NY 10024-5192
USA

Sho Kuwajima
Library
Ōsaka University of Foreign Studies
811 Aomatani-higashi
Minoo-shi
Ōsaka 562
Japan

Diana Lachatanere
Schomburg Center for Research in Black
Culture
515 Malcolm X Boulevard
New York, NY 10037-1801
USA

Danielle de Lame
Koninklijk Museum voor Midden-Afrika
Leuven 13
B-3080 Tervuren
Belgium

Frederick W. Lange
Museum
Campus Box 218
University of Colorado
Boulder, CO 80309-0218
USA

Deirdre E. Lawrence
The Brooklyn Museum Libraries and
Archives
200 Eastern Parkway
Brooklyn, NY 11238-6052
USA

Veronica Lawrence
Pitt-Rivers Museum
University of Oxford
South Parks Road
Oxford OX1 3PP
United Kingdom

Betty J. Layton
American Baptist Historical Society
P.O. Box 851
Valley Forge, PA 19482-0851
USA

Daniel J. Lenihan
Submerged Cultural Resources Unit
National Park Service
1220 South St. Francis Drive
Santa Fe, NM 87504
USA

John Leslie
Claims and Historical Research Centre
Indian and Northern Affairs Canada
Room 835
Terrasses de la Chaudière
10 Wellington St.
Hull, PQ
Canada

Jeanne L. L'Espérance
Inuit Art Section
Indian and Northern Affairs Canada
Suite 925
Terrasses de la Chaudière
Ottawa, ON, K1A OH4
Canada

Martin L. Levitt
American Philosophical Society
105 South Fifth St.
Philadelphia, PA 19106-3386
USA

Alice N. Loranth
John G. White Collection of Folklore,
Orientalia and Chess
Fine Arts and Special Collections
Department
Cleveland Public Library
325 Superior Ave.
Cleveland, OH 44114-1271
USA

Ann Lum
Natural History Museum
Cromwell Road
London SW7 5BD
United Kingdom

Nancy S. MacKechnie
Special Collections Department
Libraries
Vassar College
Campus Box 20
Poughkeepsie, NY 12601-6198
USA

Marie-Laure Manigand
International Music Collection
National Sound Archive
British Library
96 Euston Road
St. Pancras
London NW1 2DB
United Kingdom

Melissa J. Martens
Newberry Library
60 West Walton St.
Chicago, IL 60610
USA

M. Marlene Martin
Human Relations Area Files, Inc.
755 Prospect St.
New Haven, CT 06511 USA
USA

Christine Midwinter
Information Management Services
Canadian Museum of Civilization
100 Laurier St.
P.O. Box 3100, Station B
Hull, PQ, J8X 4H2
Canada

Jerald T. Milanich
Department of Anthropology
Florida Museum of Natural History
Museum Road
Gainesville, FL 32611-7800
USA

George Miller
Library
Australian National University
Menzies Building
Canberra ACT 0200
Australia

Lisa K. Miller
National Archives—Pacific Region (San Francisco)
1000 Commodore Drive
San Bruno, CA 94066
USA

Bruce P. Montgomery
Archives
University Libraries
Campus Box 184
University of Colorado
Boulder, CO 80309
USA

Barbara J. Moore
Summer Institute of Linguistics
7500 West Camp Wisdom Road
Dallas, TX 75326
USA

Robert C. Morris
National Archives—Northeast Region (New York City)
201 Varick St.
New York, NY 10014
USA

David Nathanson
Library
Harpers Ferry Center
National Park Service
Harpers Ferry, WV 25425
USA

Madeleine M. Nichols
Dance Collection
New York Public Library for the Performing Arts
40 Lincoln Center Plaza
New York, NY 10023-7498
USA

Margaret Nicholson
South-East Asia Collection
Brynmor Jones Library
University of Hull
Hull HU6 7RX
United Kingdom

Molly K. O'Donnell
Museum of Anthropology
University of Missouri
104 Swallow Hall
Columbia, MO 65211
USA

Joyce L. Ogburn
University Library
Old Dominion University
Norfolk, VA 23529
USA

Chalermsee Olson
Founders Memorial Library
Northern Illinois University
DeKalb, IL 60115
USA

Grant A. Olson
Information Technology Center
101 Watson Hall
Northern Illinois University
DeKalb, IL 60115
USA

Sheila K. O'Neill
Special Collections
National Library of Medicine
8600 Rockville Pike
Bethesda, MD 20894
USA

Luis Oporto Ordoñez
Museo Nacional de Etnografía y Folklore
Calle Ingavi no. 916
La Paz
Bolivia

R. Bruce Parham
National Archives—Pacific Alaska
Region (Anchorage)
654 West Third Ave.
Anchorage, AK 99501
USA

Neil Philip
Image Collection
National Geographic Society
1145 17th St., N.W.
Washington, DC 20036
USA

Bev Pike
Archives
Manitoba Museum of Man and Nature
190 Rupert Avenue
Winnipeg, MB, R3B ON2
Canada

Willow Powers
Museum of Indian Arts and
Culture/Laboratory of Anthropology
Museum of New Mexico
P.O. Box 2087
Santa Fe, NM 87594-2087
USA

Robin Price
Wellcome Institute Library
Wellcome Institute for the History of
Medicine
183 Euston Road
London NW1 2BE
United Kingdom

Meg Quintal
Institute of American Indian Studies
Room 12, Dakota Hall
University of South Dakota
Vermillion, SD 57069
USA

Joyce M. Raab
NPS Chaco Archives
Center for Southwest Research
University of New Mexico
General Library
Albuquerque, NM 87131-1466
USA

Angela Raspin
Archivist
British Library of Political and Economic
Science
London School of Economics and
Political Science
10 Portugal St.
London WC2A 2HD
United Kingdom

Joan Redding
National Museum of Health and Medicine
Armed Forces Institute of Pathology
Washington, DC 20306-6000
USA

Wayne V. Richter
Mongolian Studies Collection
Wilson Library
Western Washington University
Bellingham, WA 98225-9103
USA

Robert B. Marks Ridinger
Founders Memorial Library
Northern Illinois University
DeKalb, IL 60115-2868
USA

Allen Riedy
Echols Southeast Asia Collection
Kroch Library
Cornell University
Ithaca, NY 14853
USA

Cesar Rodriguez
Latin American Collection
Yale University Library
P.O. Box 208240
New Haven, CT 06520-8240
USA

Nancy B. Rosoff
Research Branch
National Museum of the American Indian
3401 Bruckner Blvd.
Bronx, NY 10461
USA

Angela Sabin
Library
School of Oriental and African Studies
Thornhaugh St.
Russell Square
London WC1H OXG
United Kingdom

Mary Mallia Samms
Arthur D. Jenkins Library of the Textile
Arts
Textile Museum
2320 S St., N.W.
Washington, DC 20008
USA

Joseph P. Sanchez
Spanish Colonial Research Center
University of New Mexico
Albuquerque, NM 87131-1466
USA

Elizabeth Sandager
Peabody Museum of Archaeology and
Ethnology
Harvard University
11 Divinity Avenue
Cambridge, MA 02138
USA

Carole Saulnier
Archives de folklore
Pavillon Jean-Charles-Bonenfant
Université Laval
Cité universitaire, PQ, G1K 7P4
Canada

Curtis Schaafsma
Museum of Indian Arts and
Culture/Laboratory of Anthropology
Museum of New Mexico
P.O. Box 2087
Santa Fe, NM 87594-2087
USA

Nicholas B. Scheetz
Special Collections Division
Georgetown University Library
37th & O Streets, N.W.
Washington, DC 20057-1006
USA

Rosemary Seton
Library
School of Oriental and African Studies
Thornhaugh St.
Russell Square
London WC1H OXG
United Kingdom

Siegfried Seyfarth
Völkerkundliche Bibliothek
Frobenius-Institut
Liebigstrasse 47
60323 Frankfurt am Main
Germany

Lisa Sherlock
E.J. Pratt Library
Victoria University
73 Queen's Park Crescent
Toronto, ON, M5S 1K7
Canada

Robert Singerman
University Libraries
University of Florida
406 Library East
Gainesville, FL 32611-2047
USA

Daniel J. Slive
John Carter Brown Library
Box 1894
Providence, RI 02912
USA

Martha Smalley
China Records Project
Yale Divinity School Library
Yale University
409 Prospect St.
New Haven, CT 06511-2108
USA

Ann L.S. Southwell
Department of Special Collections
Alderman Library
University of Virginia
Charlottesville, VA 22903-2498
USA

Cindi Steffan
Library
Manitoba Museum of Man and Nature
190 Rupert Avenue
Winnipeg, MB, R3B ON2
Canada

Richard Summerrell
Australian Archives
P.O. Box 7425
Canberra Mail Centre
Canberra ACT 2610
Australia

Anne Summers
British Library
96 Euston Road
St. Pancras
London NW1 2DB
United Kingdom

Ellen D. Sutton
Library
University of Illinois at Urbana-
Champaign
1408 West Gregory Drive
Urbana, IL 61801
USA

John Thackray
Natural History Museum
Cromwell Road
London SW7 5BD
United Kingdom

C. Eric Tull
Arctic Institute of North America Library
University of Calgary Library
2500 University Drive N.W.
Calgary, AB, T2N 1N4
Canada

D. Richard Valpy
Prince of Wales Northern Heritage Centre
Culture and Heritage Division
Department of Education, Culture and
Employment
Government of the Northwest Territories
Box 1320
Yellowknife, NT, X1A 2L9
Canada

John van Willigen
Department of Anthropology
University of Kentucky
Lexington, KY 40406
USA

Alan Ventress
Australian Research Collections
State Library of New South Wales
Macquarie St.
Sydney, NSW 2000
Australia

Honoré Vinck
Archives Aequatoria
Te Boelaerlei 11
B-2140 Borgerhout
Belgium

Cheri A. Vitez
Library
University of Illinois at Urbana-
Champaign
1408 West Gregory Drive
Urbana, IL 61801
USA

Kim Walters
Braun Research Library
Southwest Museum
234 Museum Drive
Los Angeles, CA 90065
USA

Virginia-Lee Webb
Photograph Study Collection
Department of the Arts of Africa, Oceania
and the Americas
The Metropolitan Museum of Art
1000 Fifth Avenue
New York, NY 10028-0198
USA

John M. Weeks
O. Meredith Wilson Library
University of Minnesota
309 19th Ave. S
Minneapolis, MN 55455-0414
USA

Chris Weideman
Manuscripts and Archives Collection
Yale University Library
P.O. Box 208240
New Haven, CT 06520-8240
USA

William D. Welge
Archives Division
Oklahoma Historical Society
Historical Building
2100 North Lincoln Boulevard
Oklahoma City, OK 73105
USA

Michael D. Wiant
Illinois State Museum
Research and Collections Center
1011 East Ash
Springfield, IL 62703
USA

Larry T. Wiese
Research Center
National Park Service
Mesa Verde, CO 81330
USA

Christopher Winters
Library
University of Chicago
1100 E. 57th St.
Chicago, IL 60637
USA

Organization of the Entries

Central America

South America

Europe

Middle East

Africa

Southeast Asia

East Asia

Australia and New Zealand

List of Illustrations

COVER: Betatakin Ruin, Navajo National Monument, Arizona. Photograph by George Alexander Grant, 1935. Courtesy of the Historic Photographic Collection, National Park Service, Harpers Ferry Center.

FRONTISPIECE: Portrait of William C. Farabee (1865-1925) at Marajo Island (mouth of the Amazon River), Brazil, ca. 1915. William Farabee led the University of Pennsylvania Amazon Expedition, 1913-1916. Courtesy of the University of Pennsylvania Museum of Archaeology and Anthropology (negative #S8-79900).

FIGURE 1. "Recording Eskimo music, May 1943." National Film Board of Canada Collection. Courtesy of the National Archives of Canada (negative #PA 129913).

FIGURE 2. Scene at Foula-Phong Tho, northern Indochina. Photograph by Russell W. Hendee, Field Museum Kelly/Roosevelts Expedition to northern Indochina, 1928-1929. Courtesy of the Field Museum of Natural History (negative #66339).

FIGURE 3. Edward E. Ayer beside a redwood tree, Bull Creek Forest, Mendocino County, California. Photograph by Mrs. Ayer. Courtesy of the Newberry Library.

FIGURE 4. Village scene with carabao, Leyte, Philippines, 1976. Photograph by Ethel Nurge. Courtesy of the Southeast Asia Collection, Founders Memorial Library, Northern Illinois University (#96-1936).

FIGURE 5. Dance at Suva, Viti Levu, Fiji. Alexander Agassiz Expedition. Courtesy of the Peabody Museum, Harvard University (negative #28407).

FIGURE 6. Tungus on reindeer-back crossing the Noyochan River, Siberia. Jesup North Pacific Expedition to Siberia, 1901. Photograph by Waldemar Jochelson. Courtesy of the Department of Library Services, American Museum of Natural History (negative #1590).

FIGURE 7. Portrait of Lewis Henry Morgan, ca. 1851. From a daguerreotype inset in Mrs. Morgan's copy of *League of the Ho-dé-no-sau-nee, or Iroquois*. Courtesy of the University of Rochester Library (negative #951297).

FIGURE 8. Jenichiro Oyabe with two Ainu leaders on Hokkaido Island, 1901. Courtesy of the University Museum of Archaeology and Anthropology, University of Pennsylvania (negative #S4-141810).

Anthropological Resources:
A Guide to Archival, Library and Museum Collections

The Guide

North America

Canada

The Canadian Museum of Civilization, in Hull, Québec, has been designated as a national resource for research and documentation in anthropology and related fields. The museum's archives contain an abundance of original fieldnotes, archaeological records, photographs, films and other field data from research at sites throughout Canada. Also of special interest for research in anthropology is the wealth of documentation curated in Ottawa at the National Archives of Canada. Among anthropological or related resources at the National Library of Canada (also in Ottawa), the collection of early and rare printed books in indigenous languages of Canada is of special interest.

Many Canadian libraries, archives or museums hold documentary resources of value for anthropological research. A helpful (although no longer up-to-date) guide that lists and briefly describes the printed and audio resources for First Nations, Inuit and Métis studies at 318 Canadian libraries and special collections is Nora Teresa Corley's *Resources for Native Peoples Studies* (Ottawa: 1984) (= *Research Collections in Canadian Libraries*, vol. 9).

Prominent among resources that document the culture, folklore and history of the French-speaking areas of Canada is the Archives of Folklore at Laval University in Sainte-Foy, Québec. Carole Saulnier's informative description of the Archives of Folklore collections at Laval University is included in this guide.

In recent years, a wealth of information of anthropological interest has become accessible on the World Wide Web. Many websites provide access to information on the anthropology of Canada, including documentation in ethnology, Native peoples studies, archaeology, linguistics, folklore, Northern studies and museology.

The Canadian Heritage Information Network (CHIN) is a Web resource maintained by the federal government's Department of Canadian Heritage. Artefacts Canada, which is available at CHIN, contains three national databases respectively titled: Humanities; Natural Sciences; and Archaeological Sites. CHIN's Archaeological Sites national inventory provides "information on more than 70,000 archaeological sites administered by Canadian provincial, territorial, and federal government departments and agencies." The URL of CHIN (in English- and French-language versions) is http://www.chin.gc.ca. Also at this site are hyperlinks to the useful Official Directory of Canadian Museums and Related Institutions; the Virtual List of Museums in Canada; and the Heritage Canada Directory.

The URL of the Canadian Government's Department of Indian and Northern Affairs is http://www.inac.gc.ca/index_e.html. This website provides links to additional information sources concerning the indigenous peoples of Canada. Directory information on First Nations organizations of Canada is available from Native Links (the First Nation Information Project) at http://www.johnco.com/firstnat. Researchers should contact individual First Nation associations or cultural centers, in advance of a proposed research visit, to inquire about the availability of documentary materials and the pertinent access policies.

Alberta—Calgary

Glenbow Museum. Library and Archives

Address: Glenbow Museum, 130 9th Avenue, S.E., Calgary, AB, Canada T2G 0P3.
Tel.: (403) 268-4100
Fax: (403) 232-6569
Internet address (Glenbow Museum): http://www.lexicom.ab/ca/~glenbow.
Internet address (Glenbow Archives): http://www.lexicom.ab/ca/~glenbow/archives.htm.
Public transit access: C-Train, Olympic Plaza or Centre Street stops. The Museum is readily accessible by any city bus coming into downtown.
Parking: Available at Palliser Square or City Hall.
Founded: 1954.
Major resources: Glenbow Archives; Glenbow Library.
Areas of specialization: Archival and library resources concerning the Native peoples of the Canadian prairie region. Archival resources include the Verne Dusenberry papers, Claude Schaeffer papers, George Gooderham papers, Indian Department records, John Laurie papers, Indian Association of Alberta papers, Métis Association of Alberta papers, Joseph F. Dion papers.
Archives/manuscripts: Ca. 40 linear ft. of archival materials on Native people of the prairie region of Canada.
Fieldnotes, papers, etc.: Fieldnotes by Claude Schaeffer (1901-1969), Verne Dusenberry (1906-1966) and others.
Holdings (books): Ca. 3,000 v. concerning Native people.
Visual/audio resources: The Archives has more than 10,000 black-and-white images of Native peoples, mostly from the Canadian Plains, but also from Alaska, British Columbia and Montana. The archive also has some movie footage. In 1961 the Museum produced a one-hour film on the Blackfoot Sun Dance. Audio resources include the Cree Oral History Project recordings and others.
Access: Materials are available for use by researchers and the public.
References: Hugh A. Dempsey and Lindsay Moir, *Bibliography of the Blackfoot* (Metuchen, N.J.: 1989) (= *Native American Bibliography Series*, no. 13).
Guides/catalogs: *Glenbow Archives: A Guide to Holdings* (Calgary: 1993), 2 v. Information on holdings of oral history recordings is provided in Normand Fortier, *Guide to Oral History Collections in Canada = Guide des fonds d'histoire orale au Canada* ([Ottawa?]: 1993) (= *Canadian Oral History Association = Société canadienne d'Histoire orale. Journal*, vol. 13), p. 60-65.
Artifacts of anthropological significance: Costumes, weapons and general material culture items, with an emphasis on western Canada, but including strong collections from other parts of North and South America.
Archaeological sites represented in artifact collections: None. These archaeological artifacts were given to the University of Calgary.

Description

Since its founding in 1954, the Glenbow Museum has placed great emphasis on the study of the Native people of western Canada in particular and of North America in general. This is reflected in the resources of both the library and the archive. The archive has assembled a large collection of primary and secondary material and has become a major resource for Native people doing research on their history, culture, land claims and personal ancestry. For example, the archive has microfilmed the pay sheets for all Indians in Treaties 4, 6, 8 and 9 (covering Alberta and Saskatchewan) for the period 1874 to 1899. The original records are in the Department of Indian Affairs in Ottawa.

Of particular importance among the primary documents filmed are the scattered records of the various Indian agencies in Alberta and Saskatchewan. In the 1950s the federal government carried out a program to destroy records in local Indian agencies that they believed (incorrectly) were already documented at headquarters. Instead of destroying them, a number of Indian agents turned the records over to Glenbow. The records range in date from 1884 to 1940 and include correspondence, agent and staff diaries, agriculture records, education records and normal business transactions of the agency. The collections are scattered and incomplete, ranging from agents' diaries in one agency to a continuous set of correspondence covering several decades in another. The Indian agencies represented in the collection are Blood, Blackfoot, Peigan, Sarcee, Hobbema, Lesser Slave Lake, Battleford, Edmonton and Fort McMurray.

The Glenbow also aggressively collected documents written or produced by Native people. Among these are the Joseph F. Dion (1888-1960) papers. Dion was a Cree school teacher who wrote *My Tribe the Crees* (Calgary: 1979) and also gathered considerable data on the life and customs of the Plains Cree. Smaller collections of original writings include the works of Joe Little Chief (Blackfoot); Tony Pretty Young Man (Sarcee); tape recordings in Blackfoot of George First Rider (Blood); and winter counts of Bull Plume (Peigan). The archive also holds records of the Métis Association of Alberta, 1968-1978, and of the Indian Association of Alberta, 1944-1975.

An important collection for the Blackfoot, Kutenai and Flathead are the papers of Claude Schaeffer (1901-1969). Schaeffer was an anthropologist who studied under Clark Wissler and received his Ph.D. in 1940 after extensive fieldwork among the Flathead. Schaeffer served as director of the Museum of the Plains Indian, Browning, Montana, from 1947 to 1954 and also from 1959 to 1966. The archive has his fieldnotes, typed transcripts and photographs dealing primarily with the Kutenay and Montana Blackfoot.

Another anthropological collection is that of Verne Dusenberry (1906-1966), who, at the time of his death, was Curator of Ethnology at the Glenbow. He was the author of *The Montana Cree: A Study in Religious Persistence* (Stockholm: 1962). While most of Dusenberry's papers disappeared shortly after his sudden death, the archive has some material collected from him earlier and microfilm of other records borrowed from Dusenberry's family. The collection includes research materials on the Cree, Cheyenne, Assiniboine, Kutenai, Flathead and Pend d'Oreille.

The archive has two collections from former staff members who were active in work with Native people. George H. Gooderham (1899-1977) was Indian Agent among the Blackfoot from 1920 to 1946 and Regional Supervisor of Indian Agencies for Alberta from

1946 to 1954. He then joined the Glenbow and for several years wrote his reminiscences and short articles on various people and incidents in his career. The archive also has his diaries, 1920-1976, and some personal correspondence.

An additional collection at the Glenbow Archives is that of John Lee Laurie (1899-1959), a Calgary non-Indian school teacher who became Secretary of the Indian Association of Alberta (IAA) and wrote numerous articles on the Native people of the region. He was elected to the IAA in 1944 and remained active in that association until his death. His papers contain correspondence with Native people and officials, drafts of articles and numerous photographs.

Hugh A. Dempsey

University of Calgary. Libraries. Arctic Institute of North America (AINA). Library

Address: Arctic Institute of North America Library, University of Calgary Library, 2500 University Drive, N.W., Calgary, AB, Canada T2N 1N4.
Tel.: (403) 220-5650
Fax: (403) 282-6837
E-mail: tull@acs.ucalgary.ca.
Internet address: http://www.ucalgary.ca/library/aina.html.
Internet address (University of Calgary Library): http://www.ucalgary.ca/library.
Internet address (Arctic Institute of North America): http://www.ucalgary.ca/~aina.
Internet access to on-line catalog: The address of CLAVIS is http://clavis.ucalgary.ca. Also: telnet://clavis.ucalgary.ca. CLAVIS contains records of book materials acquired after March 1978 and some earlier materials. The AINA card catalog has catalog records of the materials cataloged before 1978.
Networks, consortia: Holdings of the University of Calgary Library are reported to National Library of Canada, ISM (formerly UTLAS); OCLC; and Union List of Scientific Serials in Canadian Libraries.
Public transit access: Accessible by bus.
Founded: 1945. The library of the Arctic Institute of North America became a part of the University of Calgary Library in 1979. Prior to 1975, the AINA was located at McGill University in Montreal. The Institute was founded in 1945 by an act of Parliament.
Major resources: Materials applicable to the Arctic and polar regions, including some Antarctic materials, subarctic materials and boreal materials. Languages represented in the collection include English, French, Russian, German, Danish, Finnish, Swedish, Norwegian, Japanese, Inuktitut, Dene languages and Greenlandic.
Areas of specialization: Particular emphasis is on northern Canada, but also materials on Alaska, Greenland, Scandinavia, Russia, geology, geography, meterology, oceanography, glaciology, snow and ice, permafrost, zoology, botany, environmental impact studies, technology, energy resources, history of exploration, Native studies and Northern cultures, economic and social development, political development, Northern government. Particular strengths are in older books (pre-1900), northern pipeline and oil and gas development and

Canadian government publications. An extensive polar serial collection was obtained in exchange for Arctic and Information North.

Archives/manuscripts: A few.

Holdings (Polar Collection): More than 16,000 books, 1,000 periodical titles, 30,000 pamphlets and reprints, 3,200 maps, 16,000 government documents, 2,500 documents relating to northern pipelines, 600 microforms.

Visual/audio resources: Not held.

Access: Borrowers must have a University of Calgary Library Card unless borrowing through interlibrary loan. Materials may be used by anyone within the Library.

References: "Arctic Institute of North America Library. University of Calgary Library," in Martha Andrews, *Polar and Cold Regions Library Resources: A Directory* (3rd ed., Boulder, Co.: 1994), p. 3-4.

Guides/catalogs: Arctic Institute of North America. Library, *Catalogue of the Arctic Institute of North America* (Boston: 1968). Supplements, 1971-1980.

C. Eric Tull

British Columbia—Vancouver

University of British Columbia. Museum of Anthropology (MOA)

Address: Museum of Anthropology, University of British Columbia, 6393 Northwest Marine Drive, Vancouver, BC, Canada V6T 1W5.

Tel.: (604) 822-5087

Fax: (604) 822-2974

Internet address: http://www.moa.ubc.ca.

Founded: 1948.

Major resources: Material on Native people of the Northwest Coast.

References: Rosalind C. Morris, *New Worlds from Fragments: Film, Ethnography and the Representation of Northwest Coast Cultures* (Boulder: 1994) (= *Studies in the Ethnographic Imagination*).

British Columbia—Victoria

Royal British Columbia Museum (RBCM)

Address: Royal British Columbia Museum, 675 Belleville St., Victoria, BC, Canada V8V 1X4.

Tel.: (250) 387-3701

Fax: (250) 356-8197

Internet address: http://rbcm1.rbcm.gov.bc.ca.

Internet address (RBCM Audio-Visual Collection): http://rbcm1.rbcm.gov.bc.ca/audio-visual/aud-vis.html.

Founded: 1886.
Major resources: Anthropological Collections Section.
Areas of specialization: Native people of British Columbia.
Visual/audio resources: Information on the museum's Audio-Visual Collection is available on the museum website—see the URL, above. More than 2,800 sound recordings concerning the indigenous peoples of British Columbia and their languages are held.
References: Rosalind C. Morris, *New Worlds from Fragments: Film, Ethnography and the Representation of Northwest Coast Cultures* (Boulder, Colo.: 1994) (= *Studies in the Ethnographic Imagination*).
Guides/catalogs: Normand Fortier, *Guide to Oral History Collections in Canada = Guide des fonds d'histoire orale au Canada* ([Ottawa?]: 1993) (= *Canadian Oral History Association = Société canadienne d'Histoire orale. Journal*, vol. 13), p. 102-103.

Manitoba—Winnipeg

Manitoba Museum of Man and Nature (MMMN)
Musée de l'Homme et de la Nature du Manitoba (MHNM)

Address: Manitoba Museum of Man and Nature, 190 Rupert Avenue, Winnipeg, MB, Canada R3B ON2.
Tel.: (204) 956-2830 (Museum Reception).
Fax: (204) 942-3679
E-mail (Library): steffan@mbnet.mb.ca.
Internet address: http://www.mbnet.mb.ca/ManitobaMuseum/library.html.
Public transit access: Winnipeg Transit bus.
Parking: Available in the vicinity of the museum, downtown.
Founded: 1932 (MHNM); ca. 1970 (library); 1994 (Archives).
Major resources: Library, Archives.
Areas of specialization: Archaeology, ethnology, museology, history of Manitoba, Hudson's Bay Company, conservation, educational programming, varous natural sciences.
Archives/manuscripts: 150 linear meters of original archival records. Finding aids to the archival materials are being added to the museum website. Archaeological archives include letters, research and a biography of early archaeologist Chris Vickers. The Native Ethnology archives will be processed in 1997-1998. Another important source for anthropological archives is the Provincial Archives of Manitoba [see the following entry].
Holdings (library): More than 20,000 books and 300 journals pertaining to all areas of specialization.
Visual/audio resources: Most photos and audio tapes are housed in the Audio/Visual Department. The museum photo collection is under reorganization; departments have separate collections as well. The Library has an oral history collection, as does Native Ethnology and also Multicultural Studies. The Archaeology department has a large number of site and artifact photos documenting mostly provincial sites. The Native Ethnology department has an extensive photo collection—largely on First Nations cultures of the

prairies. The anthropological research has focused primarily on the fur trade era in Manitoba (1670-1900) and on the Red River Settlement in particular.

Access: Open to the public; Library materials are available for on-site use only. Researchers, students and the public are requested to call for an appointment before visiting the Library or the Archives.

References: After the Hudson's Bay Company Collection is cataloged in its entirety, published descriptions will be forthcoming. Katherine Pettipas, Curator of Native Ethnology, has published articles on her research. Museum archaeologists (including Leigh Syms, Brian Lenius and Leo Pettipas) have written numerous articles on prairie immigration.

Guides/catalogs: Normand Fortier, *Guide to Oral History Collections in Canada = Guide des fonds d'histoire orale au Canada* ([Ottawa?]: 1993) (= *Canadian Oral History Association = Société canadienne d'Histoire orale. Journal*, vol. 13), p. 111-113.

Artifacts of anthropological/archaeological interest: Museum holdings include the recently donated artifact collections of the Hudson's Bay Company (HBC). These are First Nations, Métis, Inuit and European-Canadian items collected by HBC personnel, beginning about 1670, in what is now Canada. Cataloging of the ca. 6,500 Hudson's Bay Company artifacts is in process. An addition to the museum is being built to house and display this important collection. Katherine Pettipas, Curator of Native Ethnology, is managing the project and the other Native collections. Related archival records of the HBC are housed at the Provincial Archives of Manitoba. The Paul Kane collection of First Nations artifacts is another important holding. Archaeology collections include those from hydro dam development sites, such as the Churchill River Diversion Project; from two 1790s North West Company forts; from ceramic, adze, spear and dart point analysis; from grassland settlement studies; from precontact Dene territories in northern Manitoba; among others. Excavations have been carried out for these and many other western sites between 1900 and the present.

Description

The Collection

The Hudson's Bay Company archival material and museum artifacts constitute much of North America's heritage and reflect a remarkable range of human creativity, perseverance and accomplishment. They have been created over the centuries by Company traders and managers, Aboriginal people, European explorers and many others. They form the world's largest and most reliable source of information on early western Canadian life and, in large measure, the history of Canada from the time of the early European explorers through Confederation.

On May 2, 1920, the Hudson's Bay Company marked the 250th anniversary of the granting of the Charter to "The Governor and Company of Adventurers of England Trading into Hudson's Bay," by King Charles II of England. The Company celebrated this event by publishing the first issue of *The Beaver* magazine, preparing a short history of the company, holding commemorative events at Lower Fort Garry National Historic Site and by contracting Francis David Wilson, a former District Manager for James Bay, "to collect historical relics, lore and souvenirs of the early history of the Company" for a museum.

The collecting of natural history specimens, human history artifacts and visual materials relating the Company's activities in North America was well established by the twentieth-century. Not only had the Company acquired materials for exhibition at its London headquarters, but many of its North American employees accumulated their own private collections. Sir George Simpson, Governor of the Northern Department from 1821 to 1826 and of the trading territories in British North America until 1860, not only acquired materials for his personal collection, but was also a patron of Canadian artist Paul Kane. He ordered Kane to bring back from his travels both artwork and "curiosities of the country" that would reflect the natural history and lives of Aboriginal nations in the western regions of Rupert's Land.

In addition to preserving a record of the Hudson's Bay Company's contribution to the development of British North America for posterity, the collections and their exhibition were considered to be the Company's legacy to all Canadians.

In June 1922 the HBC installed a major exhibition of materials at its store in Winnipeg and by 1926 the museum exhibition was housed in new quarters at the present store on Portage Avenue. The objective of the exhibition was "to depict by means of relics, pictures, documents, models, etcetera, the history of the HBC, life in the fur trade, the story of pioneer settlers and the customs, dress, and industries of the Aboriginal tribes."

The initial collections were regarded only as a beginning to future acquisitions. A general appeal was made to friends both within and outside the service of the HBC for objects to fill in the gaps. Aboriginal, Inuit and Métis items; trade goods; trading post libraries and documents; related European-Canadian artifacts and artworks found their way into the Company's holdings through donation, purchase and even trade. To date, there has been a record established for some 6,500 objects and documents. Materials were still being donated as late as the 1970s. Two major additions from the Company's other holdings were integrated into the Winnipeg collections with the transfer of materials from Vancouver in 1935 and from Beaver House in London, England, in 1972.

Some significant materials from this outstanding collection are: excellent examples of early nineteenth-century Aboriginal quillwork and ribbonwork from the Red River area; a quillwork and painted Métis frock coat; antique maps; the James Houston collection of Baffin Island stone prints (1958); and argilite carvings produced by the Northwest Coast Haida carver, Charlie Edenshaw.

In 1960, the HBC closed its Winnipeg Museum. The collection was transferred to the Province of Manitoba on permanent loan. In 1962 it was loaned to the federal Department of Northern Affairs and National Resources for exhibition and interpretation at Lower Fort Garry National Historic Site. In March 1994, the Manitoba Museum of Man and Nature was designated the new home.

The Company

The Hudson's Bay Company, one of the oldest continuously active companies in the world, was almost 200 years old when Canada was created in 1867, and had, since its inception in 1670, controlled fully one-third of present-day Canadian territory. That area, designated Rupert's Land, encompassed most of northern Ontario and northern Québec, all of Manitoba, most of Saskatchewan, the southern half of Alberta and a large part of the former Northwest Territories.

Control over this enormous domain was granted by Royal Charter following the successful voyage of the *Nonsuch* in 1686 to trade for beaver pelts with the Cree near James Bay.

What began as a simple fur-trading enterprise became a trading and exploration company that reached to the west coast of Canada and the United States, south to Oregon, north to the Arctic and east to Ungava Bay; a land development company with vast holdings in the prairie provinces; a merchandising, natural resources and real estate development company; and, today, Canada's oldest corporation and one of its largest retailers.

It was not an uneventful progression. First, the French wanted the Company out; powerful rivals emerged. The North West Company, principally Scottish-Canadian traders from Montréal, was the most formidable. The Nor'Westers, in defiance of the Charter, moved north to the Arctic and, in 1793, west to the Pacific.

However, in 1821 the North West Company was merged into the Hudson's Bay Company, and the Company's title to the land was recognized by all parties. The next half-century or so were some of the Company's best years. Under Governor Sir George Simpson, Company officers explored and traded vigorously throughout the West and North and moved south in a wide area from the sources of the Missouri to San Francisco Bay.

Not everyone liked the Company's monopoly; the Parliamentary Inquiry of 1857 found that what is now southern Alberta, Saskatchewan and Manitoba was suitable for settlement and should be ceded to Canada. This was the beginning of the end for the Company's control. By the Deed of Surrender of 1869 the Company retained its Charter, but surrendered ownership of its Rupert's Land territory. In return, it received cash and seven million acres in this fertile region which it gradually sold during the next 85 years.

By 1912 the Company had recognized that it needed a new approach to retailing and planned a chain of department stores in western Canada. By 1970 downtown department stores had been built in each of the major cities of western Canada. The rapid expansion during the 1970s strained its resources severely. In response, the Company concentrated on its retail businesses and divested itself of its Wholesale Department, Northern Stores and Fur divisions, among others.

Cindi Steffan and Bev Pike

Provincial Archives of Manitoba (PAM) including the **Hudson's Bay Company Archives** (HBCA)

Address: Provincial Archives of Manitoba, 200 Vaughan Street, Winnipeg, MB, Canada R3C 1T5.
Tel.: (204) 945-3971 (Provincial Archives of Manitoba); (204) 945-4949 (Hudson's Bay Company Archives); (204) 945-2529 (Hudson's Bay Company Photograph Collection); (204) 945-2622 (Hudson's Bay Company Cartographic Records).

Fax: (204) 948-2008 (Provincial Archives of Manitoba); (204) 948-3236 (Hudson's Bay Company Archives).

E-mail (Hudson's Bay Company Archives): hbca@archives.gov.mb.ca.

Internet address (Hudson's Bay Company Archives): http://www.gov.mb.ca/chc/archives/ hbca/index.html.

Networks, consortia: PAM provides local access to National Archives of Canada finding aids on CD-ROM.

Public transit access: PAM is centrally located in downtown Winnipeg and is easily reached by local bus lines. Visitors may call Winnipeg Transit for bus directions, if needed.

Founded: Ca. 1947 (Provincial Archives of Manitoba); 1931 (the year that the Hudson's Bay Company Archives was established in London). The HBC head office was transferred from London to Winnipeg, Manitoba, in 1970. The head office is now in Toronto, where it has been for several years. In 1974, the Hudson's Bay Company archives were transferred from London to the Provincial Archives of Manitoba. They were officially donated to the provincial government of Manitoba in 1994.

Major resources: The archives of the provincial government of Manitoba; non-official archives pertaining to Manitoba; the Hudson's Bay Company Archives; the Legislative Library of Manitoba.

Areas of specialization: Manitoba; the Hudson's Bay Company; the history of the fur trade in western and northern Canada; Native people of Canada.

Archives/manuscripts: The Hudson's Bay Company archives extend chronologically from 1671 until recent decades and consist of ca. 3,000 linear meters of archival materials. The Alexander Morris papers and the Adams G. Archibald papers are also at PAM.

Visual/audio resources (Provincial Archives of Manitoba): The Provincial Archives Photo Collection includes many photographs of Native people of Manitoba. PAM has excellent holdings of film and sound recordings of anthropological interest. The Oral History Section of PAM maintains collections of oral history recordings produced in the course of Manitoba's Oral History Grants Program. This program was begun in the early 1980s and, since 1991, has focused on the production of oral history recordings of indigenous peoples of Manitoba.

Visual/audio resources (Hudson's Bay Company Archives): The HBC photograph collection has ca. 130,000 photographic prints or negatives. The photos are mainly black-and-white and pertain to the Canadian fur trade, the Native people of northern and western Canada and other subjects of anthropological, cultural or historical interest. More than 55,000 photo images are from the Company Head Office collection. Also in the collection are some 13,500 copy images of maps, documents or other items in the HBC Archives. The Archives has some 11,000 maps and plans—see the published volume by Richard I. Ruggles (1991).

Access: Open to the public. A special HBCA Interlibrary Loan Programme, established in 1986, provides access to more than 4,000 reels of HBC records on microfilm. The HBCA Interlibrary Loan Programme finding aid (on microfilm) is available at many libraries in North America and elsewhere.

References: Peter Geller, "The HBC Archives: A Source for Aboriginal Research," *SSHARE-ERASSH* [Social Sciences and Humanities Aboriginal Research Exchange = Échange sur la recherche autochtone en sciences sociales et humaines], vol. 3, no. 1

(Spring/Summer 1995), p. 1, 8, 27-28; Tom Koppel, "Treasure-Trove of History: Three Centuries of Canada's Past Comes to Life at the Hudson's Bay Company Archives," *Canadian Geographic*, vol. 111, no. 5 (Oct.-Nov. 1991), p. 70-76; E.E. [Edwin Ernest] Rich, *Hudson's Bay Company, 1670-1870* (Toronto: 1958), 3 v.—the standard history of the HBC.
Guides/catalogs: Two microfilm reels produced in 1985 are the primary finding aids for the HBCA Interlibrary Loan Programme; these are HBCA finding aids no. 20M1 and 1MA76. In addition, some of the more recently made microfilm reels available for interlibrary loan are listed on two additional microfilm reels; Normand Fortier, *Guide to Oral History Collections in Canada = Guide des fonds d'histoire orale au Canada* ([Ottawa?]: 1993) (= *Canadian Oral History Association = Société canadienne d'Histoire orale. Journal*, vol. 13), p. 113-122; "Guide to Research Tools in the Hudson's Bay Company Archives, Provincial Archives of Manitoba"—a brief unpublished guide; Hudson's Bay Company Archives. Microfilmed Records, "Inter-Library Loan Programme Guide, 1996"—a brief unpublished guide to the HBCA ILL Programme; Richard I. Ruggles, *A Country So Interesting: The Hudson's Bay Company and Two Centuries of Mapping, 1670-1870* (Montréal: 1991) (= *Rupert's Land Record Society Series*, vol. 2).
Artifacts of anthropological significance: Among resources of the HBCA is an art collection of some 500 paintings, prints and other art objects, many of historical, cultural or ethnographic interest. The large artifact collection accumulated by the Company during its long history has been donated to the Manitoba Museum of Man and Nature (MMMN), located in Winnipeg [see the preceding entry].

Description

Hudson's Bay Company Archives

The Hudson's Bay Company is one of the oldest chartered trading companies in the world. The Company's archives contain the only known documents for many eighteenth-century settlements in Canada—including Churchill, Manitoba; Moose Factory and Albany, Ontario; Rupert House and Eastmain, Québec; Cumberland House, Saskatchewan; and Edmonton, Alberta. The records of the Company are of special value because of their continuity. For example, all of the Company Minute Books, covering a period of more than 300 years, have survived except for the years 1670-1671 and 1674-1679.

The extensive Company archives include original handwritten journals, correspondence and accounts of more than 500 trading posts (1703-1949), Company ships' logs, original maps and plans, various journals of travel and exploration and other Company or related documentation that accumulated in official files in the years since 1671. Also part of the archives is a photograph collection, an art collection and a small specialized library.

Many of the HBCA archival materials are useful for research on early contacts and trade relations (especially the fur trade) between indigenous peoples of Canada and the early Company factors. The archives include some of the earliest available census information on band settlements in western and northern Canada and an abundance of other documentation.

In 1994 the HBC archives were officially donated by the (Toronto-based) Hudson's Bay Company to the provincial government of Manitoba. They are now permanently housed at the Provincial Archives of Manitoba, where they are available for research use.

The early records of the Company have been microfilmed, while filming of more recent archives (for the years 1871-1904) and of Company maps is in progress. More than 4,000 microfilm reels of HBC archives are now available for use at the National Archives of Canada (Ottawa), as well as the Public Record Office (Kew, England). A microfilm version of the HBCA *Inter-library Loan Programme Finding Aid* is available at selected library and archival locations in Canada and the United States.

Provincial Archives of Manitoba Oral History Projects

Among the assorted Provincial Archives of Manitoba Oral History Section sound recordings on cassette tape are several groups of oral history project recordings pertaining to Native people of the Manitoba region and selected immigrant populations of Manitoba. [Quotations in the following list of Oral History Section sound recordings are excerpted from an unpublished holdings list of the Oral History Section, PAM.]

- Métis Oral History Project—29 interviews, 1984; also eighteen additional interviews, 1985. Interviews are in French or English. "The interviews are in the form of life histories. Narrators' recollections span the period from the end of the nineteenth century to the present, and provide information on family, economic and social life in rural [Métis] communities."
- Northern Manitoba Native Elders Research Project—27 interviews, 1987. Interviews are in Cree or English. Sponsored by the Ma-Mow-We-Tak Friendship Centre. "The purpose of the project was to compile tapes of Northern Manitoba's Native Elders' life experiences in six areas—education, medicine, spirituality, recreation, employment, and family lifestyles."
- Fisher River Oral History Research Project—42 interviews, 1991. Sponsored by the Fisher River Band. The project was planned "to provide an oral account of the stories of Treaty, the land, economic development and community as told through the [Fisher River Band] Elders."
- History of Fort Alexander Oral History Project—15 interviews, 1989; one interview is restricted. "The objective of the project ... was to develop an oral history of Fort Alexander for educational programming and for use in a proposed museum and cultural centre at Fort Alexander Reserve ... Topics discussed include: the native way of life from past to present, socio-economic issues from the 1800s to the present, political history, and the movement towards self-government."
- Matheson Island Community History Project—11 interviews, 1990. Sponsored by the Riverton and District Friendship Centre. This project was undertaken to record the "lifestyles and significant experiences in the lives of present and former residents of Matheson Island between 1920 and 1950 ... The tapes contain information about the social and economic life of Matheson Island and its locale. Specific topics include: transportation, the fishing industry (including the fishing cooperative), Catholic and Mennonite missions, Thomas Prince, Métis identity, Native-government relations in 1990."

- Japanese Canadians in Manitoba Oral History Project—33 interviews, 1987; three interviews are restricted. In English or Japanese. Sponsored by the Manitoba Japanese Canadians' Citizens Association. The interviews describe the "evacuation and internment of Japanese Canadians who [later] resettled in Manitoba. Topics include employment ... attitudes to Japanese Canadians ... racial discrimination, cultural institutions and organizations."

- Manitoba Chinese Historical Society Oral History Project—35 interviews, 1987; two tapes are restricted. A project of the Manitoba Chinese Historical Society "to portray and preserve the history of the Chinese ethnic community in Manitoba by collecting photographs, documents, and oral histories." "We collected many pictures from second generation Chinese whose parents or relatives were the first immigrants to Manitoba." "Some artifacts, such as water smoking pipes, leather and ceramic pillows, tiny scales for measuring medicinal herbs used by the early Chinese pioneers in Manitoba were donated or loaned to us."

Information provided by Anne Morton and Scott Reid.

Northwest Territories—Yellowknife

Prince of Wales Northern Heritage Centre

Address: Prince of Wales Northern Heritage Centre, Culture and Heritage Division, Department of Education, Culture and Employment, Government of the Northwest Territories, Box 1320, Yellowknife, NT, Canada X1A 2L9.
Location: Frame Lake North.
Tel.: (867) 873-7551
Fax: (867) 873-0205
E-mail: Archival_mail@ec&e.learnnet.nt.ca.
Internet address: http://pwnhc.learnnet.nt.ca.
Founded: 1979.
Major resources: Northwest Territories Archives Collection; Northwest Territories Geographic Names Database; Archaeology Program.
Areas of specialization: Ethnology and archaeology of the Canadian Arctic and Subarctic regions.
Archives/manuscripts: 1,200 linear ft. of textual materials. Archival holdings include oral histories and photographs that relate to the indigenous peoples of the Northwest Territories (NWT)—Inuit, Dene and Métis. The Library collection of the Archives is dedicated to the human history of the NWT. The Geographic Names database contains information on traditional names, while the Archaeology Program has a collection of unpublished reports on archaeological and ethnographic studies completed in the NWT.
Holdings (library): A library of 5,000 volumes, of which 633 volumes are classified as rare; 1,000 unpublished archaeological reports; and more than 20,000 toponymic records on the Geographical Place-Names Database.
Visual/audio resources: 250,000 photographs, including the Angulalik photo collection, are held. 5,000 oral history recordings, including the Committee for Original Peoples

Entitlement oral history collection. Also, the Fort Good Hope Dene Language Research Program audio recordings; 400 motion pictures.

Access: The resources of the Prince of Wales Northern Heritage Centre may be consulted Monday to Friday, 9:00-12:00 a.m. and 1:00-4:30 p.m., excluding statutory holidays. Some restrictions on access may apply to certain archival collections.

Guides/catalogs: Angela Schiwy and Ian Moir, *Guide to the Holdings of the NWT Archives* (Yellowknife, N.W.T.: 1994). Also available are Normand Fortier, *Guide to Oral History Collections in Canada = Guide des fonds d'histoire orale au Canada* ([Ottawa?]: 1993) (= *Canadian Oral History Association = Société canadienne d'Histoire orale. Journal*, vol. 13), p. 157-159; Government of the Northwest Territories. Education, Culture and Employment. Prince of Wales Northern Heritage Centre, *Heritage of the Northwest Territories* (Yellowknife, N.W.T.: [n.d.]).

Artifacts of anthropological interest: The Northern Heritage Centre houses and manages a diverse collection of more than 90,000 objects representing the history of people in the Territories and the regional fauna and geology. The Humanities category is divided into separate Fine Arts, History and Archaeology collections.

Archaeological sites represented in artifact collections: The Prince of Wales Northern Heritage Centre is one of two repositories in Canada for artifacts collected from archaeological sites in the NWT, under archaeological permit. The sites are very numerous.

Access to archaeological collections information: Archaeological collections information is on a database and is accessible via the Canadian Heritage Information Network (CHIN) at http://www.chin.gc.ca, or by contacting the Prince of Wales Northern Heritage Centre.

Description

The Prince of Wales Northern Heritage Centre is an institution dedicated to enhancing and preserving the culture and heritage of the peoples of the Northwest Territories. Located in Yellowknife, the facility houses the territorial museum, the territorial archives and a variety of culture and heritage programs—including Archaeology, Geographic Names, Education Extension Services, Community Programming and Exhibits.

The NWT Archives was created in 1979 to acquire, preserve and make accessible unpublished documents that record local and regional history. In 1981 it was named as the archives for the territorial government.

The Archives has more than 250,000 photographs in its holdings, with the earliest images dating from 1845; the majority of photographs, however, were taken between 1900 and 1950. Most were taken by euro-Canadians while working or visiting the north, but the Archives does have a few collections taken by Native people—one of the most notable being the Angulalik collection.

Perhaps the most significant anthropological holdings of the Archives are its oral history collections. One of the largest of these is from the Committee for Original Peoples Entitlement. In the 1960s and 1970s, a group of concerned individuals began a project to record the legends and life experiences of the Inuvialuit, Gwich'in (Loucheux) and North Slavey (Hareskin) people. Two of the leaders of this project were Nellie Cournoyea and the Oblate priest, Father Lemeur. The recordings were intended to be used in various communities as research material for school curriculum, to preserve the legends and life stories of the elders and to help promote Native language literacy. This accession consists of approximately 700 oral history recordings and 1.2 meters of transcriptions. Recordings are in Inuvialuktun, Gwich'in and North Slavey and contain life stories of elders as well as traditional legends. Languages represented include Gwich'in, Inuvialuktun, North Slavey and English.

Another important collection is the Igloolik Research Centre collection, assembled by the Igoolik Oral History Project. This accession contains both sound cassettes and transcripts generated from 276 interviews with 56 residents, conducted by Eugene Amarualik, Maurice Arnattiaq, Susan Avingaq, Paul Irngaut, John Macdonald, Rhoda Qanatsiaq, George Qulaut, Louis Tapardjuk and Therese Ukaliannuk. Subjects covered in the interviews include birth and death rituals, hunting and hunting implements, marriage, spiritual activities and supernatural events. Some of the tapes contain narrations of Inuit stories and legends. There are also examples of throat singing and music. Attitudes toward sexual activities, infanticide, child-rearing, respect for elders and the impact of southern cultural values and traditions on the traditional lifestyle of the community's residents are also discussed. The materials have been arranged into series based upon the names of the individuals interviewed; one series was created for each individual. The item list contains an alphabetical listing (by surname) of each person interviewed.

Created in 1983, the Geographic Names Program has conducted and supported community based research on traditional names for geographic features in the Territories. An on-line database has been developed that contains more than 20,000 records. Each record documents the location of a geographic feature, the origin of the names and also background information related to the feature.

Archaeological reports housed at the Prince of Wales Northern Heritage Centre have been submitted in compliance with the requirements of archaeologist permits issued under the authority of the Northwest Territories Archaeological Sites Regulations. The regulations require that a descriptive report be filed upon expiration of the permit. At a minimum these reports contain a description of the archaeological activity that took place, as well as the nature of the finds—including sites, artifacts and other archaeological remains. Some permit holders also include analysis and interpretations of the finds in their reports.

D. Richard Valpy

Ontario—Ottawa

Canadian Institute for Historical Microreproductions (CIHM)
Institut canadien de Microreproductions historiques (ICMH)

Address: Canadian Institute for Historical Microproductions, P.O. Box 2428, Station D, Ottawa, ON, Canada K1P 5W.
Tel.: (613) 235-2628
Fax: (613) 235-9753
E-mail: cihmicmh@nlo.nlc-bnc.ca.

Internet address: http://www.nlc-bnc.ca/cihm.

Founded: 1978.

Major resources: The Early Canadiana research collection, published by CIHM in microfiche format. CIHM microfilms printed materials (books, pamphlets, ephemera) with Canadian authorship, imprint or subject matter. The period covered is from the time of European contact to the early twentieth-century.

Areas of specialization: CIHM is a major and continuing microfilming project with three distinct collections now completed. The "Pre-1900 Canadian Monographs" collection comprises 62,800 titles. The subset defined as "Native Studies" consists of 1,520 titles, although there is additional relevant anthropological material throughout the larger Pre-1900 Canadian Monographs collection. Collection subsets include Native Studies as well as Anthropology. Other segments of the collection are also of potential interest to anthropologists and linguists.

Access: The complete monographs collection, including the anthropological texts, is located in 36 research libraries in Canada and in eight others abroad. Most Canadian holding libraries place records of the collection in their respective computer catalogs. Enquire for a complete list of the library locations.

References: Olive Patricia Dickason, "Tracking Down the History of Canada's First Nations," *Facsimile*, 10 (Nov. 1993), p. 2-4; David H. Pentland, "North American Languages of Canada, 1534-1900," *Facsimile*, 10 (Nov. 1993), p. 5-16.

Guides/catalogs: *Canada: the Printed Record* (Ottawa: 1995) [a COM microfiche catalog]. The bibliographic register with seven indexes consists of more than 300 fiche. The 1995 edition contains 66,000 titles microfilmed by CIHM; *Native Studies Collection Catalogue* (2nd ed., Ottawa: 1995). Also available is the CIHM semi-annual newsletter for researchers, *Facsimile*.

Description

The Canadian Institute for Historical Microreproductions is a national project established to preserve the intellectual content of Canada's printed heritage and make the resulting research collection accessible nationally and internationally. The institute is an independent non-profit corporation headed by a board composed of scholars and directors of major research libraries. Since its beginnings in 1978, CIHM has evolved into a cooperative project, working in close association with the National Library of Canada, Canadian research libraries and other Canadian institutions and associations.

The Institute traces its origin to two reports released in the 1970s: the *Report of the Commission on Canadian Studies* by Thomas H.B. Symons; and the *Report of the Consultative Group on University Research Libraries*. The Symons Report called for stronger collections of Canadian material and also encouraged the repatriation, in some form, of printed Canadiana held in foreign libraries and archives. The Library Consultative Group in its 1977 report recommended that immediate measures be taken to deal with the problem of deteriorating library collections and to facilitate access to widely scattered Canadian resource materials.

Because CIHM is not a library, materials to be filmed must first be borrowed from libraries, archives and other collections in Canada or elsewhere. The National Library of Canada and the National Archives of Canada are major lenders, and other materials for microreproduction are borrowed from as many as seventy different Canadian institutions each year. Surveys and filming have been done at the Library of Congress, Cornell University, New York Public Library and the British Library. To date, more that 200 libraries have loaned Canadiana materials, many rare and valuable, for filming.

Access to materials is afforded by a microfiche catalog, electronic tapes and printed catalogs. The records are usually placed on the computerized library catalogs at subscribing Canadian institutions, and the CIHM Internet home page allows researchers access to the complete CIHM database. CIHM records are also available on the ISM and AMICUS (National Library of Canada) databases and, in part, on OCLC.

The CIHM Native Studies Collection

The CIHM Native Studies collection contains books as well as pamphlets, reports and papers relating to Aboriginal peoples living in Canada. Government documents are not included, except in the case of reports written by an individual author commissioned by the Crown. The collection contains comprehensive primary documentation of Native North American culture from the time of contact to 1900. There are descriptions of indigenous North American legends, traditions, religions and laws, written over a period of 350 years. Included are accounts of habits and customs, major events and battles and biographies of Native leaders.

Linguistic guides and comparative studies of Native North American languages are well represented, with fifty languages from the eleven Canadian native "language families" individually documented through grammars, dictionaries and translations of prayers, hymnals and catechisms.

Pam Bjornson

Indian and Northern Affairs Canada. Departmental Library
[See the entry for this library under the heading **Québec—Hull.**]

Indian and Northern Affairs Canada. Inuit Art Section
[See the entry for this unit under the heading **Québec—Hull.**]

National Archives of Canada (NAC)
Archives nationales du Canada (AnC)

Address: National Archives of Canada, 395 Wellington Street, Ottawa, ON, Canada K1A ON3.
Tel.: (613) 992-3884 (General Information); (613) 995-5138 or 8094 (Reference Services); (613) 955-1070 (Cartographic and Architectural Sector); (613) 992-3884 (Documentary Art

and Photography Division); (613) 996-8507 (Government Archives Division); (613) 996-7374 (Manuscript Division).

Fax: (613) 995-6274 (Reference enquiries); (613) 943-8112 (Manuscript Division).

Internet address: http://www.archives.ca.

Public transit access: OC Transpo bus, routes 8 or 95; STO bus route, all lines; CTCRO (for Québec residents in the National Capital Region).

Founded: 1872.

Major resources: Records of the federal government of Canada; also many private archival collections.

Areas of specialization: Manuscripts, government archives, cartographic and architectural archives, documentary art and photography, others.

Archives/manuscripts: Special resources of anthropological interest include records relating to Indian Affairs (in Record Group 10). The immigration records of Canada are in RG 76. Records of the Multicultural Archives Program—in existence since 1972—are also available. The National Archives holds microfilm of the archives of the Hudson's Bay Company that have been filmed. The original Hudson's Bay Company Archives are at the Provincial Archives of Manitoba in Winnipeg [see the entry on the Provincial Archives of Manitoba].

Holdings: More than sixty kilometers of Canadian government records; ca. 10,000 private collections of unpublished records.

Visual/audio resources: The National Archives photo collection consists of about fifteen million items, including daguerreotypes, tintypes and large numbers of black-and-white and color negatives. Many historic photos of Inuit and other Native peoples are held. The CD-ROM, *ArchiVIA 1995*, includes a database with item-level descriptions of cataloged photographic holdings in the Archives. References to many photographs of (or pertaining to) Aboriginal people of Canada may be retrieved by means of this source. The Archives also holds many oral history collections, e.g., the Inuit Land Use and Occupancy Project interviews (140 recorded interviews).

Access: Open to the public. Readers must register and obtain a research pass. Researchers are requested to write or call in advance of a visit to enquire whether relevant research materials are available. Some additional information on access is available on the Archives' website. The National Archives maintains decentrialized reference/research units at the Provincial Archives of Manitoba in Winnipeg; at the Public Archives of Nova Scotia in Halifax; and at the Special Collections and University Archives Reading Room, University of British Columbia Library in Vancouver.

Guides/catalogs (on CD-ROM): Of special importance for access to records in the Archives concerning the Native people of Canada is the CD-ROM, *ArchiVIA: Aboriginal Peoples = Peuples autochtones* (Ottawa: ca. 1997). Also available in CD-ROM format are a guide to the archival records of the French and British colonial periods, *ArchiVIA—Colonial Archives* (Ottawa: 1997) and an earlier CD-ROM guide to National Archives resources: *ArchiVIA 1995* (Ottawa: 1995).

Guides/catalogs (other): An unpublished guide to archival records concerning the Native people of Canada is Bennett McCardle, "Archival Records Relating to Native People in the National Archives of Canada, the National Library and the National Museum of Man: A Thematic Guide" (Hull: 1985). Copies of this guide—approximately 1,000 pages in length—may be consulted at the Claims and Historical Research Center in Hull, Québec. For researchers interested in the official archival records on Native people in the Government Archives Division of the National Archives, an updated version of the McCardle guide (1995, in WordPerfect format) is available: *Archival Records Relating to Native People in the Government Archives Division of the National Archives of Canada: A Thematic Guide Prepared by Bennett McCardle ... Revised and updated by S. Barry Cottam and Theresa Redmond* (revised ed., Hull: 1995). This source describes official records in the Government Archives Division concerning First Nations, Métis and Inuit peoples. A digital copy of the 1995 McCardle guide may be obtained, in WordPerfect format, from Claims and Historical Research Centre, Indian and Northern Affairs Canada, Terrasses de la Chaudière, Ottawa, Ontario, Canada K1A OH4.

Several printed guides to National Archives holdings have been produced: Jim Burant (compiler), *Documentary Art and Photography Division* (Ottawa: 1992) (= *National Archives of Canada. General Guide Series*); Peter Gillis (general editor), *Records Relating to Indian Affairs (RG 10)* (Ottawa: 1975) (= *General Inventory Series-Public Records Division, Public Archives of Canada*, no. 1); Grace Hyam (principal author), *Manuscript Division* (Ottawa: 1994) (= *National Archives of Canada. General Guide Series*); Gilles Langelier (compiler), *National Map Collection* (Ottawa: 1985) (= *Public Archives Canada. General Guide Series*); Cynthia Lovering (compiler), *Government Archives Division* (Ottawa: 1991) (= *National Archives of Canada. General Guide Series*).

Oral history resources are described in Normand Fortier, *Guide to Oral History Collections in Canada = Guide des fonds d'histoire orale au Canada* ([Ottawa?]: 1993) (= *Canadian Oral History Association = Société canadienne d'Histoire orale. Journal*, vol. 13), p. 11-52.

Description

The National Archives of Canada is one of Canada's oldest cultural agencies. Its mission is to preserve the collective memory of the nation, of the government of Canada, and to contribute to the protection of rights and the enhancement of a sense of national identity. In carrying out its mission, the Archives has acquired, described and preserved significant archival material relating to Canadian life—literally millions of textual documents, photographs films, maps, tapes, video recordings, books, paintings, drawings, prints and electronic records.

In an effort to disseminate as widely as possible information about its holdings, the National Archives has undertaken a program of making available on CD-ROM various finding aids for records in its custody. A recent title in this series of CD-ROM guides, *ArchiVIA: Aboriginal Peoples = Peuples autochtones*, is available. Included within this product are a number of finding aids that describe a selection of the Archives' federal government records relating to Aboriginal peoples—from the seventeenth-century to the present.

FIGURE 1. "Recording Eskimo music, May 1943." National Film Board of Canada Collection. Courtesy of the National Archives of Canada (negative #PA 129913).

This CD-ROM contains information on available research sources for First Nations, Inuit and Métis people. Among the elements included are:

- A narrative historical overview of the interrelationships between Aboriginal and European peoples of Canada that provides context to the records described.
- A thematic guide to federal government textual and electronic records relating to Aboriginal peoples.
- A textual description (inventory) of records of the Department of Indian Affairs.
- A database describing 524 individual Indian treaty, surrender and agreement documents dating from 1680 to 1956.
- A textual guide to the records of the Métis Scrip Commissions, providing a historical background to both the scrip issuing process in general and the work of the various individual commissions.

Information provided by David Enns and Sarah Montgomery.

National Library of Canada (NLC)
Bibliothèque nationale du Canada (BnC)

Address: National Library of Canada, 395 Wellington Street, Ottawa, ON, Canada K1A 0N4.
Tel.: (613) 947-0828 (Michel Brisebois); (613) 943-1119 (Sandra Bell).
Fax: (613) 995-1969
E-mail: michel.brisebois@nlc-bnc.ca.
Internet address: http://www.nlc-bnc.ca.
Public transit access: OC Transpo bus, routes 16 or 18 (for Ontario residents in the National Capital Region) or CTCRO (for Québec residents in the National Capital Region).
Founded: 1953.
Major resources: Under the terms of the National Library Act, the National Library's holdings of post-1950 *Canadian* imprints, as a consequence of Legal Deposit, are comprehensive. Early books in North American Native languages (Special Collections, Rare Book Collection—contact Michel Brisebois); Canadian Indian Rights Collection (Reference and Information Services Division—contact Sandra Bell).
Visual/audio resources: See below for information on some selected early illustrated imprints in the Library.
Access: On-site consultation only for all Rare Book Collection materials is available in the Special Collections Reading Room, Monday to Friday, 8:30 a.m. to 5:00 p.m.
References: Joyce M. Banks, "Books in Syllabic Characters Printed for the Use of the Church Missionary Society in the Dioces of Rupert's Land Among the Cree, Saulteaux, Slave and Tukudh Indians, and the Eskimos of Little Whale River: 1852-1872," Ph.D. dissertation, University of London, 1988; "First Contact and Lasting Impressions," *National Library News* [National Library of Canada], vol. 25, no. 10-11 (Oct.-Nov. 1993), p. 9-11.
Guides/catalogs: Joyce M. Banks (compiler), *Books in Native Languages in the Rare Book Collections of the National Library of Canada = Livres en langues autochtones dans les collections de livres rares de la Bibliothèque nationale du Canada* (2nd rev. and enlarged

ed., Ottawa: 1985). A third edition of this work, in CD-ROM format, is forthcoming. Much of the Native-language material in the Rare Book Collection has been microfilmed by the Canadian Institute for Historical Microreproductions (CIHM); [see the separate entry in this guide on the CIHM]. Fiche are available for purchase from CIHM or may be borrowed on interlibrary loan from the National Library of Canada through institutional libraries.

Description

I. Rare Book Collection (National Library of Canada, Special Collections).

The National Library of Canada collects heavily in all areas related to the First Nations and the Rare Book Collection has strong retrospective holdings on the Aboriginal peoples, their life and customs, language and literature, complemented by accounts of early voyages and travels and works on the fur trade, settlement and other aspects of the historical development of Canadian society under the *Régime français* and in British America.

The National Library holds a good representative collection of books in Aboriginal languages. In the Rare Book Collection there are some 700 such pre-1950 imprints, including publications in about sixty Native languages or dialects. The greater part of this material was published during the nineteenth-century, but included are such early imprints as Gabriel Sagard's *Dictionaire de la langue huronne, nécessaire à ceux qui n'ont l'intelligence d'icelle, & ont à traiter avec les sauvages du pays des Hurons, situé en l'Amérique* (Paris: 1632). Also held is Roger Williams's *A Key into the Language of America, or, An Help to the Language of the Natives in That Part of America, Called New-England* (London: 1643).

The nature of printed Native-language literature up to the mid-twentieth-century was mainly evangelical. Until then, with few exceptions, books for the use of the Native people of Canada were written or translated by missionaries and printed or published by religious orders and societies. The printing of books in Aboriginal languages presupposed the existence of a literate population or of people who could easily be taught to read. Certainly, there was clear understanding that the only hope of success in proselytizing was by using indigenous languages. Wordlists, vocabularies, dictionaries, grammars and other linguistic works appeared for the use of those who lived and worked among the Native peoples, as well as for the use of linguists. During the nineteenth-century, most books printed for the use of the people were Bible translations or devotional works. In the twentieth-century, the most determined efforts of state and church to extirpate Aboriginal languages failed owing, at least in part, to the industry and efforts of early translators and publishers.

In Canada, the earliest books for Aboriginal use were printed at Québec shortly after the introduction of printing there. Prepared by Jean Baptiste de la Brosse, S.J., they include an alphabet and a primer and prayer book, *Nehiro-Iriniui aiamihe Massinahigan* ([Québec]: 1767), in the Montagnais language. This was followed by the first Mohawk book printed at Montréal: *Iontri8aiestsk8a Ionskaneks N'aieienterihag Gaiatonsera Te Gari8toraragon Ong8e on8e Ga8ennontakon* ([Montréal]: 1777). A bilingual edition of the Church of England *Book of Common Prayer* in Mohawk and English appeared in Québec in 1780, followed by *A Primer for the Use of the Mohawk Children* (Montréal) in 1781. London editions of the latter two appeared in 1787 and 1786. These titles represent nearly the entire canon of Native-language books printed for use in Canada during the eighteenth-century.

During the nineteenth-century, the Anglicans and Roman Catholics were joined in their translational labors by the Moravians, Wesleyans and Methodists, and thousands of books were printed in Canada and abroad for the use of the Native peoples. Most used the roman alphabet but other writing systems were also employed, including Micmac hieroglyphics and Duployan shorthand. Only the syllabic characters—commonly known as "Cree syllabics"—have survived. Thousands of books were printed in syllabic characters during the nineteenth-century for the use of the peoples of northern Canada [see: Joyce M. Banks, "Books in Syllabic Characters Printed for the Use of the Church Missionary Society in the Dioces of Rupert's Land Among the Cree, Saulteaux, Slave and Tukudh Indians, and the Eskimos of Little Whale River: 1852-1872," Ph.D. dissertation, University of London, 1988]. In 1993, the Canadian Aboriginal Syllabics Encoding Committee, sponsored by the Government of Canada, prepared a draft report on the standardization of syllabic character sets for the Algonquian, Athapaskan and Inuktitut syllabic repertoires. These are now being evaluated by the Unicode Technical Committee, of Unicode Worldwide Character Standard and the International Standards Organization, JTC1/SC2/WG2. Of interest is the fact that the syllabic system also appears to have been adapted for use among the Hua Miao in China.

In 1912, Canadian federal government policy made English and, in some cases, French the language of instruction. Forced acculturation of aboriginal children was attempted. The main instruments of this policy were the residential schools run by Christian missionaries that were founded prior to the twentieth-century. At the same time, practical concerns made imperative the continued use of Native languages for official publications for hunting and public health purposes and devotional works in Native languages continued to appear throughout the twentieth-century. The last residential schools were closed in the 1960s.

The Rare Book Collection also holds many pictorial materials related to Native people, including illustrations in such landmark books as Theodor de Bry's *Grands voyages* (Frankfort on Main: 1590-1630); Samuel de Champlain, *Voyages* (Paris: 1613); James Cook, *A Voyage to the Pacific Ocean ... in the Northern Hemisphere* (London: 1784); Edward King Kingsborough, *Antiquities of Mexico* (London: 1831-1848); Thomas L. McKenney, *History of the Indian Tribes of North America* (Philadelphia: 1836-1844); and Edward S. Curtis, *The North American Indian* (Cambridge: 1907-1930). [See: "First Contact and Lasting Impressions," *National Library News* (National Library of Canada), vol. 25, no. 10-11 (Oct.-Nov. 1993), p. 9-11.]

The National Library's Official Publications collection is rich in materials related to the First Nations. Among its extensive holdings, which include original antiquarian and modern French, British and American documents, are Clive Parry (editor), *The Consolidated Treaty Series* ([1648-1919/20], 1969-1981), in 231 volumes, with: Clive Parry, et al. (editors), *Index-Guide to Treaties: Based on the Consolidated Treaty Series* (1979-1986). See also the Canadian Indian Rights Collection.

II. Canadian Indian Rights Collection (National Library of Canada, Reference and Information Services Division; contact: Sandra Bell).

Address: Reference and Information Services Division, National Library of Canada, 395 Wellington Street, Ottawa, ON, Canada, K1A 0N4.
Tel.: (613) 943-1119 (Sandra Bell).
Founded: 1969.
Areas of specialization: Rights of Canadian Aboriginal peoples, land claims, social and economic conditions.
Access: The collection is available to researchers, Monday to Friday, 8:30 a.m. to 5:00 p.m.
References: *Indian Claims in Canada: An Introductory Essay and Selected List of Library Holdings = Revendications des Indiens au Canada: un exposé préliminaire et une sélection d'ouvrages disponibles en Bibliothèque* (Ottawa: 1975); *Indian Claims in Canada: Supplementary Bibliography = Revendications des Indiens au Canada: bibliographie supplémentaire* (Ottawa: 1979); "Indians, Indians, Indians"—typescript bibliography, ca. 1979, that provides subject access to the published, more selective, bibliography titled *Aboriginal People: A Selected Bibliography Concerning Canada's First People* (Ottawa: 1973); "Unpublished Materials Sent to the National Library of Canada,"—typescript, 1972, provides subject access to *A Canadian Indian Bibliography 1960-1970* (Toronto: 1974). Also see Clive Parry, et al. (editors), *Index-Guide to Treaties: Based on the Consolidated Treaty Series* (Dobbs Ferry, N.Y.: 1979-1986), 12 v.

Description

The Canadian Indian Rights Collection was founded in 1969 by the Canadian Indian Claims Commission. That commission became, in 1977, the Canadian Indian Rights Commission. The latter was dissolved in January 1979, and on February 1, 1979, the resource collection was transferred to the National Library of Canada. Two small collections, the Whiteside Collection and the Canadian Bibliography Collection, have since been housed with the Canadian Indian Rights Collection.

The Canadian Indian Rights special collection consists of three separate uncataloged collections with strengths in published and unpublished materials from the 1960s and 1970s. More recently published documents related to Canadian Aboriginal rights are part of the National Library's general and official publications collections. The three collections are:

• Canadian Indian Rights Collection—transferred from the Indian Rights Commission, it contains historical, legal and socio-economic documentation published before 1979 and relevant to Aboriginal land claims as well as comparative materials for the United States, Australia and New Zealand.
• The Don Whiteside Collection—approximately 3,800 articles and reports published in the 1960s and the early 1970s covering all aspects of Native societies are listed in Don Whiteside, *Aboriginal People: A Selected Bibliography Concerning Canada's First People* (Ottawa: 1973).

- Canadian Indian Bibliography Collection—contains 183 unpublished articles and reports concerning Native social, cultural and economic issues collected by Thomas S. Abler and Sally M. Weaver for citation in *A Canadian Indian Bibliography 1960-1970* (Toronto: 1974).

Joyce M. Banks
Updated by Michel Brisebois

Ontario—Toronto

Archives of Ontario (AO)

Address: Archives of Ontario, 77 Grenville Street, Unit 300, Toronto, ON, Canada M5S 1B3.
Tel.: (416) 327-1600 (Reception); (416) 327-1582 and (416) 327-1583 (Reference); (416) 327-1552 (Special Collections); (416) 327-1551 (Sound and Moving Images); toll-free in Ontario only: (800) 668-9933.
Fax: (416) 327-1999
Internet address: http://www.gov.on.ca/MCZCR/archives/english/homepge.htm.
Public transit access: Queen's Park subway stop on the University Avenue subway line or College subway stop on the Yonge Street subway line. Access is also provided by the Bay Street bus or the College Street streetcar.
Parking: Public parking in the area is minimal. It is recommended that visitors use public transit for convenience.
Founded: 1903.
Major resources: The archival records of Ontario, including official records of the government of Ontario and also private papers.
Areas of specialization: Records of Ontario; Native people; the papers of the Multicultural History Society of Ontario.
Archives/manuscripts: In addition to official records of Ontario, the Archives holds private papers and also some oral histories. Archival resources pertinent to Native people include the A.E. Williams/United Bands of the Chippewas and the Missisauga papers; this recent AO acquisition is an important resource of its kind. Also pertinent to Native people are the Sir Aemilius Irving papers, the Soloman Y. Chesley papers and many others. The very extensive Multicultural History Society of Ontario papers are among AO holdings.
Visual/audio resources: Most photographs are kept in Special Collections. The Archives of Ontario photographic collection contains many images of, or pertaining to, Native people of Ontario. Some of these are cited in the guide compiled by James Morrison. Notewothy among photographic holdings are the John Boyd collection, the Duncan Campbell Scott collection and the Bishop Alexander Dewdney collection. Also part of AO Special Collections are maps and drawings. Sound recordings are housed in the Sound and Moving Images Reading Room—open by appointment only.

Access: Open to the public, with limitations based on the Ontario Freedom of Information and Protection of Privacy Act for government records and donor restrictions for private papers. It is advisable, but not mandatory, to call before visiting.

Guides/catalogs: Barbara L. Craig and Richard W. Ramsey (editors), *Guide to the Holdings of the Archives of Ontario* (Toronto: 1985), 2 v.; James Morrison, *Aboriginal Peoples in the Archives: A Guide to Sources in the Archives of Ontario = Les peuples autochrones dans les archives: un guide des sources aux Archives de l'Ontario* (Toronto: 1992) (= *Archives of Ontario: Thematic Guide = Archives de l'Ontario: guide thèmatique*, vol. 1).

Other resources available to facilitate access to cultural documentation at the AO are the printed guides to the Multicultural History Society of Ontario materials. These include Nick G. Forte (compiler), *A Guide to the Collections of the Multicultural History Society of Ontario* (Toronto: 1992); Andrew Gregorovich (compiler) and Gabriele Scardellato (editor), *A Bibliography of Canada's Peoples. Supplement 1, 1972-1979* (Toronto: 1993); Andrew Gregorovich, *Canadian Ethnic Groups Bibliography: Selected Bibliography of Ethno-Cultural Groups in Canada and the Province of Ontario* (Toronto: 1972).

Description

Researchers may refer to James Morrison's detailed guide for information on many of the extensive archival resources concerning Native people—especially of the Ontario region—held at the Archives of Ontario. Morrison's guide is no longer in-print, although the Archives will provide a digital copy, without charge, to readers who send or bring a formatted 3.5″ diskette.

The extensive papers of the Multicultural History Society of Ontario (MHSO)—collected by the Society between 1976 and 1983—consist of some 508 linear feet of textual material, both originals and copy loans; 1,446 reels of microfilm; and more than 61,228 photographic images that document the social, intellectual, political, economic, religious and cultural life of Ontario's ethnocultural communities. The MHSO papers are described in a 36 volume finding aid.

Series nos. 1 through 53 of the MHSO papers consist of photographic records of Canadian peoples, arranged by ethnic or cultural group. The photographs are listed and described in a six-volume finding aid that is available for reference consultation at AO.

MHSO textual materials include documentation on numerous ethnic groups of Canada. Peoples of European origin are well represented: Polish Canadian, Lithuanian Canadian, Ukrainian Canadian, Dutch Canadian, German Canadian, Finnish Canadian and multicultural are among the many groups represented.

Information provided by the Archives of Ontario.

Royal Ontario Museum (ROM). **Libraries**
Musée royal de l'Ontario (MrO). **Bibliothèques**

Address: Libraries, Royal Ontario Museum, 100 Queen's Park, Toronto, ON, Canada M5S 2C6.

Location: The ROM Main Library is on the first floor of the Museum building. Enter by the main doors of the Museum. The H.H. Mu Far Eastern Library is on the sixth floor of the ROM Curatorial Centre. Entry is through the staff entrance of the Museum (south side, between the Planetarium and the Main Building). Sign-in through security is required for access to the H.H. Mu Library.

Tel.: (416) 586-5595 (ROM Library and Information Centre); (416) 586-5718 (H.H. Mu Far Eastern Library).

Fax: (416) 586-5863 (ROM Library and Information Centre); (416) 586-8093 (H.H. Mu Far Eastern Library).

Internet address: http://www.rom.on.ca/library.

Internet access to on-line catalog: To access UTCat, telnet to vax.library.utoronto

Networks, consortia: ROM Library holdings are included in the University of Toronto on-line catalog, UTCat.

Founded: 1912 (founding of the Royal Ontario Museum). The Royal Ontario Museum incorporates the collections of the former Royal Ontario Museum of Archaeology (ROMA) (1912-1957). The H.H. Mu Far Eastern Library (Bibliothèque H.H. Mu de l'Extrême-Orient) was established in 1937.

Major resources: ROM Library and Information Centre; H.H. Mu Far Eastern Library.

Areas of specialization: Ethnology, archaeology, palaeontology, Canadiana, decorative arts (ROM Library and Information Centre); Asian and Far Eastern archaeology and decorative arts (H.H. Mu Far Eastern Library). The H.H. Mu Far Eastern Library is also the service point for the ROM's library collections for the art and archaeology of Egypt and western Asia and for world textiles.

Archives/manuscripts: Archaeological archives are kept in several ROM curatorial departments.

Holdings: Ca. 160,000 v. (ROM Library and Information Centre); ca. 40,000 v. (H.H. Mu Far Eastern Library).

Visual/audio resources: In various locations.

Access: The library is open to the public. Library collections are non-circulating and decentralized. Hours of both libraries are Monday to Friday, 10:00 a.m. to 4:30 p.m. Access to original archaeological records in the ROM curatorial departments is limited.

References: Betty Kingston, "The Far Eastern Library: A Treasure-House of Books from the 1600s to the Present," *Canadian Collector* (Toronto), vol. 17, no. 4 (Jul.-Aug. 1982), p. 80-82.

Artifacts of anthropological significance: Many archaeological and artifact collections are held by the museum.

Information provided by Jack Howard.

University of Toronto. Department of Anthropology. Archives

Address: Department of Anthropology, University of Toronto, Room 571, 100 St. George Street, Toronto, ON, Canada M5S 1A1.
Tel.: (416) 978-6293
Fax: (416) 978-3217
Internet address (U.T. Department of Anthropology): http://www.chass.utoronto.ca:8080/anthropology.
Archives/manuscripts: Archaeological and other papers and fieldnotes of some former faculty of the Department of Anthropology. Papers of some other former faculty of the Department of Anthropology are in University Archives [see the following entry].

Information provided by John Reid.

University of Toronto. Libraries

Address: John P. Robarts Research Library, University of Toronto, 130 St. George Street, Toronto, ON, Canada M5S 1A5.
Tel.: (416) 978-2294 (John P. Robarts Library); (416) 978-4356 (Anthropology Bibliographer); (416) 978-6215 (Robarts Library Reference); (416) 978-5285 (Thomas Fisher Rare Book Library); (416) 978-5344 (University Archives). The Robarts Library has a "First Stop" telephone information line (for catalog information, etc.): (416) 978-8450.
Fax: (416) 978-1608 (Robarts Library Access and Information Department); (416) 978-1667 (Thomas Fisher Rare Book Library); (416) 978-1667 (University Archives).
Internet address: http://library.utoronto.ca.
Internet access to on-line catalog (UTCat): http://eir.library.utoronto.ca/eir/index.cfm.
Networks, consortia: UTCat.
Public transit access: Subway: St. George stop on the Bloor line.
Founded: 1891.
Major resources: Robarts Research Library; Thomas Fisher Rare Book Library; University Archives.
Areas of specialization: The Robarts Library has substantial book and journal holdings pertaining to the Native peoples of Canada and Native Americans; these are shelved with general holdings in the library—not as a separate collection. Fisher Rare Book Library holdings include the Sheldon Australiana Collection—named for collector William L. Sheldon. This collection consists of many nineteenth-century printed accounts of exploration and travel in the Pacific and Australia and also early works on the indigenous people of Australia. Fisher Library holdings also include the Charles Darwin Collection; the Hannah Collection on the History of Medicine and Related Sciences; Oriental rare books; and the Victorian Natural History Collection.
Archives/manuscripts: Papers of three former UT Department of Anthropology faculty are in University Archives. These are T.F. McIlwraith (social/cultural anthropology—Northwest Coast); R.W. Dunning (social/cultural anthropology—northern Ojibwa); and W.J. Samarin (sociolinguistics—Central Africa). Papers of some other former UT faculty are in the

Department of Anthropology Archives [see the preceding entry]. The papers of other former UT faculty who worked through the Royal Ontario Museum may have been deposited there [see the entry on the Royal Ontario Museum].

Access: Robarts Library Reference Department and Micro Texts are open to the public; Robarts Library stacks are for the use of registered readers only. Fisher Rare Book Library is open to the public.

Guides/catalogs: Nora Teresa Corley, *Resources for Native Peoples Studies* (Ottawa: 1984) (= *Research Collections in Canadian Libraries*, vol. 9), p. 135-137.

Information provided by Robin Healey.

Victoria University. E.J. Pratt Library

Address: E.J. Pratt Library, Victoria University, 73 Queen's Park Crescent, Toronto, ON, Canada M5S 1K7.
Tel.: (416) 585-4470
Fax: (416) 585-4591
Internet address: http://128.100.124.81:80/library/pratt.htm.
Networks, consortia: ISM (Information Systems Management Corporation), UTCat.
Founded: 1843.
Major resources: Manuscripts, fieldnotes, books, pamphlets in Special Collections.
Areas of specialization: Several manuscript and archival collections are important resources for the historical study of the culture, religion, language and folklore of indigenous peoples of Canada. These collections were formed by A.P. Coleman, James Evans, Peter Jones and John Maclean.
Fieldnotes, etc.: The fieldnotes of A.P. Coleman were written between 1888-1938, during his travels in Canada and throughout the world. These resources are listed in the *Guide to the Canadian Manuscript Collections in Victoria University Library* and also in Lila and Raymond Laakso, *A.P. Coleman: Geologist 1852-1939: Science, Art and Discovery: An Exhibition in the E.J. Pratt Library* (Toronto: 1994).
Holdings: The John Maclean collection of books and pamphlets (330 v. and 253 pamphlets); the A.P. Coleman collection (10 m.); the James Evans collection (88 cm.); the Peter Jones collection (1 m.); the John Maclean collection (7.5 m.).
Access: Scholars and general readers with identification may use research materials housed in Special Collections. Materials must be used in the library.
Reference: *Guide to the Canadian Manuscript Collections in Victoria University Library* (Toronto: 1988).

Description

Among the special collections housed in the E.J. Pratt Library of Victoria University in Toronto are four collections of anthropological interest.

The A.P. Coleman collection, so named for Arthur Philemon Coleman (1852-1939), is significant for the field notebooks and personal notebooks that he kept during his geological expeditions and individual journeys, in Canada and worldwide, between 1867 and 1938. Coleman, who can be variously described as a geologist, naturalist, artist and photographer, was Professor of Geology, initially at Victoria College (later Victoria University) in Cobourg, Ontario, then with the University of Toronto following the federation of Victoria University with the University of Toronto in 1891. Coleman was also Dean of the Faculty of Arts and the first Director of the Royal Ontario Museum of Geology.

The field notebooks cover a vast range of territory, most significantly the Canadian Rockies, central and eastern Canada, parts of Central and South America and Europe. These notebooks are fascinating records of Coleman's geological observations and include detailed reporting of flora and fauna and encounters with various individuals, notably indigenous peoples. The personal notebooks (dated from 1867 through 1888) record Coleman's touring of such locales as Lapland, Italy and Scandinavia and time spent as a student in Germany, with accounts of the people in these places.

James Evans (1801-1846), a Methodist minister, emigrated from England in 1822 and, after a few years in Canada, began to teach at an Indian School established by the Methodist Missionary Society. During his years as a missionary amongst Ojibwa and Cree, Evans developed a Cree written language system based on syllabic, rather than alphabetic, symbols. In 1837, he published his *Speller and Interpreter in Indian and English.*

The James Evans collection is cited for its manuscripts on the Cree language, as well as for the copies of Evans's *Cree Syllabic Handbook*, printed by him with handmade printing materials—the first book to be printed in the Canadian West. Within the category of personal material is Evans's diary—significant for its notes on Native peoples and languages. Other Evans collection materials include examples of biblical literature and hymns translated from English into Cree syllabics. The James Evans collection came to Victoria University Library through a variety of sources: from the family of Ephraim Evans, brother of James Evans; from the family of the late Egerton R. Young, who succeeded Evans at a western mission in Manitoba; from the University of Western Ontario; and from John Maclean, whose collection of books and pamphlets is described below.

Peter Jones (1802-1856), whose Ojibwa name was Kahkewaquonaby (Sacred Feathers), was born to an Ojibwa mother and a Welsh father and spent his early life with the Missisauga tribe of the Ojibwa nation, as well as among the Mohawk on the Grand River in Ontario. Jones was baptized and later worked as a Methodist missionary among the Ojibwa—the first Canadian Native to do so. Jones was also the first Canadian Native to keep a journal of his travels as a missionary and, with his brother John, was the first translator of biblical literature into such native languages as Ojibwa and Chippewa.

The Peter Jones collection is noted for the literary manuscripts of Jones's publications, *History of the Ojebway Indians,* for his autobiographical accounts of his childhood, his family and native community. The manuscripts also contain accounts of Jones's work as a missionary among the Ojibwa and contain his translations of Ojibwa and English hymns. Diaries and the journal kept by Jones include notes and anecdotes on North American Native people and—as they describe his childhood and missionary work—were likely sources for his later publications.

John Maclean (1851-1928), missionary and author, was an imigrant to Canada from Scotland who was educated at Victoria University in Cobourg, Ontario, (B.A., 1882, M.A., 1887) and at Wesleyan University, Bloomington, Illinois, (Ph.D., 1888). Following his ordination as a minister of the Methodist Church, in 1880, he served as a missionary among the Blood Indians near Macleod, Alberta, from 1880-1889. In addition to serving as a Methodist minister at various places in the Canadian West in the years following 1889, Maclean studied Aboriginal culture, lecturing frequently on the Indian tribes of Canada and wrote numerous books on the history of Methodism, western Canada and Aboriginal people.

The John Maclean papers held in the United Church Archives, Victoria University, consists of correspondence, diaries and notebooks, manuscripts, typescripts and notes of histories for his addresses and publications on the manners, customs, languages, politics and folklore of Native people in Canada. A finding aid is available to assist the user in accessing the Maclean papers.

The John Maclean collection of books and pamphlets held at the Pratt Library comprises publications by Maclean and others—primarily on the subjects of culture, religion, folklore and languages of North American Native people. A shelflist of titles within this collection is available for consultation.

Further details on resources and information on the organization of manuscript material in the Pratt Library can be found in the *Guide to Canadian Manuscript Collections in Victoria University Library* and also in individual finding aids, the records of which can be accessed through UTCat, the University of Toronto's on-line library catalog. Manuscript holdings are not entered into UTCat.

Lisa Sherlock

Québec—Hull

Canadian Museum of Civilization (CMC). **Information Management Services**
Musée canadien des Civilisations (McC). **Division des Services de Gestion de l'Information**

Address: Information Management Services, Canadian Museum of Civilization, 100 Laurier Street, P.O. Box 3100, Station B, Hull, PQ, Canada J8X 4H2.
Tel.: (819) 776-7173 (Reference); (819) 776-8431 (Archives); (819) 776-8175 (Information Access Services-Photo Archives).
Fax: (819) 776-8491
E-mail (Library): biblio@cmcc.muse.digital.ca.
Internet address (Canadian Museum of Civilization): http://www.cmcc.muse.digital.ca/cmc/cmceng/welcmeng.html.
Networks, consortia: ISM (Information Systems Management Corporation).
Public transit access: OC Transpo bus, route 8; also many bus lines from the Outaouais area.
Parking: Available at the museum (fee); also some metered parking in the vicinity.

Founded: 1842 (beginning of the Geological Survey of Canada). The museum was known as the National Museum of Man from 1967 to 1987.

Major resources: Document Collection; Audio and Visual Collections; Library collection.

Areas of specialization: Archaeology, ethnology, folk culture and social history of Canada. The Library's collection has been identified as a national resource in anthropology by the National Library of Canada.

Archives/manuscripts: Ca. 800 linear meters of archival materials are held. Included are fieldnotes, research reports, correspondence, maps and charts, etc.

Fieldnotes, papers, etc.: The Document Collection has original fieldnotes, etc., that have been filed on a continuous basis since 1910. A list of the authors of these fieldnotes and of allied unpublished materials is available on the premises. Background information is available in the respective finding aids. There is no published or unpublished catalog of fieldnotes.

Holdings: 50,000 monographs, 40,000 periodical volumes, pamphlets, photographic images, sound recordings.

Visual/audio resources: 550,000 photographic images, 7,000 videos and films, 15,000 hours of recorded sound. Holdings include the Harlan I. Smith (1872-1940) film collection and others. Some of the oral history recordings at CMC are listed in the guide compiled by Normand Fortier.

Access: Library materials may be used by scholars and general readers. No direct loans. Some archival documents are restricted.

Guides/catalogs: An unpublished guide to archival records concerning Native people of Canada is Bennett McCardle, *Archival Records Relating to Native People in the National Archives of Canada, the National Library and the National Museum of Man: A Thematic Guide* (Hull: 1985). Normand Fortier, *Guide to Oral History Collections in Canada = Guide des fonds d'histoire orale au Canada* ([Ottawa?]: 1993) (= *Canadian Oral History Association = Société canadienne d'Histoire orale. Journal*, vol. 13), p. 1-11; Linda Riley (editor), *Marius Barbeau's Photographic Collection: The Nass River* (Ottawa: 1988) (= *Canadian Museum of Civilization. Mercury Series, Canadian Ethnology Service, Paper* no. 109); various other guides and catalogs.

Artifact resources in related collections: The Canadian Museum of Civilization has a material culture collection of more than 300,000 artifacts and 2.5 million archaeological specimens related chiefly, but not exclusively, to Canada. This collection is curated by four research divisions in the fields of Human History, Ethnology, Folk Culture and New World Archaeology.

Archaeological sites represented by artifact collections: The Museum has major artifact collections from all provinces and territories of Canada. All major or significant sites of Canada are represented in the collections accessioned from the early 1900s to the present.

Published catalogs of artifacts and exhibits: Marius Barbeau, *Totem Poles* (Hull, Québec: 1950) (= *National Museum of Canada. Bulletin*, 119; *Anthropological Series*, no. 30), 2 v.; George F. MacDonald, *Haida Art* (Seattle: 1996); Judy Thompson, *From the Land: Two Hundred Years of Dene Clothing* (Hull, Québec: 1994); others.

Description

It is difficult to date the beginnings of the Canadian Museum of Civilization Library. In 1842 the Geological Survey of Canada was set up in Montréal. Its first director, William Logan, in addition to being a geologist, was also a collector. He began to accumulate specimens of Canadian flora and fauna as well as rocks and fossils. Some of the early field geologists, such as G.M. Dawson and Robert Bell, brought back items from Native cultures of the day and artifacts of earlier cultures that they unearthed.

These collections became part of the Geological Survey's museum, which in 1911 found a new home in the nation's capital at the Victoria Memorial Museum. The library for the Geological Survey was created over the years through donations, exchanges with other institutions and by internal acquisition. In 1927 the National Museum of Canada was established, and in the course of the next several decades it was placed in several different government departments. In 1967 the National Museum of Man emerged as the museum for human history and anthropology.

In 1987 the museum's name was changed from National Museum of Man to Canadian Museum of Civilization, to better reflect the collections and research regarding Canada's Aboriginal and immigrant people and folk arts and crafts. A new building for the museum was completed in 1989 in Hull, Québec, and staff and the library moved gradually into the new quarters.

The library's collection consists of printed material on the prehistory, culture and material culture of Canada's Aboriginal peoples and the history and material culture of immigrants to the country. The National Library of Canada designated the CMC library as a national resource in anthropology, and as such it is heavily used not only by the museum's researchers and staff, but also by students and researchers from other institutions, as well as the visiting public.

Subject vertical files on various topics pertaining to museum exhibits and interests are maintained in the library. The "Native Artists" file includes information on contemporary Native artists of Canada whose work is included in the museum's collections.

The Document Collection section of the library holds the archives of museum research conducted since 1910 that relates to the archaeology, linguistics, ethnology, anthropology, physical anthropology and human history of Natives and non-Natives in Canada.

The Audio and Visual Collections section is responsible for three separate collections: the Still Photography Collection, the Audio Collection and the Moving Picture Collection. The expanding content of the collections is almost exclusively the result of the endeavor of the staff in these disciplines.

The Still Photography Collection contains more than 670,000 images, the earliest of which date from the 1870s. The material in this collection consists of black-and-white negatives, color negatives and color slides and transparencies. The subject areas covered by the disciplines listed above fall into three categories: historical photos (field work photos); artifact photos (images that document the artifact collection); and event photos (images that document the life of the museum, its exhibitions, buildings, staff and major events).

The Audio Collection contains more than 15,000 hours of recorded sound. The earliest material in this collection dates from the late 1800s and is of interest in museological terms. There are examples of early recording technology such as wax cylinders, as well as magnetic tape and the latest in digital technology. Unlike the Still Photography Collection, the Audio Collection is exclusively the result of the field researchers' activities.

The Moving Picture Collection is not quite as old—although it does contain material dating from the 1920s. The material consists of film (in both positive and negative formats) as well as more contemporary media such as videotape. The films depict both historical and contemporary fieldwork as well as artifact-based research. Included are films of Aboriginal and cultural delegations examining and explaining the various historical and manufacturing details of the collections and films documenting major activities that occur in and around the museum.

Christine Midwinter

Indian and Northern Affairs Canada (INAC). **Claims and Historical Research Centre Affaires Indiennes et du Nord Canada** (MAINC). **Centre de la Recherche historique et de l'Étude des Revendications**

Address (mailing): Claims and Historical Research Centre, Indian and Northern Affairs Canada, Terrasses de la Chaudière, Ottawa, ON, Canada K1A OH4.
Location: Claims and Historical Research Center, Indian and Northern Affairs Canada, Terrasses de la Chaudière, Room 1319, 10 Wellington Street, Hull, PQ, Canada.
Tel.: (819) 994-1182 (John Leslie); (819) 997-8157 (Michelle Pelletier).
Fax: (819) 997-9873
Internet address (Indian and Northern Affairs Canada): http://www.inac.gc.ca/index.html.
Public transit access: OC Transpo bus no. 8 to the first stop in Hull.
Founded: 1973.
Major resources: The Centre seeks to provide research assistance to government agencies, Native researchers, scholars and other researchers concerning Indian treaties, claims and related topics. The Centre also maintains a vertical file collection of working papers, documents, articles and some theses on such topics as band claims, treaties with Indians or Inuit and other aspects of Indian and Northern Affairs. See the unpublished "Survey of Documents = Répertoire des documents" [revised ed., 1993], listed below under "Guides/catalogs."
Areas of specialization: Indians and Inuit of Canada; Indian or Inuit land claims; treaties; legislation; departmental history.
Archives/manuscripts: Access is provided, when available, to records of the Department of Indian and Northern Affairs. Centre staff may also refer researchers to other archival and manuscript resources—including those of the nearby National Archives of Canada, the National Library of Canada or the library and archives of the Canadian Museum of Civilization.
Access: Open to the public for research use. A researcher working on behalf of an Indian or Inuit group should have a letter of introduction or BCR authorizing that person to conduct research and to have access to departmental files pertaining to the band's business.

Researchers should also give prior notice of their arrival (preferably two weeks) and sufficient information on the nature and scope of their proposed research to enable all relevant matter to be located. Enquiries should be directed to John Leslie or Michelle Pelletier at the Claims and Historical Research Centre—telephone numbers listed above.

References: Canada, *Indian Treaties and Surrenders From 1680 to 1890* (Ottawa: 1905-1912), 3 v.

Guides/catalogs: Indian and Northern Affairs Canada. Claims and Historical Research Centre, *Survey of Documents = Répertoire des documents* (Ottawa: 1990, revised 1997); Bennett Ellen McCardle, "Archival Records Relating to Native People in the National Archives of Canada, the National Library and the National Museum of Man: A Thematic Guide," [Hull: 1985; also, an updated 1991 version]. This unpublished guide—ca. 1,000 pages in length—is available in digital form. [A copy of the updated 1991 text may be obtained on diskette in WordPerfect format from Claims and Historical Research Centre, Indian and Northern Affairs Canada, Terrasses de la Chaudière, Ottawa, Ontario, Canada K1A OH4]; Bennett Ellen McCardle, *Indian History and Claims: A Research Handbook* ([Ottawa]: 1982), 2 v.

Description

Claims and Historical Research Centre staff are available as resource people should researchers or a band or research organization need their assistance. The Centre staff will provide counsel on likely research sources and archival finding aids; the examination of available departmental files and documents; and advice on specific historical or claims situations. The Centre provides similar services to the Department, other government departments and agencies, university faculty and the staff and students of Native Studies programs.

Centre staff and their areas of specialization are as follows:

- John Leslie, Chief, tel. (819) 994-1182. Indian treaty activity in Ontario; historical situations in the Province of Québec; Indian border-crossing issues; departmental history; Indian Act legislation.
- Dennis Madill, Research Advisor, tel. (819) 997-8155. Indian treaty activity in British Columbia; historical situations in British Columbia, Yukon and the Northwest Territories, Méis history and claims.
- Michelle Pelletier, Historical Research Assistant, tel. (819) 997-8157. General historical research and facilitation.

John Leslie

Indian and Northern Affairs Canada (INAC). **Departmental Library**
Affaires indiennes et du Nord Canada (MAINC). **Bibliothèque ministérielle**

Address (mailing): Departmental Library, Department of Indian Affairs and Northern Development Canada, Ottawa, ON, Canada K1A OH4.

Location: Departmental Library, Indian and Northern Affairs Canada, 14th Floor, Terrasses de la Chaudière, 10 Wellington Street, Hull, PQ, Canada.

Tel.: (819) 997-0811

Fax: (819) 953-5491

Internet address (Indian and Northern Affairs Canada):http://www.inac.gc.ca/index.html. The Departmental Library's database is available through the website of the Department of Indian and Northern Affairs.

Public transit access: OC Transpo bus no. 8 to the first stop in Hull.

Founded: 1966.

Major resources: Books, rare books, periodicals, documents, CD-ROMs concerning Native peoples of Canada. The CD-ROMs in the library include: *Wenger Anthropological Eskimo Database* (WADE) (Alaska and Polar Regions Department, Elmer E. Rasmuson Library, University of Alaska, Fairbanks, Alaska); *PolarPac* (Fairbanks, Alaska); *Arctic and Antarctic Regions* (Baltimore: 1995).

Areas of specialization: Documentation on Aboriginal peoples in Canada, including the Canadian North.

Holdings: 42,000 book and journal titles; 900 current periodical subscriptions; 4,000 rare books; 200 commercial videos on Aboriginal themes. A microfilm copy of the department's archival Indian Affairs administration files is available on site (the originals are at the National Archives of Canada). An excellent collection of Canadian Aboriginal and Northern magazines (including many that are no longer published) is held by the library.

Video/audio resources: No photo or audio collections are maintained.

Access: The library is open to researchers and the general public. Many items in the collection are available for interlibrary loan. However, external clients must return to their home institutions to arrange these loans.

References: Indian and Northern Affairs Canada, *Schedule of Indian Bands, Reserves and Settlements Including—Membership and Population Location and Area in Hectares = Répertoire des bandes réserves et établissements Indiens—effectif population location et superficie en hectares* (Ottawa: 1992).

Description

The Department of Indian Affairs and Northern Development has a long and varied history. Its predecessor, the British Indian Office, was created in 1755. Since Confederation in 1867, responsibility for Indian Affairs and Northern Affairs has been handled by a number of government departments. The Department of Indian Affairs and Northern Development was created in 1966.

The mandate of the department is as follows:

- Fulfills the lawful obligations of the Canadian federal government to Aboriginal peoples arising from treaties, the Indian Act and other legislation.
- Administers Indian reserve lands and elections of band councils, registers entitlement to Indian status and band membership and administers band funds.
- Provides for the delivery of basic services (such as education, social assistance, housing and community infrastructure) to Indian and Inuit communities.
- Negotiates the settlement of accepted claims relating to Aboriginal title or to past non-fulfillment of government obligations.
- Supports ongoing constitutional development regarding, among other matters, the definition of rights of Aboriginal peoples in Canada.
- Provides transfer payments to the governments of the Yukon and the Northwest Territories to assist them in providing services to territorial residents.
- Supports balanced development of the North through management of natural resources, protection and management of the environment, fostering of economic and employment opportunities for Northerners and funding of social and cultural programs.
- Fosters political development of the two northern territories and coordinates federal policies and programming for the North.

The Departmental Library is an excellent source of information on the department's history and on the evolution of its relations with Aboriginal peoples in Canada and the Canadian North. The Library's collection supports the mandate of the department, changing as the department's work changes. The subject coverage includes Aboriginal history, land use patterns, legal and constitutional issues, economic development, environment assessment and protection.

Julia Finn

Indian and Northern Affairs Canada (INAC). **Indian Lands Registry**
Affaires indiennes et du Nord Canada (MAINC). **Documents et Systèmes du Registre des Terres indiennes**

Address (mailing): Indian Lands Registry, Reserves and Trusts, 17th Floor, Indian and Inuit Affairs Program, Indian and Northern Affairs Canada, Ottawa, ON, K1A OH4 Canada.
Location: Indian and Northern Affairs Canada, 17th Floor, Terrasses de la Chaudière, 10 Wellington Street, Hull, PQ, Canada.
Tel.: (819) 994-3666
Fax: (819) 997-6882
Public transit access: OC Transpo bus no. 8 to the first stop in Hull.
Founded: 1968.
Major resources: This unit of Indian and Northern Affairs Canada maintains the official registers of Indian land ownership in all provinces of Canada.

Archives/manuscripts: Reserve Land Register; Surrendered Land Leasing Register; Surrendered Land Sales Register; Crown Lands Register; Provincial General Register; Canada General Register; Reserve General Register. The Indian Lands Registry also has copies of historical and current surveys and maps of reserve lands. The original records of Indian land ownership have been electronically scanned and are now fully available in CD-ROM format.

Visual/audio resources: The Indian Lands Registry holds hard copy as well as microfiche versions of land maps for all regions of Canada.

Access: Open to the public—it is not necessary to call in advance of a visit. CD-ROM copies of the lands registry documents are available in Hull at the Indian Lands Registry. CD-ROM copies have also been provided to the thirty Canadian Native bands to which the respective land records pertain. It should be noted, however, that records of Inuit land holdings in Canada are not held by the Indian Lands Registry.

Information provided by Jacques Desroches.

Indian and Northern Affairs Canada (INAC). **Inuit Art Section**
Affaires indiennes et du Nord Canada (MAINC). **Section de l'Art inuit**

Address (mailing): Inuit Art Section, Suite 925, Terrasses de la Chaudière, Indian and Northern Affairs Canada, Ottawa, ON, Canada K1A OH4.

Location: Inuit Art Section, Indian and Northern Affairs Canada, Suite 925, Terrasses de la Chaudière, 10 Wellington Street, Hull, PQ, Canada.

Tel.: (819) 997-8311 or (800) 867-1685.

Fax: (819) 994-0106

Public transit access: OC Transpo bus no. 8 to the first stop in Hull.

Founded: About 1973.

Major resources: Library, subject and artist files on contemporary Inuit art.

Areas of specialization: Contemporary Inuit art.

Archives/manuscripts: None.

Holdings (books and journals): About 5,000 volumes on Inuit art; the library includes all available English- and French-language publications on this subject.

Visual/audio resources: More than 120,000 slides and 100,000 photographs that depict or document Inuit art.

Access: Open to the public by appointment.

References: *Biographies of Canadian Inuit Artists* (Ottawa: 1984)—pamphlet; *Canadian Inuit Sculpture* (Ottawa: 1993)—pamphlet; *Carvings from Arctic Canada* (Ottawa: 1993)—pamphlet; *Inuit Art Bibliography* (Ottawa: 1995)—pamphlet; *Inuit Art Section* (Ottawa: 1993)—pamphlet.

Description

The mission of the Inuit Art Section, Indian and Northern Affairs Canada, is to support and promote Inuit art in order to ensure its long-term stability as an art form and as an economic activity. The Inuit Art Section manages a library of books, periodicals, exhibition catalogs, as well as subject and artist files, on the topic of contemporary Canadian Inuit art, with small collections of material on the art of other circumpolar peoples and the Dorset and Thule cultures.

The Section manages a database of biographical material on more than 4,000 contemporary Inuit artists and portraits of artists. It provides reference and information services on Inuit art and culture and also distributes publications on Inuit art. The Section also supports exhibitions of Inuit art by providing free editorial and photographic services and buys exhibition catalogs for distribution.

Jeanne L. L'Espérance
Information provided by Joanne Logan.

Québec—Montréal

McGill University. Department of Anthropology

Address: Department of Anthropology, McGill University, 855 Sherbrooke Street West, Montréal, PQ, Canada H3A 2T7.
Tel.: (514) 398-4300 (reception)
Fax: (514) 398-7476
Internet address: http://www.arts.mcgill.ca/programs/anthro.
Archives/manuscripts: Original fieldnotes, papers and other documentation produced by departmental faculty are generally retained by the individual researchers.
Artifacts of anthropological interest: Many artifacts are curated in McGill University's Archaeology Research Laboratory or the Redpath Museum.

McGill University. McCord Museum
McGill University. Musée McCord

Address: McCord Museum, 690 Sherbrooke St. West, Montréal, PQ, Canada H3A 1E9.
Tel.: (514) 398-7100
Fax: (514) 398-5045
E-mail (Notman Photographic Archives): nora@mccord.can.mcgill.ca.
Internet address: http://www.mccord-museum.qc.ca.
Public transit access: Metro: McGill Metro station; bus #24, Sherbrooke.
Founded: 1919 (McCord Archives); 1956 (Notman Photographic Archives).
Major resources: McCord Archives; Notman Photographic Archives.
Areas of specialization: Canadian history and ethnology.

Archives/manuscripts: Ca. 300 meters of archival materials pertaining to Canadian history and ethnography. Materials concerning Native peoples of Canada are in various parts of the Archives.

Holdings (books and journals): About 5,000 volumes of books and journals of anthropological or related interest (in the Library).

Visual/audio resources: 400,000 photographic images (Notman Collection); 350,000 other photo images (Other Photographers Collection).

Access: Both the McCord Archives and the Notman Photographic Archives are open to the public by appointment. The library is presently closed due to a lack of funds. Library materials may be accessed through the collections manager.

References: Dorothy Harley Eber, *When the Whalers Were up North: Inuit Memories from the Eastern Arctic* (Kingston, Ont.: 1989); Roger Hall, Gordon Dodds and Stanley G. Triggs, *The World of William Notman: The Nineteenth-Century Through a Master Lens* (Toronto: 1993); J. Russell Harper and Stanley G. Triggs (editors), *Portrait of a Period: A Collection of Notman Photographs, 1856-1915* (Montréal: 1967); *Peter Pitseolak (1902-1973), chroniqueur Inuit de Seekooseelak: photographies et dessins du Cap Dorset, Terre de Baffin = Peter Pitseolak (1902-1973), Inuit Historian of Seekooseelak: Photographs and Drawings From Cape Dorset, Baffin Island* (Montréal: 1980)—an exhibit catalog; Peter Pitseolak and Dorothy Eber, *People from Our Side: An Eskimo Life Story in Words and Photographs* (Bloomington, Ind.: 1975); Stanley G. Triggs, *Le studio de William Notman: objectif Canada = William Notman's Studio: The Canadian Picture* ([Montréal]: 1992); Stanley G. Triggs, *William Notman: The Stamp of a Studio* (Toronto: 1985).

Guides/catalogs: McGill University. Archives, *A Guide to Archival Resources at McGill University = Guide des sources d'archives à l'Université McGill* (preliminary ed., Montréal: 1985), 3 v.

Description

Notman Photographic Archives

The Notman Photographic Archives documents, through its holdings, the history of Canada from the 1840s to today: the land, people, places, activities and events. The collection comprises more than 750,000 photographic prints, glass negatives, lantern slides, daguerreotypes and other works representing a range of photographic processes. Also in the collection are related archival documents, photographic equipment and a research library of approximately 2,000 books, pamphlets and catalogs dealing with the history of photography. At the core of the collection is the William Notman Collection of 400,000 photographs taken during a period of 78 years, richly documenting many facets of Canadian life. To this has been added the work of hundreds of photographers, both amateur and professional.

The William Notman Collection

The Notman Photographic Archives was formed in 1956, when the photographic work of William Notman (1826-1891) was donated to McGill University to be deposited in the

McCord Museum. The Notman Collection consists of more than 400,000 photographs taken by William Notman and his sons and staff between 1861 and 1935, and covers many facets of Canadian life. A partial list of subjects includes photographs of major cities and villages, street scenes, landscapes, river steamers, locomotives, railway construction, the lumber trade, Native people, farming, fishing, industries, costumes and the Victoria Bridge construction.

The major part of the Notman Collection consists of the portraits. Notman was widely respected as a portraitist and his premises were frequented by people of all walks of life. The prominent people of Montréal and visitors from abroad sought out his studio to have their likenesses committed to silver for posterity—some of them drawing on the talents of Notman's art department to render the image in color as a painted photograph. As well, Notman's door was not closed to those of lesser station; his prices were competitive with the popular market of the time. Thus in the Notman portraits there is a cross-section of Canadians and visitors to Montréal and an impressive display of his artistic skills.

What makes the Notman Collection unique among photograph collections are the records that he kept. From every negative an extra print was made and pasted in a picture book, in numerical order, and also identified underneath by name or title. More than 200 of these picture books cover the 78 years that the firm was in business. An alphabetical cross-file of each sitter was also kept in the "Index Books"—making it possible to trace and identify any Notman photograph taken in the Montréal studio.

Peter Pitseolak

Peter Pitseolak—an Inuk living with his wife and children and extended family in one of the larger camps on Baffin Island—realized that the old traditional way of life would soon pass. He began, about 1942, to document the passing customs and the change incurred by contact with the white man. Peter Pitseolak was totally unschooled in the mechanics of photography; it is therefore not surprising, working under unbelievable hardships as he did, that the technical quality of the negatives leaves much to be desired. Nevertheless, he intuitively understood the aesthetics of photography and produced hundreds of beautiful portraits of family and friends and exciting views of activities. The 1,600 negatives that survived the Arctic winters were discovered by Dorothy Eber, a researcher on Inuit art. These were purchased from the family in 1975 by the National Museums Council and have been deposited in the Notman Photographic Archives.

Other Photographic Holdings

Other major collections in the Notman Archives include the work of Alexander Henderson, a photographer who came to Montréal from Scotland in 1855. Calling himself a landscape photographer, he ranged widely throughout the province of Québec, including in his definition not only landscapes, but street scenes, city views, steamboats, Native people, etc., and pictorial records of many wilderness trips that he made with one or two companions. In 1872 he began a three-year project to document the construction of the Intercolonial Railway. This led to other railway projects, including the Canadian Pacific Railroad (CPR), and eventual employment by that company as the manager of the photography department. In those years he made several trips to western Canada. The

Notman Photographic Archives holds the largest collection of Henderson photographs and also several hundred letters and family papers dating back to 1760.

In 1882 W. Hanson Boorne—a young man of twenty-two—came to Canada from England as a prospective rancher and proficient amateur photographer. In 1886 he turned professional, establishing his business in Calgary. He concentrated on Native people, ranching and mountain scenery and documented the young towns of Calgary, Edmonton, Banff, Winnipeg and other smaller prairie settlements. The Archives was the recipient of four of his albums that he used for display in his studio. In this collection, purchased from the Boorne family in 1972, are other rare items, such as the manuscript of an article Boorne wrote for the *Calgary Herald* describing his successful attempt to photograph the Sun Dance in 1887; a journal he kept on his first voyage to Canada; an account of a trip he made to the Crow's Nest Pass, photographing ranches and mountain scenery; and a catalog of all his views available for purchase.

Charles Millar was another amateur photographer who had a passion for recording his family and friends and their immediate surroundings. A resident of Drummondville, he bought a camera from William Notman in 1888, received preliminary instructions from him, and was active in his hobby for the next twenty years. The surviving 188 5 x 8″ glass negatives were donated by his son, Leslie Millar, in 1974. As a bonus, and in accord with his father's passion for keeping the record, Leslie Millar spent many hours providing Museum staff with complete identification of the photographs and background information.

Some Additional Collections

The preceding brief descriptions of a few of the major collections demonstrate the wealth of material in the Notman Photographic Archives. The diversity of the photographic collections is also reflected in the following partial list of other photographic holdings:

- 500 hand-painted magic lantern slides, 1850s and 1860s.
- 4,000 photographic magic lantern slides.
- More than 100 daguerreotypes, ambrotypes and tintypes—some as early as 1845 and many made in the 1850s.
- Some 33 photographs of the Red River District in 1858, by Humphrey Lloyd Hime—the earliest known photographs of the Canadian plains.
- 34 William Bell Malloch collection photographs, taken between 1865 and 1895 in Moose Factory and the eastern shore of Hudson's Bay.
- Four collections of snapshot albums made by Arctic travelers.
- A large postcard collection.
- 14,000 photographs and postcards, mounted on cardboard sheets, of cities and villages in Canada—donated by the Redpath Library.
- Eight portfolios (of the twenty-portfolio set) of North American Indian photographs by Edward S. Curtis.
- Several photographs by Robert Flaherty.
- The Richard Smith collection, consisting of 189 dry plate glass negatives, showing scenes of the environs of Montréal.

- The work of many socially-conscious modern photographers documenting changing Canadian life in the 1970s and 1980s: Davis Miller, Brian Merrett, Clara Gutsche, Daniel Kazimierski, Gabor Szilasi, Ricardo Castro, Roger Charbonneau, Thaddeus Holowina, Claire Beaugrand-Champagne, David Marvin, Martin Lyons, Raymond and Blossom Caron.

McCord Museum Archives

The present McCord Museum archival collection on Canadian history originated from a personal collection, developed by David Ross McCord (1844-1930), on the history of Canada and related topics. The collection was presented to McGill University in 1921. The McCord Museum Archives today holds substantial original documentation on Canadian history and ethnography. Archival holdings concerning the Native people of Canada are significant, although not as extensive as those concerning other aspects of Canadian history. The museum's archival holdings have been described in *A Guide to Archival Resources at McGill University* (preliminary ed., Montréal: 1985).

Nora Hague
Information on the McCord Museum Archives provided by Mrs. Pamela Miller.

Québec—Québec City

National Archives of Québec. Archives Center of Québec and of Chaudière-Appalaches Archives nationales du Québec. Centre d'Archives de Québec et de Chaudière-Appalaches

Address: Centre d'Archives de Québec et de Chaudière-Appalaches, Archives nationales du Québec, 1210, avenue du Séminaire, C.P. 10450 Sainte-Foy, PQ, Canada G1V 4N1.
Tel.: (418) 643-8904
Fax: (418) 646-0868
Internet address: http://www.anq.gouv.qc.ca.
Public transit access: City bus system.
Founded: 1920; located in Sainte-Foy since 1980.
Major resources: Archives of Québec; other archival materials.
Areas of specialization: History of Québec and of Chaudière-Appalaches; Native people of Québec.
Archives/manuscripts: See below.
Visual/audio resources: About one million photographs from the Office de Film de Québec and also from some private photo collections.
Access: Open to the public.
Guides/catalogs: Rénald Lessard, *Copies d'archives d'origine française* (Québec: 1990) (= *Archives nationales du Québec. Guide*); Gilles-Eric Vachon, "Guide pour les usagers portant sur les Amerindiens,"—an unpublished finding aid (dated 1993) that is available for reference use at the archives.

Description

The Archives is located adjacent to the Laval University campus, in a building that was originally intended to serve as a Catholic seminary. Holdings include historical archives of the governments of Québec and Chaudière-Appalaches and also microfilm copies of many early documents reproduced from originals in the archives of France—see, for example, Lessard, 1990. For information on selected archival and manuscript documentation on Native people of the Québec region, see Gilles-Eric Vachon "Guide pour les usagers portant sur les Amérindiens."

Information provided by Rénald Lessard.

Laval University. Archives Division. Archives of Folklore of Laval University
Université Laval. Division des Archives. Archives de Folklore de l'Université Laval
(AFUL)

Address: Archives de Folklore, Université Laval, Pavillon Jean-Charles-Bonenfant, Cité universitaire, PQ, Canada G1K 7P4.
Location: Room 5164, Pavillon Jean-Charles-Bonenfant, Laval University.
Tel.: (418) 656-3722
Fax: (418) 656-3826
E-mail: Carole.Saulnier@sg.ulaval.ca.
Internet access to on-line catalog: Not available; a manual card catalog is in use.
Public transit access: City bus system.
Founded: 1944.
Major resources: 1,437 archival collections on the folklore of Québec and other French-speaking regions of North America, past and present.
Areas of specialization: The folklore of francophone North America, including traditional songs, stories, legends, beliefs, costume, pre-industrial technology and folk knowledge. The scope of the Archives extends geographically from Québec to Acadia, Manitoba, New England and Louisiana.
Archives/manuscripts: 140 linear meters of archives.
Visual/audio resources: 15,000 photos (black-and-white as well as color); color slides; more than 10,000 sound recordings on tape.
Access: Open for research. There are restrictions on access to some archival collections.
References: *Les Archives de Folklore* (Québec: 1946-1993) [26 numbers of this monographic series were published]; Carole Saulnier and Céline Savard, "Les Archives de Folklore de l'Université Laval: d'hier à aujourd'hui," *Cap-aux-Diamants*, no. 31 (1992), p. 30-33.
Guides/catalogs: Carole Saulnier, *Etat général des fonds et des collections des Archives de Folklore* (2nd éd., Québec: 1990) (= *Université Laval. Bureau du Secrétaire général. Division des Archives. Publication*, no. 14). Others: Jean du Berger, *Pour une histoire des études de folklore à l'Université Laval* ([Québec]: 1987); *Le catalogue de la chanson folklorique française* (Québec: 1977-1987) (= *Les Archives de Folklore*, vol. 18-23);

Normand Fortier, *Guide to Oral History Collections in Canada = Guide des fonds d'histoire orale au Canada* ([Ottawa?]: 1993) (= *Canadian Oral History Association = Société canadienne d'Histoire orale. Journal*, vol. 13), p. 256-291.

Artifacts of anthropological or related significance: 50,000 devotional objects, including many Catholic religious amulets, are held.

Description

On February 28, 1944, following a memorandum to the University Council by Mgr. Aimé Labrie, Dean of the Faculty of Letters, a Chair of Folklore and also the Archives of Folklore, under the direction of Luc Lacourcière, were officially established at Laval University.

The purpose of the Archives of Folklore is to:

A. Gather together in Québec the printed Canadian and French documentation, the original manuscript collections themselves or, at least, authentic copies of the actual documents. B. Organize investigations throughout the province, following the plan of Arnold van Gennep for similar studies in the provinces of France. In addition, a systematic classification of all of these documents will be developed. Information is to be disseminated to the general public by means of publications that, it is expected, will be welcomed enthusiastically in the United States and Europe as well as Canada. It is also proposed to make these treasures of our patrimony known by means of courses and conferences and to encourage students in the scientific study of our popular traditions. [Université Laval, *Annuaire général de l'Université Laval pour l'année académique 1945-1946* (Québec: 1946), no. 89, p. 261-162.]

To the first group of pioneers, among whom were Marius Barbeau, Luc Lacourcière, Félix-Antoine Savard, Conrad Laforte, Madeleine Doyon-Ferland and Roger Matton, have been added, between 1965 and 1970, other professors at the university who enlarged the program of instruction, inspired many more folklore studies and strongly encouraged the deposit of folklore collections in the Archives.

The documentary materials in the Archives are mainly the result of ethnographic investigations, scholarly studies and thesis research carried out by persons attached to Laval University—either as students, faculty or research staff. In addition, certain fonds and collections derive from individuals or organizations outside of Laval University.

As tape recording devices became portable, the collection of recorded interviews increased dramatically. The areas of folklore research interest also expanded: in addition to stories, legends, songs and music, interviews have been carried out concerning the trades, social or domestic customs, activities related to celebrations and ceremonies, popular culture, etc.

Field data has been gathered from francophone collaborators dispersed in North America from Louisiana and Maine in the United States to Manitoba, Ontario and the Atlantic Provinces of Canada. Contributions of sound recordings also multiplied; these were received from about. twenty contributors in 1961 and, during the 1970s, from several hundred contributors. The many program collaborators are former students at Laval University who, after their graduation, have continued to correspond with the Archives of Folklore and to send us their collections of folklore recordings or manuscripts.

In 1971, following recommendations of the Commission on Studies at Laval University, a new Program on Popular Arts and Traditions was created in the Department of History. This program assumed responsibility for instruction in folklore at the University.

In 1976, at the instigation of professor Jean Hamelin, responsibility for folklore research, per se, was taken over by the Center for Studies on the Language, Arts and Popular Traditions of Francophones in North America (Célat). Responsibility for publications remains with Luc Lacourcière of the Laval University Press. Twenty-six numbers of the monographic series *Archives de folklore* were published by the University Press between 1946 and 1993.

In June 1981, the Archives of Folklore was reattached to the Division of Archives of Laval University.

Holdings of the Archives of Folklore

After more than fifty years of existence, the Archives of Folklore now brings together 1,437 fonds and private collections that consist of 140 linear meters of manuscript and printed documentation, more than 6,000 hours of sound recordings and nearly 15,000 photographic negatives and prints. In addition, there are several hundred printed volumes concerning the songs, customs and costume of francophone North America and an important collection of devotional objects that serve as a witness to our religious patrimony.

Some Representative Collections and Holdings of Special Interest

● In the area of life history: the very fine film collection of cinematographer Pierre Perrault. This consists of thousands of hours of film that reflect the customs, values and trades—especially of the people of the Charlevoix region of Québec.
● In the area of oral history: the collection of Luc Lacourcière (founder of the Archives of Folklore), as well as the Bouthillier-Labrie collection; the two are concerned, to a great extent, with Acadia—especially New Brunswick.
● Some collections bearing on the spiritual domain in its ritual and pragmatic manifestations, such as the Larouche-Villeneuve collection or that of Jean Simard.
● In the area of fashion, textiles and related trades: the Jocelyne Mathieu and Madeleine Doyon-Ferland collections.
● In the area of urban ethnology: the collection of the City of Québec and of the Laboratory of Urban Ethnology at Laval University.

Carole Saulnier
[Translation from French: Lee S. Dutton.]

Saskatchewan—Regina

Saskatchewan Archives Board. Sound and Moving Images Section

Address: Sound and Moving Images Section, Saskatchewan Archives Board, University of Regina, Regina, SK, Canada S4S 0A2.
Tel.: (306) 787-3381
Fax: (306) 787-1975
Founded: Most of the oral history project recordings of Native people of Saskatchewan were made in the 1970s, although some additional oral history projects were active in the 1980s.
Major resources: Oral history recordings of Native people of Saskatchewan; also some original films or videos of Native people of Saskatchewan.
Areas of specialization: The province of Saskatchewan.
Visual/audio resources: Oral history recordings, including "Chipewyan and Métis People of La Loche," (16 audio cassettes); "Ethnocultural Groups of Saskatchewan: The First People," (129 audio cassettes); "Ethnocultural Groups of Saskatchewan: The Newcomers—the South-East Asians," (44 audio cassettes); "Métis History Research Project," (42 interviewees); "Oral History of the Wahpaton Dakota," (17 audio cassettes); other oral history archives on audio tape. Unpublished transcripts of most of the oral history recordings are available in the Sound and Moving Images Section. Some original films or videos of Native people of Saskatchewan are also held.
Access: Open to the public. There may be restrictions on the duplication of some recordings.
Guides/catalogs: Unpublished oral history project descriptions are available in the Sound and Moving Images Section; Normand Fortier, *Guide to Oral History Collections in Canada = Guide des fonds d'histoire orale au Canada* ([Ottawa?]: 1993) (= *Canadian Oral History Association = Société canadienne d'Histoire orale. Journal*, vol. 13), p. 307-349.

Information provided by Chris Gebhard.

United States

Documentary resources of importance for anthropological research are preserved at repositories in all regions of the United States—from Alaska to Florida and from Hawai'i to Massachusetts. Many academic libraries, archives or museums are key repositories for anthropological or related documentation. The federal government also maintains numerous archival and other repositories of anthropological importance. Federally-supported repositories include the National Museum of the American Indian (now in New York City and also Suitland, Maryland), the National Anthropological Archives, the Human Studies Film Archives, various other units of the Smithsonian Institution, the Library of Congress, two Washington, D.C.-area units and many regional branches of the National Archives, many others. See the **District of Columbia** section of this guide for additional information on selected federal repositories.

State-supported libraries, archives or museums (often affiliated with a local State Historical Society) are, in many cases, also important repositories for anthropological documentation. The Oklahoma Historical Society, in Oklahoma City, and the Bernice Pauahi Bishop Museum, in Honolulu, are two among many such state-level repositories.

A variety of private associations or societies (such as the American Philosophical Society, in Philadelphia, and the American Baptist Historical Society, in Valley Forge) also maintain archival, library or museum collections of anthropological significance.

Due to time limitations, information on documentary collections maintained by private individuals or Native American nations could not be included in this edition of *Anthropological Resources*. Directory information on selected tribal organizations is now becoming more accessible on the Web. A helpful guide to websites of Native American nations and organizations is Lisa Mitten's "Native American Sites" at http://www1.pitt/~Imitten/indians.html. Hyperlinks provide access to an abundance of directory and other information sources on Native American topics. Also helpful is the "American Indian Tribal Directory," available at http://www.indians.org/ tribes. An "Index of Native American Resources on the Internet" is available at http://hanksville.phast.umass.edu/misc/Naresources.html.

The National Archaeological Database is a key electronic resource for access to information on archaeological records and documentation. The URL is: http://www.cr.nps.gov/nad/nadb.htm.

Alaska—Anchorage

Anchorage Museum of History and Art

Address: Anchorage Museum of History and Art, 121 W. Seventh Ave., Anchorage, AK 99501.
Tel.: (907) 343-4326
Fax: (907) 343-6149
Founded: 1968.

Major resources: Archive, Library.
Areas of specialization: Ethnology and archaeology of Alaska.
Visual/audio resources: 200,000 photographs.

National Archives—Pacific Alaska Region (Anchorage)

Address: National Archives—Pacific Alaska Region, 654 West Third Avenue, Anchorage, AK 99501.
Location: The National Archives—Pacific Alaska Region is in downtown Anchorage; the Archives is located on West Third Avenue between F and G Streets. Use the main entrance on West Third Avenue.
Tel.: (907) 271-2443
Fax: (907) 271-2442
E-mail: archives@alaska.nara.gov.
Internet address: http://www.nara.gov/regional/anchorag.html.
Public transit access: All municipal buses, except #93, stop at the Anchorage Transit Center, which is three blocks south of the National Archives—Pacific Alaska Region. Service is limited on weekends. Call the Transit Center for route and schedule information.
Parking: Ample parking is available on the street or in nearby lots. There is no on-site parking except for two one-hour spaces for all visitors to the old Federal Building, 605 West Third Avenue, Anchorage.
Founded: The National Archives Anchorage facility first opened to the public in 1990. At that time, extensive Alaska-related records were transferred to Anchorage from the National Archives regional facility in Seattle.
Major resources: Original permanent federal records retired from government agencies in Alaska. In addition, the Anchorage facility provides storage for records scheduled for permanent retention by federal agencies in Alaska. These so-called "pre-archival records" remain the legal property of the creating agency and are not open to the public without a written letter of permission from the agency.
Areas of specialization: Alaska. The history and ethnology of Alaska are among areas represented. Holdings of anthropological or related interest include original records of the Fish and Wildlife Service (RG 22), the Bureau of Land Management (RG 49), the Bureau of Indian Affairs (RG 75), the Public Health Service (RG 90), the National Archives Gift Collections (RG 200), the General Services Administration (RG 269), the Office of Naval Research (RG 298), the National Oceanic and Atmospheric Administration (RG 370) and the Indian Arts and Crafts Board (RG 435).
Archives/manuscripts: 1,433 cubic ft. of original records; 5,818 reels of microfilm.
Visual/audio resources: Holdings include aerial photographs, photographs, slides and other images in the following record groups: Records of the Bureau of Land Management (RG 49); Records of the Bureau of Indian Affairs (RG 75); the Sir Henry S. Wellcome Collection, 1856-1936 (Donated Materials in the National Archives. WME. Sir Henry S. Wellcome Collection, 1856-1936); and the Records of the General Services Administration (RG 269). More than a dozen ethnographic (or related) photographs from Record Group 200 (National Archives Gift Collection) appear in R. Bruce Parham, "Benjamin Haldane and the Portraits

of a People," *Alaska History*, vol. 11, no. 1 (Spring 1996), p. 36-45. This article is a photo-essay on the work of Benjamin Haldane (1874-1941)—a Tsimshian photographer from Metlakatla, Alaska; the photographs depict community life in Metlakatla from the 1890s to about 1910.

Access: The great majority of holdings are open for public research. Restrictions on access to some federal records relating to individuals may be applied, in accord with exemptions in the Privacy Act of 1974.

References: L.J. Campbell, "National Archives—Alaska Region Collect the Paper of Alaska's Past," *Alaska Geographic*, vol. 20, no. 3 (1993), p. 93-94; Fern Chandonnet (editor), *Alaska at War, 1941-1945: The Forgotten War Remembered* (Anchorage: 1995)—these conference proceedings include papers relating to the relocation of the Aleuts from the Pribilof and Aleutian Islands, 1942-1945, and an extensive bibliography; Brian C. Hosmer, "'White Men Are Putting Their Hands into Our Pockets': Metlakatla and the Struggle for Resource Rights in British Columbia, 1862-1887," *Alaska History*, vol. 8, no. 2 (Fall 1993), p. 1-19; Dean Kohlhoff, *When the Wind Was a River: Aleut Evacuation in World War II* (Seattle: 1995)—Kohlhoff's book is based on Alaska Region's Pribilof Islands Program records, 1916-1970 (RG 22), that were transferred from Seattle to Anchorage in 1991.

Guides/catalogs: *Guide to Records in the National Archives—Alaska Region* (Washington, D.C.: 1997). Several pre-1990 guides contain references to Alaska-related materials—now in Anchorage—under the location for the National Archives—Pacific Northwest Region (Seattle). All records listed as held by the "Archives Branch, Federal Archives and Records Center (FARC), Seattle, Washington," in George S. Ulibarri (compiler), *Documenting Alaskan History: Guide to Federal Archives Relating to Alaska* (Fairbanks: 1982) (= *Alaska Historical Commission Studies in History*, no. 23) have now been transferred to the Alaska Region. Also now in Anchorage are Alaska-related materials listed under the location for the Federal Records Center—Seattle, in Elmer W. Lindgard (compiler), *Preliminary Inventory of the Sir Henry S. Wellcome Papers in the Federal Records Center, Seattle, Washington (Record Group 316)* (Washington, D.C.: 1963) (= *National Archives and Records Service. Preliminary Inventory*, no. 150).

Edward E. Hill, *Guide to Records in the National Archives of the United States Relating to American Indians* (Washington, D.C.: 1982); United States. National Archives and Records Administration, *American Indians: A Select Catalog of National Archives Microfilm Publications* (2nd ed., Washington, D.C.: 1995).

Description

Selected Record Groups of Anthropological Interest

- Records of the Fish and Wildlife Service (RG 22), 1870-1969, (212 linear ft.).

Administrative History: The Fish and Wildlife Service was formed on June 30, 1940, as a result of the merging of the Bureau of Fisheries (established in 1903) and the Bureau of Biological Survey (which originated in 1885). The service is responsible for administering federal laws for the control and conservation of fish, game, birds and other wildlife and for administering national wildlife refuges.

By an Act of July 27, 1868, Congress authorized the Secretary of the Treasury to protect the fur-bearing animals in Alaska and its adjacent waters. Special agents for the protection of fur seals were sent to the larger Pribilof Islands of St. Paul and St. George. Subsequently, on July 1, 1870, Congress further directed the Secretary to accept bids from private corporations for a twenty-year lease to hunt fur seals on the islands, subject to the control of the Secretary of the Treasury.

On July 1, 1903, these duties and the records of the Secretary of the Treasury relating to the Alaska Fur Seal Service were transferred to the newly created Department of Commerce and Labor. The Service was administered by that agency until December 28, 1908, when it was transferred to the Bureau of Fisheries. The Bureau of Fisheries, which lasted from 1908 until 1940, and its successor agencies (Fish and Wildlife Service, 1940-1955; Bureau of Commercial Fisheries of the U.S. Fish and Wildlife Service, 1956-1961; and the National Marine Fisheries Service) directed activities relating to the Pribilof Islands and fur seal matters until that responsibility ended in 1983.

Records Description: The Region has microfilm copies of the *Pribilof Islands Logbooks, 1872-1961* (19 reels), that were created by the resident federal agent. This person was responsible for overseeing the contract between the federal government and the private corporation which, in return for harvesting fur seals, was to provide subsistence and education for the Native population. Entries relate to a variety of subjects including fox and seal harvest statistics, Native community life, weather observations and other matters.

Also held are Pribilof Islands program correspondence files, 1923-1969, that include letters received and copies of letters sent regarding the supply program, fox and seal harvests, radio messages, medical reports, school reports and correspondence regarding scientific studies of the Arctic flora and fauna, including whale investigations. There are files on the evacuation of Pribilof Natives to Funter Bay on the Alaska mainland during the Japanese invasion of the Aleutian Islands in 1942. Also included are Special Files, Pribilof Islands, 1965-1969.

There are also records of the Fish and Wildlife Service regional office in Juneau. The records include correspondence on Alaska fisheries management and the enforcement of fisheries regulations, 1949-1959; published and unpublished annual fisheries reports, 1929-1959, (for the Central District, 1930-1959; Chignik District, 1930-1959; Ketchikan District, 1932-1959; Kodiak District, 1931-1959; Juneau District, 1929-1959; Sitka District, 1945 and 1947; Wrangell-Petersburg District, 1933-1959; Yakutat District, 1933-1959). Also held are published Alaska Fisheries and Fur Seal Industries Reports, 1897-1956; miscellaneous reports, 1884-1975; Alaska salmon statistics, 1910-1973; and records relating to the international North Pacific Salmon Fisheries Commission, 1958-1963.

The Region has records from the fisheries laboratory at Auke Bay, Alaska, that document Alaska fisheries from the late nineteenth-century to 1969. There are stream surveys, spawning ground surveys, statistical studies of the annual salmon catch and the canned salmon pack. There are also reports and unpublished studies on fisheries and fisheries biology. The Region also holds the records of the Bristol Bay Cooperative Management Project, ca. 1981-1985.

Finding Aids: Folder title lists.

Related Microfilm: Pribilof Islands Logbooks, 1872-1961 (Seattle, Washington: 1967) (= *National Archives Microfilm Publication*, A3303), 19 reels; *"Alaska File" of the Office of the Secretary of the Treasury, 1868-1903* (Washington, D.C.: 1968) (= *National Archives Microfilm Publication*, M720), 25 reels; *Public Hearings of the Commission on Wartime Relocation and Internment of Civilians* (Washington, D.C.: 1983) (= *National Archives Microfilm Publication*, M1293), 6 reels.

● Records of the Bureau of Land Management (RG 49), 1884-1988, (110 linear ft.).

Administrative History: The General Land Office (GLO) was a part of the Treasury Department until 1849, when it was incorporated into the newly formed Department of the Interior. In 1946, the GLO and the Grazing Service were combined to form the Bureau of Land Management, which remains within the Department of the Interior.

Records Description: The records held by the Alaska Region include Townsite Trustee Files, 1902-1992, from the Alaska State Office in Anchorage (264 archives boxes and forty microfilm reels of *Selected Alaska Townsite Trustees' Deeds, Deed Books, and Tract Books, ca. 1905-1992*), relating to more than 120 closed presidential townsites, railroad townsites and trustee townsites throughout Alaska. The Alaska Native Townsite Act of May 25, 1926 (44 Stat. 629; U.S.C. 733-736), provided for the survey and disposition of public lands reserved for the benefit of Alaska Natives and for the survey and disposal of lands occupied as Native towns or villages. Many townsite files pertain to the issuance of restricted deeds under the 1926 act for tracts set aside for Alaska Natives or for the issuance of unrestricted deeds under the Act of February 26, 1948 (62 Stat. 35; U.S.C. 732-737), to this group. Townsite files usually include the following: accounts files, deed files, general correspondence files, historical files, lot and block files, maps files, pending files, permit files and tract books.

Finding Aid: A list of folder titles.

Related microfilm: Alaska, *Deed Books, Tract Books Trustee Townsite Series, vol. 1-23* (Washington, D.C.: 1957-1960), 12 reels [unnumbered microfilm publication]; Alaska, *Records of Trustees Deeds, Tract Books Trustee Townsite Series, vol. 1-25* (Washington, D.C.: 1957-1960), 12 reels [unnumbered microfilm publication]; Alaska, *Tract Books, Trustee Townsite Series, volumes. 37 and 63-72* (Washington, D.C.: 1957), 4 reels [unnumbered microfilm publication]; *Deed Book[s] and Tract Book[s] Microfilmed* (Anchorage: 1968), 6 reels [unnumbered microfilm publication].

● Records of the Bureau of Indian Affairs (RG 75), 1886-1889 (1933-1977), (898 linear ft.).

Administrative History: Established in the Office of Education, Department of the Interior, the Alaska Division was created on May 17, 1884 (23 Stat. 24), and mandated by the

Secretary of the Interior to provide educational services to the children of Alaska. This legislation also enabled the General Agent for Education in Alaska to gradually expand the activities of the Alaska Division beyond education into medical care (1915) and into the field of economic assistance. Reindeer were first brought to Alaska from Siberia, in 1891, by Bureau of Education General Agent Sheldon Jackson, to provide a food supply and industry for Alaska Natives. Responsibility for reindeer herds shifted several times; in 1937 it was returned to the Alaska Division, and an Alaska Reindeer Service was established. On March 14, 1931, the Alaska Division was transferred to the Bureau of Indian Affairs by Secretary's Order 494. In the reorganization of the Bureau of Indian Affairs in 1946, Regional offices were set up to coordinate the activities of Indian Agencies and Service Districts of the Bureau. The Juneau Area Office was established to coordinate services to all Alaska Natives.

Records Description: The records are those of the Alaska Reindeer Service, 1901-1972; the Alaska Division of the Bureau of Education, Seattle, Washington, 1917-1925; the Alaska Division of the Bureau of Education, Juneau, Alaska, Office, 1928-1929; Juneau Area Office of the Bureau of Indian Affairs, 1931-1983; and the following BIA regional offices: Anchorage Agency, 1958-1973; Bethel Agency, 1946-1961; Fairbanks Native Service, 1946-1972; Fairbanks Agency, 1957-1972; Ketchikan Office, 1959-1970; Kotzebue Office, 1968-1973; Nome Agency, 1964-1966; Southeast Agency, 1960-1968; and the Juneau Area Office's Seattle (Washington) Support Center, ca. 1920-1985. Also included among the field office records of the Alaska Division is the file of Sheldon Jackson on Alaskan School Matters, 1886-1889.

The records of the Juneau Area Office, 1931-1983, including correspondence, 1912 (1933-1977)-1977, (177 linear ft.); budget and accounting records, ca. 1916-1974, (60 linear ft.); Native store records, 1939-1964, (45 linear ft.); reports and statistical records, 1955-1958, (1 foot); and photographs, ca. 1924-1971, (6,000 images). The Juneau Area Office records include correspondence, 1912 (1933-1977)-1977, regarding Native industries, education, medical care and organization of villages; and records of relocation and vocational training programs, etc. Also included are miscellaneous records, 1913 (1934-1983)-1983, (309 linear ft.), including Tlingit-Haida tribal enrollments or membership rolls and birth, marriage and death records (ca. 1890s-1976, closed in 1972); village censuses for 328 Alaska Native villages from 1912 to 1972, with the bulk dating from 1934 to 1972; and records, including individual student case files, for Mount Edgecumbe Boarding School, 1941-1983; Wrangell Institute, 1932-1975; and Goodnews Bay Day School, 1951-1977. The photographs consist of approximately 6,000 images of aerial, panoramic land and building views of BIA clinics, hospitals and schools in Alaska, 1938-1971. Also included is the Historical Album of Bureau of Education and BIA Schools in Alaska, 1925-1935. The latter records have been placed on microfilm as *National Archives Preservation Microfilm Publication*; P2010 (Seattle, Washington: 1979), 1 reel.

The records of the Alaska Division of the Bureau of Education, Juneau office, consist of general and allotment ledgers, 1928-1929, (4 inches). The records of the Alaska Division of the Bureau of Education, Seattle, Washington, office consist of disbursement and appropriation ledgers, 1917-1924; and cash books and ledgers of the Hydaburg Trading Company, 1915-1925, (3 inches). The records of the Alaska Reindeer Service and its successors, 1901-1974, (29 linear ft.) includes general correspondence; earmark registration case files; general case files for associations and districts; apprentice contracts; general information files; reindeer herd case files; monthly herd reports; village subsistence case files; hunting, fishing and fur farming correspondence; marking and counting reports; and the papers of Lawrence J. Palmer—an official of the Bureau of Biological Survey, the Fish and Wildlife Service and the Alaska Reindeer Service, 1920-1945.

The records of the Anchorage Agency consist of employment assistance case files, 1958-1973, (61 linear ft.). The records of the Bethel Agency consist of administrative files and education program decimal files, 1946-1961, (5 linear ft.). The records of the Fairbanks Native Service consist of Alaska Native village censuses, 1946-1972, (15 inches). The records of the Fairbanks Agency consist of employment assistance case files and credit operations files, 1971-1972, (10 linear ft.). The records of the Ketchikan Office consist of employment assistance case files, 1959-1970, (3 linear ft.). The records of the Kotzebue Office consist of employment assistance case files, 1968-1973, (2 linear ft.). The records of the Nome Agency consist of employment assistance case files, 1964-1966, (7 linear ft.). The records of the Southeast Agency consist of employment assistance case files, 1960-1968, (6 linear ft.). The records of the Juneau Area Office's Seattle (Washington) Support Center, 1920-1984, (121 linear ft.) relate to the Bureau of Indian Affairs' Alaska Resupply Program, that involved the transporting of fuel and cargo from Seattle to some seventy Native villages in Alaska with a combined population of about 20,000 Natives.

Finding Aid: A list of folder titles.

Related Microfilm: [Jan] *"Brøsted Project"—Selected Records of the Juneau Area Office, BIA, on Political Development of Native Communities in the Arctic Slope Region of Alaska, 1933-1971* (Seattle, Washington: [ca. 1971]), 5 reels [unnumbered]; Bureau of Indian Affairs. Alaska Division, *General Correspondence, 1908-1935* (Washington, D.C.: 1982), 54 reels [unnumbered]; Bureau of Indian Affairs. Alaska Division, *Records of the Alaska Division of the Bureau of Indian Affairs Concerning Metlakatla, 1887-1933* (Washington, D.C.: 1984) (= *National Archives Microfilm Publication*, M1333), 14 reels; *Alaskan Village Census Rolls*, 1912 (1934-1972)-1972 (Seattle, Washington: 1994) (= *National Archives Preservation Microfilm Publication*, P2286), 66 reels.

• Records of the Public Health Service (RG 90), 1948-1971, (3 linear ft.).

Administrative History: The Public Health Service operates marine hospitals, hospitals for specific diseases, medical facilities for federal penal institutions, as well as quarantine and health stations. Responsibility for providing health services for Native Americans was transferred in 1954 from the Bureau of Indian Affairs to the Public Health Service.

Records Description: Designated historical records of the Arctic Health Research Center contain background information on the establishment of the Center; annual and other reports, 1953-1967; budget records of births at the Alaska Native Health Hospital in Juneau, 1947-1957; the Juneau-Douglas village census for 1944 and 1946; and also administrative correspondence of the hospital, 1955-1958.

Finding Aid: A list of folder titles.

- National Archives Gift Collections (RG 200), Sir Henry S. Wellcome Collection, 1856-1936, (165 linear ft.).

Administrative History: The National Archives is authorized to accept documents and other material donated from private sources that relate to the organization, functions, policies and activities of the federal government.

Records Description: The records contained in the Sir Henry S. Wellcome Collection were donated to the National Archives in 1961 by the trustees of the Wellcome estate. They relate to the Tsimshian and Rev. William Duncan (1832-1918), who guided them from the time they lived in British Columbia until well after they had migrated to Annette Island, Alaska, in 1887. Duncan came to Fort Simpson, British Columbia, in 1856 as a lay missionary of the Church of England. Inability of the Metlakatla Tsimshians to gain title to their British Columbia land, and Duncan's disagreements with Church authorities, led them to seek a new home away from Canadian territory. It was at this time that Sir Henry Wellcome, a wealthy American-born British philanthropist and drug manufacturer (Burroughs-Wellcome Co.), became interested in the Metlakatla situation. The community migrated to Annette Island ("New Metlakatla") and eventually, in 1891, Congress set aside the area as a Reserve. Trouble within the settlement was evident, by 1908, as a result of two contesting forces: Duncan's ruling hand in Metlakatla affairs, based on his role as pastor, magistrate and commercial leader, and the U.S. government's initial actions toward providing education for a number of Metlakatlans who sought improved school conditions. Eventually Wellcome championed Duncan's cause and financed a program to gather documentation in support of the missionary. This collection resulted from these efforts. It is a particularly rich source of ethnographic data, accompanied by many photographs, on the Tsimshians of Alaska and British Columbia.

During the 1920s, Wellcome financed the staff of the Metlakatla Case Office to document a case against the U.S. Department of the Interior for interfering with Duncan at the settlement on Annette Island. Included are correspondence, Duncan's personal papers, copies of government documents and copies of items concerning missions from many sources. There are approximately 2,000 photographs of the settlement, its residents and buildings, various Alaskan sites, Indian artifacts and of Duncan himself. The collection also includes galley sheets for a report authored by Seattle Presbyterian minister Mark Matthews, who wrote in support of Duncan.

Finding Aids: Elmer W. Lindgard (compiler), *Preliminary Inventory of the Sir Henry S. Wellcome Papers in the Federal Records Center, Seattle, Washington* [Record Group 316] (Washington, D.C.: 1963) (= *National Archives Preliminary Inventory*, no. 150); Patricia Williams (compiler), "A List of the Photographs in the Sir Henry S. Wellcome Papers in the Federal Archives and Records Center, Seattle, Washington" (Seattle, Washington: 1976; revised by Amy Kobe, 1981) [an unpublished in-house list].

Related Microfilm: Records of the Alaska Division of the Bureau of Indian Affairs Concerning Metlakatla, 1887-1933 (Washington, D.C.: 1984) (= *National Archives Microfilm Publication*, M1333); *William Duncan Papers, 1851-1945* (Ottawa: 1964) (= *National Archives of Canada. M.G. 29, D55*, reels M-2320 - M2328 only) [on microfilm].

● Records of the General Services Administration (Record Group 269), 1964-1984, (19 linear ft.).

Administrative History: The General Services Administration (GSA) was established as an independent agency by the Federal Property and Administrative Services Act of June 30, 1949.

Records Description: The records are divided into two record series: Engineering Data Files, ca. 1964-1984, (12 linear ft.); and "Station Negatives," 1964-1984. The "Station Negatives" (7 linear ft.) consist of 35mm copy negatives of aerial views, buildings and other structures, etc., for 98 Alaskan Native towns and villages. The Engineering Data Files include reports on the condition of various buildings, power plants and other structures at each site.

Finding Aids: None.

● Records of the Office of Naval Research (RG 298), n.d., (7 inches).

Administrative History: The Naval Arctic Research Laboratory conducted studies in Barrow, Alaska, until 1980, when it was closed.

Records Description: The records in the custody of the Alaska Region consist solely of a printed copy (no. 16) of *Genealogical Record of Barrow Eskimo Families* by Edna MacLean. This 511-page work provides genealogical tracing of Barrow Eskimo (Inuit) families back, when possible, as far as the fourth generation. Information given includes the full name of the individual enumerated, current residence, date of birth, percentage, in quarters, of Eskimo (Inuit) blood and occasional other notations. The book has a surname index.

● Records of the National Oceanic and Atmospheric Administration (RG 370), National Marine Fisheries Service (Juneau, Alaska), (17.5 linear ft.).

Administrative History: The National Oceanic and Atmospheric Administration was formed October 3, 1970, by Reorganization Plan no. 4, that consolidated the Environmental Science Services Administration (ESSA) and the Bureau of Commercial Fisheries.

Records Description: The Region holds a small quantity of records from the Pribilof Islands fur seal program, including annotated charts of the islands and drawings of the buildings and town, ca. 1898-1950; telegrams from the government radio station, 1971-1975; miscellaneous office files, ca. 1960-1980s; and assorted scientific studies including a fairly complete set of the annual report, *Fur Seal Investigations*.

Finding Aids: Box contents lists.

Related Records: The Alaska Region holds both textual records and film copies of records in Record Group 22, Fish and Wildlife Service. The National Archives in Washington, D.C., has original volumes of the Pribilof Island Logbooks, 1915-1939, and related material in the Cartographic and Architectural and Still Picture Branches. The Region holds microfilm of the *Pribilof Island Logbooks, 1870-1961,* (19 reels) that are identical in content to those held by the National Archives in Washington, D.C., for the period 1915-1939. The *Pribilof Island Logbooks* are divided into two sections: one for St. Paul Island and the second for St. George Island; thereunder they are arranged chronologically. A large quantity of original records—consisting of original files, ca. late 1890s to the 1950s—remains on the island of St. Paul and in the custody of individual islanders and of the Tanadgusix (TDX) Corporation.

- Records of the Indian Arts and Crafts Board (RG 435), 1935-1983, (7.5 linear ft.)

Administrative History: The Indian Arts and Crafts Board was established by an act of August 27, 1935 (49 stat. 891), to serve Indians, Eskimos (Inuit) and Aleuts and the general public as an informational, promotional and advisory clearinghouse for all matters pertaining to the development of authentic Indian and Eskimo (Inuit) arts and crafts. It receives administrative support from the Bureau of Indian Affairs. The Alaska Field Office was responsible for fostering the traditional arts and crafts in Nome, Juneau, Sitka and Anchorage.

Records Description: Records from the Alaska Field Office, Juneau, Alaska, 1935-1983. The records consist primarily of correspondence with the Central Office of the Indian Arts and Crafts Board in Washington, D.C., other government agencies and Alaskans involved with encouraging Native arts and crafts. The records also document such special projects as the Sitka Demonstration Workshop and the Shungnak Jade Project.

Finding Aid: A list of folder titles.

- Records of the Indian Health Service (RG 513), (17 cubic ft.).

Administrative History: The federal government has provided health care services to Native Americans since the nineteenth-century. In the early history of the United States, the only federal health services available to Native Americans were those provided by military physicians assigned to forts and reservations on the frontier. In 1849, the responsibility for improving Native American health care shifted from military to civilian authority when the Bureau of Indian Affairs was transferred from the War Department to the Department of the Interior. The passage of the Snyder Act by Congress, on November 2, 1921 (42 Stat. 208), provided for the formal legislative authorization for federal health care for Native Americans. Under this general authority, Native American health care programs were administered by the Department of the Interior until 1955, when they were transferred to the Division of Indian Health in the Department of Health, Education and Welfare, pursuant to the Transfer Act (71 Stat. 370) of August 5, 1954. In 1968, the name of the Division of Indian Health was changed to the Indian Health Service (IHS). The IHS was established as an agency of the Public Health Service by an act of November 23, 1988 (102 Stat. 4824), within the Department of Health and Human Services. The IHS serves as the principal federal advocate in the health care field for Native Americans to ensure comprehensive health services for American Indians and Alaska Natives. The IHS offers hospital and ambulatory medical care, preventive and rehabilitative services and development of community sanitation facilities. The Service also facilitates and assists Indian tribes and Alaska Natives in developing and operating their health programs, coordinating health planning, utilizing health resources available through federal, state and local programs and in health program evaluation.

Records Description: Records of the Alaska Area Native Health Service, 1947-1979, (17 cubic ft.). The Alaska Region holds the program correspondence files of the Office of the Area Director, Anchorage, Alaska. Included are drafts of two manuscripts, "A Season with the Alaska Indians and Eskimos" and Robert Fortuine's "Alaska Native Medical Center: A History, 1953-1983"—Anchorage: 1986.

R. Bruce Parham

Alaska—Fairbanks

University of Alaska, Fairbanks. Alaska Native Language Center (ANLC). Library

Address: Alaska Native Language Center Library, University of Alaska, P.O. Box 757680, Fairbanks, AK 99775-7680.
Tel.: (907) 474-7874
Fax: (907) 474-6586
E-mail: fyanlp@aurora.alaska.edu.
Internet address: Not available.
Founded: 1972.
Major resources: Documentation on the Native, Aleut and Inuit languages of Alaska. The library originated from the collection of Alaskan linguistic and related materials formed by Michael Krauss.
Areas of specialization: Eskimo-Aleut, Athapaskan, Tlingit, Haida and Tsimshian languages of Alaska.
Archives/manuscripts: More than 8,000 items in and on the Native languages of Alaska. Much unpublished material is held.
Fieldnotes: The collection holds fieldnotes donated by linguistic researchers—either originals or copies.
Visual/audio resources: Ca. 1,200 audio recordings are held.
Access: Inquire.
References: *ANLC Research Papers* (Fairbanks)—issued occasionally.
Guides/catalogs: Michael E. Krauss and Mary Jane McGary, *Alaska Native Languages: A Bibliographical Catalog. Part One: Indian Languages* (Fairbanks: 1980) (= *Alaska Native*

Language Center Research Papers, no. 3). Part II of this work (Eskimo-Aleut languages) is reported to be in preparation.

University of Alaska, Fairbanks. Elmer E. Rasmuson Library. Alaska and Polar Regions Department (APR)

Address: Alaska and Polar Regions Department, Elmer E. Rasmuson Library, University of Alaska, P.O. Box 756808, Fairbanks, AK 99775-6808.
Tel.: (907) 474-7261 (APR); (907) 474-5357 (Alaska Film Archives); (907) 474-6672 (Oral History Program); (907) 474-5483 (Wenger Anthropological Eskimo Database).
Fax: (907) 474-6365
E-mail: fyapr@uaf.edu.
Internet address: http://www.uaf.alaska.edu/library/libweb/collections/apr/apr.html.
Networks, consortia: Gnosis (the University of Alaska Libraries on-line catalog), SLED (Statewide Library Electronic Doorway).
Founded: 1922.
Major resources: Alaska and Polar Regions Department; Archives; Oral History Program.
Areas of specialization: Alaska and the polar regions. Special emphasis is given to documentation on the anthropology of Alaska and other Alaska-related subjects. APR collections cover northern Canada, Greenland, northern Scandinavia, Iceland, northern Russia (Siberia and the Far East). The library, which has substantial historical and ethnological documentation on the Inuit, maintains the *Wenger Anthropological Eskimo Database*.
Archives/manuscripts: In the Manuscripts, Historical Photographs and University Archives Department. Finding aids are available for most manuscript collections.
Visual/audio resources: More than 500,000 Alaska-related photographs are in the Historical Photographs collection; films and videos are in the Alaska Film Archives; the map collection in Rare Books and Maps includes rare Alaska-related maps; the Oral History Program includes recordings of tribal elders and other Native peoples of the state; Project Jukebox provides electronic multi-media access to selected oral history documentation. Oral histories by Alaska Native peoples include:
- Fairbanks Native Association Project.
- Gates of the Arctic Project.
- Sealaska Heritage Foundation Project.
- Tanana Tribal Council Project.
- Yukon First Nations Elders Council Project.

Access: Available for research use. Some materials (including periodicals, maps, rare books and archives) are non-circulating. Additional information on Alaska-related documentation and electronic research aids is available via the APR website—see the URL, above.
Guides/catalogs: *Bibliography of Alaska and Polar Regions*—available as the *Alaska Periodical Index* on Gnosis, *Polar-PAC* and on CD-ROM; *Polar-PAC*—available on CD-ROM; *Wenger Anthropological Eskimo Database* (WADE)—a full-text database available on CD-ROM.

Information provided by Gretchen Lake.

Alaska—Juneau

Alaska. Division of State Libraries, Museums and Archives. Alaska State Library. Alaska Historical Collections (AHC)

Address: Alaska Historical Collections, P.O. Box 110571, Juneau, AK 99811-0571.
Location: 8th Floor, State Office Building.
Tel.: (907) 465-2925
Fax: (907) 465-2990
Internet address: http://www.educ.state.ak.us/lam/library/hist/hist.html.
Founded: 1900 (as the Alaska Historical Library and Museum).
Major resources: Books, government publications, periodicals, newspapers, manuscripts, photographs, maps, oral history recordings.
Areas of specialization: Alaska and arctic regions, Native peoples of Alaska.
Visual/audio resources: 110,000 historic photographs (350 collections). Holdings include the Winter & Pond photographic collection; the John Grainger Alaska post card collection; others. AHC also maintains a collection of Alaska oral history recordings.
Access: Open to the public.
References: Victoria Wyatt, *Images from the Inside Passage: An Alaskan Portrait by Winter & Pond* (Seattle and London: 1989).

Alaska State Museum (ASM)

Address: Alaska State Museum, 395 Whittier St., Juneau, AK 99801-1718.
Tel.: (907) 465-2901
Fax: (907) 465-2976
Internet address: http://www.educ.state.ak.us/lam/museum/asmhome.html.
Founded: 1900.
Areas of specialization: Native peoples of Alaska, including the Tlingit, Haida and Tsimshian tribes of southeastern Alaska.
Archives/manuscript: Archival holdings include records of the museum's European Inventory Project on Native objects from Alaska in major European museum collections.
Artifacts of anthropological significance: Many objects of Tlingit, Haida or Tsimshian origin.

Arizona—Phoenix

Heard Museum. Library and Archives

Address: Library and Archives, Heard Museum, 22 East Monte Vista Road, Phoenix, AZ 85004-1480.
Tel.: (602) 252-8840
Fax: (602) 252-9757
Internet address: http://www.heard.org/LIBRARY/HOME.HTM.
Internet address (Documentary Research Collections): http://www.heard.org/LIBRARY/ RCGUIDES/RC_GUID.HTM. Includes an annotated list of selected special collection materials at the museum; many items pertain to Native peoples of Arizona or the Southwest.
Founded: 1929.
Major resources: Library, Archives.
Areas of specialization: Native American art and culture, Native American creative writing, other Native American studies.
Archives/manuscripts: See the websites, above.
Visual/audio resources: The Byron Harvey photograph collection (ca. 1880-ca. 1970); other photo collections—see the websites mentioned above.
Access: Access to the Library and Archives is free to members and Native Americans. For other readers, access to the Library and Archives in included in the Museum admission fee.

Arizona—Tucson

Arizona State Museum (ASM)

Address: Arizona State Museum, University of Arizona, Tucson, AZ 85721.
Location: At the University of Arizona, Tucson.
Tel.: (602) 621-6281
Fax: (602) 621-2976
Internet address: http://w3.arizona.edu:180/asm.
Networks, consortia: American Association of Museums.
Founded: 1893.
Major resources: Arizona State Land Archaeological Site Files; Documentary Relations of the Southwest; Museum Archives; Museum Library; Museum Photographic Collections.
Areas of specialization: Southwestern archaeology, ethnology, ethnohistory.
Holdings: Arizona State Land Archaeological Site Files: paper and electronic files on more than 25,000 archaeological sites in the state of Arizona. Documentary Relations of the Southwest: 1,100 reels of microfilm and more than 6,000 volumes, including dictionaries, guides to archives and other research tools for the Spanish colonial period in northern Mexico and the southwestern U.S. Museum Archives: 1,300 linear ft. of paper records, approximately 1,200 hours of sound recordings and more than 9,000 maps relating to the Museum and its collections. Holdings include the ASM portion of the Doris Duke American Indian Oral History Project (1966-1972). Museum Library: Approximately 40,000 v., 1,200

journal titles and 10,000 reprints on Southwestern and general anthropology and archaeology. Museum Photographic Collections: 2,500,000 images from the late nineteenth-century to the present, documenting the anthropology and archaeology of the Greater Southwest.

Access: Arizona State Land Archaeological Site Files: open by appointment to professional archaeologists, land managers and researchers with demonstrated need. Museum Library: this non-circulating collection is open to the public. All other collections are open by appointment to researchers and scholars.

References: Thomas C. Barnes, et al., *Northern New Spain: A Research Guide* (Tucson, Ariz.: 1981); Alan Ferg (editor), *Western Apache Material Culture: The Goodwin and Guenther Collections* (Tucson, Ariz.: 1987); Bernard L. Fontana (text) and Helga Teiwes (photographs), *The Material World of the Tarahumara* (Tucson. Ariz.: 1979); James S. Griffith, *Mexican Masks from the Cordry Collection* (Tucson, Ariz,: 1982); Bradford Koplowitz, "The Doris Duke Indian Oral History Projects," *Popular Culture in Libraries*, vol. 1, no. 3 (Summer 1993), p. 23-38; Charles W. Polzer, et al., *The Documentary Relations of the Southwest: Project Manual* (Tucson, Ariz.: 1977); Charles W. Polzer, "The Spanish Colonial Southwest: New Technologies for Old Documents," *Columbian Consequences* (Washington, D.C.: 1989), vol. 1, p. 179-188. The museum publishes the *Arizona State Museum Archaeological Series* as well as occasional booklets, exhibit catalogs and brochures. In addition, ASM and others have published dozens of archaeological reports that describe collections in the museum's holdings.

Description

The Arizona State Museum was established as a unit of the University of Arizona in 1893 for the purpose of collecting, preserving and sharing with the public materials that reflect the development of human culture in Arizona and in culturally related areas. As part of its centennial year celebrations, the museum opened "Paths of Life" exhibits on Southwestern Native peoples. The permanent exhibits encompass Seri, Yaqui, Tarahumara, Tohono O'odham, Colorado River Yuman, Yavapai, Walapai, Havasupai, southern Ute, Hopi, Navajo and western Apache cultures. In recent years ASM has also mounted a number of other major exhibitions. These include Navajo pottery and potters, Tarahumara lifeways, western Apache material culture and culture change, Hopi pottery as a reflection of art and history and the history of women anthropologists in the Southwest.

The museum has outstanding Southwestern archaeological collections, including those from the Hohokam site of Snaketown, excavated in the 1930s and again in 1964-1965; from Mogollon sites excavated by the University of Arizona Field Schools, from 1938 to 1992, in the Point of Pines and Grasshopper regions; from Ventana Cave, which contains cultural materials dating from Paleo-Indian to historic times; and from the historic downtown areas of Tucson and Phoenix, excavated between the 1960s and 1990s.

It is the museum's policy to make its collections as widely accessible as is reasonably possible for research, comparative study, publication, exhibition, teaching and other educational purposes.

Arizona State Land Archaeological Site Files

The Arizona State Museum has been curating site and survey records for Arizona archaeology since the museum's first survey in 1895. Since the passage of the Arizona Antiquities Act in 1960, ASM has been charged with maintaining and managing archaeological site and survey information on state land in Arizona. While there is no centralized site file in Arizona, the Arizona State Museum Site Files Office has become by default the closest thing the State has to a centralized file. As such, land use planners and archaeological contractors often use the Site Files as the first step in doing class 1 archaeological surveys in compliance with the 1969 National Environmental Protection Act.

The Site Files Office retains site cards on approximately 25,000 sites. The site information is also entered and maintained in an automated database, AZSITE. Sites are plotted by hand on U.S.G.S. 7.5 minute topographic sheets (of which there are more than 1,900 for the State of Arizona). Surveys are plotted on mylar overlays attached to each U.S.G.S. sheet. Data for more than 3,400 surveys are maintained on Project Registration Forms. ASM has recently implemented an automated database for survey projects, AZPROJ, and a bibliographic database, BIBLIO, for inventorying the ubiquitous archaeological "gray literature."

Documentary Relations of the Southwest

The Documentary Relations of the Southwest (DRSW) is an ethnohistorical collection of research tools that includes books, typescripts and microfilm copies of documents pertaining to the Spanish colonial period of northern Mexico and the southwestern United States. The more than 6,000 volumes in the collection focus on European relations with the indigenous cultures of northern Mexico, Texas, New Mexico, Arizona and California from the first contacts to Mexican Independence in 1821. More than 600 of the collection's 1,100 reels of microfilm are part of the American Division Jesuit Historical Institute Collection, that contains documents from European archives related to Jesuit activities in the New World, especially South America, Mexico and the Philippines. The remaining microfilm collection covers documents held in archives in Mexico, Spain and the United States.

In addition to print and microfilm holdings, DRSW maintains a computer database guide (more than fifty megabytes) to various archival collections of colonial Spanish documents. The guide provides indexes to these collections by names of persons, places and ethnic groups, as well as keyword cross-referencing to summaries of more than 500,000 pages of documents.

Museum Archives

The Museum Archives, formally established in 1967, contains unique original documents, sound recordings and maps on Southwest archaeology and ethnology. Field records and personal papers of several renowned Southwest anthropologists are administered by the Archives. These include Edward Spicer (Yaqui culture, culture change), Emil W. Haury (Hohokam and Mogollon archeology, preservation legislation), Edward P. Dozier (Hopi-Tewa culture, linguistics), Grenville Goodwin (western Apache culture) and Muriel

Painter (Yaqui religion). Other collections include records from the longest running archaeological field school in the Southwest; records and manuscripts of numerous archaeological projects carried out by the museum since 1915; the files of the Gila Pueblo Foundation; fieldnotes, analyses and reports of the Arizona State Museum's Highway Salvage Program and Cultural Resource Management Division, 1964-1990; the museum's own administrative records; as well as those of the Museum Association of Arizona.

In addition, approximately 1,200 hours of sound recordings—primarily on anthropological and Native American subjects and including oral history, music, linguistic data and lectures—are available through the Archives. Most of these were produced in the course of the Doris Duke Oral History Project. They are indexed by subject matter, culture and personal name.

Museum Library

The Museum Library develops and maintains a comprehensive research collection of print materials pertaining to the anthropology and archaeology of the southwestern United States and northern Mexico. Geographical emphasis is placed on Arizona, New Mexico, Colorado, Utah, Nevada and the borderlands of California, Texas and Mexico. The collection contains a wealth of books, serials, theses, catalogs, reprints and vertical file materials relating to the classical years of anthropological study in the Southwest. In addition, the Pál Kelemen collection of Spanish colonial and pre-Columbian art and architecture is housed in the Library.

Materials on museum studies—especially as they relate to anthropological and ethnographic museum studies—are a focus of the collection. Works of general anthropology and related fields also constitute a large part of the library's holdings. Currently, the library collects published and unpublished materials including reports and professional papers in English, Spanish, French, German and southwestern Native American languages.

Since its beginnings in 1929, the library has supported the research and educational programs of the Arizona State Museum. It continues to provide access to its specialized resources, as well as reference services to the museum's staff, the University of Arizona community and the general public.

Museum Photographic Collections

The Museum Photographic Collections hold approximately 250,000 images documenting the anthropology and archaeology of the Greater Southwest, from the late nineteenth-century to the present. There are photo archives of numerous major archaeological excavations including those at Snaketown, Ventana Cave, the Naco site and the Lehner site; as well as of the University of Arizona Archaeological Field Schools at Forestdale, Point of Pines and Grasshopper and the Gila Pueblo Archaeological Foundation. Ethnographic collections include photographs of the western Apache by Grenville Goodwin; the Pima in the early twentieth-century by Daniel B. Lindermann; and Tohono O'odham, Hopi and western Apache contemporary arts and crafts and traditional agricultural methods by Helga Teiwes. Other major collections include the Forman Hanna collection, consisting of original art prints and negatives of the Native Peoples and landscapes of the Southwest; the Donald B. Cordry collection of Mexican masks and costumes; the William H. Eagle collection of South American archaeology and colonial architecture; the Pál Kelemen collection of pre-Columbian and Spanish colonial art and architecture; and the George B. Eckhardt collection on Spanish colonial missions of the Greater Southwest.

Madelyn Cook, Jan Bell, Alan Ferg, Mary Graham, Beth Grindell, Kathy Hubenschmidt, Fritz Jandry.

Central Arizona Project Repository (CAPR)

Address: Central Arizona Project Repository, 300 W. Congress Street, Tucson, AZ 85701.
Tel.: (520) 670-4807
Fax: (520) 670-4814
Founded: 1989.
Major resources: Central Arizona Project documentation, archives and artifacts.
Areas of specialization: Archaeology of the Southwest.
Archives/manuscripts: Extensive archaeological records.
Visual/audio resources: Photo documentation of CAPR field excavations.
Access: Open for research use by appointment.
Guides/catalogs: Unpublished finding aids are available.

National Park Service. Western Archaeological and Conservation Center (WACC)

Address: Western Archaeological and Conservation Center, National Park Service, 1415 N. 6th Avenue, Tucson, AZ 85705.
Tel.: (520) 670-6501
Fax: (520) 670-6525
Internet address (WACC museum collection profile): http://www.cr.nps.gov/csd/collections/wacc.html.
Networks, consortia: ANCS.
Founded: 1952.
Major resources: Archaeological research archives; photograph collections; a special library for Southwestern and Western archaeological research.
Areas of specialization: Archaeology of Arizona, New Mexico, desert portions of Texas, Utah, Colorado and California.
Archives/manuscripts: 400 linear ft.
Visual/audio resources: 160,000 photographic images—primarily archaeological and Southwestern views. Copies of photographs from all the Southwestern Region National Parks are preserved at the Center. Included are copies of photos from Canyon de Chelly National Monument and other locations.
Access: Open to scholars and the public by appointment.
Archaeological artifacts: Extensive holdings.

Information provided by Lynn Mitchell.

California—Berkeley

University of California at Berkeley (UCB)

Manuscript and archival documentation in anthropology is curated at the University's Bancroft Library and to a lesser extent at some other campus locations. See the following entry on selected Bancroft Library manuscript and archival holdings of anthropological interest. Anthropological documentation may also be found in other UCB libraries, museums or special collections. For summary information on resources at these locations (with links to available websites) see http://www.lib.berkeley.edu/ANTH/lib/libresrc.html.

Visitors to UCB may make use of the on-line UCB campus map, available at http://www.berkeley.edu/campus_map/index.html.

University of California at Berkeley. The Bancroft Library (TBL)

Address: The Bancroft Library, University of California at Berkeley, Berkeley, CA 94720.
Tel.: (510) 642-3781 (general); (510) 642-6481 (Reference desk); (510) 642-3781 (Rare Books); (510) 642-2933 (University Archives).
Fax: (510) 642-7589
Internet address: http://www.lib.berkeley.edu/BANC.
Internet address (manuscripts of U.C. Berkeley anthropologists):
http://www.lib.berkeley.edu/ANTH/research/manuscripts.html.
Internet access to on-line catalogs (GLADIS and MELVYL):
http://www.lib.berkeley.edu/Catalogs.
Networks, consortia: RLIN, OCLC, MELVYL (the University of California system-wide on-line library catalog).
Public transit access: Take BART to Berkeley station.
Founded: The library was initially developed by Hubert Howe Bancroft. It was sold to the the University of California in 1905.
Major resources: TBL holdings include books, journals, manuscripts, maps, photographs, California oral histories on tape and in transcription. Major units of the library include the Bancroft Collection of Western Americana and Latin Americana; the Rare Book Collection; the History of Science and Technology Collection; University Archives.
Areas of specialization: Bancroft Library holdings are strong in anthropological source materials. These document more than a century of ethnological, linguistic and archaeological research in the United States, Canada, South America, Africa, India, the Philippines and elsewhere. There is a particularly valuable body of ethnological resources for the study of California indigenous cultures. The collection contains both nineteenth- and twentieth-century documentation, including observations by trained as well as untrained field observers, and also transcripts of interviews with early California pioneers.

Archives/manuscripts: Ca. 32,000 linear ft. of documentation (all subject areas) spanning the period from 1870 to the late 1980s. Papers of Alphonse Louis Pinart, Alfred L. Kroeber, Robert H. Lowie, C. Hart Merriam and many others are held.

Holdings (books and journals): More than 400,000 v.

Visual/audio resources: Sound recordings of anthropological or linguistic interest are at Bancroft Library; at the Berkeley Language Center (formerly the Language Laboratory); and at the Hearst Museum of Anthropology. The Bancroft Library photo collection includes more than 1,000,000 items, some of which pertain to Native Americans or to other anthropological topics.

Access: See the Bancroft Library website for details on access.

References: *Ballena Press Publications in Archaeology, Ethnology, and History*, no. 1- (1974-   ); *Ballena Press Anthropological Papers*, no. 1- (Menlo Park, Calif.: 1973-   ); *Bancroftiana*, no. 1- (Berkeley: Mar. 1950-)*; History of Anthropology Newsletters* (various).

Guides/catalogs: Finding aids for selected TBL manuscript collections and ethnographic records are accessible via the Internet. Printed guides include Dale L. Morgan and George P. Hammond (editors), *A Guide to the Manuscript Collections of the Bancroft Library* (Berkeley: 1963-1972), 2 v. [vol. 1: *Pacific and Western Manuscripts*; vol. 2: *Mexican and Central American Manuscripts*]. The C. Hart Merriam (1855-1942) collection of notes and documentation on California Indian vocabularies is at TBL. See Robert F. Heizer, *Catalogue of the C. Hart Merriam Collection of Data Concerning California Tribes and Other American Indians* (Berkeley: 1969).

Catalogs of artifact resources: An extensive collection of exhibit catalogs on anthropological subjects is maintained at TBL. The library's strong holdings of published anthropological and related exhibit catalogs can be accessed on GLADIS. Additional exhibit catalogs on anthropological/archaeological subjects are at the Hearst Museum of Anthropology.

Artifacts of anthropological significance: The Hearst Museum holds extensive artifact collections. Many of these relate to fieldnotes or other anthropological documentation that has been transferred from Hearst Museum to the Bancroft Library.

Description

The UCB Department of Anthropology has been a leader in the study of anthropology since 1901—when a gift from Phoebe Apperson Hearst supported the university's first anthropological field studies program. In 1908 the anthropology department became the first program west of Chicago to grant a Ph.D. in this discipline.

The evolution of academic anthropology on the West Coast began at Berkeley under the leadership of Frederic W. Putnam (1839-1915), who served as the first chairman of the department (from 1902 to 1909) while also retaining his position as curator of the Peabody Museum and professor of anthropology at Harvard University. The first instructor and executive officer at Berkeley was Alfred L. Kroeber, who had been a student of Franz Boas, the father of American anthropology, at Columbia University. During the next fifty years,

Berkeley's faculty grew to include some of the most eminent anthropologists in America: Robert H. Lowie, Robert Heizer, William Bascom and David Mandelbaum, to name a few.

During the early years of anthropology at Berkeley, the primary focus of research and teaching was on the documentation and study of native Californian cultures. Thus, there is a strong regional character to the ethnological documentation in the papers of Kroeber, Lowie, Heizer, Barrett, et al. There is also, however, extensive and valuable correspondence between Berkeley anthropologists and colleagues at Harvard, Yale, Columbia, the University of Pennsylvania and other academic institutions, as well as with colleagues at the National Museum of Natural History.

The anthropology collections contain documentation of research carried out by UCB faculty and students since the beginning of the twentieth-century, providing a rich and complex documentary base for historical and cross-cultural studies in anthropology, archaeology, ethnohistory, linguistics, folklore, ethnomusicology, geography and natural resources, public health/medical anthropology, psychology and women's studies.

The anthropology collections at TBL are rich in primary source materials: correspondence, ethnological and archaeological fieldnotes, journals, grant proposals and drafts of reports, published and unpublished manuscripts, comparative linguistic data, vocabularies and grammatical notes, oral history transcripts, photographs, drawings, maps, sound recordings and films. These historical records and manuscripts contain a wellspring of information about diverse cultures, technologies, languages and ways of life that in many cases are either extinct or may soon disappear as a result of rapid and continuing culture change.

TBL houses the university's Rare Books Collection and also University Archives. The History of Western North America Collection offers valuable ethnological resources, particularly for the study of California indigenous cultures, but also cultures of Africa, Asia, North and South America. The History of Science and Technology Program at TBL, in conjunction with University Archives, has assembled a large body of anthropological documentation that includes historical manuscripts, faculty papers and the private papers of scientists who carried out ethnological work in California, as well as the records of the Department of Anthropology and those of the Lowie (now Hearst) Museum of Anthropology. There is also a substantial collection of ethnological fieldnotes that has been transferred from the Hearst Museum.

Some Manuscript Collections

● Alphonse Louis Pinart papers, 1870-1885, 24 v. Correspondence, notes, drafts and copies of articles, diaries, drawings and maps, many concerning Pinart's travels and research on linguistics and ethnology.
● Alfred L. Kroeber papers, ca. 1900-1960. Professor of Anthropology, UCB. Fieldnotes on linguistics, subject files, manuscripts of writings, correspondence, descriptions of photographed artifacts, maps—many concerning Indians of California and Indian land claim hearings.
● Robert H. Lowie papers, ca. 1893-1957. Professor of Anthropology, UCB. Correspondence, notebooks and photographs for his research on American Indians and Indian linguistics, lecture notes, diaries, manuscripts of his writings, subject files, etc.

- Robert Fleming Heizer papers, ca. 1923-1977. Professor of Anthropology (archaeology), UCB. Correspondence, subject files, research notes, manuscripts of writings, lecture notes, photographs, maps, etc., concerning research on Indians of California, their land claims, archaeological investigations and other topics.
- Lila O'Neale papers, ca. 1930-   . Anthropologist, Department of Textile Design, UCB. Fieldnotes and cyanotypes related to her research among Native American basket weavers in northern California.
- William R. Bascom papers, ca. 1930-1979. Professor of Anthropology and Director of the Lowie Museum of Anthropology, UCB. First Ph.D. student of Melville J. Herskovits at Northwestern University, in 1936, and the first American anthropologist to do field work among the Yoruba people of Nigeria. Bascom's papers relate to his lifelong work on African culture and folklore and are considered to be the most valuable documentation existing of the Yoruba at a critical historical period (colonial period to independence). Included are extensive fieldnotes and manuscripts related to his work among the Yoruba, the Kiowa of Oklahoma and the Gullah blacks of Georgia and South Carolina, as well as the peoples of Ponape in Micronesia and of Cuba.
- Samuel A. Barrett papers, ca. 1906-1963. Anthropologist. First Ph.D. from the UCB Department of Anthropology. Director Emeritus of the Milwaukee Public Museum. Fieldnotes and writings (see GLADIS catalog records).
- David G. Mandelbaum papers, ca. 1934-1987. Anthropologist, UCB. First American anthropologist to undertake ethnographic research in India. In 1932 he took the first B.A. degree in anthropology awarded by Northwestern University. At Yale University, where he received his Ph.D., he studied with the eminent linguistic scholar, Edward Sapir. University and teaching files, professional correspondence, extensive fieldnotes, photographs, audio tapes and film related to his research in India among the Tota and Kota peoples are included.
- Edward Winslow Gifford papers, ca. 1916-1950. Anthropologist, Director of the Museum of Anthropology, UCB. Mainly consists of correspondence with Edward Sapir concerning kinship terms and American Indian linguistics.

Collections also include the papers of Leslie Spier, Anna Gayton Spier, Robert Spier, Theodore McCowen, C. Hart Merriam and others. There are also ethnological and linguistic materials in the papers of botanists, geographers and explorers in Bancroft manuscript collections.

Most collections of non-book resources are cataloged under the name of the individual or the institution (e.g., University of California) and/or department (e.g., Department of Anthropology), and can be located in the various catalogs relating to manuscripts, University Archives, pictorial materials, maps, audio, microfilm and books.

Bancroft Library resources support several other historical collections of ethnological and linguistic materials on the UCB campus, such as the archives of the Archaeological Research Faculty (ARF)—at Hearst Museum; the Survey of California and Other Indian Languages—in the Department of Linguistics; the Department and Museum of Anthropology's Ethnological Documents Collections—in University Archives; and the records of the Department and Museum of Anthropology.

Sheila K. O'Neill

University of California at Berkeley. Berkeley Language Center (BLC)

Address: Berkeley Language Center, B40 Dwinelle Hall, no. 2640, University of California at Berkeley, Berkeley, CA 94720-2640.
Tel.: (510) 642-0767
Fax: (510) 642-9183
Internet address: http://www.itp.berkeley.edu/blc.
Public transit access: Take BART to Berkeley station.
Founded: Ca. 1961 (as the Language Laboratory).
Major resources: The Berkeley Language Center Language Archive and Music Archive.
Areas of specialization: Of special interest are the language and music field recordings produced as part of the Department of Linguistics' Survey of California and Other Indian Languages. Special emphasis is given to field recordings of the Indian languages of California.
Archives/manuscripts: The related fieldnotes are in the Survey of California and Other Indian Languages archives—in the Department of Linguistics, Dwinelle Hall.
Guides/catalogs: Catherine Rodriquez-Nieto, *Sound Recordings in Native American Languages: A Catalogue* (Berkeley: 1982).

Information provided by Marianne Garner.

University of California at Berkeley. Department of Linguistics. Survey of California and Other Indian Languages (SCOIL)

Address: Department of Linguistics, 2405 Dwinelle Hall, University of California at Berkeley, Berkeley, CA 94720.
Tel.: (510) 643-7621
Fax: (510) 643-5688
Internet address: http://bantu.berkeley.edu/CBOLD.html.
Public transit access: Take BART to Berkeley station.
Founded: 1956.
Major resources: Archives of the University of California Department of Linguistics Survey of California and Other Indian Languages.
Areas of specialization: Linguistic fieldnotes on the Indian languages of California.
Archives/manuscripts: American Indian-language fieldnote archives (5 vertical files).
Visual/audio resources: A related collection of tape recordings of American Indian-language field data, gathered by faculty of the Department of Linguistics since 1956, is on campus at the Berkeley Language Center.
Access: Open to the public by appointment.
Guides/catalogs: A catalog of fieldnote holdings of the Survey of California and Other Indian Languages collection is reported to be forthcoming.

Information provided by Leanne Hinton.

University of California at Berkeley. Folklore Archive

Address: Folklore Archive, 110 Kroeber Hall, University of California, Berkeley, CA 94720.
Tel.: (510) 643-7934
Fax: None.
Internet address: http://www.lib.berkeley.edu/ANTH/anth/folklore.html.
Public transit access: Take BART to Berkeley station.
Founded: 1965.
Major resources: A collection of folklore data from around the world.
Areas of specialization: Anglo-American folklore.
Archives/manuscripts: More than 500,000 folklore items are in the Folklore Archive. Since 1965, students in the Anthropology 160 class at UCB have been required to each submit forty items of folklore that are classified and placed in the archive.
Visual/audio resources: None.
Access: Materials are accessible to scholars and the public.

Description

Since its beginnings in 1965 the Folklore Archive at UCB has assembled more that one-half million items of folklore from around the world. These are arranged in alphabetical order by country or geographical area and are cataloged according to genre. Genres include *blason populaire*, counting-out rhymes, jokes, folk beliefs. Also dance, drama, folk speech, games, legends, mnemonic devices, songs and song parodies. Special classifications include religious lore, family lore and scout lore.

Information provided by the Folklore Archive.

University of California at Berkeley. George and Mary Foster Anthropology Library

Address: Anthropology Library, 230 Kroeber Hall, University of California, Berkeley, CA 94720.
Tel.: (510) 642-2400
Fax: (510) 643-9293
Internet address: http://www.lib.berkeley.edu/ANTH.
Networks, consortia: RLIN, OCLC, MELVYL (the University of California system-wide on-line library catalog).
Public transit access: Take BART to Berkeley station.
Founded: 1956.
Major resources: Books, journals and other printed materials in anthropology and related fields. Most rare books are in Bancroft Library or other UCB library locations, not in the Foster Anthropology Library.
Areas of specialization: Anthropology of California; Native Americans; folklore.

Archives/manuscripts: In Bancroft Library and certain other campus locations.
Visual/audio resources: At various other UCB locations.

University of California at Berkeley. Phoebe Apperson Hearst Museum of Anthropology

Address: Phoebe Apperson Hearst Museum of Anthropology, 103 Kroeber Hall, University of California at Berkeley, Berkeley, CA 94720.
Tel.: (510) 642-3681; (510) 643-6390 (Registration); (510) 643-1193 (Research).
Fax: (510) 642-6271
E-mail: pahma@montu.berkeley.edu.
Internet address: http://www.qal.berkeley.edu/~hearst.
Public transit access: Take BART to Berkeley station.
Founded: 1901. Formerly named the Lowie Museum of Anthropology.
Major resources: Archives, fieldnotes, photographs, slides, prints, a small library for staff use.
Areas of specialization: California Indian materials, including the California Indian Music Project; California Indian Library Collections; California archaeology.
Archives/manuscripts: A major archival/manuscript collection. The archives of the Archaeological Research Facility (ARF) are among museum holdings. Most museum accession records that pertain to objects are at Hearst Museum, while many related scholars' papers are at Bancroft Library.
Visual/audio resources: Photographs, color slides. The California Indian Music Project, 1983-1984, transferred some 1,700 hours of ethnographic field recordings of Native American music to cassette tapes. Sound and music holdings include collections of cylinder, disc, wire and tape recordings; many of these document music of California Indian tribes. Public-use copies of California Indian music recordings are in the Berkeley Language Center.
Access: Access for qualified researchers is by prior appointment only. For access to museum records, contact the Registrar. For access to objects contact the Collections Manager. See the Museum website for additional information on Hearst Museum research access policies.
Guides/catalogs: Randal S. Brandt and Jeannine Davis-Kimball (editors), *Bibliographies of Northern and Central California Indians* (Berkeley: 1994), 3 v.; Richard Keeling, *A Guide to Early Field Recordings (1900-1949) at the Lowie Museum of Anthropology* (Berkeley: 1991) (= *University of California Publications. Catalogs and Bibliographies*, vol. 6).
Artifacts of anthropological significance: Extensive collections.

Information provided by Joan Knudsen.

California—La Jolla

University of California, San Diego (UCSD). Scripps Institution of Oceanography (SIO). Library

Address (mailing): Library, Scripps Institution of Oceanography, 0175C, UCSD, 9500 Gilman Drive, La Jolla, CA 92093-0175C.

Location: Library, Scripps Institution of Oceanography, 8602 La Jolla Shores Drive, La Jolla, CA.

Tel.: (619) 534-5970 (Archives); (619) 534-4817 (Library).

Fax: (619) 534-5269.

Internet address (Scripps Institution Archives): http://scilib.ucsd.edu/sio/archives.

Internet address (Scripps Institution Library): http://scilib.ucsd.edu/sio.

Internet access to on-line catalog: Scripps Institution Library holdings on the UCSD library catalog, Roger, as well as on Melvyl, are accessible through Infopath, the UCSD campus-wide information system. Infopath may be accessed via the Web. Open a URL to http://www.ucsd.edu.

Networks, consortia: OCLC; Melvyl Catalog (University of California database system).

Public transit access: San Diego Transit bus, routes 30, 34.

Founded: 1903 (Scripps Institution of Oceanography).

Major resources: SIO Library; SIO Archives.

Areas of specialization: Oceanography, other scientific documentation—especially concerning the Pacific Ocean region. Resources of anthropological interest include a collection of nineteenth- and twentieth-century expedition reports of Pacific Ocean-area exploration and research. Also available is a collection of ships' logs, expedition photographs and the manuscripts of Scripps scientists and others who traveled extensively in the islands of the South Pacific, such as Helen Hill Raitt, Francis Shepard and Roger Revelle.

Archives/manuscripts: Manuscripts of: Helen Raitt (Tonga, Samoa,Hawai'i); Walter Munk (Samoa); Francis Shepard (Hawai'i, Truk); Roger Revelle (Tonga, Samoa); Willard Bascom (Tahiti).

Visual/audio resources: Many black-and-white prints, color photos and slides. Many photos of Pacific-area peoples are held, including those in the published *Challenger* Expedition reports.

Access: All researchers are welcome to use the UCSD Libraries. Archives hours are limited and some collections are stored off-site, so researchers are advised to call ahead for an appointment.

References (selected expedition reports): *Challenger* Expedition (1872-1876), *Report on the Scientific Results of the Voyage of H.M.S Challenger During the Years 1872-76: Under the Command of Captain George S. Nares and the Late Captain Frank Tourle Thomson* (London: 1891-), 50 v.; Danske Dubhavsekspedition Jorden Rundt (1950-1952), *The Galathea Deep Sea Expedition, 1950-1952, Described by Members of the Expedition* (London: 1956); Maud Expedition (1918-1925), *The Norwegian North Polar Expedition with the Maud, 1918-1925: Scientific Results* (Bergen, Norway: 1927-1939), 5 v. in 6.

References (others): Anton F. Bruun, *Scientific Results of the Danish Deep-Sea Expedition Round the World, 1950-1952. Galathea Report*, vol. 1 (Copenhagen: 1957-1959), p. 10; Brinton Cooper Busch, *"Whaling Will Never Do for Me": The American Whaleman in the Nineteenth-Century* (Louisville: 1994)—a history of whaling that includes a chapter on Polynesian whalingmen; William A. Lessa, "An Evaluation of Early Descriptions of Carolinian Culture," *Ethnohistory*, vol. 9, no. 4 (Fall 1962), p. 313-403; Rhys Richards, *Samoa's Forgotten Whaling Heritage: American Whaling in Samoan Waters, 1824-1878:*

A Chronological Selection of Extracts from Primary Sources, Mainly Whaling Logbooks, Journals and Contemporary News Items (Wellington, New Zealand: 1992); Harald U. Sverdrup, *Among the Tundra People* (La Jolla: 1978), p. 6—the quotation is from the English translation of Sverdrup's *Hos Tundra-Folket* (Oslo: 1938).

References (SIO expeditions): Several histories have been written on the Scripps Institution of Oceanography during the post-World War II period. Information on the Scripps Pacific expeditions of the 1950s is available in Willard Bascom, *The Crest of the Wave: Adventures in Oceanography* (New York: 1988); Henry W. Menard, *Anatomy of an Expedition* (New York: 1969); Henry W. Menard, *The Ocean of Truth: A Personal History of Global Tectonics* (Princeton, N.J.: 1986) (= *Princeton Series in Geology and Paleontology*); Henry W. Menard, *Islands* (New York: 1986) (= *Scientific American Library Series*, no. 17); Helen Hill Raitt, *Exploring the Deep Pacific* (1st ed., New York: 1956); Roger Revelle, "The Age of Innocence and War in Oceanography," *Oceans Magazine*, vol. 1, no. 3 (1969), p. 6-16; Elizabeth N. Shor, "Scripps in the 1950s: A Decade of Bluewater Oceanography," *Journal of San Diego History*, vol. 29, no. 4 (Fall 1983), p. 247-261; Elizabeth N. Shor, *Scripps Institution of Oceanography: Probing the Oceans, 1936-1976* (La Jolla: 1978).

Guides/catalogs: Eileen V. Brunton, *The Challenger Expedition, 1872-1876: A Visual Index* (London: 1994) (= *Historical Studies in the Life and Earth Sciences*, no. 2). Roger Revelle's voluminous personal papers are described in two guides: Deborah Day, *A Guide to the Roger Randall Dougan Revelle Papers (1928-1979) in the Archives of the Scripps Institution of Oceanography, Manuscript Collection 6* (La Jolla: 1985) (= *SIO Reference Series,* no. 85-26); and in Donna J. Gehres, *A Guide to the Roger Randall Dougan Revelle Papers (1909-1991) Manuscript Collection 6A* (La Jolla: 1994) (= *SIO Reference Series,* no. 94-16). Rebecca S. Smith, *A Guide to the Helen Hill Raitt Papers (1936-1985) Manuscript Collection 19* (La Jolla: 1993) (= *SIO Reference Series*, no. 93-47); Carolyn Rainey, *A Guide to the Francis Shepard Papers (1921-1985) Manuscript Collection MC 7* (La Jolla: 1993) (= *SIO Reference Series,* no. 93-4); Carol Lynn Flanigan, *A Guide to the Henry William Menard Papers (1938-1986) Manuscript Collection 18* (La Jolla: 1992) (= *SIO Reference Series*, no. 92-27). An unpublished folder list for the records of the Office of the Director of the Scripps Institution of Oceanography (Revelle), 1930-1961 (Archival Collection, 16), is available upon request from the Scripps Archives.

Description

Published Accounts of Pacific Voyages and Expeditions.

The libraries of the University of California, San Diego, include exceptional holdings of published accounts of voyages. The library of the Scripps Institution of Oceanography includes rich holdings of published oceanographic expedition reports, with nearly comprehensive holdings of nineteenth- and twentieth-century oceanographic expeditions to the Pacific. The library holds, for example, expedition reports for cruises of *Challenger*, *Galathea* and *Maud*—all mentioned below.

The Hill Collection of Pacific Voyages, at Mandeville Department of Special Collections of the University of California, San Diego, includes a spectacular collection of more than 2,000 accounts of (and commentaries on) important Pacific voyages from the sixteenth- to the mid-nineteenth-century. The Hill Collection includes extensive anthropological, botanical and zoological reports made by scientists who accompanied voyagers. The collection is especially rich in British voyages of the eighteenth-century. The Hill Collection and several other resources of anthropological interest are described in more detail in the entry [following] on selected special collections in the Social Sciences and Humanities Library, UCSD.

Ships' Logs and Related Materials at the SIO Archives.

Ships' logs and mariners' narratives are valuable primary sources for scholars interested in history, geography, natural history or ethnography. The journals of Captain James Cook's officers have long been primary sources for the early history of Hawai'i. Whaling logs, likewise, have been used by a number of historians to study Pacific people (Busch, 1994; Richards, 1992). Published accounts of voyages by naturalists, such as Charles Darwin's voyage of the *Beagle*, continue to be used by scholars interested in the history and natural history of the regions described.

Anthropologists have cited early ships' logs and seamen's narratives as documentation of Pacific cultures and of early contacts between Pacific islanders and Europeans (see, for example, Lessa, 1962). Most of these references are to eighteenth- and early nineteenth-century published narratives and expedition reports. However, the longstanding connection between ocean exploration and anthropology continues today. Researchers will find that more contemporary oceanographic expedition reports, both published and unpublished, often document the human biology, demography and ethnology of areas visited by oceanographic vessels.

The Challenger Expedition.

Oceanographers identify the *Challenger* Expedition of 1872-1876 as the first modern oceanographic expedition. *H.M.S. Challenger*, a British naval corvette converted for scientific service under the joint guidance of the Royal Society and the British Admiralty, circumnavigated the oceans, manned with Admiralty officers and seamen and accompanied by six scientists. The expedition was an oceanographic voyage because its purpose included investigations of the chemical, physical, geological and biological processes of the oceans. It was unique because the comprehensive expedition report—in fifty folio volumes—set a new standard for expedition documentation.

While the mission of the *Challenger* expedition was oceanographic, the mission instructions also required that "Every opportunity should be taken of obtaining photographs of native races to one scale." Hundreds of photographs of the peoples encountered by *Challenger* were taken as a result of this charge. The original dated and identified *Challenger* photographs are available for study only at the British Museum (Natural History) and at a few other British locations. The *Challenger* photographs have recently been described and illustrated in a "visual index" compiled by Eileen Brunton and published by the Natural History Museum in London. The SIO Library holds the printed *Challenger* Expedition report as well as Brunton's illustrated guide (1994) to the *Challenger* Expedition photographs.

Subsequent Expeditions.

Many large exploring and oceanographic expeditions followed the *Challenger* precedent and included some reference to ethnography among their scientific goals. Ethnologist Kaj Birket-Smith not only accompanied the Danish Deep Sea Expedition of 1950-1952, but was also a consulting member of the executive committee that organized *Galathea* Expedition (Bruun, 1957-1959, vol. 1, p. 10). It is therefore no surprise to find that the objects of the 1950-1952 *Galathea* Deep Sea Expedition included anthropology: "In so far as is possible without detriment to its primary purpose, the Expedition will place itself at the disposal of such scientists as may wish, in association with the Expedition, to make special studies of a biological, oceanographical, or ethnographical nature." (Bruun, 1956, p. 27.)

Some expeditions undertook anthropological research even when such research was not among the goals of the expedition. Roald Amundsen's North Polar Expedition encountered a nomadic tribe of Chukchi on the coastal ice near Ayon Island in 1919. Amundsen suggested that his chief scientist, oceanographer Harald Sverdrup, "join the Chukchi when they left to go inland ... spend the winter among them in the forest and return with them the following spring ... I was eager to go, although language and ethnography were far removed from the fields with which I felt acquainted." (Sverdrup, 1978, p. 6.) Sverdrup eventually published a book about his winter with the Chukchi, but much of the ethnographic documentation collected in the course of other oceanographic expeditions has never been published.

Scripps Institution Oceanographic Expeditions Since 1949.

The Archives of the Scripps Institution of Oceanography include substantial unpublished manuscript material documenting the Pacific peoples encountered by Scripps oceanographic expeditions since 1949—the year Scripps acquired a fleet of retired naval and other vessels capable of routine expeditions to the deep Pacific.

Several Scripps scientists first visited the Pacific as participants in "Operation Crossroads"—the 1946 American Pacific atomic test at Bikini atoll. The papers of Scripps oceanographers John Dove Isaacs (1913-1979), Roger Revelle (1909-1991) and Martin Johnson (1893-1984) at the SIO Archives include surveys of the atoll before and after the first peacetime atomic test at that site, but no information on the Bikini Islanders (a Micronesian group) who had been removed from the atoll.

Roger Revelle, director of the Scripps Institution during that period, and other oceanographers returned to the Pacific in 1949 during Mid-Pac Expedition, an expedition to begin exploration of a 50,000 square mile area in the Pacific Basin west of Hawai'i. The official documentation of this and subsequent expeditions includes ships' logs, expedition proposals, cruise plans, expedition narratives and reports, crew lists and sometimes expedition photographs. These archival records are supplemented by the papers of individual scientists and crew members that have been donated to the Archives. The papers of Roger Revelle and his records as director of the Scripps Institution of Oceanography are particularly rich sources of information on Scripps Pacific expeditions and on Revelle's own interest in and contacts with Pacific peoples. Revelle's voluminous personal papers are described in two guides: Day, 1985; Gehres, 1994.

Scripps expeditions returned regularly to the South Pacific during the 1950s and 1960s, and concentrated especially on the ocean area around the Tonga Islands, as they explored the Tonga Trench. These studies were of great scientific value and contributed to the revolution in earth science that is generally called continental drift theory. They also led to a close relationship between some oceanographers and the people of Tonga.

Helen Hill Raitt (1905-1976), accompanied her husband, Russell Raitt, on Capricorn Expedition (1952-1953). She wrote a book on the expedition, *Exploring the Deep Pacific* (New York: 1956). While her book describes the expedition and its scientific research, it includes descriptions of the people of Fiji, Tonga, Samoa, Vava'u, Tahiti and the Marquesas, and the relationships among scientists, sailors and islanders. Scripps photographer John MacFall also joined Capricorn Expedition and took hundreds of photographs of the expedition, the islands and islanders—some of these appear in Helen Raitt's book. The MacFall photos are available for use by researchers at the SIO Archives.

The Scripps Archives also holds the personal papers of Helen Hill Raitt and Russell Watson Raitt. Her papers include correspondence with Tongans, photographs, documentation of her many visits to the islands, audio recordings of Tongan dances and ceremonies and documentation of Tofua Press.

When Helen Raitt returned to Tonga in 1971, she was distressed to learn that Tongans had little access to the books documenting Tongan culture. She founded Tofua Press, in San Diego, to preserve Tongan history and legends and to make books on Tonga available to Tongans. The work of Tofua Press is documented in the Helen Hill Raitt papers at the Scripps Archives.

Like Helen Raitt, oceanographers Willard Bascom (1916-   ) and Walter Munk (1917-   ) spent periods of time living on Pacific islands. Bascom was one of the oceanographers on Capricorn Expedition. He and his family spent much of 1957 in Tahiti. His autobiography, *The Crest of the Wave: Adventures in Oceanography* (New York: 1988), includes descriptions of Capricorn Expedition and of his experiences in Tahiti. His papers at the Scripps Archives include letters, photographs and other materials that describe his Pacific travels.

During most of 1963 Walter Munk, his wife, Judith Horton Munk, and their children lived in a palm *fale* in the village of Vailoa Tai, on the southwestern coast of Tutuila in American Samoa, while they worked on a film, *Waves Across the Pacific*. The Judith Horton Munk papers at the SIO Archives include a transcription of the letters Judith Munk wrote to her parents, describing her life in Samoa. [Judith Horton Munk papers, Manuscript Accession, 93-18.]

SIO geologist Francis Parker Shepard traveled widely in the Pacific during the postwar decades. Shepard and his wife, Elizabeth Buchner Shepard, visited Guam, Truk and the Caroline Islands during Carmarsel Expedition in 1967. Shepard described his impressions of Ulul, in the Namonuito group, Truk, Toll, Pingerlap, Fefan, Moen, and the people of those and other islands, in his unpublished autobiography. (Francis P. Shepard, "Autobiography, August 1980," in Francis P. Shepard papers, Manuscript Collection MC7, "Thirty-Five Islands of Micronesia: Carmarsel Expedition," p. 168-183.) The collection also includes a log and copies of letters written by the Shepards that describe their experiences during the expedition, including notes on local dances and customs, a description of their visit to the Nan Matol ruins on Ponape Island and a description of the United Nations inspection of the Micronesian Trust Territory that occurred while they were at Moen. [Francis Parker Shepard papers, Manuscript Collection MC7, "Carmarsel Log Written by Francis P. Shepard and Elizabeth B. Shepard, Feb.-Mar. 1967"]

Scripps geologist H. William Menard (1920-1986) participated in postwar Scripps expeditions to the Pacific. Like many oceanographers before him, his correspondence and other unpublished papers at the Scripps Archives include references to the peoples of the region and the relations between them and the scientists who came to study their islands and seas (Flanigan, 1992).

Deborah Day and Samuel R. Dunlap

University of California, San Diego (UCSD). **Social Sciences and Humanities Library**
Address: Social Sciences and Humanities Library, University of California, San Diego, 9500 Gilman Drive, La Jolla, CA 92093-0175.
Tel.: (619) 534-2029 (Kathryn Creely); (619) 534-2533 (Mandeville Department of Special Collections).
Fax: (619) 534-7548 (Kathryn Creely).
E-mail: kcreely@ucsd.edu.
Internet address (Melanesian Studies): http://gort.ucsd.edu/kcreely/melanesia.
Internet address (Mandeville Library): http://orpheus.ucsd.edu/spec.coll.
Internet access to on-line catalog: The UCSD library catalog, Roger, as well as Melvyl and Special Collections finding aids are accessible through Infopath, the university's campus-wide information service. Infopath is accessible on the Web; open a URL to http://www.ucsd.edu.
Networks, consortia: OCLC, Melvyl (the University of California system-wide on-line library catalog).
Public transit access: San Diego Transit bus, routes 30, 34, 34A, 41, 50 or 301 to the UCSD campus.
Founded: 1959 (Library). The Hill Collection of Pacific Voyages was received by the library in the early 1970s. The Melanesian Archive was established in 1982, and the Melanesian Studies Resource Center was established at the library in 1983.
Major resources: Melanesian Archive; Melanesian Studies Resource Center; Kenneth E. Hill Collection of Pacific Voyages. A Middle Eastern archaeology book collection was received as a donation by the library in 1994.
Areas of specialization: Melanesia, Pacific voyages, Pacific mission materials, Middle Eastern archaeology.
Archives/manuscripts: The Melanesian Archive. Microform holdings include the Pacific Manuscripts Bureau microfilm collection, an archive of Papua New Guinea patrol reports on microfiche and many other titles.
Fieldnotes, papers, etc.: The Melanesian Archive holds papers and fieldnotes of John Layard (1891-1972), research at Vanuatu, 1914-1915. Also records of research in New Britain, 1959-1961, by A.L. and T.S. Epstein; and fieldnotes from Bruce Knauft's work in

the Western Province of Papua New Guinea, 1980-1982. Other holdings include papers of Roger Keesing's research, 1962-1991, in the Solomon Islands; Anthony Forge's work in the Sepik Region of Papua New Guinea, 1960-1990; papers of Hal and Peta Colebatch, Papua New Guinea; Edwin Cook, Western Highlands Province of Papua New Guinea, 1960s-1970s; Mary Clifton Ayres, Western Province of Papua New Guinea, 1979-1981; Stephen Leavitt, East Sepik Province, Papua New Guinea, 1984-1986; and W. Bergmann (missionary), Chimbu Province, Papua New Guinea, 1934-1968. The fieldnotes collection is still expanding, with several major gifts expected. These materials are all housed and administered through the Mandeville Special Collections Library.

Holdings (books, etc.): The Hill Collection of Pacific Voyages consists of ca. 2,000 volumes, many of these uncommonly held. The Melanesian Archive contains more than 2,600 items. The Social Sciences and Humanities Library holds thousands of titles, many in microform format.

Visual/audio resources: Some photos and audio recordings are with the fieldnotes and other manuscript materials in the Melanesian Archive. See information below on the large collection of World War II aerial photographs of Pacific islands, on microfilm.

Access: The library is open to the public. The bulk of the Melanesian collections at UCSD (that is, all non-rare books and journals) is integrated with the general collection of the Social Sciences and Humanitites Library. Hill Collection of Pacific Voyages monographs are available for use only in the Mandeville Department of Special Collections. The Melanesian Studies Resource Center will perform free database searches on request and can supply microfiche copies of many Melanesia-related manuscript materials at a nominal cost. For information about the Melanesian Archive, contact Donald Tuzin, Melanesian Archive, Department of Anthropology, 9500 Gilman Drive, University of California, San Diego, La Jolla, CA 92092-0101. For information about the Melanesian Studies Resource Center, contact Kathryn Creely.

References: Kathryn Creely, "Melanesian Studies at the University of California, San Diego," *Contemporary Pacific*, vol. 4, no. 1 (Spring 1992), p. 210-214; Donald Tuzin, "The Melanesian Archive," in Sydel Silverman and Nancy J. Parezo (editors), *Preserving the Anthropological Record* (2nd ed., New York: 1995), p. 23-34.

Guides/catalogs: Australian National University. Pacific Manuscripts Bureau, *Guide to Collections of Manuscripts Relating to the Pacific Islands* (Canberra: [1968?]-   )—an annotated looseleaf guide to the items microfilmed in the PMB Series and the PMB Document Series; Kathryn Creely, *The Melanesian Archive: A Guide to Microforms, 1983-1996* (La Jolla, Calif.: 1996); Bess Flores (editor), *Complete Annotated Catalogue, PMB Printed Document Series: Microforms PMB Doc. 1-400* (Canberra: 1991); P. Nienhuis, *Inventaris van het Rapportenarchief van het Kantoor voor Bevolkingszaken (Nederlands-Nieuw-Guinea), 1951-1962* ('s-Gravenhage: 1968); Gillian Scott (editor), *Complete Annotated Catalogue, PMB Manuscript Series: Microfilms PMB 1-1030* (Canberra: 1991); Ronald Louis Silveira de Braganza and Charlotte Oakes (editors), *The Hill Collection of Pacific Voyages* (San Diego, Calif.: 1974-1983), 3 v.

Description

The Melanesian Archive

The Melanesian Archive was launched at the University of California, San Diego, in 1982. This major archival and documentation effort was initiated by Donald Tuzin and Fitz John Poole, both faculty members at the UCSD Department of Anthropology. Presently available in the Archive are original fieldnotes deposited by Melanesian-area field researchers (or in some cases by their estates), as well as a variety of other Melanesia-related manuscripts and documentation. Finding aids or guides to the fieldnotes and papers are now available on the library's on-line catalog, Roger. An internal Melanesian Archive database presently contains records of more than 2,600 items of documentation, while cataloging of other Melanesian Archive materials is in process. Searches of the (Pro-Cite) database will be done at the request of researchers, and microfiche copies of many papers or manuscripts in the Archive may be ordered at a nominal cost.

The Archive has sought to facilitate scholarship within the Melanesian region by supplying microfiche copies, reproduced from materials in the Archive, to selected area research libraries. The National Library of Papua New Guinea, the University of Papua New Guinea, the University of Technology (Papua New Guinea), the Solomon Islands National Library Service, the Solomon Islands College of Higher Education, the University of the South Pacific (Suva, Honiara and Port Vila), the South Pacific Commission (New Caledonia), the Vanuatu Cultural Centre and the Universitas Cenderawasih (Irian Jaya) libraries all receive complimentary sets of Melanesian Archive microfiche on a continuing basis.

Melanesian Studies Resource Center

The Melanesian Studies Resource Center was established at the UCSD Library in 1983. The Center acquires and provides access to books, journals and other materials that support and supplement the resources of the Melanesian Archive. Holdings at UCSD have been described in a 1992 article by Kathryn Creely. Prominent among these is the large collection of pre- and post-World War II Papua New Guinea patrol reports on microfiche. Thousands of pre-World War II patrol reports have been filmed at the Australian Archives, and copies are now available for use (in microfilm format) at the Center. Filming of more than 30,000 post-World War II patrol reports at the National Archives and Public Records Service of Papua New Guinea is about 75 percent complete. Patrol reports of Bougainville, Central, Chimbu, Eastern Highlands, East New Britain, East Sepik, Gulf, Madang, Manus, Northern, West New Britain, Milne Bay, Morobe and New Ireland provinces are now available. Still to be filmed are patrol reports for Southern Highlands, West Sepik, Western Highlands and Western provinces. Indexing of patrol reports is being done by Center staff, and the patrol report indexes are being made available on the Internet and in print format.

Also at La Jolla are microfilm copies of 921 Dutch-language reports reproduced from documents in the archives of the Netherlands New Guinea Bureau of the Advisor on Native Affairs (Kantoor voor Bevolkingszaken). These reports cover the years 1951-1962. The

Center also has a microfiche set of IDC's *Indonesia: Memories van Overgave, 1900-1969*, reproduced from the original reports in the General State Archives in The Hague.

Microfilm copies of a very large archive of World War II aerial photographs of the islands of the Pacific have been obtained by the Center from the Bernice Pauahi Bishop Museum in Honolulu. About half of this set consists of aerial photos of Melanesian islands. The full microfilm set reproduces approximately 64,000 World War II-era aerial photographs of islands throughout the Pacific.

Microfilm holdings at the Resource Center also include copies of extensive archival materials filmed at the National Archives of Fiji.

The UCSD library holds a full set of the Pacific Manuscripts Bureau microfilms. This is one of only two PMB sets in the United States—the other being at the Hamilton Library, the University of Hawai'i. Since 1968, the Pacific Manuscripts Bureau has worked to locate and preserve, in microform format, "manuscript (private and official) or semi-published material" of value for Pacific-area studies. Annotated catalogs of PMB manuscript and printed document series have been produced by the Bureau. These catalogs are available on the Internet. The URL of the Pacific Manuscripts Bureau is http://sunsite.anu.edu.au/spin/RSRC/PMB.

Most materials in the Melanesian Studies Resource Center collection are cataloged, and information on these holdings may be accessed via Roger, Melvyl or OCLC.

Kenneth E. Hill Collection of Pacific Voyages

The Kenneth E. Hill Collection of Pacific Voyages was donated to the UCSD library in the early 1970s. This collection consists of some 2,000 printed volumes that are kept in the library's Mandeville Department of Special Collections. The Hill Collection contains a wealth of published accounts of Pacific voyages, from the sixteenth- to the mid-nineteenth-centuries. The three-volume printed catalog of this collection, with annotations, is available in many libraries. In addition, records of Hill Collection holdings are included on Roger, the UCSD library catalog, and also on Melvyl and OCLC. Roger may be accessed via the Internet.

Missionary Materials

The library has a very strong collection of missionary materials for the Pacific, including microfilmed archival records of the major mission groups in the Pacific, microfilms of many unpublished missionary diaries, etc., and very good holdings of published missionary works, such as mission journals, memoirs, etc. These records are an important source of early ethnographic descriptions, for genealogical records, etc.

Kathryn Creely with Lee S. Dutton

California—Laguna Niguel

National Archives—Pacific Region (Laguna Niguel)

Address: National Archives—Pacific Region, 24000 Avila Road, Laguna Niguel, CA 92677-6719.
Location: Laguna Niguel is 65 miles south of Los Angeles and 70 miles north of San Diego.
Tel.: (949) 360-2641
Fax: (949) 360-2641
E-mail: archives@laguna.nara.gov.
Internet address: http://www.nara.gov/regional/laguna.html.
Parking: On-site parking is available.
Founded: 1969.
Major resources: Original federal records retired from government agencies in Arizona, southern California and Clark County, Nevada. Also microfilm copies of some other National Archives records.
Areas of specialization: Archival holdings include 3,310 cubic ft. of records from the Bureau of Indian Affairs (BIA).
Archives/manuscripts: 28,000 cubic ft. of original records and 60,000 rolls of microfilm.
Access: The great majority of holdings are open for public research. Restrictions on access to some federal records may be applied in accord with exemptions in the Freedom of Information Act.
Guides/catalogs: Edward E. Hill, *Guide to Records in the National Archives of the United States of America Relating to American Indians* (Washington, D.C.: 1981).

Information provided by National Archives—Pacific Region (Laguna Niguel).

California—Los Angeles

Southwest Museum. Braun Research Library

Address: Braun Research Library, Southwest Museum, P.O. Box 41558, Los Angeles, CA 90041-0558.
Location: In the Southwest Museum, 234 Museum Drive, Los Angeles, CA 90065.
Tel.: (213) 221-2164, ext. 255.
Fax: (213) 224-8223
Internet address: http://www.annex.com/southwest/braun.htm.
Networks, consortia: OCLC.
Public transit access: The best public transit access to the Museum is by taxi. Visitors are not generally encouraged to take the bus to the museum.
Parking: On-site parking is available.
Founded: 1907 (Southwest Museum). The Braun Research Library building opened in 1977.
Major resources: Library and Archives.
Areas of specialization: Native American cultures.

Archives/manuscripts: Some 750 manuscript collections, several of which include diaries and fieldnotes of anthropological significance. There is almost 300 linear ft. of archival or manuscript material of anthropological or related interest. Noteworthy among the archival collections are:

- Archaeological Institute of America. Southwest Society (1903-1915)—includes correspondence, brochures, published reports and annual reports that incorporate the financial statements for the Southwest Society and membership lists.
- Diana Meyers Bahr (1930-   )—papers and sound recordings. This collection includes oral history tapes of Cupeño women for Bahr's book *From Mission to Metropolis: Cupeño Indian Women in Los Angeles* (Norman: 1993).
- Elizabeth Crozer W. Campbell (1893-19[?]) and William H. Campbell (1895-1938)—papers; includes correspondence and archaeological site reports for Pinto Basin site, Dry Lakes, Lake Mojave (Soda Lake) and Lake Mojave (Silver Lake).
- Frank Hamilton Cushing (1857-1900)—papers dated between1876 and 1900; includes his correspondence, notes, Zuni-language material, illustrations and manuscripts. These documents include information about Cushing's five-year residency at Zuni Pueblo, 1879-1884; material and fieldnotes about the Hemenway Southwestern Archaeological Expeditions; and the Pepper-Hearst Expedition to Florida. The archaeological material for the Hemenway Expedition is held by the Peabody Museum of Archaeology and Ethnology. The Huntington Free Library (Bronx) also holds correspondence that relates to the Hemenway Expedition. The University of Pennsylvania Museum holds the archaeological material recovered during the Pepper-Hearst Expedition.
- Frances Densmore (1867-1957)—papers dated between 1876 and the 1930s; includes correspondence, notes, diaries and manuscripts about her ethnomusicology research. There is also melodic analysis for her work on Cheyenne and Arapaho songs and Santo Domingo songs.
- George Bird Grinnell (1849-1938)—papers dated between 1876 and the 1930s; includes correspondence, notes, diaries and manuscripts—all relating to the Plains Indians. Very important for the study of Plains Indian cultures and the early reservation period. This relates to the Grinnell collection held by Yale University.
- John P. Harrington (1884-1961)—papers; includes correspondence and some notes on southern California Indians.
- Mark R. Harrington (1882-1971)—papers dated primarily to the 1930s; includes correspondence, archaeological fieldnotes—primarily for the survey work done in Nevada by the Southwest Museum—and clippings.
- Frederick W. Hodge (1864-1956)—papers dated between the 1880s and 1956; includes his correspondence, notes, diaries, manuscripts and clippings. The collection covers his work with the Hemenway Southwestern Archaeological Expedition; the Smithsonian Institution; the various positions he held at the Bureau of American Ethnology; the Museum of the American Indian—Heye Foundation; the Hendricks-Hodge Expedition; and the Southwest Museum. The documents also include the various books and serials that he edited, such as *American Anthropologist*; *Benavides Memorial*; *Handbook of American Indians North of Mexico* (Washington, D.C.: 1907-   ), 2 v.; Edward S. Curtis, *North American Indian* (Cambridge: 1907-1930), 20 v.; and others.

- George Wharton James (1858-1923)—papers dated between the 1890s and the 1930s; includes correspondence, notes, manuscripts, diaries, clippings and scrapbooks.
- Charles F. Lummis (1859-1928)—papers dated between the 1880s and 1928; includes Lummis's correspondence, journals, diaries, Isleta vocabulary, manuscripts of his published and unpublished works. In addition, it includes documents from the Southwest Society, the Landmarks Club, the Sequoya League, *Land of Sunshine* and *Out West* magazines and the Los Angeles Public Library.
- Walter McClintock (1870-1949)—papers; includes manuscripts, clippings and typed copies about his lectures. The library also holds a large collection of his hand-colored photographs of Blackfoot Indians. Yale University also holds a collection.
- Washington Matthews (1843-1905)—papers; includes a scrapbook, miscellaneous clippings and correspondence.
- Alanson B. Skinner (1886-1925)—papers; includes correspondence, manuscripts (anthropological and fiction). The main focus of the collection is on the eastern and midwestern tribes.
- Edwin F. Walker (1872-19[?])—papers; includes fieldnotes for archaeological work in southern California.
- Frances E. Watkins (1899-1986)—papers; includes papers and articles on various subjects about Native Americans. There is a report on excavations done at Tecolate in New Mexico.
- T.A. Willard (1862-1943)—papers; includes correspondence and manuscripts that relate to his Mayan studies. Several hundred photographs from this collection are in Photo Archives.
- Toshio Yatsushiro—papers dated from the 1950s to the 1960s—includes research notes and manuscripts on Inuit of the Frobisher Bay area.

Holdings (books and journals): More than 50,000 titles. The majority are of anthropological or historical interest.

Visual/audio resources: More than 137,000 photographs, 900 wax cylinder recordings, the Frances Densmore collection (recordings of Cheyenne, Arapaho, Maidu and San Ildefonso music), the Walter McClintock collection (Blackfoot recordings), other Native American recordings, the Charles F. Lummis collection of early California Hispanic folksongs (dating from 1895 to 1907).

Access: Open to the public. Researchers should call one month in advance of a visit to arrange access to archival materials, including photographs.

Guides/catalogs: *Charles F. Lummis Manuscript Collection (MS.1): Correspondence Series (MS.1.1) Finding Aid* (Los Angeles: 1993), 3 v. Finding aids for the papers and correspondence of Frederick W. Hodge and Frank Hamilton Cushing are in preparation.

Artifacts of anthropological significance: The Southwest Museum holds large collections of material culture and archaeological artifacts from the Americas.

Archaeological sites for which the museum has artifact collections: Some of the important ones include the Stall site, Little Lake, Mesa House, Gypsum Cave, several sites on San Nicolas Island, Borax Lake, Casa Grande and Tule Springs. There is no published catalog of the artifact collections although many of the site reports were published in the *Southwest Museum Papers* series. Upon request we can provide computer printouts of the collection.

University of California, Los Angeles (UCLA)

Resources of anthropological interest are maintained in a number of UCLA archives, libraries and departments.
- Information on the Institute of Archaeology is available at http://www.ioa.ucla.edu.
- For information on the UCLA Folklore and Mythology Archives, see http://www.humnet.ucla.edu/humnet.folklore/content1.
- The URL of the UCLA Library is http://www.library.ucla.edu.

University of California, Los Angeles (UCLA). Fowler Museum of Cultural History (FMCH)

Address: Fowler Museum of Cultural History, Haines Hall, University of California, Los Angeles, CA 90024-1549.
Location: The museum is west of Royce Hall on the UCLA campus. See the "Map to the Museum," on the FMCH website, for travel, parking or related information.
Tel.: (310) 825-4361
Fax: (310) 206-7007
E-mail (library): library@fmnh.ucla.edu.
Internet address: http://www.fmch.ucla.edu/welcome.html.
Founded: In 1963, as the UCLA Museum and Laboratories of Ethnic Arts and Technology; later renamed the Fowler Museum of Cultural History.
Major resources: The Kitnick-Alexander Library; archives; photographic documentation.
Areas of specialization: Ethnic art, ethnology, material culture, Indonesian textiles. The Center for the Study of Regional Dress (CSRD) was established in 1993.
Archives/manuscripts: Yes.
Holdings (library): Ca. 7,500 volumes.
Visual/audio resources: Photographic holdings include the Arnold Rubin photographs and slides of tattoos and body markings.
Access: Library materials are for on-site use only. See the website for information on research access to archival or photographic materials.
Catalogs of artifacts: Jerome Feldman, *Arc of the Ancestors: Indonesian Art from the Jerome L. Joss Collection at UCLA* (Los Angeles, Calif.: 1994); Roy W. Hamilton (editor), *Gift of the Cotton Maiden: Textiles of Flores and the Solor Islands* (Los Angeles: 1994).

California—San Bruno

National Archives—Pacific Region (San Francisco)

Address: National Archives—Pacific Region (San Francisco), 1000 Commodore Drive, San Bruno, CA 94066-2350.
Tel.: (650) 876-9001
Fax: (650) 876-0920
E-mail: center@sanbruno.nara.gov.
Internet address: http://www.nara.gov/regional/sanfranc.html.
Public transit access: San Mateo County Transit (SamTrans) bus 5L stops within a few blocks of the archives. The archives is not directly accessible by BART.
Parking: On-site parking is available.
Founded: 1969.
Major resources: Original federal records retired from government agencies in northern California, Nevada (except Clark County), Hawai'i, American Samoa, Guam and the Trust Territory of the Pacific Islands. Microfilm copies of many National Archives records held in Washington, D.C., are also available.
Areas of specialization: Holdings include Bureau of Indian Affairs (BIA) records for northern California and Nevada (except Clark County).
Archives/manuscripts: Ca. 45,000 cubic ft. of original records and 55,000 reels of microfilm. 2,770 cubic ft. of Bureau of Indian Affairs records are held.
Visual/audio resources: Photographs of Chinese and Chinese American individuals and family groups, Native American individuals—including a few photos involving traditional activities—and other photographs are interfiled with the textual records of federal agencies involved with these groups. There are no separate collections of anthropological photographs nor are there indexes or item lists of photographs in Pacific Region (San Francisco) holdings. A few drawings made by Native American students are held.
Access: The great majority of holdings are open for public research. Restrictions on access to some federal records may be applied in accord with exemptions in the Freedom of Information Act.
Guides/catalogs: *Guide to Records in the National Archives—Pacific Sierra Region* (Washington, D.C.: 1995); Edward E. Hill, *Guide to Records in the National Archives of the United States of America Relating to American Indians* (Washington, D.C.: 1981); *Records in the National Archives—Pacific Sierra Region for the Study of Ethnic History* (San Bruno, Calif.: 1994) (= *National Archives and Records Administration. Reference Information Paper,* 83).

Description

The Pacific Region (San Francisco) Archives serves as the depository for federal records created in northern California, Nevada (with the exception of Clark County),Hawai'i, American Samoa, Guam and the Trust Territory of the Pacific Islands. The approximately 55,000 reels of microfilm at the Region can be divided into two groups. Most are National

Archives microfilm publication copies of records held by the National Archives in Washington, D.C., (such as the decennial census schedules) that relate to the Pacific Region (San Francisco) geographic area, or to the United States as a whole. Some of the microfilm was produced at this branch or was acquired directly from federal agencies within the Pacific Region (San Francisco) geographic jurisdiction. These reels often are not published or duplicated elsewhere in the National Archives system. Records of federal agencies held at the Region contain information pertinent to many ethnic groups, including Native American, African American, Asian Indian, Chinese and Chinese American, Filipino, Hispanic, Japanese and Japanese American.

Records of the Bureau of Indian Affairs (BIA)

Holdings of records of the Bureau of Indian Affairs (RG 75) consist of 2,770 cubic feet of records created from 1859 to 1974. The bulk of these are from the twentieth-century. The records were created by the following area offices, agencies and schools: California Agency, Carson Agency, Carson/Stewart School, Digger Agency, Fallon Subagency, Fort Bidwell School and Agency, Fort McDermitt Subagency, Greenville School and Agency, Hoopa Valley Agency, Nevada Agency, Pyramid Lake Subagency, Reno Agency, Roseburg Agency, Round Valley Agency, Sacramento Agency, Sacramento Area Office, Special Agency of Nevada, Tule River Agency, Upper Lake-Ukiah Agency, Walker River Agency, Western Nevada Agency and Western Shoshone Agency. Also available are records of the Supervisor of Indian Education (Sacramento, California); Special Agent at Large (Reno, Nevada); records of Indian clinics and health centers in Alturas, Fresno and Ukiah, California; and records of the Berkeley Outing Center.

These records pertain to all aspects of administration and operation of agencies and schools—such as agricultural extension projects, home demonstration programs, irrigation and land management activities, construction of homes and roads, emergency relief programs conducted in the 1930s, health care programs and law enforcement activities. A draft inventory of the records of each California agency is available. In addition to the draft inventories of BIA units in California, the Region has series title and date lists for the Nevada BIA units. BIA records at the Region include some land allotment case files, probate case files and the 1933 and 1955 rolls of California Indians, all of which are useful ethnographic sources.

In addition to these original records, the Region has a large collection of microfilm representing Bureau of Indian Affairs records held at the National Archives in Washington, D.C. Among microfilm holdings at San Bruno are 65 reels of *Indian Census Rolls, 1884-1940* (Washington, D.C.: 1967) (= *National Archives Microfilm Publications*, M595). A total of 692 reels of the *Indian Census Rolls* have been produced. The 65 reels of this series held at San Bruno cover California and Nevada BIA agencies only.

Immigration and Naturalization Records

Other large collections of records of potential anthropological interest include the records of the Immigration and Naturalization Service (RG 85). The RG 85 holdings were created by the Angel Island Immigration Station, the San Francisco District Office and the

Honolulu District Office, from 1882 to 1955. Totaling more than 2,200 cubic feet, they document Chinese Exclusion Acts arrival and departure cases. These case files (concerning individual Chinese and non-Chinese immigrants) contain information about the families, homes and towns from which they emigrated, usually in the form of transcripts of interrogations, village maps, witness statements and other records. Other case files contain information about individuals leaving the U.S.—such as merchants traveling on business. The arrival and departure files contain information about ethnic communities existing in the United States.

The Region also holds records of the Honolulu and San Francisco Offices of the Immigration and Naturalization Service pertaining to Chinese immigration. These document ship passages, arrivals and departures and exclusion and deportation cases of individuals, as well as business activities of individuals and firms. The bulk of the records are case files created during the enforcement of the Chinese Exclusion Acts, 1882-1943. Nearly all records generated at Angel Island Immigration Station are included. In general, case files contain the subject's name, place and date of birth, family information, occupation, descriptions of interrogations, statements of witnesses, photograph of the subject and sometimes of family members, and exhibits. With the exception of business partnership case files, most of the records concern individuals and may be protected by privacy restrictions. The Chinese partnership lists contain records for individual Chinese businesses throughout California, as well as maps of San Francisco's Chinatown.

The U.S. District Courts had jurisdiction over naturalization, equity and *habeas corpus* cases (*habeas corpus* cases were heard both in civil and admiralty courts). Records of such cases, as well as Court Commissioner's files, provide extensive documentation of Chinese immigration and immigrants for San Francisco and Hawai'i.

The late nineteenth-century correspondence of the San Francisco Collector of Customs includes letters relating to the enforcement of the Chinese Exclusion Acts.

The records of the Public Health Service's Angel Island Quarantine Station in San Francisco Bay pertain to Chinese and Japanese passengers quarantined between 1896 and 1948. Some of these records are protected by privacy restrictions.

Filipinos' applications for Certificates of Citizenship for the Hawai'ian Islands, 1934-1944, can be found among the records of the Immigration and Naturalization Service.

The records of the district courts include microfilm copies (and some original records) of land grant cases, 1852-1910, in which former Mexican citizens of California sought to regain land held by them under Spanish and Mexican land grants prior to annexation of California by the United States. Other records pertaining to land grants are on microfilm in the Records of the Bureau of Land Management.

Records of the Hawai'i Office of the Immigration and Naturalization Service contain case files of Japanese immigrants, including picture ID cards, 1924-1928, and appeals for Japanese immigrants, 1919-1940. San Francisco records include case files for Japanese picture brides, 1907-1912.

The Government of American Samoa

The records of the Government of American Samoa (RG 284) consist of 200 cubic feet of records created from 1899 to 1966. They pertain to district and village affairs, emigration and immigration, census data, native agreements, court and *Fono* (Congress) proceedings, etc. The records of the U.S. Naval Station at American Samoa contain information on the Fita Fita Guard Unit, as well as other administrative records concerning the Navy's period of governance, 1919-1951.

Records on Migratory Labor in California

Also of interest are several collections containing information about migratory labor in California, including Farm Security Administration records relating to the Dust Bowl migrants, 1934-1947 (RG 96); records of the regional War Manpower Commission office concerning Mexican nationals who worked for railroads and agricultural enterprises in California during World War II (RG 211); and records of the regional solicitor of the Department of Labor, concerning the bracero program, 1950-1965 (RG 174).

Other Records of Ethnic or Related Interest

The Region's most extensive sources for a variety of ethnic populations are the records of the Federal Courts. Court records cannot be accessed by subject, except in the broadest terms. To locate a particular case file, it is necessary to know either the case name or number. In addition to case files of the Federal Courts, less extensive files that relate to Native Americans (or other ethnic populations) may be found among the records of U.S. Attorneys and Marshals, the Bureau of Land Management, the National Park Service, the Fair Employment Practices Committee and the Bureau of Mines.

These are probably the largest groups of records of anthropological interest, but many smaller series of records available at the Region may also be of interest.

Lisa K. Miller

California—San Marino

Henry E. Huntington Library, Art Collections and Botanical Gardens

Address: Henry E. Huntington Library, 1151 Oxford Road, San Marino, CA 91108.
Tel.: (818) 405-2190
Fax: (818) 449-5720
Internet address: http://www.huntington.org.
Networks, consortia: RLIN.
Founded: 1919.
Major resources (of anthropological interest): The materials of anthropological significance may be found primarily in four collections: the Mary (Hunter) Austin collection, the Sir Richard F. Burton library, the Grace Nicholson collection and the Horatio Nelson Rust collection. Each of those collections has a finding aid or an index.
Holdings (manuscripts): Mary Austin collection: 5,456 pieces; Grace Nicholson collection: ca. 3,000 pieces; Horatio N. Rust collection: 1,229 pieces.

Holdings (books): 2,700 books and pamphlets in the Richard Burton library.

Visual/audio resources: There are photographs from the Mary Austin and Grace Nicholson collections that have been transferred to the Huntington's Photographic Archives. Some of those photos depict Native Americans or aspects of their material culture.

Access: The Huntington Library is a private institution and its collections are accessible only to scholars who possess doctoral degrees in its primary fields of British or American history and literature, or who have been advanced to candidacy for such a degree, or who can demonstrate substantial experience in the use of rare original materials, as well as a specific project requiring the consultation of such materials. The collections are not open to the general public.

Guides/catalogs: Readers interested in the scope of the Huntington's holdings should consult one of the following volumes, depending upon their scholarly pursuits: Henry E. Huntington Library and Art Gallery, *Guide to American Historical Manuscripts in the Huntington Library* (San Marino, Calif.: 1979); Henry E. Huntington Library and Art Gallery, *Guide to British Historical Manuscripts in the Huntington Library* (San Marino, Calif.: 1982). The Richard Burton library is described in B.J. Kirkpatrick (editor), *A Catalogue of the Library of Sir Richard Burton, K.C.M.G., Held by the Royal Anthropological Institute* (London: 1978).

Artifacts: The Huntington Library has no collections of artifacts in any field of study.

Description

Since its founding in 1919, the Henry E. Huntington Library has emphasized the fields of British and American history and literature since the sixteenth-century as its primary collecting areas. Within those fields, the library has acquired extensive holdings that document the contact of European and Euro-American civilizations with Native peoples in the Americas, Asia and Africa. Although in the course of its institutional development the library has never collected the papers of professional anthropologists or original archaeological artifacts, the Huntington has accumulated some eclectic resources for anthropological study. Outside of a scattering of individual documents, such as diaries or single letters, four significant collections would assist research in two broad areas: the study of Native peoples in the Pacific Northwest and the Southwest and of the indigenous peoples of Africa and the Middle East. Those collections include the papers of Americans Mary Austin, Grace Nicholson and Horatio Nelson Rust, as well as the library of the British explorer, Sir Richard F. Burton.

Of these four individuals, the one who bears the closest resemblance to a trained anthropologist probably would be Sir Richard F. Burton (1821-1890). Often overshadowed, both then and now, by his exceptionally outspoken utterances on matters such as religion and his fellow Victorian-era explorers, Burton's remarkable linguistic skills and his impressive expeditionary record reflected the vast storehouse of knowledge about indigenous peoples and cultures that he gathered over his lifetime. In his library are more than 2,700 books, pamphlets, maps and documents (placed on permanent deposit at the Huntington Library in 1986 by the late Allen Christensen and the Christensen Fund). Burton's terse and forceful annotations, as well as the correspondence he exchanged with other scholars and authors, demonstrate the breadth and depth of that knowledge. Burton, as seen through his library, exemplifies many of his age's most admirable and most deplorable traits in exploration and in the study of "alien" peoples and cultures.

Unlike Burton, the other three individuals mentioned here were essentially amateurs motivated by a compelling personal passion, such as collecting art and artifacts or ensuring the preservation of a cultural heritage. The author Mary Austin (1868-1934), for example, cultivated a passion for the landscape of the southwestern deserts (as demonstrated by her 1903 volume, *Land of Little Rain*) that extended to a fascination with the culture of its indigenous inhabitants and the folklore of the early Hispanic settlers. Her collection of more than 5,400 pieces includes letters from authors, folklorists and students of anthropology such as Charles F. Lummis and Frederick W. Hodge, transcriptions of many different examples of Hispanic folk literature and both correspondence and essays focusing upon the causes of Indian rights, Indian education and the preservation of Indian crafts in the early twentieth-century.

Like Mary Austin, Grace Nicholson (1877-1948) engaged in the detailed study of many Native American cultures, including their mythology and languages. Nicholson's interest arose, however, from her unrelenting pursuit of Indian artifacts, such as basketry and jewelry. An extremely diligent and well-informed collector, she established ties with tribes, and in some cases with individual artisans, in the Southwest and the Pacific Northwest. Her reputation led various institutions, such as the University of Pennsylvania and the Smithsonian Museum, to engage her services as a buyer. At the same time, she obtained accounts detailing different legends and folkways from various Native informants. In later life, Nicholson also became an equally successful collector of Asian art objects and the founder of the institution that became the Pacific Asia Museum in Pasadena, California, but it is the material that she assembled on Native Americans that forms the bulk of her 2,500-piece manuscript collection and constitutes the most valuable material for anthropological research.

Nicholson and Austin, in their distinctive careers, mirrored the growing appreciation of twentieth-century America for the American Indian. Horatio Nelson Rust (1828-1906), a New Englander transplanted to southern California in 1882, pursued concurrent careers as a collector of archaeological specimens and a fervent advocate of Indian rights against the background of a still-powerful national sense of ambivalence about Native peoples. Rust himself expressed assimilationist views about the fate of Native peoples that later generations would repudiate. Among the 1,229 pieces in his collection, however, are numerous letters from such leading scientists and writers as Frederick W. Hodge, Alfred L. Kroeber, William H. Holmes and Spencer F. Baird; manuscripts and letters concerning his work as Indian Agent; and diaries recounting his archaeological expeditions in the Southwest.

For further details about the Richard Burton library, interested researchers should consult B.J. Kirkpatrick, *A Catalogue of the Library of Sir Richard Burton, K.C.M.G.* (London: 1978); the Nicholson and Rust collections are described briefly in *A Guide to American Historical Manuscripts in the Huntington Library* (San Marino, Calif.: 1979), while more detailed finding aids (known as "Summary Reports") are available for the Austin, Nicholson and Rust papers, from the Manuscripts Department, Huntington Library, 1151 Oxford Road, San Marino, CA 91108.

Peter J. Blodgett

California—Santa Barbara

Santa Barbara Museum of Natural History (SBMNH)

Address: Santa Barbara Museum of Natural History, 2559 Puesta del Sol Road, Santa Barbara, CA 93105.
Tel.: (805) 682-4711
Fax: (805) 569-3170
E-mail (library): library@sbnature.org.
Internet address: http://www.sbnature.org.
Networks, consortia: The library's anthropological holdings are on OCLC.
Parking: Available.
Founded: 1916.
Major resources: Channel Islands archives, Chumash collection, John P. Harrington collection, Local History collection.
Areas of specialization: Chumash and other California tribes, including history, culture and language; California rock art; archaeology of the Southwest, California and the Channel Islands.
Holdings: 80 linear ft. of archival or manuscript materials; 4,500 book and journal vols. in the fields of archaeology, anthropology and linguistics; 300 reels of microfilm; 150 audio cassette tapes; 1,300 slides; 1,000 photographs.
Manuscripts:
- John P. Harrington (1884-1961)—notes, photographs and recordings, 1915-1954.
- David Banks Rogers (1868-1954)—fieldnotes and photographs, 1923-1937.
- Phil C. Orr (d. 1991)—papers, fieldnotes and photographs, 1941-1968.
- Stephen Bowers (1832-1907)—archaeological journals, 1875-1889.
- D. Travis Hudson (1942-1985)—research files on California Indians, 1973-1986.
- W.I. (Wilbur Irving) Follett (1901-1992)—papers in archeoicthyology, 1950-1970.
- Madison Scott Beeler (1910-1989)—California Indian linguistic manuscripts and lexical files, 1960-1980.
- Campbell Grant (1909-1992)—rock art notes, drawings and slides, 1960-1987.
- Georgia Lee (1926-   )—Chumash rock art research papers, 1978-
- John W. Cawley—rock art research papers, 1970-1980.
- Robert F. Heizer (1915-1979)—research notes on Leon de Cessac's collections from the Santa Barbara area in 1877-1879.
Fieldnotes, etc.: Madison S. Beeler, Stephen Bowers, Campbell Grant, D. Travis Hudson, Phil C. Orr, David Banks Rogers, Arthur Woodward.
Visual/audio resources: Photographic prints and negatives of early archaeological excavations by David Banks Rogers and Phil C. Orr on the Channel Islands and the Santa Barbara mainland, and of John P. Harrington's California fieldwork, are deposited in the museum. Photographs, negatives, slides and colored drawings in the Campbell Grant archives document rock art sites in the western United States, Mexico, Canada, France and

Africa, with emphasis on California. Audio collections include copies of original Chumash linguistic recordings (both music and text) from John P. Harrington's field work (60 cassette tapes) and of Juan Justo's recordings in Chumash and Spanish (90 cassette tapes).

Access: Library resources, except for some site specific or culturally sensitive materials, are accessible to general readers for library use. Much of the collection is available through interlibrary loan. Archival materials are available to qualified researchers by appointment.

References: Campbell Grant, *The Rock Paintings of the Chumash: A Study of a California Indian Culture* (Santa Barbara: 1993)—first published 1965; Marie S. Holmes and John R. Johnson, *The Chumash and Their Predecessors: An Annotated Bibliography* (Santa Barbara, Calif.: 1998) (= *Santa Barbara Museum of Natural History. Contributions in Anthropology*, no. 1).

Artifacts of anthropological significence: Archaeological collections are mostly from the Santa Barbara mainland and northern Channel Islands, with more than 70,000 items representing all major periods in prehistory from at least 8,000, B.C., to the era of European colonization. Additional collections feature nearly 5,000 ethnological objects from numerous other western North American Indian cultures. The majority of artifacts were obtained from excavations by the museum's first two curators, David Banks Rogers and Phil C. Orr. Other principal holdings are the James-Abels collection from the Cuyama region; Santa Barbara City College collections; the W.I. Follett collection of archaeological specimens of fish remains and marine archaeological finds. The museum also curates the Los Padres National Forest anthropological collections. The museum houses the world's largest collection of Chumash basketry, fiberwork, wood and other perishable artifacts, including thirty Chumash baskets and several hundred other California baskets.

Archaeological sites represented in artifact collections: The museum has significant numbers of items from many sites on the northern Channel Islands, Santa Barbara and Ventura Counties coastal and inland areas, dating from the excavations of 1923 onward.

Catalogs of artifact resources: Santa Barbara Museum of Natural History, *North American Indian Basketry and Textiles in the Anthropology Collection of the Santa Barbara Museum of Natural History* (Santa Barbara, Calif.: 1975) (= *Culture Resource Records*, no. 1); Santa Barbara Museum of Natural History, *Pacific Northwest Coast Indian Materials in the Anthropology Collection of the Santa Barbara Museum of Natural History* (Santa Barbara, Calif.: 1977) (= *Culture Resource Records*, no. 2). The above publications are now out-of-date; however, work in progress on computerization of all records will facilitate both publication of guides and on-line access.

Description

The Santa Barbara Museum of Natural History holds an extensive archival and library reference collection focusing on the archaeology and anthropology of the western United States, with special emphasis on south central California—particularly the region occupied by the Chumash Indians. Important collections include:

• Extensive unpublished fieldnotes of David Banks Rogers and Phil C. Orr, the museum's first two curators of anthropology, whose collections of artifacts from their excavations on the Santa Barbara mainland and the northern Channel Islands are also at the museum.

- A small, but significant, portion of the unpublished papers and personal library of John P. Harrington—includes original fieldnotes, research notes, drafts of published and unpublished manuscripts, correspondence, photographs, transcripts and photostats of archival material, books and other miscellaneous items. A guide to this collection will be published in 1999. The photo negatives and prints in the collection include an almost complete set from Harrington's fieldwork in California in 1931; a considerable number of photographs taken about 1924 in and around Santa Barbara; documentation of his archaeological investigations at Burton Mound; and also personal photographs. Microfilm copies of Harrington's original papers in the Smithsonian Institution may also be consulted at the museum.

- The archaeological journals of Stephen Bowers, who excavated sites throughout the entire Chumash region in the 1870s—a time when the sites were still relatively intact.

- California Indian linguistic manuscripts and Chumash lexical files compiled by Madison S. Beeler.

- Copies of the fieldnotes of Arthur Woodward (1898-   ).

- Rock art site records, drawings and photographs from around the world, donated by Campbell Grant, author of the seminal work on Chumash rock art.

- Other resources include extensive research files on Chumash social organization and genealogies and on Chumash ethnobotany, compiled by the current curators, John R. Johnson and Jan Timbrook.

The museum library's collection includes 4,500 volumes in archaeology, anthropology and linguistics of the Western Hemisphere, with an emphasis on southwestern United States and California Indian tribes. In addition to standard books and periodicals, the library holds archaeological and cultural research reports, dissertations and publications of local historical and archaeological societies. Its many published reports from the late eighteenth- and early nineteenth-centuries (from such sources as the Carnegie Institution, the Smithsonian Institution, the Bureau of American Ethnology, the Bureau of Indian Affairs, the U.S. National Museum and the U.S. Geological Survey) document cultural and archaeological material that has since been lost or destroyed.

The Chumash and their Predecessors: An Annotated Bibliography, by Marie S. Holmes and John R. Johnson, was published in 1998 as the museum's *Contributions in Anthropology*, no. 1.   This reference volume serves as a key to information on the Chumash, from the account of Cabrillo's visit in 1542 to the latest publications in 1998. More than 1,200 annotated entries are cited.

For access to the archival or anthropological collections of the museum, call (805) 682-4711, or use the library's Internet address (above) to ask for an appointment.

Marie S. Holmes

California—Stanford

Stanford University. Hoover Institution on War, Revolution and Peace. Library and Archives

Address: Library and Archives, Hoover Institution on War, Revolution and Peace, Stanford University, Stanford, CA 94305.
Tel.: (650) 723-2058 (Main Collection); (650) 725-3435 (East Asia Collection); (650) 723-3563 (Archives).
Fax: (650) 725-4655 (Main Collection); (650) 723-1687 (East Asia Collection); (650) 725-3445 (Archives).
E-mail (Main Collection): molloy@hoover.stanford.edu; wheeler@hoover.stanford.edu.
E-mail (East Asia Collection): tung@hoover.stanford.edu (Chinese); findley@hoover.stanford.edu (Japanese).
E-mail (Archives): leadenham@hoover.stanford.edu.
Internet address: http://www-hoover.stanford.edu/homepage/library.html.
Public transit access: For information on Caltrain, VTA or SamTrans, see http://www-facilities.stanford.edu/transportation/traninfo.html.
Founded: 1919.
Major resources: Hoover Institution: Main Collection; East Asia Collection; Hoover Institution Archives.
Areas of specialization: East Asia; Africa; the Americas; Europe; the Middle East; Russia/Commonwealth of Independent States.
Access: Open to the public. See the website for additional information on access. Visitor maps are available at http://www.stanford.edu/home/visitors/map.html.

Information provided by Carol A. Leadenham.

Stanford University. Libraries

Address: Cecil H. Green Library, Stanford University, Stanford, CA 94305.
Tel.: (650) 723-9108
Fax: (650) 725-4902
Internet address: http://www-sul.stanford.edu.
Public transit access: For information on Caltrain, VTA or SamTrans, see http://www-facilities.stanford.edu/transportation/traninfo.html.
Founded: 1892.
Major resources: Special Collections.
Areas of specialization: Mexican American manuscript collection (ca. 5,000 linear ft.); Asian American manuscripts; gender studies.
Access: Open to the public.

Colorado—Boulder

University of Colorado. Museum

Address: Museum, Campus Box 218, University of Colorado, Boulder, CO 80309-0218.
Tel.: (303) 492-6892
Fax: (303) 492-4195
Internet address: http://stripe.Colorado.EDU/~ucm/Home.html.
Founded: 1902.
Major resources: Anna O. Shepard archive; Earl H. Morris archive; Joe Ben Wheat archive; general anthropology/archaeology research and reference collections.
Areas of specialization: Southwestern archaeology and ethnology (with special focus on textile research); Plains ethnology; Paleo-Indian archaeology; ceramic materials research.
Archives/manuscripts: Anna O. Shepard (48 linear ft.); Earl H. Morris (24 linear ft.); Joe Ben Wheat (40 linear ft.).
Fieldnotes: Earl H. Morris, Anna O. Shepard, Joe Ben Wheat.
Holdings (books and journals): 44 linear ft.
Visual/audio resources: The Earl H. Morris collection has more than 9,000 photographic images that include glass and film negatives, prints, lantern slides and movie film that primarily record expeditions to the Southwest and the Maya area, excavations, camp life and Southwestern scenery. The Anna O. Shepard collection contains more than 2,900 prints and negatives of archaeological and ethnological research, as well as on experimental ceramic firing and some glass-plate spectrographs from her ceramic analyses. The Joe Ben Wheat collection contains thousands of slides and black-and-white images of field excavations and archaeological and ethnological specimens.
Access: The general library is available to the public and university students. Archives are available to scholars (including students enrolled at the University of Colorado and other institutions). Because of space limitations, two months advance notice is required for archival researchers. Photocopies of many photographic prints have been placed in ring binders for scholarly access. Users of the photographic images are required to pay for use negatives, as the loan or use of originals is not permitted.
References: Ronald L. Bishop and Frederick W. Lange (editors), *The Ceramic Legacy of Anna O. Shepard* (Niwot, Colo.: 1991); Frederick W. Lange and Holley R. Lange, "The Interactive Value of the Earl H. Morris Collection, University of Colorado Museum," in M.S. Duran and D.T. Kirkpatrick (editors), *Collected Papers in Honor of Robert C. and Florence H. Lister* (Albuquerque, N.M.: 1989) (= *Papers of the Archaeological Society of New Mexico*, 15), p. 153-163; Frederick W. Lange and Diana Leonard, "The University of Colorado Museum's Anthropology Collections: A Legacy from Joe Ben Wheat," in Meliha S. Duran and David T. Kirkpatrick (editors), *Why Museums Collect: Papers in Honor of Joe Ben Wheat* (Albuquerque, N.M.: 1993) (= *Papers of the Archaeological Society of New Mexico*, 19), p. 137-151; Anna Osler Shepard, *Ceramics for the Archaeologist* (Washington. D.C.: 1956) (= *Carnegie Institution of Washington. Publication*, vol. 609).
Artifacts: Southwestern archaeology and ethnology; Plains ethnology; Paleo-Indian archaeology; ceramic materials research.

Archaeological sites represented in artifact collections: La Plata District, Gobernador area (northern New Mexico) and Mimbres area (southern New Mexico); Yellow Jacket, Olsen-Chubbuck, Jurgens, Falls Creek Cave, Dinosaur National Monument (Colorado); Kawaika-a, Canyon de Chelly and Canyon del Muerto (Arizona).

Catalogs of artifact resources: Robert H. Lister and Florence C. Lister, *The Earl H. Morris Memorial Pottery Collection: An Example of Ten Centuries of Prehistoric Ceramic Art in the Four Corners Country of Southwestern United States* (Boulder: 1969) (= *University of Colorado Studies. Series in Anthropology*, no. 16); also see Lange and Leonard, 1993.

Description

There are three principal archival collections of anthropological interest at the University of Colorado. These collections represent the lifetime research and curation activities of Earl H. Morris (1889-1956), Anna O. Shepard (1903-1973) and Joe Ben Wheat (1916-1997). The three archival data bases are historically linked: Morris was one of Shepard's strongest supporters, frequently intervening on her behalf with A.V. Kidder and others. Much of her early Southwestern analysis was for Morris's Aztec and La Plata projects, and there was significant correspondence between Morris and Shepard. Most importantly, preliminary inspection shows that there are letters from Morris to Shepard, where there is no copy in the Morris archive, and vice versa. Wheat joined the University of Colorado faculty in part to work with Morris, and in some of his earliest research continued Morris's emphasis on Basket-Maker culture pit-houses in southwestern Colorado. He also was a research colleague of Anna Shepard.

The Earl H. Morris Archival Collection

Morris carefully recorded field data in notes and photographs and was a constant correspondent with numerous colleagues. His papers, which focus on the period from the late 1920s to the 1950s, are numerous and detailed, and have been divided into correspondence and miscellaneous files. The collection was reorganized after it was received by the museum, and an unpublished finding aid for the papers (container inventories that approach item-level listings) has been compiled. A microfiche copy of the Morris archive is also available through the National Park Service Office in Denver, Colorado. The collection is wide-ranging, documenting excavations from across the Four Corners area: from Aztec, the La Plata region, Canyon de Chelly, Canyon del Muerto, Gobernador and the Durango region.

Morris's correspondents included contemporary archaeologists and various individuals involved in his archaeological expeditions and research. Some of the more important persons or recognizable names include Alfred V. Kidder, Anna O. Shepard, Sylvanus G. Morley, Emil Haury, Harold S. Gladwin, Alfred M. Tozzer, Jesse L. Nusbaum, Gustav Stromsvik, Clark Wissler, Marie Wormington, Charles L. Bernhiemer, John Otis Brew, Junius Henderson, Nels C. Nelson and Laura Gilpin. There is also considerable correspondence with "amateur" archaeologists and others who knew about interesting sites or unusual artifacts. Personal letters are much fewer in number. There are also some letters of a purely routine nature.

In addition to the correspondence, numerous miscellaneous files contain a wide variety of materials, grouped generally by site. Fieldnotes and notebooks, site reports, artifact lists, additional correspondence, loose photographs and photograph albums, manuscripts and maps and diagrams are all part of these files and provide a key resource in understanding Morris's research.

Morris worked in an era in which the photographic record was often better than the written record, and he took hundreds of photographs of excavations at numerous sites. He was well-known for his architectural restoration of archaeological sites, and the photographic collections include unique records of restoration steps taken at Canyon de Chelly, Canyon del Muerto, Aztec and Chichén Itzá. Many images duplicate or nearly duplicate each other, but overall they record the careful progression of excavation or restoration and amplify data and contextual information that is only briefly mentioned in written notes. Most are identified, at least according to site and field season, and there are prints of most negatives in a reference collection. Given past storage and the preservation limitations of the photographic images, their condition is good. However, deterioration is quite severe in some cases, and can be anticipated to progress throughout the collection in coming years.

This archive has been rearranged at least twice since it became part of the University Museum collection and does not retain its original organizational integrity. Current storage is in two metal filing cabinets with four drawers each. The originals of the three rolls of movie film have been donated to the Smithsonian Institution and donor copies are retained by the University of Colorado Museum.

The Anna O. Shepard Archival Collection

Anna O. Shepard conducted research in chemistry, physics, mathematics, geology, mineralogy and microchemical spectroscopy, and applied these diverse fields to archaeological ceramics. She brought not only a unique perspective, but also the highest professional standards to her research efforts. Further, she was able to articulate problems of interest to anthropologists and archaeologists with the tools of these sciences. Her success may be attributed to the fact that she was first an archaeologist, not a petrographer or chemist, as she has occasionally been characterized. She gained excavation experience in the North American Southwest and undertook ethnographic and linguistic fieldwork there.

Her pioneering research and the records and the data bank she left have provided a significant collection from a wide variety of locations, but most extensively from the North American Southwest and Mesoamerica. Finally, her extensive correspondence provides a unique perspective from which to view the development of anthropology and archaeology.

The Anna O. Shepard paper and photograph archive records the beginnings of technical and instrumental analyses of archaeological ceramics in the early 1920s, with her research continuing until the early 1970s. Shepard pioneered technical research on archaeological ceramics, culminating in her landmark *Ceramics for the Archaeologist* (1956, submitted 1954). Access to her manuscripts, unpublished research, experimental records and photographs is becoming increasingly important to modern research in materials analysis. In addition, her lengthy correspondence with a wide variety of professional colleagues provides unique insights on the role of women during the developing years of the archaeological profession, the role of ceramic analysis in archaeological research, and the development of archaeology as a discipline.

The Anna O. Shepard collection consists of 48 linear feet of paper archives (75 percent professional correspondence, 25 percent manuscripts and reports) and an extensive book and reprint library related to her research. Many of the volumes have marginal notations relating the publications to research projects. Also in the collection are 2,920 prints, negatives and glass-plate spectrographs. This archive has been rearranged since it became a part of the University Museum collections and does not retain its original organizational integrity.

The paper archives (ca. 40,000 items) are currently stored in four filing cabinets with four drawers each. The research library is currently stored on bookshelves in two offices and in two laboratory/storage areas. The photographic negatives and most prints and spectrographs are stored in filing cabinets with paper archives. Most photographs have been placed in acid-free negatives and boxes.

The Joe Ben Wheat Archival Collection

Joe Ben Wheat was active in research prior to his death in 1997; this summary represents the recent status of the archival materials that he assembled in the course of many years. The archives include correspondence, fieldnotes, maps, student reports, theses and dissertations that reflect more than forty years of archaeological research in the North American Southwest and national service at the highest levels of the archaeological profession with the Society for American Archaeology. There are also extensive notes on Southwestern textile research (history, techniques, dye analysis). Because research on textiles and the Yellow Jacket site is ongoing, research resources in this collection are located in different offices and laboratories of the University Museum and Department of Anthropology at the University of Colorado.

General Library Resources

The general anthropological resources of the University of Colorado Museum cover more than forty linear feet of library space in various offices of the Anthropology Section and include the books and monographs from Anna Shepard's research library. Holdings include almost the complete series of *American Antiquity, American Anthropologist*, the annual reports of the Bureau of American Ethnology; and specialized reference materials (books, monographs, reprints) pertaining to ceramic analysis and to cultural areas and artifact classes represented in the Anthropology Section's artifact collections.

Summary

All three major archival collections consist of photographic and textual materials and also contain an archaeological element. At present the archival and object collections are stored in different locations in the University Museum, primarily because of environmental and space considerations. The cross-referencing of these elements is essential for full utilization of the resources, and efforts are proceeding to meet this goal.

As a result of the NAGPRA (Native American Graves Protection Act) legislation, the University of Colorado Museum has begun consultations with various Native American groups whose cultural heritage is represented in the collections of the museum. In some cases where, in the view of the Native American groups, the archival collections contain descriptions or images of sensitive materials (human interments and associated objects), these archival materials may also be subject to repatriation at some future date, or may only be accessible under more stringent guidelines than are currently being applied.

Frederick W. Lange

University of Colorado, Boulder. University Libraries. Archives

Address: Archives, University Libraries, Campus Box 184, University of Colorado, Boulder, CO 80309.
Tel.: (303) 492-7242
Fax: (303) 492-1881
Internet address: http://www-Libraries.colorado.edu/ps/arv.frontpage.htm.
Networks, consortia: CARL, OCLC.
Founded: 1876 (founding of the University).
Major resources: Archives, papers.
Areas of specialization: Omer Stewart papers, peyote ritual.
Archives/manuscripts: 375 linear ft.
Access: Open for research with restrictions. Access to Tri-ethnic Research Project case files and fieldnotes is currently restricted. Materials must be used in the Archives.
References (Omer Stewart papers): Richard Jessor, et al., *Society, Personality, and Deviant Behavior: A Study of a Tri-ethnic Community* (New York: 1968); Martha C. Knack and Omer C. Stewart, *As Long as the River Shall Run: An Ethnohistory of Pyramid Lake Indian Reservation* (Berkeley: 1984); Omer C. Stewart, *Peyote Religion: A History* (Norman: 1987) (= *The Civilization of the American Indian Series*, vol. 181); Omer C. Stewart and David F. Aberle, *Peyotism in the West* (Salt Lake City: 1984).
Guides: An inventory of the Omer Stewart papers is available.

Description

The Omer Stewart Papers

The Archives at the University of Colorado, Boulder, Libraries houses the papers of Omer Stewart (1908-1991), professor of anthropology, who pioneered research on Peyotism and the Native American Church. Stewart also conducted the Tri-ethnic Research Project—a community study of Hispanic Americans, Anglos and Native Americans in southern Colorado.

Born of a Mormon family in 1908 in Provo, Utah, Stewart served as a Mormon missionary in Switzerland and France from 1928 to 1930. In 1933 he began graduate studies in anthropology at the University of California, Berkeley, where he studied under Alfred L. Kroeber and Robert H. Lowie, both leading figures in the ethnography of the Great Basin and the Plains. In 1945 Stewart accepted a faculty position in anthropology at the University of Colorado at Boulder. He remained there for the rest of his career, broadening his interests in Peyotism, Indian claims cases and various ethnic communities in southern Colorado.

Stewart was a leading expert on the history of Peyotism and its formal organization, the Native American Church—a subject in which he first developed an interest during the 1930s as a graduate student at the University of California at Berkeley. Stewart directed his work on the "trait list"—a comparative study of the presence or absence of numerous elements in the peyote ceremony among various practicing tribes. As a participant-observer and with the assistance of other researchers, he compiled these lists for many of the tribes that engaged in the peyote ritual. Stewart's research was bolstered in the late 1950s, when he received the peyote files of James Sydney Slotkin, after the latter's death in 1958. Slotkin was an "actionist" anthropologist, who also served as the official secretary of the Native American Church of North America. Along with Slotkin's files, Stewart inherited his place as a knowledgeable defender of the Native American right to freely practice the centuries-old peyote religion, and he began appearing as an expert witness in court cases on behalf of the Native American Church, a service he continued throughout the remainder of his career.

Stewart wrote numerous articles on the origins of Peyotism and the history of the Native American Church, which was first incorporated in Oklahoma in 1918 around the practice and theology of Peyotism. In 1945 the organization changed its name to the Native American Church of the United States and then again, in 1945, to the Native American Church of North America. By 1961 the church was incorporated in twelve other states and one Canadian province. Peyote, from the Aztec word *peyotl*, is a small spineless cactus that grows in northern Mexico and southern Texas, on both sides of the Rio Grande, in the vicinity of Larado, Texas. Since early Spanish times, American Indians and Mexican mestizos have digested the mild intoxicant as a sacred medicine and as a source of divine knowledge, in spite of its prohibition in 1620 by the Inquisitor of New Spain. The Huichol Indians in the Sierra Madra Occidental in Mexico preserved intact the pre-Columbian practice of Peyotism, including the 300-mile pilgrimage to the peyote garden near San Luis Potosí. Although anthropologists have had difficulty establishing a close cultural connection among some forms of Peyotism, both American and Mexican tribes emphasize the existence of an intimate relationship with animals, plants, fire, sun, moon, stars, wind and other forces of nature. Since the 1880s a number of tribes have continued to practice the peyote ritual, including the Kiowa, Comanche, Kiowa-Apache, Caddo, Wichita, Cheyenne and others.

The Stewart papers contain considerable documentary evidence on the history of Peyotism, as well as correspondence, tribal peyote files, individual peyotist records, fieldnotes, court testimony, subject files, photographs and other materials that Stewart compiled in the course of more than forty years of research. The collection constitutes one of the most complete archives in existence relating to the history, theology and practice of Peyotism. The files are extensively cross-referenced and served as the source for Stewart's major publication on the subject, *Peyote Religion: A History* (1987).

In the 1950s, Stewart also began testifying as an expert witness in Indian Claims Commission cases. In preparing for these cases, Stewart undertook extensive research concerning native resources prior to the American appropriation of Indian lands, as well as detailed studies of tribal and band boundaries. One result of this work was a book jointly written by Stewart and Martha Knack, *As Long as the River Shall Run* (1981), describing the efforts of the northern Paiute to regain water rights for Pyramid Lake. Stewart's research produced numerous files documenting the claims cases of the Ute, Shoshone, Chippewa, Ottawa, Arapaho, Klamath and those of other tribes. These papers comprise correspondence, transcripts of testimony, court document exhibits, research files, general publications and a variety of other materials.

At the same time, Stewart began the Tri-ethnic Research Project, carried out between 1958 and 1964—an extensive community study of Anglos, American Hispanics and Native Americans in a small town in southwestern Colorado. With a grant from the National Institute of Mental Health (NIMH), he produced a vast wealth of documentation, providing an extraordinary profile of the living conditions, habits and life styles of community residents. His research led to another community study on the causes and effects of alcoholism.

The more than 200 linear feet of Tri-ethnic Project research files comprise an extensive array of data, including historical documents dated from 1540 to 1964, covering the study area; fieldnotes, surveys of inhabitants based on gender and ethnicity, maps and charts, subject files and study reports, progress reports and memoranda on the project's methodology and intellectual orientation. The files also contain extensive data on area communions, baptisms, marriages, burials, welfare cases, corrections, court cases, educational attainment, voter registration, traffic violations, alcoholism, sexuality, living habits, property and earnings and other facets of the intimate lives of community residents. Because of the sensitive nature of some of this information, the files have restricted access.

Bruce P. Montgomery

Colorado—Colorado Springs

Colorado College. Hulbert Center for Southwestern Studies

Address: Hulbert Center for Southwestern Studies, Colorado College, 14 E. Cache la Poudre, Colorado Springs, CO 80903.
Tel.: (719) 389-6649
Fax: (719) 634-4180
Founded: 1975 (founding of the Hulbert Center).
Major resources: The Rubén Cobos collection of Indo-Hispanic Folklore. A partial collection of tapes from the Robb collection.
Areas of specialization: Spanish New Mexican folklore, including music, poetry, prayers, riddles, reminiscenses, proverbs, stories, life histories, children's games and descriptions of other aspects of culture from 1944-1974.
Visual/audio resources: 358 seven-inch reels of audio tape recordings are in the Rubén Cobos collection.
Access: Available for use by scholars and general readers. Contact Judith A. Pickle, program coordinator, at the Hulbert Center.

References: Victoria Levine, "Two Colorado Sources of Spanish New Mexican Music," *American Music Research Center Journal*, vol. 3 (1993), p. 65-77.

Guides/catalogs: Two notebooks describing the taped material in the Cobos Collection and also two books of transcripts of Robb Collection tapes are available.

Information provided by the Hulbert Center for Southwestern Studies.

Colorado—Denver

Denver Museum of Natural History (DMNH)

Address: Denver Museum of Natural History, 2001 Colorado Boulevard, Denver, CO 80205-5798.

Location: In Denver City Park.

Tel.: (303) 370-8353 (Archivist); (303) 370-6362 (Library); (303) 370-8250 (Photo Archives).

Fax: (303) 331-6492

E-mail: haglund@dmnh.org (Archivist and Photo Archivist); kgully@dmnh.org (Librarian).

Networks, consortia: OCLC.

Public transit access: The RTD bus stops at Montview and Colorado Blvds., adjacent to the museum.

Founded: 1900.

Major resources: Archives (1,100 cubic ft.); Photo Archives (300,000 items); Library (25,000 v.). All three collections include many archaeological and ethnographic resources.

Areas of specialization: Anthropology, archaeology, astronomy, earth sciences, museum studies, zoology.

Archives/manuscripts: Papers of Ruth M. Underhill (ethnology), H. Marie Wormington (archaeology), Betty Huscher (archaeology), Mary W.A. and Francis V. Crane (collectors), Robert Easterday (archaeology), Charles A. Mantz (archaeology), Jesse D. Figgins (archaeology), Harvey C. Markman (archaeology), Sarah J. Workman (ethnology), Walter Austin (archaeology), Jessee H. Bratley (ethnology), Paul L. Hoefler (Africa, ethnology), Stephen Olop (ethnology), Michael Taylor (ethnology). Also, Lindenmeier site files (archaeology).

Visual/audio resources: Photographs from Walter Austin, Jesse H. Bratley, Mary W.A. and Francis V. Crane, Robert Easterday, Paul L. Hoefler, Charles A. Mantz, Stephen Olop, Aaron Manning Phelps, Roland W. Reed, Gertrude Van Roekel and others; a few oral histories.

Access: Open 9:00 a.m.-5:00 p.m. weekdays; an appointment is required.

Artifacts of anthropological/archaeological significance: Contact the museum's Anthropology Department at (303) 370-6388.

Kristine A. Haglund

Denver Public Library. Western History/Genealogy Department

Address: Western History/Genealogy Department, Denver Public Library, 10 West 14th Avenue Parkway, Denver, CO 80204-2731.
Tel.: (303) 640-6291
Fax: (303) 640-6298
Internet address: http://www.denver.lib.co.us.
Networks, consortia: OCLC.
Internet access to on-line catalog: CARL through the library home page.
Public transit access: Most major bus lines stop within two blocks of the library.
Founded: 1889 (Denver Public Library); 1935 (Western History Department).
Major resources: Books, journals, manuscripts, original photographs.
Areas of specialization: Colorado, the Rocky Mountain region and the Trans-Mississippi West.
Archives/manuscripts: Extensive.
Holdings (books and journals): 75,000 books and pamphlets; Western journals; 5,000 maps and atlases.
Visual/audio resources: More than 500,000 photographs.
Access: Open to the public. Materials in this department are for reference use only.
Guides/catalogs: Denver Public Library. Western History Department, *David F. Barry: Catalog of Photographs* (2nd ed., Denver: [19 ?]).

Description

The Photograph Collection

The Photograph Collection contains more than 500,000 images of the American West. Of these, some 10,000 images depict Native Americans, their clothing, artifacts and material culture. 107 Native American tribes are represented. The Dakota tribe is frequently depicted, while Crow, Cheyenne, Pueblo, Ute, Apache and Arapaho are also represented. The collection includes many portraits and studio poses of Native Americans by commercial photographer David F. Barry. A list of 946 glass negatives made by Barry is available.

Information provided by Western History/Genealogy Department.

National Archives—Rocky Mountain Region

Address: National Archives—Rocky Mountain Region, Denver Federal Center, Building 48, P.O. Box 25307, Denver, CO 80225-0307.
Location: In Building 48 at the Denver Federal Center.
Tel.: (303) 236-0804
Fax: (303) 236-9297
E-mail: center@denver.nara.gov.

Internet address: http://www.nara.gov/regional/denver.html.
Parking: On-site parking is available.
Founded: 1969.
Major resources: Holds original records retired from federal government agencies in Colorado, Montana, New Mexico, North Dakota, South Dakota, Utah and Wyoming. Holdings include some original Bureau of Indian Affairs (BIA) records. Also holds microfilm copies of many National Archives records.
Holdings: More than 35,000 cubic ft. of original records.
Visual/audio resources: The Region has photographs from the Bureau of Reclamation, the Bureau of Indian Affairs and other federal agencies. No audio holdings.
Access: The great majority of holdings are open for public research. Restrictions on access to some federal records may be applied in accord with exemptions in the Freedom of Information Act.

Information provided by National Archives—Rocky Mountain Region.

Colorado—Mesa Verde

Mesa Verde National Park

Address: Research Center, Mesa Verde, CO 81330.
Tel.: (970) 529-4510
Fax: (970) 529-4498
Internet address (Mesa Verde National Park museum collection profile): http://www.cr.nps.gov/csd/collections/meve.html.
Founded: 1906.
Major resources: Excavation documentation and reports of archaeological work conducted within Mesa Verde National Park.
Areas of specialization: Southwest archaeology.
Archives/manuscripts: More than 300 linear ft. of archives.
Visual/audio resources: Black-and-white excavation and stabilization photographs; some object photographs.
Access: Open to scholars and general readers. A research proposal must be submitted and approved by the Mesa Verde Research Committee, and materials must be used in the Research Center.
References: George S. Cattanach, Jr., *Long House, Mesa Verde National Park, Colorado* (Washington D.C.: 1980) (= *U.S. Department of the Interior. National Park Service. Wetherill Mesa Studies. Publications in Archeology*, no. 7H); James A. Lancaster, Jean M. Pinkley, Philip F. Van Cleave and Don Watson, *Archaeological Excavations in Mesa Verde National Park, Colorado, 1950* (Washington, D.C.: 1954) (= *U.S. Department of the Interior. National Park Service. Archeological Research Series*, no. 2); Gustaf Nordenskiold, *The Cliff Dwellers of the Mesa Verde, Southwestern Colorado: Their Pottery and Implements.* English translation by D. Lloyd Morgan (Stockholm and Chicago: 1893); Arthur H. Rohn, *Mug House, Mesa Verde National Park—Colorado* (Washington, D.C.: 1971) (=

U.S. Department of the Interior. National Park Service. Archeological Research Series, no. 7-D).

Guides/catalogs: 90 percent of the object collection has been cataloged. However, only 10 percent of these catalog records have been entered into a data base (the Automated National Catalog System—a National Park Service dBaseIII+ cataloging system). Inventories have been prepared for the majority of archaeological field reports, maps and reports. None of these finding aides have been published.

Artifacts: A collection of approximately two million objects—the great majority from the Wetherill Mesa Archeological Project (WMAP) and from excavations conducted by the University of Colorado, Boulder.

Description

Mesa Verde National Park, established in 1906, is the largest archaeological preserve in the United States and contains the greatest number of cliff dwellings ever found. Nearly 4,000 sites have been located within the park, and more than 600 of these are cliff dwellings. The combination of a semi-arid environment and the inaccessible location of the cliff dwellings has been responsible for the preservation, not only of the structures of the prehistoric inhabitants, but also of artifacts representative of their material culture. These artifacts—the textiles, pottery, baskets and other articles produced by the ancestral Pueblos, as well as foodstuff and flora specimens—are vital to the understanding of the cliff dwelling occupants.

Mesa Verde was the center of the northern ancestral Pueblo ("Anasazi") culture that existed in the Four Corners area for more than 1,000 years. For nearly a century, archaeological investigations have taken place at Mesa Verde—varying from simple records kept by the Wetherill family (the first Anglos to conduct investigations in the Mesa Verde area), to very detailed excavations and technical reports by scientists from universities and other institutions.

The Museum collection has experienced several periods of rapid growth. During the late 1920s several excavations produced artifacts; by 1934 the quantity of museum objects on hand prompted the initiation of a museum records system. The Wetherill Mesa Archeological Project (WMAP) continued from 1958 to 1965 and contributed more than 40,000 artifacts and associated excavation documentation to the collection. WMAP artifacts were processed as archeological research specimens and have remained in the project laboratory after the conclusion of the project.

In 1965 the National Park Service and the University of Colorado signed an agreement creating the University of Colorado Archaeological Research Center in Mesa Verde. The Center undertook archaeological survey work and excavations that produced substantial additions to the museum collection.

In 1974 the park established the Division of Research and Ruins Stabilization—now the Division of Research and Resource Management. In September 1978 Mesa Verde was designated as the first World Heritage Cultural Park in the United States, in recognition of the significance of the ancient Pueblo culture that flourished here between the sixth- and thirteenth-centuries.

Larry T. Wiese

Connecticut—New Haven

Human Relations Area Files, Inc. (HRAF)

Address: Human Relations Area Files, Inc., 755 Prospect St., New Haven, CT 06511.
Tel.: (800) 520-4723 or (203) 764-9501.
Fax: (203) 764-9404
E-mail: hrafmem@minerva.cis.yale.edu.
Internet address: http://www.yale.edu/hraf/home.htm.
Founded: 1949.
Major resources: Human Relations Area Files Collections.
Areas of specialization: Ethnographic texts.
Holdings: As of January 1, 1996, the HRAF Collections of Ethnography on microfiche consisted of 6,529 documents containing 826,881 text pages, on 23,381 microfiche, covering about 350 cultural groups. eHRAF contained 85,459 pages, approximately 40,000 of which are available only in electronic format, and the remaining 45,000 were converted from the microfiche collection.
Manuscripts: HRAF has some fieldnotes and manuscripts, especially of translations. They are not listed or cataloged in any way.
Access: HRAF is a consortium with membership open to nonprofit educational, research and cultural organizations and government agencies. There are several kinds of membership. Sponsoring members are institutions that have complete sets of the collections and are entitled to one seat and one vote on HRAF's Board of Directors. Associate members hold all or some portion of the collections. Associate members may be active (i.e., holding a complete set of the collections and receiving annual updates) or inactive (i.e., holding an incomplete set of the collections). The materials just described are available in two ways:

a. At HRAF in New Haven, Connecticut, where the collection is available to scholars and the general public. Material must be used in HRAF, and users should make appointments.

b. The HRAF Collections are distributed to, and available at, approximately 300 member institutions around the world. Access to the collection in these institutions is subject to each institution's rules and regulations.
CD-ROMs: *Electronic HRAF* (*eHRAF*) (New Haven: 1994-   ); *Cross Cultural CD* (New Haven: 1989-   ).
References: Carol R. Ember and Melvin Ember, *Guide to Cross-Cultural Research Using the HRAF Archive* (New Haven, Conn.: 1988); Josephine Z. Kibbee, "Human Relations Area Files (HRAF)," in her *Cultural Anthropology: A Guide to Reference and Information Sources* (Englewood, Colo.: 1991), p. 93-96; David Levinson, "The Human Relations Area Files," in *RSR: Reference Services Review,* vol. 17, no. 3 (Fall 1989), p. 83-86; David Levinson, *Instructor's and Librarian's Guide to the HRAF Archive* (New Haven, Conn.: 1988); Ellen D. Sutton, "The Human Relations Area Files and Cross-Cultural CD: Enhanced

Access to Selected Subjects," in *RSR: Reference Services Review,* vol. 19, no. 1 (Spring 1991), p. 57-70.

Bibliography: George P. Murdock, et al., *Outline of Cultural Materials* (New Haven, Conn.: 1982); George P. Murdock, et al., *Outline of World Cultures* (New Haven, Conn.: 1983).

Description

HRAF's mission is to encourage and facilitate the comparative study of human culture, society and behavior. The mission is accomplished through the HRAF Collections—a collection of ethnographic texts that is indexed by culture and subject. Sociologist Herbert Spencer's efforts in the late nineteenth-century to collect and organize information on the cultures of the world, and later William Graham Sumner's more systematic efforts along the same lines, constitute the intellectual foundation of HRAF. In the 1930s George Peter Murdock, Clelland S. Ford and their colleagues created the "Cross-Cultural Survey" at Yale University's Institute of Human Relations. HRAF incorporated as an inter-university consortium in 1949, with five sponsoring members. Today, the HRAF Collections and annual updates are distributed to a membership of more than 300, in the United States and 25 other nations.

The HRAF Collections provide information on a broad range of culture types, including non-industrialized cultures, Native North American cultures, national cultures, cities and urban cultures, American ethnic minorities and pre-industrial civilizations. The collection does not cover all of the cultures of the world and does not contain all available information on the cultures covered. In the early years, HRAF staff made decisions about what to include largely on the basis of the priorities of its financial supporters. HRAF now solicits recommendations from the scholarly community regarding the cultures and the literature to include in the Collections. While the number of documents included for each ethnic group varies, the average number is twenty. This means that HRAF staff must select documents from what is often a much larger corpus available on a culture. Experts are asked for advice, and thorough bibliographic searches of the available literature are made. There are several general criteria in document selection. First, a search is made for general descriptive studies (i.e., ethnographies) and historical overviews of the culture. This practice insures that a wide range of subjects is included. Second, reports on specific topics, such as art, music, family life, the legal system, and so on, are included. Such subject focusing is dependent on the dominant interests of researchers of specific cultures. For example, in the collection on the Trobriand Islanders, there is a large amount of information on the *Kula*, a system of ceremonial exchange, because the Kula is a subject that has interested most of the researchers on the Trobrianders. In short, an effort is made to include some information on many different subjects, although there is no guarantee that all subjects will be described completely or equally.

There is considerable variation in the time range of the information in the HRAF Collections. HRAF seeks first-hand primary information, and (to the extent possible) time and place foci are identified. HRAF is currently updating two existing cultures per year as part of the regular annual installment, and at least one new document is added to each of ten existing cultures being converting to electronic format. It is important to understand that

108

anthropology is not a current events subject, and there are several considerations that mitigate requests for up-to-date information. An ethnography from 1910 may be an excellent source of information and provide a baseline from which to track changes. Such an ethnography may be of significant value in itself, among other things, as a thorough description of a particular culture at a particular point in time, or even the only description that exists. Other factors to consider in time coverage are: first, that some cultures, such as the Ona, have become extinct, and it is impossible to update the information; and, second, many cultures have been described by only a single observer whose fieldwork comprises a finite segment of time, and thus is also impossible to update.

While a collection of this size and scope is significant, HRAF's unique value as a research and teaching resource is based on its indexing of the information. The cultures that HRAF selects to include in the Collections are defined in terms of the controlled vocabulary *Outline of World Cultures* (OWC) (Murdock, et al.: 1983), and the documents in the HRAF Collections are indexed for subjects using the controlled vocabulary *Outline of Cultural Materials* (OCM) (Murdock, et al.: 1982). The *Outline of Cultural Materials* lists approximately eighty broad terms and more than 700 narrower terms that are used to index the texts. Indexers at HRAF analyze each page and apply three-digit subject codes for the subjects described on the page, with as many code numbers entered as there are different subjects on the page. The average number of subjects per page is 5.5. For the microfiche version, the pages were duplicated for the number of subjects and filed in the appropriate subject sections of the Collections. In the electronic versions of the HRAF Collections, users may search by the subject codes, the culture codes, as well as do free-text searching.

People have used the HRAF Collections as an important source of information for hundreds of scholarly books, doctoral dissertations, journal articles and conference papers. For cross-cultural researchers, the HRAF Collections provide at least three benefits. First, the Collections provide a universe of cases from which to draw a sample for comparative research. Second, the Collections provide a volume of information that is unattainable from any other single collection. Third, the Collections provide information for more than one point in time for many of the cultures, allowing for both diachronic and synchronic analysis. Educators in the social sciences and humanities find the HRAF Collections valuable because they serve as a resource for correcting biased views of human culture, clarifying materials introduced in the classroom, encouraging a deeper appreciation of other viewpoints and studying the effects of contemporary social forces, such as modernization and urbanization.

In its early years, HRAF distributed the Collections on paper slips. In 1958 HRAF began to reproduce the Collections on microfiche. In 1989 an effort to computerize the Collections began with the *Cross-Cultural CD*, a series consisting of a selection of ten subject areas for a subsample of sixty cultures. In 1994 HRAF ceased microfiche reproduction and distribution and began to issue the annual installments in electronic format.

The HRAF Collection of Ethnography contains books, dissertations, government reports, journal articles and other formats. HRAF commissioned the translation of approximately 10 percent of the documents from fifteen different languages. The HRAF Collection of Ethnography is updated and expanded each year by approximately 20,000 pages (about 100 documents) through the addition of new documents, both on cultures already covered and on cultures new to the Collections. Beginning in 1994, each annual installment includes the conversion to electronic format of ten to twelve existing cultures—an additional 20,000 pages.

M. Marlene Martin

Yale University. Library

Address: Yale University Library, 130 Wall Street, P.O. Box 208240, New Haven, CT 06520-8240.
Tel.: (203) 432-1818 (Library Administration); (203) 432-1775 (Sterling Memorial Library Reference); (203) 432-3439 (Kline Science Library Reference).
Fax: (203) 432-7231
Memberships: RLG, OCLC, CRL, ARL.
Internet address: http://www.library.yale.edu.
Internet access to on-line catalog: Access to the Yale Library on-line catalog, Orbis, is available at orbis@yalevm.cis.yale.edu; Gopher: yaleinfo@yalevm.cis.edu. Access to basic descriptions of some of the library collections is available on-line through the Yale Libraries and Collections Web pages at http://www.library.yale.edu/guide1.htm.
Founded: 1701.
Holdings: Library holdings include approximately 10,000,000 print volumes, 3,400,000 microforms, 45,000 linear ft. of manuscripts and 860,512 photographs. The library has also collected thousands of music scores, maps, exhibition catalogs, clay tablets, coins, prints, recordings and slides.
Access: Access is made available to scholars and other qualified persons.
References: There is no written guide to anthropological resources at the library. Guides are written for specific collections and are noted, where applicable, in the following descriptions of library collections.
Artifacts of anthropological significance: Artifactual material is housed primarily in the Peabody Museum of Natural History. The Peabody collections in the Anthropology Division contain more than 267,000 cataloged lots—see the separate description of Peabody Museum resources in this guide.

Description

The Yale University Library houses one of the premier research collections in the world. The Library consists of the central libraries—Sterling Memorial Library, Cross Campus Library, Beinecke Rare Book and Manuscript Library and Seeley G. Mudd Library (storage facility and Government Documents Center)—and twenty school and department libraries, as well as small collections within each of the twelve residential colleges. Second largest among the university libraries in the United States, the Yale Library contains more than 10,000,000 volumes, more than one-third of which are in the Sterling Library (major humanities, social science and area studies collections) and the Cross Campus Library (primarily an undergraduate intensive-use collection). Each year the Yale Library adds approximately 150,000 new volumes, as well as numerous maps, sound recordings, microforms, manuscripts, coins, musical scores, art works and computer files.

Descriptions of the holdings may be found in Orbis, the library's on-line catalog, in its card catalogs and RLIN—the on-line database of the Research Libraries Group.

There are also many other rich collections in the University, including those at the Peabody Museum of Natural History (ethnographic, archaeological and skeletal material; fieldnotes, photographs, correspondence and manuscripts); the Center for British Art (rare prints and watercolors); and the Collection of Musical Instruments (gathered from around the world).

The anthropology collections reside primarily in two libraries. The Kline Science Library houses the Anthropology Library, which is primarily a print collection of more than 20,000 volumes. The collection emphasizes physical anthropology, archaeology and some area studies materials, particularly on Oceania and Mesoamerica. Anthropological materials are also collected at the Sterling Memorial Library, which houses the manuscript and archive collections for anthropology, the area studies collections, microforms and general social science and humanities resources. The Sterling collections consist of the more general anthropology, socio-cultural and humanities-based materials; anthropology titles related to the area studies collections (Africa, East Asia, Judaica, Latin America, Near East, Slavic and Southeast Asia) are likely to be found at Sterling Library. Other materials that support research in anthropology are located at many other libraries, including the Beinecke Rare Book and Manuscript Library, the Divinity Library and the Economic Growth Center. Reference services for anthropology are provided by the Kline Science Library staff and the Reference Department of Sterling Memorial Library.

Joyce L. Ogburn

African Collection

Address: African Collection, Yale University Library, 130 Wall Street, P.O. Box 208240, New Haven, CT 06520-8240.
Tel.: (203) 432-1883
Fax: (203) 432-7231
Major resources: Published and manuscript materials relevant to research in the humanities and social sciences that document the history and culture of (mainly) sub-Saharan Africa and the Indian Ocean and Atlantic islands, with particular strengths in southern, anglophone western and eastern Africa.
Holdings: 100,000 monographs and serials held throughout the library system.
Access: Open to scholars and other qualified persons.

Description

Systematic collecting on Africa seems to have started at the Yale Library in the 1920s. Several masters degrees and at least one history Ph.D. were awarded before 1930. The collection of printed books and journals on African ethnography is now among the most extensive in North America. Books and pamphlets on folklore and customary law, published in Africa, are systematically collected. These include items in African languages. Official publications by colonial government anthropologists, administrators and military or police officers that deal with indigenous peoples are still being actively acquired. Collections of African materials are primarily located in the Sterling Memorial Library, but some may be found in other Yale libraries.

Besides original manuscript collections, there are very extensive holdings of private papers and archives of organizations in microform. The preponderance of these deal with southern Africa, Nigeria, Kenya and Zaire (now the Democratic Republic of Congo), but there is at least one such collection on almost every other country. Among the most significant collections are the following:

- Vivien F. Ellenberger papers, 1920-1969, [microfilm, 1 reel]. Resident magistrate in Bechuanland. Includes reports, notes, correspondence and newspaper clippings. (Sterling Memorial Library, Microform Reading Room.)
- Edward C. Baker, Tanganyika papers, 1914-1957, [microfilm, 2 reels]. The papers contain tribal histories, extensive notes on social life and customs, genealogies, vocabulary lists and a typed manuscript on the North Mara, 1935, written and compiled by Edward Conway Baker. (Sterling Memorial Library, Microform Reading Room.)
- Machakos District (Kenya) Records, 1904-1915, [microfilm, 3 reels]. The files include correspondence, reports and memoranda by British administrators on questions of land policy, forest boundaries, settlement of Swahilis, and other problems of local government in Ukamba province in Kenya. Prominent among the officials is John D. Ainsworth, Acting Deputy Commissioner. (Sterling Memorial Library, Microform Reading Room.)
- Tanganyika District Books, 1922-1966, [microfilm, 28 reels]. The Tanganyika District Books were compiled between 1922 and 1966, using 22 subject headings for recording information on courts, treasuries, population, economic and social conditions, tribal history and legends, language, customs, prehistory and archaeology and the history of the districts. (Sterling Memorial Library, Microform Reading Room.)
- Hubert Frank Mathews papers, 1912-1961, [microfilm, 5 reels]. The papers consist of letters sent by Mathews to his parents describing his work in Nigeria. Also included are official correspondence and reports, manuscripts of writings, notes and printed matter. (Sterling Memorial Library, Microform Reading Room.)
- Simon Ottenberg collection, 1923-1967, [microfilm, 14 reels]. A collection of pamphlets, serials and other publications assembled by Simon Ottenberg of the University of Washington. The publications are principally from the eastern provinces of Nigeria and relate mainly to the Igbo tribe. (Sterling Memorial Library, Microform Reading Room.)

There are at least six pamphlet collections (including some manuscript material) on Nigeria. These include the Simon Ottenberg collection on eastern Nigeria and the University of Ibadan Library's Nigerian pamphlets (includes several private collections loaned for filming); the latter is particularly strong on western Nigeria and the Yoruba in particular.

Similar collections containing ethnographic material are held on Gambia, Ghana, Liberia, Sierra Leone and several other countries.

Ethnographic photographs are held by the Divinity Library, the Sterling Memorial Library's Manuscripts and Archives and by the Anthropology Division of the Yale Peabody Museum. Notable is the Basel missionary Friedrich R. Ramseyer's album on the Ashanti Kingdom. There are also large postcard collections showing costumes, domestic architecture, ceremonies, weapons and the like.

Moore Crossey
Joyce L. Ogburn, general editor.

China Records Project

Address: China Records Project, Yale Divinity School Library, 409 Prospect Street, New Haven, CT 06511-2108.
Tel.: (203) 432-5301
Fax: (203) 432-3906
Founded: The archival and manuscript collections of the Yale Divinity School Library include papers collected by the China Records Project, which was begun by the National Council of Churches in 1968. The Yale Divinity School Library was designated by the Council as a repository for papers of former missionaries to China solicited by the Project. Following an initial five-year period funded by the National Endowment for the Humanities, the Divinity School Library has continued to seek out and acquire collections documenting the era of intensive Protestant missionary activity in China, 1830-1950.
Holdings: 950 linear ft. of manuscript material related to Protestant mission work and the Christian church in China.
Access: Open to scholars and other qualified persons.
References: A fairly detailed description of the Divinity Library's China-related collections can be found in Archie R. Crouch (editor), *Christianity in China: A Scholars' Guide to Resources in the Libraries and Archives of the United States* (Armonk, N.Y.: 1989). Seven manuscript groups have been added to the China Records Project collection since the compilation of the Crouch guide. Collection level records describing manuscript groups in the China Records Project are entered in Orbis, and selected full finding aids are available through the Special Collections Web page of the Yale Divinity Library at http://www.library.yale.edu/ div/speccoll.htm.

Description

Records of more than 300 former China missionaries are represented in this archive. Not all of these collections are of anthropological interest, but some of the missionaries took a particular interest in documenting the language, customs and art of the Chinese people, particularly of the ethnic groups living on the western borders of China. One example of such a missionary is Daniel Sheets Dye, who taught at West China Union University from 1910 to 1949. As an avocation, Dye recorded and analyzed window lattice and woven belt patterns throughout West China. He was a founder of the West China Border Research Society and of the West China Union University Museum. Hundreds of lattice and woven belt patterns recorded by Dye and his Chinese assistants are available in his papers, as well as photographs and slides that illustrate costumes, artwork and architecture of West China.

Another collection of interest is the archives of the Border Service Department of the Church of Christ in China. This department concentrated its work among the Nosu (Lolo, now Yi), Ch'iang and Chia-rung national minorities in West China. Writings and photographs document the culture of these peoples. The papers of YMCA missionary Lyman Hoover contain significant material about the Muslim population of China, including photographs. The Campbell family papers include documentation of work among the Hakka people of South China. Also of interest are the archives of the United Board for Christian Higher Education in Asia, which include records of thirteen colleges and universities in China sponsored by Protestant mission agencies. Some of these schools had institutes or museums relating to Chinese culture, including the Ferguson Collection of Chinese art and artifacts and the Institute of Chinese Cultural Studies at the University of Nanking. Photographs and films in this archival collection document a range of subjects from a Sung dynasty gravesite in Shaowu to tribespeople of Sikiang.

The Yale Divinity Library also has a strong collection of manuscripts, books and periodicals that document the history of missionary work in areas other than China. Photographs, engravings, letters, journals and writings in the Library's collections document cultures in a wide range of geographical areas and time periods.

Martha Smalley
Joyce L. Ogburn, general editor.

Economic Growth Center Collection

Address: Economic Growth Center Collection, Yale University, 140 Prospect Street, P.O. Box 208263, New Haven, CT 06520-8263.
Tel.: (203) 432-3301
Fax: (203) 432-6976
Founded: 1961.
Major resources: Foreign governments' statistical publications, development plans and censuses, with a focus on developing countries.
Areas of specialization: Statistical economic data.
Holdings: 60,000 volumes, 3,900 active serial titles.
Access: Open to scholars and other qualified persons.

Description

The Economic Growth Center Collection, which is part of the Social Science Library, is composed of 60,000 volumes of international data, with a focus on materials relating to statistics, economics and planning in more than 100 countries. More than 3,900 serials issued by foreign governments, research institutions and intergovernmental organizations are received currently. Of special interest to anthropologists are the collections of statistics on agriculture, economics and religion, demographic survey reports and censuses—particularly those with linguistic and ethnographic tables.

The Collection is the library for the Economic Growth Center, which was established in 1961 by the Yale Economics Department, with the primary mission to advance understanding, through both theoretical and empirical analysis, of the processes of economic development within the developing countries and of the relationships between these countries and the economically advanced nations. Mary T. Reynolds was the first librarian of what was then called the Economic Growth Center Library. In 1972 the library became administratively part of the newly established Social Science Library and was renamed the Economic Growth Center Collection. The Economic Growth Center Collection is one of the most comprehensive collections of its kind in the United States. It has its own unique classification—by region and country first and then by subject. Access to the library is extended to those doing research from outside of Yale. Specialized reference service is provided by the Social Science Library, and interlibrary loans are transacted with other universities and institutions, notably through the Research Libraries Group (RLG).

Edita R. Baradi
Joyce L. Ogburn, general editor.

Latin American Collection

Address: Latin American Collection, Yale University Library, P.O. Box 208240, New Haven, CT 06520-8240.
Tel.: (203) 432-1835
Fax: (203) 432-7231
Areas of specialization: Research material in the humanities and social sciences that document the history and cultures of South America, Mexico, Central America and the Caribbean.
Holdings: 375,000 printed volumes, including monographs, serials, newspapers and government documents. In addition to printed matter, the collection is rich in manuscript material, as well as such non-book resources as photographs, documentary film, sound recordings, sheet maps, musical scores, archaeological artifacts and paintings.
Access: Open to scholars and other qualified persons.

Description

Yale's first published catalog of library holdings, printed by T. Green in New London, Connecticut, in 1743, shows two Latin American items: Garcilaso de la Vega, *The Royal Commentaries of Peru* (London: 1688) and a copy of Hans Sloane's *A Voyage to the Islands of Madera, Barbados, Nieves, S. Christopher's and Jamaica* (London: 1707-1725).

By 1907, however, Prof. Hiram Bingham, III—historian, explorer, politician and curator of Yale's Collection of Latin American History, 1908-1930—was able to state that the Yale Library had one of the best collections of Latin American material in the U.S. Today this statement remains true. As one of the oldest Latin American collections in the United States, it offers a wide variety of research opportunities, and is one of the leading U.S. resource centers for Latin American studies.

The most anthropologically interesting components of the collection are its manuscripts, the largest of which is the Yale Peruvian Expedition Papers (16.25 linear ft., Sterling Memorial Library, Manuscripts and Archives). The Yale Peruvian expeditions of 1911, 1912 and 1914-1915 were organized and led by Hiram Bingham, III (1875-1956), professor of Latin American history at Yale. These expeditions performed extensive archaeological, geological and topographical exploration and conducted important studies of Peruvian flora, fauna and native inhabitants. The most significant accomplishments of the expeditions were the discovery, excavation and investigation of the Inca city at Machu Picchu. The collections are rich with documentation about the former inhabitants of Machu Picchu and the nearby region. In the course of exploring Inca roads near Machu Picchu, Bingham and his colleagues discovered and examined other ruins, revealing that the city had been the center of a densely populated region. Studies of birds and animals in the region produced additional information about the living conditions of the Incas and anthropometric measurements of the Quechua and Machiguenga natives revealed anthropological characteristics of the descendants of the Incas. The collections also contain the papers relating to the organization of each expedition; the daily records of activities for most members of the expeditions; the original journals of the prominent scientists and scholars detailing their observations and findings; and photographs, glass slides, maps and scrapbooks that provide a wealth of information on the Quechua, their crafts and artifacts and the region they inhabited.

Other manuscript collections with substantial documentation of interest to anthropologists include the Latin American Manuscript Collection (microfilm, 100 reels, Sterling Memorial Library, Manuscripts and Archives), that contains an extremely rich and varied assortment of original documents detailing the history and culture of the Native peoples of Latin America. It contains many private memoirs, official accounts of expeditions, as well as a great many letters from people in all walks of life, describing Native cultures and their relations with the newly-arrived Europeans.

The Latin American Pamphlet Collection (128 linear ft., Sterling Memorial Library, Manuscripts and Archives) provides first-hand documentation of the social, political and economic conditions in Latin America from the seventeenth- to the early twentieth-century. The pamphlets offer a vivid picture of what life was like in Latin America for 300 years. These times come alive in original reports and personal accounts, government records, economic reports, histories, biographies, political broadsides, scholarly theses, speeches by religious and civic leaders and even playbills.

The Benjamin Lee Whorf papers (6 linear ft., Sterling Memorial Library, Manuscripts and Archives) consist of correspondence and his writings on linguistics, including drafts of published works, unpublished manuscripts and research notes on his trip to Mexico in 1930; and on Maya, Hopi and other Indian languages.

In addition to these and other manuscript collections, the Latin American Collection contains substantial secondary editorial production published in Latin America in the fields of physical anthropology, cultural anthropology, linguistic anthropology, ethnology, ethnohistory, archaeology, folklore and mythology, folk medicine, folk religions, ethnobotany, peasant cultures, community studies and urbanization.

Cesar Rodriguez
Joyce L. Ogburn, general editor.

Manuscripts and Archives Collection

Address: Manuscripts and Archives Collection, Yale University Library, P.O. Box 208240, New Haven, CT 06520-8240.
Tel.: (203) 432-1744
Fax: (203) 432-7231
Archives/manuscripts: 32,000 linear ft. of manuscript material; 300,000 photographs.
Access: Open to scholars and other qualified persons.
References: The *Guide to the Primary Sources for the Study of Native Americans, Including: Indians of North America and South America, Hawaiians, and Eskimos* (New Haven: 1985) is available for purchase ($7) from the department. In addition, collection level descriptions of our holdings are continuously entered into the Archives and Manuscripts Control File of the Research Libraries Information Network (RLIN) bibliographic database of the Research Libraries Group. There the researcher will find descriptions of collections with materials related to anthropology.

Description

The Manuscripts and Archives collection contains numerous resources of value to research in anthropology. Resources include archival material and also many microfilm editions of unique collections. The most notable collections are described below:

- African Collection, 1850-1987 (52.75 linear ft.). An artificial collection of pamphlets, printed material, correspondence, manuscripts, photographs, postcards, posters, calendars and microforms relating to Africa and South Africa.
- American Indian Collection, 1647-1940 (.75 linear ft.). An artificial collection of correspondence, writings, photographs and miscellanea relating to American Indians, including the Mohegan Indians of Connecticut, 1740-1750.
- William Sully Beebe papers, 1844-1898 (.75 linear ft.). Largely writings on Biblical subjects and on the Indians of South and Central America to support Beebe's theory that "a great philosophical cult once occupied all the Americas, originating in Peru," and that there is a relationship between the phonetic values of Indian pictographs and those of the Semitic languages. He also believed that their legends resemble those of the Genesis cycle which, Beebe thought, had their origin in America.

• Beecher Family papers, 1704-1964 (40 linear ft.). Includes the papers of Annie Beecher Scoville (1866-1953), teacher and worker, that contain an extensive collection of photographs of Native American family life.

• Millicent Todd Bingham papers, 1865-1968 (82 linear ft.). Emily Dickinson scholar, teacher of French and geographer, particularly of Peru. Papers related to her work on Emily Dickinson; correspondence, research notes, publications and other papers on her professional life, including her work on Peru; personal papers, including journals, diaries, notebooks and scrapbooks; papers on nature conservation.

• Bingham Family papers, 1811-1974 (48.50 linear ft.). Correspondence, diaries, journals, manuscripts, notebooks, sermons, writings, legal and financial records, photographs, printed material and miscellanea documenting the personal lives and professional careers of four generations of the Bingham family. Includes materials documenting Hiram Bingham (1789-1869) and his missionary work in Hawai'i; Hiram Bingham (1831-1908) and his missionary work in the Gilbert Islands, his literary efforts and family matters; and Hiram Bingham (1875-1956) and his academic career, his South American explorations, including the discovery of the ruins of Machu Picchu in 1911, and his political career as Lieutenant Governor, Governor and U.S. Senator from Connecticut.

• Leonard Bloomfield papers, 1909-1950 (2 linear ft.). Correspondence, writings and notebooks entirely related to Bloomfield's professional interest in languages and linguistics. The largest part of the papers consists of a sequence of 44 notebooks, each devoted to a language or linguistic problem. The phonology and morphology of 21 languages are covered in these volumes.

• John Collier papers, 1910-1987 (52.25 linear ft.). Collier was a specialist in American Indian Affairs. Correspondence, subject files, writings, memoranda and reports, research materials and miscellanea.

• Maurice Rea Davie papers, 1914-1975 (5.5 linear ft.). Sociologist, specialist in child welfare, immigration and William Graham Sumner. Correspondence (primarily with Albert G. Keller), writings, subject files and photographs.

• Dwight Family papers, 1713-1937 (5.5 linear ft.). Included are the travel journals of Timothy Dwight, that form a comprehensive survey and collection of historical observations of Indian culture in New England in the early eighteenth-century.

• Edwin Rogers Embree papers, 1903-1956 (4 linear ft.). Embree was an executive officer with the Rockefeller Foundation and the Julius Rosenwald Fund. Personal and professional correspondence; family journals, 1918-1949, of trips to Europe, China, Samoa, Java and Central America; and articles, book reviews and speeches on cultural anthropology (particularly on the Pacific), education, medicine, American race relations and philanthropic institutions.

• John Fee Embree papers, 1908-1950 (2 linear ft.). Sociologist and anthropologist. Miscellaneous papers, including two journals of trips to the Far East, 1926 and 1947-1948.

• Evarts Family papers, 1753-1960 (24 linear ft.). Correspondence, writings, legal and financial material, congressional papers, family memorabilia and other papers of various members of the Evarts family of Vermont, Boston and New York. Includes papers of Jeremiah Evarts and his work and writings on Congregational orthodoxy, his travels for the American Board of Foreign Missions and his efforts on behalf of American Indians.

- Wilfred Thomason Grenfell papers, 1855-1986 (31.50 linear ft.). Grenfell was a medical missionary to Newfoundland and Labrador, 1892-1940; established the Labrador Medical Mission and the International Grenfell Association. Correspondence, diaries, ships' logs, notebooks, writings, speeches and legal and financial papers.
- George Bird Grinnell papers, 1859-1939 (16.5 linear ft.). Editor-in-chief of *Forest and Stream* magazine; conservationist; authority on the Blackfoot, Cheyenne and Pawnee; and prolific writer on Indian folklore and life. Letterbooks, correspondence, subject files, photographs and writings.
- Harold D. Gunn papers, 1918-1982 (9 linear ft.). Anthropologist. Reports and memoranda from the files of the British colonial administration in Nigeria, used in an ethnographic survey of Africa south of the Sahara, for the International African Institute.
- Elizabeth Merwin Page Harris papers, 1808-1978 (53.25 linear ft.). Author. Correspondence, family papers, writings, printed works, photoprints and other materials, including extensive materials on the International Grenfell Association; also data on the inhabitants of the White Bay area in Newfoundland.
- Loomis Havemeyer papers, 1886-1971 (14 linear ft.). Professor of anthropology and geology at Yale University. Correspondence, account books, diaries, 1904-1970, writings, photographs, official records and printed matter related to Yale.
- Ellsworth Huntington papers, 1876-1952 (136 linear ft.). Geographer, professor of Geology-Geography at Yale University, author. Correspondence, writings, notes and notebooks covering his numerous fieldtrips around the world, clippings, printed matter and other papers.
- Albert Galloway Keller papers, 1874-1956 (26.5 linear ft.). Sociologist, author and student and colleague of William Graham Sumner. Correspondence, writings, student and teaching files and miscellanea.
- Raymond Kennedy papers, 1935-1950 (5 linear ft.). School teacher in the Philippines, field representative for General Motors in Java and Sumatra, taught sociology at Yale University, served with Military Intelligence, consultant to the Department of State and the Office of Strategic Services, author. Writings, maps, photographs and teaching and field trip materials relating to Southeast Asia, and particularly to Indonesia, including notes and drafts for his unpublished four-volume work, "Peoples and Cultures of Indonesia."
- Latin American Manuscripts Collection, 1521-1975 (29 linear ft.). An artificial collection of correspondence, government documents (including reports, commissions, decrees and awards), church documents and essays, poems, engravings, volumes and miscellanea from the Latin American region, on civil, military, religious and social topics.
- Latin American Pamphlet Collection, 1568-1949 (128 linear ft.) A collection of pamphlets from Mexico, Peru, Argentina, Bolivia, Brazil, Chile, Colombia, Cuba, Ecuador, Guatemala, Haiti, Honduras, Martinique, Panama, Paraguay, Puerto Rico, El Salvador, Uruguay, Venezuela, the West Indies and other Latin American and South American countries. The pamphlets document the agricultural, economic, legal, military, political, religious and social activities in these countries.
- Anne Morrow Lindbergh papers, 1906-1988. Access restricted. (111.5 linear ft.) An observer of various indigenous cultures. Correspondence, diaries, writings, childhood, school and college materials, housekeeping and social records, reports, memoranda and correspondence from the many organizations in which she took an active interest.

- Charles Augustus Lindbergh papers, 1830-1987. Access restricted. (534.25 linear ft.). An observer of various indigenous cultures. Correspondence concerning his political and scientific activities; files in military and civilian aviation; correspondence and related materials on conservation; a large file of writings, speeches, statements and diaries; and family correspondence.
- Charles Templeman Loram papers, 1779-1940 (5 linear ft.). Educator and professor of education in South Africa and at Yale. Correspondence, articles, reports, notes, lectures, memorabilia and other papers.
- Bronislaw Malinowski papers, 1869-1946. Access restricted. (12 linear ft.). Malinowski (1884-1942) was a cultural anthropologist, teacher and author. Correspondence, manuscripts of writings and lectures, fieldwork notebooks, photographs, memorabilia and other papers.
- Morse Family papers, 1779-1868 (8 linear ft.). Includes papers of Jedidiah Morse (1761-1826), minister, educator, missionary, author of *Geography Made Easy* (many editions), with documentation of his missionary work among the Indians and his concern for their condition.
- Page Family papers, 1828-1948 (15.5 linear ft.). Includes papers of Elizabeth Merwin Roe Page, author of *In Camp and Tepee* (New York: 1915), which described the Indian mission activities of the Women's Board of Domestic Missions of the Reformed Church in America; and of her daughter, Elizabeth Merwin Page Harris, teacher, Y.M.C.A. volunteer in World War I, employee of the International Grenfell Association and author.
- Theophil Mitchell Prudden papers, 1872-1925 (2 linear ft.). Prudden (1849-1924) was a pathologist and bacteriologist. Chiefly correspondence relating to medicine, public health and details on laboratory techniques at the turn-of-the-century; also includes a notebook from a scientific expedition to the West in 1873.
- Helen Heffron Roberts papers, 1916-1963 (8 linear ft.). Ethnomusicologist and research assistant in anthropology at Yale University. Correspondence, research materials, notebooks, musical scores and transcripts, photographs and printed material.
- Roe Family papers, 1802-1977 (77.25 linear ft.). Includes the papers of Henry Roe Cloud (1886-1950), a Winnebago Indian and adopted son of Mary and Walter Roe, graduated from Yale University in 1910 and received a B.D. from Auburn Theological Seminary in 1913. He founded and headed the Roe Indian Institute, 1915-1930; was special regional representative for the Office of Indian Affairs, 1931-1933; served as superintendent of Haskell Institute, 1933-1936; and was assistant supervisor of Indian education-at-large, 1936-1947.
- Michael Ivanovitch Rostovzeff papers 1870-1952 (13.25 linear ft.). Rostovzeff (1870-1952) was professor of ancient history at the University of Wisconsin and Yale University, where he also served as director of archaeological research and curator of ancient art. Includes extensive works on the Dura Europos excavations in Syria. Contains manuscripts, notes, lectures, photographs and miscellanea.
- Southeast Asia Collection, 1912-1984 (9.75 linear ft.). An artificial collection of pamphlets, papers, letters, speeches, songs, printed material, posters, photographs and miscellanea relating to the politics, culture and life of the Southeast Asian region.

- William Graham Sumner papers, 1863-1946 (60.25 linear ft.). Sociologist, professor at Yale University. Correspondence, writings, notes and research materials, clippings, memorabilia, photographs and financial records.
- Terry Family papers, 1795-1939 (5 linear ft.). Family papers, including correspondence and military papers related to the Indian campaigns (1870s) and drawings supposedly done by Sitting Bull.
- Richard Christian Thurnwald papers, 1895-1936 (2 linear ft.). Thurnwald (1869-1954) was a German sociologist. Correspondence, writings, printed material relating to Thurnwald's foreign expeditions, teaching positions and literary works.
- James Hammond Trumbull papers, 1649-1897 (1.5 linear ft.). Historian, philologist, bibliographer. Correspondence, writings, notes and other papers pertaining to Connecticut and New England history and American Indians.
- Herman Landon Vaill Collection, 1821-1952 (.25 linear ft.). Papers concerning Elias Boudinot, an Indian whose original name was Galagina, or Buck Oowatie, and who became editor of the *Cherokee Phoenix* (New Echota, Cherokee Nation). Early correspondence relates chiefly to Boudinot's marriage to Harriet Gold and the Gold family controversy over intermarriage with an Indian. Other correspondence relates to the dispute between the Cherokee Nation and the state of Georgia, the Supreme Court decision of 1832, President Jackson's refusal to halt Georgia's annexation of the Cherokee Nation and Boudinot's support of John Ridge, who favored withdrawal of the Cherokee Nation to the West.
- Victor Wolfgang Von Hagen papers, 1932-1954 (5.5 linear ft.). Von Hagen was an author and explorer (1908-   ). Correspondence, research materials, typescripts and galley proofs for ten books written by Von Hagen, relating to Central and South American history.
- Benjamin Lee Whorf papers, 1914-1957 (6 linear ft.). Whorf (1897-1941) was a linguist. Correspondence; writings on linguistics, science and religion; miscellaneous biographical material; and lantern slides.
- Yale Miscellaneous Manuscripts Collection, 1701-1987 (27.50 linear ft.). An artificial collection of correspondence, writings, diaries and memorabilia relating to Yale University, its officials and employees, faculty, students and related topics. Includes the journals of John Henry Lefroyo on Native Americans in the Northwestern Territories of Canada, 1843-1844.
- Yale Peruvian Expedition (1911) papers, 1908-1948 (16.25 linear ft.). Correspondence, administrative records, scientific reports, writings and illustrative material on the three expeditions to Peru sponsored by Yale University, 1911-1915.
- Yale University. Anthropology Club Records, 1901-1917 (.25 linear ft.). Correspondence, minutes of meetings, accounts and lists.
- Yale University. Institute of Human Relations Records, 1928-1960 (26 linear ft.). Established in 1929 as an interdisciplinary center for cooperative research on problems of human welfare. Administrative and subject files, annual reports, financial records, publications and correspondence.

Chris Weideman
Joyce L. Ogburn, general editor.

Collection of Western Americana

Address: Beinecke Rare Book and Manuscript Library, P.O. Box 208240, New Haven, CT 06520-8240.
Tel.: (203) 432-2958
Fax: (203) 432-4047
Founded: The Yale Collection of Western Americana opened in 1952, moved to its current quarters in the Beinecke Rare Book and Manuscript Library in 1963.
Areas of specialization: The history and culture of Native American communities, as well as the European and American exploration, settlement and development of the trans-Mississippi West, from Mexico to the Arctic Circle.
Holdings: 40,000 printed works, 2,000 cataloged manuscript collections, thousands of vintage photographs and hundreds of prints, watercolors and paintings.
Access: Open to scholars and other qualified persons.
References: The collection is described in *The Beinecke Rare Book & Manuscript Library: A Guide to the Collections* (New Haven: 1994). Two catalogues of the manuscript collections have been published: Mary C. Withington, *A Catalogue of Manuscripts in the Collection of Western Americana Founded by William Coe* (New Haven: 1952); and Jeanne M. Goddard and Charles Kritzler (compilers), *A Catalogue of the Frederick W. & Carrie S. Beinecke Collection of Western Americana* (New Haven: 1965), vol. 1: *Manuscripts*. Though outdated, these remain useful guides. Most Western Americana materials are listed in Orbis. Additionally, many finding aids for Western Americana manuscript collections are accessible through the Beinecke Web pages at http://www.library.yale.edu:80/beinecke/blgw.htm.

Description

The collection's anthropological interest lies in its documentation of the full range of Indian-white relations west of the Mississippi. The history and culture of Native Americans are detailed in the official accounts of government-sponsored expeditions and in the private memoirs and autobiographies of missionaries, traders and government agents. In addition to early ethnographic works, the collection has many of the first Indian grammars, dictionaries and texts. It features an extensive collection of Cherokee and Creek imprints from Indian Territory, as well as numerous mission imprints from the Pacific Northwest. Among the manuscripts in the collection is a series of notebooks collected by the anthropologist Jack Kilpatrick that contain hundreds of Cherokee medical formulas in the Sequoyan syllabary. The collection also includes the papers of George Bent (267 items), that document the creation and history of Bent's Fort, a major trading post on the southern plains; the papers of Richard Henry Pratt (43 boxes and 60 v.), the founder of Carlisle Indian School; and the personal archive of Felix Cohen, the legislative architect of John Collier's "Indian New Deal."

Graphic materials in the collection provide an often stunning visual record of Western peoples, cultures and landscapes. Among the collection's most valuable holdings are sketches, paintings, prints and books by artists and writers such as George Catlin, Karl Bodmer, Alfred Jacob Miller, James Otto Lewis and the brothers Edward and Richard Kern.

Early photographs of Native Americans by photographers such as Julius Vannerson, Samuel Cohners, Zeno Shindler, Alexander Gardner, William Soule, William Henry Jackson, John K. Hillers and Edward S. Curtis supplement the papers of Yale alumnus Walter McClintock, who spent nearly fifteen years among the Blackfoot of Montana; and whose collection includes more than 2,000 photographs, extensive fieldnotes and the texts to accompany lantern slide lectures. The McClintock papers range in date from 1874 to 1946, with the bulk of the photographs taken between 1896 and 1910.

In addition to material about Native Americans, the Western Americana Collection contains accounts of Pacific voyages, especially those of the United States Exploring Expedition, 1838-1842. Expedition commander Charles Wilkes (1798-1877) made stops on several South Seas islands, most notably Samoa, and his reports include descriptions of Native laws, languages and customs. Unofficial journals of crew members supplement the official reports.

Bridget Burke
Joyce L. Ogburn, general editor.

Yale University. Peabody Museum of Natural History (PMNH)

Address: Peabody Museum of Natural History, Yale University, 170 Whitney Avenue, P.O. Box 208118, New Haven, CT 06520-8118.
Tel.: (203) 432-3770
Fax: (203) 432-9816
Internet address: Portions of collections data may be accessed by gopher client: gopher.peabody.yale.edu, port 70; or by Web browser client. The URL is
gopher://gopher.peabody.yale.edu
Founded: 1866.
Areas of specialization: Documentation that supports the artifact collections.
Holdings: 1,300 monographs and serials; 120 linear ft. of manuscript and archival material, including photographs, maps, films, fieldnotes and correspondence.
Access: Open to scholars and other qualified persons.
Guides/catalogs: There is no written guide to anthropological, non-artifactual, resources at the Peabody Museum of Natural History.

Description

Established in 1866, the Yale Peabody Museum of Natural History is one of the largest university natural history museums in the United States. It houses more than ten million specimens in the fields of anthropology and the natural sciences, and also provides facilities for collection-based teaching and research. The museum collections offer students and scholars a primary resource for the study of the history and diversity of life, both cultural and biotic. Through exhibits and public education programs, the museum also serves the wider regional community in which it resides. The Division of Anthropology subsumes the archaeological, ethnological and human osteological collections of the Peabody. Acquired through the donations of Yale's alumni and friends, and the scientific expeditions of Yale faculty and students, the holdings of the division number more than 267,000 cataloged lots.

The majority of the Division's holdings is New World in origin, composed of extensive type collections in North American archaeology, comprehensive excavated collections from the Caribbean Basin region, and also significant collections from South America and Mesoamerica. George Grant MacCurdy's Old World archaeological study collections are also housed in the division. An added dimension is brought to the collection by a small, but rich, ethnological collection of objects made or used by Native American peoples. The ethnological collections contain significant contemporary material from Southeast Asia and are particularly strong in the cultures of the Philippine Cordillera. A broad and representative collection of ethnological objects from Oceania rounds out the holdings.

The Division maintains a library of approximately 600 volumes and 700 serials related to archaeology. Aside from this resource, material held by the Division is directly related to the artifact collections, such as fieldnotes and collector lists of artifacts and inventories of collections. Material of this kind is represented by such archives as: the teaching, research files and correspondence of Wendell C. Bennett, 1930-1952 (11 linear ft.) comprising photos, drawings, notes, maps and fieldnotes related to his teaching and field work in South America; site maps and photographs related to Hiram Bingham's excavations at Machu Picchu, 1911-1916 (38 linear ft.); records of the town-by-town survey of Connecticut archaeological sites conducted by Froehlich Rainey in the 1920s; field and research notes of Adam Garson pertaining to the La Calzada archaeological project, La Betania, Estado Barinas, Venezuela, from 1967 to 1978; a narrative by George Langford detailing his excavations at the Fisher Site on the Des Plaines River near Joliet, Illinois, between 1906 and 1927; Gary Vescelius's papers, including field and research notes on the archaeology, history and ecology of St. Croix, the Virgin Islands and the Caribbean, through 1977; and fieldnotes from excavations conducted at the Old Lyme site in Connecticut in 1939.

Also included in the archives is a small amount of material that was acquired with artifact collections that is of general interest to ethnographers, such as T.F. Clark's photographs and travel memorabilia from his travels through Europe, Asia and the Pacific from 1911 to 1919; Ethel M. Klemm's memorabilia collected in Alaska and northern and northwestern North America, between 1930-1939, while teaching and traveling among the Alaskan Inuit and the Sioux of South Dakota; and the photographs and notes of T. [Theophil] Mitchell Prudden, who conducted archaeological surveys in the American Southwest between 1899 and 1902.

Martha Hill
Joyce L. Ogburn, general editor.

District of Columbia

Many Washington, D.C.-area museums, archives and libraries contain documentation of exceptional value for research in anthropology. Prominent among these are selected museums and libraries of the Smithsonian Institution. Several Smithsonian repositories are located beside the National Mall in Washington. These include the National Anthropological Archives, the Human Studies Film Archives, the National Museum of African Art, the Arthur M. Sackler Gallery and the Office of the Smithsonian Institution Archives. The National Anthropological Archives and the Human Studies Film Archives are units of the Department of Anthropology, National Museum of Natural History, which in turn is part of the Smithsonian Institution.

The National Museum of the American Indian (NMAI), also a part of the Smithsonian Institution, is in New York City. By the year 2002, a new NMAI gallery is to be opened in Washington, on the National Mall at Maryland Avenue. The NMAI derives from the former Museum of the American Indian—Heye Foundation, which was established in Manhattan in 1916. For information on the NMAI George Gustav Heye Center (located in **New York City**), see the entry in this guide by Nancy Rosoff. Information on the important archival resources of the NMAI Research Branch (now in the **Bronx, New York**, but to be relocated in 1999 to the new NMAI Cultural Resources Center in Suitland, Maryland) is provided in an additional entry in this guide by Nancy Rosoff.

The Smithsonian Institution maintains several specialized research libraries of significance for anthropological research. Of particular importance is the Anthropology Branch Library (in the **District of Columbia**), which curates the former library of the Bureau of American Ethnology (BAE), and other specialized library collections in anthropology. See the entry in this guide by Margaret R. Dittemore on the Smithsonian Institution Libraries. Among other Smithsonian libraries pertinent to anthropology are the African Art Branch (also in the **District of Columbia**); the Museum Support Center Branch (in **Suitland, Maryland**); and the Smithsonian Tropical Research Institute Branch (in **Panama City, Panama**). The latter library holds materials in Central and South American anthropology.

Research access to information on Smithsonian Institution collections is available on-line, via the SIRIS system, at http://www.siris.si.edu. Included in SIRIS are catalogs of Smithsonian library holdings, art inventories, archives and manuscripts, research/bibliographies and a Smithsonian chronology. SIRIS provides access to some 1,021,000 Smithsonian records—including records of 97,000 items in the National Anthropological Archives collections. Researchers interested in Native American topics should note that records of the important National Museum of the American Indian research collections are not accessible via SIRIS.

Other major Washington-area repositories of special interest for anthropological research are the Library of Congress and the two Washington-area sites of the National Archives. The American Folklife Center (AFC), a unit of the Library of Congress, is of special importance in the fields of American folklife and folklore.

Many other federal government departments and agencies maintain libraries, collections or archives that may be of potential interest for research in anthropology. The National Park Service (NPS) curates important archival collections at its regional research centers and at many of the individual U.S. National Parks and Sites. The NPS also maintains the National Archaeological Database and the National Register of Historic Places. A central NPS photographic archive, the NPS Historic Photographic Collection, initially came into being at National Park Service headquarters in Washington, D.C., but is now at Charles Town, West Virginia—see the entry under the **West Virginia** heading.

Hyperlinks to the steadily increasing array of U.S. federal websites are available via the Federal Web Locator (operated by the Center for Information Law and Policy) at http://www.law.vill.edu/Fed-Agency/fedwebloc.html.

Washington-area universities, privately-endowed museums, organizations and associations are also repositories of documentation of potential anthropological interest. An important privately-operated photo archive, the Image Collection, is maintained by the National Geographic Society at its Washington headquarters. Also in the **District of Columbia** are the Organization of American States' Columbus Memorial Library and Harvard University's Dumbarton Oaks Research Library (Pre-Columbian Studies Library and Byzantine Studies Library). The Columbus Memorial Library is open to the public; research access to the Dumbarton Oaks libraries is quite limited.

Researchers planning to visit District of Columbia-area museums, libraries or archives may wish to consult one or more volumes in the *Scholars' Guide to Washington, D.C., Series*, published with support of the Woodrow Wilson International Center for Scholars. Several volumes in the series have an area studies focus, such as Michael Grow and Craig VanGrasstek's *Scholars' Guide to Washington, D.C., for Latin American and Caribbean Studies* (2nd ed., Washington, D.C.: 1992) (= *Scholars' Guide to Washington, D.C.*, no. 2). Also in this series are guides to Washington-area resources for African studies, East Asian studies, Middle Eastern studies, South Asian studies, Southeast Asian studies, others. Many of the guides in this series are no longer up-to-date, although most remain helpful.

American Folklife Center (AFC)

Address: American Folklife Center, Thomas Jefferson Building, LJ G17, Washington, DC 20540-8100.
Location: In the Thomas Jefferson Building of the Library of Congress—in the Capitol Hill area of Washington.
Tel.: (202) 707-6590 (Administrative); (202) 707-5510 (Public Reference); (202) 707-1740 (Federal Cylinder Project).
Fax: (202) 707-2076
Internet address: http://lcweb.loc.gov/folklife. This site contains selected AFC publications, including *Folklife Center News* and *Folkline*.
Networks, consortia: OCLC, IFLA.
Public transit access: Metro: Orange Line or Blue Line to Capitol South station or Red Line to Union Station.
Founded: 1928 (Archive of Folk Culture); 1928 (Archive of Folk-Song); 1976 (American Folklife Center); 1979 (Federal Cylinder Project).
Major resources: Archive of Folk Culture; Archive of American Folk-Song; Federal Cylinder Project. American Folklife Center holdings include photographs, fieldnotes, music

and sound recordings, moving images, ephemera and manuscripts. Resources are worldwide in scope, but with primary emphasis on the folklife and folk culture of the United States.

Areas of specialization: The American Folklife Center and its Archive of Folk Culture have been active for many decades in preserving and disseminating information on American folklife. Projects carried out under American Folklife Center auspices include the Federal Cylinder Project, which seeks to preserve, document, reproduce and disseminate the historic field cylinder recordings that accumulated in federal agencies in the course of many decades. The Archive of American Folk-Song has been developed continuously since 1928. The Blue Ridge Parkway Folklife Project was carried out in 1978 by the American Folklife Center, in cooperation with the National Park Service. More recent projects include the Montana Folklife Survey (1979); the Rhode Island Folklife Survey (1979); the Pinelands Folklife Project (Pinelands National Reserve, New Jersey, 1983); the Grouse Creek Cultural Survey (Northwest Utah, 1985); and the Lowell Folklife Project (Lowell, Massachusetts, 1987-1988).

Holdings: More than one million items in all formats.

Archives/manuscripts: Preserved in the Archive of Folk Culture.

Visual/audio resources: Photographs, slides, films and documentation in other formats. AFC holdings include the Fahnestock South Sea collection (film footage, sound recordings and photographs) from the 1940 and 1941 expeditions led by Bruce and Sheridan Fahnestock.

Access: Services are available to anyone beyond high school who is doing serious research.

References: Peter T. Bartis and Hillary Glatt, *Folklife Sourcebook: A Directory of Folklife Resources in the United States* (2nd ed., Washington, D.C.: 1994) (= *Publications of the American Folklife Center*, no. 14); Thomas Carter and Carl Fleischhauer, *Grouse Creek Cultural Survey: Integrating Folklife and Historic Preservation Field Research* (Washington, D.C.: 1988) (= *Publications of the American Folklife Center*, no. 13); Mary Hufford, *One Space, Many Places: Folklife and Land Use in New Jersey's Pinelands National Reserve* (Washington, D.C.: 1986); Ormond H. Loonis (coordinator), *Cultural Conservation: The Protection of Cultural Heritage in the United States; A Study by the American Folklife Center, Library of Congress, Carried Out in Cooperation with the National Park Service, Department of the Interior* (Washington, D.C.: 1983) (= *Publications of the American Folklife Center*, no. 10).

Guides/catalogs: Lyntha Scott Eiler, Terry Eiler and Carl Fleischhauer (editors), *Blue Ridge Harvest: A Region's Folklife in Photographs* (Washington, D.C.: 1981) (= *Publications of the American Folklife Center*, no. 7); *Ethnic Recordings in America: A Neglected Heritage* (Washington, D.C.: 1982) (= *Studies in American Folklife*, no. 1); *The Federal Cylinder Project: A Guide to Field Cylinder Collections in Federal Agencies* (Washington, D.C.: 1984-) (= *Studies in American Folklife*, no. 3) [vols. 1, 2, 3, 5 and 8 have been published at this time]; *Folk Recordings Selected from the Archive of Folk Culture, Motion Picture, Broadcasting and Recorded Sound Division, Library of Congress* (Washington, D.C.: 1989); Stephanie A. Hall, *Ethnographic Collections in the Archive of Folk Culture: A Contributor's Guide* (Washington, D.C.: 1995) (= *Publications of the American Folklife Center*, no. 20); *An Inventory of the Bibliographies and Other Reference and Finding Aids Prepared by the Archive of Folk Culture* (rev. ed., Washington, D.C.: 1991).

Description

Created by an act of Congress in 1976, the American Folklife Center (which absorbed the older Archive of Folk-Song, originally established in the Library of Congress Music Division in 1928) is perhaps the most valuable resource for research in cultural anthropology within the Library of Congress system. Under its charge to preserve and disseminate information on American folkways, specific attention has been devoted to assembling comprehensive collections covering folk music, the narrative arts, dance and occupational lore in all formats. Holdings number more than one million items ranging from manuscripts and ephemera to books and sound recordings. It is in this latter area that the Center has made a major impact on the preservation of the American cultural heritage.

Notable projects done under the Center's aegis include the Blue Ridge Parkway Folklife study of 1978; a study of folklife of the Wiregrass region of south-central Georgia; exploration of the ranching community of Paradise Valley, Nevada; and examination of ethnic language and heritage schools throughout the United States. Other Center projects studied maritime occupational traditions from Florida; artistic expression in Chicago's ethnic communities; and Acadian traditions of northern Maine. More recent folklife projects include a cultural resources survey in the New River Gorge area of West Virginia and a study of occupational folklore in Paterson, New Jersey.

The Federal Cylinder Project, one of the more notable of Center endeavors, was begun in 1979. This project is concerned with the duplication of early wax cylinder recordings made of the songs of various cultures in the late nineteenth- and early twentieth-centuries, through 1940, by fieldworkers employed by the Bureau of American Ethnology and other federal agencies. Beginning with the first recordings of the Passamaquoddy Indians of Maine done by Jesse Walter Fewkes in March 1890, the collections include recordings made by John P. Harrington, Frances Densmore, Frederica De Laguna, Edward Sapir, Charles F. Lummis, Alice Fletcher, Francis LaFlesche and Helen Roberts. The majority of Library cylinder holdings are recordings of Native American vocal music being performed by a single person, usually without accompaniment. Additional regions or countries represented by cylinder holdings include Polynesia, Britain, Denmark and many others. The cylinders are overwhelmingly recordings of song—very few contain the spoken word. Researchers planning to utilize this section of the library will find it necessary to consult *The Federal Cylinder Project: A Guide to Field Cylinder Collections in Federal Agencies*. This eight-volume set (not yet complete) was initiated in 1984 and provides catalogues of recordings of Native American groups from the Northeast, Great Basin, Northwest Coast, Arctic, California, Southwest; and Central and South America.

Recent additions to the Center include such collections as 400 wax recordings of blind and sighted village musicians of Ukraine, made between 1904 and the late 1930s, and field recordings of Hispanic music and Pentecostal church services made in Puerto Rico in 1967 by Henrietta Yurchenco. Finding aids for some AFC resources are accessible via LC Marvel, the Library's on-line information service.

Robert B. Marks Ridinger
Information provided by Judith Gray.

Department of the Interior. National Park Service. See **National Park Service**

Department of the Interior. Natural Resources Library (NRL)

Address: Natural Resources Library, 1849 C Street, N.W., M.S. 1151, Washington, DC 20240.
Location: In the White House area at C Street, N.W.
Tel.: (202) 208-5815
Fax: (202) 219-1434
Internet address: http://ios.doi.gov/nrl.
Internet access to on-line catalog: Natural Resources Library holdings cataloged since 1975 are on the library's local on-line catalog, STILAS. Earlier holdings are accessed by a card catalog.
Networks, consortia: OCLC.
Public transit access: Metro: Orange Line or Blue Line, Farragut West station—the library is eight blocks west of this station.
Founded: 1949.
Major resources: A U.S. document depository library. Most, but not all, official publications of the U.S. Department of the Interior and of its ca. ten bureaus are held. The library holds official publications and some non-official publications on Native Americans, the National Parks, conservation, land management, territorial affairs and other topics.
Areas of specialization: Most official publications of the Bureau of Land Management, the Bureau of Indian Affairs, the National Park Service, the Bureau of Reclamation and other bureaus within the Department of the Interior are held. Special holdings include bulletins of U.S. Indian Schools published between 1900 and 1945.
Holdings (books and journals): Ca. 1,000,000 book and journal volumes.
Access: Open to the public for reference and on-site use. Interlibrary loan service is available through OCLC to federal government libraries only.
Guides/catalogs: U.S. Department of the Interior, *Dictionary Catalog of the Departmental Library* (Boston: 1967), 37 v. Four supplements, 1969-1975.

Description

   The Natural Resources Library serves the staff of the U.S. Department of the Interior and other federal government researchers. Holdings include most publications of the Department of the Interior and of its various bureaus. Department of the Interior archives and manuscript materials are not at this location; they are either among holdings at the National Archives (including the Regional Archives) or possibly at some other locations. Resources of significance for anthropology include the printed documents and other materials pertaining to the Bureau of Indian Affairs, the National Park Service, the Bureau of Land Management and the Bureau of Reclamation. The library also holds printed materials concerning the administration of U.S. territorial affairs in Puerto Rico, Guam, American Samoa and the Northern Marianas (Commonwealth of the Northern Mariana Islands).

Information provided by Harriet Rusin and Lisa Kosow.

Department of the Interior. Office of the Solicitor. Library

Address: Library, Office of the Solicitor, Department of the Interior, 1849 C Street, N.W., M.S. 7100W, Washington, DC 20240.
Location: In the White House area at C Street, N.W.
Tel.: (202) 208-4571
Fax: (202) 219-1434
Internet address (Office of the Solicitor): http://www.doi.gov/sol.
Internet access to on-line catalog: Not available; the library's holdings are on the local catalog, STILAS.
Public transit access: Metro: Orange Line or Blue Line, Farragut West station—the library is eight blocks west of this station.
Founded: Established when selected legal and related material was separated from other printed material then in the Natural Resources Library.
Major resources: Published material on Native American law and other legal topics.
Areas of specialization: Most Native American codes and constitutions; also Indian Claims Commission, *Decisions* and *Reports.*
Access: Open to the public for on-site use only.

Information provided by Harriet Rusin.

Dumbarton Oaks Research Library and Collection

Address: Dumbarton Oaks Research Libraries, 1703 32nd St., N.W., Washington, DC 20007.
Location: In the Georgetown area.
Tel.: (202) 342-3265 (Pre-Columbian Studies Library); (202) 342-3241 (Byzantine Studies Library).
Fax: (202) 342-3207
Internet address: http://www.doaks.org/index.html.
Networks, consortia (library): OCLC, HOLLIS.
Public transit access: See the website for details.
Founded: The Dumbarton Oaks house, gardens and Byzantine studies library were donated to Harvard University in 1940 by art collectors Robert Woods Bliss and Mildred Bliss. A library on pre-Columbian art was later donated by Robert Woods Bliss.
Major resources: Pre-Columbian Studies Library; Byzantine Studies Library.
Areas of specialization: Pre-Columbian art and archaeology; Byzantine art and archaeology.
Archives/manuscripts: Yes.
Holdings: Ca. 22,000 v. (books and journals) in the Pre-Columbian Studies Library; ca. 123,000 v. (books and journals) in the Byzantine Studies Library.

Access: The Pre-Columbian Studies Library and the Byzantine Studies Library are open to qualified researchers by application only. Not open to the public. The Dumbarton Oaks Museum is open to the public, Tuesday-Sunday, 2:00-5:00 p.m.

Artifacts: Extensive pre-Columbian and Byzantine art and archaeology collections are curated by the Dumbarton Oaks Museum.

Catalogs of museum collections (selected): Elizabeth Hill Boone, *Andean Art at Dumbarton Oaks* (Washington, D.C.: 1996) (= *Pre-Columbian Art at Dumbarton Oaks*, no. 1), 2 v.; Michael D. Coe, *Classic Maya Pottery at Dumbarton Oaks* (Washington, D.C.: 1975); Dumbarton Oaks, *Handbook of the Robert Woods Bliss Collection of Pre-Columbian Art* (Washington, D.C.: 1963). Supplement, 1969. See the Dumbarton Oaks museum website for information on additional Dumbarton Oaks publications.

Information provided by Dumbarton Oaks, Pre-Columbian Studies.

Georgetown University. Library. Special Collections Division

Address: Special Collections Division, Georgetown University Library, 37th & O Streets, N.W., Washington, DC 20057-1006.

Location: In the Georgetown area.

Tel.: (202) 687-7444

Fax: (202) 687-7501

Internet address: http://gulib.lausun.georgetown.edu/dept/speccoll. The finding aid to the Fitzhugh Green papers is accessible at this site by clicking on the collection's title in the list of collections with electronic databases.

Networks, consortia: OCLC.

Public transit access: Metro: to Dupont Circle station, then take a cab or the G2 bus to Georgetown University; a map and travel directions are on the website.

Founded: 1789 (founding of Georgetown University).

Major resources: The Fitzhugh Green papers (19 boxes) in Special Collections.

Visual/audio resources: 93 glass color slides of the Crocker Land Expedition are part of the Fitzhugh Green collection.

Access: Open to the public, 9:00 a.m.-5:00 p.m., Monday-Friday, except holidays.

References: Fitzhugh Green, *Peary: The Man Who Refused to Fail* (New York: 1926); Donald Baxter MacMillan, *Four Years in the White North* (rev. ed., Boston, New York.: 1925).

Guides/catalogs: *Special Collections at Georgetown—A Descriptive Catalogue* (Washington, D.C.: 1989).

Description

The Fitzhugh Green Papers

Through his journals and notebooks, Fitzhugh Green, Sr. (1888-1947) provides firsthand accounts of his experiences in the Arctic regions, his contacts with the Inuit (Eskimo), their customs and culture, as well as of the terrible beauty of the Arctic landscape. The Green collection documents—through journal and notebook reports, correspondence and printed materials—the expedition led by Donald B. MacMillan (from 1913 to 1917) to Greenland and beyond, in search of Crocker Land, which had purportedly been sighted by Robert E. Peary at the end of an expedition in 1907.

The Fitzhugh Green papers consists of Green's correspondence, diaries and notebooks, manuscripts of articles and books, reprints of articles and papers, newspaper and magazine clippings and photographic material, including 93 glass color slides from the Crocker Land expedition. Green's journal and notebook accounts of his experiences traversing the Arctic region and Greenland are of interest for their impressions of Inuit customs and culture.

Four scrapbooks (consisting of correspondence between Green, MacMillan and other members of the expedition, as well as with equipment supply companies) provide a unique source of information on the technical preparations for the expedition. The collection contains correspondence from or material about each member of the expedition.

Nicholas B. Scheetz

Howard University. Founders Library. Moorland-Spingarn Research Center (MSRC)

Address: Moorland-Spingarn Research Center, Founders Library, Howard University, 500 Howard Place, N.W., Washington, DC 20059.
Location: The Main Campus of Howard University is in the 2500 block of Georgia Avenue, in the Ledroit Park area of Washington. The Moorland-Spingarn Research Center is in the university's Founders Library building.
Tel.: (202) 806-7239 (Administration); (202) 806-7480 (Manuscript Division); (202) 806-7266 (Library Division).
Fax: (202) 806-6405
Internet address: http://www.founders.howard.edu.
Networks, consortia: ARL, RLIN.
Public transit access: Metro: Green Line or Yellow Line to Shaw-Howard Univ. station. The university is a fifteen-minute walk north on Georgia Avenue, N.W. Look for the clock tower above the Founders Library building.
Founded: 1867 (founding of Howard University); 1914 (date the Rev. Jesse Edward Moorland (1863-1940) book and manuscript collection was donated to Howard University). In 1946 the University purchased the Arthur B. Spingarn (1878-1971) book collection that included books authored by black men and women in many languages. In 1973 the

Moorland-Spingarn Collection was reorganized and renamed the Moorland-Spingarn Research Center.

Major resources: Library Division; Manuscript Division (includes the Manuscript Department, the Prints and Photographs Department, the Oral History Department and the Music Department); Howard University Archives; Howard University Museum.

Areas of specialization: African American studies, Africana, Pan-Africanism, African diaspora, Caribbean studies, Latin American studies.

Archives/manuscripts: 6,000 linear ft. of manuscripts are preserved in the Manuscript Department. Manuscripts of anthropological interest include the archives of the Association of Black Anthropologists; also the Eslanda Robeson (1896-1965) papers. Robeson was an anthropologist who wrote on Africa. Papers and photos of the Haitian diplomat, Dantès Bellegarde (1877-1966), concerning Haiti are held (unprocessed), as well as the Mark Hanna Watkins (1905-1977) papers. Watkins was a Howard University anthropologist. The Watkins papers consist of 43 boxes of manuscripts (unprocessed). The Zora Neale Hurston (1891-1960) papers include selected correspondence and writings. Hurston was an anthropologist and folklorist as well as a writer of fiction. The papers of Thomas Narven Lewis (1892-1931), a Liberian physician, include samples of the Bassa-language alphabet as well as photographs of Liberia. The Center also has a large and important collection of manuscripts pertaining to African American history and culture. Catalog records of manuscript resources at MSRC are partially available on RLIN, and additional catalog records are being added.

Holdings (books and journals): 150,000 book volumes; 3,000 journal titles. Library Division holdings of books and journals on African and African American subjects are extensive. Also available are the Spingarn and Moorland collection of African authors; the Jon Bonk collection of Ethiopian materials; other book collections.

Visual/audio resources: Many photographs, sound recordings, music scores and oral history transcripts are held. Photographic resources include the Griffith Davis photo collection (images of Liberia and other areas), the Dantès Bellegarde photos (Haiti) and others.

Access: Open to the public. It is recommended that researchers call in advance to arrange access to manuscript materials.

References: Thomas Battle, "Moorland-Spingarn Research Center, Howard University," *Library Quarterly*, vol. 58, no. 2 (Apr. 1988), p. 143-163; Betty M. Culpepper, "Moorland-Spingarn Research Center: Legacy of Bibliophiles," in Elinor Des Verney Sinnette, W. Paul Coates and Thomas C. Battle (editors), *Black Bibliophiles and Collectors: Preservers of Black History* (Washington, D.C.: 1990), p. 103-114; Arthur B. Spingarn, "Collecting a Library of Negro Literature," *The Journal of Negro Education*, vol. 7, no. 1 (Jan. 1938), p. 12-18.

Guides/catalogs: Greta S. Wilson, *Guide to Processed Collections in the Manuscript Division of the Moorland-Spingarn Research Center* (Washington, D.C.: 1983) [a reference copy of this guide, with unpublished updates, is available at MSRC]. Also available, although no longer current, are the *Dictionary Catalog of the Arthur B. Spingarn Collection of Negro Authors* (Boston: 1970), 2 v.; and the *Dictionary Catalog of the Jesse E. Moorland Collection of Negro Life and History* (Boston: 1970), 3 v. Supplement, 1977, 3 v.

Artifacts of anthropological interest: The Howard University Museum (a part of the Moorland-Spingarn Research Center) has many artifacts made by or pertaining Africans and African Americans.

Information provided by Moorland-Spingarn Research Center.

Library of Congress (LC)

Address: Library of Congress, Washington, DC 20540.
Location: In the Capitol Hill area.
Tel.: (202) 707-5000; National Reference Service: (202) 707-5522; Main Reading Room (Anthropology): (202) 707-4773; African and Middle Eastern Reading Room: (202) 707-7937; African Reading Room: (202) 707-5528; American Folklife Center: (202) 707-5510; Asian Reading Room: (202) 707-5420; Geography and Map Reading Room: (202) 707-6277; Hispanic Reading Room: (202) 707-5400; Manuscript Reading Room: (202) 707-5387; Motion Picture, Broadcasting and Recorded Sound Division, Recorded Sound Reference Center: (202) 707-7833; Motion Picture and Television Reading Room: (202) 707-8572; Music Division: (202) 707-5507; Prints and Photographs Reading Room: (202) 707-6394; Rare Book and Special Collections Reading Room: (202) 707-5434; South/Southeast Asia Section: (202) 707-7711.
Fax: Library of Congress: (202) 707-5844; African and Middle Eastern Division: (202) 252-3180; American Folklife Center: (202) 707-2076; Asian Division: (202) 707-1724; Geography and Map Division: (202) 707-8531; Hispanic Division: (202) 707-2005; Humanities and Social Sciences Division: (202) 707-1957; Manuscript Division: (202) 707-6336; Motion Picture, Broadcasting and Recorded Sound Division: (202) 707-2371; Music Division: (202) 707-0621; Prints and Photographs Division: (202) 707-6647; Rare Book and Special Collections Division: (202) 707-4142.
E-mail (African and Middle Eastern Division): amed@loc.gov.
E-mail (Asian Division): asian@loc.gov.
E-mail (Hispanic Division): hispref@loc.gov.
E-mail (Humanities and Social Sciences Division): hssref@loc.gov.
E-mail (Manuscript Division): mss@loc.gov.
Internet address: http://lcweb.loc.gov.html.
Networks, consortia: OCLC, IFLA.
Public transit access: Metro: Orange Line or Blue Line to Capitol South Station, or Red Line to Union Station.
Founded: 1800 (Library of Congress). The American Folklife Center was created in 1976. The Archive of Folk Culture, founded at the Library of Congress in 1928, became a part of the American Folklife Center in 1978.
Major resources: Collections are universal in scope.
Areas of specialization: Resources of anthropological interest are housed in many divisions, including the Manuscript Division (papers of Margaret Mead and others), the Prints and Photographs Division (many photographs and films of Native Americans), Music Division, Geography and Map Division, Asian Division, Hispanic Division, etc. The American Folklife Center and its Archive of Folk Culture have been active in preserving and disseminating information on American folklife. The Hawai'ian Imprint Collection (in The Rare Book and Special Collections Division) consists of some 353 early and rare Hawai'ian imprints that (in 1927) were transferred from the library's general stacks to the Rare Book

Room. The collection includes Hawai'ian wordlists printed by Elisha Loomis, the first printer in the Hawai'ian Islands, and other early imprints from Oahu.

Manuscripts, papers, etc.: Manuscripts are housed in the Manuscript Division. Some additional manuscripts are in the Folklife Center or elsewhere at LC.

Holdings (books and other materials): Library of Congress holdings occupy some 532 miles of shelves that contain more than 110 million items in all subject areas. About two-thirds of items are in non-book format collections.

Visual/audio resources: In the Motion Picture, Broadcasting and Recorded Sound Division; the Prints and Photographs Division; the Music Division; the Archive of Folk Culture; other divisions.

Access: Services are available to anyone beyond high school who is doing serious research.

Selected references: *Global Resources: The International Collections of the Library of Congress* ([Washington, D.C.: 1997?])—an undated pamphlet; Beverly A. Gray, "Africana Acquisitions at the Library of Congress," in Julian W. Witherell (editor), *Africana Resources and Collections: Three Decades of Development and Achievement: A Festschrift in Honor of Hans Panofsky* (Metuchen, N.J.: 1989), p. 62-76; "Library of Congress (LC)," in Michael Grow and Craig VanGrasstek, *Scholars' Guide to Washington, D.C. for Latin American and Caribbean Studies* (2nd ed., Washington, D.C.: 1992) (= *Scholars' Guide to Washington, D.C.*, no. 2), p. 33-43, 146-148; "Library of Congress (LC)," in Ralph E. Ehrenberg, *Scholars' Guide to Washington, D.C. for Cartography and Remote Sensing Imagery* (Washington, D.C.: 1987) (= *Scholars' Guide to Washington, D.C.*, no. 12), p. 25-65.

Guides/catalogs: Jennfier Brathovde, *American Indians on Film and Video: Documentaries in the Library of Congress* (Washington D.C.: 1992); Barbara Bryant, "Native American Images: Collection Documents a Period in Nation's History," *Library of Congress Information Bulletin*, vol. 52, no. 15 (July 26, 1993), p. 302-305; Patrick Frazier, *Portrait Index of North American Indians in Published Collections* (Washington, D.C.: 1992); Debra Newman Ham, et al., *The African-American Mosaic: A Library of Congress Resource Guide for the Study of Black History and Culture* (Washington, D.C.: 1993 [i.e., 1994]); Irene Heskes, *Yiddish American Popular Songs, 1895-1950: A Catalog Based on the Lawrence Marwick Roster of Copyright Entries* (Washington, D.C.: 1992); Abrahan J. Karp, *From the Ends of the Earth: Judaic Treasures of the Library of Congress* (Washington, D.C.: 1991); Library of Congress, *Many Nations: A Library of Congress Resource Guide to the Study of Indian and Alaska Native Peoples of the United States* (Washington, D.C.: 1996) (= *Library of CongressResource Guide*); Library of Congress. Reference Department. General Reference and Bibliography Division. African Section (compiler), *Africa South of the Sahara: Index to Periodical Literature, 1900-1970* (Boston: 1971), 4 v., Supplements: 1973, 1982 and 1985; Karen C. Lund, *American Indians in Silent Film: Motion Pictures in the Library of Congress* (Washington, D.C.: 1992); A. Kohar Rony, "Malay Manuscripts and Early Printed Books at the Library of Congress," *Indonesia*, no. 52 (1991), p. 123-134; Aloha South, *Guide to Non-Federal Archives and Manuscripts in the United States Relating to Africa* (London: 1989), vol. 1, p. 146-341.

Description

As the national library of the United States, the Library of Congress has been placed in a unique position with regard to the discipline of anthropology. From its creation in 1800, its holdings reflected the intellectual currents of the scientific disciplines such as anatomy and ethnology that would contribute to the later birth of anthropology as a distinct field of study. Beginning with the foundation of the first academic department of anthropology in the United States by Franz Boas at Columbia University in 1896, the collections of the institution quickly expanded to include the varied contributions made to the new discipline by field researchers, government officials and the general public. Strengths of the Library lie in reports of fieldwork issued in the publications of professional societies, government departments, colleges and universities and museums, as well as in various materials on indigenous peoples of the Americas, Africa, Asia, Europe and the Arctic regions, documentation of federally funded archaeological excavations and materials in the general topics of anthropology, archaeology and ethnology in formats ranging from maps and musical recordings to microforms and photographs. Weaknesses in LC resources are an absence of significant numbers of local archaeological journals—particularly those produced in Great Britain and Ireland—and works on medical anthropology and agricultural practices.

While much of the purely historical documentation of the evolution of American anthropology is housed in the National Anthropological Archives at the Smithsonian Institution, certain divisions of the Library of Congress possess materials of significant value. These include the Manuscript Division, the American Folklife Center with the Archive of Folk Culture (formerly the Archive of American Folk-Song), the Prints and Photographs Division, the Asian and Hispanic Divisions and the Music Division.

Manuscript Division

The Manuscript Division (established as a separate entity at LC in 1897) houses several major collections of the papers of anthropologists representing a wide range of subdisciplines and eras. Examples are the papers of physician Anita Newcomb McGee (1864-1940) relating to the foundation of the Women's Anthropological Society of America and her studies of the Shaker, Oneida and Bethel communities; an extensive body of material by Ephraim George Squier (1821-1888) tracing his careers as diplomat, ethnologist and archaeologist, including drafts of published articles, the manuscript of his 1848 book *Ancient Monuments of the Mississippi Valley* and correspondence; and more than 500,000 items comprising the Margaret Mead papers and the South Pacific Ethnographic Archives. The Mead collection includes personal, family and professional papers covering Mead's highly diverse and influential career, with particular emphasis on her correspondence between 1914 and 1979 with such associates as Franz Boas, Ruth Benedict, Rhoda Métraux and husbands Gregory Bateson, Reo Fortune and Luther Cressman. Mead's own system of organization has been retained. The South Pacific Ethnographic Archives covers the period from 1925 to 1978 and contains original fieldnotes from expeditions to Bali, Manus and the Admiralty Islands, as well as Mead's famous work in American Samoa. Separate series of the records of the Institute for Intercultural Studies and special working groups with which Mead was associated, such as the Committee for National Morale, 1940-1944, are also included, as is a complete file of her publications.

In 1994 a digital image project was initiated to salvage 35,000 photographic negatives taken on the Mead-Bateson field trips to New Guinea and Bali, to be accompanied by an electronic reproduction of Bateson's fieldnotes, the first major collection of visual anthropological images to be preserved in this fashion. Films from the Admiralty Islands and Bali ventures are also available.

American Folklife Center

[Information on the extensive documentary resources of the American Folklife Center is presented separately under the heading "American Folklife Center."]

Robert B. Marks Ridinger
Information provided by Judith Gray and others.

National Archives and Records Administration. National Archives, Washington, D.C.

Address: National Archives, Eighth Street and Pennsylvania Avenue, N.W., Washington, DC, 20408.

Location: In the Federal Triangle area. [A second Washington, D.C.-area facility is the National Archives at College Park, in Maryland.]

Tel. (National Archives, Washington, D.C.): (202) 501-5400 (general information); (202) 501-5395 (Bureau of Indian Affairs records).

Tel. (National Archives at College Park, Maryland): (301) 713-6800 (general information—College Park); (301) 713-7250 (Textual Reference—College Park); Special Media telephone numbers at College Park include: (301) 713-7040 (Cartographic Branch); (301) 713-6795 (Still Picture Branch); (301) 713-7060 (Motion Picture, Sound and Video Branch); (301) 713-6645 (Center for Electronic Records).

E-mail (for general inquiries): inquire@arch2.nara.gov

Internet address: http://www.nara.gov.

Internet address (list of NARA regional facilities): http://www.nara.gov/regional/quicklst.html.

Public transit access: Metro: Green Line or Yellow Line to Archives-Navy Memorial station. The Archives building is across Pennsylvania Avenue from the Metro station. The following Metrobuses stop in front of the Archives building on Pennsylvania Avenue: 30, 32, 34, 53, A42, A46, A48, P1, P2, P4, P17 and W13.

Founded: 1934 (the National Archives Building in Washington, D.C.); 1994 (opening of the National Archives at College Park, Maryland).

Major resources: Many National Archives records have been transferred from Washington, D.C., to the newer National Archives at College Park building. Important among materials that remain in Washington, D.C., are many records of genealogical importance (censuses, passenger arrivals, etc.) and also the records of Congress and the Supreme Court.

Areas of specialization: The National Archives Building, Washington, D.C., and the National Archives at College Park are major repositories for federal records and documentation. Census reports, Bureau of Indian Affairs records and many other federal records are available at the Washington, D.C., building. The Archives also holds many collections of "Donated Materials" that have been received as gifts of private individuals or of non-governmental organizations.

Visual/audio resources: The National Archives holds large collections of historic still pictures, films and videos.These have been transferred to the College Park facility.

Access: Open to the public.

Guides/catalogs: The Center for Electronic Records' "Title List: A Preliminary and Partial Listing of the Data Files in the National Archives and Records Administration" is available via the NARA homepage; U.S. National Archives and Records Administration, *Guide to the Federal Archives in the National Archives of the United States* (Washington, D.C.: 1996), 3 v.—The text of this guide is accessible on the National Archives' website. Other published guides include Edward E. Hill, *Guide to Records in the National Archives of the United States of America Relating to American Indians* (Washington, D.C.: 1981); Laura E. Kelsay, *Cartographic Records of the Bureau of Indian Affairs* (Washington, D.C.: 1977) (= *National Archives and Records Service. Special List*, 13); John H. Martin, *List of Documents Concerning the Negotiation of Ratified Indian Treaties, 1801-1869* (Washington, D.C.: 1949) (= *National Archives and Records Service. Special List*, no. 6); Richard S. Maxwell and Evans Walker (compilers), *Records of the Office of Territories* (Washington, D.C.: 1963) (= *National Archives and Records Service. Preliminary Inventories*, no. 154); George S. Ulibarri and John P. Harrison (compilers), *Guide to Materials on Latin America in the National Archives* (Washington, D.C.: 1987).

Description

The National Archives assists researchers and the general public from two Washington, D.C.-area locations: the National Archives Building on Pennsylvania Avenue and the newer National Archives at College Park (Maryland). In addition, there are Regional Archives (formerly known as Regional Branches) at locations throughout the United States.

National Archives records pertaining to American Indians have been described in the guide compiled by Edward Hill (1981) and in other guides and inventories. Important among the National Archives holdings still in Washington are many records of the Bureau of Indian Affairs (BIA). This agency was created in 1824 as an office of the War Department and was transferred to the Department of Interior in 1849, when that department was established. Records of the Bureau of Indian Affairs, 1793-1989, amount to 54,988 cubic feet of documentation (RG 75). Some 13,546 cubic feet of Bureau of Indian Affairs (BIA) records are now stored at the Washington National Archives Building. The remaining original BIA records are distributed among the various Regional Archives.

Records of historical significance for Native Americans also include: Records of the Indian Division of the Office of the Secretary of the Interior (RG 48—at College Park); Records of the Indian Territory Division of the Office of the Secretary of the Interior (RG 48—at College Park); and Records of the Indian Arts and Crafts Board (RG 435—many at the Washington National Archives Building, but some others are kept at the Regional Archives). The original federal government treaties with Indian tribes are preserved in Record Group 11 (General Records of the U.S. Government).

While many Archives record groups remain in Washington, D.C., a large portion of National Archives records are now in College Park or at the various Regional Archives. The four National Archives units that house "special media" are at College Park. These are Cartographic and Architectural Records; Motion Picture, Sound and Video Records; Still Picture Records; and Electronic Records.

[See the separate entry in this guide on the National Archives at College Park (Maryland) for additional information. Entries on NARA's Regional Archives are arranged in this guide by geographic location.]

Information provided by the Users Service Division, National Archives at College Park and by Robert M. Kvasnicka.

National Geographic Society (NGS)

Address: National Geographic Society, 1145 17th Street, N.W., Washington, DC 20036.
Location: In the Dupont Circle area.
Tel.: (202) 857-7783 (NGS Library); (202) 857-7503 (Image Collection); (202) 857-7510 (Records Library); (202) 857-7659 and (202) 828-6660 (Television/Film Library); (800) 434-2244 (photo orders).
Fax: (202) 775-6141 (general); (800) 363-9422 (Image Collection); (202) 429-5755 (Television/Film Library).
Internet address: http://www.nationalgeographic.com.
Internet address (NGS Resources Index): http://www.nationalgeographic.com/resources/ngs/publications/explore.html.
Public transit access: Metro: Farragut North.
Founded: 1888.
Major resources: Image Collection; Television/Film Library; NGS Library.
Areas of specialization: Natural history, human geography, archaeology, cartography. The Library maintains a complete set of NGS publications.
Archives/manuscripts: Summary information on many NGS-sponsored expeditions was published in *National Geographic Society Research Reports* (Washington, D.C.: 1955-1984)—continued as *National Geographic Research and Exploration* (Washington, D.C.: 1985-1994). The original field documentation from NGS-sponsored expeditions was not deposited with the Society, however.
Visual/audio resources: The Image Collection curates natural history and related photographs in many formats: color slides, black-and-white prints (ca. 500,000 items), negatives, cut film and glass-plate images. Artwork and paintings are also in this archive. Many of the Image Collection photos derive from NGS-sponsored research expeditions. Among photo collections of anthropological interest are the E. Wyllys Andrews photos—974 black-and-white prints from the Yucatán in the 1950s; the Hiram Bingham photos—ca. 12,000 black-and-white prints and 7,800 negatives from the expeditions to Peru and Machu

Picchu, 1912-1915; photos from the 1954 archaeological studies of Dorset culture, Southampton Island, led by Henry B. Collins (many of these photos were taken by Eugene Ostroff or W.E. Taylor); the Edward S. Curtis collection—more than 700 pictures of American Indians, 1900-1930; photos from Neil Merton Judd's work on Indian cultures in Arizona and Colorado, 1922-1948; the Leakey family field photographs, Africa, 1959- ; more than 6,000 prints from the Robert E. Peary arctic expeditions—includes images of Inuit (Eskimo) people; the Joseph Rock photos—ca. 3,000 black-and-white prints from China in the 1920s and 1930s; Matthew W. Stirling (who was associated with NGS from 1937-1969) led expeditions to South America that yielded valuable information on Olmec sites; other photo collections of anthropological interest. Image Collection photo resources also include the Autochrome collection (ca. 14,500 early twentieth-century glass-plate images from around the world); the Russia lantern slide collection (early photographs of Tsarist Russia); others.

Access: The NGS Library is open with restrictions (reference use). The Image Collection operates on a commercial basis and can be contacted by phone or fax.

References: C.D.B Bryan, *The National Geographic Society: 100 Years of Adventure and Discovery* (New York: 1997); Catherine A. Lutz, *Reading National Geographic* (Chicago: 1993).

Description

The Image Collection

In 1919 the National Geographic Society organized a Photographic Library to house a few thousand illustrations submitted for publication in its magazine. Today the Image Collection consists of more than ten million color and black-and-white photographs and original artwork from staff and other sources. The collection includes images submitted for *National Geographic* magazine and other Society products—including *Traveler* magazine, adult and children's books, *Explorer* and other television programming.

Pictures in the Image Collection fall into two categories—published and unpublished—available for both publication and reference. The published image collection dates back to 1896 and an on-line record and published location history for each picture is maintained.

NGS picture editors and Image Collection editors review the unpublished film from a coverage and choose pictures, called "file selects," for future use. Original staff photographs are kept by the Society; the unpublished pictures not chosen as file selects are filed by photographer and coverage, along with the photographer's caption notes written while on assignment. Unpublished original film shot by nonstaff photographers is returned to the photographer after publication of the assigned project.

Published and file select pictures are cataloged and available on the collection's Digital Image Archiving System (DIAS)—one of the most comprehensive photo retrieval systems in the world. DIAS, which currently contains more than 500,000 images, is constantly updated and enhanced with new images. Individual photographs can be retrieved by search criteria such as subject (specific subjects are preferred over broad ones), location, photographer, assignment, picture ID, orientation (horizontal or vertical), medium and copyright status.

Neil Philip
Information provided by Susan Riggs.

National Museum of Health and Medicine (NMHM)

Address: National Museum of Health and Medicine, Armed Forces Institute of Pathology, Washington, DC 20306-6000.
Location: NMHM is a part of the Walter Reed Army Medical Center—located east of Rock Creek Park in Washington.
Tel.: (202) 782-2200 (NMHM); (202) 782-2212 (Chief Archivist).
Fax: (202) 782-3573
Internet address (Armed Forces Institute of Pathology): http://www.afip.mil.
Public transit access: Metro: Red Line, Takoma Park station. The museum is a fifteen -minute walk from this station; or take a taxi.
Founded: 1862 (as the Army Medical Museum).
Major resources: Otis Historical Archives; Anatomical Photographs, Contributed Photographs, Curatorial Records, Morris Steggerda Collection.
Areas of specialization: Anthropometry; Native Americans.
Archives/manuscripts: 95 cubic ft.
Fieldnotes and papers: Records of Carnegie Institution anthropologist Morris Steggerda.
Visual/audio resources: Some photographs are held; see collection descriptions below.
Access: Accessible to all researchers.
Artifacts of anthropological interest: A small quantity of Native American medicine bags and weapons; Sri Lankan medicine boxes; anthropometry equipment.

Description

The Army Medical Museum (now the National Museum of Health and Medicine) was founded by the Union Army in 1862 as a repository of medical artifacts and remains, for the purpose of research in military medicine. In the late nineteenth-century the museum was engaged for a time in anthropological research, primarily related to Native Americans. When the museum discontinued this research, most of its collections and related records were transferred to the Smithsonian Institution, where they can be found in the National Anthropological Archives. However, many institutional records related to this research remain in the museum's archives. Additionally, the archives holds the personal papers of anthropologist Morris Steggerda. The collections are described individually below, with internal referencing system notations.

● Anatomical Photographs, 1870s. (4 boxes; finding aid available, arranged, inactive, unrestricted.) A set of photographs of 32 crania collected by the museum for anthropological study. In the late nineteenth-century the museum was involved in anthropological research on American Indians, but subsequently left the field and transferred much of its collection (including these crania) to the Smithsonian Institution. Related documents are located in Washington at the National Anthropological Archives.

- Contributed Photographs, 1862-1918. (39 boxes; finding aid available, arranged, inactive, unrestricted.) More than 4,000 photographs sent to the museum by various donors. Provides a survey of nineteenth-century medicine; especially strong on the Civil War and Western forts. The photographs are numbered consecutively—although many are missing. Copies of some of the series were bound in thirteen volumes.

- Curatorial Records: Incoming Correspondence (loose), 1862-1894. (5 boxes; no finding aid, arranged, inactive, unrestricted.) Correspondence, arranged alphabetically, that was not entered into the museum's internal referencing system (see Curatorial Records: Numbered Correspondence). Includes letters sent to curators John Brinton, George A. Otis, D.L. Huntington, John S. Billings and Walter Reed.

- Curatorial Records: Letterbooks of the Curators, 1863-1921. (17 boxes; no finding aid, arranged, inactive, unrestricted.) Bound volumes of outgoing correspondence by curators John Brinton, George A. Otis, D.L. Huntington, John S. Billings, Walter Reed, James Carroll, F.F. Russell, Eugene R. Whitmore, C.C. McCulloch, Jr., William O. Owen, Charles F. Craig and G.R. Callender.

- Curatorial Records: Numbered Correspondence, 1894-1917. (30 boxes; partial finding aid, arranged, inactive, unrestricted.) Correspondence and accompanying documents numbered according to a system used in the late nineteenth- and early twentieth-centuries that assigned a distinct number to particular topics or correspondents. Includes correspondence of curators Walter Reed, James Carroll, F.F. Russell, Eugene R. Whitmore and C.C. McCulloch, Jr.

- Curatorial Records: Outgoing Correspondence (loose), 1862-1894. (1 box; no finding aid, arranged, inactive, unrestricted.) Correspondence, arranged alphabetically, that was not entered into the museum's internal referencing system (see Curatorial Records: Numbered Correspondence). Includes correspondence of curators John Brinton, George A. Otis, D.L. Huntington, John S. Billings and Walter Reed.

- Curatorial Records: Reports to the Curator, 1885-1892. (1 box; no finding aid, arranged, inactive, unrestricted.) Work reports to curators George A. Otis and John S. Billings, including reports on anthropometry and fire procedures from Assistant Surgeon Washington Matthews; weekly work reports from photographer C.F. Blacklidge; monthly reports from several departments; and an ethnological report from Assistant Surgeon H.C. Yarrow to Bureau of Ethnology director John Wesley Powell.

- Curatorial Records: Smithsonian Correspondence, 1867-1887. (1 box; finding aid available, arranged, inactive, unrestricted.) Incoming correspondence, mostly from Smithsonian Secretaries Joseph Henry and Spencer F. Baird, relating primarily to the exchange of specimens between the museum and the Smithsonian. George A. Otis, D.L. Huntington and John S. Billing were curators of the museum during this time. (See Museum Records: Accession Records and Curatorial Records: Letterbooks of the Curators, for related correspondence.)

- Curatorial Records: Special Correspondence, 1862-1887. (2 boxes; no finding aid, arranged, inactive, unrestricted.) Box 1: Correspondence relating to photography and photographic services at the museum between 1862 and 1885. Includes correspondence of curators George A. Otis, D.L. Huntington and John S. Billing and Surgeon General Joseph K. Barnes. Box 2: Correspondence relating to the craniology collection and craniometric/anthropometric measurement at the museum between 1862 and 1887, mostly sent to curators Otis and Billings.

- Steggerda Collection, 1910-1940. (87 boxes; no finding aid, part arranged, inactive, unrestricted.) Anthropometric records collected by Carnegie Institution anthropologist Morris Steggerda. Includes photographs, measurements, hair samples, palm prints and dental records of American Indians, Jamaicans, Tuskeegee College students and white Americans.
- Mexican Anthropology Photograph Album, ca. 1920s. (1 box; no finding aid, arranged, inactive, unrestricted.) An album of anthropological photographs of Mexico, showing people, agriculture and other activities, buildings and skulls. No captions.

Joan Redding

National Museum of the American Indian. (Smithsonian Institution). See Smithsonian Institution. National Museum of the American Indian. George Gustav Heye Center under the geographic heading **New York—New York City—Manhattan**

National Park Service (NPS)

The NPS website (http://www.nps.gov) provides hyperlinks to the National Archaeological Database, the National Register of Historic Places Collection and other important Web resources. For summary profiles of the National Park Service museum collections see http://www.cr.nps.gov/csd/collections/parkprof.html.

National Park Service. Archaeological Assistance Division. National Archaeological Database (NADB)

Address: Archaeological Assistance Division, National Park Service, P.O. Box 37127, Washington, DC 20013-7127.
Tel.: (202) 343-4101
Fax: (202) 523-1547
Internet address: The National Archaeological Database (NADB) is accessed by telnet: nadbcast.uark.edu. Login: nadb.
Founded: 1992.
Major resources: On-line data on U.S. archaeological investigations.
Holdings: The NADB contains more than 100,000 citations of mainly unpublished archaeological reports and documentation.

National Park Service. National Register of Historic Places Collection

Address: National Register Reference Desk, National Park Service, P.O. Box 37127, Mail Stop 2280, Washington, DC 20013-7127.
Location: The National Register Collection is in Room LL99, 800 North Capitol Street, in the Capitol Hill area of Washington.
Tel.: (202) 343-9559
Fax: (202) 343-9522
E-mail: nr_reference@nps.gov.
Internet address: http://www.cr.nps.gov/nr/nrhome.html.
Networks, consortia: The NRIS (National Register Information System) is the official database of the National Register of Historic Places and is the index to the National Register Collection. The URL of NRIS is http://www.nr.nps.gov. NRIS contains a complete index of National Register listings and is updated weekly.
Public transit access: Metro: Union Station. The National Register Collection is located three blocks from the Union Station Metro.
Founded: 1966 (date of National Historic Preservation Act; amended 1980).
Major resources: The National Register Collection; NRIS.
Areas of specialization: The National Register Collection contains documentation on historic structures, buildings, sites or objects throughout the U.S., as well as in Guam, American Samoa, the Marshall Islands, Micronesia and Puerto Rico. Many National Register listings are sites or objects of particular ethnic or cultural significance. Approximately 8 percent of National Register listings are archaeological sites—including many prehistoric or historic Native American sites.
Holdings: The National Register Collection consists of about 67,000 listings that are represented by some 1.2 million documentary resources—such as archaeological site reports, etc.
Archives/manuscripts: Nomination files for each Register site are maintained in the National Register Collection. The documentation consists of the "National Register Registration Forms" for each listing, together with associated reports, photographs, maps or other materials. Most documents in the Collection were compiled by Historic Preservation Offices in the respective states or territories of the U.S.
Visual/audio resources: Most National Register Collection files contain photographs of the listed structures, building(s), sites or objects.
Access: The NRIS database is available to the public via the Web URL cited above. The National Register Collection is open to the public for reference use, Monday-Friday, 9:00 a.m.-3:00 p.m., except federal holidays.
References: A list of publications is available from the National Register. Also, selected National Register publications are available on the Web at http://www.cr.nps.gov/nr/nrhome.html.

Information provided by Jeff Joeckel.

Organization of American States (OAS). **Columbus Memorial Library**

Address: Columbus Memorial Library, 19th Street and Constitution Avenue, N.W., Washington, DC 20006-4499.
Location: On the National Mall at 19th Street.
Tel.: (202) 458-6040
Fax: (202) 450-3914
Internet address (OAS): http://www.oas.org.
Networks, consortia: OCLC (since 1980).
Public transit access: Metro: Orange Line or Blue Line, Farragut West station—the library is a fifteen-minute walk from this station.
Founded: 1890 (founding of both the OAS and the Columbus Memorial Library).
Major resources: The Columbus Memorial Library is the official depository and library of the Organization of American States. Holdings include substantial book, periodical, rare book, document, archival and photograph collections concerning Latin America and the Caribbean.
Areas of specialization: Latin America and the Caribbean; Inter-American relations. The most comprehensive available collection of OAS official documents, archives, records and manuscripts. Publications of the International Bureau of the American Republics and the Pan American Union are held. Also publications of the Inter-American Indian Institute, the Pan American Health Organization, the Inter-American Commission of Women and the Pan American Institute of Geography and History; other special resources.
Holdings: Extensive holdings in several divisions or collections. The Rare Book Collection contains about 10,000 volumes.
Archives/manuscripts: In the Archives Collection; the Library; and the Records Center.
Visual/audio resources: Ca. 45,000 black-and-white photographs of Latin American and Caribbean subjects—in the Photograph Collection. Photos depicting Latin American antiquities, peoples, village life and other subjects of cultural, anthropological or related interest are held.
Access: Open to the public. Books do not circulate except to staff. Interlibrary loans are available (fee).
Guides/catalogs: *Guide to the Columbus Memorial Library* (3rd ed., Washington, D.C.: 1991) (= *Documentation and Information Series*, no. 12). Also available are Columbus Memorial Library, *Index to Latin American Periodical Literature, 1929-1960* (Boston: 1962), 8 v.; *Indice general de publicaciones periódicas latino americas: humanidades y ciencias sociales = Index to Latin American Periodicals: Humanities and Social Sciences* (Metuchen, N.J.: 1961-1970), 10 v.; Thomas L. Welch, *The Aztecs: A Bibliography of Books and Periodical Articles* (Washington, D.C.: 1987) (= *Hipólito Unánue Bibliographic Series*, 3); Thomas L. Welch, *The Incas: A Bibliography of Books and Periodical Articles* (Washington, D.C.: 1987) (= *Hipólito Unánue Bibliographic Series*; 1); Thomas L. Welch, *The Indians of South America: A Bibliography* (Washington, D.C.: 1987) (= *Hipólito Unánue Bibliographic Series*, 2); Thomas L. Welch, *The Mayas: A Bibliography of Books and Periodical Articles* (Washington, D.C.: 1991) (= *Hipólito Unánue Bibliographic Series*, 8); Thomas L. Welch and Myriam Figueras, *Travel Accounts and Descriptions of Latin America and the Caribbean, 1800-1920: A Selected Bibliography* (Washington, D.C.: 1982).

Artifacts of anthropological interest: In the Museo de Arte de las Américas, 201 18th Street, N.W., Washington, DC.

Information provided by Columbus Memorial Library.

Smithsonian Institution. Freer Gallery of Art and Arthur M. Sackler Gallery. Library

Address: Library, Freer Gallery and Arthur M. Sackler Gallery, Smithsonian Institution, Washington, DC 20560.
Location: In the Arthur M. Sackler Gallery, 1050 Independence Avenue, S.W.,—on the National Mall.
Tel.: (202) 357-4880, ext. 343 (Library reference); (202) 357-4880, ext. 341 (Archives).
Fax: (202) 786-2936
Internet address (Freer and Sackler galleries): http://www.si.edu/organiza/museums/freer/homepage/about.html.
Internet address (Freer Gallery research and study): http://www.si.edu/resource/research/resmus/rfreer.htm.
Networks, consortia: RLG, RLIN.
Public transit access: Metro: Blue or Orange Line to Smithsonian Station. Use either the Mall or the Independence Avenue exits. The Freer Gallery is one block east of either exit.
Founded: 1923 (Charles Lang Freer Gallery); 1987 (Arthur M. Sackler Gallery).
Major resources: The (combined) Freer Gallery and Arthur M. Sackler Gallery Library and Archives.
Areas of specialization: Asian art and culture (including Chinese, Japanese, Korean, South and Southeast Asian, Near Eastern and Eastern Mediterranean art); also American art of the late nineteenth-century. About one-half of library holdings are in Chinese, Japanese and other non-English languages.
Archives/manuscripts: The Archives holds the records of the Freer and Sackler Galleries as well as some seventy other manuscript collections—many concerning aspects of Asian art and archaeology. Archival holdings include the Carl Whiting Bishop papers (archaeological work in China in the 1920s); Charles Lang Freer (1856-1919) papers; Li Chi (1896-1979) archaeological reports; Tz'u-hsi, Empress Dowager of China (1935-1908) photographs; Ernest Herzfeld (1879-1948) papers (records and fieldnotes of archaeological excavations in Iran and the Near East); Myron Bement Smith (1897-1970) collection; others.
Visual/audio resources: 73,000 color slides; 100,000 photographs. Photographic holdings include the Antoin Sevruguin photographs. Sevruguin (active 1860s-1920s) was an official photographer of the Imperial Court of Iran.
Access: Open for research use. Library hours are Monday-Friday, 10:00 a.m.-5:00 p.m. Archives hours are Tuesday, Thursday and Friday, 10:00 a.m.-5:00 p.m. Appointments to use the Archives should be made in advance.
References: Sarah L. Newmeyer, "The Carl Whiting Bishop Photographic Archive in the Freer Gallery of Art: A Resource for the Study of Chinese Architecture, Archaeology, Geology, Topography, Flora, Fauna, Customs and Culture," *Committee on East Asian Libraries Bulletin*, vol. 82, no. 8 (Sept. 1987), p. 23-28.

Guides/catalogs: Freer Gallery of Art. Library, *Dictionary Catalog of the Freer Gallery of Art, Smithsonian Institution* (2nd ed., Boston: 1991)—on microfiche; *Guide to Photographic Collections at the Smithsonian Institution* (Washington, D.C.: 1989-   ), v. 3, p. 140-192.

Smithsonian Institution. Libraries (SIL)

Address: Libraries, National Museum of Natural History, 10th Street & Constitution Avenue, N.W., Washington, DC 20560.

Location: Many of the Smithsonian Institution libraries are in museum facilities on the National Mall. The Anthropology Branch Library is in the Anthropology Department of the National Museum of Natural History—on the National Mall at 10th Street.

Tel.: (202) 357-2240 (Office of the Director); (202) 357-1819 (Anthropology Branch Library).

Fax: (202) 357-2690 (Office of the Director); (202) 357-1896 (Anthropology Branch Library).

E-mail: libmail@sil.si.edu.

Internet address: http://www.sil.si.edu. This site has the Smithsonian Institution Libraries *User Guide* as well as information from the SIL branch libraries. The SIL Electronic Editions, an on-line publications project begun in 1996, is also available here.

Internet access to on-line catalog: www.siris.si.edu. Holdings are also cataloged in OCLC and RLIN.

Networks, Consortia: ARL, OCLC, FLICC (Federal Library Information Center Committee), RLG ShaRes member and special member, participant in the Reciprocal Faculty Borrowing Program of OCLC.

Public transit access: Metro: Orange Line or Blue Line to Smithsonian or Federal Triangle station.

Founded: The Smithsonian Institution Libraries (SIL) were formally organized in 1968 when a library system was established uniting many of the existing Smithsonian Institution museum and research center special libraries into a single organization. The eighteen branches of the SIL currently serve the Institution and the public with support of Smithsonian curatorial, research, exhibition, educational and other program activities. In 1980, as part of the celebration of the centennial of the Bureau of American Ethnology, SIL's Anthropology Branch library was renamed the John Wesley Powell Library of Anthropology.

Major resources: Various, including: Anthropology Branch; Museum Support Center Branch (in Suitland, Maryland); the Museum of African Art Branch; and the Smithsonian Tropical Research Branch (in Panama City, Panama). See areas of specialization and branch descriptions below.

Areas of specialization: Various; for anthropology: Native American history, culture and linguistics; a very extensive collection of works focusing on North American Indian languages and linguistics; an extensive collection of facsimiles of codices; history of American anthropology; Asian cultural history; physical anthropology—especially skeletal biology, paleo-pathology and human variation; African art and material culture; museum conservation and associated laboratory analyses.

Holdings: The SIL collections number approximately 1.2 million volumes; holdings include more than 15,000 journal titles. The Anthropology Branch itself has approximately 75,000 volumes, including more than 400 serials, 800 rare books, a considerable amount of microform materials and a growing collection of CDs and other electronic media. The number of anthropological holdings in SIL libraries other than the Anthropology Branch is unknown, but significant.

Access: The Smithsonian Institution Libraries is open to scholars and general readers by appointment only. Materials must be used on-site.

References: [Margaret R. Dittemore], "Smithsonian Anthropology Library: A National Resource," *ASW Newsletter* [Anthropological Society of Washington] (Jan. 1995), p. 11-13; pamphlets and brochures produced by SIL.

Guides, catalogs: *Smithsonian on Disc: Catalog of the Smithsonian Institution Libraries on CD-ROM* (New York: 1994-   ).

Description

Anthropological materials in the Smithsonian Institution Libraries (SIL) are found primarily in the Anthropology Branch Library, and secondarily in several other branch libraries—most notably at the Museum Support Center (MSC) Branch, the Museum of African Art Branch and the Smithsonian Tropical Research Institute (STRI) Branch in Panama City, Panama. As with the rest of SIL's collections, these materials support the programs, exhibitions, research and publication activities of the Smithsonian Institution (SI). The SI has been central to the development of American anthropology during the last century, and research and publication by Institution staff in this area are held in high esteem worldwide.

Anthropology Branch Library

The Anthropology Branch, also known as the John Wesley Powell Library of Anthropology, is housed within the Anthropology Department in the National Museum of Natural History. It consists of approximately 75,000 volumes, including more than 400 serials, 800 rare books and a large number of microform materials.

The core of the collection is the library of the Bureau of American Ethnology (BAE), established by Congress in 1879 within the SI, initially as the Bureau of Ethnology. The purpose of the BAE was to continue the "anthropologic researches among the North American Indians," [Bureau of Ethnology, *1st Annual Report* (Washington, D.C.: 1881), p. xi] that had previously been conducted by various geological and geographical surveys.

The Bureau library was developed very broadly, and a significant portion of its holdings came through gifts and exchanges. Many Bureau members and supporters donated books and other materials from their personal collections. John Wesley Powell—who was in charge of the Bureau's precursor, the Geological Survey, and who initially managed the Bureau—contributed some materials. Frederick W. Hodge donated materials as well. Hodge organized the Bureau library collection during its early years, before he succeeded BAE Chief William H. Holmes. (The bulk of Hodge's personal library was sold to the Museum of the American Indian, however.)   Other donors included Frank R.R. Roberts, John Swanton, Neil Judd, Otis Mason, Charles Rau and Aleš Hrdlička. Extensive exchange programs with national and international learned societies and other scholarly organizations, the acquisition of relevant government documents, and the collection of a large offprint and pamphlet collection have significantly enriched the collection.

The BAE library grew quickly during its early years. By the early 1930s it contained 30,391 volumes, about 16,993 pamphlets and several thousand unbound periodicals [Bureau of American Ethnology, *50th Annual Report* (Washington, D.C.: 1933), p. 6]. Because the collection grew primarily through gifts and exchange, the quantity of incoming material varied considerably from year to year. The growth of the collection was also affected by the Depression (1930s) and by both world wars.

From 1910 until 1965, the BAE and its library were located in the original Smithsonian Building (known as "The Castle")—a very prominent and visible place. During those years the BAE library was arguably the best resource available for the study of Native Americans. The library was regularly used by SI personnel and, in addition, reference assistance was provided to "investigators and students" outside the institution, according to the annual reports of the Bureau.

In 1965, when the BAE was abolished, its library was joined with those of the museum anthropology divisions and was moved to its present location, where it became a branch of the Smithsonian Institution Libraries system. The merger of the BAE library and the division libraries resulted in a collection estimated at the time of merger to consist of about 52,000 volumes, of which about 35,000 volumes were from the former BAE library.

The division libraries consisted of materials concerning the anthropology and archaeology of the Old World—specifically Asia, Africa and the Middle East—as well as of Oceania and Latin America. However, because the BAE collection had a unique classification system, the recataloging and integration of the two collections into a single Library of Congress cataloging sequence was completed only in 1989.

The collection today is the product of careful development during the last century in support of museum collections and of the pursuits of SI curatorial staff. It continues to expand as a result of gifts and exchanges, as well as through purchases. More than 150 regular exchange partners add valuable publications—especially from developing countries—that would not otherwise be readily available.

Coverage is broad, including materials from the four subfields of American anthropology, but is somewhat uneven. The Anthropology Branch's greatest overall strength lies in its holdings of early materials, including national and international journals. The emphasis throughout the collection is on research materials, many of which have a strong material culture emphasis.

Holdings remain especially strong in Native American culture history for all of North America and the Arctic rim. There is a very extensive collection of works on North American Indian languages. Materials focusing on cultural and linguistic development in Mexico and Central and South America are represented as well. The Anthropology Branch continues to collect research materials on Native Americans—especially in the fields of anthropology, archaeology, history and linguistics.

A diverse body of physical anthropological and biomedical literature supports research in skeletal biology, paleo-pathology and human variation. In addition, the library has research materials concerning the study of human origins in Africa, and also of early humans in the Americas. A research-level collection is being developed, together with the branch library of the Museum Support Center, to support the archaeobiology program that was established in 1992.

The last decade has also seen significant growth in the Asian Cultural History Collection. The core of this resource is the former personal library of the late Cornell University linguist and Indonesian-language specialist, John M. Echols. This resource has been further developed as a result of the dedication and generosity of the current Asian Cultural History Program.

Another very strong collection is the Alexander Easter Island Collection of books and pamphlets donated by Robert Alexander. Materials on the Near East, Oceania, Africa and the New World diaspora are also represented.

The reasonably strong reference collection includes complete sets of the *Catalogue of the Library of the Peabody Museum of Archaeology and Ethnology, Harvard University* (Boston: 1963-1979); Cornell University Libraries, *Southeast Asia Catalog* (Boston: 1976-1983); Musée de l'Homme. Bibliothèque, *Catalogue systématique de la section Afrique* (Boston: 1970); Newberry Library, *Dictionary Catalog of the Edward E. Ayer Collection of Americana and American Indians* (Boston: 1961); Huntington Free Library and Reading Room, *Dictionary Catalog of the American Indian Collection* (Boston: 1977); U.S. Department of the Interior, *Biographical and Historical Index of American Indians and Persons Involved in Indian Affairs* (Boston: 1966); *Ethnographic Bibliography of North America* (New Haven, Conn.: 1975-1990); and *Handbook of Middle American Indians* (Austin, Texas: 1964-1976) and its supplements.

Reference holdings also include all of the Bureau of American Ethnology publications, as well as more recent SI publications such as the *Catalog to Manuscripts at the National Anthropological Archives* (Boston: 1975); *Guide to the National Anthropological Archives* (Washington, D.C.: 1990), as well as the current on-line catalog of that archive; *Smithsonian Contributions to Anthropology* (Washington, D.C.: 1965-   ); and the *Handbook of North American Indians* (Washington, D.C.: 1978-   ).

In addition to both the print and on-line versions of *Anthropological Literature* (Tozzer Library, Harvard University) the library has *Anthropological Index* (Royal Anthropological Institute of Great Britain and Ireland) and a number of other geographical and topical indexes. The library has a small CD-ROM collection that includes HRAF, *Cross Cultural CD* (Boston: 1989-   ); *Polar Pac* (Fairbanks: 1990-   ); *Bibliography of Native North Americans on Disc* (Santa Barbara, Ca.: 1992); *The American Indian: A Multimedia Encyclopedia* (New York: 1993); and Archivo General de la Nacion, *Argena* (Mexico: 1993-   ).

The Anthropology Branch receives approximately 400 journals, about one-half of which are acquired through exchange. They range from complete runs of core titles to more ephemeral serials such as newsletters of state and local associations and museums. A number of international journals are received as well.

A retrospective collection of government documents pertaining to Native Americans is also held. This collection includes early Congressional reports, War (and later Interior) Department publications and those of various special boards and commissions.

The small but distinguished rare book collection contains many important early works of exploration and study, especially in the Americas. Included are works by Adolph Bandelier, Thomas McKenney, James Hall and Henry R. Schoolcraft. An extensive collection of facsimiles of codices—important for understanding Mesoamerican ethnohistory—is found. A number of Native American-language materials—some published by small missionary presses and printed on poor quality paper—are among rare book holdings.

The microform collection in the Anthropology Branch contains materials from a variety of sources. Examples include: British Museum. Museum of Mankind Library, *Museum of Mankind Library Subject Catalogue and Periodicals Index* (Bath, England: 1989); the *Rasmuson Library Catalog* (Fairbanks: 1975-1985); the Museo de Etnologia y Antropologia de Chile publications; *Djawa: Tijdschrift van het Java-Institut* (Weltevreden: 1921-1941); *Iroquois Indians: A Documentary History of the Diplomacy of the Six Nations and Their League* (Woodbridge, Conn.: 1984); and Indian Claims Commission materials. *The Professional Correspondence of Franz Boas* (Wilmington, Del.: 1972), and Indian-language collections from Alaska and the Pacific Northwest are also available and are currently housed in the National Anthropological Archives.

The library works closely with the National Anthropological Archives (NAA), as many of the library's published materials support and/or derive from NAA's archival holdings. One of the goals of the Anthropology Branch is to strengthen its holdings in the history of American anthropology, as the NAA has become the repository for the archival records of many professional associations in the field. Among these are the American Anthropological Association and the Society for American Archaeology.

The library has constructed an Anthropology home page advertising many of the resources related to anthropology that are on the Internet. A pilot project is making several BAE publications, including its *Bulletin* no. 200 (1971)—the last BAE publication and the index to all previous numbers—available electronically from an SIL server.

Other SIL Branch Libraries

Library materials related to the study of anthropology may also be found in several other SI branches:

• The Museum Support Center Branch Library [see the brief entry under the heading **Maryland—Suitland**] has information supporting the management of museum collections, including their conservation, restoration, preservation; and a number of different laboratory facilities, including archaeometry, archaeozoology and archaeobiology. This Branch Library is located in Suitland, Maryland.

• The African Art Branch Library [see the following entry] focuses on the visual arts of Africa with supporting collections in the archaeology and ethnology of Africa. Its collection (approximately 25,000 book volumes) is considered one of the best in the world.

• In Panama City, Panama, the Smithsonian Tropical Research Institute Branch Library [see the brief entry under the heading **Panama—Panama City**] holds materials on Central and South American anthropology and archaeology.

Smithsonian Institution. Libraries. African Art Branch Library

Address: African Art Branch Library, 950 Independence Avenue, S.W., MRC 708, Washington, DC 20560.
Location: In the National Museum of African Art building—on the National Mall at Independence Avenue, S.W.
Tel.: (202) 357-4600, ext. 286.
Fax: (202) 357-4879
E-mail: libmail@sil.si.edu.
Internet address: http://www.sil.si.edu/afahp.htm.
Internet access to on-line catalog: Cataloged African Art Branch Library holdings may be accessed on the Web at www.siris.si.edu. Holdings are also on OCLC and RLIN. Indexing of the Branch's journal holdings was published beginning in 1990 in annual volumes of *The Arts of Africa: An Annotated Bibliography.* More recently, journal indexing is added by the African Art Branch to the Smithsonian's SIRIS online catalog.
Public transit access: Metro: Orange Line or Blue Line to Smithsonian station, Mall or Independence Avenue exit.
Founded: 1964 (Smithsonian Museum of African Art); 1971 (African Art Branch Library).
Major resources: Books and journals on the visual arts of Africa and related topics.
Areas of specialization: African art, folklore and ethnography; supporting library collections on African history, archaeology, religion, oral traditions, music and literature.
Holdings (books and journals): Ca. 25,000 books and 400 journals.
Visual/audio resources: A large photographic collection on African arts is maintained in the nearby Eliot Elisofon Photographic Archives [see the following entry on this resource].
Access: Open to the public.
Guides/catalogs: Smithsonian Institution. Libraries. National Museum of African Art Branch, *Catalog of the Library of the National Museum of African Art Branch of the Smithsonian Institution Libraries* (Boston: 1991) (= *Smithsonian Insitution Libraries. Research Guide*, vol. 7), 2 v.; Janet L. Stanley, *African Art: A Bibliographic Guide* (New York: 1985) (= *Smithsonian Institution Libraries. Research Guide*, no. 4); Janet L. Stanley (compiler), *The Arts of Africa: An Annotated Bibliography* (Atlanta, Ga.: 1990-   ).
Artifacts of anthropological significance: The National Museum of African Art has rich collections of African art—including sculpture, woodcarvings, textiles and other objects.

Information provided by Nancy L. Matthews and Janet L. Stanley.

Smithsonian Institution. National Museum of African Art. Eliot Elisofon Photographic Archives

Address: Eliot Elisofon Photographic Archives, National Museum of African Art, MRC 708, 950 Independence Avenue, S.W., Washington, DC 20560.

Location: In the National Museum of African Art building—on the National Mall at Independence Avenue, S.W.
Tel.: (202) 357-4600, ext. 280, 281, 282, 283.
Fax: (202) 357-4879.
E-mail: afaem016@sivm.si.edu.
Internet address: http://www.si.edu/nmafa/resource/archives.htm.
Public transit access: Metro: Orange Line or Blue Line to Smithsonian station, Mall or Independence Avenue exit.
Founded: 1973.
Major resources: Ca. 300,000 photographic images organized by collection name; film and video collections; maps and engravings.
Areas of specialization: African art history, African history, African studies, visual anthropology, anthropology of art, history of colonialism.
Archives/manuscripts: Some of the collections are accompanied by supplementary materials, such as fieldnotes and/or annotations—among them the Eliot Elisofon collection of field photographs, the Gulla Kell-Pfeffer collection, the Andrew and Martha Ruch collection and the Henry John Drewal and Margaret Thompson Drewal collection. There are no published guides to these collections.
Visual/audio resources: Approximately 300,000 images organized by collection; 220 films and videos; 270 maps and engravings.
Access: Open by appointment to scholars for research and to the general public. A few collections may not be accessible due to their fragile nature, state of preservation or incomplete classification. Materials are classified according to the Archives classification system. Records for ca. 40,000 field slides have been entered into a local database.
References: "The Classification Systems for Field and Art Images"—this brochure will be mailed on request; "The Eliot Elisofon Photographic Archives"—this brochure will be mailed on request; Diane Vogt O'Connor (editor), *Guide to Photographic Collections at the Smithsonian Institution* (Washington, D.C.: 1989-   ), vol. 3, p. 30-70; Aloha South, *Guide to Non-Federal Archives and Manuscripts in the United States Relating to Africa* (London: 1989), vol. 1, p. 341-352.
Artifacts of anthropological significance: The adjacent National Museum of African Art has rich collections of African art, including sculpture, carvings, textiles and other objects.

Description

The National Museum of African Art is dedicated exclusively to the collection, study and exhibition of African art. The museum's primary aim is to foster public understanding and appreciation of the diverse cultures and arts of Africa. As part of the museum, the Eliot Elisofon Photographic Archives is a research and reference center for visual materials, devoted to the collection, preservation and dissemination of visual resources that encourage and support the study of the arts, peoples and history of Africa. Archives staff conduct picture research in the fields of African art and cultural history, and research on the history of photography in Africa. In addition, the staff works with art historians, photographers, anthropologists, filmmakers and other interested specialists in the acquisition and preservation of visual resources.

Eliot Elisofon (1911-1973), for whom the Archives is named, was an internationally known photographer and filmmaker. He created an enduring visual record of African life during the years from 1947 to 1973. Some of Elisofon's work was published in magazines such as *Life* and *National Geographic*. As a filmmaker, he worked on projects such as a four-part Westinghouse documentary on Africa and an ABC television series on the same subject.

Elisofon began his association with what was then called the Museum of African Art, as a founding trustee, in 1964. Upon his death in 1973, he bequeathed to the museum his African materials. These comprised more than 50,000 black-and-white photographs, 30,000 color transparencies and 120,000 feet of unedited film. The bequest became the foundation for the Eliot Elisofon Photographic Archives, which was funded in part by a generous grant from the Samuel H. Kress Foundation.

Since 1973, the holdings have increased to more than 180,000 color transparencies and 80,000 black-and-white photographs. In recent years, rare historical collections of original glass negatives, lantern slides, stereographs and postcards, dating from the 1870s to the 1940s, have been acquired. The archives also maintains a collection of engravings and maps dating from the sixteenth- to the nineteenth-centuries, more than 100 documentary feature films that are used for study purposes, and a collection of documentary and educational videotapes.

The holdings are divided into two major categories: art photographs that show African works of art in museum and gallery settings, and field photographs that depict life and art in Africa. The art portion of the holdings consists of photographs of objects in the permanent collection of the National Museum of African Art. Also included are photographs of holdings from other collections, public and private, throughout the world that may be consulted for study purposes. Among the special collections within this category are Eliot Elisofon's systematic survey of African art objects in the United States and abroad, photographed in 1965. Also included within the art portion of the holdings is one of the most interesting portfolios on African art, created in 1935 by the well-known documentary photographer, Walker Evans. It contains images of art works that were part of the landmark exhibition, "African Negro Art," held at the Museum of Modern Art in New York in the same year.

The field section, which comprises more than 100 collections, contains images of art and culture taken in Africa, most of which reflect the work of particular photographers. Among the outstanding field collections are Eliot Elisofon's photographs, focusing on art and life in West and Central Africa. They portray African leaders, such as traditional rulers in Ghana, Côte d'Ivoire, Nigeria and Zaire. They also depict masquerades, indigenous architecture, artists at work and many other subjects.

Some collections, such as the White Fathers (Pères blancs) Mission collection from Rwanda and Burundi (ca. 1903 to 1924), contain the photographic work of missionaries in Africa. American missionaries Andrew and Martha Ruch photographed in Kenya from 1922 to 1925, and Wilhelm Schneider, a German missionary, worked in Cameroon from 1930 to 1940. Other photographs were taken by well-known art historians or anthropologists. William B. Fagg, a British specialist on Nigerian art, photographed in Nigeria from 1949 to 1959. Eva L.R. Meyerowitz, a German-born anthropologist, documented her studies in Bénin and Burkina Faso in the 1930s. Of equal interest are the images that Gulla Kell-Pfeffer, another anthropologist, created in Nigeria and Cameroon between 1927 and 1932. A recent addition to the archives is a collection of more than 10,000 35mm transparencies depicting Yoruba art and culture that were taken by the American art historian Henry John Drewal and his wife, Margaret Thompson Drewal, a specialist in performance studies.

The archives also holds extensive collections of images produced by professional European and African photographers between 1870 and 1940. Among these are postcard collections grouped by either photographer or by publishing company. The Fortier postcard collection, for example, was created by the French photographer François-Edmond Fortier, who maintained a studio and postcard publishing business in Dakar (Senegal) from 1900 to 1928. Other postcard producers include Sierra Leonian-born photographer Alphonso Lisk-Carew, who was active from 1905 (when he established his studio in Freetown) well into the 1950s. The Polish photographer Casimir d'Ostoja Zagórski lived and worked in Léopoldville (now Kinshasa, Democratic Republic of Congo) until 1949. In 1926, he traveled through Central Africa and photographed an important series of postcards entitled "L'Afrique qui disparait."

Use and Access to the Collections

The staff of the Eliot Elisofon Photographic Archives includes the Curator of the archives, a cultural anthropologist and specialist in African studies; the Archivist; and two Archives Technicians. The Archives serves the staff of the Smithsonian Institution, government agencies, professional associations, publishers, scholars, students and the general public who require access to specialized visual resources. The Archives staff can also provide information about photographic resources within the Smithsonian Institution and other repositories in the Washington, D.C.-area and elsewhere.

The collections of the Smithsonian Institution Libraries, National Museum of African Art Branch, located adjacent to the archives, but administered separately, complement the visual resources of the archives. For more information about that library's collections and services, contact the library at (202) 357-4600, ext. 286.

The Archives is open to the public, by appointment only, Monday through Friday, 10:00 a.m. to 4:00 p.m., and is closed on federal holidays. For appointments and more information about the Archives, contact either the Curator or the Archivist at (202) 357-4600, exts. 280 and 283. For scholars interested in extended research at the Archives, the Smithsonian Office of Fellowships and Grants (OFG) provides different types of research awards for projects that make use of Smithsonian collections. In addition to discussing such projects with the Curator of the Archives, individuals should contact the Office of Fellowships and Grants, at (202) 357-3271, for additional information.

Christraud M. Geary

Smithsonian Institution. National Museum of Natural History. Department of Anthropology. Arctic Studies Center (ASC)

Address: Arctic Studies Center, National Museum of Natural History, 10th Street and Constitution Ave., N.W., Washington, DC 20560.

Location: In the National Museum of Natural History—on the National Mall at Constitution Ave., N.W.

Tel.: (202) 357-2682 (main office); (907) 343-4326 (Anchorage office).

Fax: (202) 357-2684 (main office); (907) 343-6149 (Anchorage office).

E-mail: arctics@nmnh.si.edu.

Internet address: http://www.nmnh.si.edu/arctic.

Networks, consortia: Smithsonian Institution Research Information Service (SIRIS)—now available on the Web.

Public transit access: Metro: Orange Line or Blue Line to Smithsonian or Federal Triangle station.

Founded: 1988 (Arctic Studies Center). However, circumpolar research was carried out for many decades prior to 1988 by Smithsonian and other governmental units or agencies. Records from that research are in the National Anthropological Archives or other federal government repositories in Washington.

Major resources: Research documentation on the anthropology of the circumpolar region.

Areas of specialization: Northern peoples of Eurasia and North America, archaeology, Arctic history and biology, Alaska.

Archives/manuscripts: Older anthropological documentation for the circumpolar region is mainly preserved at the National Anthropological Archives [see the separate entry on that repository], while more recent records are at ASC.

Visual/audio resources: Extensive Arctic photo collections (color slides, black-and-white negatives and prints, videos, etc.)—either at ASC or the National Anthropological Archives. In addition, hundreds of hours of video documentation of ASC research are stored in New York City at Spofford Films. For information on the ASC videos at Spofford Films, contact Ted Timreck, tel. (212) 685-1134.

Access: Contact the National Anthropological Archives to request research access to older anthropological documentation on circumpolar peoples. Contact ASC regarding research access to more recent circumpolar records, documentation and ethnological and archaeology collections.

References: Valérie Chaussonnet, *Crossroads Alaska: Native Cultures of Alaska and Siberia* (Washington, D.C.: 1995); William W. Fitzhugh and Valérie Chaussonnet (editors), *Anthropology of the North Pacific Rim* (Washington, D.C.: 1994); William W. Fitzhugh and Aron Crowell, *Crossroads of Continents: Cultures of Siberia and Alaska* (Washington, D.C.: 1988); William W. Fitzhugh, *Inua: Spirit World of the Bearing Sea Eskimo* (Washington, D.C.: 1982). The *Arctic Studies Center Newsletter* is a continuing publication of ASC.

Information provided by William W. Fitzhugh.

Smithsonian Institution. National Museum of Natural History. Department of Anthropology. Human Studies Film Archives (HSFA)

Address: Human Studies Film Archives, National Museum of Natural History, Room E307 MRC 123, 10th Street and Constitution Ave., N.W., Washington, DC 20560.
Location: In the National Museum of Natural History—on the National Mall at Constitution Ave., N.W.
Tel.: (202) 357-3356
Fax: (202) 357-2208
E-mail: hsfa@nmnh.si.edu.
Internetaddress:http://www.nmnh.si.edu/gopher-menus/HumanStudiesFilmArchives.html.
Internet access to on-line catalog: www.siris.si.edu.
Networks, consortia: Smithsonian Institution Research Information Service (SIRIS)—available on the Web.
Public transit access: Metro: Orange Line or Blue Line to Smithsonian or Federal Triangle station.
Founded: 1975.
Major resources: Various; more than 1,008 named collections of film and video.
Areas of specialization: Visual anthropology, ethnographic film, colonial documentaries, amateur and professional travelogues, the history of anthropology, African, Arctic, Oceanic and Himalayan studies.
Archives/manuscripts: Approximately 30 percent of HSFA film and video collections are accompanied by some supplementary materials such as manuscripts, fieldnotes, photographs and/or annotations. No published guide to these exists, except a note in the HSFA catalog, *Guide to the Collections of the Human Studies Film Archives* (Washington, D.C.: 1995). The main Smithsonian Institution collection of anthropological manuscripts and photographs is the very large collection housed in the National Anthropological Archives (NAA).
Holdings (film and video): More than 1,000 named film and video collections—more than eight million ft. total.
Access: Collections are, with special exceptions, accessible to all who need to use them. Approximately 30 percent of film and video collections are accompanied by supplementary materials such as manuscripts, fieldnotes and/or annotations.
Guides/catalogs: Pamela Wintle and John P. Homiak, *Guide to the Collections of the Human Studies Film Archives: 100th Anniversary of Motion Pictures, Commemorative Ethnographic Edition* (Washington, D.C.: 1995). The on-line version of this guide is available to the public at the HSFA website mentioned above; the guide may be downloaded as needed. Also available is Deanna Kingston, *Guide to the Edited Films of Father Bernard Hubbard, S.J.* (Washington, D.C.: 1993).

Description

The Human Studies Film Archives is administered as part of the Department of Anthropology, National Museum of Natural History, Smithsonian Institution. The holdings of the Archives presently consist of approximately eight million feet of film and video (approximately 75 percent 16mm color and black-and-white film and 25 percent video in various formats). During the past five years the collections have grown at a rate of some 200,000 feet per year. The oldest collection dates to 1908 (film shot in Crow Agency, Montana) and the most recent was produced in 1996 (video shot in Jamaica). Collections vary from a single roll of silent footage to extensive anthropological film projects produced with field sound and accompanying documentation. The subject matter of collections is related to cultures from around the world and an attempt is made to acquire materials of broad ethnographic and historical significance. The collection includes materials created by various well-known anthropologists, ethnographic and documentary filmmakers and others.

The intellectual roots of the HSFA can be traced to a small, but determined, cohort of anthropologists who established themselves in the 1960s as a committee within the broader structure of the American Anthropological Association. Under the heading of the Program in Ethnographic Film (PIEF) (and later the Society for the Anthropology of Visual Communications [SAVICOM]), this group sought to establish a recognized place for the use of film and other visual media in anthropological teaching and research. Figures of particular significance within this original circle included Margaret Mead, Sol Worth, John Adair, Walter Goldschmidt, Conrad Arensberg, Alan Lomax, Paul Hockings, Edmund Carpenter, Colin Young, Robert Gardner, Gordon Gibson, Asen Balikci, Timothy Asch, John Marshall, David MacDougall and Karl Heider. It was largely through the efforts of this interested group of anthropologists—who incorporated themselves as members of the Anthropological Film Research Institute (AFRI)—that, in the early 1970s, funding was sought for the creation of a National Anthropological Film Research Archives. The ultimate result was the creation of the National Anthropological Film Center at the Smithsonian in 1975. This was renamed the Human Studies Film Archives in 1981.

Although the original purposes of this Center were manifold, the HSFA continues a number of the functions intended by AFRI: the ongoing acquisition of a world ethnographic film sample, the cataloging of film materials, the preservation of these visual materials and the facilitating of access by researchers. A number of the most significant collections in the HSFA were produced by the charter members of AFRI. These include: the Yanomami Film Project, 1968-1972 (100,000 ft. by Timothy Asch—from which 37 Yanomami films have been edited); the !Kung San Film Project, 1950-1978 (700,000 ft. by John Marshall—from which nineteen !Kung films have been edited); the Pashtoon Nomad Film Project, 1975-1976 (95,000 ft. by Asen Balikci and Timothy Asch—from which the film *Sons of Haji Omar* has been edited); the Jie and Turkana Film Projects, 1968-1974 (54,000 ft., David and Judith MacDougall—from which *To Live with Herds* and *Turkana Conversations: A Trilogy* have been edited). From 1975 to 1982, the National Anthropological Film Center also funded a number of field projects that produced extensive research films. These included projects in Nepal, India, Micronesia (the western Caroline Islands), Melanesia (New Guinea and the New Hebrides) and northwest Mexico.

Although the archives originally formed around a number of anthropologists who themselves made films (and therefore incorporated their materials), it has always had as its mandate the preservation and study of visual materials associated with all forms of anthropological research. Other figures of interest whose materials form part of the HSFA collections include Franz Boas (footage on Kwakiutl from Fort Ruppert, British Columbia, 1929); Paul Wirz (footage from the Lake Sentani region of New Guinea, 1919); Melville J.

Herskovits (research footage shot in Dahomey and the Gold Coast, 1931, and Haiti, 1934); George E. Simpson (footage shot in Haiti, 1936); Robert Zingg (footage on the Huichol and Tarahumara, 1933); Scudder McKeel (footage shot on the Rosebud Reservation, Lakota Sioux, 1930); Matthew Stirling (footage from Dutch New Guinea, 1926); and Colin Turnbull (footage on the Mbuti of Zaire, 1954-1972, and on the Ik of Uganda, 1972).

In addition to the records of film projects by ethnographic and independent filmmakers and the research footage of various anthropologists, the HSFA has preserved a wealth of historical footage shot by travelers and explorers that is of ethnographic interest. A unique collection of early film materials has been amassed on areas such as Africa, South America, the Arctic and Oceania in this way. This includes uncut footage as well as early edited "scenics" and travelogues—e.g., Pathé Science Series, Castle Films, Burton Holmes travelogues.

The HSFA also distributes a collection of particular interest to students of anthropology, "Video Dialogues in the History of Anthropology," a project jointly sponsored by the Wenner-Gren Foundation for Anthropological Research and the University of Florida. Information about the contents and prices for this series can be obtain by writing to or calling the HSFA, as indicated below.

Use of and Access to the Collections

The HSFA staff includes a cultural anthropologist, two film archivists and a media resource specialist. The staff encourages the scholarly use of its resources and makes its collections available for screening by researchers and other patrons of the Film Archives. All accessioned collections are cataloged at a minimal descriptive level. Approximately 35 percent of the HSFA materials are more intensively cataloged, using index terms from the Human Relations Area Files publication, *An Outline of Cultural Materials*. Index searching is done on the Smithsonian Institution Research Information System (SIRIS) database for archives.

Appointments for screening of materials can be made by contacting Pamela Wintle, (202) 357-3349, or Mark White, (202) 357-3356. The HSFA staff recommends giving 48 hours notice for requests to screen materials. For scholars interested in extended research with the collections, the Smithsonian Office of Fellowships and Grants (OFG) provides awards in amounts up to $2,000 for projects that make use of Smithsonian Institution collections. Prior contact should be made with the HSFA for approval concerning such projects. For further information, individuals should contact Bruce Morrison, Program Specialist, OFG, at (202) 287-3271.

Scholars interested in materials for teaching purposes should be aware that HSFA materials do not, as a rule, circulate outside the Smithsonian. Independent and/or commercial filmmakers interested in stock footage should be aware that reproduction of materials depends upon existing agreements with filmmakers who have deposited their collections. Information on reproduction and use fees can be obtained by calling (202) 357-3356. A copy of the guide to the HSFA collections can be obtained by writing to Pamela Wintle, Senior Film Archivist, Human Studies Film Archives, Room E-307, MRC 123, Natural History Building, Smithsonian Institution, Washington, D.C. 20560.

John P. Homiak
Information provided by Pamela Wintle.

Smithsonian Institution. National Museum of Natural History. Department of Anthropology. National Anthropological Archives (NAA)

Address: National Anthropological Archives, Room 60-A, MRC 152, National Museum of Natural History, 10th Street and Constitution Avenue, N.W., Washington, DC 20560.
Location: In the National Museum of Natural History—on the National Mall at Constitution Ave., N.W.
Tel.: (202) 357-1986
Fax: (202) 633-8049
Internet address (Smithsonian Institution Department of Anthropology): http://www.nmnh.si.edu/departments/anthro.html.
Internet access to on-line catalog: www.siris.si.edu.
Networks, consortia: Smithsonian Institution Research Information Service (SIRIS)—available on the Web. NAA has approximately 95,000 records on SIRIS, including descriptions of the manuscript collection of the former Bureau of American Ethnology, more than 400,000 photographs, maps, the John P. Harrington sound recording collection, more than 20,000 items of artwork, as well as collection-level descriptions of all its collections.
Public transit access: Metro: Orange Line or Blue Line to Smithsonian or Federal Triangle station.
Founded: 1879; as successor to the archives of the Bureau of American Ethnology: 1968.
Major resources: Official records of the Smithsonian Institution, including records of the Bureau of American Ethnology; the Division of Anthropology, U.S. National Museum; the Center for the Study of Man; the Department of Anthropology; the Institute for Social Anthropology; and River Basin Surveys.
Areas of specialization: American Indian linguistics and ethnology; North American archaeology; physical anthropology; the history of anthropology.
Archives/manuscripts: Ca. 6,600 linear ft. of official records and manuscript collections.
Fieldnotes, papers, etc.: Listed in the *Guide to the National Anthropological Archives, Smithsonian Institution.*
Visual/audio resources: The collection includes ca. 400,000 photographs from around the world—many of North American Indians, North American archaeological sites and physical anthropology specimens. All motion picture material received by NAA is sent to the Smithsonian Institution Human Studies Film Archives (HSFA). Sound recordings include aluminum discs recorded by John P. Harrington in his work with Alaska, California and Northwest Coast Indians.
Access: The NAA is open to all who need to use it. Some collections have donor-imposed restrictions. It is necessary to contact the Archives in advance of a visit to obtain information on the use of specific material and to schedule an appointment; hours and days open to the public vary.
References: Curtis M. Hinsley, *The Smithsonian and the American Indian: Making a Moral Anthropology in Victorian America* (Washington, D.C.: 1994). [Originally published as

Savages and Scientists: The Smithsonian Institution and the Development of American Anthropology, 1846-1910 (Washington, D.C.: 1981)]; Mary Elizabeth Ruwell, "The National Anthropological Archives," in Sydel Silverman and Nancy J. Parezo (editors), *Preserving the Anthropological Record* (2nd ed., New York: 1995), p. 17-21; Aloha South, *Guide to Non-Federal Archives and Manuscripts in the United States Relating to Africa* (London: 1989), vol. 1, p. 396-405.

Guides/catalogs: James R. Glenn (compiler), *Guide to the National Anthropological Archives, Smithsonian Institution* (rev. ed., Washington, D.C.: 1996). A detailed catalog of the manuscript collection of the Bureau of American Ethnology has been published as National Museum of Natural History, *Catalogue of Numbered Manuscripts at the National Anthropological Archives* (Boston: 1975), 4 v.

Some papers have finding aids. Records of many are included in the catalog published by G.K. Hall: *Catalogue of Numbered Manuscripts at the National Anthropological Archives* (Boston: 1975), 4 v.

Artifacts of anthropological significance: All artifacts received with archival materials are transferred to the Processing Lab, Department of Anthropology, Smithsonian Institution. No catalogs of artifacts are available in the NAA.

Archaeological sites represented by artifact collections: The NAA has material for sites worked by Smithsonian personnel, including those sites explored and recorded by the Bureau of American Ethnology Division of Mound Surveys; and the River Basin Surveys. Also available is a set of the periodical reports on archaeological work by the U.S. Work Projects Administration (WPA).

Description

In 1879 John Wesley Powell founded the Bureau of Ethnology—later the Bureau of American Ethnology (BAE)—a research unit of the Smithsonian Institution devoted to the study of American Indian cultures. The BAE immediately acquired manuscript material from two sources: the Smithsonian Institution, which had collected linguistic manuscripts since the 1850s, and from the Powell, Hayden and Wheeler surveys, which had collected manuscripts during the 1870s. These materials, described in James C. Pilling's "Catalogue of Linguistic Manuscripts in the Library of the Bureau of Ethnology," *First Annual Report of the Bureau of American Ethnology, 1880* (Washington D.C.: 1881), formed the beginning of what would later become the National Anthropological Archives, one of the largest collections of anthropological materials in the United States.

From 1879 to 1965 the archival collections expanded largely through the addition of fieldnotes, letters, circular forms, works of art, manuscripts of writings, cartographic items and other materials produced or collected by BAE staff and collaborators. The scope of the collection also expanded when, during the 1880s, the BAE undertook a survey of mounds and other structures east of the Rocky Mountains, thus bringing archaeology within its purview.

Among the contributors to the Archives were some of the outstanding figures in the early institutional development of American anthropology, including John Wesley Powell, Franz Boas, W.J. McGee and William Henry Holmes. Later heads of the BAE who would join these ranks included Jesse Walter Fewkes, Matthew W. Stirling, Frank H.H. Roberts and Henry B. Collins.

Other contributors were known primarily for their work in the field. These included Albert S. Gatschet (in his day, according to Franz Boas, the best-trained linguist in America), J. Owen Dorsey (a Sioux specialist), James Mooney (a Cherokee and southern Plains specialist), John R. Swanton (Northwest Coast and Southeast ethnologist), Truman Michelson (Algonquian linguist and ethnologist), John P. Harrington (California, Northwest and Southwest linguist and ethnologist) and Philip Drucker (Northwest Coast, Micronesia and Mexico specialist). Among these scholars were several women, including Erminnie Smith (an Iroquois specialist), Matilda Coxe Stevenson (Pueblo specialist), Alice C. Fletcher (Omaha-Winnebago-Nez Perce specialist) and Frances Densmore (an ethnomusicologist). Also included were two American Indian anthropologists: the Tuscarora, J.N.B. Hewitt, an Iroquianist with a particular interest in the League of the Iroquois; and Francis LaFlesche, an Omaha who was a specialist in the cultures of the Omaha and the Osage.

The BAE had a special relationship with Franz Boas and several of his early students. For a time Boas was the BAE honorary philologist, and he and some of his early students enjoyed one of the larger commitments of the BAE budget in exchange for their field materials or finished manuscripts. In addition, some of Boas's students, including Swanton and Michelson, were employed by the BAE after they completed their studies. Thus, materials of researchers Alfred L. Kroeber, Robert H. Lowie, Paul Radin, Harry Hull St. Clair, Leo J. Frachtenberg and others were acquired, along with some of Boas's papers. This arrangement—together with the use of temporary appointments and contracts with other anthropologists—considerably extended the list of contributors to the Archives.

In 1965, the BAE was merged with the Department of Anthropology in the Smithsonian's United States National Museum to form the Smithsonian Office of Anthropology. The Archives—then named the SOA Archives—began to acquire the documents that had accumulated in the Department, including miscellaneous manuscripts and papers of the ethnologists Otis T. Mason, Walter Hough, Neil M. Judd and Herbert W. Krieger; archaeologists Charles Rau, Thomas Wilson, Herbert W. Krieger and Frank M. Setzler; and physical anthropologists Aleš Hrdlička, J. Lawrence Angel and T. Dale Stewart.

A further change took place in 1968, as part of an effort to create Smithsonian programs concerned with broad problems. The SOA Archives was renamed the National Anthropological Archives and was given the mission to collect papers of American anthropologists and records of American anthropological organizations. Following this, in a resolution of November 1968, the American Anthropological Association urged members to consider NAA as a depository for their papers, if they had no other commitments.

As NAA, the Archives has become the repository for the records of the American Anthropological Association, the American Association of Physical Anthropologists, the American Dermatoglyphics Association, the American Ethnological Association, the American Society for Conservation Archaeology, the American Society for Ethnohistory, the Anthropological Society of Washington, the Central States Anthropological Society, the Committee on Anthropological Research in Museums, the Council for Northeast Historical Archaeology, the Northeastern Anthropological Association, the Society for American Archaeology, the Society for Applied Anthropology, the Society for Medical Anthropology, the Society for Visual Anthropology, the Southern Anthropological Association and the Southwestern Anthropological Association.

NAA also has the records relating to anatomical collections transferred from the United States Army Medical Museum, periodic reports on archaeological work by the WPA (Works Progress Administration) during the 1930s and 1940s, and U.S. General Accounting Office records compiled in its study of the effectiveness of federal legislation regarding antiquities. In addition, it also has a collection of about 1,500 reports produced by contract archaeologists in compliance with laws concerning archaeological work on federal land. Among other NAA holdings are records of Indian-interest organizations, including the Indian Rights Association (on microfilm), the National Tribal Chairmen's Association and the National Congress of American Indians. Also held are the U.S. Army-captured anthropological materials produced by the Institut für Deutsche Ostarbeit in its attempt to identify Poles of German origin.

Examples of personal collections from anthropologists are papers of Ethel M. Albert, J. Lawrence Angel, Homer G. Barnett, Ralph L. Beals, Leonard Bloomfield, William E. Carter, William A. Caudill, Henry B. Collins, Carleton S. Coon, John L. and Ann M. Fischer, James A. Ford, O.R. Gallagher, James Geary, Esther S. Goldfrank, Marcus S. Goldstein, Joel M. Halpern, R. King Harris, Robert F. Heizer (regarding work at La Venta), M. Inez Hilger, John J. Honigmann, James H. Howard, Charlene James-Duguid, Frederick Johnson, Carol F. Jopling, Eugene I. Knez, Weston La Barre, Ruth S. Landes, Anthony Leeds, Donald J. Lehmer, Dorothea C. Leighton, William A. Lessa, William Lipkind, Frances C. Macgregor, Gordon Macgregor, Robert F. Mahar, Leonard Mason, Washington Matthews (including microfilm), Philleo Nash, Jesse L. Nusbaum, Frans Olbrechts (Cherokee material), Edward Palmer, Conrad C. Reining, F.L.W. Richardson, Louise Robbins, Géza Róheim, Harold K. Schneider, William H. Sheldon, Mary S. Slusser, Albert Spaulding, T. Dale Stewart, William Duncan Strong, Sol Tax, Walter W. Taylor, Laura Thompson, Sara Jones Tucker, W.W. Turner, Waldo R. and Mildred M. Wedel and Alfred F. Whiting.

The Archives has also acquired the records of several special Smithsonian Institution units. The River Basin Surveys conducted archaeological work in federal reservoir areas during the period 1947-1969. The Institute for Social Anthropology (ISA), 1943-1952, led by Julian H. Steward, aimed to help train Latin American anthropologists, while sponsoring research in that area. The Center for the Study of Man (CSM), 1968-1983, was concerned with broad problems that confronted mankind. From both the ISA and CSM, the Archives mainly received administrative materials.

NAA also holds a collection of photo negatives of American Indians that was begun by Ferdinand V. Hayden and William Blackmore during the 1860s. That collection, joined with negatives and prints of anthropological researchers—ethnologists, archaeologists and physical anthropologists—and material produced by many professional photographers, number about 400,000 different images. These images document cultures from many regions of the world. The archives also holds an important collection of sound recordings, including those made by John P. Harrington among the natives of Alaska, California and the Northwest Coast.

John Wesley Powell, the first director of the BAE, was in effect the first keeper of the Archives, for he maintained the manuscript collection in his office, together with his library. Much of the actual work with the archives, however, was carried out under Powell's chief administrative assistants, James C. Pilling, Henry W. Henshaw and W.J. McGee.

At first, classification of individual or small groups of manuscripts by language family provided control of the collection. This choice grew from the involvement of many BAE staff members with Powell's project to classify American Indian languages "genetically," and the fact that many new acquisitions were used for that purpose. Although abandoned in the 1930s, the former classification scheme has left many marks on the collection and its finding aids.

In spite of this arrangement, disorder was chronic during the 1880s and 1890s, owing largely to the lack of an effective keeper, the self-service by staff members and the haphazard refiling that accompanied it. Further confusion came from loaning manuscripts to researchers without an adequate tracking system, a practice that continued for many decades. The enduring result was that some losses did occur.

In 1894 McGee initiated an effort to improve matters by arranging the manuscripts in two fire-proof vaults, and he assigned J.N.B. Hewitt the task of describing them. Hewitt later claimed that, after he had all but completed his catalog, a clerk discarded it. Thus, when a Smithsonian investigation into BAE administration was conducted in 1903, the state of the Archives—considered the BAE's most valuable property—became a major concern. Following a negative report, Hewitt was officially placed in charge of the Archives and, largely through the work of the clerical staff, a book-type catalog was completed in 1910.

During the next four decades, several organizational improvements were made. Powell's project having been completed, language family names became less important for control purposes. Replacing them for physical control was a numerical scheme and, for intellectual control, tribal names. The book catalog was indexed through a card file and eventually it was completely discarded and its descriptive data were included in the card catalog.

Controls were extended over the BAE sound recordings (these were eventually transferred to the Library of Congress) and the photographic materials that had previously been under the control of the BAE photographer. With the receipt of these photographs the Archives received a great treasure depicting American Indians on glass negatives, and a great miscellany of historical prints. By the last decade of this period, the archivist undertook studies that considerably improved the description of both manuscripts and photographs. Since 1972, the Archives has come to depend on inventories, registers and a computerized catalog using the MARC-AMC format as the basic finding aids for newer collections. Many of the older methods of control, however, remain in use for parts of the collection. In 1992 a *Guide to the National Anthropological Archives, Smithsonian Institution* was published and distributed to several hundred libraries throughout the world. The *Guide* attempts to overcome some of the complexities of control and to facilitate use of the collection. A revised and expanded edition of the *Guide* was published in 1996.

Appointments and inquiries can be made by calling (202) 357-1986 or by writing John P. Homiak, Director, National Anthropological Archives.

James R. Glenn
Information provided by John P. Homiak and Robert S. Leopold.

Smithsonian Institution. Office of Smithsonian Institution Archives

Address: Office of Smithsonian Institution Archives, 900 Jefferson Drive, S.W., Room 2135, Washington, DC 20560.
Location: In the Smithsonian Institution Arts and Industries Building, Room 2135—on the National Mall at Jefferson Drive, S.W.
Tel.: (202) 357-1420
Fax: (202) 357-2395
Internet address: http://www.si.edu/organiza/offices/archive/start.htm.
Internet access to on-line catalog: www.siris.si.edu.
Public transit access: Metro: Orange Line or Blue Line to Smithsonian station.
Founded: Ca. 1967 (Smithsonian Institution Archives).
Major resources: Official archives of the Smithsonian Institution; other research papers and manuscripts.
Areas of specialization: Many scientific disciplines.
Archives/manuscripts: Ca. 20,000 cubic ft., some part of which is of potential anthropological or related interest. Records and papers of Secretaries Joseph Henry and Spencer F. Baird document the Institution's early interest in and support of anthropology—including the work of Ephraim George Squier, E.H. Davis, George Gibbs and others. Manuscripts and oral histories of anthropological interest also include interviews with Henry B. Collins, T. Dale Stewart and John C. Ewers; and papers of C. Malcolm Watkins and William Henry Holmes. Other materials at this location include: United States National Museum. Permanent Administrative Files, 1877-1975; and Records of the Ethnographic Board, 1942-1945. Many additional Smithsonian Institution-related manuscripts and papers of anthropological interest are curated nearby in the National Anthropological Archives (NAA).
Visual/audio resources: A very small amount.
Access: Call in advance. Some restrictions on access apply.
Guides/catalogs: *Guide to the Smithsonian Archives* (Washington, D.C.: 1983, 1996).
Artifacts of anthropological significance: Many such artifacts are in the very large collections of the various Smithsonian Institution museums; also in some other Washington, D.C.-area collections.

Information provided by William Cox.

Textile Museum. Arthur D. Jenkins Library of the Textile Arts

Address: Arthur D. Jenkins Library of the Textile Arts, 2320 S Street, N.W., Washington, DC 20008.
Location: The library is on the third floor of the Textile Museum—in the Dupont Circle area of Washington.
Tel.: (202) 667-0441
Fax: (202) 483-0994

Public transit access: Metro: Red Line, exit at Dupont Circle station, north exit. The Textile Museum is a few minutes walk from the Dupont Circle station.

Founded: 1926 (Textile Museum); 1976 (Jenkins Library).

Major resources: Books, journals, pamphlets, ephemera, slides and videos on textiles and related topics.

Areas of specialization: Textiles of pre-Columbian cultures of the Americas, the Islamic Middle East, India, Southeast Asia (including Indonesia) and other areas.

Holdings (books and journals): 15,000 v.; more than 100 journal titles; 15 file drawers of pamphlets and ephemera.

Visual/audio resources: The library contains some slides and video cassettes on the arts, cultures, costume, textiles and textile techniques of non-European peoples and cultures.

Access: Materials are for reference use only. Stacks are open. No appointment is necessary. The library is open to the public Wednesday through Saturday, 10:00 a.m. to 2:00 p.m.

Guides/catalogs: Textile Museum. Arthur D. Jenkins Library, *Rug and Textile Arts: A Periodical Index, 1890-1982* (Boston: 1983).

Catalogs of textile resources (selected): Mattiebelle Gittinger, *Master Dyers to the World: Technique and Trade in Early Indian Dyed Cotton Textiles* (Washington, D.C.: 1982); Mattiebelle Gittinger and H. Leedom Lefferts, Jr., *Textiles and the Tai Experience in Southeast Asia* (Washington, D.C.: 1992); Ann Pollard Rowe, *Costumes & Featherwork of the Lords of Chimor: Textiles from Peru's North Coast* (Washington, D.C.: 1984); others.

Artifacts of anthropological or related significance: The Textile Museum has extensive collections of textiles, rugs and costumes from numerous non-European cultures. Special strengths include Oriental carpets, Coptic and Islamic textiles and archaeological textiles from pre-Columbian Peru.

Description

The Textile Museum was founded in 1925 by George Hewitt Myers, who began his life-long avocation of collecting rugs and textiles with the purchase of a single Oriental rug, while a student at Yale University's School of Forestry. A successful investment banker, Myers established the Textile Museum with a collection of 275 rugs and sixty textiles produced by the Islamic peoples of Spain, the Middle East and Central Asia. The collections are housed in two early-twentieth-century buildings in the Dupont Circle area of Washington, a neighborhood of museums and galleries, embassies and historic homes. The museum consists of Myers's home—a handsome building designed for him by John Russell Pope in 1913—and an adjoining residence that was later purchased for the growing collection and linked to the original structure. From a modest collection of Islamic textiles and Oriental rugs, the museum's collections have grown to include more than 1,400 rugs and 14,000 textiles from non-European cultures the world over. What began as one man's private collection, open only by appointment, has become an internationally known museum that sponsors exhibitions, publications, symposia, educational programs, textile festival days, an annual Rug Convention and Celebration of Textiles Day.

The Arthur D. Jenkins Library of the Textile Arts is located on the third floor of the gallery building, overlooking the museum's formal gardens and the skyline of Washington.

The library is named for midwesterner Arthur D. Jenkins, an attorney and newspaper publisher who was at one time President of the museum's Board of Trustees. Jenkins was a discerning rug collector and scholar who also began collecting Oriental rugs while in his early twenties. In the 1970s Jenkins's fine collection of 1,000 books and ephemera was added to that of Myers to form the nucleus of the present library. A generous benefactor, Jenkins supported the library until his death.

The library maintains a collection of literature and visual resources that reflect the museum's collections and the broader field of textile studies. Because contemporary textile scholarship examines textiles within the social and economic context of a people's culture, the library is an excellent source of ethnographic information about the traditional cultures of the Americas, Asia, Africa, the Middle East and the Pacific Rim. The Jenkins Library's holdings include books, dissertations, serials, pamphlets, slides and video cassettes. Since the library participates in an international exchange relationship with more than 130 museums and cultural institutions, its collection includes museum journals, exhibition catalogs and ephemera published around the world. These resources enable the researcher to view textiles as expressions of cultural values, reflections of gender issues, products of technology, objects of trade and works of art. Of special significance is the library's collection of materials on Oriental rugs, pre-Columbian art and textiles of the Americas, as well as textiles and costume of the Middle East, India, China, Japan, as well as Indonesia and other nations of the Southeast Asian region.

Due to the unique nature of the collection, the library's holdings are classified using a modified Dewey Decimal system and are cataloged with Library of Congress subject headings. Books are arranged in broad subject areas (i.e., rugs, textiles and costume, textile techniques, art history, cultural history) and are then subdivided by geographic area. Cultural history literature includes material in anthropology, archaeology, history, religion and travel accounts. While the library's primary focus is on textiles, the anthropologist is also able to explore the landscape, rituals, mythology and daily life of a people through slides, video cassettes, journal articles, travelers' tales and scholarly monographs.

Since 1991 library acquisitions have been entered into an on-line catalog that is accessible only within the museum. Articles about rugs and textiles from the library's periodicals are indexed in this on-line catalog. At present the card catalog is the only complete record of the library's holdings and will continue to be for the foreseeable future.

The Jenkins Library is visited each year by more than 1,000 museum visitors and scholars of all ages and degrees of expertise. Although the library is for reference use only, its open stack policy, photocopying facilities, slide projectors, video player and card catalog assist the researcher in using the many valuable resources.

Textile Museum publications that are available in the library are the *Textile Museum Workshop Notes*, the *Textile Museum Journal*, the *Irene Emery Roundtable Proceedings* on ethnographic and archaeological textiles, the quarterly *Textile Museum Bulletin*, scholarly catalogs published to accompany exhibitions and scholarly monographs written by the museum's curators and research associates.

Mary Mallia Samms

Florida—Gainesville

Florida Museum of Natural History. Anthropological Archives

Address: Department of Anthropology, Florida Museum of Natural History, Museum Road, Gainesville, FL 32611-7800.
Location: In Dickinson Hall, on the University of Florida campus.
Tel.: (352) 392-6563
Fax: (352) 392-3698
Internet address (Museum): http://www.flmnh.ufl.edu.
Founded: 1917.
Areas of specialization: Pre-Columbian and colonial period archaeology and zooarchaeology, especially of Florida, Georgia and the Caribbean region.
Archives/manuscripts: Approximately 65 linear ft., not including site files.
Fieldnotes, papers, etc.: Fieldnotes and/or research correspondence from a number of archaeologists are in the archives, including Ripley P. Bullen (1902-1976)—various Florida sites, 1953-1976; Charles H. Fairbanks (1913-1984)—various sites in Florida and Georgia, 1963-1984; James A. Ford (1911-1968)—for Veracruz only, 1964-1965; E. Thomas Hemmings (1937-)—various sites in Florida, 1971-1974; William H. Sears (1920-) —various sites in Florida, 1955-1964. Fieldnotes and files of Florida Park Service archaeologists John Griffin (1919-1993); Ripley P. Bullen (1902-1976), for 1948-1976; and Hale G. Smith (1918-1977), for 1946-1952 are also on file.
Visua/audio resources: A cataloged negative file of about 2,000 black-and-white images—largely compiled by Florida Park Service archaeologists—is organized by site. Other photographs and slides relative to specific sites are being cataloged.
Access: Open to scholars with prior arrangement; materials may be copied.
Artifact collections: Artifacts from ca. 2,000 archaeological sites in Florida, the Southeast United States, the Caribbean and South America are cataloged in the museum.

Description

For more than 75 years the Florida Museum of Natural History has served as a repository for collections and information on the natural history of Florida and surrounding regions, especially the southeast United States and the Caribbean. Anthropological collections and accession data, including archival materials, date from the museum's founding in 1917. Some early records (prior to 1970) are filed in the past museum directors' files. Most, however, are in the accession files of the Department of Anthropology, a part of the Anthropological Archives. The accession file lists names of donor or researchers, site numbers, the catalog and—in many instances—site names.

The Department of Anthropology as a distinct entity within the museum was founded in 1952. At the same time, the records and collections of the Florida Park Service's Archaeology Division, 1946-1952, were transferred to the museum. Those files include the site files, fieldnotes, reports, the photograph archive and correspondence of Park Service archaeologists John Griffin, Hale G. Smith and Ripley Bullen.

At the time of the transfer, Ripley Bullen was hired as the first museum archaeologist. His wife, bioanthropologist Adelaide Kendall Bullen, received a courtesy appointment to the museum curatorial staff. All of the existing notes and correspondence spanning their Florida careers are in the archive. In 1955 William H. Sears joined the Bullens, serving as curator in archaeology. Since that time, to the present, other anthropological curators in the museum have included James A. Ford, William Bullard, S. Jeffrey, K. Wilkerson, E. Thomas Hemmings, William R. Maples, Jerald T. Milanich, Kathleen A. Deagan, Brenda J. Sigler-Eisenberg, William F. Keegan, William H. Marquardt and Elizabeth S. Wing. Field and laboratory notes and archival materials generated by the research projects undertaken or supervised by these curators during their employment at the museum are in the archive. The bulk of the materials focus on the pre-Columbian and colonial period archaeology and archaeobiology of Florida, coastal Georgia, the Caribbean and selected sites in South America.

From 1970 to 1976 Ripley Bullen was editor of the *Florida Anthropologist*—the journal of the Florida Anthropological Society. He was succeeded by Jerald Milanich, 1976-1979. Information relevant to some archaeological sites featured in that journal—especially sites in South Florida—consequently has found its way into the archive.

In the early 1970s the archaeological collections and archival materials stored in the University of Florida's Department of Anthropology were transferred to the museum's department of the same name. Those extensive materials encompass a host of Florida archaeological sites investigated and/or recorded by John M. Goggin (1916-1963), who worked in Florida from the late 1930s until his death. Most of Goggin's fieldnotes are housed at the University of Florida's P.K. Yonge Library of Florida History. However, some correspondence and research notes are in the museum archive. Notable are Goggin's county maps showing site locations, his bibliographies on 3 x 5″ cards and paper slips and his Florida archaeological site file. Many of the bibliographic entries correspond to author names and years cited in the site file. The thorough bibliography includes nineteenth- and twentieth-century popular and academic publications. Goggin's site file, kept on 5 x 8″ cards (with added notations and slips) has been combined with the museum site file kept by Bullen and a third file previously in the University of Florida Department of Anthropology. Although a computer-inventoried Master Site File was begun in the late 1970s in Florida, that file does not include many of the notations and the information various archaeologists—especially Goggin and Bullen—added to the files they curated. Goggin's unpublished ca. 700-page typescript manuscript synthesizing the archaeology of South Florida is among the materials in the archive.

Following the death of Charles Fairbanks, his personal papers and fieldnotes also were transferred to the museum archive. Materials (and collections) relevant to Florida and Georgia sites that he investigated were included in the transfer. Those sites include the plantation, pre-Columbian and early colonial-period sites excavated by Fairbanks and Milanich and their students on St. Simons Island, Georgia. Especially important are the materials from Couper Plantation and Taylor Mound.

In the early 1980s William Sears transferred to the museum the complete collections, fieldnotes, data records and photography and slide archive that he collected at the Fort Center site in South Florida in the late 1960s and 1970s. Later in that decade the complete data record and collections from the massive King's Bay archaeological project in southeastern

Georgia also were made a part of the museum's holdings. That project—the survey and/or excavation of a number of pre-Columbian and plantation period sites—was undertaken by William Adams and other archaeologists and students working through the University of Florida.

In addition to the fieldnotes, reports and other information relevant to site investigations compiled by museum and University of Florida archaeologists, the archive includes similar materials written by their students. Such student-generated records continue to result from archaeological field schools, cultural resource management projects and thesis and dissertation research projects. Because hundreds of the archaeological sites in Florida first were recorded by student archaeologists working with Goggin, these student reports provide location and other data that are often more detailed than the summary information in the Florida Master Site File. Student reports are filed by name of student, but they are also referenced by county in the archive site files. In addition, names of site recorders appear on site forms, providing another entrée into the student files.

Published reprints and unpublished reports written by Florida archaeologists and pertinent to specific sites and related archival materials are filed by author. A reprint file compiled by Goggin and containing pertinent articles on the anthropology and natural history of Florida and the southeast United States, published in the 1930s, 1940s, 1950s and early 1960s is similarly filed by author.

The Department of Anthropology has completed a computerized inventory of the archaeological sites represented by its collections. Because many of the anthropological archival materials are intimately tied to those sites and their collection, that inventory and the accession and site number or site name files are important starting points for scholars wishing to use the anthropological archive and collections. It is recommended that scholars wishing to use any of these materials first write to the appropriate curator for information.

Jerald T. Milanich

University of Florida. Samuel Proctor Oral History Program

Address: Oral History Program, 104 Anderson Hall, University of Florida, P.O. Box 115215, Gainesville, FL 32611.
Tel.: (352) 392-7168
Fax: (352) 846-1983
Internet address: http://www.clas.ufl.edu/history/oral.
Founded: 1967 (Oral History Program).
Major resources: The University of Florida Doris Duke American Indian Oral History Project recordings and transcripts.
Areas of specialization: Recorded Doris Duke Project oral history interviews with Native Americans of the Southeast—including Seminole, Cherokee and Creek; other Native American recordings made by Harry A. Kersey.
Holdings: Among holdings are the transcripts (and the archived original recordings) of more than 900 University of Florida Doris Duke Project oral history interviews.

Visual/audio resources: Hundreds of slides and photographs of all tribes of the Southeast—mainly Seminole and Catawba; the archived University of Florida Doris Duke Project oral history recordings; recorded Native American chants.

Access: Materials (including the Doris Duke Project transcripts) are available for on-site use by researchers and other interested persons.

References: C. Gregory Crampton, "The Archives of the Duke Project in American Indian Oral History," in Jane F. Smith and Robert M. Kvasnicka (editors), *Indian-White Relations: A Persistent Paradox* (Washington, D.C.: 1972) (= *National Archives Conferences*, vol. 10), p. 119-128; Bradford Koplowitz, "The Doris Duke Indian Oral History Projects," *Popular Culture in Libraries*, vol. 1, no. 3 (1993), p. 23-38; Harry A. Kersey, *An Assumption of Sovereignty: Social and Political Transformation Among the Florida Seminoles, 1953-1979* (Lincoln: 1996) (= *Indians of the Southeast*); Harry A. Kersey, *Pelts, Plumes, and Hides: White Traders Among the Seminole Indians, 1870-1930* (Gainesville: 1975).

Information provided by Julian M. Pleasants.

University of Florida. George A. Smathers Libraries

Address: University Libraries, University of Florida, Gainesville, FL 32611-2048.
Tel.: (352) 392-0361 (Humanities and Social Science Services).
Fax: (352) 392-7251
Internet address: http://www.uflib.ufl.edu/uflib.html.
Internet access to on-line catalog: LUIS is at http://www.uflib.ufl.edu or telnet nermvs.nerdc.ufl.edu.
Networks, consortia: OCLC, RLIN.
Founded: 1853.
Major Resources: Books, serials, scholars' papers and manuscripts.
Areas of specialization: Monographs and serials supporting anthropology are conservatively estimated to exceed 20,000 volumes, with particular strength in the ethnology of Africa, the Latin American/Caribbean area and Native Americans of the United States, with emphasis on Southeastern archaeology and tribes.
Archives/manuscripts: Charles Wagley papers (11 boxes); Donald Pierson papers (10 boxes); Mary Elmendorf papers (more than 40 boxes—held by University Archives, Department of Special Collections); Florida Anthropological Society papers (eight boxes); John M. Goggin papers (fifteen boxes and nine boxes of notecards, with a finding aid—held by the P.K. Yonge Library of Florida History, Department of Special Collections); Lawrence K. Carpenter papers (held by University Archives).
Holdings (books and journals): More than 20,000 volumes in anthropology and related subject areas.
Access: Library materials, except for holdings in the Department of Special Collections, circulate freely to University of Florida faculty, staff and students. Manuscripts and non-circulating collections are available to researchers and general readers for in-building use only.

References: Donald Pierson, *Cruz das Almas: A Brazilian Village* (Washington, D.C.: 1948) (= *Smithsonian Institution. Institute of Social Anthropology. Publication*, no. 12); Donald Pierson, *O homem no Vale do São Francisco*, translated by M.A. Madeira Kerberg and R. Jungmann (Rio de Janeiro: 1972), 3 v.; Charles Wagley, *Amazon Town: A Study of Man in the Tropics* (New York: 1953); Charles Wagley, *Welcome of Tears: The Tapirapé Indians of Central Brazil* (Prospect Heights, Ill.: 1977).

Description

Resources of Anthropological Interest in the George A. Smathers Libraries

• Charles Wagley (1913-1991)—Tapirapé Indians (Brazil), field notebooks and more than 700 related ethnographic photographs, 1939-1965. Included in the Wagley papers are his fieldnotes as well as those of Eduardo and Clara Galvão, on Gurupá, a river town, called Itá in Wagley's *Amazon Town: A Study of Man in the Tropics* (1953) and in Galvão's doctoral dissertation, "The Religion of an Amazon Community," Columbia University, 1952. Wagley's work on the Tapirapé resulted in a monograph, *Welcome of Tears*: *The Tapirapé Indians of Central Brazil* (1977). The Gurupá project files have been microfilmed and there is a finding aid to the Wagley papers.

• Donald Pierson (1900-   )—professional papers, lecture notes, drafts, correspondence, etc., related to social anthropology and race relations in Brazil, 1940s-1950s, and social etiquette and national self-image in Portugal, Spain and Brazil (completed questionnaires, 1960s). In addition to the manuscripts of Pierson's *Cruz das Almas: A Brazilian Village* (1948), the collection holds the manuscript of his "Life in a Brazilian Valley,"—published only in Portugese translation, *O homem no Vale do São Francisco* (1972). A finding aid for the collection is available.

• Mary Lindsay Elmendorf (1917-   )—more than forty boxes of fieldnotes, journals, trip reports, household surveys, taped interviews, films, slides, statistical data, photographs, correspondence, etc., related to changing roles of Maya women at Chan Kom, 1968-1971, and subsequent projects at Chan Kom with Deborah Merrill or Alfonso Villa Rojas, in the 1970s, to study the socio-economic impact of development and changing patterns of family planning, fertility, childbearing, birthing, etc., among the Maya of the Yucatan. Mary Elmendorf's project work for the World Bank, 1977-1980, on appropriate technology for sanitation improvement and human waste disposal in developing countries—particularly in Guatemala, Mexico and Nicaragua—is documented in the collection. Overall, the collection is important for the study of women and social change, and more specifically, on Maya women in Chan Kom, a village now famous in the ethnographic literature through the early work of Robert Redfield. An extensive finding aid is available.

• Florida Anthropological Society papers (1947-1990)—minutes of annual and executive committee meetings; reports of officers; general correspondence; a set of the Florida Anthropological Society *Newsletter* and other publications of the Society; material related to chapters and affiliated regional archaeological or anthropological societies in Florida; Florida Anthropological Society Board Minutes, 1974-1990 (on cassette tapes); slides. A finding aid is available.

- John M. Goggin (1916-1963)—archaeological site surveys in the Bahamas (Andros Island), Florida, Colombia and Venezuela; correspondence with William C. Sturtevant, John R. Swanton, Charles H. Fairbanks, etc.; clippings, scrapbooks, field notebooks and photographs. The Goggin materials are especially strong on Seminole and Creek ethnology. Of special note is documentation related to Goggin's role as an expert witness on Seminole land claims. Goggin's early interest in underwater archaeology of Florida rivers is also documented here. Fieldnotes and photographs on the Choctaw, furnished by William C. Sturtevant, round out the Goggin collection.

- Lawrence K. Carpenter papers, 1973-1988—notebooks, transcripts and tape cassettes of Ecuadorian Quechua spoken in Imbabura Province and other regions, based on field informants. Card files containing Quechua linguistic data are correlated to the notebooks and tapes. Also included are tapes of Andean festivals; videotapes pertaining to Carpenter's fieldwork in Ecuador, Bolivia and Peru; photographs and slides. Carpenter's Peace Corps journal, January-July 1973; and a notebook of the Yoruba, 1976-1977, are among items in the collection. A preliminary inventory is available, but final processing has not yet been completed.

Robert Singerman

Florida—Tallahassee

National Park Service. Southeast Archaeological Center (SEAC)

Address: Southeast Archaeological Center, National Park Service, Box 7, Suite 120, Johnson Building, 2035 E. Paul Dirac Drive, Tallahassee, FL 32310.
Location: The SEAC entrance is from the back of the Johnson Building.
Tel.: (904) 580-3011
Fax: (904) 561-2884
Internet address: http://www.cr.nps.gov/seac.
Internet address (SEAC collection profile):
http://www.cr.nps.gov/csd/collections/seac.html.
Internet access to on-line catalog: ANCS (the database that contains records of all National Park Service museum collections) is accessed by telnet: nadbcast.uark.edu. Login: nadb.
Networks, consortia: ANCS.
Parking: On-site parking is available.
Founded: 1966. From its begining until 1972 the Center was located at Ocmulgee National Monument in Macon, Georgia.
Major resources: SEAC is the repository of archives and photographs from some 47 National Park Service units in the Southeast Region. In addition, substantial Work Projects Administration (WPA) archives and photographs are held. Much of this material documents the archaeological work of the WPA in Georgia during the 1930s.
Areas of specialization: National Park Service archaeological records and photos for the Southeast Region (Kentucky, Tennessee, Alabama, Mississippi, Georgia, North Carolina, South Carolina, Florida, Louisiana, the Virgin Islands and Puerto Rico) are held.

Archives/manuscripts: Ca. 1.2 million archival items.
Fieldnotes, etc.: Fieldnotes from archaeological investigations at National Park sites in the Southeast Region are held.
Visual/audio resources: Many black-and-white negatives and some color slides of archaeological work at NPS sites in the Southeast Region. Photographic holdings also include WPA archaeological photos—mainly from sites in Georgia.
Access: Contact John Ehrenhard, SEAC Chief, by mail or phone in advance of anticipated research.
Archaeological artifacts: Approximately six million archaeological objects from National Park Service sites in the Southeast Region.

Information provided by Richard Vernon.

Georgia—East Point

National Archives—Southeast Region (Atlanta)

Address: National Archives—Southeast Region, 1557 St. Joseph Avenue, East Point, GA 30344-2593.
Tel.: (404) 763-7477
Fax: (404) 763-7033
E-mail: archives@atlanta.nara.gov.
Internet address: http://www.nara.gov/regional/atlanta.html.
Founded: 1969.
Major resources: Holds original federal records retired from government agencies in Alabama, Florida, Georgia, Kentucky, Mississippi, North Carolina, South Carolina and Tennessee. Also holds microfilm copies of some other National Archives records.
Access: The great majority of holdings are open for public research. Restrictions on access to some federal records may be applied in accord with exemptions in the Freedom of Information Act.

Hawai'i—Honolulu

Bernice Pauahi Bishop Museum (BPBM)

Address: Bernice Pauahi Bishop Museum, 1525 Bernice Street, P.O. Box 19000A, Honolulu, HI 96817-0916.
Tel.: (808) 848-4147
Fax: (808) 841-8968
Internet address: http://www.bishop.hawaii.org.
Internet address (Bishop Museum Archives): http://www.bishop.hawaii.org/bishop/archives/arch.arch.html.

Internet address (Bishop Museum Library on-line catalog): http://www.bishop.hawaii.org/ bishop/library/libdata.html. Four Bishop Museum databases are accessible via the University of Hawai'i's UHCARL catalog. These are *Bishop Museum Archives/Library Catalog*; *Bishop Museum Mele (Chant & Song) Index*; *Bishop Museum Visual Materials Catalog*; and *Bishop Museum News and Information*.

Networks, consortia: OCLC.

Public transit access: Take the #2 bus from Kuhio Avenue in Waikiki. The museum is a two-block walk from the nearest bus stop. For bus route information, call The Bus, (808) 848-5555.

Founded: 1889. The Bishop Museum has been designated as the Hawai'i "State Museum for Cultural and Natural History."

Major resources: Bishop Museum Archives; Library.

Areas of specialization: Natural and cultural history of Hawai'i and the Pacific Islands.

Archives/manuscripts: 300 cubic ft. of papers and manuscripts. Also oral histories, photographs, artwork, maps.

Holdings (library): 90,000 book volumes, journals, an important collection of retrospective Hawai'ian newspapers.

Visual/audio resources: Holdings include audio recordings of Hawai'ian and Pacific Island music and sound. Recordings are on wax cylinders, tapes and in other formats. There is a large Hawai'ian photograph collection. Significant art and map collections for Hawai'i and the Pacific are held.

Access: See the website.

References: Roger G. Rose, *A Museum to Instruct and Delight: William T. Brigham and the Founding of Bernice Pauahi Bishop Museum* (Honolulu: 1980) (= *Bernice P. Bishop Museum Special Publication*, 68).

Guides/catalogs: Bernice Pauahi Bishop Museum. Library, *Dictionary Catalog of the Library* (Boston: 1964), 9 v. Supplementary volumes of the *Dictionary Catalog* were published in 1967 and 1969. The 1969 supplement is a catalog of the A.W.F. Fuller Library, developed by Captain Alfred Walter Francis Fuller and Mrs. Fuller—an extensive collection of books on the Pacific region. The Fuller's collection of Pacific region artifacts (6,500 objects) was purchased by the Field Museum (Chicago) in 1958. See Roland W. Force and Maryanne Force, *The Fuller Collection of Pacific Artifacts* (London: 1971), for a description of the Fuller artifact collection.

Hawai'i. Department of Accounting and General Services. Hawai'i State Archives (HSA)

Address: Hawai'i State Archives, Iolani Palace Grounds, Honolulu, HI 96813.

Location: Kekauluohi Building, Iolani Palace Grounds, Honolulu, Hawai'i.

Tel.: (808) 586-0329 (reference desk); toll free from the Neighbor Islands only: (800) 486-4644.

Fax: (808) 586-0330

Internet address: http://www.state.hi.us/dags/archives/welcome.html.

Public transit access: The bus stops within one block of the Archives. For bus route information call The Bus, (808) 848-5555.

Parking: Some metered parking is in the vicinity of the Archives.

Founded: 1905.

Major resources: Archives of the State and Territorial governments of Hawai'i, the Republic of Hawai'i and the Hawai'ian Kingdom. Also some private papers of prominent Hawai'ians; historic photographs; the Captain Cook Memorial Collection; the Paul Markham Kahn Collection.

Area of specialization: Official government records of Hawai'i.

Archives/manuscripts: More than 10,000 cubic ft. of Hawai'ian government records. The State Archives also holds 480 collections of private papers on Hawai'ian history and culture.

Visual/audio resources: More than 100,000 historic photographs of Hawai'ian people and scenes; 1,800 maps.

Access: Open to the public—see the website (the URL is above) for regulations on use of the State Archives.

References: "The Archives of Hawaii" ([Honolulu]: 1977); Patrick V. Kirch and Marshall Sahlins, *Anahulu: the Anthropology of History in the Kingdom of Hawai'i*, vol. 1, *Historical Ethnography* (Chicago: 1992).

Guides/catalogs: Descriptive inventories and archival finding aids are available for in-house use, but are not published or available for sale.

Information provided by Jolyn G. Tamura

University of Hawai'i at Mānoa. Hamilton Library

Address: Hamilton Library, University of Hawai'i, 2550 The Mall, Honolulu, HI 96822.

Tel.: (808) 956-8264 (Hawai'ian Collection); (808) 956-8264 (Pacific Collection); (808) 956-2311 (Asia Collections); (808) 956-6673 (Archives and Manuscripts).

Fax: (808) 956-5968

Internet address: http://www2.hawaii.edu/lib.

Internet address (Hawai'ian Collection): http://nic2.hawaii.edu/~speccoll/h.html.

Internet address (Pacific Collection): http://nic2.hawaii.edu/~speccoll/p.html.

Internet address (Asia Collections): http://nic2.hawaii.net/~asiaref.

Networks, consortia: OCLC, CARL.

Founded: 1927 (Hawai'ian Collection); 1959 (Pacific Collection); 1962 (Asia Collections); 1968 (Archives and Manuscripts).

Major resources: Hawai'ian Collection; Pacific Collection; East, Southeast and South Asia Collections.

Areas of specialization: Hawai'ian Islands; the Pacific (including Polynesia, Micronesia and Melanesia); East, Southeast and South Asia. The Pacific collection holds a numerous printed Pacific voyages. The UHCARL catalog offers several databases of Hawai'ian and Pacific interest: *Hawai'i Pacific Journal Index*; *Hawai'i [Sheet] Music Index*.

Archives/manuscripts: The *Trust Territories of the Pacific Islands Archives* (2,169 reels) is a microfilm version of the records of the U.S. administration of Micronesia. Also held are

Micronesian photograph, map and audiovisual collections. The Hamilton Library holds a full set of Pacific Manuscripts Bureau microfilms.

Holdings (books and journals): More than 118,000 v. (Hawai'ian Collection); more than 75,000 v. (Pacific Collection); more than 600,000 v. (Asia Collections).

Visual/audio resources: Audio resources include the Hawai'ian Oral History Collection; also some recordings of traditional Southeast Asian music on cassettes.

Access: Open to the public.

Idaho—Moscow

University of Idaho. Alfred W. Bowers Laboratory of Anthropology

Address: Alfred W. Bowers Laboratory of Anthropology, University of Idaho, Moscow, ID 83844-1111.

Tel.: (208) 885-6123

Internet address: http://www.uidaho.edu/LS/Anth-Lab.

Internet address (Asian American Comparative Collection): http://www.uidaho.edu/LS/AACC.

Founded: 1968.

Major resources: Laboratory collections in archaeology, ethnohistory, linguistics, physical anthropology.

Archives/manuscripts: Pacific Northwest Anthropological Archives; Don Crabtree Lithic Collection Library.

References: Priscilla Wegars, *The Ah Hee Diggings: Final Report of Archaeological Investigations at OR-GR-16, the Granite, Oregon "Chinese Walls" Site, 1992 through 1994* (Moscow, Id.: 1995) (= *University of Idaho Archaeological Reports*, no. 97); Priscilla Wegars (editor), *Hidden Heritage: Historical Archaeology of the Overseas Chinese* (Amityville, N.Y.: 1993) (= *Baywood Monographs in Archaeology*).

Artifacts: Various, including the Asian American Comparative Collection (AACC).

Illinois—Chicago

Center for Research Libraries (CRL)

Address: Center for Research Libraries, 6050 South Kenwood Avenue, Chicago, IL 60637-2804.

Tel.: (773) 955-4545 or (800) 621-6044. For information on any of the six special foreign area microform projects, see the CRL website, or contact Marlys Rudeen at CRL, extension 324.

Fax: (773) 955-4339

Internet address: http://wwwcrl.uchicago.edu. Scroll down the home page to Area Studies, where there are pointers to the Brazilian documents, to CAMP, and to other area projects. The CAMP pointer is to a list of African newspapers currently received by U.S. libraries.

Internet address (CRL foreign newspapers list): http://wwwcrl.uchicago.edu/~paper/ Foreign_newspapers.html.

Internet access to on-line catalog: CRLCATALOG contains on-line records of 98 percent of cataloged CRL holdings. Internet users can telnet to crlcatalog.uchicago.edu (128.135.73.2). When the log-in prompt appears, enter: guest. A self-explanatory menu then displays. CRLCATALOG is an Innovative Interfaces, Inc., system and has a menu-driven user interface. The address of the CRL listserv is CRLONLINE@crlmail.uchicago.edu.

Networks, consortia: OCLC, RLIN.

Public transit access: #6 bus or Metra Electric from the Loop; walk west on 60th Street to Kenwood Avenue, then south one block.

Founded: 1949 (as the Midwest Inter-Library Center).

Major resources: Infrequently held, expensive, or otherwise uncommon research materials of many types.

Areas of specialization: Among resources of anthropological or related interest are extensive holdings of foreign (non-U.S.) newspapers, dissertations and documents; many categories of microforms (including the six special foreign area microform programs); Special Foreign Currency (previously known as PL 480) Program materials; others.

Holdings: 3.7 million book and journal volumes; 1.2 million microforms (including microfilm, microfiche and microcards); 6,200 foreign newspaper titles; 695 U.S. ethnic newspaper and periodical titles.

Archives/manuscripts: Some archival and manuscript resources are held. These are mainly in microform format.

Access: CRL serves the faculty, students and patrons of subscribing U.S. and Canadian research libraries. Materials are usually made available for use through interlibrary loan. In keeping with CRL's mission, the stacks are closed and many holdings are stored on compact shelving. A small reading room is available to the public, without charge, for on-site use of materials. Call in advance to arrange for the on-site use of materials.

References: David L. Easterbrook, "The Archives-Library Committee and the Cooperative Africana Microform Project: A Brief History," in Julian W. Witherell (editor), *Africana Resources and Collections: Three Decades of Development and Achievement: A Festschrift in Honor of Hans Panofsky* (Metuchen, N.J.: 1989), p. 18-38.

Guides/catalogs: Center for Research Libraries, *Handbook* (Chicago: 1996).

Description

The Center for Research Libraries is a cooperative institution that is supported primarily by its U.S. and Canadian research library membership. CRL is located in Hyde Park, on Chicago's South Side, not far from the campus of the University of Chicago. Records of nearly all of CRL's cataloged holdings are now accessible on-line. In accord with CRL policies, many categories of holdings are not individually cataloged; these are listed and described in the CRL *Handbook*. On-line access to the CRL listserv, CRLONLINE and the website are now available.

Since its beginning in 1949 CRL has acquired many types of infrequently used research materials. Of special significance for anthropological studies are the extensive holdings of foreign (non-U.S.) newspapers, foreign (non-U.S. and non-Canadian) dissertations and foreign government documents. Archival resources on microfilm and many other categories of materials are also held.

Newspapers

CRL's extensive newspaper holdings (usually on microfilm) include newspaper titles published in cities throughout the world. More than 6,200 non-U.S. newspaper titles are held. See the Web URL, above. More than 695 U.S. ethnic newspapers and periodicals are also held. In the latter group are newspapers in Norwegian, Italian, German, Yiddish, Japanese and other languages of U.S. immigrant populations. Some twenty African American newspapers are also available.

Foreign Area Microform Projects

Six special area microform programs are headquartered at CRL: the Cooperative Africana Microfilm Project (CAMP); the Latin American Microform Project (LAMP); the South Asia Microform Project (SAMP); the Southeast Asia Microform Project (SEAM); the Middle East Microform Project (MEMP); and the Slavic and East European Microform Project (SEEMP). For additional information on these projects, see the Center's website.

Archives Aequatoria Manuscripts

A microfiche set of Archives Aequatoria manuscripts and documentation, from the Centre Aequatoria, in Bamanya, Democratic Republic of Congo, is among CAMP materials available at CRL. The Centre Aequatoria archive has been reproduced on 2,459 microfiche. For the assistance of researchers, a catalog of the collection (*Catalogue des Archives Aequatoria*) is available on diskette (Microsoft Word, 6.0 format).

SAMP Projects

The National Endowment for the Humanities (NEH) funded a project to preserve 2,000 nineteenth-century South Asian publications in Hindi, in the British Library's Oriental and India Office Collections. Microfilm service copies of all titles have been added to the SAMP/CRL collections.

A project to preserve 2,880 nineteenth-century Hindustani books held in the British Library's Oriental and India Office Collections was funded by NEH. Microfilm service copies of all titles will be added to the SAMP/CRL collections.

Preservation on microfilm of 8,000 early twentieth-century Indian publications in Marathi, Gujarati, Sindhi, Konkani and English—the major languages of western India—was supported by NEH. Microfilming is being done at the University of Bombay Library and at the Library of Congress Field Office in New Delhi; microfilm service copies of all titles will be added to the SAMP/CRL collections.

Resources of research value to South and Southeast Asianists include relatively complete sets of the Library of Congress' large South and Southeast Asia microfiche collections. A majority of the documents in the Southeast Asia microfiche set consist of Indonesian-language materials acquired by the LC Jakarta Field Office.

Lee S. Dutton
Information provided by Marlys Rudeen.

Field Museum of Natural History (FMNH)

Address: Field Museum of Natural History, Roosevelt Road at Lake Shore Drive, Chicago, IL 60605-2498.
Tel.: (312) 922-9410, ext. 282 (Library); ext. 248 (Photography Department); ext. 213 (Museum Archives); ext. 442 (Anthropology Department Archives).
Fax: (312) 427-7269 (Library; Museum Archives; Anthropology Department Archives; Museum); (312) 922-7440 (Photography Department).
E-mail (Museum Archives): esai@fmppr.fmnh.org.
E-mail (Photography Department): photo@fmnh.org.
Internet address: http://www.fmnh.org.
Internet address (Department of Anthropology): http://www.fmnh.org/candr/anthro/anthro.html.
Networks, consortia: OCLC (Library catalog records have been added to OCLC since 1977).
Public transit access: CTA bus #146 or 6, south from the Loop. For transit information call the RTA Travel Center Hotline: (312) 836-700.
Parking: At the Museum and Soldier Field lots (fee).
Founded: 1893.
Major resources: Books, journals, some archives (in the Library, also in Special Collections); additional archives (in Museum Archives and the Anthropology Department Archives); photographs, slides, films (in the Photography Department).
Areas of specialization: Anthropology (especially Indians of the Americas), archaeology, botany, geology, museology, paleontology, zoology. Geographic coverage of these subjects is global in scope, but strongest for the regions on which the museum's research has traditionally focussed: the Americas, the Far East and Oceania.
Archives/manuscripts: Archival/manuscript materials of anthropological interest are in several locations. Museum administrative and accession files and other institutional records are in Museum Archives. Additional manuscripts and papers, as well as expedition records and fieldnotes, are in Anthropology Department Archives. Other papers, manuscripts, fieldnotes, clippings, etc., of anthropological interest are in Special Collections.
Holdings (books and journals): 250,000 volumes in many disciplines (Library). Included in this number are 39,000 volumes in the Anthropology Library.

Visual/audio resources: The Photography Department holds photos of artifacts, field and exhibit photographs of Native America, the Pacific, Africa and China. Between 100,000 and 200,000 black-and-white photographic negatives are held.

Access: The library is open to the public; the stacks are closed. The Anthropology Library is not open to the public, although books may be paged from that location for on-site use. Interlibrary loan service is available to museum libraries, libraries in the Midwest and to other U.S. libraries for research use. On-site access to images in the Photography Department is decided on a case-by-case basis. A detailed project description is required.

References: G.L. Dybwad and Joy V. Bliss, *Annotated Bibliography: World's Columbian Exposition, Chicago, 1893* (Albuquerque: 1992), also a "Draft Supplement," 1996; Ann Elizabeth Koopman, "Archives in a Museum Environment," M.A. thesis, Graduate Library School, University of Chicago, 1981; Frank C. Lockwood, *The Life of Edward E. Ayer* (Chicago: 1929); E. Leland Webber, "Books, Business and Buckskin," *Field Museum of Natural History Bulletin*, vol. 55, no. 7 (July-Aug. 1984), p. 5-25; Benjamin W. Williams and W. Peyton Fawcett, "Field Museum of Natural History Library," *Science and Technology Libraries,* vol. 6, no. 1-2 (Fall 1985-Winter 1985/86), p. 27-33.

Artifact resources: Specimen and artifact collections in all areas of scientific activity: more than 20,000,000 items. Among these are some 608,383 anthropology/archaeology artifacts.

Some selected catalogs of artifact resources: Roland W. Force and Maryanne Force, *The Fuller Collection of Pacific Artifacts* (London: 1971); Donald W. Lathrop, Donald Collier and Hellen Chandra, *Ancient Ecuador: Culture, Clay and Creativity = El Ecuador antiguo: cultura, cerámica y creatividad* (Chicago: 1975); Anne Leonard and John Terrell, *Patterns of Paradise: The Styles and Significance of Bark Cloth Around the World* (Chicago: 1980); *México: la visión del cosmos = Three Thousand Years of Creativity* (Chicago: [1992]); Michael E. Moseley, *Peru's Golden Treasures; An Essay on Five Ancient Styles* (Chicago: 1978).

Description

The Field Columbian Museum of Chicago originated in the wake of the World's Columbian Exposition, held at Chicago in 1893. A wealth of cultural and ethnographic objects and artifacts, assembled from around the world, were displayed at that event. The anthropological exhibits were prepared under the direction of Frederic W. Putnam, curator of Harvard University's Peabody Museum, with the aid of his assistants Franz Boas and George A. Dorsey. In 1894 many of these ethnographic collections were transferred to the newly incorporated Field Columbian Museum—now known as the Field Museum of Natural History. Museum collections were stored in the Palace of Fine Arts Building, on the grounds of the Columbian Exposition, until May 1921, when the large new Field Museum of Natural History building was opened to the public in Grant Park.

The museum's scientific staff is organized in four principal departments: Anthropology (including Archaeology), Botany, Geology and Zoology. Several long-standing journals disseminate research findings of Museum staff. *Fieldiana: Anthropology* is an ongoing journal of the Department of Anthropology.

Prominent among early museum administrators were George A. Dorsey (North American ethnology), who was chief curator of anthropology, 1896-1915. Berthold Laufer (Asian ethnology) succeeded Dorsey as chief curator of anthropology, 1915-1934. Other anthropologists/archaeologists associated with the museum include Alfred L. Kroeber (American archaeology), Fay-Cooper Cole (Malayan ethnology), A.B. [Albert Buell] Lewis (Melanesian ethnology), Ralph Linton (North American ethnology), William Duncan Strong (North American ethnology and archaeology), Henry Field (physical anthropology) and John Eric Thompson (Central American archaeology).

During its first century, the museum organized and carried out scientific expeditions to Oceania, East Asia, South America and other areas of the world. Today the Field Museum continues to develop artifact and related collections and maintains ongoing research, curatorial, and educational programs in anthropology and the natural sciences.

Museum Archives

The institutional records preserved in Field Museum Archives span more than a century—from the beginnings of the museum to the present time. Among the archival materials in this office are the administrative records of the museum. The museum accession records have been recorded on cards by successive Registrars since 1893. The accession records, which are filed by department and accession number, sometimes contain correspondence between curators in the field and administrators, as well as other records of historical interest. Some fragmentary correspondence and records from the World's Columbian Exposition are also in Museum Archives. The historical records in Museum Archives have not yet been cataloged, although an inventory is in preparation. Additional museum archives and records of anthropological interest are in Special Collections and also in the Department of Anthropology Archives.

Department of Anthropology Archives

Fieldnotes, correspondence and other records of the Department of Anthropology are in both Anthropology Archives and in Special Collections (Library). Among archives of anthropological interest (with locations) are:

- George A. Dorsey (1868-1931)—notes and papers (North American ethnology)—in Anthropology Archives.
- Henry Field (1902-)—papers in physical anthropology and the archaeology of Iraq, 1909-1983—in Special Collections.
- A.W.F Fuller (1882-1961)—some of Fuller's papers, notes and other documentation (Pacific ethnology)—in Special Collections.
- William Jones (1871-1909)—Jones's manuscript diary, Philippine Islands, 1907-1909—in Anthropology Archives.
- Berthold Laufer (1874-1934)—extensive papers (East Asian ethnology)—in Special Collections.
- A.B. (Albert Buell) Lewis (1867-1940)—(Melanesian anthropology); holdings include notebooks, fieldnotes and other documentation—in Anthropology Archives.

- Charles Staniland Wake (1835-1910)—diaries and manuscripts—in Anthropology Archives.
- Department of Anthropology. Expedition Files, 1900-1939; also other Department of Anthropology records and archives—in Anthropology Archives.

Some additional information on holdings of papers, fieldnotes and other documentation of anthropological interest is provided in the thesis by Ann Koopman (1981).

Library

The present Field Museum Library originated from the library of the World's Columbian Exposition. The handwritten catalog of the World's Columbian Exposition Department of Ethnology Library—compiled about 1893 by Charles Staniland Wake—is still in library holdings. This source lists the donors of publications to the fledgling Exposition library. Many of those items, the catalog shows, were loaned or donated by Frederic W. Putnam or Franz Boas. The Museum Library today holds some 250,000 book and journal volumes, with subject emphasis in the areas of specialization of the museum's scientific staff: anthropology, botany, zoology, geology, paleontology and related areas.

Library materials are housed in the General Library, in Special Collections and also the Mary W. Runnells Rare Book Room. Also at the museum are separate Anthropology, Botany and Geology departmental libraries.

Runnells Rare Book Room

The Runnells Rare Book Room has collections of printed voyages and journals of early explorers, travelers and ethnographers. Noteworthy among the rare book holdings of ethnographic interest are the collections formed (respectively) by Stanley Field and Berthold Laufer. The latter is part of the larger "Berthold Laufer Collection," which is kept in several units and locations at the museum.

The Stanley Field collection consists of some sixty titles of early, rare and important voyages, journals and accounts of exploration, printed between 1671 and 1901. Many of these chronicle the travels and discoveries of British explorers—including captains James Cook and George Vancouver. Also in this collection are illustrated volumes such as George Henry Mason's *The Costume of China* (London: 1800) and Thomas Williamson's *The Costume and Customs of Modern India* (London: 1813).

Berthold Laufer was recruited by Franz Boas in 1897 to carry out field research in Siberia with the Jesup North Pacific Expedition. Laufer collected artifacts and books in China from 1901 to 1904, on behalf of the American Museum of Natural History. The 114 volumes of the Laufer rare book collection date mainly from the sixteenth- to the eighteenth-centuries and include works of ethnographic or related scholarly interest in many languages. Among these are voyages or travels by Karl Peter Thunberg, Wouter Schouten and Nicolas Gervaise. Also in the collection is Antonio Pigafetta's *Première voyage autour du monde* (Paris: 1801). Many volumes in this collection have penciled marginal notes or index annotations by Laufer.

Special Collections

Museum library resources include several special collections and archives. The extensive Berthold Laufer collection of books on China, Japan, India, Southeast and Central Asia has yet to be cataloged. The Laufer book collection—originally Laufer's personal library—was formed during Laufer's years in the museum's Anthropology Division. Included are early books in European and East Asian languages related to the anthropology and archaeology of China, Japan, Korea and Mongolia. Also noteworthy are the Chinese printed books gathered by Laufer—these occupy about 56 shelves. An unusual Mongolian book collection, also formed by Laufer, is in the Anthropology Library.

Anthropology Library

Most anthropology and related library materials (including all ethnographic materials in (modified) Library of Congress D, E and F classifications) are in the Anthropology Library, which is not open to the public.

Photography Department

• *Native American Photographs*

Between 1895 and 1910 most of the museum's Native American ethnological and archaeological material was collected to augment the objects obtained from the World's Columbian Exposition. Between 1897 and 1898 free-lance photographer Edward Allen and museum curator George Dorsey documented the daily activities, ceremonies and peoples of the Pacific Northwest Coast and of the plains, plateau and desert regions of the western United States.

In 1899 Charles H. Carpenter was hired as the museum's first full-time professional photographer. He remained in that position until his retirement in 1947. Carpenter went with curators on several early expeditions, including the 1900 Stanley McCormick-sponsored expedition that produced more than 1,200 photo negatives of the Hopi tribes. Carpenter and H.R. Voth—a missionary to the Hopi from 1893 to 1902 and ethnologist for the Field Columbian Museum—photographed daily activities and life of the villagers. Voth lived with the Hopi for more than ten years and was witness to several important religious ceremonies and activities. Photographer Summer Matteson, under the direction of George A. Dorsey, added other photographs of the Hopi to the collection.

John W. Hudson spent his life as a collector-scholar and amassed a significant number of California Indian baskets that are now held by Field Museum. Photographs in the museum's possession document the native Pomo, Yurok, Miwok and Hupa from 1900 to 1905, when Hudson collected artifacts under Dorsey's leadership. Hudson visited more than twenty tribes, and photographed traditional activities such as basket-making, acorn-grinding and other rapidly disappearing arts. In many cases, these photographs are the only visual record of such activities. The Hudson photo collection contains more than 450 negatives. Other strengths in the collection of Native American culture include Dorsey and Carpenter's documentation of two Cheyenne dances in 1901 and 1903, Matteson's prints of the Blackfoot tribe and S.C. Simms's Crow and Cheyenne photographs.

- *Carpenter and the Louisiana Purchase Exposition*

In 1904, the City of St. Louis was host to an exposition held to celebrate the centennial of the Louisiana Purchase. More than 47 acres of exhibits of Philippine and Native American tribes (including Pawnee, Pueblo, Pima, Kwakiutl, Eskimo, Oglala and Rosebud Sioux) recreated ceremonies and native habitats on the fairgrounds. This fair was Carpenter's last field assignment for the museum, and he made more than 3,000 negatives, including portraits of Geronimo and Pacific Northwest Coast natives Bob Harris and Charles Nowell.

- *A.B. Lewis and Melanesia*

From 1909 to 1913 Museum curator A.B. Lewis became the first American to conduct systematic ethnological field research in Melanesia. In the course of his travels Lewis collected more than 12,000 examples of Melanesian ethnological material. This is the largest American collection of such material, and is one of the world's largest collections from that area of the Pacific. His more than 2,000 photographs represent some 100 different societies in Melanesia and have been used to catalog and interpret his collections of artifacts.

- *West African Grassfields—Cameroon*

The Field Museum contains one of the finest collections of Cameroon artifacts from the West African grassfields. In the 1920s Jan Kleykamp, representing the J.F.G. Umlauff Company in Hamburg, sold a collection of artifacts to the Field Museum. The purchase included 332 ethnological photographs taken in 1912. These have been attributed to a man named "Schroeder." Like the A.B. Lewis photographs, Schroeder's photos consist of village scenes and portraits that illustrate the use and social context of the artifacts.

- *The Dean C. Worcester Photo Collection*

During the 1920s, curator Fay-Cooper Cole visited the Philippine Islands and Indonesia. Through the former Philippine government official, Dean C. Worcester, Cole obtained more than 200 Philippine prints taken by Worcester's personal photographer. Cole also took more than 400 photographs while visiting the Philippines and areas of Indonesia, including Nias.

- *The Berthold Laufer Photo Collection*

Berthold Laufer spent three years in China and Tibet in the 1920s, while laying the foundation for the museum's highly regarded collection of Asian material. The collection of negatives that Laufer made while in the Far East includes images of ceremonies, daily life and portraits.

FIGURE 2. Scene at Foula-Phong Tho, northern Indochina. Photograph by Russell W. Hendee, Field Museum Kelly/Roosevelts Expedition to northern Indochina, 1928-1929. Courtesy of the Field Museum of Natural History (negative #6639).

- *The Kelley-Roosevelts Expedition (1928-1929)*

In 1929 members of the museum's Kelley-Roosevelts Expedition traveled into remote areas of northern Indochina in search of the giant panda and other rare mammals. Russell W. Hendee, a mammologist, documented the journey through Tonkin and Laos with his camera. Hendee's field photos depict the daily life of Meo, Lü and other peoples encountered in the journey.

- *Henry Field Photo Collection*

Henry Field spent the years 1928 to 1934 excavating and collecting material from the Sumerian-Akkadian capital of Kish. Nearly 5,000 photographs of excavations and portraits of villagers were produced by Field or his associates. He also took photographs of prehistoric caves in France and Spain.

- *1950 to the Present*

In the late 1950s curators began to maintain their own collections of slides of field trips. In the 1990s staff photographer James Bolodimas made two trips to Senegal and Tahiti for the "Africa" exhibit and for revisions to "Traveling the Pacific." More than 1,000 color slides were made in Senegal and approximately 200 color negatives were made in Tahiti. The Photography Department maintains those two collections.

Information provided by W. Peyton Fawcett, Michele Calhoun, Benjamin W. Williams, Nina Cummings and Armand Esai.

National Archives—Great Lakes Region (Chicago)

Address (mailing): National Archives—Great Lakes Region, 7358 South Pulaski Road, Chicago, IL 60629.
Location: The facility street entrance is on West 75th Street.
Tel.: (773) 581-7816
Fax: (312) 353-1294
E-mail: archives@chicago.nara.gov.
Internet address: http://www.nara.gov/regional/chicago.html.
Public transit access: CTA bus 53A (the South Pulaski Road route) stops at South Pulaski Road and West 75th Street.
Parking: On-site parking is available.The facility street entrance is on West 75th Street—one block west of Pulaski Road.
Founded: 1969.
Major resources: Original records retired from federal agencies in Illinois, Indiana, Michigan, Minnesota, Ohio and Wisconsin. Microfilm copies of many National Archives records are also held.

Areas of specialization: Holdings include original Bureau of Indian Affairs (BIA) records (RG 75) and Indian Arts and Crafts Board records (RG 435) for the Great Lakes Region. Also Chinese Exclusion Act records (RG 85) for the Great Lakes Region.

Archives/manuscripts: Original records: more than 64,000 cubic ft.; Bureau of Indian Affairs records: 75 cubic ft.; Chinese Exclusion records: more than 83 cubic ft.

Holdings (microfilm): Ca. 52,000 reels.

Visual/audio resources: Some photographs of potential ethnographic interest (e.g., Chinese Exclusion Act photos) are held.

Access: Most holdings are open for public research. It is strongly recommended that readers call a few days in advance of a planned visit to arrange for the availability of needed materials.

References: Francis Paul Prucha (editor), *Documents of United States Indian Policy* (Lincoln, Neb.: 1990); John R. Swanton, *The Indian Tribes of North America* (Washington, D.C.: 1969).

Guides/catalogs: "American Indian-Related Records in the National Archives—Great Lakes Region" [Chicago: 1994]; Edward E. Hill, *Guide to Records in the National Archives of the United States of America Relating to American Indians* (Washington, D.C.: 1981); Edward E. Hill (compiler), *Preliminary Inventory of the Records of the Bureau of Indian Affairs (Record Group 75)* (Washington, D.C.: 1965).

Description

The National Archives—Great Lakes Region (Chicago) is located on the South Side of Chicago, about two miles southeast of Midway Airport, in a mixed use (commercial, residential and light industrial) area. Also in the same large building is the Chicago Federal Records Center, which, like the regional archive, is a unit of the U.S. National Archives and Records Administration. Among records of anthropological interest at the Great Lakes Region are the Chinese Exclusion Law materials. These include correspondence, certificates and other information on applicant's occupation, period of residence in the United States and other biographical details. Identification photographs of many of the immigrants from China are preserved along with these records.

Archived federal records that pertain to Native Americans of the Great Lakes Region are in several record groups. A one-page reference sheet, *"American Indian-related Records in the National Archives—Great Lakes Region"* (Mar. 1994), lists these resources. The most extensive of Native American-related records are in Record Group 75 (the Bureau of Indian Affairs). Great Lakes Region Bureau of Indian Affairs records include those of Indian agencies such as Lac du Flambeau Agency and School, 1892-1949; the Consolidated Chippewa Agency, 1913-1935; and others. Indian Arts and Crafts Board records are preserved in RG 435. Records concerning the Hopewell Culture National Historical Park are part of National Park Service records in RG 79.

Additional records relating to Native Americans, and possibly other topics of anthropological interest, may be found in the large body of records in two Judicial Branch record groups (RG 21: Records of the District Courts of the United States; and RG 276:

Records of U.S. Courts of Appeals) and perhaps in other Executive Branch record groups. There is no comprehensive index to these records.

Lee S. Dutton
Information provided by Scott Forsythe and Donald W. Jackanicz.

Newberry Library

Address: Newberry Library, 60 West Walton Street, Chicago, Illinois 60610.
Tel.: (312) 943-9090
Internet address: http://www.newberry.org.
Networks, consortia: OCLC, ILLINET Online.
Public transit access: CTA #151 bus; subway: Dan Ryan-Howard line—exit at Chicago or Clark/Division.
Founded: 1887.
Major resources: Edward E. Ayer Collection, William B. Greenlee Collection, Prince Louis-Lucien Bonaparte Collection.
Areas of specialization: Ayer Collection: Western Europe, North America, South America, Central America, Latin America, Hawai'i, the Philippines, Native American culture, linguistics, seventeenth-century Americana, Philippine printed books, Latin Americana and ethnohistory. Greenlee Collection: social life and customs of Portuguese colonies, Portuguese overseas expansion and the overseas expansion of Brazil, Africa, Goa and Macau. Bonaparte Collection: historical linguistics.
Archives/manuscripts: Ayer Collection: 1,006 linear ft.; Greenlee Collection: 8 linear ft.; Bonaparte Collection: no archival or manuscript materials. The Ayer Collection includes some 2,500 manuscripts from the fifteenth- to the twentieth-centuries, relating to five areas: North America; Spanish America; the Philippine Islands; the Hawai'ian Islands; and linguistics. Many of these are of potential interest to anthropologists. Much of this material is described in the checklist by Ruth Lapham Butler—cited below. Important manuscript holdings also include: the principal text of the Popol Vuh of the Quiché Maya of present-day Guatemala—a sacred text and a fundamental source for Mayan cosmography, history and linguistics; extensive transcripts from the Archives of the Indies in Seville and the Mexican, Nacogdoches and Matamoros archives; the John Howard Payne papers on the Cherokee.
Fieldnotes, papers, etc.: The Ayer collection also includes the personal papers, fieldnotes and research materials of several twentieth-century historians, anthropologists and activists interested in Native American cultures, including:
● Thomas L. Ballenger (1882-)—6 boxes and other papers primarily related to Cherokee genealogy.
● John S. Gray (1910-1991)—81 notebooks relating to the history of the Great Plains.
● Jane Richardson Hanks (1908-)—1 box of fieldnotes relating to Oklahoma Kiowa, 1935.
● Solon Toothaker Kimball (1909-1982)—23 boxes of papers related to the Navajo between 1936-1942, and to rural Ireland in the early 1930s.

- D'Arcy McNickle (1904-1977)—17 boxes containing diaries, personal correspondence, drafts of books and articles and copies of his publications.
- Carlos Montezuma (1866-1923)—7 boxes of correspondence, newspaper articles, notes for speeches and interviews with Montezuma's mother.
- Peter Nabokov (1940-   )—more than 5 boxes of correspondence and manuscripts on Native American culture.
- Elmo Scott Watson (1892-1951)—16 boxes of material containing correspondence and various materials related to Indian wars.
- Erminie Wheeler-Voegelin (1903-1987)—published material such as books, leaflets, pamphlets, dissertations, offprints and journals. Unpublished docket material related to Indian Claims Commission reports, research material, scholarly papers, personal correspondence, notecards and notes.

Holdings (books and journals): Ayer Collection: 100,000 v., Greenlee Collection: 10,000 v., Bonaparte Collection: 14,000 v.

Visual/audio resources: Approximately 6,000 photographs of American Indians and Western views by such prominent photographers as William Henry Jackson, John K. Hillers and Alexander Gardner. Approximately 8,000 photographs of people and scenes in the Philippine Islands. About 3,500 drawings, paintings and engravings relating to Native Americans and the American West.

Access: The Newberry Library is free and open to readers who are at least sixteen years old and who are conducting research requiring use of the collections. A reader's card must be obtained. The Newberry is a closed-stack, non-circulating library.

References: Ruth Lapham Butler, "The Filipiniana of the Ayer Collections: the Rizaliana," *Journal of History* [Philippine National Historical Society], vol. 10, no. 1 (Mar. 1962), p. 42-55; Frederick E. Hoxie, "Businessman, Bibliophile, and Patron: Edward E. Ayer and His Collection of American Indian Art," *Great Plains Quarterly*, vol. 9, no. 2 (Spring 1989), p. 78-88; Frank C. Lockwood, *The Life of Edward E. Ayer* (Chicago: 1929); Newberry Library, "General Guide to the Collections in the Newberry Library," [unpublished]; Lawrence W. Towner, *An Uncommon Collection of Uncommon Collections: The Newberry Library* (Chicago: 1971).

Guides/catalogs: Ruth Lapham Butler (compiler), *A Check List of Manuscripts in the Edward E. Ayer Collection* (Chicago: 1937); Victor Collins, *Attempt at a Catalog of the Library of the Late Prince Louis-Lucien Bonaparte* (London: 1894); Newberry Library, *A Bibliographical Check List of North and Middle American Indian Linguistics in the Edward E. Ayer Collection* (Chicago: 1941), 2 v.; Newberry Library. Edward E. Ayer Collection, *Dictionary Catalog of the Edward E. Ayer Collection of Americana and American Indians* (Boston: 1961), 16 v., Supplements, 1970-1980, 7 v.; Newberry Library. William B. Greenlee Collection, A *Catalogue of the Greenlee Collection* (Boston: 1970), 2 v.

Description

The vast majority of the Newberry Library's anthropological holdings are contained within the Edward E. Ayer Collection. Edward E. Ayer was a member of the first Newberry Library Board of Trustees, established under a charter granted by the State of Illinois in

1892. While Ayer had little formal education, he was a successful Chicago businessman who was prominent in the lumber trade. He became interested in history by reading William H. Prescott's *Conquest of Mexico*. In the course of a forty-year period he collected a personal library documenting the encounters between Indians and Europeans in the Americas.

In 1911 he gave his library, which then contained more than 17,000 items, to the Newberry Library. Between that time and his death, Ayer endowed the collection so it would continue to grow. When Ayer died in 1927 he bequeathed the rest of his collection, along with funds for a curator, binding, cataloging and for future purchases. Ayer was the first donor to make such a gift to the Newberry, and this collection did, in fact, lead to the establishment of the library's Department of Special Collections. The collection also had a significant impact on later donors; the Ayer collection today contains more than 100,000 books, many thousands of pages of manuscripts and hundreds of maps, drawings and paintings. Most of the items within the Ayer collection are relevant to anthropological research.

The culture of the Indians of the Western Hemisphere is highly represented throughout the Ayer Collection. In archaeology, the collection is exceptionally strong in Mayan and Mexican materials; in southwestern United States archaeology; and Midwestern tribes. Ayer spent several years after 1911 actively collecting all ethnological sources relating to North America, as well as some sources on Middle and South America. Since other Chicago institutions collect in this field, the Newberry has not concentrated its collecting efforts in this area. There is extensive material relating to Indian linguistics in books, manuscripts, manuscript reproductions, and in Mayan and Mexican codices. For the first twenty to thirty years, the emphasis was on grammars, dictionaries and texts prepared by missionaries working with the tribes.

Also of anthropological interest are Ayer Collection materials relating to the history and development of the Western Hemisphere. Special attention is devoted to the relations between Indians and whites, to discovery and exploration, colonization and early political and social developments. There is a nice balance of materials between original and modern works. The Newberry Library also selectively collects current secondary sources, such as anthropological journals and museum publications, to complement its historical holdings.

The Ayer collection is housed in the Special Collections Department of the Newberry Library, and is widely used by national and international scholars. The holdings of the Ayer Collection are complemented by some of the anthropological materials within the Greenlee and Bonaparte collections. The Newberry Library is also home to the D'Arcy McNickle Center for the History of the American Indian. The Center's mission is to promote research into Native American cultures using the resources of the library.

Melissa J. Martens
Assistance and information provided by John Aubrey, Hjordis Halvorson, Margaret Kulis and Robert Karrow.

FIGURE 3. Edward E. Ayer beside a redwood tree, Bull Creek Forest, Mendocino County, California. Photograph by Mrs. Ayer. Courtesy of the Newberry Library.

University of Chicago. Library

Address: Library, University of Chicago, 1100 E. 57th Street, Chicago, IL 60637.
Tel.: (773) 702-7874 (Reference Department); (773) 702-8147 (Bibliographer of Anthropology); (773) 702-8705 (Department of Special Collections); (773) 702-8430 (Southern Asia Collection); (773) 702-9537 (Oriental Institute Research Archives).
Fax: (773) 702-6623
Internet address: http://www.lib.uchicago.edu.
Internet address (anthropology collection): http://www.lib.uchicago.edu/LibInfo/ SourcesBySubject/Anthropology.
Internet address (Special Collections): http://www.lib.uchicago.edu/LibInfo/Libraries/SpCl.
Internet address (Southern Asia Collection): http://www.lib.uchicago.edu/LibInfo/ SourcesBySubject/SouthAsia.
Internet address (Oriental Institute): http://www.oi.uchicago.edu/OI/default.html.
Internet access to on-line catalog: Internet access to the library's on-line catalog (which includes most materials cataloged since 1975) is available. Telnet: libcat.uchicago.edu.
Networks, consortia: OCLC, CIC.
Public transit access: #6 bus or Metra Electric from the Loop; walk west on 56th or 57th Street.
Founded: 1890 (opened in 1892).
Major resources: Anthropology collections are integrated into the general collections as well as those of departmental libraries.
Areas of specialization: Social and cultural anthropology; materials from or about South Asia and the Middle East; papers of University of Chicago anthropologists.
Fieldnotes, papers, etc.: Special Collections holds papers of numerous University of Chicago anthropologists. These include fieldnotes, correspondence and other materials as follows:
- Frederick Starr (1858-1933)—fieldnotes on Congo, Liberia, Asia, Latin America; correspondence with numerous contemporaries.
- William Jones (1871-1909)—fieldnotes on the Philippines.
- Fay-Cooper Cole (1881-1961)—correspondence.
- Robert Redfield (1897-1958)—fieldnotes on Middle America (e.g., on Tepoztlán, Yucatán); correspondence with colleagues, students, family and institutions; classnotes.
- Sol Tax (1907-1995)—fieldnotes on Middle America (especially Guatemala) and on North American Indians as well as on action anthropology; correspondence with numerous colleagues and students and with many organizations; classnotes.
- Fred Eggan (1907-1991)—fieldnotes on American Indians of the Great Basin, Northwest Coast and Southwest; materials on the Philippines and on the writings of Edward Sapir and A.R. Radcliffe-Brown.
- Milton Singer (1912-1994)—fieldnotes on India; other material.
- Gitel Steed (1914-1977)—fieldnotes and other material on South Asia.
- Lloyd Fallers (1925-1974)—fieldnotes on eastern and southern Africa and Turkcy.

Access to manuscript holdings is provided through finding aids in Special Collections.

The Oriental Institute Archives holds the papers of James Henry Breasted (1865-1935).

Holdings: No separate count of anthropological materials is available. The Library held some 6,200,000 book volumes as of 1998. (These figures do not include materials at the Oriental Institute Research Archives.)

Visual/audio resources: There is quite a good map collection and a very small video collection.

Access: There are some restrictions on use of the collection by persons not affiliated with the University of Chicago; check with the library's Cashier/Privileges Office, tel. (773) 702-8782. Special conditions apply to the use of certain archival materials.

References: The most important sources of information about the holdings of the University of Chicago Library are its catalogs. The on-line catalog includes references to most books and serials (but to hardly any of the archival materials or non-codex publications) acquired since 1975; the card catalog lists most earlier book and serial acquisitions. Published (and quasi-published) sources of information include M. Llewellyn Raney, *The University Libraries* (Chicago: 1933) (= *The University of Chicago Survey*, vol. 7); George W. Stocking, Jr., *Anthropology at Chicago: Tradition, Discipline, Department: An Exhibition Marking the Fiftieth Anniversary of the Department of Anthropology, October 1979-February 1980* (Chicago: 1979)—deals with the Department of Anthropology, not the Library.

References to the Oriental Institute include: Chicago. University. Oriental Institute. Library, *Catalog of the Oriental Institute Library, University of Chicago* (Boston: 1970), 16 v.; Charles E. Jones, *The Research Activities of the Oriental Institute: Introduction and Guide* ([Chicago: 1993]); John Larson, *The Collections Management Policy of the Oriental Institute Research Archives* ([Chicago: 199?]).

Artifacts: The Library itself holds no artifacts, but the Oriental Institute has a major collection of Middle Eastern artifacts.

Archaeological sites represented in artifact holdings: The Oriental Institute has artifacts from sites throughout the Middle East, particularly Egypt, Iraq and Syria.

Catalogs of artifact resources: Only an unpublished registry of Oriental Institute artifactual holdings is available.

Description

The University of Chicago has been an important center of anthropological research since the founding of the Department of Anthropology in 1929. Among those associated with the department during its first decades were Robert Redfield, Fred Eggan, Sol Tax, William Lloyd Warner, Fay-Cooper Cole, Robert Braidwood and Milton Singer. Numerous others taught at the University of Chicago, at least briefly—e.g., Edward Sapir and A.R. Radcliffe-Brown.

The work of the department's scholars is documented by archival materials held at the University of Chicago Library's Department of Special Collections. The activities of the department have been supported by the library's general collection, now largely held at Joseph Regenstein Library. Elsewhere on campus, the Research Archives of the Oriental Institute maintains a fine ancient Middle East collection. The Research Archives also holds archival material connected with the Oriental Institute.

The General Collection

The University of Chicago Library holds what is probably one of North America's better anthropology collections. The collection does have strengths and weaknesses. The comparatively late founding of the University in the early 1890s, for example, certainly had some effect on the nature of the collection. In an effort to make up for lost time, the library evidently spent as much money on books as any other North American university library in many of its first thirty years. But, because of the late start, some runs of older periodicals remain incomplete.

The late founding of the Department of Anthropology, however, probably had little effect on collecting practices. Anthropology played a subsidiary role in a joint Sociology-Anthropology Department until 1929, but had enough of a presence even before that to assure that the library would acquire what were felt to be the most significant publications as well as subscriptions to most major serials—including the publications of most of the learned societies in anthropology in North America and of ethnology and (oddly) folklore in Western Europe.

Until after World War II, selection was very Eurocentric and, more specifically, Germanocentric. This is not surprising given that the University was to a large extent modeled after German universities. As a result, there is a great deal of older "minor" European material in the library stacks—and comparatively little pre-World War II material from what is now called the Third World.

Beginning in the 1920s, library selection, as elsewhere in North America, gradually fell into the hands of subject specialists called "bibliographers." (The University of Chicago Library is said to have been the first library at which this term was used in this sense.) Although overall expenditures on new materials since the 1930s have not ranked as high as they did in the library's first decades, the library's aloofness from approval plans has, in theory, allowed selection to be oriented to the institution's needs. In the case of anthropology, this has often meant, among other things, a focus on cultural and social, rather than physical anthropology.

Since World War II, acquisition of materials from the Third World has improved dramatically, in part because it has increasingly been managed by area specialists (although Latin American, African and Oceanian materials have remained the responsibility of the Anthropology Bibliographer). Since about 1960 the library has developed an extensive collection of South Asian materials, not only acquiring nearly everything that the PL 480 program has offered, but also making a special effort in certain areas, such as Sanskrit studies. The Middle East collection is also one of the best in North America—its offerings of Ottoman materials and older materials on the ancient Middle East are particularly strong. (There is a G.K. Hall catalog of the book and journal holdings at the Oriental Institute that were incorporated into the general library collections in 1970.) The collections of materials on East Asia, Eastern Europe and Latin America are also quite good. The sub-Saharan African and Southeast Asian holdings are much weaker.

Until 1970 the library was highly decentralized. There were numerous departmental libraries, including a small one at the Department of Anthropology and the large one at the Oriental Institute. The general collections were kept at the overcrowded Harper Library. Virtually all of these materials have been consolidated at the Joseph Regenstein Library, which opened in 1970. Since that time the University of Chicago Library has been among the more centralized of major North American university libraries.

A second major event occurred in the early 1980s when the collections of the formerly separate John Crerar Library were added to those of the University of Chicago Library, and a separate science library (still called the John Crerar Library) was opened. The Crerar collections include (among much other material) numerous older expedition reports and "natural-science" materials, many of which are important documents for those with an interest in the early history of anthropology.

Special Collections

Most of the unique holdings of the library re:˙ le at the Department of Special Collections. Special Collections holds the papers of Frederick Starr, Robert Redfield, Sol Tax, Fred Eggan, Milton Singer, Gitel Steed and Lloyd Fallers. These sets of papers typically include both fieldnotes and correspondence. Finding aids are available for all of these collections In addition, the department holds the papers of David M. Schneider and Cora DuBois, for which preliminary inventories are available.

Special Collections also holds the records of the Department of Anthropology from its inception in 1929 until 1970, as well as of the Philippine Studies Program, which functioned under the aegis of the Department of Anthropology, starting in the 1950s. The departmental records include the files of Fay-Cooper Cole; the Philippine Study Program's records include the correspondence and fieldnotes of William Jones.

Special Collections also holds records of the Robert Redfield Ford Foundation Cultural Studies Project, 1951-1961; of the journal *Current Anthropology*, 1960-1970; of the 29th International Conference of Americanists, Chicago, 1949; and of the IXth International Conference of Anthropological and Ethnological Sciences, Chicago, 1973.

A Title II-C grant was awarded in 1993 for the purpose of creating on-line records for much of Special Collections' archival materials in the social sciences.

In addition, many of the University's rare books (including those brought by the John Crerar Library merger) are held by Special Collections. Some of these remain uncataloged.

The Oriental Institute

The study of anthropology and the study of the ancient Middle East have generally been quite separate academic enterprises. This has to some degree been true at the University of Chicago as well, but there have been several figures at the University (e.g., Robert J. Braidwood and Robert McC. Adams) who have been associated both with the Anthropology Department and with the Oriental Institute and who have done important academic work on the anthropological implications of the growth of "civilization" in the ancient Middle East.

The Oriental Institute's ambivalent relationship with the rest of the University could be said to be reflected in its complicated library arrangements. Although (as noted above) its older collection was merged into the general library collection in 1970, the Oriental Institute still maintains a separate Archives. In part this consists of the Research Archives—an excellent special library of published materials on the ancient Near East. This facility is not part of the University of Chicago Library. It has its own quite separate on-line catalog. It also publishes a catalog of new acquisitions that includes indexing of journal articles.

The Oriental Institute also maintains its own Archives proper, a repository of material generated or collected by faculty and staff at the Institute. The Archives includes field records of the Institute's expeditions, particularly those of the 1920s and 1930s. Photographs made during the course of these expeditions constitute the most frequently consulted material at the Archives. There are also the papers of deceased Oriental Institute staff members (e.g., James Henry Breasted) and the records of the Institute's administration.

Christopher Winters, in part on the basis of information supplied by Daniel Meyer, Charles E. Jones and John Larson.

Illinois—DeKalb

Northern Illinois University. Founders Memorial Library. Southeast Asia Collection

Address: Southeast Asia Collection, Founders Memorial Library, Northern Illinois University, DeKalb, IL 60115-2868.
Tel.: (815) 753-1819 (Office); (815) 753-1808 (Reference—Island Southeast Asia); (815) 753-1809 (Reference—Mainland Southeast Asia).
Fax: (815) 753-2003
Internet address: http://lib.ws66.lib.niu.edu.
Networks, consortia: ILLINET Online, OCLC, CRL, SEAM.
Public transit access: The DeKalb O'Hare Limousine Service (a private carrier, tel. 815 758-0631) provides shuttle service, by appointment only, between O'Hare Airport and DeKalb locations.
Parking: A visitors' parking lot is on Carroll Avenue, west of Founders Memorial Library (fee). Some metered parking is available in the small lot east of Carroll Avenue.
Founded: 1964.
Major resources: Books, periodicals, newspapers, documents, pamphlets, microforms, maps, recordings and manuscripts from or about Southeast Asia.
Areas of specialization: Southeast Asia. Most of the diverse ethnic and linguistic groups of the Southeast Asian region are represented (to a greater or lesser extent) in the book, journal and other library collections.
Archives/manuscripts: Southeast Asia-related manuscripts and fieldnotes are in Special Collections.

Fieldnotes, papers, etc.: Ethel Nurge (fieldnotes—Leyte, Philippines), Donn V. Hart (fieldnotes—Cebu, Philippines); Gordon P. Means (Karo Batak project papers—Sumatra, Indonesia); Robert Wessing (fieldnotes—West Java, Indonesia).

Holdings (books and journals): Books: 74,200 v.; periodicals: 767 titles. The former personal libraries of Paul J. Bennett (Burma), Gordon P. Means (Malaysia/Indonesia), Kenneth W. Berger (Philippines), Donn V. Hart (Philippines) and Willis E. Sibley (Philippines) are among library holdings. An excellent collection of colonial-era journals from Indochina and Vietnam was donated by Gerald C. Hickey.

Holdings (microfilm): 5,000 reels.

Visual/audio resources: An excellent collection of early printed maps of Southeast Asia is held—in Special Collections. Photographic holdings include the Irvin E. Winship and Peter G. Gowing field photographs (southern Philippines, 1964); black-and-white photographs by William A. Hammond (Philippines, ca. 1898); numerous stereograph cards illustrating Philippine life in the early 1900s; a documentary video on the Semai (Sengoi) of peninsular Malaya, by Gordon P. Means. Audio resources include Javanese gamelan performances and many other Southeast Asian music recordings on cassettes or CDs (in the Music Library).

Access: Most Southeast Asia Collection materials are available for on-site use by visitors, and interlibrary loans are provided. Catalog records of nearly all Southeast Asia holdings are on OCLC and Illinet Online.

References: Lee S. Dutton, "Southeast Asian Research Materials: Report on a Field Trip," *Southeast Asia Library Group Newsletter* (Hull, Yorkshire, U.K.), no. 6 (Apr. 1971), p. 1-5.

Guides/catalogs: Lee S. Dutton, "Some Ethnic and Regional Studies Journals of the Philippines," *Serials Review*, vol. 16, no. 3 (Fall 1990), p. 23-28; Lee S. Dutton, "Stereograph Cards of the Philippines,"—an unpublished finding aid, 1998.

Artifacts of anthropological interest: The Burma Gallery (in Altgeld Hall) curates the Burma Studies Foundation collection of art objects, including early bronze drums and Buddha images from Burma. The Anthropology Museum (in Cole Hall) maintains object collections from Southeast Asia, Oceania and other regions.

Description

The Southeast Asia Collection was established in the Northern Illinois University Libraries in 1964. Library materials were first acquired in the field by Donald Clay Johnson, in the course of his 1966 acquisitions trip to the region. During the formative decades beginning in 1969, Lee S. Dutton managed the expansion of the collections and also consolidated Southeast Asia holdings as a separate unit within the library. Library resources were greatly enhanced by means of individual purchases, field trips to the region, standing orders and gifts. Participation in the National Program for Acquisitions and Cataloging (NPAC) program for Indonesia was inaugurated in 1969, and the following year NPAC program coverage was extended to include Malaysia, Singapore and Brunei. Library holdings on Burma were enhanced in 1989, when the extensive personal library of Paul J. Bennett was received as a bequest.

A Title II-C grant, awarded in 1984, made possible the retrospective conversion of catalog records for all Southeast Asia Collection holdings.

FIGURE 4. Village scene with carabao, Leyte, Phillippines, 1976. Photo by Ethel Nurge. Courtesy of the Southeast Asia Collection, Founders Memorial Library, Northern Illinois University (#96-1936).

Areas of present collection strength (in Western and national languages of the region) include Malaysia, Singapore, Indonesia, the Philippines, Burma (Myanmar) and Thailand. Holdings for Brunei, Cambodia, Laos and Vietnam are less extensive, although significant. Special holdings include rare books and manuscripts; early accounts of travel and exploration; dictionaries and linguistic studies; early maps of the area; Thai-language cremation volumes; local publications from Bali, Indonesia; also books and journals deposited by the Burma Studies Foundation.

Among Southeast Asia-related manuscripts (housed in Special Collections) are the fieldnotes of Ethel Nurge (Leyte, Philippines); Donn V. Hart (Cebu, Philippines); and Gordon P. Means (Karo Batak project papers, Sumatra, Indonesia).

Several collections of Southeast Asian photographs are held. The William A. Hammond photographs document Philippine life at the time of the Spanish-American War. Photos from Leyte, Philippines, accompany the Ethel Nurge fieldnotes. The Irvin E. Winship and Peter G. Gowing photographs document daily life in Moro areas of Mindanao in the 1960s.

Periodical holdings include scholarly and some popular journals from or about the region. Among periodicals of anthropological interest are society and museum publications such as the *Journal of the Siam Society*, the *Sarawak Museum Journal* and others. Holdings of Philippine ethnic and regional studies journals (*Ilocos Review*, *Kinaadman*, *Mindanao Journal*, others) have been described in an article by the author (Dutton, 1990). Gerald C. Hickey's welcome gift of colonial-era periodicals from Indochina included the *Revue Indochinoise* (1914-1944) and other uncommon titles. Southeast Asia-related newsletters (*Caraka: Newsletter for Javanists*, *Orang Asli Studies Newsletter*, many others) are also held. Serials are received currently from Malaysia, Singapore and Indonesia via the NPAC program. Periodicals published for a popular readership include the Malay-language *Gila-Gila*, and others.

Lee S. Dutton

Illinois—Evanston

Northwestern University. Library. Melville J. Herskovits Library of African Studies

Address: Melville J. Herskovits Library of African Studies, Northwestern University Library, 1935 Sheridan Road, Evanston, IL 60208-2300.
Tel.: (847) 467-3084 (reference desk); (847) 491-7684 (office).
Fax: (847) 491-8306
E-mail: africana@nwu.edu.
Internet address: http://www.library.nwu.edu/africana.
Networks, consortia: OCLC, RLG, CAMP, CIC.
Public transit access: From Chicago, on weekdays at rush hours, take the CTA Express to Evanston. Exit there at Foster Street. The campus is a short walk to the east. At other times, when the CTA Express is not scheduled, take the CTA train to Howard Street in Chicago. Change there to take the CTA to the Foster Street stop in Evanston.

Founded: 1954 (establishment of the African Studies Library).

Major resources: Books, journals, manuscripts, maps, pamphlets, photographs, videos.

Area of specialization: Africa—in particular, Africa south of the Sahara.

Archives/manuscripts: Africana manuscripts and papers are preserved in several locations on campus—among these are the Herskovits Library; the Northwestern University Library's Special Collections Department; and also in University Archives. Africana and related manuscript holdings include: the Abdullah Abduraham Family papers, 1906-1962; African Studies Association papers, 1957-1980; Black Sash papers, 1928-1963; Melville J. Herskovits papers, 1906-1963; Lorcnzo D. Turner papers, 1913-1973; and others. The papers of the Asante Collective Biography Project (about three vertical file cabinets of material) are also on campus—inquire at the Herskovits Library for the current location of Asante Project materials or to request research access to them.

Holdings (books and journals): 245,000 v.; 2,800 current serials; 10,500 books in 300 African languages; extensive collections of ephemera, maps, posters, videos and electronic resources for the study of Africa. A large uncataloged collection of books and other published materials in African languages—many printed in small editions—is available.

Visual/audio resources: The Herskovits Library has a collection of video recordings about Africa and/or produced in Africa. These are detailed in the "Guide to the Africana Video Collection"—available on request from the Library.

Access: Anyone interested in the study of Africa is welcome to use the resources of the Herskovits Library, regardless of academic or institutional affiliation. Access to the University Library is restricted during certain hours of the week to readers with valid Northwestern University identification or to readers who have previously arranged for library access. For further information contact the library prior to visiting for the first time.

References: Descriptions of selected Herskovits Library reources appear in Aloha South, *Guide to Non-Federal Archives and Manuscripts in the United States Relating to Africa* (London: 1989), vol. 1, p. 448-456; and also in Jean E. Meeh Gosebrink, *African Studies Information Resources Directory* (Oxford: 1986), p. 232-237. For background information on the Asante Collective Biography Project, see Ivor Wilks, *Asante in the Nineteenth-Century: The Structure and Evolution of a Political Order* (London: 1975).

Moore Crossey, "Hans Panofsky: Biographical Notes and Bibliography," in Julian W. Witherell (editor), *Africana Resources and Collections: Three Decades of Development and Achievement: A Festschrift in Honor of Hans Panofsky* (Metuchen, N.J.: 1989), p. 9-17; David L. Easterbrook, "International Library and Archival Cooperation: America," in *African Studies* (London: 1986), p. 153-160.

References (Melville J. Herskovits): For concise information on the life of Melville J. Herskovits, see Alan P. Merriam, "Melville Jean Herskovits, 1895-1963," *American Anthropologist*, vol. 66, no. 1 (Feb. 1964), p. 83-109. This article includes a detailed bibliography of Herskovits's professional writings. Also available is James W. Fernandez, "Herskovits, Melville J. (Melville Jean)," in Christopher Winters (general editor), *International Dictionary of Anthropologists* (New York: 1991) (= *Garland Reference Library of the Social Sciences*, vol. 638), p. 285-287.

Guides/catalogs: Full retrospective conversion of the library's collections has made use of the published collection catalogs generally unnecessary. The published catalogs are: Melville J. Herskovits Library of African Studies, *Catalog of the Melville J. Herskovits Library of*

African Studies, Northwestern University Library (Evanston, Illinois) and Africana in Selected Libraries (Boston: 1972), 8 v., supplement (1978), 6 v. The Herskovits Library has published since 1962 the bimonthly *Joint Acquisitions List of Africana* (Evanston)—a listing of current acquisitions at Northwestern and other selected major Africana collections.
Artifacts of anthropological significance: The Herskovits Library has no artifact collections.

Description

Established in 1954, the Melville J. Herskovits Library of African Studies is the largest separate Africana collection in the world. The library's collections include more than 245,000 volumes, 2,800 current serials, 300 current African newspapers, as well as comprehensive collections of sheet maps and atlases, and many research materials in microform. The collection has about 10,500 books in African languages, an extensive and indexed vertical file collection, major collections of rare books, archival and manuscript collections, videotapes and also various forms of electronic information.

Africana Manuscripts

Fieldnotes and correspondence relating to research and publication are found in a number of Herskovits Library archival and manuscript collections. Those of particular anthropological interest include the Vernon Anderson papers, the Melville J. Herskovits papers (the latter papers also include copies of fieldnotes of a number of Herskovits's students), the Polly Hill papers, the Lorenzo D. Turner papers, and also the microfilms of the Meyer Fortes and Robert Sutherland Rattray materials. An inventory is available for each of these collections.

The Melville J. Herskovits papers span the years from 1906 to 1963, and include some fieldnotes, correspondence and drafts of publications as well as photographs. The Herskovits papers were received at Northwestern in 1963 as a gift from Frances S. Herskovits and Jean Herskovits. It should be noted that many of the original fieldnotes of Melville and Frances Herskovits are in the New York Public Library Schomburg Center for Research in Black Culture.

The ethnographic focus of the Anderson papers is on the Baluba in Zaire (now the Democratic Republic of Congo). Anderson was a Presbyterian minister in Zaire from 1921 to 1949. [Additional information on the Anderson papers may be found in James Sanders, "The Vernon Anderson Papers," *History in Africa*, vol. 8 (1981), p. 361-364.] The Polly Hill papers span the years from 1946 to 1988, and include fieldnotes from Ghana, Nigeria and India. The Lorenzo D. Turner papers cover the years from 1923 to 1973, and include fieldnotes of his research into Gullah on the islands off the southeast coast of the U.S.

There are microfilm copies of two sets of personal papers that are of anthropological significance: the Meyer Fortes papers relating to the Ashanti Social Survey (9 reels) from the African Studies Center, Cambridge University; and the Robert Sutherland Rattray papers (6 reels) from the Museum of Mankind, the British Museum, London. Both the Meyer Fortes and Robert Sutherland Rattray microfilms focus on Ghana.

Information provided by Northwestern University Library.

Illinois—Springfield

Illinois Archaeological Research: Illinois State Museum (ISM), **Research and Collections Center** and **Dickson Mounds Branch Museum**

Address: Illinois State Museum, Research and Collections Center, 1011 East Ash, Springfield, IL 62703; Dickson Mounds Museum, 10956 North Dickson Mounds Road, Lewistown, IL 61542.
Tel.: (217) 785-0134 (Illinois State Museum); (309) 547-3149 (Dickson Mounds Branch Museum).
Internet address (Illinois State Museum): http://www.museum.state.il.us.
Founded: 1877 (ISM); 1972 (Dickson Mounds Branch).
Major resources: Notes, maps, illustrations, photographs, manuscripts, reports, published monographs and articles; and artifacts from archaeological research in Illinois and the midwestern section of North America; an affiliated library with 20,000 volumes.
Areas of specialization: Native American culture history and material culture; eighteenth- and nineteenth-century Euroamerican and American material culture.
Holdings: More than 250 linear ft. of notes, maps, illustrations and photographs; and 7,500,000 objects that chronicle Native American, Euroamerican and American lifeways and the evolution of archaeological science.
Visual/audio resources: Photo resources include the University of Chicago Photographic File from the 1930s and 1940s that documents archaeological excavations in fifteen states, including Illinois. The museum also has a working contact print file and photo documentation from photograph and negative albums.
Access: Library: open to scholars and general readers daily; borrowing privileges are available. Archives: open to scholars by appointment; loan privileges to qualified institutions. Collections: open to scholars by appointment; loan privileges to qualified institutions.
References: Joan Megan Jones, *Native Basketry of Western North America: The Condell Collection of the Illinois State Museum* (Springfield, Ill.: 1978) (= *Illinois State Museum, Springfield. Handbook of Collections*, no. 3); Sissel Schroeder, *Masterpieces of the Past: Prehistoric Art in Illinois* (Springfield: 1984)—a catalog to accompany a 1984 exhibition at the Illinois State Museum; B.W. Styles and M.J. Bade, "The University of Chicago Photography File," *Living Museum*, vol. 50, no. 2 (1988), p. 19-22.
Artifact collections: 7.5 million objects, including extensive holdings of prehistoric chipped and ground stone artifacts, ceramics, plant and animal remains and human skeletal remains, from more than 4,500 prehistoric and historic Native American sites; and Euroamerican and American artifacts dating to the eighteenth- and nineteenth-centuries. Other significant collections include: 1.) the Cutler-Blake Ethnobotany Collection—primarily carbonized plant remains from prehistoric Native American sites that chronicle the domestication of a variety of native species; and 2.) the Dan Frost Trade Bead collection—71 sample cards showing various bead types that were in use during the mid-nineteenth to early twentieth-century. In

addition, important artifact collections have been donated to the museum by the University of Chicago, the Peoria Academy of Science, Lakeview Museum, William McAdams, George and Ethel Schoenbeck, Donald Wray, Patrick Munson and Alan Harn and Kelvin Sampson. Ethnographic collections (more than 3,000 items) include late nineteenth- to twentieth-century Native American materials such as baskets from western North America, Pueblo pottery from the southwestern United States, clothing, apparel and armament from the Great Plains.

Guides/catalogs: There is no comprehensive published catalog of artifact resources. Selected artifacts and their catalog numbers are illustrated in two publications: Jones: 1978; Schroeder: 1984.

Description

The Illinois State Museum curates the results of more than a century of archaeological research in Illinois and the American Midwest. The collection includes extensive holdings of artifacts and research documents (fieldnotes, journals, illustrations and manuscripts) from research on American Indian sites that pre-date 1400 A.D.; from American Indian and Euroamerican sites, ca. 1675-1845; and from nineteenth- and twentieth-century American sites. These materials are housed in the museum's Research and Collection Center—a state-of-the-art 100,000 square foot curation and research facility—and at the Dickson Mounds Museum. Significant site collections include the Cahokia Mounds in Madison and St. Clair counties; Modoc Rock Shelter and Fort de Chartres in Randolph County; Rogers Shelter in Benton County, Missouri; Zimmerman site; and sites in the Starved Rock vicinity in La Salle County; sites in the FAP-408 project area, located in the lower Illinois River Valley (e.g., Smiling Dan and Napoleon Hollow sites); sites of the Riverton Culture in the Wabash River Valley (Riverton, Swan Island and Robeson Hills sites); the Rench site in Peoria County; and the Morton Village, Norris Farms, Crable, Larson, Myer-Dickson and Dickson Mounds sites in Fulton County. These documents and artifacts chronicle human culture during a 12,000-year period and the history of archaeological research in Illinois.

Michael D. Wiant

Illinois—Urbana

University of Illinois at Urbana-Champaign (UIUC). **Department of Anthropology. Doris Duke American Indian Oral History Project Archive**

Address: Department of Anthropology, University of Illinois at Urbana-Champaign, 109 Davenport Hall, 607 South Mathews Avenue, Urbana, IL 61801.
Tel.: (217) 333-3616
Fax: (217) 244 3491
E-mail: anthro@uiuc.edu.

Major resources: The Doris Duke American Indian Oral History Project at the University of Illinois was one of seven distinct, but related, Doris Duke American Indian Oral History Projects funded, beginning in late 1966, at seven U.S. universities. The Duke Project at Urbana was directed by Edward Brunner and involved faculty and graduate students of the university's Department of Anthropology. All of the Duke projects had ended by 1972.

Areas of specialization: Recorded oral history interviews with informants in several Native American communities.

Archives/manuscripts: The UIUC Doris Duke Project Archive consists of approximately 16,000 pages of fieldnotes, papers and reports based on oral history recordings made in the late 1960s.

Visual/audio resources: Duke Project oral history recordings; black-and-white photographs and color slides.

Access: In compliance with the conditions of the research, access to materials in the project archive is limited. Requests for access to the project materials may be sent to the Chair, Department of Anthropology, UIUC, where they will be considered on a case-by-case basis.

References: C. Gregory Crampton, "The Archives of the Duke Project in American Indian Oral History," in Jane F. Smith and Robert M. Kvasnicka (editors), *Indian-White Relations: A Persistent Paradox* (Washington, D.C.: 1972) (= *National Archives Conferences*, vol. 10), p. 119-128; Bradford Koplowitz, "The Doris Duke Indian Oral History Projects," *Popular Culture in Libraries*, vol. 1, no. 3 (1993), p. 23-38.

Guides/catalogs: An unpublished index to the Duke Project archive at Urbana, in loose-leaf volumes, was compiled.

Information provided by the Department of Anthropology, UIUC.

University of Illinois at Urbana-Champaign (UIUC). Library

Address (library): Library, University of Illinois at Urbana-Champaign, 1408 West Gregory Drive, Urbana, IL 61801.

Tel.: Library: (217) 333-0790 (Office of the University Librarian); (217) 333-2305 (Education and Social Science Library); (217) 333-2290 (Information Desk/Reference Library); (217) 333-0798 (University Archives); Music Library: (217) 333-1173.

Fax: Library: (217) 244-0398; (217) 244-6649; Music Library: (217) 244-9097.

Internet address: http://www.library.uiuc.edu/default.htm.

Internet access to on-line catalog: Telnet to illinet.aiss.uiuc.edu.

Networks, consortia: OCLC, ILCSO, CRL, CIC, ARL, CODSULI.

Founded: 1868.

Major resources: An outstanding collection of general anthropology resources that covers all four of the major subdisciplines of the field (cultural anthropology, physical anthropology, archaeology and linguistic anthropology); the Human Relations Area Files (the entire collection); archives of former members of the faculty of the University of Illinois at Urbana-Champaign Department of Anthropology—most notably Joseph B. Casagrande, Oscar Lewis and Julian H. Steward. The Music Library houses a wide range of materials on ethnomusicology and other topics related to music that are relevant to anthropology.

Areas of specialization: A superb collection of Slavic anthropological materials. Strong holdings of materials on Latin American anthropology and the archaeology of the Americas (particularly North America, Mexico, Central America and the Andean countries of South America), linguistics and ethnomusicology. There are also strong holdings of sociocultural materials from South and East Asia and sub-Saharan Africa. The East Asian, Latin American, Slavic and African collections support expanding academic programs related to those areas.

Archives/manuscripts: The University Archives' anthropological holdings consist of approximately 170 cubic ft. of materials—all but a small portion of which is printed matter. The Music Library and the School of Music house several archival collections related to ethnomusicology. [Also see the following entry for the University of Illinois at Urbana-Champaign School of Music.]

Fieldnotes, papers, etc.: University Archives holds papers of several University of Illinois anthropologists. These include correspondence, publications, fieldnotes and other materials, as noted in the following brief descriptions:

- Douglas S. Butterworth (1930-   )—5 cubic ft. of correspondence, manuscripts, publications and other materials on Mexican Americans and the Lower Rio Grande Valley of Texas.
- Joseph B. Casagrande (1915-1982)—43.2 cubic ft. of correspondence, manuscripts, fieldnotes, diaries and numerous other materials related to the field of anthropology, linguistics, highland Indians of Ecuador and the Chippewa and Comanche tribes.
- Arthur Randolph Kelly (1900-1979)—6 cubic ft. of correspondence, reports and other printed matter concerning Indian sites in southeastern Illinois, including papers concerning the Illinois Archaeological Survey of Southern Counties.
- Oscar Lewis (1914-1970)—approximately 75 cubic ft. of correspondence, fieldnotes, manuscripts and other materials related to research in Mexico, Cuba and Puerto Rico. Includes edited tape recordings of interviews with informants. (Written permission from Ruth M. Lewis, wife of the late Oscar Lewis, must be secured prior to using these materials.)
- Demitri Shimkin (1916-1993)—19 cubic ft. of correspondence, notes and notebooks, manuscripts, publications and other materials on a wide range of anthropological topics, including medical anthropology, related to North American Indians, African Americans, Africa, Central Asia, Eastern Europe and other areas.
- Julian H. Steward (1902-1972)—16.3 cubic ft. of correspondence, fieldnotes, publications, manuscripts and other materials related to a wide variety of anthropological topics; and on North and South American Indian culture. Includes papers related to his association with numerous institutions, including his position as Associate Anthropologist in the Smithsonian Institution Bureau of American Ethnology.

The University Archives has produced written finding aids for collections of personal papers. Photocopies of these may be requested from the University Archives.

Holdings (books and journals): Due to the integration of anthropological materials into the general library collection, volume count can only be estimated. More than 100,000 volumes (books and journals) are of direct relevance to the work of anthropologists. Many of these volumes are concentrated in the Dewey Decimal ranges 303-306, 572-573 and 900-999 (historical works of particular countries, including archaeological investigations, are classified by geographic area). The bulk of the anthropology collection is housed in the Main Stacks; most current English-language anthropology materials are housed in the Education and Social Science Library. Area studies collections are housed primarily in the Main Stacks—although there are specific area studies libraries (such as the Slavic and East European Library) that provide reference services related to those collections. The Music Library holds more than 5,000 volumes of books and serials on ethnomusicology and related topics; holdings of specific types of materials are described (below) in the separate section on the Music Library.

Visual/audio resources: The Media Center of the Undergraduate Library houses hundreds of anthropological videotapes and films and numerous other audiovisual materials relevant to anthropology. The Music Library houses more than 7,000 cataloged and 1,000 uncataloged ethnomusicological recordings (cassettes, compact discs and records) and approximately thirty videotapes. In addition, University Archives contains tapes of interviews within its collections of personal papers and a small number of archaeological conference proceedings.

Access: Area studies libraries and a number of other departmental libraries—including the Education and Social Science Library—are located in the Main Library building. Access to most campus library units is open to all persons. Access to the Main Library book stacks is limited to UIUC faculty, graduate students and official Visiting Scholars. Most stacks materials circulate to all holders of valid borrowers' cards and are available for interlibrary loan. A number of the most valuable resources owned by the library (certain rare Mesoamerican codices, for example) are housed in the Rare Book Room. The University Archives is open to all researchers. Researchers should write or call in advance to arrange for use of archival materials.

References: The on-line catalog (ILLINET Online) is the most authoritative source of current holdings information on the library's cataloged collections. The serials card catalog contains information on serial holdings that was never entered in its entirety into the on-line catalog. University Archives' holdings do not appear in the library's on-line or card catalogs. Archival holdings are entered into a locally-accessible data-processing system.

Published or locally produced sources of information include Maynard Brichford, "The Illiarch," *Illinois Libraries*, vol. 52, no. 2 (Feb. 1970), p. 182-204; Robert B. Downs (editor), *Guide to Illinois Library Resources* (Chicago: 1974); Jean Geil and Richard Burbank, "The Kasura Collection," *News from the Music Library* [University of Illinois at Urbana-Champaign] (Fall 1993), p. 2-4, and (Spring 1994), p. 2, 5; Joseph Robert Hanc, "Sources for the History of Anthropology: The Julian H. Steward Papers," *History of Anthropology Newsletter*, vol. 6, no. 1 (1979), p. 3-6; William J. Maher, "The Illini Archives in the 1980s," *Illinois Libraries*, vol. 69, no. 8 (Oct. 1987), p. 584-587; *Preliminary Checklist and Index of Ensemble Music in the Walter J. Kasura Collection of Russian Folk Music* (Urbana: 1994).

Description

The General Collection

The University of Illinois at Urbana-Champaign Library has an outstanding general collection in anthropology and also several prominent special collections of anthropological importance. Anthropology teaching and research occurred at the university for many years before a separate Department of Anthropology was created in 1960. Prior to that year, anthropology had been taught in the Department of Sociology and Anthropology since 1948. In 1960 the library created a separate book fund for anthropology, and more emphasis was placed on the systematic collection of anthropological materials. Anthropology faculty have played a very active role in the selection of anthropological materials, particularly before the appointment of an anthropology subject specialist by the library in 1975. In 1980 the addition of the Sweitzer Endowment provided the library with sufficient funds to continue its efforts to build a strong anthropology collection. At the present time, it is considered one of the best collections of anthropological publications in the United States.

The collection that was developed prior to 1960 is quite good—due in part to the fact that numerous works in anthropology were published in museum series that were especially well represented in the library's collection. The *International Directory of Anthropological Institutions*, published by the Wenner-Gren Foundation in 1952, described the University of Illinois Library's collection as "excellent in anthropology." The library holds complete runs of numerous series and periodicals from museums throughout the world and from numerous anthropology educational and research institutions in North America. Series of other major organizations and learned societies outside the United States are also well represented in the collection. The library's publisher-based approval plans bring in all monographs classed as anthropology from university and major scholarly U.S. and British presses, and the separate anthropology materials budget purchases monographs from other presses. The library currently has standing orders to approximately 300 anthropology journals and other non-monographic serials. The Music Library subscribes to an additional fifty series relevant to anthropology.

In addition to the anthropology subject specialist and anthropology faculty, area specialists have contributed to the collection of anthropological materials for many years. The library's holdings include numerous English-language and vernacular materials from throughout the world, but the areas best represented are the Americas, South and East Asia, Slavic and Eastern European countries and Africa.

The library has received a large number of materials from South Asia via the PL 480 program. This program brings in materials on a broad range of topics, including anthropology, archaeology, religion and women's studies, many of which are in English. The Asian Library has collected quite heavily in East Asian vernacular monographic materials, particularly Chinese and Japanese publications, and purchases serials in Western as well as Asian languages. Recently, the library has increased its program for the collection of Korean materials. The East Asian collection is especially rich in languages and literatures, but art and archaeology, anthropology, music, religious studies and sociology are also among subjects actively collected. Middle Eastern materials have received less emphasis. Southeast Asian materials have not been collected extensively because of the strength of the Southeast Asia

Collection at Northern Illinois University, with which the UIUC Library has direct borrowing arrangements through ILLINET Online.

The UIUC Library's collection is historically strong in a broad range of Latin American materials, including general anthropology, archaeology and ethnohistory. Because a number of UIUC anthropologists and students have done research in Mexico, Central America and the Andean countries of South America, holdings in those areas have been particularly well developed. The library actively collects materials from numerous Latin American countries and has blanket orders and exchange agreements with government, educational and research institutions.

Anthropology and related subjects are very well represented in the Africana collection. The Africana bibliographer routinely collects materials in English, French, German and the following African languages: Bambara, Hausa, Lingala, Swahili, Wolof and Zulu. (Arabic-language materials on African subjects are purchased by the Asian Library, but the bulk of these materials have not yet been cataloged.) Collection development efforts of the Africana subject specialist target African countries south of the Sahara: Burkina Faso, Côte d'Ivoire, Ethiopia, Gambia, Kenya, Mozambique, Nigeria, Senegal, South Africa, Tanzania, Democratic Republic of Congo and Zimbabwe. The library has a number of exchange arrangements for the receipt of Africana materials, primarily with University Libraries and Africana research institutes. Standing orders for a particular subject profile (which includes anthropology) have been established with major vendors of Africana materials.

The library's collection of Slavic and Eastern European materials is considered to be one of the two best in the U.S. Holdings of Russian and East European publications on anthropology, archaeology, geological history (including paleontology and related subjects) and Russian cultural history are extremely rich. Numerous anthropological serials and monographs arrive through the many purchasing and exchange arrangements the library has with Slavic and East European studies institutions and with commercial vendors, as well as through donations.

Traditionally excellent science holdings have supplemented the anthropology collection, as numerous relevant works in paleontology, geology and botany have been acquired as parts of scientific series that have been purchased on standing order for many years. The library's collections of ethnomusicology and linguistics materials are also very good, due to the strength of those two areas of teaching and research at the University.

University Archives

The most important anthropology archival holdings are the sets of papers from prominent UIUC anthropologists. Additionally, archival holdings include various Department of Anthropology publications (including its *Research Reports* series), papers and publications issued by the Illinois Archaeological Survey and tape recordings of two regional archaeological conferences held in 1956. The collections in the University Archives are not cataloged. The Archives has produced "control cards" and printed finding aids for the collections it has processed. Also, control of the materials is maintained by a local automated database.

The Music Library at UIUC has a wide range of holdings supporting ethnomusicology instruction and research at the doctoral level. In addition to published books and journals in the field, in English and other Western languages, Music Library holdings include a broad selection of folk song collections and other printed music sources, recordings in several formats, videotapes and several collections of scores and parts for Russian folk instrument ensemble.

Library materials in the field of ethnomusicology (as strictly defined) are also complemented by extensive holdings in historical musicology, popular music and jazz. A collection of more than 100,000 items of nineteenth- and early twentieth-century American vocal and piano sheet music is supplemented by several thousand published folios of relatively recent popular music (largely 1960s to the present).

Catalog records for the Music Library's collection of more than 7,000 Western and non-Western commercially-issued ethnomusicological recordings (33 1/3 rpm records, cassettes and compact discs) include access points reflecting the geographical region or cultural group, as derived from George Murdock's *Outline of World Cultures*, developed for Human Relations Area Files, Inc. Among these recordings are more than 2,500 cassettes of popular and film music from India, Pakistan and Bangladesh, received largely via the PL 480 program, as well as about fifty 33 1/3 rpm records of Egyptian popular music of the 1970s, acquired to support dissertation research.

Among audio resources that remain uncataloged at present are about 1,000 78 rpm, 45 rpm and 33 1/3 rpm commercial recordings from the personal collection of Frank Scheibenreif, who, for several decades beginning in the mid-1940s, broadcast a program entitled *Slovak American Radio Review* on Station WSBC in Chicago. Many of these records were issued in Czechoslovakia and elsewhere in Eastern Europe before World War II. Besides Czech and Slovak folk music, the repertory includes Gypsy music and music of other Eastern European ethnic groups.

Also uncataloged at present are about 150 78 rpm records of commercially-issued popular music and field recordings from other areas of the world, including South Asia, West Africa, various regions within the former USSR, Japan and Greece. *Songs of France*—a series of radio programs produced by the French Broadcasting System in North America—is reproduced on about 200 16″ discs and about fifty 12″ discs. These programs include folk music and popular songs from various regions of France, Canada and other areas of French cultural influence, as well as art songs and excerpts from stageworks. Holdings of this series in the Music Library are incomplete.

To supplement ethnomusicological and anthropological holdings in the Media Center of the Undergraduate Library, the Music Library has a collection of about thirty videotapes in VHS format. Music Library holdings include folk music and blues of the United States, African popular styles and also musical traditions of a number of other specific countries and cultural groups.

Printed resources include more than 1,000 published collections of folk songs of North America and other regions, including a number of song collections published in Russia and in non-Russian areas of the former USSR. The Music Library houses copies of more than fifty master's and doctoral theses and dissertations, completed in the field of ethnomusicology at the University of Illinois since the School of Music's program was established in 1965, as well as microfilms of numerous other dissertations in ethnomusicology completed at other institutions.

The Music Library's Special Collections Unit houses manuscripts, pre-twentieth-century materials, uncataloged sheet music and other rare, fragile or unique items (including much material described above). It holds two extensive collections of performance material from New York-based Russian folk instrument ensembles. The personal collection of Alexander Kutin, director of the Balalaika Symphonic Orchestra, consisting of more than 700 scores and part sets, is uncataloged at the present time; a handwritten repertory list may be consulted. The collection of Walter J. Kasura, director of the Balalaika and Domra Society Orchestra, is described below. In addition, the library has received several smaller collections from other donors of solo and ensemble music for Russian folk instruments.

The Walter J. Kasura Collection of Russian Folk Music

Walter J. Kasura was a virtuoso prima domra performer and was for many years a leading proponent of Russian folk music in the United States. After his death in 1983, Kasura's manuscript arrangements for the Balalaika and Domra Society Orchestra (along with many thousands of other manuscripts from his library and from the libraries of Mark Selivan and other U.S. performers, directors and arrangers) were acquired by the Music Library. Also received were published music, books about Russian music and Kasura's collection of photocopied materials numbering many thousands of items. The collection as a whole consists of approximately 2,700 cataloged titles, including books as well as published and manuscript music for Russian folk orchestra, smaller ensembles or solo works; about 11,000 pieces of music that have not received full cataloging; and miscellaneous archival materials, including programs, correspondence, posters and photographs.

Published material includes about 500 scores and books on musical subjects, as well as 700 pieces of sheet music. All are fully cataloged and available for in-library use or for copying. The photocopies and clippings of published music are not fully cataloged, but have been arranged by title in several categories: vocal music (mostly voice and a piano)—about 8,000 items, for which a brief composer/title card catalog is being compiled; instrumental folk music for solo or small ensembles—452 folders; Russian popular and classical music arranged for small ensembles of traditional Russian instruments—669 folders; and scores for folk, popular and classical Russian and Soviet music arranged for traditional Russian orchestra—716 folders.

The Kasura Collection manuscripts are stored in more than 1,500 folders. Nearly all of the manuscript material is arranged for some form of Russian folk orchestra (domra, balalaika, bayan or gusli, with an occasional solo instrument such as violin, guitar, etc.). Most of the music in the Kasura Collection is folk music or is based on folk themes (e.g., Glinka's and Varlamov's settings of folk songs). Other significant types of music represented are the "Gypsy" songs of the late nineteenth-century, other popular music of the late nineteenth- and early twentieth-centuries, and Soviet popular music, especially of the 1920s and early 1930s. There are also many pieces of folk and popular music published by the Russian emigré communities in Harbin (China), Turkey, Bulgaria, Slovenia, Poland, France, Canada and the United States.

A printed guide to this collection [see References, above] is available for use in the Music Library and may be borrowed through interlibrary loan.

Ellen D. Sutton, Jean Geil, Cheri A. Vitez, David Bade

University of Illinois at Urbana-Champaign. School of Music. Ethnomusicology Archive

Address: School of Music, University of Illinois at Urbana-Champaign, 2136 Music Building, 1114 W. Nevada, Urbana, IL 61801.
Tel.: (217) 333-2620
Fax: (217) 244-4585
Internet address (Music Library): http://www.library.uiuc.edu/mux.
Founded: 1895 (School of Music); ca. 1970 (Ethnomusicology Archive).
Major resources: Materials to support instructional and research programs in ethnomusicology; music for performance on Russian folk instruments.

Description

The Ethnomusicology Archive (established about 1970) includes approximately 250 collections, each consisting of from one to 150 tapes, with corresponding fieldnotes or other documentation. Areas of emphasis—reflecting research interests of present and former faculty and graduate students of the School of Music—include the Middle East, India, Plains Indians, Africa and Latin America. A card catalog provides access by subjects (instruments, geographic areas, etc.) as well as by names of collectors and performers. The School of Music also holds about twenty 16mm films focusing on particular folk or jazz performers or introducing the musics of various cultural groups. A collection of performance material—approximately 500 score and parts sets—is maintained by the University of Illinois Russian Folk Orchestra. Access is by appointment only.

Jean Geil

Indiana—Bloomington

Indiana University. Archives of Traditional Music (ATM)

Address: Archives of Traditional Music, Room 120, Morrison Hall, Indiana University, Bloomington, IN 47405-2501.
Tel.: (812) 855-4679
Fax: (812) 855-6673
Internet address: http://www.indiana.edu/~libarchm.
Networks, consortia: IUCAT, OCLC, CIC.

Founded: 1936, at Columbia University; moved to Indiana University in 1948.

Major resources: An extensive collection of music and sound recordings of cultural and ethnological interest; also many other audio materials. Resources include field and commercial recordings in many formats, vocal and instrumental music, oral histories, recorded folktales; also any associated fieldnotes, correspondence or other documentation (when available).

Areas of specialization: One of the largest U.S. collections of ethnic and traditional music. Early field recordings of Native North American music and song are among ATM holdings. Also recordings of the Center for African Oral Data, the Edward S. Curtis collection of American Indian music, the Berthold Laufer collection of wax cylinder recordings (China, 1901-1902), linguistic data from the Archives of the Languages of the World, others.

Holdings: Approximately 7,000 wax cylinders, 250 wire recordings and many thousands of disc, tape and cassette recordings.

Fieldnotes, papers, etc.: As provided by the collectors. Many of these (when available) are simple notes or jottings that may identify the place and/or something of the context in which one or more field recordings were made.

Access: Available for on-site use with limitations. Unless otherwise restricted, copies of field recordings may often be purchased from the Archives for educational or research use only.

References: Marilyn Graf, "The Papers of George Herzog," *Resound: A Quarterly of the Archives of Traditional Music*, vol. 5, no. 1 (Jan. 1986) [2 p.]; "Herzog, George," in Stanley Sadie (editor), *The New Grove Dictionary of Music and Musicians* (London: 1980), vol. 8, p. 527-528; George Herzog, "The Collections of Phonograph Records in North America and Hawaii," *Zeitschrift für vergleichende Musikwissenschaft*, vol. 1 (1933), p. 58-62; Carol F. Inman, "George Herzog: Struggles of a Sound archivist," *Resound: A Quarterly of the Archives of Traditional Music,* vol. 5, no. 1 (Jan. 1986), [5 p.]; Aloha South, *Guide to Non-Federal Archives and Manuscripts Relating to Africa* (London: 1989), vol. 1, p. 465-471; Bonnie Urciuoli, "Preserving the Archives of the Languages of the World," *Resound: A Quarterly of the Archives of Traditional Music*, vol. 6, no. 3 (July 1987), [p. 1, 3-5]. The ATM publication *Resound: A Quarterly of the Archives of Traditional Music* (Bloomington, Ind.: 1982-) is useful for current information on resources at the ATM.

Guides/catalogs: *A Catalog of Phonorecordings of Music and Oral Data Held by the Archives of Traditional Music—Archives of Traditional Music, Folklore Institute, Indiana University, Bloomington, Indiana* (Boston: 1975); Anthony Seeger and Louise S. Spear (editors), *Early Field Recordings: A Catalogue of Cylinder Collections at the Indiana University Archives of Traditional Music* (Bloomington, Ind.: 1987); Ruth M. Stone and Frank J. Gillis, *African Music and Oral Data: A Catalog of Field Recordings, 1902-1975* (Bloomington, Ind.: 1976); Dorothy Sara Lee, *Native North American Music and Oral Data: A Catalogue of Sound Recordings, 1893-1976* (Bloomington, Ind.: 1979); Bonnie Urciuoli, *Catalog of the C.F. and F.M. Voegelin Archives of the Languages of the World* (Bloomington, Ind.: 1988), 8 v.

Description

The "Archives of Folk and Primitive Music" was initiated at Columbia University in 1936 by George Herzog (1901-1983). Herzog's early career included study at the Royal Academy of Music in Budapest and at Berlin University. He was an assistant to Erich M. von Hornbostel at the Berlin Phonogramm-Archiv, 1922-1924, and subsequently studied with Franz Boas at Columbia University. His dissertation (on Pueblo and Pima music) was completed at Columbia in 1937.

In the mid-1930s Herzog was encouraged by Boas to begin development of the Archives of Folk and Primitive Music, drawing upon the former's knowledge, and experience gained while working with von Hornbostel and the Berlin Phonogramm-Archiv. Herzog encountered major difficulties in advancing this project during the Depression years, but continued the effort to assemble a unique collection of field cylinder recordings. His work to develop the archive of field recordings has been described in an article by Carol Inman: "George Herzog: Struggles of a Sound Archivist."

In 1939 major funding was secured that enabled Herzog to establish the Archive at Columbia University. Included in this developing collection were all of the wax cylinder field recordings made in the 1890s by researchers at the American Museum of Natural History, as well as cylinders transferred from Columbia University, from the Field Museum of Natural History in Chicago and other institutions.

In 1948 Herzog was appointed to a professorship in anthropology at Indiana University, and the Archives accompanied him when he moved to Bloomington in that year. While the wax cylinders under Herzog's care received needed conservation in Bloomington, some other wax cylinders—including those at the University Museum in Philadelphia—were only transferred to Bloomington about 1956. Many of the latter, due to prolonged lack of attention, had deteriorated beyond the possibility of restoration by the time they were transferred to Bloomington.

The Archives has experienced several organizational and administrative changes since its transfer in 1948 to Indiana University. In 1964 it was renamed as the Archives of Traditional Music. Published catalogs of ATM holdings now include a general catalog of recordings (1975—indexed, but not annotated), as well as specialized catalogs of African (1976) and Native North American (1979) recordings.

A National Science Foundation grant enabled the Archives to carry out, between 1983 and 1985, a major project to clean, preserve and re-record the wax cylinders (some 7,000 items) on high-quality magnetic tape. At that time, many of the cylinders were found to be in poor condition, having cracks, mold, inadequate documentation, or other technical problems. The cylinder project sought to reconstruct any remaining collector documentation, making use of such resources as original cylinder boxes, fieldnotes, spoken collector announcements on the cylinders, or published or unpublished transcriptions. An annotated catalog of the cylinder project recordings (*Early Field Recordings: A Catalogue of Cylinder Collections at the Indiana University Archives of Traditional Music*) was published in 1987. This volume provides detailed indexes by personal names (of collectors, etc.), culture group, subject and geographical names.

Archives holdings include—in addition to early recordings of North American Indian songs—early African, South Asian and other field recordings. Also in the Archives is a special collection known as the Center for African Oral Data. Catalog records of the ATM music and oral recordings have been added to OCLC and are also accessible on-line, through the Indiana University Library catalog, IUCAT.

Lee S. Dutton
Information provided by Mary Bucknam and Marilyn Graf.

Indiana University. University Library. Folklore Collection

Address: Folklore Collection, Indiana University Library, Tenth Street and Jordan Avenue, Bloomington, IN 47405.
Tel.: (812) 855-1550
Fax: (812) 855-8068
Internet address (Special Collections): http://www.indiana.edu/~libsalc/speccoll.html.
Internet address (Folklore Institute): http://www.indiana.edu/~folklore.
Internet access to on-line catalog: IUCAT contains records of Indiana University Library holdings, including those of the Folklore Collection. IUCAT can be accessed at http://www.indiana.edu/~libweb.
Networks, consortia: OCLC, CIC, INCOLSA.
Founded: Ca. 1928 (Folklore Collection).
Major resources: Folklore Collection; Folklore Archives; Archives of Traditional Music.
Areas of specialization: Folklore, ethnomusicology.
Archives/manuscripts: Some 8,062 items in the Stith Thompson manuscript collection are preserved in the Lilly Library. Olso at Lilly Library is the Richard Dorson manuscript collection—65,000 items. The Dorson manuscripts include correspondence relating to his academic research, his service as chair of the Indiana University Folklore Department and Institute and as a reviewer of proposals and books. The original drafts of Dorson's books can be found, as well as papers read at professional meetings (and not published) and copies of his remarks before federal committees.
Fieldnotes, papers, etc.: More than 40,000 field collections of folklore from Indiana, Michigan, Ohio and Kentucky are kept in the Folklore Archives. Special collections include the Joseph T. Hall limerick collection; Roger Mitchell's Micronesian folktales; and urban folklore from the Calumet, Indiana, region.
Holdings (books and journals): Approximately 93,000 book and journal titles; 949 journal and monograph series titles (includes 263 titles on current subscription). The library holds complete runs of most journal/series titles.
Visual/audio resources: Many sound recordings are nearby on campus at the Archives of Traditional Music.
Access: The Collection is open to all scholars and visitors for in-house use. Indiana University students and residents of Indiana may borrow most book titles. Most books may also be borrowed through interlibrary loan.
Guides/catalogs: "Journal and Monograph Series in the Folklore Collection, September 1995,"—unpublished; "Motif-Index of Folk-Literature: Bibliography and Abbreviations, 1976,"—unpublished.

Description

The research component of the Folklore Institute at Indiana University is divided by format: sound recordings are in the Archives of Traditional Music, manuscript holdings are in the Folklore Archives and the Lilly Library, and all published research is in the separate Folklore Collection of the main library.

The Folklore Collection was originally organized and nurtured by the eminent folklorist, Stith Thompson (1885-1976). His attention and devotion to the quality of the collection began in the late 1920s, and throughout the next three decades he purchased books for the collection when traveling and working with folklorists in many parts of the world. He searched for monographs and journals in bookstores, purchased some private collections (for example from Russian emigrés in Paris), and received many titles as gifts. Thompson donated most everything he received from scholars around the world—so there is not a separate Stith Thompson book collection. All of the books and related materials collected by Thompson are included in the Folklore Collection.

Thompson's early concern for a repository of folklore research materials is continued today by the collection policies. The consistency of these collecting endeavors has created one of the best collections of its kind in the world, attracting many researchers to use the collection's resources in person, or to inquire by phone or mail.

The general purpose of the Folklore Collection is to support upper division undergraduate and graduate teaching and research to the Ph.D. level, as well as individual faculty research. The collection reflects the theories, techniques and history of folkloristics.

Every effort is made to collect, as comprehensively as possible, all pertinent material in the following genres: folk speech and speech play (graffiti, proverbs, riddles, speech events); folk narratives (folk histories, tales, jokes, legends, myths, personal experience narratives and tall tales); folk poetry (ballads, epic poetry, folk song); folk oratory (preaching, ethnographies of orally performed narrative events); music and dance (blues, bluegrass, country, popular and musical instruments); folk medicine; witchcraft; ethnic folklore; community rites and festivals; folk drama; games, play and practical jokes; rites of passage; urban folklore; cultural geography; folk art (body art, yard art, folk sculpture, textile art); vernacular architecture; cultural conservation; costume; food; handwork; occupational lore; public and applied folklore; and the uses of folklore in nationalism, media and the schools.

Material is collected in most languages and from most areas of the world. Special microfilm collections are also purchased—for example, the Opie Collection of Children's Literature. In 1955 and 1984, the Archives of the Finnish Folklore Society (*Kansanrunousarkisto*) were filmed for the Folklore Collection.

In recent years the staff has participated with the journal indexing for the "Folklore" volume of the *International Bibliography*, sponsored by the Modern Language Association. In 1994 the indexing of edited publications was included as part of this project. The journal holdings and other strengths of the Folklore Collection have enhanced the value of this important bibliographic resource, which is now accessible on-line in most research libraries.

Polly S. Grimshaw

Indiana University. Glenn A. Black Laboratory of Archaeology

Address: Glenn A. Black Laboratory of Archaeology, 9th and Fess Streets, Indiana University, Bloomington, IN 47405.
Tel.: (812) 855-9544
Fax: (812) 855-1864
Internet address: http://www.gbl.indiana.edu/home.html.
Founded: 1965.
Major resources: The Archive (includes the Ohio Valley-Great Lakes Ethnohistory Archive, as well as other archaeological records and papers); the Library.
Areas of specialization: The Archaeology of Indiana. The Ohio Valley-Great Lakes Ethnohistory Archive contains documentation on Native American land claims in the Great Lakes region (the region extending from Pennsylvania to Illinois and from Minnesota to Indiana).
Archives/manuscripts: The Ohio Valley-Great Lakes Ethnohistory Archive was formed between 1953 and 1966, in a project directed by Indiana University historian Erminie Wheeler-Voegelin. The Ethnohistory Archive consists of: photocopies of primary and secondary documents preserved at various repositories, including the U.S. National Archives and some European archives. Other manuscript holdings include archaeological papers of Glenn A. Black, James H. Kellar, Eli Lilly and others; archaeological records received from the Indiana Historical Society. Some descriptive information on these archival collections is on the Web at http://www.gbl.indiana.edu/publ.html.
Visual/audio resources: Archaeological photographs.
Guides/catalogs: David R. Miller, "A Guide to the Ohio Valley-Great Lakes Ethnohistory Archive"—this text is on the Web at http://www.gbl.indiana.edu/abstracts/intro1.html. Finding aids for access to the Tribal History Documents Collection, the Microfilm Collection, the Indian Claims Commission Collection and the General Collection are available.
Archaeological site reports: Archaeological site records for sites throughout Indiana—especially the southern area of the state—are in Laboratory collections. Published archaeological site reports are in both the main Indiana University Library and in the Library of Glenn A. Black Laboratory.
Access: Write to the Laboratory director several weeks in advance, with a research synopsis, to request research access to manuscript or archival materials. Not open to the public.
Artifacts: Artifact collections from many archaeological sites in Indiana are held.

Information provided by Noel D. Justice.

Kentucky—Lexington

University of Kentucky. Margaret I. King Library. Special Collections and Archives

Address: Special Collections and Archives, Margaret I. King Library, University of Kentucky, Lexington, KY 40506-0039.

Tel.: (606) 257-8611 (Reference Desk); (606) 257-8371 (Office of the Director).
Fax: (606) 257-8379
Internet address (Special Collections and Archives): http://www.uky.edu/Libraries/Special.
Internet address (Applied Anthropology Documentation Project): http://anthap.oakland.edu/sources1.htm.
Networks, consortia: OCLC, SOLINET, CRL.
Founded: 1978 (Applied Anthropology Documentation Project).
Major resources: The Applied Anthropology Documentation Collection.
Areas of specialization: The Applied Anthropology Documentation Collection is focused on documentation of applied and practicing anthropology from any geographic region.
Archives/manuscripts: More than 1,920 cataloged items, chiefly consisting of technical reports or conference papers. In addition, there are small numbers of reprints, journal issues, proposals, legal briefs, brochures, pamphlets, etc.
Access: Materials are available for on-site use at Special Collections and Archives in King Library and may be borrowed through Interlibrary loan.
References: John van Willigen, *Anthropology in Use: A Source Book on Anthropological Practice* (Boulder, Colo.: 1991) (= *Westview Special Studies in Applied Anthropology*); John van Willigen, "The Records of Applied Anthropology," in *Preserving the Anthropological Record* (2nd ed., New York: 1995), p. 135-142.

Description

Applied anthropology has characteristically been poorly documented, and access to the written products of applied anthropologists is limited. Yet non-academically employed applied anthropologists do produce much written material in the course of their work. Many of these "naturally occurring" documents are valuable as a means of understanding both the problem addressed in the applied project and the role of the applied anthropologist. For the most part these documents, however useful, become fugitive.

In response to these and other concerns, in the years since 1978, the Applied Anthropology Documentation Project at the University of Kentucky has developed a collection of fugitive or gray literature produced by applied and practicing anthropologists. The collection includes technical reports, research monographs, conference papers, practicum and internship reports, legal briefs, proposals and other materials. Areas of special strength, within the field of applied anthropology, of the King Library collection include agricultural anthropology, medical anthropology and curriculum development. There is a rather complete collection of technical reports of the Bureau of Applied Research in Anthropology (BARA) of the University of Arizona and of its antecedents.

Catalog information on project holdings is available through OCLC, and materials that have been cataloged may be borrowed through interlibrary loan. Many projects from which submitted applied anthropology materials are derived are profiled in a regularly appearing section of the quarterly, *Practicing Anthropology*. This section is entitled "Sources." Also, an anthology of project profiles published before 1991 appears as *Anthropology in Use: A Source Book on Anthropological Practice* (1991).

The Applied Anthropology Documentation Project is sponsored by the Society for Applied Anthropology, the Washington Association of Professional Anthropologists, the Society for Applied Anthropology in Canada, the National Association for the Practice of Anthropology and the Society for Medical Anthropology. Anthropologists interested in documenting their work may mail submissions to: John van Willigen, Applied Anthropology Documentation Project, Special Collections and Archives, King Library, University of Kentucky, Lexington, KY 40506.

John van Willigen
Information provided by Nancy L. DeMarcus.

Maryland—College Park

United States. National Archives and Records Administration. National Archives at College Park (Archives II)

Address: National Archives at College Park, 8601 Adelphi Road, College Park, MD 20740-6001.
Tel.: (301) 713-6800 (General Information); (301) 713-7250 (Textual Reference); (301) 713-7040 (Cartographic Branch); (301) 713-6660 (Still Picture Branch); (301) 713-7060 (Motion Picture, Sound and Video Branch); (301) 713-6645 (Center for Electronic Records).
Fax (National Archives fax-on-demand): (301) 713-6905.
E-mail (general inquiries): inquire@arch2.nara.gov.
Internet address: http://www.nara.gov.
Parking: A visitor parking structure is adjacent to the Archives building.
Founded: 1934 (National Archives); 1994 (National Archives at College Park).
Major resources (National Archives at College Park): Textual Records; Cartographic and Architectural Records; Motion Picture, Sound and Video Records; Still Picture Records; Electronic Records; Library; Microforms.
Areas of specialization: Various. Among many records of anthropological interest are Indian Division and Indian Territory Division records, housed with the records of the Office of the Secretary of the Interior (RG 48). Also at College Park are archival records of the National Park Service (RG 79), the Government of the Virgin Islands (RG 55), the Smithsonian Institution (RG 106), the Office of Territories (RG 126), the Office of Inter-American Affairs (RG 229), and the Bureau of Insular Affairs (RG 350).
Visual/audio resources: More than 8,000,000 photographic images. Most National Archives photographic resources are preserved in the Still Picture Branch and also in the Motion Picture, Sound and Video Branch. Both of these units are at College Park. Photo resources in the Still Picture Branch include photographs by William Henry Jackson, taken during the Hayden Survey (1867-1879)—also known as the U.S. Geological and Geographical Survey of the Territories (RG 57.1); photographs by E.O. Beaman, James Fennemore and John K. Hillers taken during the Powell Survey (1871-1879)—also known as the U.S. Geographical and Geological Survey of the Rocky Mountain Region (RG 57.2); photographs by Timothy O'Sullivan taken during the King Survey (1867-1879)—also known as the Geological

Exploration of the Fortieth Parallel (RG 77.7); stereographs and other images by William Bell and Timothy H. O'Sullivan taken during the Wheeler Survey (1871-1879)—also known as the U.S. Geographical Surveys West of the 100th Meridan (RG 77.8).

Access: Open to the public. Researchers may use personal laptop or notebook computers, approved personal cameras and certain other personal research equipment. An on-site cafeteria and storage lockers are available for public use.

Guides/catalogs: U.S. National Archives and Records Administration, *Guide to Federal Records in the National Archives of the United States* (Washington, D.C.: 1996), 3 v. The text of this guide is now accessible on National Archives' websites; Barbara Lewis Burger (compiler), *Guide to the Holdings of the Still Picture Branch of the National Archives* (Washington, D.C.: 1990). This text is also available on National Archives' websites. Burger's guide covers photographs in the National Archives at College Park, Maryland, only—not those in the Regional Archives.

Description

The National Archives at College Park opened for public service in 1994. Many record groups have been transferred to College Park, both from the National Archives Building in Washington and from storage at the Washington National Records Center in Suitland, Maryland. Reference and other public services are available at both the National Archives Building in Washington, D.C., and at the National Archives at College Park. U.S. archival records of anthropological and related interest can be found at both the Washington, D.C., and the College Park Archives. The extensive records of the Bureau of Indian Affairs (RG 75), for example, remain at the National Archives, Washington, while Indian Division and Indian Territory Division records (RG 48) have been relocated to College Park. The latter materials are contained within the records of the Office of the Secretary of the Interior. Also at College Park are archival records of the National Park Service (RG 79) that contain materials of archaeological and anthropological interest.

The four National Archives units that house "special media" are at College Park. These are Cartographic and Architectural Records; Motion Picture, Sound and Video Records; Still Picture Records; and Electronic Records. While some photographs remain with the textual records to which they pertain, a majority of National Archives' still picture holdings are now in the Still Picture Branch at College Park.

The *Guide to Federal Records in the National Archives of the United States* will assist researchers in the identification of pertinent National Archives record groups. Many specialized guides and finding aids (published or unpublished) are also available. Information on National Archives holdings is increasingly available on the National Archives websites.

Information provided by Users Service Division, National Archives at College Park and by Robert M. Kvasnicka.

Maryland—Suitland

Smithsonian Institution. Libraries. Museum Support Center (MSC) **Branch**

Address: Museum Support Center Branch, Smithsonian Institution Libraries, Room C2000, MRC 534, 4210 Silverhill Road, Suitland, MD 20746.
Location: In Suitland Maryland—six miles southeast of the Smithsonian museums on the Mall in Washington, D.C.
E-mail: libmail@sil.si.edu.
Tel.: (301) 238-3666
Fax: (301) 238-3667
Internet address: http://www.sil.si.edu/mschp.htm.
Internet access to on-line catalog: http://www.siris.si.edu.
Public transit access: Call or e-mail the Branch Library for information.
Parking: On-site parking is available.
Access: Open to the public by appointment only.

[Also see some references to the **Museum Support Center Branch Library** under: **Smithsonian Insitution. Libraries** (District of Columbia).]

Massachusetts—Cambridge

Harvard University

Special research collections are maintained at some ninety Harvard University libraries, most of which are located in Cambridge or Boston. The URL of the Harvard University Libraries is http://www.harvard.edu/home.library.html. Harvard University's Tozzer Library (formerly the Peabody Museum Library) holds extensive book and journal collections in anthropology and related fields. Many Harvard University manuscript and archival resources in anthropology are curated on campus at the Peabody Museum of Archaeology and Ethnology (founded in 1866) and also at University Archives. The Dumbarton Oaks Research Libraries—which consist respectively of the Pre-Columbian Studies Library and the Byzantine Studies Library—are Harvard University facilities that are located in Washington, D.C. A brief entry on the Dumbarton Oaks libraries is included under the **District of Columbia** geographic heading in this guide. Research access to the Pre-Columbian Studies Library or the Byzantine Studies Library is limited and is by application only.

Harvard University. Loeb Music Library. Archive of World Music

Address: Archive of World Music, Loeb Music Library, Harvard University, Cambridge, MA 02138.
Tel.: (617) 495-2794

Fax: (617) 496-4636
Internet address: http://www.rism.harvard.edu/MusicLibrary/AWM/AWM.html.
Major resources: Ethnic and folk music recordings from throughout the world.
Areas of specialization: Areas of collection strength include field and commercial recordings from Asia and the Middle East.

Harvard University. Peabody Museum of Archaeology and Ethnology

Address: Peabody Museum of Archaeology and Ethnology, Harvard University, 11 Divinity Avenue, Cambridge, MA 02138.
Tel.: (617) 496-2994 (Archives); 495-3329 (Photographic Archives).
Fax: (617) 495-7535
Internet address: http://www.peabody.harvard.edu.
Internet access to on-line catalog: HOLLIS can be accessed at hollis.harvard.edu
Networks, consortia: HOLLIS, RLIN.
Public transit access: Red Line from Boston. Exit at Harvard Square.
Founded: 1866.
Major resources: Archives; Photographic Archives.
Areas of specialization: Many resources, including records of Harvard expeditions, the Carnegie Institution of Washington collection of archives and photographs.
Archives/manuscripts: Paper archives: ca. 760 linear ft. Also oversize maps, drawings, works of art on paper, etc.
Visual/audio resources: About 500,000 photo negatives and prints, including some 34,000 photo negatives; 140,000 mounted historical photographic prints of ethnographic interest; more than 600 4 x 5″ color transparancies. Also, about 16,000 35mm color slides. The Carnegie Institution Division of Historical Research Photo Collection contains some 42,000 photo negatives and corresponding prints.
Access: Available for research and public use. On-site visits are by appointment, at least two weeks in advance.
References: Curtis M. Hinsley, "From Shell-Heaps to Stelae: Early Anthropology at the Peabody Museum," in George W. Stocking, Jr. (editor), *Objects and Others: Essays on Museums and Material Culture* (Madison, Wis.: 1985) (= *History of Anthropology*, vol. 3), p. 49-74; Curtis M. Hinsley, "The Museum Origins of Harvard Anthropology, 1866-1915," in Clark A. Elliott and Margaret W. Rossiter (editors), *Science at Harvard University: Historical Perspectives* (Bethlehem, Pa.: 1992), p. 121-145; Charles Coleman Sellers, *Mr. Peale's Museum: Charles Willson Peale and the First Popular Museum of Natural Science and Art* (New York: 1980).
Guides/catalogs: Melissa Banta and Curtis M. Hinsley, *From Site to Sight: Anthropology, Photography, and the Power of Imagery: A Photographic Exhibition from the Collections of the Peabody Museum of Archaeology and Ethnology and the Department of Anthropology, Harvard University* (Cambridge, Mass.: 1986); Melissa Banta, et al., *A Timely Encounter: Nineteenth-Century Photographs of Japan: An Exhibition of Photographs from the Collections of the Peabody Museum of Archaeology and Ethnology and the Wellesley College Museum* (Cambridge, Mass.: 1988); "The Peabody Museum of Harvard University;

Photographic Resources," [folded brochure, undated]; Peabody Museum of Archaeology and Ethnology, Hillel S. Burger (photographer), Ian W. Brown (photographic annotator), Barbara Isaac (editor), *The Hall of the North American Indian: Change and Continuity* (Cambridge, Mass.: 1990); Elisabeth Sandager, *Guide to African-American and African Primary Sources at Harvard University and Radcliffe College* (Cambridge, Mass.: 1992). Also see finding aids on-line on the museum webpage.

Artifacts: Collection strengths include North, Central and South American Indian cultures. Also held are ethnographic materials from Africa and Oceania. Museum holdings of ethnographic objects number about 200,000 items, including some 75,000 Native North American objects, 36,000 Central and South American objects, 28,000 Oceanic objects and 25,000 African objects. Holdings of archaeological artifacts are very extensive.

Catalogs of artifacts: Garth Bawden and Geoffrey W. Conrad, *The Andean Heritage: Masterpieces of Peruvian Art from the Collections of the Peabody Museum* (Cambridge, Mass.: 1982); Hillel Burger (photographer), *Masterpieces of the Peabody Museum, Harvard University* (Cambridge, Mass.: 1978).

Description

Founded in 1866, the Peabody Museum of Archaeology and Ethnology is one of the oldest museums in this hemisphere devoted entirely to the disciplines of archaeology and ethnology. The Peabody houses collections of prehistoric and historic cultures from throughout the world. The largest collections focus on North, Central and South American indigenous cultures, with important ethnographic collections from Africa and Oceania as well. The museum archives includes accession files, expedition records, papers of individual anthropologists, exhibition materials and curatorial files in a wide range of formats and media. These documents reflect the activities of the museum, its affiliates and other well-known institutions and organizations.

Accession Files

The accession files and catalog entries are the Peabody's major source of information on the provenance of its collections. Accession file materials date to the museum's founding, 1866, and include correspondence, maps, charts, drawings, vocabularies, field notebooks, original inventory lists, unpublished research manuscripts, newspaper clippings, diaries, field photographs and studio views of artifacts from anthropological and archaeological expeditions. Historical museum exhibit labels (and corresponding artifacts) from the early Peale Museum of Philadelphia, as well as from the Peabody, also are preserved in the files. The accession files typically contain information on how an object was obtained, why it was sold or donated, what was known about it, the value the donor attributed to the object, and reference requests about it, among other things. Some of this information is restricted to museum staff.

FIGURE 5. Dance at Suva, Viti Levu, Fiji. Alexander Agassiz Expedition. Courtesy of the Peabody Museum, Harvard University (negative #28407).

Major supporting documentation exists for the following artifactual collections (dates reflect the approximate date span of documentation, not of the objects): American Antiquarian Society collection, 1890-1976; David I. Bushnell collection, 1923-1944; Mark R. Harrington collection, 1903-1910; Mary Hemenway Southwestern Archaeological Expedition, 1887-1894; Harriet and C.B. Cosgrove's Mimbres Valley Expeditions, New Mexico, 1924-1933; Grace Nicholson-Lewis Farlow collection, 1902-1946; Peale Museum/Boston Museum collection, 1804-1899; Edward Palmer collection, 1875-1880; Frederic W. Putnam papers (including Peabody Museum's expeditions to Ohio, 1879-1911, and collecting organized by Putnam for the World's Columbian Exposition of 1893); Patrick Putnam collection from the Belgian Congo, 1927-1963; E.H. Thompson collection from Chichén Itzá, 1890-1920; expeditions to Copán, 1892-1900; Awatovi (Arizona) Expedition, 1935-1939; Southwest Africa (Marshall) Expeditions, 1950-1959.

The Peabody's accession files therefore constitute an artifact of the record-keeping practices of a "scientific" museum. They not only illuminate a changing concept of what types of information were thought important to gather and preserve, but also provide significant insights into the emotional, intellectual and monetary values attached to objects. The accession files are an invaluable artifact of intellectual history as they relate to both the history of American museums and the scope and emphasis of the field of anthropology throughout the nineteenth- and twentieth-centuries.

Archival and Manuscript Collections

The archival collections of the Peabody Museum constitute a central resource for the histories of the various subfields of anthropology in the United States during the past century and for the institutional and social history of the Harvard University community as well. Early letterbooks of incoming correspondence to museum directors, 1866-1879, total several thousand letters. Supplementing these are daybooks kept by Jeffries Wyman (the first curator, 1866-1874) and Frederic W. Putnam (Wyman's successor, 1875-1915), as well as original trustee minutes. Documentary holdings relating specifically to archaeological collections include correspondence and drawings concerning the Mary Hemenway Expedition and the museum's work on the so-called "Moundbuilder" sites between the 1860s and the 1890s. Taken together, the records for the years until 1890 provide a detailed picture of the internal operations of the country's first museum of anthropology and, externally, of the nature of the anthropological community of the late nineteenth-century.

Beginning in the 1890s, the museum expanded the scope of its research to embrace Central America. The archives grew accordingly in size and variety. An example can be found in the correspondence and notebooks of Charles Pickering Bowditch, 1890-1921, which not only monitor the evolution of the Peabody Museum into Harvard Anthropology, but also trace, institutionally and theoretically, the formative years of Central American archaeology.

Among the protégés of Bowditch (a central figure in Harvard Anthropology until 1950) was Alfred M. Tozzer (1877-1954). His papers (e.g., correspondence, diaries, scrapbooks, covering the years from 1900 to 1948) span virtually the entire anthropological profession (e.g., William Gates, Frans F. Blom and J.E.S. Thompson). In addition, the papers of Herbert J. Spinden and Edward H. Thompson (regarding the latter's work for the museum in Yucatán, from 1890 to 1920) are included. Other noteworthy collections include Adela C. Breton's watercolors of murals at Chichén Itzá, and correspondence, 1904-1923; and Tatiana Proskouriakoff's research notebooks, correspondence, unpublished manuscripts and watercolors, 1935-1985. The records of the Carnegie Institute of Washington, 1914-1958, constitute a substantial part of the museum's archives. Types of materials range from original diaries and notebooks of Sylvanus G. Morley and others, to works of art on paper.

Documentary holdings relating to Harvard's archaeological research in Europe and Asia are limited in scope, but nonetheless significant because they record initial efforts by Americans in this area. They include correspondence and catalogs from Gabriel de Mortillet regarding his systematic collection of Neolithic and Bronze Age artifacts, 1860s; extensive papers of Hallam L. Movius, especially from his fieldwork in Burma, 1937-1940, and at La Colombière, 1948-1950, and the Abri Pataud, 1953-1963, France; correspondence and other research papers of Hugh O'Neill Hencken relating to the Harvard Irish Survey, 1930-1936; and project records of Robert W. Ehrich and Vladimir J. Fewkes's excavations at Homolka and other Neolithic sites in Bohemia, 1929-1940. Other European materials include catalog data and acquisition records, 1908-1940, for the Duchess of Mecklenburg's Iron Age collection from Slovenia.

In addition, the Peabody preserves the administrative and research records of the American School of Prehistoric Research (ASPR), a multi-institutional consortium of Old World scholars that includes noted Harvard archaeologists such as Hallam L. Movius (European Paleolithic), Hugh O'Neill Hencken (Iron Age Europe and North Africa), Robert W. Ehrich (Eastern European archeology and ethnology), C.C. Lamberg-Karlovsky (Near East and Western Asia), Lauriston Ward (East Asia) and K.C. Chang (East Asia). Other ASPR holdings include papers of non-Harvard scholars Henry Field (Near East) and George Grant MacCurdy (European Paleolithic).

There are also several small but significant holdings reflecting African ethnographic collecting and archaeological fieldwork. Included are correspondence, copies of fieldnotes, reports and other records of the Lorna and Laurence Marshall, 1950-1959, and John Yellen Expeditions, 1968-1970, to southwest Africa; ethnographic notes and correspondence from George Schwab and George Harley's "Harvard Expedition to Liberia" in 1928, and correspondence, manuscripts, research notes, etc., concerning the work of Lloyd Cabot Briggs among the Tuareg people of Algeria and on the prehistory of northwest Africa.

Archival holdings that document archaeological work in North America include papers of former museum directors: comprehensive field survey data from Donald Scott's work on petroglyphs in Africa and the southwestern United States, 1934-1967; excavation data for John Otis Brew's expeditions to Awatovi, 1935-1939, the Upper Gila region of Arizona, 1938, and southwest Utah, 1931-1933; and published and unpublished data from Stephen Williams, Jeffrey Brain and Ian Brown's work with the Lower Mississippi Survey, 1954-1990.

The subfield of physical anthropology at Harvard is well documented in the Archives. This tradition began in the late nineteenth-century with the relatively unknown work of a Harvard physician, D.A. Sargent, who collected somatological data on various populations, and continued with the well-publicized efforts of Earnest A. Hooton (1887-1954) in the first half of the twentieth-century. His research—which is represented in the Archives by extensive correspondence, manuscripts and anthropometric data—culminated in many scholarly as well as popular publications. During the 1920s, physiological and sociological information on families of mixed race was gathered by Caroline Bond Day, under Hooton's direction. Albert Damon carried on with studies of Harvard athletes and a longitudinal study of child health and development. His research went largely unpublished due to his untimely death. Most recently, W.W. Howells's project records from expeditions to the Solomon Islands in 1966, 1968 and 1970, and other research papers have been added to the Archives.

All or parts of some archival collections are closed for reasons of privacy or while processing is underway. Please consult the Archivist on issues of access.

Photographic Archives

The Photographic Archives house what is estimated to be at least 500,000 images, ranging in date from 1850 to the present, and in all media from daguerreotypes to safety film. The collection includes a series of black-and-white negatives consisting of both glass and safety film, a series of 4 x 5" color transparencies, a series of 35mm slides and two series of mounted prints. In addition, there are discrete collections, such as the Carnegie photographic negatives and mounted prints, and more than 300 inventoried boxes consisting of mixed media and albums.

The photo collections reflect the intellectual interests represented by the other museum holdings. They embody some of the earliest uses of photography for the purposes of anthropology. In addition to supporting the archives and manuscript collections mentioned above, the Photographic Archives include the following: an extensive photographic record of J.O. Brew's excavations at Awatovi in the 1930s, and also relating to Steven Williams's work on the Lower Mississippi Survey, from the 1940s to the present. Holdings from Meso-America include eleven albums reflecting the research of John G. Owens and George Byron Gordon during the first Honduras Expedition of the late nineteenth-century; and negatives taken by Teoberto Maler in Petén and Usumacinta Valley, Guatemala, 1892-1907.

The field of physical anthropology is represented by many images originally collected by Louis Agassiz—principal antagonist of Charles Darwin in the United States—and his son, Alexander, who succeeded him as director of the Museum of Comparative Zoology, Harvard. Significant collections include fifteen daguerreotypes of African-born slaves, photographed in South Carolina in the 1850s; two albums depicting residents of Manaus, Brazil, in 1865; and numerous *cartes-de-visite* from around the world.

Holdings relating to social/cultural anthropology are similarly varied. One of the earliest in-depth collections is that of W. Cameron Forbes, Governor-General of the Philippines, 1909-1913. Two major collections (more than 3,000 negatives each) were created by Owen Lattimore and Frederic Wulsin, both while traveling in Inner Mongolia in the 1920s. Cora Alice DuBois, a former Harvard professor of anthropology, donated 900 negatives taken during her fieldwork in Indonesia in the 1930s. Another significant body of photographs was produced as a result of the Chiapas Project, under the direction of Evon Vogt. This project entailed an ambitious aerial survey, covering 6,400 square miles of southeastern Mexico, that was taken in 1963.

In addition to the photographic resources in the Photo Archives, additional photographic documentation, much of which depicts artifact or material culture holdings of the museum, is preserved in the Archives Department, described above. Any visitor researching a particular topic of interest should contact each of the museum archives in order to make sure that no relevant documentation is overlooked. Contact the Photo Archivist at (617) 495-3329. Please contact the Collections Department Archivist at (617) 496-2994 for information about museum accession files and other archival and manuscript collections.

Elizabeth Sandager and Barbara Isaac
Information provided by Sarah Demb.

Harvard University. University Archives

Address: University Archives, Pusey Library, Harvard University, Cambridge, MA 02138.
Tel.: (617) 495-2461
Fax: (617) 495-8011
Internet address: http://hul.harvard.edu/huarc.
Internet access to on-line catalog: Descriptions of holdings of the Harvard University Archives have been entered in HOLLIS, which can be accessed at hollis.harvard.edu.
Networks, consortia: Harvard University Library, with which the University Archives is associated, participates (in varying ways) in OCLC and RLIN. Descriptions of the Archives' holdings (as of about 1986) are accessible through RLIN; for a more up-to-date catalog, HOLLIS (Harvard On-Line Library Information System) should be used.
Public transit access: Subway: Red Line from Boston—exit at Harvard Square.
Founded: Preservation of the historical records of the university began in the mid-nineteenth-century. In 1939 the Governing Boards of the university formally established the Archives as a unit of the library.
Major resources: See below.
Areas of specialization: The Harvard Archives is the repository for official records of the university, papers of tenured members of the university faculty and other materials that are related to the history of Harvard. Sources relating to anthropology and cognate fields are collected within the scope of this mandate.
Archives/manuscripts: The total holdings of the University Archives is about 65,000 linear ft.
Visual/audio resources: See below.
Access: The University Archives is opened to all researchers; they are required to register upon entry to the repository. Some materials are restricted. Official university records less than fifty years old require permission of the current department or office head for access. Terms of access to faculty collections vary, depending on the wishes of the donors. A substantial portion of the Archives' holdings are stored off campus and require 24 hours for retrieval. All users are urged to contact the Archives prior to a research visit.
References: Clark A. Elliott, "The Further Study of Harvard Science (1636-1945): Sources and Suggestions," in Clark A. Elliott and Margaret W. Rossiter (editors), *Science at Harvard University: Historical Perspectives* (Bethlehem, Pa.: 1992), p. 301-330; Clark A. Elliott, "Sources for the History of Science in the Harvard University Archives," *Harvard Library Bulletin*, vol. 22 (Jan. 1974), p. 49-71; Harvard University. Archives, *User's Guide*. [This

and several other guides on particular aspects of the Archives are available from the repository.]

Description

In addition to official records of the university, University Archives collections include personal and professional papers of faculty members, records of student and other affiliated clubs and organizations and printed material by and about the university. There are also small unpublished manuscript items relating to various topics. Types of materials found among the holdings include minutes, correspondence, financial and student records, notes and manuscripts and a range of other types of textual documents, as well as photographs, motion pictures and audio and video tapes.

The resources of the University Archives are directed toward the support of historical research, and the disciplines of anthropology, archaeology and cognate areas are encompassed to the degree that they have been practiced within the university. Generally, the University Archives defers to the university's Peabody Museum of Archaeology and Ethnology for the collection and preservation of fieldnotes and other data.

Sometimes potentially useful pieces of information might show up in unexpected places. For example, in the American colonial era and in the early republic, Harvard supported work among Native American groups, and reports of the missionaries are found among the Archives' holdings. These represent incidental happenings. It was not until 1866 that a substantial gift from George Peabody led to the establishment of the museum named for him. Thereafter, the records of the Peabody Museum and the papers of its teaching faculty and curators represent the primary documentary source for the history of anthropology and ethnology at Harvard. The University Archives shares with the Peabody Museum responsibility for preservation of this historical record—the museum itself generally retaining records that document its artifact holdings. The divisions of effort are not absolute, however, and researchers should consult both repositories.

The records of the Peabody Museum, as found in the University Archives, include minutes of the Trustees and other bodies, beginning with the museum's establishment in 1866. Especially important are holdings of the correspondence of early curators/directors: Jeffries Wyman (1814-1874), Asa Gray (1810-1888), Frederic W. Putnam (1839-1915) and Charles C. Willoughby (1857-1943), covering the period 1866-1928. The Archives' holdings for the museum directors after that date are sparse. Other records for the Peabody Museum include miscellaneous financial records, as well as catalogs of the museum's collections (duplicates of those maintained by the museum). Records of the museum library are extensive and cover the years 1884-1984.

The official records of the university also include those of the academic Department of Anthropology, which is administratively separate from the Peabody Museum. These departmental records date from 1890, the period of its establishment, but overall are rather miscellaneous in character. They include correspondence, budgetary material and student records (restricted). The department materials also incorporate course records, including syllabi and other items, for the years 1955-1984. The Department of Social Relations, in existence from 1946-1972, encompassed some aspects of anthropology, and the Archives has its records. Furthermore, the Archives' general collection on the curriculum will contain materials relating to anthropology and cognate areas (e.g., there are anthropology course reading lists for the years 1926-1974). Small amounts of miscellaneous material on the Anthropological Society (established 1898) and the Folklore Club (established 1897) are with the collections on Harvard clubs and societies.

Among the chief sources for the history of anthropology are the personal and professional papers of individual faculty members. For the nineteenth-century, the papers of Frederic W. Putnam are the major source; these complement his records as head of the Peabody Museum. While some of Putnam's correspondence and other papers relate to the museum, they also contain much about other professional concerns, including the anthropology exhibits at the World's Columbian Exposition (1893), which Putnam headed; the American Museum of Natural History; the University of California at Berkeley; his teaching and research and other activities.

Faculty collections of the twentieth-century include those of Alfred M. Tozzer (1877-1954), especially relating to his teaching (e.g., undergraduate superstitions). The papers of Alfred V. Kidder (1885-1963) include Kidder's diaries, covering 1896-1963, and relate to his field work in the American Southwest and Mexico. One of the most important collections for the history of anthropology is the papers of Clyde K.M. Kluckhohn (1905-1960), which covers the years 1930-1960. In addition to general professional correspondence, the Kluckhohn collection contains material relating to the Values Study and Navaho Study (Ramah Project), including fieldnotes of Kluckhohn and others. The papers of John Otis Brew (1906-1988), covering the years 1936-1977, include series relating to persons and organizations (e.g., the Massachusetts Archaeological Society), to Brew's Lowell Institute lectures on museums in New England (1959), and to the Values Study. [Extensive research materials relating to the Ramah Project are at the Laboratory of Anthropology, Museum of New Mexico, Santa Fe. Additional J.O. Brew papers are at the Museum of Anthropology, University of Arizona.]

The Harvard Archives has small collections of several other faculty members in anthropology, including Cora Alice DuBois (1903-1991), although the bulk of her papers are at the Peabody Museum; Earnest A. Hooton (1887-1954); and Donald Scott (1879-1967), who was director of the Peabody Museum. The papers of professor of anthropology Evon Vogt (1918-   ), and professor of archaeology Gordon Willey (1913-   ) are also in the University Archives. The teaching materials of professor of anthropology Stephen Williams (1926-   ) also have been accessioned.

The field of archaeology is represented among the Archives' holdings by correspondence, memoranda, reports and other records of the Archaeological Exploration of Sardis—an excavation project in Turkey jointly sponsored by Harvard and Cornell University; the records cover the period 1956-1981. A related source in the Archives is the substantial collection of personal and professional papers of George M.A. Hanfmann (1911-1986), who directed the Sardis project. The Hanfmann papers, covering the period 1927-1985, contain correspondence, reports, field notebooks and other materials relating to Sardis and other topics and concerns—such as his teaching; and to Harvard and other institutions, e.g., the Boston Museum of Fine Arts.

Other collections in archaeology held by the Archives include the papers of George Chase (1874-1952) in classical archaeology—e.g., correspondence relating to the

Archaeological Institute of America; Ernst Kitzinger (1912-   ), who was professor of Byzantine art and archaeology; and a small collection of the papers of Egyptologist George A.R. Reisner (1867-1942). The Archives' holdings also include records of the Harvard Semitic Museum—especially for the period 1891-1935—and the papers of David Gordon Lyon (1852-1935), who was curator of the Semitic Museum.

Clark A. Elliott

Harvard University. Tozzer Library

Address: Tozzer Library, Harvard University, 21 Divinity Ave., Cambridge, MA 02138.
Tel.: (617) 495-2253 (Public Services)
Fax: (617) 496-2741
Internet access to on-line catalog: Records of nearly all book holdings are accessible on HOLLIS at hollis.harvard.edu.
Public transit access: Subway: Red Line from Boston—exit at Harvard Square.
Founded: 1866. Formerly the Peabody Museum Library.
Holdings: Ca. 185,000 v.

Massachusetts—Waltham

National Archives—Northeast Region (Boston)

Address: National Archives—Northeast Region, 380 Trapelo Road, Waltham, MA 02154.
Location: At the Federal Records Center in Waltham, Massachusetts—10 miles from downtown Boston.
Tel.: (781) 647-8100
Fax: (781) 647-8460
E-mail: archives@waltham.nara.gov.
Internet address: http://www.nara.gov/regional/boston.html.
Founded: 1969.
Major resources: Archived federal records for the New England Region, consisting of Connecticut, Maine, Massachusetts, New Hampshire, Rhode Island and Vermont.
Holdings: More than 24,000 cubic ft. of original federal records; also additional federal records on microfilm. A limited number of records may be of anthropological interest.
Access: The great majority of holdings are open for public research. Restrictions on access to some federal records may be applied in accord with exemptions in the Freedom of Information Act. It is strongly recommended that readers call a few days in advance of a visit to arrange for the availability of needed records.

University of Michigan. Harlan Hatcher Graduate Library. Special Collections Library
University of Michigan. Bentley Historical Library

Address: Harlan Hatcher Graduate Library, University of Michigan, Ann Arbor, MI 48109-1612; Michigan Historical Collections, Bentley Historical Library, University of Michigan, 1150 Beal Avenue, Ann Arbor, MI 48109-2133.

Tel.: (313) 764-9356 (Southeast Asia, Harlan Hatcher Graduate Library); (313) 764 3482 (Bentley Historical Library).

Fax: (313) 763-5080 (Harlan Hatcher Library); (313) 936-1333 (Bentley Historical Library).

Internet address (Special Collections Library): http://www.lib.umich.edu/libhome/SpecColl.lib/spec_coll.html.

Internet address (Graduate Library. Southeast Asia Division): http://www.lib.umich.edu/libhome/Area.Programs/Southeast.Asia/index.html.

Internet address (Bentley Historical Library): http://www.umich.edu/~bhl/bhl/bhlmenu.htm.

Internet address (Museum of Anthropology): http://www.umma.lsa.umich.edu.

Internet address (Kelsey Museum of Archaeology): http://www.umich.edu/~kelseydb.

Internet access to on-line catalog (MIRLYN): http://www.lib.umich.edu/libhome.mirlyn.mirlynpage.html.

Networks, consortia: RLIN, OCLC, CIC, CRL, VEL, MRLT.

Founded: 1817 (founding of the University of Michigan).

Major resources: The Worcester Philippine Collection (located in Rare Books and Special Collections, 711 Harlan Hatcher Graduate Library); Thai (Gedney) Collection (in Hatcher Graduate Library); Asian Division (in the Museum of Anthropology, 4009 Museums); Kelsey Museum of Archaeology (434 South State Street).

Areas of specialization: Philippine, Thai and other Southeast Asian ethnology, archaeology, literature, religion, folklore, linguistics, government and history.

Holdings: 30,000 volumes (books and journals) in Hatcher Graduate Library; 1,250 titles (books and journals) in Hatcher Special Collections Library; 14 linear ft. of archival materials in Hatcher Library Archives. The Worcester papers (4 linear ft.) are in Bentley Historical Library.

Archives/manuscripts: Worcester Philippine Collection; Thai (Gedney) Collection.

Visual/audio resources: See below.

Access: Open to the public.

References: Karl L. Hutterer, "Dean C. Worcester and Philippine Anthropology," *Philippine Quarterly of Culture and Society*, vol. 6, no. 3 (Sept. 1978), p. 125-156; Giok Po Oey, *Survey of Southeast Asian Collections, November 1977-January 1978* (Ithaca, N.Y.: 1982); David K. Wyatt, "Report of Appraisal: William J. Gedney Collection, Ann Arbor, MI. Submitted to the Center for South and Southeast Asian Studies, January 1973," unpublished report.

Guides/catalogs: Marjorie Barritt (compiler), *American-Philippine Relations: A Guide to the Resources in the Michigan Historical Collections* (Ann Arbor: 1982); Thomas Powers, *Balita Mula Maynila = News from Manila* (Ann Arbor: 1971) (= *Michigan Historical*

Collections. Bulletin, no. 19; *Center for South and Southeast Asian Studies. Special Publication*, no. 1); Fe Susan Go, et al., *The Thai (Gedney) Collection of the University of Michigan Library: A Union Catalogue* (Ann Arbor: 1987); Langolm Warner, "Mr. Worcester's Recent Finds in the Philippines," [an article published in Philadelphia, 1922—the journal title not identified], p. 9-15; David K. Wyatt, "Checklist of Thai-Language Serials in the William J. Gedney Library, the University of Michigan,"—an unpublished report, 1969.

Artifacts of anthropological significance: The Asian Division of the Museum of Anthropology holds all of the university's artifact collections from Asia. Most notable is the Philippine Collection, which encompasses not only artifacts collected during various archaeological excavations, but also a variety of artifacts in the divisions of Paleontology and Zoology. The artifacts in the latter two divisions date as early as the first (1899) University of Michigan expedition to the Philippines, led by Carl E. Guthe. Resources in the Herbarium supplement the collections in the Museum of Anthropology. The Museum of Art has a sizable collection of art from Thailand, Cambodia and Indonesia. The Stearns Collection, located in the School of Music, consists of musical instruments from various parts of Asia. Instrumental resources include a complete gamelan ensemble, various old Philippine musical instruments, and also some collections of musical instruments from Thailand, Laos and Cambodia.

Archaeological sites represented in collections: The Museum of Anthropology houses the major artifact collection on campus. Sites represented here include the burial caves in Luzon, where Carl E. Guthe carried out excavations, and also the Negros Oriental excavation site that was investigated in the early 1980s by a group lead by Karl Hutterer. There is also a complete field catalog, 1922-1925, of the University of Michigan Philippine Expedition.

Selected catalogs of artifact resources: H. Otley Beyer and Evett D. Hester, *Preliminary Catalog of the Hester Collection of Ceramic Wares* (Manila: 1937)—this work describes the historical development of the Hester ceramics collection; Evett D. Hester, *Catalog of the Hester Collection of Ceramic Wares: Jeffersonville Section* (Chicago: 1957)—the E.D. Hester ceramics collection was formed while Hester was in the Philippines as a member of the High Commission—the ceramics were found in Luzon between 1930 and 1945; Aga-Oglu Kamer, *The Williams Collection of Far Eastern Ceramics* (Ann Arbor: 1972).

Description

The Worcester Collections

There are two Worcester Collections at the University of Michigan. One is in the Special Collections Library, a unit of the Harlan Hatcher Graduate Library, while the other is on North Campus at the Michigan Historical Collections—otherwise known as the Bentley Historical Library. Each collection is distinct, but each should be used in combination with the other for a wider view of Dean C. Worcester (1866-1924) and his role in the evolutionary development of the Philippines under American rule. The following discussion describes the Worcester Philippine Collection in the Special Collections Library. The Bentley Worcester Collection on North Campus has been fully described in two published guides: *Balita Mula*

Maynila = News from Manila, by Tom Powers; and *American-Philippine Relations*, compiled by Marjorie Barritt.

The Worcester Philippine Collection in Special Collections at Hatcher Library is the rubric within which several different collections that pertain to American involvement in the Philippines are grouped.

The development of the Worcester Collection at the university began in 1914, when Dean C. Worcester donated part of his personal library to the Graduate Library. This collection has subsequently been expanded through donations and purchases. The emphasis of the collection is on the American role in Philippine history during the period from 1890 to 1930, although seventeenth-century Jesuit letters from their mission, reports of an expedition to the "wild tribes" of the Philippines, and other materials are also held.

The Philippine manuscript collection at the university also began in 1914, with the donation of personal manuscripts by Dean C. Worcester. The Philippine manuscript collection now consists of three components: the Worcester papers, the H.H. Bartlett collection and the Lanzar-Carpio collection.

Within the Worcester papers is the original Worcester collection that spanned the period from 1834 to 1915; and also the Worcester family papers that extend chronologically from ca. 1740 until 1940. The family papers are primarily records of Worcester family activities as gleaned through correspondence, diaries, sermons and photographs. These materials span several generations of Worcester family history—from Dean C. Worcester's great grandparents to his children.

Dean Worcester's first field experience in Asia occurred in 1887. While still an undergraduate at the University of Michigan, he accompanied a zoological expedition to the Philippines under the direction of Joseph B. Steere. Worcester returned to the Philippines in 1890 as a member of the Louis Menage expedition that was directed by Frank S. Bourns. Worcester's first-hand experience in the Philippines, and his visibility following the publication of his first book, *The Philippine Islands and Their People* (New York: 1898), led to his appointment by William McKinley as a member of the High Commission that investigated and decided the future of the Philippines. He subsequently served as Secretary of the Interior of the Insular Government.

The bulk of the manuscript collection concerns the period from 1899 to 1913. The Worcester Collection in the Graduate Library consists of 1,700 printed items and manuscripts that relate to all phases of Philippine life and history. The manuscripts are bound into 24 volumes and include such topics as "Slavery and Peonage," "Voting in the Philippines," etc. The "Slavery and Peonage" topic includes Worcester's investigation of who in the Philippines owned "slaves" and what differing concepts of "slavery" existed in the Philippines. This section also covers the papers and photographs that Worcester used to produce his two-volume work, *The Philippines Past and Present* (New York: 1914).

The collection also includes the unpublished ethnographic survey of the Philippines, submitted by anthropologists who were commissioned by, and worked for, Worcester. It is one of the most valuable ethnographic surveys ever made in the Philippines. This documentation is also a good source for tracking down early anthropologists, and for study of the research methodologies that they used.

Also of importance is the slide and photograph collection that was assembled by Worcester himself. These resources (in the Museum of Anthropology) consist of more than

5,000 negatives gathered by Worcester. The photo collection, described in an article by Karl Hutterer (1978), documents the everyday life of the Filipinos, including the rural and mountain peoples of Luzon, depicting their various cultures and habitats. The slides and photos give a glimpse of everyday life in the Philippines, incorporating the indigenous as well as Spanish and American influences.

The H.H. Bartlett collection, ca. 1899-1916, and other manuscripts have been added to the collection. The Bartlett collection (one box) is primarily typescript copies of articles and reports concerning political and military events and social issues of the period. The Bartlett Special Collections materials complement the Bartlett journals in the Michigan Historical Collection. These contain intensive observations on the same topics. A large collection of printed Southeast Asian materials, of interest for studies in languages, linguistics and other topics, was collected by Bartlett (1886-1960) during his career. This collection is now at the American Philosophical Society in Philadelphia.

The collection under the name of Maria Lanzar-Carpio consists of the Lanzar-Carpio papers, the Herbert Welsh papers, 1895-1913, and the Winslow Anti-Imperialist League papers, 1903-1922. These collections were named after Lanzar-Carpio, since she was the person who collected the various materials.

The Herbert Welsh papers consist of 765 items. Included are correspondence and documents relating to the efforts of the Anti-Imperialist League—a group that was opposed to the American occupation of the Philippines. The correspondence, mainly from League members, gives insight into the character of the Anti-Imperialist League.

The Winslow papers, named after Alfred E. Winslow, who was Anti-Imperialist League secretary, further document the activities of the Anti-Imperialist movement. Winslow's personal correspondence with well-known American educators and politicians (such as Moorfield Storey, Elihu Root and Charles Francis Adams) offers further insights into the discourse of the Anti-Imperialist League movement. The correspondence spans the years 1903-1922.

The Thai (Gedney) Collection

The Thai (William J. Gedney) Collection consists of 6,038 monographic and serial titles dating as far back as 1837, when printing in Thailand was in its infancy. The collection also contains 73 manuscripts. This collection was formed by professor Gedney in the course of his teaching career at the university, and during his research (much of it in the field) on the Thai language and Tai linguistics. The main emphasis of the Gedney Collection falls between 1920 and 1954—years during which the Thai printing industry flourished. The subject matter spans all aspects of Thai life, but with special concentration on Theravada Buddhism, folklore, history and literature. A majority of the monographs are cremation volumes—i.e., books that usually contain biographical information on the life of the deceased person, followed by one or more texts reprinted from traditional literary or religious classics. Cremation volumes are good sources for biographies and also for hard-to-find literary or religious classics.

Sermons of prominent Buddhist monks, and their interpretations of the meaning of the Tripitaka in daily life figure, prominently in the Gedney monographic collection. The development of Buddhism in Thailand, and the patterns of Thai politics, government and daily life, are also documented in these imprints. The collection also bears witness to the literary and linguistic development of the Thai people. The works are mostly in a poetic style called *klon* (a style which is fast disappearing in modern Thai poetry), and topics include Thai folk beliefs, culture and morals.

A collection of accordion-folded manuscripts written in ink or chalk, mostly during the nineteenth-century, is also held. The themes of these accordion manuscripts concentrate on the Tripitaka, on medical techniques and various herbal medicines to be applied to the body. All of these manuscripts are in the old Thai style of writing.

The Thai (Gedney) serials collection consists mostly of scattered issues of Thai journals and newspapers published during the years before World War II. Most of these are unavailable elsewhere, even in Thailand itself. A checklist of these serials was compiled by David K. Wyatt in 1969.

Aside from books and serials, the Gedney Collection also includes documentation of William J. Gedney's unpublished linguistic research that includes tape recordings, field notebooks and an index of the notebooks on 3 x 5" slips. These fieldnotes and related materials will be transferred to the Hatcher Special Collections Library when editorial work with them has been completed.

The Gedney fieldnotes contain documentation on the languages and dialects of the Tai language family that extends over much of Mainland Southeast Asia, as well as into southeastern China. In his field research, Gedney was meticulous in documenting his informants' use of the particular language. He elicited tonal sounds and also cultural and historical information about each language in the Tai language group. As examples of particular languages in context, Gedney recorded folktales, songs and poetry. Data on each language was entered in a journal that he kept, and each new word he encountered was indexed, syllable-by-syllable, on 3 x 5" slips.

Languages that were studied in depth include the Yay, Saek, Lü, Western Nung and the Tai dialect of Lunming, China. Other languages that were studied, and for which there are significant data, are Shan, Tai dialects from Kwangsi, White, Black and Red Tai. Most of Gedney's research on Yay, Saek, Lü and Western Nung has been published in five volumes of the Michigan Papers on South and Southeast Asia monograph series, edited by Thomas J. Hudak.

Fe Susan Go

Minnesota—Minneapolis

University of Minnesota, Twin Cities. Institute of International Studies and Programs. Refugee Studies Center (RSC)

Address: Refugee Studies Center, University of Minnesota, 104 Nicholson Hall, 216 Pillsbury Drive, S.E., Minneapolis, MN 55455.
Tel.: (612) 625-5535
Fax: (612) 626-1730
E-mail: refugee@maroon.tc.umn.edu.

Internet address: http://www.isp.acad.umn.edu/RSC/rsc.html.

Catalog: A small database of references to documentation on Hmong and other Asian refugee groups in the U.S. is maintained. Searches can be made by appointment with program staff.

Public transit access: Call the Center for public transit information.

Founded: In 1980, as the Southeast Asian Refugee Studies Project (SARS).

Major resources: The Southeast Asian Refugee Studies Archive—includes on-line records of about 4,700 articles, monographs and other information sources on Southeast Asian refugees in the U.S.

Areas of specialization: The program's initial focus was on Hmong refugees from Laos—many of whom resettled in the Twin Cities area in the 1970s. Information on other Southeast Asian refugee groups (Lao, Cambodian, Vietnamese, Burmese and Tibetan) is included in the Archive, and efforts are underway to include within RSC programs newly-arriving refugees from Bosnia, Somalia, the former Soviet Union and Sudan.

Holdings: Ca. 4,700 books, manuscripts and articles; newspaper clippings.

Visual/audio resources: A few videos of local (Twin Cities-area) Hmong New Year observances are held.

Access: Open to researchers by appointment. Materials must be used on the premises.

Guides/catalogs: Laura M. Boyer, *The Older Generation of Southeast Asian Refugees: An Annotated Bibliography* (Minneapolis, Minn.: 1991) (= *Southeast Asian Refugee Studies Occasional Paper*, no. 11); Marjorie A. Muecke, *Bibliography, Nursing Research and Practice with Refugees* (Minneapolis, Minn.: 1990) (= *Southeast Asian Refugee Studies Occasional Paper*, no. 10; *University of Minnesota. Center for Urban and Regional Affairs. Publication*, no. CURA 90-13); J. Christina Smith, *The Hmong, 1987-1995: A Selected and Annotated Bibliography* (Minneapolis, Minn.: 1996) (= *University of Minnesota. Refugee Studies Center. Occasional Papers* Series); J. Christina Smith, *The Hmong: An Annotated Bibliography, 1983-1987* (Minneapolis, Minn.: 1988) (= *Southeast Asian Refugee Studies Occasional Paper*, no. 7; *University of Minnesota. Center for Urban and Regional Affairs. Publication*, no. CURA 88-6). The Center publishes a newsletter, *Refugee Review*, which lists recent Center activities.

Description

The Refugee Studies Center at the University of Minnesota promotes multidisciplinary collaborations among faculty, students, service providers and educators interested in refugee populations and their resettlement. The Center database includes records of the 4,700 items in the RSC Archive. A collection of newspaper clippings from the Twin Cities area documents the resettlement of Cambodian, Hmong, Lao, Vietnamese and Tibetan refugees in Minnesota and elsewhere in the U.S.

Jane Bennett

University of Minnesota, Twin Cities. Libraries

Address: O. Meredith Wilson Library, University of Minnesota, 309 19th Avenue South, Minneapolis, MN 55455-0414.

Tel.: (612) 624-4520 (Wilson Library); (612) 624-4857 (Ames Library of South Asia, S-10 Wilson Library); (612) 624-1528 (James Ford Bell Library, 462 Wilson Library); (612) 624-0562 (University Archives, 10 Walter Library).

Fax: (612) 626-9353

Internet address (Ames Library of South Asia): http://www.lib.umn.edu/ames.

Internet address (James Ford Bell Library): http://www.bell.lib.umn.edu.

Networks, consortia: RLG, RLIN, OCLC, CIC, NOTIS, MINITEX, MULS, CONSER.

Public transit access: Available from downtown Minneapolis and St. Paul.

Founded: 1851.

Major resources: Ames Library of South Asia; James Ford Bell Library; University Archives.

Areas of Specialization: South Asia (Ames Library); history of European expansion prior to 1800 (Bell Library).

Holdings: Ames Library of South Asia: 150,000 v., 1,600 rare books, 220 manuscript collections, 1,600 pamphlets; James Ford Bell Library: 15,000 v., 2,500 manuscripts, 2,000 maps.

Archives/manuscripts: The University Archives contains a few items of anthropological interest, such as the personal papers, 1945-1947, 1949-1956 and 1958-1964, of Helen P. Mudgett (1900-1962)—including fieldnotes and recordings relating to the Red Lake Band of the Chippewa (29 folders); the professional papers, 1927-1934, of Albert E. Jenks (1869-1953), Chair of the Department of Anthropology between 1918 and 1938—includes fieldnotes relating to research in North Africa, Europe and the United States (1 box); field notebooks (42 v.) of the Geological and Natural History Survey of Minnesota, conducted between 1893 and 1918. The Wilford Archaeology Laboratory (S-48 Ford Hall) contains field notebooks of J.V. Brower, J. Clark, H. Colby, L. Hakkerup, T.H. Lewis, C. McLennan, L.A. Wilford and R. Wing pertaining to archaeological research at Galaz site in New Mexico, 1929-1933, and the midwestern United States—especially in Minnesota and adjacent states. There is also an extensive collection of cultural resource management reports.

Access: Materials are accessible to general readers and to scholars for research use. Materials must be used in the library.

Reference: *James Ford Bell and His Books: The Nucleus of a Library* (Minneapolis, Minn.: 1993).

Guides/catalogs: Ames Library of South Asia, *Catalog of the Ames Library of South Asia, University of Minnesota* (Boston: 1980), 16 v.; James Ford Bell Library, *The James Ford Bell Library: An Annotated Catalog of Original Source Materials Relating to the History of European Expansion, 1400-1800* (2nd ed., Minneapolis: 1994).

Artifacts: The Wilford Archaeology Laboratory, tel. (612) 625-1062, maintains a teaching collection of archaeological materials from the Galaz site in New Mexico, 1929-1933, and the midwestern United States—especially Minnesota and adjacent states. Smaller collections are available from Ghila Kazan in Pakistan, southern Jordan and the Veraguas region of Panama.

Archaeological sites associated with artifact holdings: Galaz site, New Mexico, 1929-1933.

Catalogs of artifact resources: Selected specimens from the Galaz Mimbres pottery collection are illustrated in J.J. Brody, Catherine J. Scott and Steven A. LeBlanc, *Mimbres Pottery: Ancient Art of the American Southwest: Essays* (New York: 1983). Two graduate theses are based on the Galaz site materials: Robert W. Keyser, "The Architecture of the Galaz Site," M.A. thesis, Department of Anthropology, University of Minnesota, 1965; and James Provinzano, "The Osteological Remains of the Galaz Mimbres Amerinds," M.A. thesis, Department of Anthropology, University of Minnesota, 1968.

Description

The University of Minnesota Libraries maintains a general anthropology collection to support teaching and research by the Department of Anthropology. The Ames Library of South Asia and the James Ford Bell Library offer special collections of interest to anthropologists.

The Ames Library of South Asia collects material on the social sciences and humanities of South Asia, including Afghanistan, Bangladesh, Burma, India, Nepal, Pakistan and Sri Lanka. Charles Lesley Ames, a St. Paul publisher, began the collection in 1908, and by 1961, when it was donated to the University of Minnesota, his collection had grown to about 25,000 volumes. At present the collection includes some 150,000 volumes. Some areas of specific strength are the Indian Mutiny, Portuguese India, the East India Company, regimental histories, Tibet, Warren Hastings (1732-1818), Mahatma Gandhi (1869-1948), Jawaharlal Nehru (1889-1964), Rabindranath Tagore (1861-1941) and Munchi Premchand (1880-1936). All major Western languages are represented, as well as several South Asian languages, among which Bengali, Hindi, Sanskrit and Urdu are the strongest.

The Ames collection grew to its present size largely through the acquisition of material from India, Pakistan, Nepal and Sri Lanka on the Special Foreign Currency Program (formerly Public Law 480) of the Library of Congress. The Ames Library has a manuscript collection of seventeen linear feet, a section of rare books and pre-1800 imprints, a lithograph collection, a collection of eighteenth- and nineteenth-century pamphlets and some Oriental and Sanskrit series. Special collections include the Abdus Salam Salam Sandilvi (1919-   ) collection of more than 500 volumes on history, language and literature in Urdu and Persian; the Nilakanta Shastri collection of several hundred volumes on South India; and the Hector Bolitho (1898-   ) collection of manuscripts, typescripts, clippings, photographs and books.

The James Ford Bell Library, established at the University of Minnesota in 1953, had its origins in the interests of Bell (1879-1961), a Minneapolis industrialist. Bell's collecting interests emphasized his mercantile vocation; he acquired books, maps and manuscripts to document and explain the origins and development of the international commercial network. Such sources illustrated also the ways in which European cultural influences expanded world-wide, as well as the impact non-Western cultures had in Europe. The library documents European expansion in contemporary accounts of exploration and discovery in the generation of Columbus, Vespucci and Magellan, along with commercial expansion into Asia under the Portuguese flag. Various types of religious, political and economic institutions emerged to manage the missions and trade, while propelling them further through continued exploration. These are documented in reports of governors, missionaries, explorers, colonists and merchants.

Concentrating on the period from 1400 to 1800, the James Ford Bell Library has an interest in all regions of the world known or discovered outside of Europe in that period, and its materials are distributed among Western European national and linguistic divisions appropriate to their overseas interests.

John M. Weeks

Minnesota—St. Paul

Minnesota Historical Society (MHS). Research Center

Address: Research Center, Minnesota Historical Society, 345 Kellogg Boulevard West, St. Paul, MN 55102-1906.
Tel.: (212) 296-2143
Fax: (212) 297-7436
Internet address: http://www.mnhs.org/index.html.
Networks, consortia: OCLC, RLIN.
Public transit access: Bus routes #12 or #21, west from downtown St. Paul; or #16 or #94, east from downtown Minneapolis.
Founded: 1849 (the beginning of the Society).
Major resources: The Minnesota Historical Society Research Center building contains the Minnesota Historical Society Library; Archives; Manuscripts; Audio-Visual; Newspapers; Art Collection; and Maps.
Areas of specialization: The culture, history and peoples of the Upper Midwest and the Great Lakes area, with concentration on Minnesota.
Archives/manuscripts: Many manuscripts that relate to Native North Americans, including the Gilbert and Frederick Wilson collection. The Alan R. Woolworth papers will be transferred to MHS Archives.
Holdings (books and journals): 550,000 volumes (all subject areas). It is not possible to estimate the percentage of these that relate to Native Americans or to anthropology. Book and journal holdings on Native Americans are extensive.
Visual/audio resources: In Audio-visual, Archives, Manuscripts. Many Native North American photo collections are part of the ca. 500,000 photos in the Research Center. An Indian Photographs Database on videodisk contains 3,000 images of Native Americans.
Access: Open to the public. Hours are Mon.-Sat., 9:00 a.m.-5:00 p.m., Thurs. evening until 9:00 p.m. Closed legal holidays.
References: Gary Clayton Anderson and Alan R. Woolworth (editors), *Through Dakota Eyes: Narrative Accounts of the Minnesota Indian War of 1862* (St. Paul: 1988); June

Drenning Holmquist (editor), *They Chose Minnesota: A Survey of the State's Ethnic Groups* (St. Paul: 1981) (= *Publications of the Minnesota Historical Society*); Gordon Allan Lothson, *The Jeffers Petroglyphs Site: A Survey and Analysis of the Carvings* (St. Paul: 1976) (= *Minnesota Prehistoric Archaeology Series*, no. 12); Mary Jane Schneider, "A Guide to the Wilson Collections," in Carolyn Gilman and Mary Jane Schneider, *The Way to Independence: Memories of a Hidatsa Indian Family, 1840-1920* (St. Paul: 1987) (= *Museum Exhibit Series*, no. 3), p. 348-351; Alan R. Woolworth, "Contributions of the Wilsons to the Study of the Hidatsa," in Carolyn Gilman and Mary Jane Schneider, *The Way to Independence: Memories of a Hidatsa Indian Family, 1840-1920* (St. Paul: 1987), p. 340-347.

Guides/catalogs: General guides to MHS manuscript collections have been published in 1935, 1955 and 1977. Also available is Carolyn R. Anderson (compiler), "Sources for Researching Dakota Family History at the Minnesota Historical Society,"—an unpublished finding aid, 1994; Lila Johnson Goff and James E. Fogerty (compilers), *The Oral History Collections of the Minnesota Historical Society* (St. Paul: 1984); Alan R. Woolworth, "Biographical Sketches Written by Alan R. Woolworth,"—lists 147 biographical accounts of Indians, traders and frontiersmen of the Minnesota and Dakota region; Alan R. Woolworth (compiler), "Research Notebooks of the Santee Dakota Indians,"—an unpublished finding aid.

Artifacts of anthropological importance: Extensive archaeological or ethnological collections are held by the Society. Many of these are listed on PALS. Some of the Hidatsa Indian artifacts are illustrated in Carolyn Gilman and Mary Jane Schneider, *The Way to Independence: Memories of a Hidatsa Indian Family, 1840-1920* (St. Paul: 1987).

Description

The contemporary granite and limestone History Center building of the Minnesota Historical Society houses the Society's primary museum, as well as its conservation and administrative facilities. Also at this location is the MHS Research Center, which preserves and provides public access to documentation previously housed at several locations. The Research Center holds books, journals, newspapers, maps, manuscripts, state archives, photographs, recordings and other resources that pertain to Native Americans—particularly the Ojibwa (Chippewa), Dakota (Sioux) and Hidatsa tribes. Also at the Research Center are materials on Minnesota folklore, oral history recordings of Dakotas, Hmong and Cambodians in the Twin Cities area, music and sound recordings and other documentation of anthropological interest.

The Library

The Research Center Library has extensive holdings of books and journals concerning Native Americans of the Upper Midwest, the Great Lakes area and the adjacent regions of Canada. Library holdings include accounts of travel and exploration in the Midwest and Canada and early editions of Indian-language dictionaries. Several early monographs of ethnographic interest, including Frederic Baraga's *A Dictionary of the Ojibway Language* (first printed in 1853), have been reprinted by the Society.

Manuscripts

Numerous manuscript collections concerning tribes of Minnesota and the surrounding region are preserved at the Research Center. The Gilbert L. and Frederick N. Wilson collection has been described by Mary Jane Schneider (1987). The papers and notebooks of Alan R. Woolworth on the Dakota will be transferred to Research Center archives. Among other manuscript holdings is the Dakota Conflict of 1862 manuscript collection, which includes first-person accounts by Dakotas, as well as by settlers in the region.

Photographs

A large collection of archival photographs, including portraits and other images of Dakotas, is in the Research Center Photo Collection.

Oral Histories

Several oral history projects have been carried out under the auspices of the society. Tapes and transcripts of the Hmong Oral Histories Project are available for use, and other Southeast Asian oral history materials are in preparation. Dakota oral histories at the Research Center include a 1954 recording of songs, stories and reminiscences, recorded at Lower Sioux; a 1976 interview with Rose Whipple Bluestone; a 1965 interview with Elizabeth Wakeman Lawrence; a ca. 1958 interview with Harry Lawrence; and a 1980 interview with Mary Myrick Hinman LaCroix.

The Jeffers Petroglyphs Site

The Jeffers Petroglyphs Site in southern Minnesota has been owned and maintained by the Society since 1966. This site was surveyed in 1971, and has been described in a monograph by Gordon A. Lothson (1976).

Lee S. Dutton
Information provided by Alan R. Woolworth and Denise E. Carlson.

Missouri—Columbia

University of Missouri. Museum of Anthropology

Address: Museum of Anthropology, University of Missouri, 104 Swallow Hall, Columbia, MO 65211.
Tel.: (573) 882-3764
Fax: (573) 884-5450

Internet address: http://www.missouri.edu/~anthmjo/musm15.html.

Parking: Available to the public at the Museum Support Center on the University of Missouri campus.

Founded: 1939.

Major resources: The archaeological collections housed at the Museum of Anthropology, University of Missouri—Columbia, are the largest and best documented holdings of prehistoric and protohistoric materials from the state.

Areas of specialization: Carl H. Chapman collection, Robert T. Bray collection, Naylor collection and the American Archaeology Division collection.

Archives/manuscripts: The museum's total collection is approximately 500 linear ft. of textual documents, 6,000 maps and drawings and more than 50,000 photographic images. Archives and collections are housed at the Museum Support Center (MSC) on the University of Missouri campus.

Fieldnotes, papers, etc.: The Museum of Anthropology Archives contains, almost exclusively, documentary records generated by the research activities of the American Archaeology Division. Original fieldnotes and manuscripts constitute a large part of the collection. All of the original notes of Carl Chapman (1916-1987) are in the archives. A large portion of his fieldwork was conducted at prehistoric rock shelter, cave and mound sites in the state of Missouri, few of which exist today. Important sites include Graham Cave, Towasaghy; also historic Osage and Missouri Indian sites. Fieldnotes date back to 1935. Only an unpublished partial catalog of fieldnotes exists.

The records and fieldnotes of the Robert T. Bray collection, 1925-   , are primarily historical in nature, including more than thirty sites. Important sites include the Battle of Lexington State Historic Site; the state's first capital in St. Charles; Boone's Lick in central Missouri; and Nauvoo, Illinois. Prehistoric sites include Utz and the Button Cairn site.

The American Archaeology Division collection contains fieldnotes, maps, etc., from excavations in 114 counties in Missouri, dating from the 1940s to the present. Major sites include Ste. Genevieve—the oldest Euroamerican settlement in the state, Arnold Research Cave, Old Monroe and the Shriver site.

Visual/audio resources: More than 50,000 photographic images are held.

Access: Materials in the archives are available to scholars for research.

Artifacts of anthropological significance: The archaeological collection consists of millions of artifacts, both prehistoric and historic. The collection covers the entire history of occupation in the state of Missouri.

Archaeological sites represented by artifact collections: Every major site in Missouri is represented in the collection.

Catalogs of artifacts: There is no published or unpublished catalog of artifact or archaeological resources.

Description

Archaeological collections housed at the University of Missouri—Columbia Museum of Anthropology, the result of more than fifty years of intensive fieldwork throughout Missouri, constitute the largest and best-documented holdings of prehistoric and protohistoric materials in Missouri. The museum is administered by the American Archaeology Division and serves as the official repository for all collections generated by research activities of the Department of Anthropology, the American Archaeology Division, the Missouri Archaeological Society and the U.S. Army Corps of Engineers, St. Louis District. Four major archive collections exist in conjunction with the artifact collections: the Carl H. Chapman collection, the Robert T. Bray collection, the Naylor collection and the American Archaeological Division collection. Together, they comprise the entire non-federal holdings of the Museum of Anthropology Archives, involving approximately 202 linear feet of textual materials, 1,900 maps and drawings and 18,000 descriptive catalog cards. Including federally-owned collections, the current estimate is that the total collection encompasses more than 500 linear feet of textual documents, 6,000 maps and drawings and more than 50,000 photographic images. Not all of the collection has been inventoried.

Carl H. Chapman is considered by the archaeological community to be the "Father of Missouri Archaeology." His research documents the state's prehistoric and early historic occupation and serves as the foundation for all current archaeological interpretation. All of the records documenting his archaeological career are in the Museum of Anthropology Archives, including fieldnotes, photos, maps and other related work. Much of the work remains unpublished.

The records in the Robert T. Bray collection are primarily historical in nature, since Bray's studies focused on the early Euroamerican settlement of Missouri. Documentation of more than thirty excavations is included in the archive. Also included is the documentation of his excavation at Nauvoo, Illinois, and the other early Mormon settlements of that area.

The Naylor collection consists of more than eighty linear feet of textual materials, 5,000 descriptive catalog cards and approximately 1,000 site maps and excavation profiles. The collection documents the Mississippian occupation of the southeastern region of Missouri from ca. 1275 to ca. 1325.

The remainder of the archives, the American Archaeology Division collection, consists of numerous document files from surveys and excavations in 114 counties in Missouri, dating from the 1940s to the present. The files contain approximately 44 linear feet of textual items, 300 maps and drawings and 3,000 descriptive catalog cards. Taken as a whole, this collection provides a valuable database for the formulation of geographical and comparative hypotheses relating to the prehistory and protohistory of Missouri.

Molly K. O'Donnell

Missouri—Kansas City

National Archives—Central Plains Region (Kansas City)

Address: National Archives—Central Plains Region, 2321 East Bannister Road, Kansas City, MO 64131.
Tel.: (816) 926-6272
Fax: (816) 926-6982
E-mail: archives@kansascity.nara.gov.

Internet address: http://www.nara.gov/regional/kansas.html.
Founded: 1969.
Major resources: Original federal records retired from agencies in Iowa, Kansas, Missouri, Nebraska and parts of Minnesota, North and South Dakota. Also microfilm copies of many National Archives records.
Areas of specialization: Original records of the U.S. District Court; Corps of Engineers; Bureau of Indian Affairs; National Park Service; and more than seventy other U.S. government agencies. Bureau of Indian Affairs records, 1860-1971, (RG 75) account for 5,139 cubic ft. Holdings include records of the Mid-Continent Mapping Center of the U.S. Geological Survey, Central Region (RG 57).
Archives/manuscripts: More than 35,000 cubic ft. of original records. These include more than 5,000 cubic ft. of primary historical material on Indians of the northern Great Plains.
Holdings (microfilm): More than 58,000 reels of government records. Among microfilm holdings are *Old Settler Cherokee Census Roll, 1895, and Index to Payment Roll, 1896* (Washington, D.C.: 1966) (= *United States. National Archives and Records Service. Microfilm Publications*, no. T 985), 2 reels; United States. Office of Indian Affairs, *Records of the Choctaw Trading House, Under the Office of Indian Trade, 1803-1824* (= *National Archives Microfilm Publications, Microcopy* no.T 500), 6 reels.
Visual/audio resources: Many record groups contain significant numbers of photographs. Photograph lists are available for several Bureau of Indian Affairs field units.
Access: The great majority of holdings are open for public research. Restrictions on access to some federal records may be applied in accord with exemptions in the Freedom of Information Act.

Information provided by National Archives—Central Plains Region.

Montana—Helena

Montana Historical Society

Address: Montana Historical Society, 225 North Roberts St., Helena, MT 59620-1201.
Tel.: (406) 444-2681 (Library); (406) 444-4775 (Archives); (406) 444-4714 (Photo Archives); (406) 444-7717 (State Historic Preservation Office).
Fax: (406) 444-4704
Internet address: http://www.his.mt.gov.
Networks, consortia: WLN (Library and Archives). Catalog records from the mid-1980s are on-line.
Parking: On-site parking is available.
Founded: 1865.
Major resources: Library, Archives, Photo Archives.
Areas of specialization (Archives and Library): Montana; the American West.
Archives/manuscripts: Some archival materials on the tribes of Montana and on Indian-white relations are held; these include a few recorded oral histories and some other documentation.

Visual/audio resources: The Society's large Photo Archives collection includes many archival photographs of Montana-area Indians and related subjects.
Access: Open to the public.
Artifacts of anthropological interest: Many objects are in the museum collections pertain to Native Americans.

Information provided by Ellie Arguimbau.

Nebraska—Lincoln

National Park Service. Midwest Archaeological Center (MWAC)

Address: Midwest Archaeological Center, National Park Service, Federal Building, Room 474, 100 Centennial Mall North, Lincoln, NE 68508-3873.
Tel.: (402) 437-5392
Fax: (402) 437-5098
Internet address (Midwest Archaeological Center museum collection profile): http://www.cr.nps.gov/csd/collections/mwac.html.
Internet access to on-line catalog: ANCS (the database that contains records of all National Park Service museum collections) is accessed by telnet: nadbcast.uark.edu. Login: nadb
Founded: 1969.
Major resources: Archaeological artifacts and the associated records and fieldnotes from some 65 National Park Service parks and sites in the Midwest Region.
Areas of specialization: The Midwest Archaeological Center conserves archaeological artifacts and associated records from excavations (mainly post-1969) at National Park sites in Ohio, Indiana, Michigan, Illinois, Iowa, Minnesota, North Dakota, South Dakota, Nebraska, Missouri, Kansas, Colorado and Wyoming.
Archives/manuscripts: Many.
Visual/audio resources: Site excavation records are usually accompanied by color and black-and-white photographs.
Access: Access to archaeological records is available to qualified researchers only. A research design is required.

New Hampshire—Hanover

Dartmouth College. Library. Special Collections

Address: Special Collections, Dartmouth College Library, Hanover, NH 03755.
Tel.: (603) 646-2037
Fax: (603) 646-3702
Internet address: http://www.dartmouth.edu/~library/thelibs/speccoll.html.
Networks, consortia: RLIN; a tape loading member of OCLC.
Founded: 1769 (Dartmouth College).

Major resources: The Stefansson Collection on Polar Exploration.

Areas of specialization: Polar regions.

Archives/manuscripts: The Stefansson Collection holds 522 linear ft. of manuscripts and 52 linear ft. of vertical file materials.

Fieldnotes, etc.:

• Fieldnotes and diaries of Vilhjalmur Stefansson from the Anglo-American Polar Expedition, 1906-1908. Notes from the Mackenzie River Delta include measurements of Inuit peoples as well as linguistic notes. A typescript guide to the Stefansson papers is available.

• Fieldnotes and diaries of Vilhjalmur Stefansson from the Stefansson-Anderson Arctic Expedition, 1908-1912, to Coronation Gulf, Herschel Island and Victoria Island contain studies of Inuit diet, language and other ethnological observations. A typescript guide to the Stefansson papers is available.

• Fieldnotes and diaries of Vilhjalmur Stefansson from the Canadian Arctic Expedition, 1913-1918, to the western Canadian Arctic archipelago contain linguistic notes on the Inuit. A typescript guide to the Stefansson papers is available.

• Fieldnotes and diaries of Charles W. Furlong (1874-1967), from his expedition to Tierra del Fuego, 1907-1908, include studies of language and music of the Ona and Yahgan peoples. A typescript guide to the Furlong papers is available.

Holdings (monographs in the Stefansson Collection): 5,000 v.

Visual/audio resources: More than 24,000 photographs. The Charles W. Furlong papers contain photographs and recordings (from wax cylinders that have been transcribed to tape cassettes) of Yahgan and Ona culture from Furlong's expedition to Tierra del Fuego in 1907-1908. The Stefansson papers contain photographs of Inuit clothing, tools, boats and homes from the Canadian Arctic Expedition of 1913-1918.

Access: The collection is open to use by all researchers. Materials must be used in the reading room.

Guides/catalogs: Philip N. Cronenwett, "The Stefansson Collection: Past, Present and Future," *Proceedings of the Twelfth Northern Libraries Colloquy* (Boulder, Co.: 1988) (= *INSTAAR Special Publication. Report*, GD-22), p. 167-174—provides an historical introduction to the collection as well as information on activities and acquisitions; *Dictionary Catalog of the Stefansson Collection of the Polar Regions in the Dartmouth College Library* (Boston: 1967), 8 v.—this catalog represents the collection as of 1962; *Polar Notes: An Occasional Publication of the Stefansson Collection*, nos. 1-14, (1959-1975)—contains information on holdings and acquisitions.

Description

The Stefansson Collection on Polar Exploration was created by Arctic explorer and anthropologist Vilhjalmur Stefansson (1879-1962) as his private research library. After returning from five years in the Arctic as leader of the Canadian Arctic Expedition, 1913-1918, Stefansson began to write and lecture about his experiences and his views of the Arctic. For this purpose he needed resources not readily available to him in New York City, and he thus began to develop a very large collection of monographs, serials, photographs and manuscripts relating to these polar interests.

Stefansson began his association with Dartmouth College in 1929, when he gave a series of lectures to the student body. He returned to Hanover periodically to lecture and advise, and in 1947 he was asked to consult on the development of a Northern Studies Program at the College. In 1951 Stefansson moved (with his library) from New York City to Hanover, and he soon became associated with the Dartmouth College Library as a consultant. In the same year, through the generosity of an alumnus, the College offered to purchase the collection. Stefansson agreed, but with the proviso that he be permitted to donate one-half of the collection as his gift to Dartmouth. Since that time the collection has grown significantly.

In 1965 an acquisitions policy for the collection was drafted. Events prior to 1925 and north of 60° North latitude were the chronological and geographical bounds for Arctic materials, and 1940 and 60° South latitude were the bounds for Antarctic materials. This policy permits the collection to concentrate on the exploration of the two polar regions; more contemporary materials are acquired by other units of the library system.

A 1981 grant from the U.S. Department of Education provided funds for the much-needed preservation treatment of Stefansson Collection materials and for the complete revision of intellectual access points. All materials were recataloged into MARC-format records, and all manuscript collections were reprocessed. Currently the collection consists of some 5,000 monographs, 220 manuscript collections totaling 522 linear feet, 52 linear feet of vertical file materials and more than 24,000 photographs. Additions to the collection of both primary and secondary materials are made frequently.

While the collection concentrates on the geographical exploration of the polar regions, there are also several manuscript collections that contain important anthropological resources. First among these are the papers of Vilhjalmur Stefansson. Stefansson did graduate work at Harvard University, initially at the Divinity School and later in anthropology, before leading three Arctic expeditions: the Anglo-American Expedition, 1906-1908; the Stefansson-Anderson Expedition, 1908-1912; and the Canadian Arctic Expedition, 1913-1918. In his papers are diaries, fieldnotes and manuscripts that detail his encounters with the Inuit. Included are detailed studies of Inuit language, physical measurements, diet and culture. These papers are accompanied by photographs. There is a typescript guide to his papers (100 linear ft.), as well as a complete name index to his correspondence (162 linear ft.). The latter contains correspondence with explorers, scientists, archaeologists and anthropologists.

A second anthropological collection is the papers of Robert Addison McKennan (1903-1982). This collection (twelve linear ft.) contains McKennan's research notes and manuscripts relating to his fieldwork with the Athapaskan peoples of the upper Tanana River in Alaska, 1929-1930; and the Chandalar Kutchin peoples in Alaska, 1933. Also included are papers relating to the development of the Northern Studies Program at Dartmouth College—a program that concentrated on the social sciences as well as physical scientific research and training in the Arctic. A typescript guide to this collection is available.

A third major collection is the papers of Charles W. Furlong (1874-1967). Although more an explorer and adventurer than an anthropologist, Furlong worked extensively in Patagonia and Tierra del Fuego, 1907-1908, studying and photographing the peoples of those areas. Included in the (thirty linear feet) collection are notes and manuscripts, recordings on wax cylinders (now transcribed to tape cassettes) and also dermatoglyphs with both foot and hand prints of Fuegian peoples. A typescript guide to this collection is available.

Philip N. Cronenwett

New Mexico—Albuquerque

Chaco Culture National Historical Park. Museum Collections. Chaco Archives

Address: NPS Chaco Archives, Center for Southwest Research, University of New Mexico, General Library, Albuquerque, NM 87131-1466.
Tel.: (505) 277-7189
Fax: (505) 277-0874
E-mail (Curator's office): chcu_curation@nps.gov.
Internet address (Chaco Culture National Historical Park): http://www.chaco.com/park.
Internet access to on-line catalog: The Chaco Archives are not accessible on Libros at this time. Libros (which is located at the General Library, University of New Mexico) can be accessed via the Internet.
Founded: The Chaco Canyon National Monument was established by presidential proclamation in 1907. The University of New Mexico General Library was founded in 1926. Chaco Canyon National Monument became Chaco Culture National Historical Park (NHP) in 1980, and a World Heritage Site in 1987.
Major resources: Publications, manuscripts, photographs, negatives, maps, slides, site files and notes from the Chaco Project.
Areas of specialization: Southwest archeological and ethnological data collected during the Chaco Project.
Holdings: 1,000 publications/manuscripts; 150 linear ft. of records, correspondence, site files; 35,000 black-and-white photographs; 30,000 photo negatives; 6,200 color slides; 2,500 maps. Unpublished indexes of the publications/manuscripts collection and a finding aid for the map collection are available in the Archives Office. The authors of original documents include David Brugge, Cathy Cameron, W. James Judge, Stephen H. Lekson, F. Joan Mathien, Thomas C. Windes, H. Wolcott Toll, Gordon Vivian and many others. The years are primarily those covered by the Chaco Project, 1969-1986. There is a manual finding aid—e.g., cards and an index to materials in the Vivian Archives. Databases have been completed for the manuscript, map and slide collections, but are not available as an on-line catalog.
Visual/audio resources: Black-and-white photographs and photo negatives, color slides and maps that depict site excavations in Chaco Canyon, and the related artifacts and personnel. The photographs date from the 1890s to the present.
Access: Open to scholars, students and general readers. Materials must be used in the library. Copies of most materials can be provided at the researcher's expense.
References: David M. Brugge, *Tsegai: An Archeological Ethnohistory of the Chaco Region* (Washington, D.C.: 1986) (= *Publications in Archaeology*, 18c); Wendy J. Bustard, "Space

as Place: Small and Great House Spatial Organization in Chaco Canyon, New Mexico, A.D. 1000-1150," Ph.D. thesis, University of New Mexico, Albuquerque, 1996; John Kantner, "Political Competition Among the Chaco Anasazi of the Southern San Juan Basin, New Mexico," M.A. thesis, Dept. of Anthropology, University of California, Santa Barbara, 1994; F. Joan Mathien, "Exchange Systems and Social Stratification Among the Chaco Anasazi," in Jonathon E. Ericson and Timothy G. Baugh (editors), *The American Southwest and Mesoamerica: Systems of Prehistoric Exchange* (New York: 1992) (= *Interdisciplinary Contributions to Archaeology*); Thomas C. Windes, *Investigations at the Pueblo Alto Complex, Chaco Canyon, New Mexico, 1975-1979* (Santa Fe, N.M.: 1987) (= *Publications in Archaeology, 18F. Chaco Canyon Studies*), 4 v.

Artifact collections: The Chaco Archives are related to the Chaco Culture National Historical Park Museum Collection, which includes 65,000 catalog records (1.5 million artifacts) for the archaeological collection from Chaco Canyon sites primarily excavated during the Chaco Project. Artifacts in the collection include ceramics, ground stone, lithics, faunal, botanical, pollen and soil samples, mineral, architectural, fossils, dendro samples, woven vegetal materials, charcoal, ornaments and historic objects.

Archeological sites represented: These include Pueblo Bonito, Pueblo Alto, Chetro Ketl, Pueblo del Arroyo and other great houses; smaller contemporary pueblo sites, Navajo and historic. Most of the materials are related to the fieldwork of the Chaco Project from 1971-1979, but include items from earlier work.

Catalog of artifacts: There is a published catalog of artifacts: *Chaco Museum Collection Guide* (Chaco Culture NHP: 1995). This catalog was compiled by Chaco Culture NHP Museum Collection staff; distribution of the catalog is limited. A computerized database consisting of more than 65,000 catalog records of artifacts—representing more than 1.5 million cataloged items—is also available.

Description

The arid northwestern desert of New Mexico harbors the relics of a Neolithic agricultural society in Chaco Canyon National Historical Park. Architectural remnants and bits and pieces of material culture tell a story of the archaic, Basket-Maker and Pueblo peoples who struggled to survive here in the distant past. More recent remains tell tales of their successors, the Navajo and also the Euroamericans who came to learn more about the past occupation of the canyon.

The earliest mention of Chaco Canyon was by early Spanish explorers. The first specific mention of the extensive ruins was by José Antonio Vizcarra in 1823. In 1849 First Lt. James H. Simpson, on a survey for the U.S. military, spent some time recording data about the ruins when he first encountered the prehistoric remains at Chaco Canyon.

Archaeological Excavations at Chaco Canyon

The very earliest excavations at Chaco Canyon were conducted by Richard Wetherill and George H. Pepper, as part of the Hyde Exploring Expedition, at Pueblo Bonito in 1896. Prior to 1920, Earl H. Morris of the American Museum of Natural History and Nels Nelson succeeded the Hyde Exploring Expedition and also worked at Pueblo Bonito. In 1921 Neil Judd, sponsored by the National Geographic Society, began excavations at Pueblo Bonito and Pueblo del Arroyo, and began to consider natural aspects of the canyon and of numerous other Chacoan archeological sites. The National Geographic Society supported these excavations through 1929.

The School of American Research/University of New Mexico Field Schools were conducted at Chaco Canyon National Monument in the 1930s, under the direction of Edgar Hewett, with excavations at Chetro Ketl. There was little archeological activity in the canyon during World War II. The final University of New Mexico Field School was conducted in 1947.

Many of the students who participated in these endeavors became noted leaders in the field of archaeology. Among these were John Corbett, Robert Lister, Gordon Vivian and Alden Hayes—all of whom were involved with Chaco Canyon later in their lives. Gordon Vivian headed the Ruins Stabilization Program (initiated at the park in 1933) and later became Park Archaeologist. John Corbett, as the National Park Service Archaeologist, conceived the idea of the Chaco Project. He induced Robert Lister to become head of the project. Alden Hayes became the supervisory archaeologist for field research, and James Judge (later to become director of the Chaco Project) led the general surveys of the canyon from 1971 to 1976. The project supervisor for remote sensing was Tom Lyons.

The Chaco Project

The Chaco Project (1969-1986) involved a cooperative agreement between the National Park Service and the University of New Mexico, and employed many students. In doing so, it produced a new cadre of archaeologists who went on to become professionals in archaeology. Thomas C. Windes and Joan Mathien, who worked for the Chaco Project, are now preparing the publications that are being produced from the resulting research and analysis.

The goal of the Chaco Project was to conduct a comprehensive investigation of Chaco Canyon, while employing and testing the latest archaeological methodology. One of the main objects was to produce a management plan for eventual use in the maintenance and preservation of the park's resources. The survey identified 2,220 sites within and adjacent to the park boundary. Eventually more than 4,000 sites were identified. These included sites from 2900 B.C. to 1250 A.D., Navajo sites from the early 1700s to the present, as well as rock art and historic sites. The existence of the Chacoan roadway system was confirmed by the use of remote sensing and aerial photography. The result was a comprehensive study of the complex culture that flourished in this arid and isolated region.

Because of the new information that resulted from the Chaco Project, research by numerous scholars continues to examine topics related to the Chaco phenomenon.

The Chaco Archives

The National Park Service Chaco Archives is a component of the Chaco Culture National Historical Park (NHP) Museum Collection. The archives are housed at the University of New Mexico General Library as an affiliated program of the Center for

Southwest Research, while the NPS Chaco Culture NHP Museum Collection operates under a memorandum of understanding with the University of New Mexico Maxwell Museum of Anthropology, in Albuquerque.

The original documents, site files, research library, negatives, photographs, maps and slides were organized for use by the employees of the Chaco Project, but were not cataloged. An archivist has been appointed to manage the Chaco Archives, to catalog and update prior records, and to bring the collection up to date and make it more accessible to researchers.

Joyce M. Raab

University of New Mexico. General Library. Center for Southwest Research (CSWR)

Address: Center for Southwest Research, General Library, University of New Mexico, Albuquerque, NM 87131-1466.
Tel.: (505) 277-6451 (Center for Southwest Research); other units: Chaco Archives Collection (505) 277-7189 or (505) 766-3780; Spanish Colonial Research Center (505) 766-8743.
Fax: (505) 277-6019
E-mail: cswrref@unm.edu.
Internet address: http://www.unm.edu/~cswrref.
Internet access to on-line catalog: Telnet to libros2.unm.edu.
Networks, consortia: OCLC, ARL.
Public transit access: Bus or taxi via Central Avenue.
Founded: 1889.
Major resources: CSWR has extensive archival, manuscript, book, journal and audio holdings and collects publications on the tribes of New Mexico and the Southwest.
Areas of specialization: The Doris Duke American Indian Oral History Archives at UNM; the Bell Collection (a library collection named for Thomas Bell); the New Mexicana and Southwest Library Collection; the John D. Robb Archive of Southwestern Music; Manuscripts; Photoarchives; Chaco Archives Collection (a National Park Service project); the Spanish Colonial Research Center (a joint project of the National Park Service and the University of New Mexico).
Archives/manuscripts: The Doris Duke American Indian Oral History Archives at New Mexico-UNM (27 cubic ft.); the Michael Steck papers (7 cubic ft.). The CSWR also has additional collections of manuscripts on American Indians that are not listed here—see Libros.
Fieldnotes, papers, etc.: CSWR has original interviews and tapes of Doris Duke oral histories done by New Mexicans. The Center also has the University of Oklahoma Doris Duke collection on fiche cards.
Holdings (books and journals): Extensive holdings of books and journals dealing with Indians of the Southwest.
Visual/audio resources: Ten Native American-related photograph collections are described below. The Doris Duke American Indian Oral History Collection (New Mexico) is also

described below. The Oral History Project (OHP) has moved to the Continuing Education Division, UNM.

Access: The Doris Duke Collection (New Mexico) and the Steck papers are open to scholars visiting the CSWR. The Doris Duke transcripts have been microfilmed and are available for purchase. The photo collections are open to visitors to the CSWR.

References: C. Gregory Crampton, "The Archives of the Duke Projects in American Indian Oral History," in Jane F. Smith and Robert M. Kvasnicka (editors), *Indian-White Relations: A Persistent Paradox* (Washington, D.C.: 1981) (= *National Archives Conferences*, vol. 10), p. 119-128; Richard N. Ellis, "The Duke Indian Oral History Collection at the University of New Mexico," *New Mexico Historical Review*, vol. 48, no. 3 (July 1973), p. 259-263; Bradford Koplowitz, "The Doris Duke Indian Oral History Projects," *Popular Culture in Libraries*, vol. 1, no. 3 (1993), p. 23-38.

Guides/catalogs: An 8-reel microfilm index to the Doris Duke Collection from the University of Oklahoma Western History Collection is available at the CSWR. Transcripts from the Doris Duke Oral History Collection, University of Oklahoma, are available on fiche cards (310 cards) at the CSWR. Three printed guides to microfilmed transcripts of the University of New Mexico Doris Duke American Indian Oral History Project materials are available and can be purchased.

Artifacts of anthropological significance: See the information on the Chaco Archives Collection—a division of the CSWR—below.

Description

Center for Southwest Research

Among manuscript collections at the University of New Mexico of interest to anthropological scholars are the New Mexico-UNM Doris Duke American Indian Oral History Collection, and the Michael Steck papers. From 1966 to 1972, the late Doris Duke of New York generously granted funds to seven major state universities, including the University of New Mexico (UNM), to conduct oral histories among Native American groups.

Doris Duke American Indian Oral History Collection

The Doris Duke oral histories done by the University of New Mexico concentrate on the Navajos, the majority of the New Mexico Pueblos, and the White Mountain Apaches. In addition, there is a large section entitled "Miscellaneous" that contains a myriad of materials on varied subjects.

The Center for Southwest Research now holds more than 27 cubic feet of transcriptions, plus 900 original tapes of the interviews conducted under the university's Duke Project. The tapes must be transferred to cassettes for listening; three working days notice must be given for duplication. The duplicate tapes must be used at the CSWR; they do not circulate and cannot be loaned. However, the transcripts of the majority of the interviews (i.e., those for the Navajo, Pueblos and "Miscellaneous") have been microfilmed and are available for purchase (on sixteen reels) [from Southwest Micropublishing, Inc.,

2627 E. Yandell Drive, El Paso, TX 79903; tel. (800) 367-1273]. Three separate printed guides to the microfilmed transcripts—Navajo, Pueblo and "Miscellaneous"—may be purchased from the Center for Southwest Research.

The University of New Mexico has transcribed oral histories from most pueblos, with a substantial body of material on Isleta and Laguna, and smaller collections on San Juan, Santa Ana and Taos. Santo Domingo is not represented in the pueblo collection, but there are a few interviews pertaining to that pueblo in the "Miscellaneous" set. Transcripts are not available for all Navajo-language tapes, although many of the tapes have been translated and transcribed.

Topics discussed in the interviews include personal and family history, traditions, hunting, agriculture, ranching, mining, traders, land and water claims, military service, the Bureau of Indian Affairs, rural and urban living and working experiences, boarding school education, the Pueblo Revolt, relations with the Spanish, Comanches and Utes and with the U.S., pueblo government, the Long Walk, etc. Controversial issues of the 1960s—such as the formation of the All Indian Pueblo Council, the Blue Lake Controversy, the Alcatraz Island incident, the founding of the Navajo Community College, the Indian Civil Rights Act, the Rough Rock Demonstration School, and the Red Power Movement—are also discussed.

The Doris Duke oral histories classified as "Miscellaneous" also cover important issues in the lives of many Native American groups. Included here are additional interviews with the New Mexico Pueblos, Navajo, Hopi and Apache, as well as with the northern Diegueño and desert Cahuilla tribes of California, the Clallam and Yakima of Washington, Alaskan Inuit and Indians, the Blackfoot, Flathead, Crow and northern Cheyenne of Montana. A few interviews were made with Creek and Yavapai individuals, too.

Oral histories funded by Doris Duke were also collected at the Universities of Arizona, Florida, Utah, Oklahoma, Illinois and South Dakota. Arizona and Utah also have collections of interviews from the New Mexico pueblos, especially Zuni. The UNM Library has a set of microfilm called the *Doris Duke American Indian Oral History Collection Index* (on eight reels), which is an index to the Oklahoma oral histories, as filmed by Johnson Associates. The CSWR also has the companion set of 310 fiche cards that contain the transcripts of the Oklahoma collection. The microfilm consists of alphabetical catalog index cards for the persons and groups that were interviewed as part of the Doris Duke oral histories at the University of Oklahoma. This index is also available at other universities.

Michael Steck Papers

The other collection at the CSWR related to Native Americans is the Michael Steck papers. The Steck papers (seven cubic feet) have been microfilmed on seven reels. Steck was the Indian Agent to the Mescalero Apaches in 1852, in southeastern New Mexico, and was Superintendent of Indian Affairs for New Mexico in 1863. In 1865 he was appointed Superintendent of the New Mexico Mining Company. Four boxes of his papers contain important information about the Apaches, Navajos, U.S. officials and U.S. Indian policy for the 1850s and 1860s, as well as information on other Southwestern tribes. The other four boxes deal with mining and Steck's personal business concerns. A number of the letters in both sets were addressed to or from Hispanics in New Mexico and are in Spanish. The collection is available for purchase on microfilm from Southwest Micropublishing, Inc., El Paso.

Chaco Archives

Chaco Culture National Historical Park, a World Heritage Site, is located in the northwest corner of New Mexico and is administered by the Department of the Interior, National Park Service. It was established to preserve and protect the impressive archaeological sites of the Chaco Canyon area that flourished in the Four Corners area 1,000 years ago. The evidence that remains includes sites such as Pueblo Bonito, Pueblo Alto, Chetro Ketl and many others; millions of sherds, stone and bone artifacts and more fragile items. The Chaco Archives is the result of years of research that reveals the technical accomplishments, environment, lifestyle and artistry of Chaco Canyon.

The Chaco Archives consists of approximately 1,000 manuscripts, 35,000 black-and-white photographs, 30,000 negatives, 6,200 slides, 2,500 maps and ca. 150 linear feet of associated project documentation, notes, archives and site files, resulting from excavations in Chaco Canyon. The manuscripts component represents a collection of papers, reports, research and publications on the archaeology, anthropology and physical sciences of the prehistoric Southwest. The photographs, negatives and slides document site surveys, excavations and artifacts of Chaco Canyon National Historical Park. The map component of the collection consists of detailed drawings from the 1890s to the 1980s. The majority of the documentation originated from the Chaco Project (1969-1981). Written materials include site files and notes from the Chaco Project, the Vivian Archives, site survey cards and computer-generated data sheets and printouts.

The Vivian Archives, named after noted archaeologist Gordon Vivian, represent many years of fieldnotes, journals, maps, reports, photographs and correspondence from earlier archaeological projects at Chaco Canyon.

The Chaco Archives are a component of the Chaco Culture National Historical Park Museum Collection. Hours are 8:00 a.m. to 4:30 p.m., daily. Information is available from Joyce Raab, Archivist, tel. (505) 277-7189. The Museum Collection Curator is Philip LoPiccolo, tel. (505) 766-3780.

Native American Photographs

• Taos Pueblo Photographic Project collection. Photographer Nancy Wood documented life at Taos pueblo between 1983 and 1986, in black-and-white photographs that focus on the people and their everyday lives, as well as on celebrations and dances. Collections consists of 150 contact sheets, 236 working prints, 25 master prints and a handmade book containing twenty master prints. These items are available for research and educational use only.

• Charles F. Lummis (General File Collection). 215 cyanotype prints made by writer/photographer/promoter of the Southwest, Charles F. Lummis (1859-1928) between ca. 1890 and 1906. The collection consists largely of images made in the various pueblos of New Mexico, as well as in Navajo and Hopi communities. Many of the photographs were made at Isleta pueblo.

- Indians of North America (General File Collection). The collection contains folders for photographs relative to the following peoples and communities: Acoma, Apache, Havasupai, Hopi, Isleta, Laguna, Navajo, Santa Clara, Santo Domingo, Taos, Yuman, Zuni, Sioux and other Plains Indians. There is also a folder containing photos of pottery. This is a dynamic collection; images are added as appropriate. The collection presently contains approximately eighty black-and-white photographs, including card-mounted albumen prints, that date from ca. 1880 to 1960. Photographers represented include C.S. Fly (Tombstone, Arizona) and Ben Wittick (New Mexico).
- The North American Indian (Folios). The complete set of twenty folios containing prints by Edward S. Curtis accompanies the twenty-volume book series, *The North American Indian*. This rare collection contains all of Curtis's original images reproduced by the photogravure process.
- George Wharton James (General File Collection). Photographs from the collection of California writer and promoter of the West, George Wharton James. Most photographs were taken by James, others by Frederick Maude and C.C. Pierce. Subjects represented include views of pueblos, as well as feast day events, ceremonies and dances at pueblos and Navajo and Hopi communities, arts and crafts, domestic activities and agriculture. Some photographs show interaction between Indian, Hispanic and Anglo-American communities. The collection presently contains approximately thirty prints, many on printing-out paper, ca. 1890-1909.

Other photo collections containing notable photographs of American Indian subjects:

- The Elizabeth Dehuff collection consists of albums with captioned prints and hand-tinted glass lantern slides, shown at the La Fonda Hotel to tourists participating in the Indian Detours auto tours, associated with the Fred Harvey Company.
- The Atlantic & Pacific Railroad collection consists of albums containing cyanotypes and unbound prints documenting life along the A&P Railway as it was constructed, between 1881 and 1883, from Albuquerque to California. This collection includes photographs taken at the Acoma and Laguna pueblos and of Mojave Indians in California.
- The Roy Rosen collection. This collection includes approximately 150 color prints made by photographer Roy Rosen, of Pueblo Indians, arts and crafts and dances in the 1960s and 1970s.
- The Laurens C. Bolles collection. Contains small albums with well-documented black-and-white photographs of Pueblo Indian communities, people, arts and crafts, agriculture and family life. Photographs were made between 1936 and 1938 for the U.S. Soil Conservation Service.
- The Horatio Oliver Ladd collection. Three folders of this collection contain nineteenth-century images of Jicarilla and Navajo Indians, students and teachers at the Romona Indian School.

Photographs of, or related to, Native Americans can be found in many other collections in the Photoarchives. These may be located by means of the index finding aid.

Robb Archive of Southwestern Music

The John D. Robb Archive holds nearly 33,000 individual selections contributed by some three dozen collectors. John D. Robb, a dean of the College of Fine Arts, collected New Mexican, Southwestern and Latin American folk music for more than forty years. The Archive preserves a rich heritage of the area's music, including Native American, black, Hispanic and Mexican music, the music of fiestas, festivals and others.

Spanish Colonial Research Center (SCRC)

This program—a joint project of the National Park Service and the University of New Mexico—holds ca. 80,000 pages of microfilmed Spanish documents, and 4,500 maps, architectural plans and sketches. The Spanish Colonial Research Center has developed a database of transcriptions, translations and interpretive materials from this collection. The Center publishes the *Colonial Latin American Historical Review* (CLAHR), which has a world-wide distribution. As a scholarly quarterly, CLAHR is dedicated to articles and historical manuscripts that deal with Spanish colonial history, ethnohistory and culture.

Nancy Brown, Stella De Sa Rego, Joyce Raab and Joseph P. Sanchez.

University of New Mexico. Maxwell Museum of Anthropology

Address: Maxwell Museum of Anthropology, University of New Mexico, University and Ash Streets, N.E., Albuquerque, NM 87131.
Tel.: (505) 277-4405
Fax: (505) 277-1547
Internet address: http://www.unm.edu/~maxwell.
Founded: 1932.
Major resources: A small library; part of the Chaco Archive; photo archive; other archival materials.

New Mexico—Santa Fe

Museum of New Mexico. Museum of Indian Arts and Culture/Laboratory of Anthropology (Library)

Address (mailing): Museum of Indian Arts and Culture/Laboratory of Anthropology, Museum of New Mexico, P.O. Box 2087, Santa Fe, NM 87594-2087.
Location: 708 Camino Lejo, Santa Fe, NM 87501.
Tel.: (505) 827-6344
Fax: (505) 827-6497
Internet access to on-line catalog: Catalog access will be available through the New Mexico State Library's union catalog of New Mexico libraries, SALSA.

Networks, consortia: OCLC member through AMIGOS.

Founded: 1927.

Major resources: Library; the personal library of Sylvanus G. Morley; Archives of the MIAC/Lab; Archaeological Records Management Section (ARMS).

Areas of specialization: Southwestern anthropology (including archaeology, ethnology, linguistics, physical anthropology), Mesoamerican archaeology and ethnohistory, all archaeological sites reported in the state of New Mexico, the administrative history of the Laboratory of Anthropology.

Archives: 1,300 linear ft.

Fieldnotes, etc.: There are many fieldnotes. Lists can be prepared from the computerized file of the Archaeological Records Management Section.

Holdings (library): 25,000 v.

Access: All library materials are available to the public for research use during library hours. Archival materials are available during working hours by appointment. Some restrictions apply to the use of some materials. Use of Archaeological Records Management Section materials is restricted by the National Historic Preservation Act of 1966, as amended; the New Mexico Cultural Properties Act of 1969, as amended; and the Archaeological Resource Protection Act.

Artifacts: There are major archaeological and ethnographic materials of Native American cultures in New Mexico and the Greater Southwest.

Catalogs of artifacts: Stewart Peckham, Mary Peck (photographer), *From This Earth: The Ancient Art of Pueblo Pottery* (Santa Fe, N.M.: 1990); Museum of New Mexico. Laboratory of Anthropology, Andrew Hunter Whiteford, et al., *I Am Here: Two Thousand Years of Southwest Indian Arts and Culture* (Santa Fe, N.M.: 1989) (= *Museum of New Mexico Press Series in Southwestern Culture*).

Archaeological site collections: Extensive collections from several hundred sites and smaller collections from several thousand sites, mostly in New Mexico, excavated from ca. 1910 to the present.

Description

The Laboratory of Anthropology, Inc., was founded in 1927 as a private research institution for "anthropological research, public education, welfare of the native races in the Southwest, and publication." A committee of anthropologists headed by Alfred V. Kidder was active in formulating the original goals of the Lab, Inc. Jesse L. Nusbaum was the first director, opening the Lab in 1931 with a new facility, field school programs, collections, library and a publications program. Many of the holdings derive from the period 1931-1934. Extensive ethnographic collections were added in that era. Funding was a problem after the original support from John D. Rockefeller, Jr., ended in 1934. The Depression and World War II, among other factors, made it difficult to find support, but a dedicated staff, led by Kenneth M. Chapman—who had been active in the Lab from the earliest stages—carried on.

In 1947, having failed to find independent funding, the Laboratory of Anthropology became a unit of the Museum of New Mexico, a state-funded institution. Sylvanus G. Morley became the director of the combined institutions. In the following decades the Lab became a national leader in salvage archaeology. Extensive archival and collection holdings derive from this work. The current Office of Archaeological Studies, now a separate unit of the Museum of New Mexico, engages in archaeological survey and excavation projects statewide, performs specialized laboratory analysis services, such as ethnobotany and archaeomagnetic dating, and maintains an active outreach program.

In 1987 the Museum of Indian Arts and Culture opened as the public programs and exhibit facility. The Museum of New Mexico now includes the Palace of the Governors, the Museum of Fine Arts, the Museum of International Folk Art, the Museum of Indian Arts and Culture/Laboratory of Anthropology and six State Monuments around New Mexico. The Museum of New Mexico is administratively part of the Office of Cultural Affairs. One of the first programs to be established was the Archaeological Survey, under Harry P. Mera, who had already begun his own survey of the Rio Grande drainage archaeological sites and started his own sherd collection. This has grown into the Archaeological Records Management Section, with computerized records for the 104,000 reported sites and 45,000 surveys in New Mexico.

Mera's survey collections and the Type Sherd Collection provide one of the bases for pottery typology in Southwestern archaeology. And the Lab currently is the primary curatorial facility for records, reports and collections for all contract archaeologists working in the state. This material and its associated records provide an invaluable database for contemporary and future research.

The Archive contains the institutional files of the Lab from its founding in 1927. In addition, there are special collections, including Mabel Morrow's notes and sketches, Ina Sizer Cassidy's correspondence relating to the Indian Defense League of the 1920s, the Dorothy Dunn Kramer papers, photographs relating to the Lab's work and collections, the Harvard Values Study fieldnotes, and archaeological papers and manuscripts. The collections are cataloged and indexed.

The Library specializes in the study of Southwestern American Indian cultures. Holdings include archaeological reports, published and unpublished ethnological studies, complete sets of many professional journals and series, and many hard-to-find publications, essays and reports. The library's catalog is computerized and includes indexing of books, journal articles and papers.

Laura Holt, Willow Powers and Curtis Schaafsma

National Park Service. Southwest Cultural Resources Center. Branch of Archaeological Data Management

Address: Branch of Archaeological Data Management, National Park Service—Southwest Region, 1220 S. St. Francis Drive, Santa Fe, NM 87504.
Tel.: (505) 988-6832
Fax: (505) 988-6876
Founded: Ca. 1991.
Major resources: Archaeological archives.

Areas of specialization: Records of archaeological data from National Park and other sites in the Southwest Region.

Visual/audio resources: Ca. 70,000 photographs, including about 8,000 photo images on photo CDs.

Access: Limited access.

References: James E. Bradford, *Archaeological Survey, Gila Cliff Dwellings National Monument* (Santa Fe, N.M.: 1992) (= *Southwest Cultural Resources Center Professional Papers*, no. 21); James E. Ivey, *Presidios of the Big Bend Area = Los presidios del area de Big Bend* (Santa Fe, N.M.: 1990) (= *Southwest Cultural Resources Center Professional Papers*, no. 31); Robert H. Lister and Florence P. Lister, *Aztec Ruins National Monument: Administrative History of an Archaeological Preserve* (Santa Fe, N.M.: 1990) (= *Southwest Cultural Resources Center Professional Papers*, no. 24); Frances J. Mathien, Charlie R. Steen and Craig D. Allen, *The Pajarito Plateau: A Bibliography* (Santa Fe, N.M.: 1993) (= *Southwest Cultural Resources Center Professional Papers*, no. 49); Peter Russell, *Gila Cliff Dwellings National Monument: An Administrative History* (Santa Fe, N.M.: 1992) (= *Southwest Cultural Resources Center Professional Papers*, no. 48).

Guides/catalogs: There are several catalogs of Southwest Region archives (on paper).

National Park Service. Submerged Cultural Resources Unit (SCRU)

Address: Submerged Cultural Resources Unit, National Park Service, 1220 S. St. Francis Drive, Santa Fe, NM 87504.

Location: In the Intermountain Cultural Resource Center, Santa Fe, NM.

Tel.: (505) 988-6750

Fax: (505) 988-6876

E-mail: icrc_submerged_resources@nps.gov.

Internet address: http://www.nps/scru.

Founded: 1980 (Submerged Cultural Resources Unit). The unit was based, in part, on earlier (1975-1980) work of the National Reservoir Inundation Study.

Major resources: The unit is concerned with submerged cultural resources at National Park Service and other locations in the U.S. Also within scope of the unit are submerged cultural resources on nationally-owned public lands, on Indian reservations in the U.S., and within island territories under U.S. administration.

Areas of specialization: Resources include records and photographs (mainly color slides) that document underwater surveys of cultural artifacts and structures, including submerged vessels, inundated Native American sites, historic dock sites, etc.

Archives/manuscripts: A small accumulation of fieldnotes, etc., is kept at this office.

Visual/audio resources: Ca. 15,000 color slides that document aspects of submerged cultural resources.

Access: The unit is a small and active research entity. Research assistance is available mainly to National Park Service staff and to professionals engaged in submerged cultural resources research.

References: Publications reporting on the unit's research work include Toni Carrell (editor), *Submerged Cultural Resources Assessment of Micronesia* (Santa Fe, N.M.: 1991) (=

Southwest Cultural Resources Center. Professional Papers, no. 36); James P. Delgado and Stephen A. Haller, *Submerged Cultural Resources Assessment: Golden Gate National Recreation Area, Gulf of the Farallones National Marine Sanctuary and Point Reyes National Seashore* (Santa Fe, N.M.: 1989) (= *Southwest Cultural Resources Center. Professional Papers*, no. 18); Larry E. Murphy, *8SL17: Natural Site-Formation Processes of a Multiple-Component Underwater Site in Florida* (Santa Fe, N.M.: 1990) (= *Southwest Cultural Resources Center. Professional Papers*, no. 39); Larry E. Murphy (editor), *Dry Tortugas National Park Submerged Cultural Resources Assessment* (Santa Fe, N.M.: 1993) (= *Southwest Cultural Resources Center. Professional Papers*, no. 45). For detailed information on the National Reservoir Inundation Study, see Daniel J. Lenihan, et al., *Final Report of the National Reservoir Inundation Study* (Santa Fe, N.M.: 1981), 2 v.

Artifacts: These are in the National Park Service regional repositories.

Description

Submerged Cultural Resources Unit staff conduct underwater archaeological research operations, including underwater remote sensing and submerged site mapping and photo/video documentation. The unit has full self-contained diving capabilities. At the present time, the unit's work is primarily on historical shipwrecks, but staff were previously heavily involved in reservoir research dealing primarily with the impact to prehistoric and historic sites of water impoundment projects. The unit has a staff of six permanent and varying numbers of temporary personnel.

Daniel J. Lenihan

New York—Ithaca

Cornell University. Kroch Library. Asia Collections

Address: Asia Collections, Kroch Library, Cornell University, Ithaca, NY 14853.
Tel.: (607) 255-4189 (Asia Collections); (607) 255-3530 (Division of Rare and Manuscript Collections).
Fax: (607) 255-8438 (Asia Collections); (607) 255-9524 (Division of Rare and Manuscript Collections).
Internet address: http://www.library.cornell.edu/Asia.
Internet access to on-line catalog: The "Cornell On-line Catalog" can be accessed at notis@library.cornell.edu.
Networks, consortia: RLIN.
Founded: 1867 (founding of the university).
Major resources: The Charles W. Wason Collection on East Asia; the John M. Echols Collection on Southeast Asia; the South Asia Collection.
Areas of specialization: Asia.
Archives/manuscripts: 300 cubic ft. of archival/manuscript materials on Asia.

Fieldnotes, papers, etc.: The most significant ones are noted below.

Holdings (books and journals in the Asia Collections): More than 1,015,000 v.

Visual/audio resources: Asia-related video holdings are not substantial. For the musicologist, holdings of audio tapes of folksongs/folkmusic are significant.

Access: Materials are generally available to scholars for research and to general readers. Rare and Manuscript Collections materials must be used on-site. Some archival materials have restrictions on use.

References (Asia Collections): *The Carl A. Kroch Library* (Ithaca: 1992); Cornell University Libraries, *Report of the Curator and Archivist* (Ithaca: 1942-1966); Cornell University Libraries. Department of Manuscripts and University Archives, *Documentation Newsletter* (Ithaca: 1975-1990).

Guides/catalogs (Asia Collections): Paul P.W. Cheng (compiler), *The Catalog of the Wason Collection on China and the Chinese, Cornell University Libraries* (Washington, D.C.: 1978-1985) (= *Center for Chinese Research Materials, Association of Research Libraries. Bibliographical Series*, no. 17a), 9 v.; Giok Po Oey (compiler), *Southeast Asia Catalog* (Boston: 1976-1983), 10 v.

Artifact resources: The university's Herbert F. Johnson Museum of Art has collections of Asian and indigenous art, including the Alexander B. Griswold collection of Asian art.

Description

Asia Collections

The Cornell University Library system consists of eighteen libraries. Ethnographic materials on Asia are found primarily in the Asia Collections of Kroch Library, in the Division of Rare and Manuscript Collections of Kroch Library and in the Mann Library, which has significant holdings in rural sociology and education. The Asia Collections of Kroch Library are composed of the Charles Wason Collection on East Asia; the John M. Echols Collection on Southeast Asia; and the South Asia Collection. The three collections are administratively separate, but the materials of the three are intershelved in the Kroch Library stacks. Archival, manuscript and rare materials belonging to the three collections are housed in the Division of Rare and Manuscript Collections. This narrative describes only the collections in Kroch Library, chiefly those in the Division of Rare and Manuscript Collections.

Cornell University's involvement with Asia dates back almost to the university's founding in 1867. The class of 1872, for example, included Japanese national Yatabe Ryokichi, who later became the first Director of the Tokyo Imperial Museum. During the 1920s and 1930s the Crop Improvement Project sponsored jointly by Cornell and Nanking University drew a number of Cornell faculty and researchers to China for extended periods. In fact, during the first half of this century, 3,500 students from China attended Cornell, fully 12 percent of all Chinese students who studied in the U.S. during that period.

The Cornell University Library's Asia Collections have their genesis in Cornell's early interest in Asia. In 1914 William Eliot Griffis (1843-1928), who lived in Japan from 1870 to 1874 and was the first American employee of the Japanese government, donated

2,000 volumes of Japanese-language books, periodicals and maps to the library. In 1918 Charles William Wason, for whom the East Asia Collection is named, donated 9,000 volumes on China and the Chinese. These two donations formed the basis of Cornell's Wason Collection on East Asia, which now totals almost 1.5 million volumes.

As regular travelers to Asia, Cornell alumni, faculty and students have, over the years, created a considerable body of material on Asia. The letters they wrote, the diaries they kept and the photographs they took constitute a valuable ethnographic portrait of the peoples of the region. A number of these materials now reside in the archives of the library. Archival collections on China and Japan number 79 and 27, respectively. Of these, perhaps 30 or 40 percent would be of interest to ethnographers. The materials in these collections consist of photographs, missionary accounts, fieldnotes of professionals in education, law, agriculture, entomology and other fields, and letters from travelers. Missionary accounts of life in China are numerous. Of particular note are the papers of William Reginald Wheeler, who was both missionary and army officer in China during the 1920s and 1930s. Other noteworthy missionary collections are those of Augustus Loomis Ward and his wife, and of John Heard, who lived in China in the mid-nineteenth-century. The Leslie R. Severinghaus papers are a splendid example of the ethnographic information available from the observant traveler. Severinghaus lived in China in the 1920s, and his many letters and photographs vividly record the life of the Chinese people during that turbulent era. A particularly interesting collection on China and Southeast Asia is that of petroleum engineer Robert Jackson Belknap, who worked in China during World War II. The collection contains not only his diary, various notebooks and photographs, but also five reels of 8mm movie film taken in various areas of China from 1942 to 1944. The papers of entomologist James G. Needham, educator John R. TeWinkel and lawyer George Jarvis Thompson, among others, are also worth consulting for their insights on various aspects of pre-World War II Chinese society.

Archival sources on Japan are not nearly so numerous, but there are items of interest. The papers of William Eliot Griffis, noted above, reside in the Cornell Archives, as do those of Alice Hanson Cook, an industrial labor relations specialist who lived in Japan for a number of years in the 1960s and recorded her observations of Japanese life and society.

Anthropological resources on Southeast Asia are uncommonly rich. The John M. Echols Collection on Southeast Asia was established in 1953. In 1977 it was named for Cornell linguist and bibliophile John M. Echols, a tireless bibliographer whose efforts and guidance have made this the premier Southeast Asia collection outside of Southeast Asia. Its considerable resources contain much of interest to the anthropologist. Of special note is the exceptional body of materials produced by European travelers, adventurers, scholars and colonial administrators who visited or lived in the region from the eighteenth- to the mid-twentieth-century. For the linguist, the collection contains more than 100,000 volumes written in the languages of the region, as well as virtually everything published in the West on these languages.

Archival collections at Cornell on Southeast Asia number more than 100. The archives contain more than 100,000 photographs of the region. Among the more significant photographic collections are those of Yale geographer Karl J. Pelzer (Indonesia and Philippines, pre- and post-World War II), Dutch photographer Niels A. Douwes Dekker (Indonesia, ca. 1900), French naval physician François-Jules Harmand (Vietnam, late nineteenth-century), Paul Hartmann (Indochina, pre-1954), Joel M. Halpern (Laos, late 1950s), journalist Claire Holt (Indonesia, 1930s), photographer Hedda Morrison (Sarawak, ca. 1950-1985), photojournalist Carol Rubinstein (Sarawak, 1970s), James David Givens (Philippines, 1898-1901) and Charles A. Blue (Philippines, early twentieth-century). The collection also contains several unattributable photograph albums of Indonesia in the late nineteenth- and early twentieth-centuries, of Burma in the last decade of the nineteenth-century and of Thailand from the turn-of-the-century.

Collections of interest to linguists and folklorists include the Richard D. Cushman papers on the Yao (with audio tapes of Yao music); a manuscript of Bahnar tales compiled prior to World War II by French priest Paul Guilleminet; and the Balinese Manuscript Project, a collection of more than 3,000 typed transcriptions of Balinese palm-leaf manuscripts, principally tales from Hindu epics and legends of Balinese kings. A collection stunning for its physical beauty as well as its intrinsic linguistic and ethnographic value is the 38-volume Shan/Northern Thai, Khmer Manuscript Collection. This collection contains palm-leaf, mulberry and *saa* paper folding-book manuscripts on Buddhism, local rituals, astrology, astronomy and magic. Many of the covers of these lovely manuscripts are heavily ornamented in gold with colored glass.

The Archives hold several collections containing the fieldnotes and observations of academics, professionals and colonial administrators. Among the more noteworthy are those of anthropologists Richard D. Cushman (southern China, northern Thailand), Lauriston Sharp (Thailand) and Joel M. Halpern (Laos); geographer Karl J. Pelzer (Indonesia, Philippines); rural sociologist Milton Barnett (Indonesia, Malaysia, Philippines); art historian Alexander B. Griswold (Thailand, Burma, Indochina); U.S. colonial administrator Edward Bowditch (Philippines, especially ethnic groups of Mindanao); François-Jules Harmand (Indochina) and educator Paul Hartmann (Indochina). The papers of journalist Claire Holt are especially interesting for materials on Indonesian dance dating from ca. 1930.

Some of the more interesting miscellaneous items in the archives are the records of the Governor of Cochinchina on the Moi, 1887-1938; certificates of enfeoffment of local spirits issued by Vietnam's Nguyen Dynasty, 1802-1945; genealogical charts of Mandon nobility and aristocracy in Balanipa Mandar, Indonesia; and the 62-reel microfilm collection of the American Baptist Foreign Missionary Society records relating to its activities in Burma.

While archival collections on Southeast Asia number more than 100, a single collection may have more than one country focus. For this reason, the number of collections, when listed by country, is more than 200. When arranged by country the numbers of Southeast Asian archival collections are: Burma (11), Cambodia (12), Indonesia (46), Laos (9), Malaysia (11), Philippines (47), Singapore (6), Thailand (28), Vietnam (38).

The South Asia Collection is the fourth largest in the United States. The collection was established in 1868, when Cornell president Andrew Dickson White acquired the 5,000-volume library of German Sanskritist and philologist, Franz Bopp. The collection contains numerous eighteenth- and nineteenth-century German, Dutch and French works on the Subcontinent, a comprehensive body of ethnographic materials on all of the countries of the region (Nepal is particularly well covered), as well as substantial language and linguistic holdings in eleven languages of the region.

While South Asian archival sources are not plentiful, there are items of interest. The records of missionaries Hervey DeWitt Griswold (Pakistan, early twentieth-century), Hervey Crosby Hazen (Madras, late nineteenth-, early twentieth-century), Helen Isabel Root (Sri Lanka, India, early twentieth-century) and Daniel Poor (Sri Lanka, early nineteenth-century) all describe aspects of life in the regions where they were active. The diaries, notebooks and photographs of agricultural consultants Dana Reynolds (India) and Nicolaas Luykx (India, Pakistan), who were active in the 1960s, contain information on Indian rural society. The diaries and letters of Louise Spieker Rankin, the wife of Everett Rankin, a Standard Oil executive in India during the 1930s, record her observations of Indian life. Among the items in Cornell's Rudyard Kipling collection is an album of photographs of India dating from 1888.

Allen Riedy

New York—New York City—Bronx

Huntington Free Library and Reading Room (This library currently serves as the library for the National Museum of the American Indian.)

Address: Huntington Free Library and Reading Room, 9 Westchester Square, Bronx, NY 10461.
Tel.: (718) 829-7770
Fax: (718) 829-4875
E-mail: hflib1@metgate.metro.org.
Public transit access: Subway 6 to Westchester Square and East Tremont Ave.
Founded: 1892; the anthropologial collections were added in 1930.
Major resources: The Marshall H. Saville book collection; the Frederick W. Hodge book collection.
Areas of specialization: Indians of North America, South America and Central America. Includes volumes on archaeology, ethnology, history, languages, art, government relations and current issues of the Native peoples of the Americas.
Archives/manuscripts: 90 cubic ft.
Fieldnotes, papers, etc.:
● Reginald Pelham Bolton (1856-1942)—fieldnotes and photographs, Bronx and Manhattan, N.Y., 1889-1936.
● Joseph Alfred Borome—research papers, primarily on Venezuela, 1944-1960.
● Charles Carr—field and research notes, Wampanoag burial sites at Burr's Hill, Warren, Rhode Island, 1913.
● Frank Hamilton Cushing (1857-1899)—letterpress books of Cushing's correspondence, 1886-1896. Unpublished calendar (see also: Hemenway Southwestern Archaeological Expedition).
● Edward H. Davis—fieldnotes and sketch books on Indians of southern California, ca. 1912-1944.

- Constance DuBois—research notes and correspondence on Luiseño and Diegueño Indians in southern California, 1897-1909. Published guide: Mary B. Davis (compiler), *Papers of Constance Goddard DuBois in the Huntington Free Library: A Guide to the Microfilm Edition* (Bronx: 1994).
- Hemenway Southwestern Archaeological Expedition—records, 1886-1891. Directed by Frank Hamilton Cushing. Published guide: Mary B. Davis (compiler), *Papers of the Hemenway Southwestern Archaeological Expedition in the Huntington Free Library: A Guide to the Microfilm Edition* (Bronx: 1987).
- Hendricks-Hodge Expedition, 1917-1923. Directed by Frederick W. Hodge. Published guide: Brenda Shears (compiler), *Field Notes and Maps of the Hendricks-Hodge Archaeological Expedition, 1917-1923: A Guide to the Microfilm Edition* (Bronx: 1987).
- Joseph Jones (1833-1896)—papers on mound builders of Louisiana and Tennessee, 1868-1888.
- Joseph Keppler—correspondence and papers relating to twentieth-century Iroquoian people, 1882-1944. Published guide: Mary B. Davis (compiler), *The Joseph Keppler Iroquois Papers in the Huntington Free Library: A Guide to the Microfilm Edition* (Bronx: 1994).
- Joseph Laurent—manuscripts and publications in the Abnaki language from St. Francis Abnaki Reservation, Odanak, Québec, 1806-ca. 1830. Published guide: Mary B. Davis (compiler), *The Wabanaki Collection and the William Wallace Tooker Papers in the Huntington Free Library: A Guide to the Microfilm Edition* (Bronx: 1991).
- Samuel K. Lothrop (1892-1965)—fieldnotes and diaries of excavations in Chile, 1929-1930.
- José Toribio Medina (1852-1930)—proof sheets for published bibliography on Quechua and Aymara languages, 1930.
- Warner D. Miller—papers for his Lakota research, 1931-1945.
- Clarence B. Moore (1852-1936)—fieldnotes for Moore's southeastern United States archaeological expeditions, 1891-1918. Published guide: Mary B. Davis (compiler), *Field Notes of Clarence B. Moore's Southeastern Archaeological Expeditions, 1891-1918: A Guide to the Microfilm Edition* (Bronx: 1987).
- Bonita Wa Wa Calachaw Nuñez (1888-1972)—photocopies of diaries, sketches and journals of a California Indian who was adopted by Mary Duggan.
- Passamaquoddy Indians. Records, 1775-1912. Published guide: Mary B. Davis (compiler), *The Wabanaki Collection and the William Wallace Tooker Papers in the Huntington Free Library: A Guide to the Microfilm Edition* (Bronx: 1991).
- Marshall H. Saville (1867-1935)—research notes on Mound-Builders of Ohio, ca. 1920.
- Rodolfo R. Schuller (1873-1932)—papers on languages of Mexico, Central and South America, ca. 1912-1935.
- Alanson B. Skinner (1886-1925)—fieldnotes on New York City archaeological sites, 1918-1919.
- De Cost Smith (1864-1939)—manuscript and papers dealing with Lakota language and people. Some sketch books and painting, 1881-1945.

- Stockbridge papers, 1735-1916—papers of the Stockbridge Indians. Published guide: Mary B. Davis (compiler), *Stockbridge Indian Papers in the Huntington Free Library: A Guide to the Microfilm Edition* (Bronx: 1987).
- William Wallace Tooker (1848-1917)—papers and texts concerning Algonquian languages, especially of New York and the coastal Atlantic. Published guide: Mary B. Davis (compiler), *The Wabanaki Collection and the William Wallace Tooker Papers in the Huntington Free Library: A Guide to the Microfilm Edition* (Bronx: 1991).
- United States. War Department—typescript copies of internal correspondence, primarily concerned with attempts to remove Indians, 1811-1913.
- Philipp Johann Josef Valentini (1818-1899)—research notes, notebooks and other papers concerning the Maya, 1858-1898.
- Women's National Indian Association records, 1880-1951. Published guide: Mary B. Davis (compiler), *Papers of the Women's National Indian Association in the Huntington Free Library: A Guide to the Microfilm Edition* (Bronx: 1994).

The National Museum of the American Indian holds in its archives—located at the Museum Research Branch, in the Bronx, *not* the Library—papers and manuscripts from many of the noted anthropologists, other scholars and collectors associated with the Museum of the American Indian, throughout its existence.

Holdings (books and journals): 45,000 v.

Visual/audio resources: The Huntington Free Library does not hold these. The National Museum of the American Indian has a large photo collection and a film and video department that is establishing a collection of films and videos about the First Peoples of the Western Hemisphere.

Access: The library is open to both scholars and the public by appointment. The collection is non-circulating. Access to rare books and manuscripts is limited to those with a demonstrated need.

Reference: Mary B. Davis (editor), *Native America in the Twentieth-Century: An Encyclopedia* (New York: 1994) (= *Garland Reference Library of the Social Sciences*, vol. 452).

Guides/catalogs: Huntington Free Library and Reading Room, New York, *Dictionary Catalog of the American Indian Collection, Huntington Free Library and Reading Room, New York* (Boston: 1977), 4 v.; Francis R. Kowsky, "The Huntington Free Library and the Van Schaick Free Reading Room," *Journal of the Bronx County Historical Society*, vol. 7, no. 1 (Jan. 1970), p. 1-7; Ruth N. Wilcox, "The Huntington Free Library and Reading Room," *Indian Notes*, vol. 8, no. 3 (Summer 1972), p. 102-103.

Description

Nestled in tree-covered grounds in the northeast part of the Bronx, in New York City, the Huntington Free Library and Reading Room has served as the library for the Museum of the American Indian since 1930. The Huntington Free Library's history began in 1880, when an area resident and local philanthropist, Peter C. Van Schaick, left money in his will to erect a free reading room, to be donated to the citizens of the village of Westchester upon its completion. The library, designed by the well-known architect, Frederick C. Withers, was erected in 1882. However, attempts to present the library to the citizens failed because the town fathers of Westchester were unwilling to pay the building maintenance costs.

In 1890 Collis Potter Huntington, the founder of the Southern Pacific Railroad, was persuaded to purchase the vacant library. He expanded the building and endowed its operations. In 1892 Huntington transferred the deed of the library to its trustees, who continue today to operate the library as a non-circulating general collection, open to the public.

The library's role expanded significantly in 1930, when the trustees of the Museum of the American Indian made an agreement with Archer M. Huntington, Collis Huntington's adopted son, in which Huntington, a good friend of museum founder George G. Heye, agreed to erect an addition to the reading room in the Bronx, to house the museum's growing book collection.

This book collection had its origins in the private libraries of noted anthropologists Frederick W. Hodge and Marshall H. Saville. Hodge's primary interest was in North America, while Saville concentrated on Latin America. Both were excellent bibliophiles, collecting not only core items for a given people or area, but ephemeral materials as well. Anthropologists on the museum's staff, they convinced George G. Heye of the necessity of a library for the budding museum. They turned to trustee James B. Ford, a connoisseur of rare books, who agreed in 1926 to finance the purchase of their personal libraries for the museum. By 1928 the James B. Ford Library was assigned space in the basement of the Museum of the American Indian. Its librarian was Ruth B. Gaines.

Heye soon discovered that the area allotted the library was insufficient for acceptable library operations. Discussions ensued with Archer M. Huntington, and in 1930 the trustees of the Museum of the American Indian transferred the museum's book collection to the Huntington Free Library, to be housed in a new addition constructed by the library for that purpose. The trustees of the library assumed responsibility for the collection's care and maintenance, operating the library from its endowment, which was newly supplemented by Huntington.

The trustees of both institutions envisioned close cooperation between the library and the museum: George G. Heye served as the Vice-President of the library's Board of Trustees until his death in 1957, and Edwin K. Burnett—Librarian from the end of the 1930s until the 1960s—held a joint appointment on the museum's staff. The library's trustees authorized new acquisitions—making occasional purchases of rare materials, such as two treaties with the Iroquois and Delaware, negotiated by William Johnson in the colonial period.

From its start the library subscribed to the standard periodicals and other serial publications relevant to a collection on the Native peoples of the Western Hemisphere. This strong serials collection includes all of the *Bulletins* and *Annual Reports* of the U.S. Bureau of American Ethnology and entire runs of the *American Anthropologist* and *American Antiquity*. Holdings are international in scope, including such diverse periodicals as *Ñemity*, a Guaraní-language publication from Paraguay; *Mexikon*, published in Germany; and *Recherches amérindiennes au Québec* from Canada.

Anthropological studies are a major strength of the library's collection. They range from early works of pioneers in the field, such as Adolph Bandelier's *Final Report of Investigations Among the Indians of the Southwestern United States* (Cambridge, Mass.:

1890) and Lewis Henry Morgan's *League of the Ho-dé-no-sau-nee, or Iroquois* (New York: 1851), to more recent studies such as Napoleon Chagnon's *Yanomamo: The Fierce People* (New York: 1968) and Karen I. Blu's *The Lumbee Problem* (Cambridge, Mass.: 1980).

Collections such as the *Reports of the Commissioner of Indian Affairs*; *Jesuit Relations and Allied Documents: Travels and Explorations of the Jesuit Missionaries in New France, 1610-1791* (Cleveland: 1896-1901); and the reports and papers of the Indian Rights Association help form the backbone of the library's history collection. Twentieth-century history is not neglected. Mary B. Davis, the current librarian, edited *Native America in the Twentieth-Century: An Encyclopedia* (New York: 1994), drawing heavily on the library's holdings for bibliographic information. The library also receives a significant number of Congressional documents, including Congressional hearings, legislation and committee reports on Indian matters. The area of government relations is augmented by an outstanding offprint and pamphlet collection. Another important acquisition was the *Decisions and Expert Testimony Before the Indian Claims Commission* (Clearwater Publishing Co., microfiche edition).

Contemporary affairs of Native Americans are well documented in this collection. The library subscribes to more than fifty current newspapers and journals issued by Indian organizations. Holdings range from *Indian Country Today*, published in South Dakota, to *Causa Indigena* from Peru's Shipibo Indians. Its retrospective collection in this area, published in conjunction with Princeton University and the Newberry and Smithsonian Libraries, is available on microfiche.

The Huntington Free Library was the library for the Museum of the American Indian until 1990, when the museum became a branch of the Smithsonian Institution, the National Museum of the American Indian. Although the library was not part of the transfer to the Smithsonian, it currently serves as the library for the New York staff of the new museum. It continues to collect materials pertinent to the study of America's Native peoples.

Mary B. Davis

Smithsonian Institution. National Museum of the American Indian (NMAI). Research Branch

Address: Research Branch, National Museum of the American Indian, 3401 Bruckner Boulevard, Bronx, NY 10461.
Tel.: (212) 825-4481 (general); (212) 825-8456 (Archives).
Fax: (212) 825-4489
E-mail: General: gaines@ic.si.edu; Archives: jeffrey@ic.si.edu.
Internet address (NMAI): http://www.si.edu/nmai. This useful website offers news on programs and services of the museum and provides links to other Native websites.
Public transit access: Subway: Buhre Ave. station of the Lexington Ave. IRT (train 6). Express Bus: Jarvis Ave./Bruckner Blvd. stop on the Pelham Bay Express Bus line (bus travels north on Madison Ave., with its last stop in Manhattan at Third Ave. and 88th Street).
Founded: 1916 (Museum of the American Indian—Heye Foundation); 1922 (opening of the museum at 155th St. and Broadway in Manhattan); 1926 (opening of the museum's Research

Branch in the Bronx); 1989 (the MAI collection was transferred to the Smithsonian, and the National Museum of the American Indian was established as part of the Smithsonian Institution); 1994 (opening of the NMAI George Gustav Heye Center in Manhattan); 1999 (scheduled opening of the NMAI Cultural Resources Center in Suitland, Maryland); 2002 (scheduled opening of the NMAI on the National Mall in Washington, D.C.).

Major resources: Archives, artifacts.

Areas of specialization: Indigenous peoples of North, Central and South America.

Archives/manuscripts: The Archives of the National Museum of the American Indian, Smithsonian Institution, consists of approximately 300 linear ft. of records dating from the 1860s to the present. Preserving the history of what was once the Museum of the American Indian (MAI)—Heye Foundation, the Archives collections include correspondence; exhibition planning materials; Board of Trustees meeting minutes; annual reports of the museum, as well as its various departments; museum publications; financial reports; legal documents; records of field expeditions sponsored by George G. Heye and the Heye Foundation; and public relations materials such as press packages, exhibition brochures, invitations and museum newsletters. The holdings also contain information concerning museum objects and collectors. These materials consist of published and unpublished manuscripts; fieldnotes containing original drawings, site diagrams and maps; scrapbooks; photographs; notes and letters. Other materials include catalogue notes and object lists; acquisition records relating to gifts, purchases, loans, exchanges; and objects acquired as a result of museum-sponsored expeditions. Noted anthropologists, scholars and collectors associated with MAI throughout its existence include Reginald Pelham Bolton, Donald A. Cadzow, Frances Densmore, Lt. George T. Emmons, William N. Fenton, Alberto V. Fric, Marion E. Gridley, Alfred I. Hallowell, Mark R. Harrington, Fred Harvey, Frederick W. Hodge, Joseph Keppler, Samuel K. Lothrop, Clarence B. Moore, John Louw Nelson, William C. Orchard, George H. Pepper, Marshall H. Saville, Alanson B. Skinner, Frank G. Speck, Thomas Henry and Susette La Flesche Tibbles, A. Hyatt Verrill and William Wildschut. The Archives will eventually be moved to the NMAI Cultural Resources Center in Suitland, Maryland.

Holdings (books and journals): A collection of more than 200 books, journal volumes and exhibition catalogues (many of which are out of print), published by the Museum of the American Indian—Heye Foundation. Also, see information on the library resources of the Huntington Free Library, located in the Bronx.

Access: Contact the Archives staff by phone, fax or e-mail to discuss research strategy.

Artifacts: The museum's Research Branch contains approximately one million objects from the Western Hemisphere. There are collections from all major culture areas of the Americas, for virtually all tribes of the United States, most of those from Canada, and a smaller number from Mexico, Central and South America and the Caribbean. Chronologically, the collection includes artifacts from the Paleo-Indian period to contemporary arts and crafts. Object types range from strictly utilitarian to masterworks of Native American art. Many have great historical and/or aesthetic importance. Highlights of the collection include eighteenth-century Great Lakes material; Plains clothing, feather bonnets and painted and quilled hides; Northwest Coast masks and carvings; California basketry; Amazonian featherwork; ceramics from Mexico, Panama and Ecuador; gold ornaments from central Mexico, Colombia and Peru; the Clarence B. Moore collection from the southeastern United States; and Navajo weavings showing a broad range of early types. Caribbean archaeology is extraordinarily well represented. Works on paper include Plains ledger drawings, as well as contemporary prints and paintings.

Archaeological sites for which the museum has artifacts: The museum holds artifacts from archaeological sites throughout the Western Hemisphere. The following represent a small sample of the excavations for which NMAI has collections:

- Burr's Hill, Warren, Rhode Island, 1913—excavated by Charles Carr.
- Cocle Province, Panama, 1920s—excavated by A. Hyatt Verrill and Frederick W. Hodge.
- Hawikuh, New Mexico, 1917-1923—excavated by H.W. Hendricks.
- Las Mercedes, Costa Rica, 1916-1917—excavated by Alanson B. Skinner.
- Lovelock Cave, Nevada, 1924—excavated by Mark R. Harrington and Llewellyn Loud.
- Manabi, Ecuador, 1906-1908—excavated by Marshall H. Saville.
- Clarence B. Moore's Southern Archaeological Expeditions, 1891-1918.

Catalogs of exhibitions and/or of artifacts (Museum of the American Indian): Over the years the Museum of the American Indian (MAI) published several exhibition catalogs highlighting artifacts from its collections. The following books, while not wholly catalogs of the museum's collection, are illustrated largely from the museum's holdings: Frederick J. Dockstader, *Indian Art in America: Arts and Crafts of the North American Indian* (Greenwich, Conn.: 1961); Frederick J. Dockstader, *Indian Art in Middle America* (Greenwich, Conn.: 1964); Frederick J. Dockstader, *Indian Art in South America* (Greenwich, Conn.: 1967); Frederick J. Dockstader, *Indian Art of the Americas* (New York: 1973).

Catalogs of exhibitions (Museum of the American Indian): Lee A. Callander and Ruth Slivka, *Shawnee Home Life: The Paintings of Earnest Spybuck* (New York: 1984); Mary Jane Lenz, *The Stuff of Dreams: Native American Dolls* (New York: 1986); Anna Curtenius Roosevelt and James G.E. Smith (editors), *The Ancestors: Native Artisans of the Americas* (New York: 1979); James G.E. Smith, *Arctic Art: Eskimo Ivory* (New York: 1980).

Catalogs of exhibitions and/or artifacts and other publications and media (National Museum of the American Indian): *All Roads Are Good: Native Voices on Life and Culture* (Washington, D.C.: 1994); José Barreiro (editor), *Native American Expressive Culture* (Washington, D.C.: 1994); Eulalie H. Bonar (editor), *Woven by the Grandmothers: Nineteenth-Century Navajo Textiles from the National Museum of the American Indian* (Washington, D.C.: 1996); *Creation's Journey: Native American Music Presented by the National Museum of the American Indian* (Washington, D.C.: 1994); Charlotte Heth (editor), *Native American Dance: Ceremonies and Social Traditions* (Washington, D.C.: 1992); Tom Hill and Richard W. Hill, Sr., *Creation's Journey: Native American Identity and Belief* (Washington, D.C.: 1994); Tim Johnson (editor), *Spirit Capture: Photographs from the National Museum of the American Indian* (Washington, D.C.: 1998); Clara Sue Kidwell and Richard W. Hill, Sr., *Treasures of the National Museum of the American Indian, Smithsonian Institution* (New York: 1996); *This Path We Travel: Celebrations of Contemporary Native American Creativity* (Golden, Colo.: 1994).

Description

[See the description of the **Smithsonian Institution. National Museum of the American Indian. George Gustav Heye Center** under the heading **New York—New York City—Manhattan.**]

Nancy B. Rosoff
Acknowledgements: Lee Davis, Mary B. Davis, Allison Jeffrey.

New York—New York City—Brooklyn

Brooklyn Museum of Art (BMA). Libraries and Archives

Address: Brooklyn Museum of Art Libraries and Archives, 200 Eastern Parkway, Brooklyn, NY 11238-6052.
Tel.: (718) 638-5000, ext. 307.
Fax: (718) 638-3731
Internet address (BMA): http://www.brooklynart.org.
Networks, consortia: RLIN, METRO. Library and Archival records are available on RLIN with the library identifier NYBA.
Public transit access: Subway 2, 3 to Eastern Parkway.
Founded: In 1823, as the Brooklyn Apprentices' Library Association. In 1842 renamed the Brooklyn Institute, which in 1890 evolved into the Brooklyn Institute of Arts and Sciences. The Institute was the parent of the Museum, which in 1997 was renamed the Brooklyn Museum of Art.
Major resources: Museum Libraries and Archives.
Areas of specialization: Art, anthropology and ethnology of the Americas.
Archives/manuscripts of anthropological significance: Ca. 100 linear ft. of correspondence, fieldnotes, sketches and documentary photographs.
Fieldnotes, papers, etc., of anthropological significance:
- Stewart Culin (1858-1929)—fieldnotes for 1871-1929 (includes United States, 1901-1911, 1917; Vancouver, 1908, 1911; Asia, 1912-1914; and Europe, 1920-1928).
- Frank Hamilton Cushing (1857-1900)—fieldnotes (including sketches), 1881-1890.
  In addition, documents on the museum's archaeological and ethnographic collections contain information of related significance. Unpublished finding aids and lists of manuscripts and fieldnotes can be generated.
Visual/audio resources: Visual collections include documentary photographs, original field sketches, photographic postcards—mostly relating to Native American cultures. Additional material can be found on the cultures of Mexico and Central and South America.
Holdings (books and periodicals of anthropological significance): 30,000 v.
Access: The Libraries and Archives are open to the public by appointment. This is a reference collection and materials are made available, when possible, through interlibrary loan to other libraries. Special permission may be required for the reproduction of some visual and textual material on Native American culture that may be deemed sensitive.

References: *Brooklyn Museum of Art* (Brooklyn, N.Y.: 1997); *Converging Cultures: Art & Identity in Spanish America* (Brooklyn, N.Y.: 1996); Diana Fane, Ira Jacknis and Lise Breen, *Objects of Myth and Memory: American Indian Art at The Brooklyn Museum* (Brooklyn, N.Y.: 1991); Deirdre E. Lawrence, "Culin: Collector and Documentor of the World He Saw," *Orientations*, vol. 20, no. 7 (July 1989), p. 20-27; Deirdre E. Lawrence, *The Stewart Culin Library and Archives at the Brooklyn Museum* (Brooklyn, N.Y.: 1991).

Guides/catalogs: *Latin American Colonial Art from the Brooklyn Museum Collections: Finding Aid to Documentary Resources in the Museum Libraries & Archives* (Brooklyn, N.Y.: 1993); Deirdre E. Lawrence and Deborah Wythe, *Guide to the Culin Archival Collection* (Brooklyn, N.Y.: 1996)—this publication contains information on the Stewart Culin archival collection (including the related Frank Hamilton Cushing material) held at the Brooklyn Museum of Art and in other repositories.

Collections of artifacts of anthropological significance: The Brooklyn Museum of Art is the second largest fine arts museum in the city and state of New York, and seventh largest in North America. Important objects of anthropological significance can be found in the museum's collection under the following curatorial areas: the Arts of Africa, the Americas and the Pacific; the Asian Art Department; and Egyptian, Classical and Ancient Middle Eastern Art.

Description

The Brooklyn Museum of Art Libraries and Archives contain a substantial amount of research material of anthropological significance due to the encyclopedic scope of the museum's object collections. The museum evolved out of a library association that was established in 1823. The research collections have subsequently expanded in number and subject and in geographic scope—as has the museum's object collection. Today the Libraries and Archives offer more than 200,000 volumes (in addition to textual and visual documents) that provide information on the history of the museum and its collections, as well as on the more general areas of art and cultural history.

The research collections have been built over the years by the librarians and curators who have either purchased or arranged for the donation of important materials. One highly significant part of the department is the Culin Archives and Library. The Brooklyn Museum established the Department of Ethnology in 1903, and appointed Stewart Culin (1858-1929) as its founding curator. Before coming to the museum, Culin held several positions at the University of Pennsylvania and had published two seminal works: *Korean Games, With Notes on the Corresponding Games of China and Japan* (Philadelphia: 1895) and *Games of the North American Indians* (= *Bureau of American Ethnology Report, 1902-1903*). After his arrival at the Brooklyn Museum, Culin immediately launched a series of expeditions through the Southwest, California and the Northwest Coast regions, and, by 1911, he had brought back more than 9,000 Native American objects. He later turned his attention to the cultures of Africa, Asia and Eastern Europe. His ground-breaking African Art exhibition of 1923 was one of the first to display African artifacts as art objects. Culin maintained a working relationship with leading designers and design students and encouraged them to use the museum's collections as an influence for their costume and textile creations.

Culin's contemporaries and correspondents included Franz Boas, Frank Hamilton Cushing, Frederic W. Putnam and George Dorsey. He was a founder of the American Anthropological Association and the American Folklore Society, and a member of many other professional organizations.

After Culin's death, the museum acquired his research collection, which includes the documentation he amassed from the beginning of his professional studies in Philadelphia through his career at the Brooklyn Museum, 1875-1929. This also included his personal library (more than 6,000 titles) that contains many rare or unique publications of anthropological interest. The Culin Archival Collection contains expedition reports, research files, departmental records and reports, object documentation and illustrative study material, including documentary photographs and sketches. The depth and range of the information available in the Culin Archival Collection make it a critical resource for the study of cultural anthropology, the development of ethnology as a discipline, the role of museums in presenting and interpreting objects and cultures and the social and economic consequences within Native communities of large-scale systematic collection.

Expositions were central to the development of the science of anthropology, and Culin was known to have organized exhibitions for at least six expositions. Three expositions are documented in the Culin Archival Collection: the Columbian Historical Exposition, Madrid (1892-1893); the World's Columbian (1893); and the Philadelphia Sesquicentennial (1926).

Aside from the Culin Archival Collection, material of anthropological significance can also be found in the Archives, in the curatorial department records. In particular, the records of the Department of the Arts of Africa, the Americas and the Pacific (formerly known as the Department of Ethnology, with various subsequent titles) includes information on the object collection, exhibitions, field expeditions, research activities and correspondence files from 1929 onwards. Other areas of anthropological interest may be found in the records of the Asian Art Department, and of the Department of Egyptian, Classical and Ancient Middle Eastern Art.

Deirdre E. Lawrence

Kurdish Library

Address: Kurdish Library, 144 Underhill Ave. (corner of Park Place), Brooklyn, NY 11238.
Tel.: (718) 783-7930
Fax: (718) 398-4365
Public transit access: Subway 2 or 3 to Grand Army Plaza; Subway D to 7th Ave.
Founded: 1981 (beginning of the Kurdish program); 1986 (Kurdish Library); 1988 (Kurdish Museum).
Major resources: Kurdish Library; Kurdish Museum.
Areas of specialization: The Kurdish Library holds documentation in several formats on the history, culture and contemporary affairs of the Kurds.
Holdings: Ca. 2,500 books in various languages, including Kurdish, English, French, Swedish and Hebrew. Books in Western languages are cataloged in the Library of Congress

classification system. Books in Kurdish languages (approximately 1,200 volumes) are arranged by type, but are not yet cataloged. Holdings of Kurdish-language books include works of poetry, publications on Kurdish political history and others. Kurdish-language journal holdings include, among others, the Archibald Roosevelt, Jr., collection of periodicals from Mahabad (Kurdish Republic).

Visual/audio resources: A substantial photograph collection (black-and-white as well as color photos) is maintained. Included are the Dana Adams Schmitt photographs taken about 1968. Some 1,500 color slides of Kurdish people and locales are also held, including a group of about 300 slides taken in Kurdistan in 1965 by Ismet Cherif Vanly. There is a map collection (current and retrospective maps) and about sixty posters. Approximately 100 videos are held, including some thirty Kurdish oral histories and also videos of Kurdish dance (in PAL format). Recordings of Kurdish music are on cassette tape.

Access: Open to the public, Monday through Thursday, 10:00 a.m.-3:00 p.m. Books and other materials may be used on-site, but do not circulate outside of the library or via interlibrary loan.

Artifacts: The Kurdish Museum, located at the same address as the Kurdish Library, holds a variety of Kurdish artifacts, jewelry, textiles and costumes. The museum presents two exhibits annually.

Description

Both the Kurdish Library and the Kurdish Museum are in a brownstone building in Brooklyn. The Library and Museum seek to enhance public and scholarly knowledge of Kurdish culture and history. The Kurdish Library publishes the *International Journal of Kurdish Studies* (Brooklyn)—formerly titled *Kurdish Times* (Brooklyn); and *Kurdish Life: A Quarterly Analysis of News, Views of Historical and Geopolitical Significance* (Brooklyn).

Information provided by Vera Beaudin Saeedpour.

New York—New York City—Manhattan

American Museum of Natural History (AMNH)

Address: American Museum of Natural History, 79th St. and Central Park West, New York, NY 10024-5192.
Tel.: (212) 769-5400 (Department of Library Services); (212) 769-5419 (Department of Library Services Special Collections, Photographs, Film, Manuscripts, Art & Realia); (212) 769-5375 (Department of Anthropology); (212) 769-5879 (Department of Anthropology Archives).
Fax: (212) 769-5009 (Department of Library Services); (212) 769-5334 (Department of Anthropology).
Internet address: http://www.amnh.org.
Internet address (Department of Anthropology): http://pearl.amnh.org.

Networks, consortia: OCLC.

Public transit access: Subway: 1 or 9 to 79th Street; B, C or K to 81st Street; bus: M7, M10, M11, M79 or M104.

Founded: 1869 (American Museum and Library); 1873 (Department of Anthropology).

Major resources: Department of Anthropology Archives; Special Collections and Manuscripts, Department of Library Services (includes the Photographic Collection and the Film Collection); Main Library.

Areas of specialization: Archives; artwork pertaining to AMNH publications in anthropology (in the Department of Anthropology Archives); photographs (in the Photographic Collection); films (in the Film Collection); books and serials on anthropology and natural history (in the Library).

Archives/manuscripts: Approximately 654 linear ft. of archives (in the Department of Anthropology Archives); Artifact Catalog (in the Department of Anthropology Archives): 115 volumes. The Department of Anthropology Archives include accession documentation, catalogs and fieldnotes related to the collections and also departmental correspondence from 1894 to the present.

Fieldnotes, papers, etc.: The Department of Anthropology Archives is a major resource for fieldnotes related to the archaeology of the Americas. Also in this location are miscellaneous ethnographic fieldnotes—largely unpublished. In general, field data do not exist for ethnographic research published prior to 1970.

Visual/audio resources: The Department of Anthropology's photographic and film collections are incorporated into Special Collections, Department of Library Services. The personal photograph collection of Franz Boas is an exception; it is in the Department of Anthropology. The Department of Anthropology's collection of 2,500 sound recordings (1900-1935)—primarily of North American Indians and indigenous peoples of Siberia—is on deposit with the Archives of Traditional Music, Indiana University, which releases tape copies with permission of the (AMNH) Department of Anthropology. [See the separate entry on the sound and music collections at the Archives of Traditional Music, Indiana University, Bloomington, Indiana.]

Access: The Collections and Archives of the Department of Anthropology are open to scholars, by written appointment, Monday-Friday, 10:00 a.m. to 5:00 p.m. See the "Guidelines for Study in the Collections and Archives of the Department of Anthropology, American Museum of Natural History," for more detailed information on access to Department of Anthropology archival resources. Library hours are Tuesday-Friday, 11:00 a.m. to 4:00 p.m. A prior written request to the Special Collections Librarian is required. Department of Library Services materials must be used on-site.

References: Bella Weitzner, "A Year-by-Year Summary of the Department of Anthropology Based on the *Annual Reports* of the American Museum of Natural History from 1871 through 1952,"—a manuscript on file in the Department of Anthropology Archives, AMNH; A.E. Parr, "Filling the Gaps of Knowledge. I," American Museum of Natural History, *Eighty-Fourth Annual Report, July 1952-June 1953* (New York: 1953), p. 7-33; Stanley A. Freed and Ruth S. Freed, "Clark Wissler and the Development of Anthropology in the United States," *American Anthropologist*, vol. 85, no. 4 (Dec. 1983), p. 800-825; Ira Jacknis, "Franz Boas and Exhibits: On the Limitations of the Museum Method of Anthropology," in George W. Stocking, Jr. (editor), *Objects and Others: Essays on Museums and Material Culture*

(Madison: 1985) (= *History of Anthropology*, vol. 3), p. 75-111; *Guide to Historical Resources in New York County (Manhattan) Repositories*, vol.III, *American Museum of Natural History* ([Ithaca]: 1989), p. 1-13. Also useful are American Museum publications in Anthropology, including: AMNH, *Memoirs*, vols. 2-8, 10-15 ([1898-1930]); AMNH, *Anthropological Papers*, vols. 1-77 (1907-1995); AMNH, *Bulletin*, vols. 8-10, 12-21, 35, 48, 58, 67 ([1896-1934]); and miscellaneous AMNH publications. On the AMNH Library, see Nina J. Root, "American Museum of Natural History Library," *Science and Technology Libraries*, vol. 6, no. 1-2 (Fall 1985/Winter 1985-1986), p. 1-7.

Guides/catalogs: *Guide to Historical Resources in New York County (Manhattan) Repositories*, vol. III, *American Museum of Natural History* ([Ithaca]: 1989); Nina J. Root (editor), *Catalog of the American Museum of Natural History Film Archives* (New York: 1987) (= *Garland Reference Library of the Humanities*, vol. 723).

Artifacts of anthropological significance: Major artifact collections are in the archaeology of the Americas; ethnology of Asia, Africa, North America and the Pacific.

Archaeological sites represented in artifact collections: Numerous, including Pueblo Bonito and Aztec Ruin, New Mexico; Ipiutak site, Point Hope, Alaska; Mitla and Cuilapa, Oaxaca State, Mexico; Lambayeque and Huaca Prieta, Peru; Fell's Cave, Chile.

Catalogs of artifact resources: American Museum of Natural History, *Ancient Mexico and Central America* (New York: 1970); N.C. Christopher Couch, *Pre-Columbian Art from the Ernest Erickson Collection at the American Museum of Natural History* (New York: 1988); Walter Ashlin Farservis, *Asia: Traditions and Treasures* (New York: 1981); William W. Fitzhugh and Aron Crowell, *Crossroads of Continents: Cultures of Siberia and Alaska* (Washington, D.C.: 1988); Carolyn Gilman and Mary Jane Schneider, *The Way to Independence: Memories of a Hidatsa Indian Family, 1840-1920* (St. Paul: 1987) (= *Minnesota Historical Society. Museum Exhibit Series*, no. 3); Aldona Jonaitis (editor), *Chiefly Feasts: The Enduring Kwakiutl Potlatch* (Seattle: 1991); Aldona Jonaitis, *From the Land of the Totem Poles: The Northwest Coast Indian Art Collection at the American Museum of Natural History* (New York: 1988); David H. Murdoch, *North American Indian* (New York: 1995); Enid Schildkrout and Curtis A. Keim, *African Reflections: Art from Northeastern Zaire* (New York: 1990); Enid Schildkrout, "Art as Evidence: A Brief History of the American Museum of Natural History African Collection," in Center for African Art, *ART/artifact* (New York: 1988), p. 153-192.

Description

Department of Anthropology Archives

The Department of Anthropology was formed in 1873, four years after the American Museum was founded. During the next two decades Albert C. Bickmore (1839-1914), Superintendent of the Museum, administered the collections, which were acquired more or less at random to fill the exhibition halls. Although a number of accessions were accompanied by the collector's personal catalogue—notably George T. Emmons's collection of Tlingit material purchased in 1888—no systematic method of record-keeping was in force.

Sources of documentation for this period consist of annual reports, the minutes of trustee meetings and miscellaneous correspondence housed in the Department of Library Services.

In an effort to put the collections on a "scientific" footing in 1890, the Trustees hired Frederick Starr on a one-year contract to catalogue miscellaneous holdings. This stepping-stone to Starr's career at the University of Chicago is the basis for the present artifact catalogue of 115 handwritten ledgers encompassing a half-million entries.

Archaeology collections, primarily from the Americas, presently account for approximately two-thirds of total entries. The ethnographic collections, representing one-third of entries, focus on Asia, North America, Africa and the Pacific, in that order. Significant collections in physical anthropology also exist.

The cataloguing system, whereby a series of numerators designate date and provenance of accession, general provenience (North America, Asia, Africa, etc.) and type of collection (ethnology, archaeology or physical anthropology) is of historical interest in that it remains a legacy of the Putnam/Boas era. Databases also exist, at present, for the Inuit (Eskimo), Siberian, African, Northwest Coast Indian and North American Indian ethnographic catalogues, with Asian ethnography in process.

Digital images of the Inuit and Northwest Coast Indian collections also exist. Printout quality—both black-and-white and color—is excellent for record purposes and adequate for certain publications. Printouts may be purchased from the department, depending on the availability of staff to process orders. Imaging of the North American Indian collection is in process.

Accession files were established beginning in 1891, when the department became a distinct division of the museum. James Terry, a businessman from Hartford, Connecticut, was appointed its first Curator, in conjunction with the purchase of his extensive collection of North American archaeology.

Terry's correspondence with the cross-country network of amateur archaeologists from whom he acquired artifacts characterizes the kind of documentation subsequent accession files contain. They may also include original labels, bills of lading and shipping receipts, newspaper clippings, photographs, press releases and curatorial directives with respect to expeditions the department has mounted.

These materials tend to document the administrative history of an accession, not necessarily of specific artifacts. Depending on the accession, these may range from one to several thousand items. Accession records also serve as a major resource in illuminating the scope and direction of the department's collecting policy after it was systematized by Frederic W. Putnam (1839-1915), who was joint Curator at the Peabody Museum, Harvard, and at the AMNH from 1894 to 1903.

On his appointment, Putnam presented Museum President Morris K. Jesup with a comprehensive scheme for developing the collections that was predicated on field research and a scientific staff to implement it. While the emphasis was to be on the indigenous peoples of the Americas, whose traditional cultures Putnam perceived were fast disappearing, he also proposed to investigate their prehistory and to build collections from all other parts of the world as opportunities arose. Publishing the results of fieldwork was an integral part of the program.

FIGURE 6. Tungus on reindeer-back crossing the Noyochan River, Siberia. Jessup North Pacific Expedition to Siberia, 1901. Photograph by Waldemar Jochelson. Courtesy of the Department of Library Services, American Museum of Natural History (negative #1590).

Curatorial correspondence (1894-present), in association with accession records, reflects the administrative activities of the staff in pursuing these objectives, beginning with Marshall H. Saville, 1894-1907, and Harlin I. Smith, 1897-1910, in archaeology; and Franz Boas, 1896-1905, in ethnology.

As a result of Putnam's arrangement with the AMNH, which required him to be in New York only one week a month, Boas was delegated with the department's day-to-day business and soon developed his own agendas. Correspondence through 1905 reflects the energy and vision Boas brought to bear on Putnam's initiative, through enterprises such as the Jesup North Pacific Expeditions (1897-1902), Huntington California Expedition (1899-1903), East Asiatic Expedition (1901-1904) and North American Indian fieldwork—begun in 1899 with Alfred L. Kroeber's studies of the Arapaho and completed twenty years later under Clark Wissler.

Friction with Putnam during his curatorship, and with the museum's administration when Boas himself was appointed Curator, led to Boas's resignation in 1905 to take up a full-time professorship at Columbia University.

Papers that provide insights into Boas's rejection of museum anthropology in favor of academia include memoranda to Putnam, President Jesup and Director Herman Bumpus; correspondence pertaining to the New York Bureau of Missions and the East Asiatic Committee—which was formed to support Berthold Laufer's work in China; and to publications that Boas remained under contract to bring out after his departure from the museum. (The concluding volume to the Jesup series never materialized, nor did the results of Laufer's fieldwork. The extensive library of Chinese books Laufer acquired for reference in writing up the collections is an exceptional resource, however—now housed in the Department of Library Services.)

On succeeding Boas as Curator in 1907, Clark Wissler's first act was to establish the *Anthropological Papers* as a separate series under his direction. Wissler (1870-1947) proved to be an able administrator in the area of publications. Despite his reputation as a quiet individual, the correspondence files also reveal Wissler as a major force in museum anthropology through World War II.

Comprehensive studies in North American Indian culture gained focus and momentum with the deployment of numerous fieldworkers, including J.R. Walker, D.C. Duvall, Gilbert Wilson and James R. Murie; and the appointment of Robert H. Lowie, 1908-1920, Pliny Earle Goddard, 1909-1927, and Alanson B. Skinner, 1909-1915, to the staff.

Southwest archaeology, initiated at Pueblo Bonito under George H. Pepper (Hyde Expeditions, 1896-1900), expanded, beginning in 1911, to include N.C. Nelson's studies of chronology in the Galisteo Basin, Earl H. Morris's excavation of Aztec Ruin, and later explorations of Canyons del Muerto and de Chelly—conducted during the 1920s in association with A.V. Kidder of the Peabody Museum, Phillips Academy.

Herbert J. Spinden's preliminary surveys of Central and South American sites, 1917-1920, were followed by George Vaillant's work in central Mexico in the 1930s. During this period, major work in Arctic archaeology was also underway, culminating in the discovery of Ipiutak culture by Froelich Rainey, in association with Helge Larsen of the Danish National Museum.

Wissler's interest in physical anthropology led to the appointment of Louis R. Sullivan in 1916 as the department's first curator in that field. Sullivan's analyses of race in

Polynesia—conducted in association with the Bernice Pauahi Bishop Museum—were continued after his death in 1925 by Harry L. Shapiro, who was departmental chair from 1942 to 1970. Wissler was also instrumental in making the science of anthropology increasingly accessible to the public through his support of temporary exhibitions, popular lecture series, and the department's participation in events such as an Industrial Arts Exposition, held at the Museum in 1919, and the 1939 NY World's Fair.

Under Harry L. Shapiro (1902-1990) the department sought innovative ways to further its educational role. A ground-breaking exhibit, "Men of the Montana," acquainted museum-goers with the ethnology of the Amazon—a new direction for the department that brought Harry Tschopik, Jr., to the staff from 1946-1956. CBS's "Adventure" television series—produced in cooperation with the department—helped to make anthropology a household word. No one was more influential in this area than Margaret Mead.

In formally acknowledging her appointment as Assistant Curator of Ethnology in January 1926, Mead wrote, "I am sure that I shall thoroughly enjoy my association with the Museum." That relationship—which continued for more than fifty years—is reflected in the Mead material that remained in the department after the bulk of her papers were transferred to the Library of Congress, following her death in 1978. The materials that remained with the museum include Mead's correspondence with the staff in the course of her numerous field trips, and inter-office memoranda that focus on her activities as curator, specifically with respect to the Pacific Collections and the permanent exhibition hall devoted to them.

From 1912 into the 1960s, the correspondence files and all other departmental records were managed by Bella Weitzner, who joined the staff as Clark Wissler's assistant, and was later promoted to the rank of curator in recognition of her long-time editorship of the department's publications. For reasons that remain unclear, it appears more than likely that Weitzner discarded the bulk of ethnographic field data once it was edited. At least, in most instances, original field notebooks, etc., do not exist in the department, and almost nothing of the kind is known to exist in other repositories.

The department's fieldnote and manuscript collection in the area of ethnography is therefore limited to material that appears in publications other than the AMNH *Memoirs* and *Anthropological Papers*, or remains unpublished. Among the latter are Robert H. Lowie, Hopi notes, 1915-1916; Claude E. Schaeffer, Kutenai/Flathead notes, 1934-1937; "Notes on the Rio Grande Pueblos, 1909-1913," MS. by Herbert Spinden; and "Ethnical and Geographical Study of the Tsimsiyan Nation," MS. by William Beynon, 1954. Also noteworthy is "Beitrage zur Völkerkunde des Westlichen Südsee,"—a manuscript in the original German by nineteenth-century ethnographer Otto Finsch, from whom Boas purchased a collection from New Guinea, New Ireland and the Marshall Islands in 1898. The manuscript is accompanied by 200 watercolor plates and numerous line drawings by Finsch's wife, Elisabeth.

On the other hand, AMNH publications can be considered a reliable guide to the archaeological data that exists in the department. In addition to the fieldnotes, the records generally include photographs, site plans, maps, etc. The papers of Marshall H. Saville and Nels C. Nelson (personal and professional in both instances) are major resources for the archaeology of Mexico and the American Southwest, respectively.

In addition to AMNH-related materials, the Saville archive includes his reprint collection and manuscripts and notes up to 1932, when Saville retired as a staff member of the Heye Foundation—now the National Museum of the American Indian. These papers came to the Department in 1951 through the efforts of Gordon F. Ekholm, Curator of Meso-American Archaeology at the time.

The Nelson papers also include notes on European archaeology and material connected with Nelson's participation as field archaeologist on the AMNH Central Asiatic Expedition (1926-1927), led by paleontologist Roy Chapman Andrews.

The Boas Collection

At the time he closed his office at Columbia University in 1943, Boas deposited a portion of his personal papers with the department. The collection includes drawings by Northwest Coast Indian artists—some of which are published in his *Primitive Art* (1927); photographs taken by Boas, Waldemar Jochelson and others during the course of the Jesup Expeditions—some of which are not duplicated in the AMNH Library's photographic collection; and anthropometric records, consisting of data on indigenous peoples of North America and Siberia. These are currently on long-term loan to the Department of Anthropology, University of Tennessee, for analysis. Additional anthropometric data connected with Boas's immigrant studies was recently transferred to the National Park Service, Ellis Island Immigration Museum.

Junius Bird Laboratory of South American Archaeology

The Lab was founded in memory of Junius B. Bird (1907-1982), a pioneer in the study of pre-Columbian textiles and curator of South American archaeology, 1939-1973. Located in Bird's former office in the department, it houses his library, slide collection and papers, in particular with respect to excavations at Fell's Cave and Palli Aike Cave in southern Chile, between 1934 and 1937, and at Huaca Prieta in northern Peru from 1946 to 1947. The Lab is also the repository for all other departmental records associated with South American archaeology, including the notes and journals of Adolph Bandelier from 1892 to 1900, and of Wendell C. Bennett, curator from 1931 to 1937. These cover the sites of Surco and Pachacamac, Peru, and Tiwanaku, Bolivia, among many others.

In addition, the Bird Lab serves as current curator Craig Morris's base for ongoing research in connection with his previous work at the site of Huanuco Pampa and present studies involving Inca frontier expansion in Bolivia; and the Chincha archaeological project on Peru's south-central coast.

Other Records

Other divisions of the museum that house records related to the department's activities include the Department of Library Services; Special Collections; and the Archives of the Departments of Mammalogy and Ornithology. The Archives of Traditional Music, Indiana University, houses the Department of Anthropology's collection of wax cylinder recordings dating to 1901. The American Philosophical Society, Philadelphia (Franz Boas papers), and the Harvard University Archives (Frederic W. Putnam papers), are repositories for additional material related to Boas's AMNH career. Clark Wissler's personal papers are in the Library, Ball State University, Muncie, Indiana.

Belinda Kaye

Columbia University. Department of Music. Center for Ethnomusicology

Address: Center for Ethnomusicology, 417 Dodge Hall, Columbia University, New York, NY 10027.
Tel.: (212) 854-1247
Fax: (212) 854-1309
Internet address: http://www.music.columbia.edu/~cecenter.
Public transit access: Subway: 1 or 9 to 116th Street-Columbia University; bus: M4, M5, M11 or M104.
Founded: 1967.
Major resources: Archives of the Center for Ethnomusicology.
Areas of specialization: Ethnomusicological recordings from throughout the world.
Visual/audio resources: 50,000 tape recordings, 300 videos.
Access: Open for research and public use on a very limited basis.
Guides/catalogs, etc.: Information on selected African recordings at the Center is in Aloha South, *Guide to Non-Federal Archives and Manuscripts in the United States Relating to Africa* (London: 1989), vol. 2, p. 691-694.

Metropolitan Museum of Art (MMA). Department of Egyptian Art

Address: Department of Egyptian Art, The Metropolitan Museum of Art, 1000 Fifth Avenue, New York, NY 10028-0198.
Tel.: (212) 570-3770
Fax: (212) 570-3752
Public transit access: Subway: 4, 5 or 6 to 86th Street; bus: M1, M2, M3, M4, M79 or M86.
Founded: 1870 (MMA);1906 (Department of Egyptian Art).
Major resources: Library and Archives of the Department of Egyptian Art.
Areas of specialization: Egyptian art and archaeology.
Archives/manuscripts: The Research Archive, derived from excavations: ca. 550 linear ft.
Fieldnotes, papers, etc.: The department has the fieldnotes and other expedition records from its excavations in Egypt. These records cover the years from 1907 to 1936—a period when the museum had uninterrupted excavations in progress in Egypt at Thebes, Lisht, Hierakonpolis, the Khargeh Oasis and the Wadi Natrun. In 1984 the museum resumed excavations at Lisht, and in 1990 began excavation at Dahshur. Publication of these excavations has been ongoing since 1916 in the series cited below.

Field Directors and authors of these publications are Albert M. Lythgoe (1868-1934), Herbert E. Winlock (1884-1950), Arthur C. Mace (1874-1928), Harry Burton, (1879-1940), William C. Hayes (1903-1963), Ambrose Lansing (1891-1959), H.G. Evelyn White

(1884-1924), Charles. K. Wilkinson (1898-1986), Norman deGaris Davies (1865-1941), Nina Davies (1881-1965), Caroline Ransom Williams (1874[?]-1952), Dieter Arnold (1936-), Dorothea Arnold (1935-), Peter Dorman (1948-) and Felix Arnold (1972-).

Holdings (books and journals): The Research Library in Egyptology holds ca. 10,000 v.

Visual/audio resources: The department holds approximately 70,000 photographs, 2,000 slides and a set of 16mm films from its excavations (kept in the museum's Film Department).

Access: The library is a non-circulating curatorial library for use by the department staff. Outside researchers use duplicate materials in the museum's main Watson Library. Archives are primarily accessible to staff and collaborating scholars who are publishing the excavations.

References: Preliminary reports on the museum's excavations were published in the *Bulletin of The Metropolitan Museum of Art* (New York) from 1907 to 1939. Final publication is made in the series *Publications of The Metropolitan Museum of Art Egyptian Expedition*, vol. 1- (New York: 1916-). [This series has now reached 25 volumes.] Results of the department's Graphic Expedition, which copied and published Egyptian tombs, are found in a subseries: Metropolitan Museum of Art (New York). Egyptian Expedition, *Robb de Peyster Tytus Memorial Series* (New York: 1917-1927), 5 v.; William Christopher Hayes, *The Scepter of Egypt: A Background for the Study of the Egyptian Antiquities in The Metropolitan Museum of Art* (rev. ed., New York: 1990), 2 v.

Artifacts: The Egyptian Collection of The Metropolitan Museum of Art is the largest collection of Egyptian artifacts in the United States and one of the major collections in the world. The display of these objects is unique: all of the department's holdings (except for objects removed for study, conservation or loan) are on exhibit at all times in a combination of main galleries and adjacent small study galleries. Since much of the material is derived from the museum's early excavations, groups of material and their accompanying documentation are very complete—a situation more normally found in history museums than in art museums.

Archaeological sites represented in the departmental artifact collections:

Museum excavations:
- Thebes, 1907-1936.
- Lisht, 1907-1909, 1911-1914, 1916-1918, 1920-1925, 1931-1934, 1984-1989, 1991-
- Khargeh Oasis, 1908-1910, 1927-1928, 1930-1931.
- Wadi Natrun, 1910-1912, 1920-1921.
- Hierakonpolis, 1934-1935.
- Dahshur, 1990, 1992-

Catalogs of artifacts: There is no separate catalog of the Egyptian Collection. It is published and discussed, however, in William C. Hayes, *The Scepter of Egypt: A Background for the Study of the Egyptian Antiquities in The Metropolitan Museum of Art*, first published in 1953-1959. A convenient guide to the work of the Graphic Expedition in Thebes is available in Charles K. Wilkinson, *Egyptian Wall Paintings: The Metropolitan Museum's Collection of Facsimiles* (New York: 1983).

Description

The scope and scale of the excavations in Egypt during the early part of this century by the Egyptian Department, The Metropolitan Museum of Art, are unequaled, then or now, by any other American institution. The department's Egyptian work is comparable to that of the major foreign archaeological institutes in Egypt. Economic conditions, however, and subsequently World War II, put a halt to these excavations. Many years have been needed to conserve and catalog the objects and data produced by thirty years of excavations.

In the 1970s and 1980s the field archives were organized and stored properly so that work on publication could be initiated. New excavations that resumed at Lisht in 1984 are designed to clarify and update the materials from the earlier excavations, so that they can be published according to modern archaeological standards. Three volumes on Lisht have now been published and two are in preparation. Unpublished material from the Khargeh Oasis is also in preparation, as well as material from some of the Theban tombs. A publication on the excavations at Hierakonpolis is forthcoming.

In 1983 the reinstallation of the museum's Egyptian Collection was completed, making it fully accessible to the public. Material on display is available to scholars for study and for publication (unless otherwise committed) by application to the Curator in Charge. The department also answers written requests for information from scholars and the public (within the limits of staff resources). The department is currently preparing a computerized catalog of its collection; there are no plans at this time to take it on-line.

Susan J. Allen

Metropolitan Museum of Art. Department of the Arts of Africa, Oceania and the Americas. Photograph Study Collection (PSC)

Address: Photograph Study Collection, Department of the Arts of Africa, Oceania and the Americas, Metropolitan Museum of Art, 1000 Fifth Avenue (at 82nd Street), New York, NY 10028-0198.
Tel.: (212) 879-5500 (main Museum number); (212) 650-2823 (Photograph Study Collection).
Fax: (212) 570-3879
Public transit access: Subway: 4, 5 or 6 to 86th Street; bus: M1, M2, M3, M4, M79 or M86.
Founded: The Photograph Study Collection was founded with the "Museum of Primitive Art" in 1957.
Major resources: 120,000 photographs in many formats.
Areas of specialization: Photographs of African, Oceanic, Native and pre-Columbian American objects in public and private collections. Exterior contextual photographs made in Africa and Oceania.
Archives/manuscripts: The archives of the Department of the Arts of Africa, Oceania and the Americas. This archive contains various records of the former Museum of Primitive Art, New York.

Fieldnotes and related materials: Manuscripts and notes of Edward H. Dodd, Paul Fejos, Douglas Fraser, Paul Gebauer, Frederick A. Peterson and Michael C. Rockefeller.

Access: Open to scholars with a pass from an Information Desk, 10:00 a.m. to 4:30 p.m., Tuesday to Friday. Appointments are necessary for use of special collections or for detailed research projects. Closed during August.

References (general): "The Photograph Study Collection,"—a 1991 brochure; Virginia-Lee Webb, "Collected Images: A Research File of Photographs of Art," *Curator,* vol. 30, no. 1 (Mar. 1987), p. 77-83; Virginia-Lee Webb, "The Photographs of Paul Gebauer," *African Arts,* vol. 20, no. 2 (Feb. 1987), p. 46-51.

References (about specific items in the collection): Christraud Geary and Virginia-Lee Webb (editors), *Delivering Views: Distant Cultures in Early Postcards* (Washington, D.C.: 1998); Virginia-Lee Webb, "The Crane Pacific Expedition, 1928-29: The Sepik River Photographs," *Pacific Arts,* no. 1-2 (Jan.-July 1990), p. 91; Virginia-Lee Webb, "Fact and Fiction: Nineteenth-Century Photographs of the Zulu," *African Arts,* vol. 25, no. 1 (Jan. 1992), p. 50-59, 98.

Artifacts of anthropological interest: Objects in the collection of the Department of the Arts of Africa, Oceania and the Americas are on view in the museum's Michael C. Rockefeller Wing.

Artifact catalogs: Object collections are documented in many publications. See, for example, Metropolitan Museum of Art (New York), *The Pacific Islands, Africa and the Americas* (New York: 1987).

Description

The Photograph Study Collection is a research collection of photographs dedicated to the arts of Africa, the Pacific Islands and Native and pre-Columbian America. The collection—a part of The Metropolitan Museum of Art's Department of the Arts of Africa, Oceania and the Americas—seeks to promote the understanding of, and research on, the traditional arts and cultures of these areas through visual media. Both nineteenth- and twentieth-century images are included, among them photographs of art in public and private collections from around the world. Holdings of The Metropolitan Museum of Art are represented among them. Photographs taken in exterior locations, showing the art in its larger cultural context, are also part of the Photograph Study Collection. The collection contains more than 120,000 images in a wide variety of photographic formats.

Photographs by art historians, anthropologists, commercial photographers, missionaries, scholars and explorers, among others, form the collection. Documentation in varying degrees of detail and complexity is provided by the photographers. Several unique archives are available for study. These include photographs taken in 1961 by Michael C. Rockefeller in Asmat villages in Irian Jaya, on the island of New Guinea; the more than 11,000 images made by Paul Gebauer, who lived in Cameroon (central West Africa) with his family from 1935 to 1962; Merle Greene Robertson's detailed documentation of the Maya site of Palenque in Mexico; Frederick A. Peterson's photographs of Mexican ceramic art; the archive of published and unpublished annotated manuscripts on Polynesian art by Edward H. Dodd; Pál Fejos's photographs of ancient Peruvian architectural sites and

Indonesian communities; Anthony Forge's photographs of the traditional architecture and art of Papua New Guinea; Mervyn Meggitt's photographs of the Enga people of Papua New Guinea; Sidney Shurcliff and Murry N. Fairbank's photographs on the Crane Pacific Expedition; and William B. Fagg's photographs made while living in Nigeria and studying the local art and architecture.

Photograph albums with gelatin silver prints by Anthony Wilkin, made on the 1898 Cambridge Anthropological Expedition to Torres Strait, are possibly the only copies outside of Great Britain available for study. A selection of 900 annotated photographs made in various locations in New Guinea by Swiss ethnologist Paul Wirz documents the inventive and prolific artistic cultures of the island. Nineteenth-century albumen print collections contain exterior and studio photographs made by commercial photographers in New Zealand, Samoa, Fiji, New Guinea and various African countries.

Approximately 5,000 photographic postcards are also available for study. Many nineteenth-century exterior photographs of African and Pacific communities were altered and reissued in the twentieth-century on postcards. Images by commercial photograph studios and amateur photographers comprise a major part of the holdings. Also included in the postcard collection are images produced in conjunction with missionary activity, World Fairs and Expositions.

The Photograph Study Collection originated at the Museum of Primitive Art in 1957, was transferred to The Metropolitan Museum of Art in the 1970s, and is now housed in the Michael C. Rockefeller Wing. The archives of the Department of the Arts of Africa, Oceania and the Americas is a special collection of documents, correspondence, installation photographs and related ephemera documenting the exhibitions and presentations at the Museum of Primitive Art, New York. Installation photographs, primarily by Charles Uht, show the exhibitions presented at the museum.

A brochure concerning the Photograph Study Collection is available free of charge by contacting the Department. Appointments are not necessary during public hours, but are recommended. Application for research in the archive must be submitted in advance, in writing, with a description of the proposed project. Advance appointments are required for any project involving fragile or detailed archival material.

Virginia-Lee Webb

Metropolitan Museum of Art. Department of the Arts of Africa, Oceania and the Americas. Robert Goldwater Library

Address: Robert Goldwater Library, Metropolitan Museum of Art, 1000 Fifth Avenue (at 82nd Street), New York, NY 10028-0198.
Tel.: (212) 570-3707
Fax: (212) 472-2872
Networks, consortia: The Goldwater Library is beginning to enter current catalog records of its holdings in RLIN. Retrospective catalog records are not yet on-line.
Public transit access: Subway: 4, 5 or 6 to 86th Street; bus: M1, M2, M3, M4, M79 or M86.
Founded: 1957 (as the Library, Museum of Primitive Art, New York).

Major resources: Books and journals on indigenous art, archaeology and ethnology of Africa, Oceania and the Americas.
Areas of specialization: Africa, Oceania and the Americas.
Holdings (books and journals): Ca. 35,000 v.
Visual/audio resources: Many photos are in the department's Photograph Study Collection (PSC) [see the preceding entry].
Access: Available for graduate and undergraduate students and for research use.
Guides/catalogs: Metropolitan Museum of Art. Robert Goldwater Library, *Catalog of the Robert Goldwater Library, The Metropolitan Museum of Art* (Boston: 1982), 4 v.
Artifacts: Extensive collections of art objects and artifacts are in the museum's Department of the Arts of Africa, Oceania and the Americas.

Metropolitan Museum of Art. Thomas J. Watson Library

Address: Thomas J. Watson Library, Metropolitan Museum of Art, 1000 Fifth Ave. (at 82nd Street), New York, NY 10028-0198.
Tel.: (212) 879-5500
Fax: (212) 570-3847
E-mail: watsonlibrary@metmuseum.org.
Internet address: http://www.metmuseum.org.
Networks, consortia: RLIN, RLG.
Public transit access: Subway: 4, 5 or 6 to 86th Street; bus: M1, M2, M3, M4, M79 or M86.
Founded: 1880.
Major resources: Books and journals on art, archaeology and architecture.
Archives/manuscripts: These are in the departments—see, for example, the entry for the museum's Department of Egyptian Art.
Holdings (books and journals): 400,000 book vols.; 5,000 periodical titles.
Access: Available for graduate students and qualified researchers.

National Archives—Northeast Region (New York City)

Address: National Archives—Northeast Region, 201 Varick Street, New York, NY 10014.
Tel.: (212) 337-1300
Fax: (212) 337-1306
E-mail: archives@newyork.nara.gov.
Internet address: http://www.nara.gov/regional/newyork.html.
Public transit access: Subway 1 to Houston Street, or PATH to Christopher Street.
Founded: 1969.
Major resources: Records of federal courts and agencies in New York, New Jersey, Puerto Rico and the U.S. Virgin Islands. Holdings include original records of District Courts of the United States, including naturalizations (RG 21); U.S. Courts of Appeals (RG 276); U.S. Attorneys and Marshals (RG 118); the Immigration and Naturalization Service, including case files generated under the Chinese Exclusion Acts (RG 85) and the Puerto Rico

Reconstruction Administration (RG 323). On microfilm, the National Archives—Northeast Region also has *Passenger Lists of Vessels Arriving at New York, N.Y., 1820-1957*. Detailed information from the Chinese Exclusion case files, 1882-1960, has been entered in an electronic database.

Areas of specialization: Regional and national history of the United States from 1685 to the present.

Holdings: 63,000 cubic ft. of original records; more than 40,000 reels of microfilm.

Visual/audio resources: The Chinese case files include photographs of individuals and a few places of business. Some photographs were taken in China.

Access: Most records related to anthropology are open for public use, although some Chinese Exclusion records are subject to Privacy Act restrictions.

References: Robert C. Morris, "Chinese Immigration Database at the National Archives—Northeast Region," *The Record*, vol. 1, no. 2 (Nov. 1994), p. 5-6.

Description

Chinese Case Files. Records of the Immigration and Naturalization Service. 1882-1960. (RG 85).

Immigration and Naturalization Service case files at the National Archives—Northeast Region were generated under the Chinese Exclusion Acts. A result of anti-Chinese sentiment on the West Coast, the first such legislation in 1882 prohibited the immigration of Chinese laborers for a period of ten years. Subsequent acts further tightened restrictions—prohibiting the entry of all except merchants, teachers, students and visitors; barring laborers visiting China from returning unless they had a family in the United States or property worth at least $1,000; and in 1924 excluding foreign-born wives and children of citizens. Enforcement of these laws between 1882 and their repeal in 1943 generated more than 18,500 files for the New York-New Jersey area. In addition to standard documents associated with these acts, files often include such useful records as interrogations, depositions, inspector's reports, photographs and even some information supplied by informants. Several files contain coaching books used to prepare for interrogations.

Although the Exclusion Acts led to widespread falsification of information about an immigrant's true identity, much of the data in these files is reliable. Late in 1956 the Immigration and Naturalization Service instituted the Chinese Confession Program, which assisted those who admitted they were in the country illegally to adjust their status "if at all possible under the law." Some case files thus include corrections as to actual identities and family relationships.

A database for every file includes the following information: name, Chinese home town, date and place of birth, sex, age, occupations, date and port of entry, addresses in the United States, documents in the case file and disposition of the case.

Also held at the Northeast Region are:

- Records of District Courts of the United States, 1685-1973, (RG 21).

District Courts (and Circuit Courts until 1911) exercise jurisdiction over naturalization, and their records often include Declarations of Intention and Petitions for Naturalization. Naturalization records in the National Archives—Northeast Region include:

- Petitions for Naturalization filed in federal, state and local courts located in New York City, 1792-1906.
- Petitions for Naturalization filed in U.S. District Court for the Southern District of New York, 1824-1940.
- Petitions for Naturalization filed in U.S. Circuit Court for the Southern District of New York, 1846-1876, 1906-1911.
- Petitions for Naturalization filed in U.S. District Court for the Eastern District of New York, 1865-1957.
- Petitions for Naturalization filed in U.S. District Court for the Western District of New York, 1907-1966.
- Petitions for Naturalization filed in the U.S. District Court for the District of New Jersey. Newark Office.

U.S. District Court for Puerto Rico:

- Naturalizations for the U.S. District Court for Puerto Rico.
- Declarations of Intention and Naturalization Records, 1898-1972.
- Petitions for Naturalization, 1917-1929.
- Armed Forces Naturalization Petitions, 1944-1956.
- Declarations of Persons who Retained Spanish Nationality.
- Petitions for Naturalization Denied, 1929-1962.
- Records of the Puerto Rico Reconstruction Administration, 1935-1953, (RG 323).

The Puerto Rico Reconstruction Administration was established in the Department of the Interior, under the Emergency Relief Appropriation Act of 1935, to provide relief, increase employment and rehabilitate the agricultural economy in Puerto Rico. The records are described in Mary Jane Schmittou and Mario D. Fenyo (compilers), *Preliminary Inventory of the Records of the Puerto Rico Reconstruction Administration,* (Washington, D.C.: 1963) (= *Preliminary Inventory*, no. 152).

Robert C. Morris

New-York Historical Society (N-YHS)

Address: New-York Historical Society, 170 Central Park West, New York, NY 10024-5194.
Tel.: (212) 873-3400
Fax: (212) 875-1591
Networks, consortia: RLIN, RLG. An OPAC is in the reading room; there is a separate database of the flat-map collection.
Public transit access: Subway: 1 or 9 to 79th Street, B or C to 81st Street.

Founded: 1804.
Major resources: Library and Manuscripts Division; Department of Prints and Photographs.
Areas of specialization: American history; substantial printed and manuscript documentation on some Native American groups—particularly those in the New York area. Holdings include significant numbers of so-called "Indian captiviy" narratives, Bibles translated into Native American languages, studies of Native American languages and colonial manuscripts documenting relations with Native Americans.
Holdings (all subject areas): 650,000 books; 2 million manuscripts; 10,000 newspaper titles.
Archives/manuscripts: In the Manuscript Department.
Visual/audio resources: The Map Collection (in the Library) has extensive holdings of historical maps of North America. Historical photographs are in the Department of Prints and Photographs.
Access: Open to the public. No appointment is needed to visit the Library (which includes the Manuscript Department). A prior appointment is needed for access to the Department of Prints and Photographs.
Guides/catalogs: Donald Glassman and Stephen Fadden (compilers), "A Partial Bibliography of N-YHS Library Holdings (Including Books, Manuscripts & Periodicals) That Bear on Native American History,"—an unpublished 1992 draft list that is available for reference use in the library.

Information provided by the New-York Historical Society.

New York Public Library (NYPL). **Central Research Library**

Address: Central Research Library, New York Public Library, Fifth Avenue at 42nd Street, New York, NY 10018-2788.
Tel.: (212) 930-0826 (general); (212) 930-0716 (Oriental Collection); (212) 930-0845 (Slavic Collection); (212) 930-0714 (Jewish Collection); (212) 930-0601 (Latin American Collection); (212) 930-0837 (Photography Collection); (212) 930-0740 (Special Collections).
Fax: (212) 921-2546
Internet address: http://www.nypl.org. This website provides information on resources of the Research Libraries within the NYPL system.
Internet access to on-line catalog: Access to CATNYP is available at nyplgate.nypl.org. Logon: nypl.
Networks, consortia: CATNYP contains catalog records of the Research Libraries from 1972.
Public transit access: Subway: 1, 2, 3, 6, 9, N, R or S to Times Square; 7 to Fifth Ave.; B, D, F or Q to 42nd St.; bus: M1, M2, M3, M4, M5, M6, M7, M42, M104 or O32.
Founded: 1895.
Major resources: The New York Public Library is a very large research library system that serves the general public as well as specialist researchers and scholars. The landmark Central Research Library at 42nd Street and 5th Avenue is the locale of the Center for the Humanities. Important area research collections at this location include the Jewish, Slavic,

Oriental and Latin American Collections. The Central Research Library has extensive book and journal holdings pertaining to Native Americans, some materials on aboriginal people of Australia, Gypsy and Ainu-related publications. The extensive holdings of the NYPL Schomburg Center for Research on Black Culture (at 135th Street in Manhattan) are described separately in this guide. Also of anthropological significance is the New York Public Library for the Performing Arts [at Lincoln Center Plaza in Manhattan; see the following entry].

Areas of specialization: Many area and other specialized collections are maintained at the Research Libraries. The Oriental, Jewish, Slavic and Latin American Collections are prominent among resources of anthropological research interest. Central Research Library holdings include PL 480 materials from India, Pakistan and Egypt. The James Legge (1815-1897) collection of Chinese rare books is a special resource of the Oriental Collection.

Archives/manuscripts: In several NYPL locations.

Holdings (all subject areas): 11,867,000 cataloged books; 38,834,000 items, including books and non-print materials.

Visual/audio resources: In the Prints and Photographs Division and in other departments.

Access: The four major NYPL Research Libraries serve as reference libraries for researchers, while branch libraries in the NYPL system meet the needs of general readers. Materials in the Central Research Library are for on-site use only.

Guides/catalogs: Sam P. Williams, *Guide to the Research Collections of The New York Public Library* (Chicago: 1975). Several specialized catalogs of NYPL holdings have been published. For information on retrospective NYPL holdings on the history of Native peoples in the Americas, see New York Public Library. Reference Department, *Dictionary Catalog of the History of the Americas* (Boston: 1961), 28 v., Supplement, 1974.

Artifacts: A collection of African art and artifacts is maintained at the New York Public Library Schomburg Center for Research in Black Culture—[see the separate entry on the Schomburg Center].

New York Public Library for the Performing Arts

Address: New York Public Library for the Performing Arts, 40 Lincoln Center Plaza, New York, NY 10023-7498.

Tel.: (212) 870-1657 (Dance Collection); (212) 870-1663 (Rodgers and Hammerstein Archives of Recorded Sound); (212) 870-1650 (Music Division); (212) 870-1639 (Billy Rose Theatre Collection); (212) 870-1630 (general Performing Arts information).

Fax: (212) 799-7975 (Dance Collection); (212) 496-5196 (Performing Arts).

Internet address: http://www.nypl.org/research/lpa.

Networks, consortia: RLIN, Dance Heritage Coalition.

Public transit access: Subway 1 or 9 to 66th St./Lincoln Center; bus: M5, M7, M10, M11, M57, M66 or M104.

Founded: The Dance Collection became a NYPL division in 1964, when the Performing Arts collections were moved from The New York Public Library's 42nd Street building to the new Lincoln Center complex.

Major resources: Dance Collection; Rodgers and Hammerstein Archives of Recorded Sound; Music Division; Billy Rose Theatre Collection.

Areas of specialization: The performing arts, including dance and music. The Dance Collection is the most comprehensive archive on its subject in the world. It is the only one devoted solely to collecting and preserving the literature and iconography of every kind of dance: ballet, modern, social, jazz, tap, ethnic, folk and national.

Archives/manuscripts:

• Claire Holt papers, ca. 1928-1970—Indonesian court dance, dance drama, temples and sculpture. Sixteen boxes of papers, 9,000 photographic prints, 3,500 photographic negatives and three 1938 films of Sumatra, Java and Bali-Celebes.

• Tassilo Adam films, 1921-1928—dances, shadowplay, dance drama, ceremonies of Indonesia. The film negatives have been edited into three coherent sequences, and a positive print has been made. Approximately 90 minutes.

• Encyclopaedia Cinematographica films—the Dance Collection owns 140 films from this ethnographic series, representing dance of every continent, produced by the Institut für Wissenschaftlichen Film of the University of Göttingen.

• Eleanor King papers, 1931-1991—Korea, Japan, Burma, Sri Lanka and American Indian. Five boxes of research notes, book and article manuscripts and lecture/demonstration scripts.

• Mura Dehn papers on African American social dance, ca. 1869-1987, and *The Spirit Moves* films, 1950-1986. Five boxes of manuscript writings on jazz dance; seven films of jazz dance—including lindy at the Savoy Ballroom of Harlem and break dance.

• Denishawn Dance films, 1925-1926—dancers of India, Japan and Indonesia performing their own traditional works for members of the first American dance company to tour Asia.

• Centro de Trabalho Indigenista, Brazil, 1980s—videotapes of rituals of Nambicuara Indians (recorded by Vincent Carelli); and men's initiation rituals of Xavante Indians (recorded by Paolo César Soares). Tapes are edited; each is 20 minutes.

• Javanese Dance, Yoganese style, 1980—filmed by William Terry Start at dance academy Pamulangan Beksa Ngayakarta. 13 hours.

• Classical Khmer Ballet of Cambodia, 1971—filmed in New York City by the Dance Collection. 3 1/2 hours.

Fieldnotes of anthropological significance: Claire Holt (1901-1970)—the collection is analyzed in an unpublished finding aid.

Holdings (Dance Collection): 32,700 books and 710 periodical titles. The periodicals of particular interest to anthropologists include *Journal for the Anthropological Study of Human Movement*; *Journal of the Association of Graduate Dance Ethnologists*; and *Dance Research Journal* (CORD)—which publishes frequent anthropological articles; as well as *Dance Studies*—an anthropologically-based journal published in the United Kingdom. Also in the Dance Collection are 270,000 photographic prints and negatives, 762 linear ft. of manuscripts, 3,130 hours of oral history, 2,070 original stage and costume designs, 6,050 engravings and lithographs, 1,740 reels of microfilm, 24,400 files of newspaper clippings and 21,000 reels of film and videotape.

Visual/audio resources: See below.

Access: The Dance Collection and other departments are open to the public. No special qualifications are required, nor are advance appointments needed. A small percentage of Dance Collection films and manuscript collections require prior permission from their donors or from producing organizations. All of the research collections in the performing arts are located on the third floor and are non-circulating.

References: For a description of the Asian materials in the Dance Collection, see Sal Murgiyanto, "For the Dance of Tomorrow: Documentation and Research," *Performing Arts* (Singapore), no. 4 (Dec. 1987), p. 40-47. Several photographs from the Claire Holt Collection and a summary description by Nancy Shawcross are published in "The Claire Holt Collection," *Dance Research Journal* (CORD), vol. 19, no. 1 (Summer 1987), p. 25-35. One of the largest manuscript units covering a dance company's activities is described by Amy Taylor Alpers in "Sergei Denham, 1896-1970: Records of the Ballet Russe de Monte Carlo, ca. 1936-1978," Society of Dance History Scholars, *Proceedings, 11th Annual Conference* (Riverside, Ca.: 1988), p. 158-162. A general description of the Dance Collection is in Sam P. Williams (compiler), *Guide to the Research Collections of The New York Public Library* (Chicago: 1975), p. 150-156.

Guides/catalogs: *Dance on Disc: The Complete Catalog of the Dance Collection of The New York Public Library on CD-ROM* (version 3.0, Boston: 1995) [one laser optical disc].

Description

The Dance Collection

The Claire Holt collection richly documents Indonesia from the period 1920 through 1960. The Holt collection comprises approximately 9,000 photographs and 61 notebooks (totaling 8,500 pages) on choreography and art, personal observations, letters, articles and manuscripts. Dominant are Miss Holt's two special fields of interest: dance and art history. Photographs documenting the dance classes that she took with the daughters of the Sultan of Surakarta, Mankunagara VII, are juxtaposed with the sculptural dance reliefs of Tjandi Prambandan and the Borobodur. The journeys to Sumatra, Borneo, Bali, Nias, the Celebes, Timor and New Guinea, undertaken in the 1930s with Rolf de Maré and Hans Evert, to film all of the dances in these islands, are extensively recorded. The lives and thoughts of the performing and visual artists are notated in detail in the form of biographical sketches. Also captured is the atmosphere of Miss Holt's circle of friends, including Jaap Kunst, Walter Spies, Beryl de Zoete, Margaret Mead, Jane Belo, Cora DuBois, Mankunagara VII and Sukarno. Holt's papers include the manuscript for her book, *Art in Indonesia: Continuities and Change* (Ithaca, N.Y.: 1967) and two unpublished book manuscripts: "The Dance in Java and the Dances of Bali" and "Dances of Sumatra and Nias." Prints of the films recorded in the 1930s by Claire Holt, Rolf de Maré and Hans Evert supplement this collection.

The Tassilo Adam film collection encompasses approximately 10,000 feet of film shot in the 1920s in Indonesia. The bulk of the collection is of Central Java, comprising court ceremonies and dance dramas at the palaces of Jogyakarta and Surakarta, as well as village performances and rituals in the surrounding area. Of special interest is the *wayang wong* that Tassilo Adam filmed in 1923, produced by the Sultan of Jogyakarta to celebrate the 25th anniversary of the coronation of Queen Wilhelmina of The Netherlands. This four-day performance was a return to the nineteenth-century practice of multi-day wayangs and is said to have been the first presented in more than two decades. Also notable are films of the *bedoyo*, a ritualistic women's dance, considered to be a holy object of mystical power owned by a court. The dedicated groups of girls who performed the bedoyo have since disappeared, as the court structures have changed in the present century.

Tassilo Adam was a German-born ethnographer who was appointed official Ethnologist of the Dutch East Indies by the Governor General of Java. Originally filmed in 35mm, the Asia Society possessed 16mm reduction prints, that, because of their damaged condition, could not be projected or studied. The Dance Collection produced a negative and print of the films, and these have been organized, edited and cataloged by Deena Burton, a specialist in Indonesian dance. The resulting compilation films are available for viewing in the Dance Collection. These historical films have been returned to Indonesia by the Collection. With the assistance of funds from the Asian Cultural Council, they have been donated to three arts educational institutions in Indonesia and to the current Sultans of Surakarta and Jogyakarta. The Dance Collection also owns a ninety-minute audiotape interview recorded in 1988 with Lilo Gottschalk, daughter of Tassilo Adam, in which she describes her early dance studies at the Javanese court and her father's work.

Where documents do not exist, the Dance Collection acts to create them. During the past thirty years more than 600 major dance works have been filmed and videotaped, and more than 380 oral history interviews have been recorded and transcribed. The Collection has recently videotaped an eight-hour Tibetan folk opera, *Sukyi Nima*, performed by the Chaksampa Company, as well as classes, workshops, performances and ceremonials during Tibet Week, hosted by Cross Cultural Resources, in Flagstaff, Arizona.

In 1993 the Dance Collection collaborated with the Smithsonian Institution to videotape approximately thirty hours of the Festival of American Folklife. A sampling of folkloric dances of Saudi Arabia was recorded during a 1990 U.S. exposition. In 1971, at the height of the devastation in Cambodia, nearly four hours of a performance by the Classical Khmer Ballet were recorded in Brooklyn—and a tradition threatened by oblivion was captured. In the Collection's rapidly expanding film and videotape archive, the tools are immediately available for dancers to study and compare dance styles and traditions.

The Claire Holt and Tassilo Adam collections are the only substantial groups of materials organized by individuals with formal anthropological training. However, the Dance Collection is rich in documentary collections of producing organizations, dance companies and individuals that could be used for anthropological analysis. Some of these collections document early performance tours by artists such as Uday Shankar, companies like the Moiseyev or the National Dance Company of Senegal, and resident artists such as Michio Ito. The Collection also records the work of dancers who were intrigued by non-Western traditions and who studied their dances in depth. These include choreographer Eleanor King, who worked in several East Asian traditions.

A dance company can be conceived as a kind of tribe; company members are performers of highly ritualized events, initiates who have been prepared by many years of specialized physical and artistic training. The Collection has among its manuscript holdings the papers of dance companies, including the Ballet Russe de Monte Carlo, the American

Ballet Theatre, the José Limón Dance Company and Ruth St. Denis and Ted Shawn's Denishawn.

The Dance Collection on-line catalog, now available via the Internet, provides access to indexing of articles by dance anthropologists in the dance periodicals. These citations do not appear in other humanities indexes. The on-line catalog also contains a series of subject headings for "Ritual and Ceremonial Dancing"—subdivided by country or area—that captures hundreds of citations.

At a recent conference of dance scholars, a speaker remarked that anthropologists have traditionally tended to describe a feast in detail regarding kinship, child-rearing practices, foods consumed, utensils used, and concluded the account with "and then they danced." Pioneering and contemporary dance anthropologists such as Gertrude Kurath, Adrienne Kaeppler, Drid Williams and Joann Kealiinohomoku are working to provide those missing descriptions.

Madeleine M. Nichols

New York Public Library. Schomburg Center for Research in Black Culture

Address: Schomburg Center for Research in Black Culture, 515 Malcolm X Boulevard (at 135th Street), New York, NY 10037-1801.
Tel.: (212) 491-2200
Fax: (212) 491-6760
Internet address: http://www.nypl.org/research/sc/sc.html.
Networks, consortia: RLIN, OCLC.
Public transit access: Subway: 2 or 3 to 135th Street; bus: M1, M2, M7, M102 or BX33.
Founded: 1925.
Major resources: Library resources on African, African American and Afro-Caribbean culture, including folktales, traditional medicine, language, music, folk art, cuisine, religion, dance and expressive and symbolic aspects of the lives of ordinary African peoples.
Areas of specialization: May Mandelbaum Edel papers, Melville and Frances Herskovits papers, photograph and artifacts collection, José Vigo papers. Catalog records of each of the preceding three collections are available on-line on RLIN and OCLC.
Holdings: Ca. 130,000 vols. of books and journals in all Schomburg Center collections; 50 linear ft. of manuscript materials in the Edel, Herskovits and Vigo collections.
Fieldnotes, papers, etc.: Fieldnotes and papers of Melville J. Herskovits (1895-1963) and Frances Herskovits (1898-1972); May Mandelbaum Edel (1909-1964); and José Vigo (1950-1987) are held.
● Herskovits papers: Surinam, 1925-1929; Dahomey, Gold Coast, Nigeria, 1931; Haiti, 1936; Trinidad, 1939; Brazil, 1941-1942.
● May Edel papers: western Uganda, 1933-1934.
● José Vigo papers: Samana, Dominican Republic, 1979, 1982-1983.
Unpublished finding aids are available for all of the above collections, which are housed in the Manuscripts, Archives & Rare Book Division.
Visual/audio resources: Nearly 1,000 long-playing phono-disc recordings and approximately fifty motion picture films/videos are held. In the Photographs and Prints

Division is a collection of photographs documenting African, African American and Afro-Caribbean religion and dances and also the Melville and Frances Herskovits photographs that depict West African traditional village life. In the Moving Image and Recorded Sound Division is a substantial collection of anthropological documentary films and music recordings from Africa, the Caribbean, South America and the Southern states of the United States. Subject strengths include religion, art, music and an overview of various societies.

Access: Open to scholars and general readers. Materials must be used in the Center. Interlibrary loan (excluding rare books) is available for books and periodicals only for RLG (Research Libraries Group) members.

Guides/catalogs: Schomburg Collection of Negro Literature and History, *Dictionary Catalog of the Schomburg Collection of Negro History and Literature* (New York: 1962). Three supplements were published from 1967 to 1976; Schomburg Center for Research in Black Culture, *Bibliographic Guide to Black Studies* (New York: 1975-   ); *Black Studies on Disc* (New York: 1995-   ); *Kaiser Index to Black Periodicals* (Brooklyn, N.Y.: 1992).

Artifacts of anthropological significance: The African art and artifacts collection consists of traditional masks, pottery, musical instruments, games, reliquary statuary, religious objects, implements and utensils, weaponry, gold weights and adornments. The objects document the aesthetic and ethnographic dimensions of traditional African societies and African cultures in the Caribbean and South America. The collection consists of more than 3,000 items from the following countries: Niger, Burkina Faso, Mali, Nigeria, Liberia, Ivory Coast, Ghana, Zaire (now Democratic Republic of Congo), South Africa, Tanzania, Somalia, Gabon, Cameroon, Kenya, Ethiopia, Zimbabwe, Sierra Leone, Haiti and Surinam. Represented ethnic groups include the Dogon, Songhai, Lobi, Igbo, Hausa, Dan, Ngere, Senufo, Baule, Kuba, Zande, Luba, Kongo, Yaka, Pende, Lozi, Mende, Duala, Yoruba, Kota, Chokwe, Songe, Ashanti, Ekoi, Fon, Mossi, Bushongo, Mangbetu, Basa Bateke, Fang, Falasha and Guro.

Catalog of selected artifact resources: "Schomburg Center Issue," *Bulletin of Research in the Humanities* (New York), vol. 84, no. 2 (Summer 1981), p. 137-[261].

Description

- *May Mandelbaum Edel Papers, 1928-1965*

An anthropologist and author of *The Chiga of Western Uganda* (New York: 1957), Edel was a student of Franz Boas and did her fieldwork among the Chiga in western Uganda in 1933-1934. The collection documents Edel's fieldwork through her notebooks, vocabulary and wordlists, notes on kinship and religion and collected stories and tales. There are published and unpublished writings, including several drafts of "The Bachiga of East Africa"—an unpublished work that describes the culture of the Chiga people. Also drafts of individual chapters and page proofs for *The Chiga of Western Uganda*. Included are letters to Edel from Ugandans in the Bantu dialect of the Chiga.

- *Melville and Frances Herskovits Papers*

Organization: personal papers, 1902-1963; research materials, 1925-1957; writings, 1920-1963; Frances S. Herskovits files, 1937-1972; general file, 1920-1971; Northwestern University, 1930s-1960s; Jean F. Herskovits files, 1937-1968. Research materials document all phases of the Herskovits's work: fieldnotes written on cards, in notebooks and in typescript; and drafts, typescripts and published articles. The fieldnotes were collected during trips to Surinam, Dahomey, Gold Coast, Nigeria, Haiti, Trinidad and Brazil. There are also notes and diaries from later trips to Africa in 1953 and 1956-1957.

The Frances Herskovits files include research materials and writings and contain notes from her 1968 Brazil trip, a follow-up to the initial field research conducted between 1941 and 1942, and her Haiti and Trinidad diaries.

A Herskovits collection finding aid is available for purchase. Additional Herskovits papers are preserved at the Northwestern University Library in Evanston, Illinois.

- *José Vigo Papers, 1967-1987*

These consist of material relating to Vigo's dissertation "Language Maintenance and Ethnicity: A Sociolinguistic Study of Samana, Dominican Republic." The study dealt with the processes of language maintenance and language shift among the descendants of a nineteenth-century colony of freedmen from the United States. There are fieldnotes collected in 1979, 1982-1983, and articles written by other scholars pertaining to the history of Samana, linguistics, Creole language and bibliographies.

Diana Lachatanere

Smithsonian Institution. National Museum of the American Indian (NMAI). George Gustav Heye Center (GGHC)

Address: George Gustav Heye Center, National Museum of the American Indian, Alexander Hamilton U.S. Custom House, One Bowling Green, New York, NY 10004.
Tel.: (212) 825-6700 (operator); (212) 825-8118 (Resource Center); (212) 825-4459 (Photo Archives); (212) 825-6894 (Film and Video Center).
Fax: (212) 825-8180 (Resource Center); (212) 825-8356 (Photo Archives); (212) 825-8180 (Film and Video Center).
E-mail (Resource Center): nin@ic.si.edu.
E-mail (Photo Archives): dewey@ic.si.edu.
E-mail (Film and Video Center): robert@ic.si.edu.
Internet address (National Museum of the American Indian): http://www.si.edu/nmai. This useful website offers news on programs and services of the museum and provides links to other Native American-related sites on the Internet.
Networks, consortia: Smithsonian Institution Research Information System (SIRIS).
Public transit access: Subway: Bowling Green station of the Lexington Ave. IRT (trains 4 and 5); Whitehall Street station of the BMT (trains N and R); South Ferry station of the Broadway-7th Ave. IRT (trains 1 and 9); bus: South Ferry stop on the M1, M6 and M15 buses.

Founded: 1916 (Museum of the American Indian—Heye Foundation); 1922 (opening of the museum at 155th Street and Broadway in Manhattan); 1926 (opening of the museum's Research Branch in the Bronx); 1989 (the MAI collection was transferred to the Smithsonian and the National Museum of the American Indian was established as part of the Smithsonian Institution); 1994 (opening of the NMAI George Gustav Heye Center in Manhattan); 1999 (scheduled opening of the NMAI Cultural Resources Center in Suitland, Maryland); 2002 (scheduled opening of the National Museum of the American Indian on the National Mall in Washington, D.C.).

Major resources: Resource Center; Photo Archives; Film and Video Center.

Areas of specialization: Indigenous peoples of North, Central and South America.

Holdings (books, journals, etc.): The Resource Center has a collection of about 3,000 books—including juvenile titles (coloring, picture and reference books) and adult titles (Native American-produced curriculum, reference books and fiction); twenty periodicals—including several tribal newspapers and publications of Indian interest (*Indian Country Today*, *Akwe:kon*, *Winds of Change*, *Akwesasne Notes*, etc.); public information files covering a variety of subjects, from Indian kissing in pre-Columbian times to articles on repatriation and reburial. Also available at the Resource Center is public access to the museum collection's database; four interactive multimedia programs; SIRIS, the Smithsonian's on-line catalogue; and a handling collection.

Visual/audio resources: The Photo Archives has a collection of more than 75,000 images depicting nearly all aspects of Native American life in the Western Hemisphere. The collection includes historic studies, portraits and field photographs of the museum's ethnographic and archaeological expeditions; and studio photographs of the museum's collection of artifacts from North, Central and South America. The chronological span of the collection ranges from early daguerreotypes to contemporary prints. Represented in this collection are the works of prominent historic photographers such as Edward S. Curtis, Sumner W. Matteson and William Henry Jackson, as well as notable field workers, such as George H. Pepper and A. Hyatt Verrill.

The Film and Video Center (FVC) has a study collection of approximately 1,500 films, videotapes and radio programs, predominantly by independent media makers. These works, dating from 1979 to the present, have been produced in North, Central and South America and the Pacific Rim. Approximately 40 percent of this collection consists of works by Native American producers. The center also houses footage and audiotape documentation, produced by the museum since 1990, of events and interviews with Native American artists, curators and media makers. A smaller collection of works and footage produced before 1950 exists, including films about the Crow and Zuni made in the 1920s. The museum's collection is for use by researchers, programmers and the general public, and is also utilized in the museum's own public programs and daily screenings. The media library is available for individual viewing in the Resource Center. The FVC also maintains information on Native media makers and tribal media projects throughout the Americas, and extensive files on media productions. A published guide, *Native Americans on Film and Video, Volume II* (New York: 1988) listing 400 works in distribution, can be purchased from the Center. A description of works shown in the Center's Native American Film and Video Festival is accessible through the FVC's Web page. A database of media in the Resource Center is complete. Databases currently under development describe the museum's media collection and Native media organizations worldwide.

The Resource Center has a small collection of 100 videos—including children's stories and documentaries; and 100 audio recordings of music, children's stories and Native languages.

Access: Contact the individual departments by phone, fax or e-mail to discuss research strategy.

Description

Beginning in 1897, George Gustav Heye (1874-1957) traveled and collected extensively, accumulating a collection of Native American artifacts that is one of the finest and most comprehensive in the world. The Museum of the American Indian—Heye Foundation was founded by Heye on May 10, 1916. In 1989 the collections of the Heye Foundation were transferred to the Smithsonian Institution, and the National Museum of the American Indian was established as part of the Smithsonian Institution.

George Gustav Heye

George G. Heye was the son of Carl Friederich Gustav Heye—a German immigrant who accumulated his wealth in the petroleum industry—and Marie Antoinette Lawrence Heye of Hudson, New York. George G. Heye graduated from Columbia College in 1896 with a degree in electrical engineering. He began collecting Native American artifacts in 1897, when he went to Arizona to supervise the construction of a railroad line. Some of the laborers were Navajos, and one night Heye noticed the wife of one of the foremen chewing the seams of her husband's deerskin shirt to kill the lice. He bought the shirt, and thus began his life-long passion for collecting.

In 1901 Heye began a career in investment banking and helped form the firm of Battles, Heye and Harrison, which had offices in Philadelphia and New York. Heye continued to collect Indian artifacts as a hobby—picking up single pieces during his travels. In 1903 he purchased his first large collection: several hundred pottery vessels from Tularosa canyon, Socorro County, New Mexico. By 1906 he had acquired more than 30,000 objects, and in 1914 he withdrew from his banking firm completely, in order to spend all his time collecting Indian cultural materials. During the remainder of his life, Heye devoted all his energy and a fortune of approximately ten million dollars to accumulating the largest private collection of Native American objects in the world.

Even before the Museum of the American Indian was founded, Heye was an avid sponsor of archaeological expeditions and of the publication of field research. From 1904 on, he sponsored expeditions in Mexico, Guatemala, Honduras, Costa Rica, Panama, the Caribbean and Ecuador. A large number of prehistoric sites in the United States were also studied. For example, archaeological work was conducted in Michigan, New York, New Jersey, Georgia, Arkansas, Nevada and New Mexico.

Early ethnological studies were undertaken among the Menominee, Havasupai, Crow, Sioux, Blackfoot, Shoshone, Arapaho and tribes of the Puget Sound, as well as among the people of the MacKenzie River Delta in Canada, the Penobscot, Nanticoke, Assiniboine, Cree, Bungi, northern Piegan, Montagnais, Mistassini and Naskapi of Labrador. In Mexico, Central and South America early ethnographic expeditions were undertaken among the Seri of Mexico, Maya of Chiapas and Guatemala, Bribrí of Costa Rica, Guajiro of Colombia, Chachi of Ecuador, Mapuche of Chile and various groups of Patagonia and Tierra del Fuego.

Museum of the American Indian—Heye Foundation

Heye's collection was initially stored in his Madison Avenue apartment in New York City, and later in a rented room in a building on Fifth Avenue. In 1910 Heye lent a portion of his North American ethnology collection to the University Museum at the University of Pennsylvania, where it was placed on exhibit in three large halls. His collections continued to grow, and he finally had to rent a floor in a building on 33rd Street in Manhattan. When his mother died in 1915, Heye then had full control of the family fortune and was in a position to realize his great ambition: to create his own museum in New York City. Heye withdrew his collection from the University Museum and established the Museum of the American Indian (MAI)—Heye Foundation in 1916. The land for the new museum was located at 155th Street and Broadway, in an elegant neighborhood in upper Manhattan. In late 1917 Heye's rapidly expanding collection was moved into the newly constructed museum, but the opening was delayed by World War I; the American Geographical Society was using the building to make maps for the Navy. The museum officially opened to the public in 1922.

The collection quickly outgrew the museum's facilities at 155th Street and Broadway and, in 1926, a storage and research facility was built in the Bronx—later referred to as the Research Branch. Heye's personal collection of Native American artifacts became the basis of the National Museum of the American Indian (NMAI) collection, which is considered to be the largest and most comprehensive collection of its kind. The collection consists of more than one million objects, with a geographic range that extends from the Arctic to Tierra del Fuego. There are collections from all major culture areas of the Americas, for virtually all tribes of the United States, most of those of Canada and a smaller number from Mexico, Central and South America and the Caribbean. Chronologically, the collection includes artifacts from the Paleo-Indian period to contemporary arts and crafts.

Approximately 80 percent of the collection is archeological and 20 percent is ethnographic; 65 percent is from the United States, 4 percent from Canada, 1 percent from Greenland and Siberia, 12 percent from Mexico and Central America, 12 percent from South America and 6 percent from the Caribbean.

Highlights of the collection include eighteenth-century Great Lakes material; Plains clothing, feather bonnets and painted and quilled hides; Northwest Coast masks and carvings; ivory carvings from the Arctic; pottery from the Southwest; California basketry; Amazonian featherwork; ceramics from Mexico, Panama and Ecuador; gold ornaments from central Mexico, Colombia and Peru; the Clarence B. Moore collection from the southeastern United States; and Navajo weavings showing a broad range of early types. Caribbean archaeology is extraordinarily well represented. Works on paper include Plains ledger drawings, as well as contemporary prints and paintings.

In the years following the opening of MAI, Heye employed and commissioned a remarkable number of noted anthropologists. Among these pioneers were Samuel A. Barrett, Theodoor de Booy, Donald A. Cadzow, Edward H. Davis, Mark R. Harrington, Thomas Huckerby, Frederick W. Hodge, Samuel K. Lothrop, Jesse L. Nusbaum, William C. Orchard, George H. Pepper, Foster H. Saville, Marshall H. Saville, Alanson B. Skinner, Frank G. Speck, A. Hyatt Verrill, Thomas T. Waterman and William Wildschut.

During the 1930s the impact of the Depression on the museum was severe. The staff was reduced in size, and the volume of fieldwork and publication was greatly affected. Heye nevertheless continued to purchase objects and to secure them by exchange. He remained the leading spirit of the museum, serving as director from 1916 until late 1956, when failing health forced him to retire. He died the following year.

Transfer to the Smithsonian Institution

The Museum of the American Indian—Heye Foundation collection was transferred to the Smithsonian Institution in 1989, when President George Bush signed legislation to establish the National Museum of the American Indian, Smithsonian Institution. A new building to house the museum is scheduled to open in 2002 on the National Mall—just east of the National Air and Space Museum.

Cultural Resources Center, Suitland, Maryland

In addition to the Mall Museum, a Cultural Resources Center has been built in Suitland, Maryland—about six miles from Washington, D.C. The Center, which will open in 1999, will house the bulk of NMAI's collections and will also accommodate associated activities such as research, collections care and management, conservation, repatriation, exhibition support functions and outreach services.

George Gustav Heye Center, New York

The George Gustav Heye Center (GGHC) of the National Museum of the American Indian is located in the historic Alexander Hamilton U.S. Custom House—adjacent to Battery Park in lower Manhattan. When the Heye Center opened in 1994, the museum facility at 155th Street and Broadway was closed. The Heye Center is NMAI's permanent exhibition and education facility in New York City.

Huntington Free Library

In the late 1920s Museum of the American Indian trustee James B. Ford established a library for the museum by purchasing the personal libraries of Marshall H. Saville and Frederick W. Hodge. These major acquisitions could not be assimilated into the museum's existing space, so trustee Archer M. Huntington provided funds for the construction of a building to house the entire book collection, serial publications and manuscripts, as an adjunct to the Huntington Free Library and Reading Room in the Bronx—about a mile from the museum's Research Branch. Huntington also created an endowment intended to maintain and expand the library, a non-circulating collection intended primarily for scholarly research.

Although the Huntington Free Library was not part of the transfer of the museum to the Smithsonian Institution, it continues to serve as the library for the New York staff of the new museum and to collect materials pertinent to the study of America's Native peoples. [An entry by Mary B. Davis on Native American-related library resources of the Huntington Free Library is under the heading **New York—New York City—Bronx.**]

Nancy B. Rosoff
Acknowledgments: Lee Davis, Mary B. Davis, Pamela Dewey, Marty de Montaño and Elizabeth Weatherford.

Union Theological Seminary. Burke Library

Address: Burke Library, Union Theological Seminary, 3041 Broadway (at 121st St.), New York, NY 10027.
Tel.: (212) 280-1501
Fax: (212) 280-1456
Internet address: http://www.uts.columbia.edu/burke2.html.
Networks, consortia: RLIN, OCLC. However, most printed materials in the Missionary Research Library collection are not cataloged in either RLIN or OCLC.
Public transit access: Subway: 1 or 9 to 116th St.-Columbia University; bus: M4, M5, M11 or M104.
Founded: 1838 (Union Theological Seminary Library); ca. 1910 (Missionary Research Library).
Major resources: Library collections in theology, missions and related fields.
Areas of specialization: The Missionary Research Library is one of the largest U.S. collections documenting the history of Protestant missionary activities in mission fields throughout the world.
Holdings: Burke Library: more than 700,000 items. Of these, some 100,000 items are in the Missionary Research Library collection.
Archives/manuscripts: An unpublished guide to archival holdings is available for consultation at the library. Catalog records of archival collections formed by individual missionaries are accessible on RLIN.
Visual/audio resources: Burke Library has a small collection of photographs of Chinese scenes and locales.
Access: The library is accessible to serious researchers; please call in advance. A letter of reference is required for use of special collections (i.e., archives, pre-1861 books, etc.)
Guides/catalogs: Archie R. Crouch, *Christianity in China: A Scholar's Guide to Resources in the Libraries and Archives of the United States* (Armonk, N.Y.: 1989); Missionary Research Library (New York, N.Y.), *Dictionary Catalog of the Missionary Research Library, New York* (Boston: 1968), 17 v.

Description

The Missionary Research Library collection consists of books, pamphlets, archival materials, etc., originally gathered by a group of American Protestant mission boards and now preserved and maintained by the Burke Library. The collection documents Protestant missionary activity in China, Africa and other mission fields. China mission materials in the collection are described in Archie R. Crouch, *Christianity in China: A Scholar's Guide to Resources in the Libraries and Archives of the United States* (Armonk, N.Y.: 1989).

Seth Kasten

New York—Poughkeepsie

Vassar College. Libraries. Special Collections Department

Address: Special Collections Department, Libraries, Vassar College, Campus Box 20, Poughkeepsie, NY 12601-6198.
Tel.: (914) 437-5799
Fax: (914) 437-5864
Internet address: http://iberia.vassar.edu/vcl/information.special-collections/special_collections.html.
Internet access to on-line catalog: The libraries' on-line catalog has no name. It can be accessed either through the Web at http://iberia.vassar.edu/vcl/index.html, or via telnet at telnet vaslib.vassar.edu. Type "library" at login.
Networks, consortia: OCLC.
Founded: 1861.
Major resources: Ruth Fulton Benedict papers.
Area of specialization: Ruth Benedict.
Archives/manuscripts: Benedict papers (130 linear ft.).
Access: Vassar's Special Collections department is open to scholars and general readers. All materials must be used in the Special Collections reading room.
References: Margaret M. Caffrey, *Ruth Benedict: Stranger in This Land* (Austin: 1989) (= *American Studies Series*); Nanako Fukui, *From "Japanese Behavior Patterns" to "The Chrysanthemum and the Sword"* (Kansai: 1995); Pauline Kent, "Ruth Benedict's Original Wartime Study of the Japanese," *International Journal of Japanese Sociology,* no. 3 (1994), p. 81-97; Judith Schachter Modell, *Ruth Benedict: Patterns of a Life* (Philadelphia: 1983).

Description

Ruth Fulton Benedict, an American cultural anthropologist, was born in the city of New York in 1887 and died there in 1948. She graduated Phi Beta Kappa from Vassar College in Poughkeepsie, New York, in 1909, was a social worker for a year, then spent three years teaching. In 1919 she began taking courses—first at Columbia University with

John Dewey and then at the New School for Social Research with Elsie Clews Parsons, whose course in ethnology of the sexes kindled Benedict's interest in anthropology. Under the guidance of Franz Boas, Benedict received her doctorate in 1923 from Columbia, where she remained throughout her career. In 1948 she was promoted to full professor in the Faculty of Political Science, the first woman to achieve such status.

Benedict's fieldwork was done among the Serrano in California and with the Zuni, Cochiti and Pima in the Southwest. Student training trips took her to the Mescalero Apache in Arizona and to the Blackfoot in the Northwest. From her work in the field, several of her books were developed: *Tales of the Cochiti Indians* (New York: 1931); *Zuni Mythology* (New York: 1935); and *Patterns of Culture* (Boston: 1934). The latter book became a best seller and influenced American life in that it explained the idea of "culture" to the layperson.

During World War II, Benedict worked for the Office of War Information (OWI), applying anthropological methods to the study of contemporary cultures. A study of Japan was her final assignment. The outgrowth of her work on Japan for the OWI was her book, *The Chrysanthemum and the Sword: Patterns of Japanese Culture* (New York: 1946), which became a bestseller at the time and ultimately a classic work in the study of Japanese culture. It is still in print today.

After Ruth Benedict's death, on September 17, 1948, her executor and sole legatee, Ruth Valentine, did preliminary sorting of Benedict's professional and personal papers located in her home and office. The papers were sent to Margaret Mead's office at the American Museum of Natural History, where they were further arranged into categories by Benedict's friend and former undergraduate student, Marie Eichelberger, for use by Mead in *An Anthropologist at Work: Writings of Ruth Benedict* (Boston: 1959).

Early in 1959 the Benedict papers were shipped to the Vassar Libraries by Mead. The collection comprises the largest number of Benedict's known personal and professional papers and consists of correspondence, manuscripts of published and unpublished works, notebooks, lecture and research notes, diaries, photographs, financial papers and clippings. A register is available in Special Collections and may also be purchased. The Benedict papers served as the basis for two biographies: Judith Schachter Modell, *Ruth Benedict: Patterns of a Life* (Philadelphia: 1983) and Margaret M. Caffrey, *Ruth Benedict: Stranger in This Land* (Austin: 1989). Benedict's work on Japan is currently being revisited by scholars in Japan. Among scholarly publications are Pauline Kent's article, "Ruth Benedict's Original Wartime Study of the Japanese," (1994); and Nanako Fukui's *From "Japanese Behavior Patterns" to "The Chrysanthemum and the Sword"* (Kansai: 1995).

Correspondence accounts for nearly a third of the Benedict papers, and includes a large number of letters from colleagues, friends, family, acquaintances and students—along with many carbon copies of Benedict's responses, ranging from 1916 until her death. It is arranged chronologically, with some exceptions. A project is underway to index the names of the correspondents and, if letterhead was used, their organizations. Organizational correspondence is arranged alphabetically by organization name, and includes the American Anthropological Association, the New York Academy of Sciences, the Council Against Intolerance in America, the National Research Council and the Progressive Education Association, among others.

From 1925 until 1940, Benedict was editor of the *Journal of American Folk-Lore*. Consequently, there is a large series of correspondence relating to the journal, from 1923 to

1944. Correspondence from Franz Boas to Benedict covers the period from 1922 to 1940. Another series of correspondence, formerly restricted by Margaret Mead, Benedict's original literary executor, is now freely accessible. This series includes letters to Benedict from some of her students, colleagues and informants.

The collection contains many Benedict manuscripts, published and unpublished articles, book reviews, speeches and lectures, as well as numerous drafts of her unpublished biographical essay on Mary Wollstonecraft; a partial unpublished book manuscript, "The Religion of the North American Indians," and drafts and other materials relating to some of her books, including *Race: Science and Politics* (New York: 1940) and *The Chrysanthemum and the Sword*. During the 1920s Benedict published sonnets, mainly in journals such as *Poetry*, under the pseudonym of Anne Singleton. Many of her poetry manuscripts are in the collection, along with the stories that she wrote as a child and young adult.

There are a large number of Indian subject files, deriving from Benedict's fieldwork and other research, especially regarding mythology, as well as material from some of her students' fieldwork. Numerous culture area files from her OWI days, and correspondence and reports from her work for the government are in the papers; also her diaries (mainly from the 1920s) and notebooks; drafts of *An Anthropologist at Work*; and teaching and lecture notes.

Photographs in the collection include many of Benedict and her family, photos of her taken by Stanley Benedict, the family farm in Norwich, Benedict's homes and a few of Benedict in the Southwest. Some of these have been published in various works about her.

Margaret Mead served as Benedict's literary executor until her death in 1978. In a letter to Vassar's librarian in 1959, Mead noted that certain materials were still in existence, but had not been included in the collection: Benedict's letters to Mead and Mead's letters to Benedict—now located in the Mead papers at the Manuscript Division of the Library of Congress; and Edward Sapir's letters to Benedict. Mead further stated that most of Stanley Benedict's letters to Ruth were destroyed by Ruth Benedict's executor, Ruth Valentine, and no trace of her letters to Edward Sapir had been found.

In addition to her personal and professional papers, a portion of Ruth Benedict's personal anthropological library was given to the Vassar College Libraries after her death, by the executor of her estate, Ruth Valentine. When they were donated to Vassar in 1948, the decision was made to incorporate her books into the main library collection. In her letter dated November 16, 1948, to Sarah Gibson Blanding, then President of Vassar, Valentine expressed the hope that the books would be to those who read them "what they were to [Benedict]. Not only a record of others' research and thinking, but a stimulus to go ahead and further . . . enrich scholarship as a living force in the world."

Nancy S. MacKechnie

New York—Rochester

University of Rochester. Rush Rhees Library. Department of Rare Books and Special Collections

Address: Department of Rare Books and Special Collections, Rush Rhees Library, University of Rochester, Rochester, NY 14627-0055.
Tel.: (716) 275-4477
Fax: (716) 273-1032
Internet address: http://www.lib.rochester.edu/rbk/rare.htm.
Networks, consortia: OCLC.
Public transit access: A line of the city bus system goes to campus. One stop on this line is at the library.
Founded: 1850.
Major resources: Manuscripts, special collections.
Areas of specialization: Lewis Henry Morgan papers; includes Morgan's research on the Iroquois.
Archives/manuscripts: 12 ft. of anthropological and related manuscripts are in Special Collections.
Holdings (books and journals): An estimated 30,000 book and journal volumes on anthropological subjects are in the Main Library.
Access: Materials are available for research and public use. An appointment to use Special Collections/Rare Books materials is recommended and appreciated.
Guides: Thomas R. Trautmann and Karl Sanford Kabelac, *The Library of Lewis Henry Morgan* (Philadelphia: 1994) (= *Transactions of the American Philosophical Society*, vol. 84, pt. 6-7).

Description

Lewis Henry Morgan, the American anthropologist, was born near Aurora, New York, in 1818. He graduated from Union College in Schenectady, New York, in 1840, studied law and moved to Rochester, New York, in 1844. In Rochester his law practice and investments gave him the financial security to pursue anthropological research and writing. His published books were *League of the Ho-dé-no-sau-nee, or Iroquois* (Rochester: 1851), *The American Beaver* (Philadelphia: 1868), *Systems of Consanguinity and Affinity of the Human Family* (Washington: 1871), *Ancient Society* (New York: 1877) and *Houses and House-Life of the American Aborigines* (Washington: 1881). He was the first anthropologist elected president of the American Association for the Advancement of Science (1879). Morgan died in Rochester late in 1881, and his estate was left for the life use of his widow and son. As provided in his will, after the death of Morgan's son in 1905, the estate came to the University of Rochester. Included in this bequest were his manuscripts, library and collection of artifacts.

The manuscript collection consists of correspondence, fieldnotes, drafts of several of his books, diaries of his European trip and other material. A register of the collection is available in the Special Collections Department. The collection was the basis of two book-length biographies of Morgan: Bernhard J. Stern, *Lewis Henry Morgan, Social Evolutionist* (Chicago: 1931) and Carl Resek, *Lewis Henry Morgan, American Scholar* (Chicago: 1960).

A fair amount of Morgan's incoming professional correspondence survives, and, in addition, the library has acquired photostats and xerographic copies of Morgan's correspondence as found in other repositories. The correspondence is arranged in chronological order, and a card index, arranged by name of letter writer, is available in the department. Thus a researcher can approach it either by time period or by name of correspondents.

Morgan had his fieldnotes bound in six volumes that he entitled "Manuscript Journals." The six volumes contain 75 different sets of notes, 1845-1876, and are a rich source of information. The notes of his Midwestern trips were edited by Leslie White and were published as *The Indian Journals, 1859-62* (Ann Arbor: 1959). A selection of those of his Iroquois research has been edited by Elisabeth Tooker and published as *Lewis H. Morgan on Iroquois Material Culture* (Tucson: 1994).

Preliminary and final drafts for Morgan's *The American Beaver, Systems of Consanguinity . . .* and *Ancient Society* are found in the papers, as are his preliminary and final drafts of the tables of kinship terms for *Systems*. In addition, many of the lengthy questionnaires filled in and returned to Morgan from various parts of the world—from which he compiled the detailed kinship tables—are extant in the collection, including some he did not use. Morgan's own copies of *League* and *Ancient Society*, with his manuscript additions, corrections and notes, also survive. Thomas R. Trautmann's *Lewis Henry Morgan and the Invention of Kinship* (Berkeley: 1987) is a study of *Systems*.

Morgan and his wife and son took an extended trip to Europe in 1870 and 1871. Morgan's travel diaries from July 9, 1870, to August 13, 1871, survive in six manuscript volumes, and Mrs. Morgan's from June 21, 1870, to August 13, 1871, survive in five volumes.

Parts of Morgan's account were edited by Leslie White and have been published as "Extracts from the European Travel Journal of Lewis H. Morgan," in volume 16 (1937) of the Rochester Historical Society's *Publication Fund Series*.

Other materials in the collection include 130 individual manuscripts by Morgan and others. About a third of these relate to the Grand Order of the Iroquois, the fraternal group of young white men in upstate New York in the 1840s in which Morgan was active, and which led to his scholarly interest in the Iroquois. Also in this group is Lorimer Fison and A.W. Howitt's manuscript draft of *Kamilaroi and Kurnai*, which was published in Melbourne in 1880.

The final materials in the collection include printed and manuscript papers relating to Morgan's business interests, photographs of Morgan and his family, material related to the American Association for the Advancement of Science annual meeting in Boston in 1880—the year Morgan served as president—and twentieth-century articles about Morgan and reviews of his books as acquired by the library.

FIGURE 7. Portrait of Lewis Henry Morgan, ca 1851. From a daguerreotype inset in Mrs. Morgan's copy of *League of the Ho-dé-no-sau-nee, or Iroquois.* Courtesy of the University of Rochester Library (#95127).

Morgan's library also came to the University of Rochester. As there was no Special Collections area then, it went to the general stacks, but over the years the surviving volumes have been transferred to the present-day Department of Rare Books and Special Collections. A number of the volumes contain his annotations; typically he would draw a line in pencil next to a passage of special interest to him and then make an index of such passages on the rear free flyleaf of the book. A knowledge of his library is important to an understanding of his reading, research and intellectual development. To this end, Thomas Trautmann and Karl Kabelac have bibliographically reconstructed Morgan's library, and their study, with its detailed introduction by Trautmann, appeared as *The Library of Lewis Henry Morgan* (Philadelphia: 1994).

Morgan made three collections of artifacts during his life. His personal collection, which came to the University of Rochester by the terms of his will, is now, by gift from the University, at the Rochester Museum and Science Center. A second collection, for the New York State Museum in Albany, was largely destroyed in their disastrous fire of March 1911. The third and much smaller collection, for which Morgan acted as acquisition agent, was made for the Danish Royal Museum in Copenhagen (now the National Museum of Denmark), where it is found today.

Karl Kabelac

North Carolina—Durham

Duke University. Special Collections Library

Address: Special Collections Library, Duke University, Box 90185, Durham, NC 27708.
Tel.: (919) 660-5820
Fax: (919) 684-2855
Internet address: http://odyssey.lib.duke.edu.
Internet address (Duke Papyrus Archive): http://odyssey.lib.duke.edu/papyrus.
Networks, consortia: OCLC.
Founded: 1931 (Manuscript Department).
Major resources: Manuscripts, rare books.
Areas of specialization: Southern Americana—especially the Southeast, Native Americans, African American studies, Duke Papyrus Archive.
Archives/manuscripts: More than 9,500,000 manuscript and archival items in all subject areas. Manuscript holdings concerning Native Americans have been described in a guide compiled by Kirsten Fischer (1991).
Visual/audio resources: Some photographs of Native Americans.
Access: The Special Collections Library is open to scholars and general readers. There are restrictions on use of some collections.
Guides/catalogs: Richard C. Davis and Linda Angle Miller (editors), *Guide to the Cataloged Collections in the Manuscript Department of the William R. Perkins Library, Duke University* (Durham, N.C.: 1980); Kirsten Fischer (compiler), and Linda McCurdy

(editor), *Indians of North America: A Guide to the Sources on Native Americans in the Special Collections Department of Perkins Library* (Durham, N.C.: 1991).

Information provided by William R. Erwin, Jr.

North Carolina—Raleigh

North Carolina. Division of Archives and History. Archives and Records Section

Address: Archives and Records Section, North Carolina Division of Archives and History, 109 East Jones Street, Raleigh, NC 27601-2807.
Tel.: (919) 733-3952
Fax: (919) 733-1354
Internet address: http://www.ah.dcr.state.nc.us/archives.arch.archhp.htm.
Founded: 1903.
Major resources: The Archives' collection policy is to serve as the official repository of permanently valuable North Carolina state and local government records and private papers of public officials or families active in public life.
Areas of specialization: Of particular anthropological interest are the Archives' extensive holdings of official and non-official records pertaining to Indians of North Carolina and the adjacent areas. A brief guide to Indian-related records in the Archives—from the colonial period to 1876—was compiled by Donna Spindel (1979).
Archives/manuscripts: Ca. 36,000 ft. of original records and manuscripts and 150,000 reels of microfilm in all subject areas.
Visual/audio resources: The Archives has a significant collection of audiovisual materials, including sound and video recordings, and some 600,000 photographic negatives, some of which may be of anthropological significance.
Access: Available for use by scholars and the general public with proper identification.
Guides/catalogs: Donna Spindel, *Introductory Guide to Indian-Related Records, to 1876, in the North Carolina State Archives* (Raleigh, N.C.: 1979).

Information provided by North Carolina Division of Archives and History.

North Dakota—Bismarck

State Historical Society of North Dakota. North Dakota Heritage Center

Address: North Dakota Heritage Center, State Historical Society of North Dakota, 612 East Boulevard Avenue, Bismarck, ND 58505-0830.
Tel.: (701) 328-2666 (State Historical Society of North Dakota); (701) 328-2668 (State Archives and Historical Research Library).
Fax: (701) 328-3710
Internet address: http://www.state.nd.us/hist/hcenter.htm.

Networks, consortia: OCLC.
Founded: 1895 (State Historical Society of North Dakota).
Major resources: State Archives and Historical Research Library; Archaeology and Historic Preservation Division.
Areas of specialization: Native Americans of North Dakota and the northern Great Plains; archaeology; historic preservation.
Archives/manuscripts: In the State Archives and Historical Research Library and the Archaeology and Historic Preservation Division. Archives at the former location include the papers of Harold Case—a Congregational missionary at Fort Berthold Reservation.
Holdings: Manuscripts, archives, books, periodicals, maps, newspapers, photographs.
Visual/audio resources: The photograph collections include photos of Native Americans. Among holdings are the Frank B. Fisk photos taken at Stony Rock Agency.
Access: The State Archives and Historical Research Library is open to the public. Research access to the Archaeology and Historic Preservation Division is by appointment only.
Guides/catalogs: *A Traveler's Companion to North Dakota State Historic Sites* (Bismarck, N.D.: 1996).
Artifacts: Artifact collections are in the History, Natural History, Archeology and Ethnology Sections of the Museum Division.

Information provided by Jim Davis.

Ohio—Cleveland

Cleveland Public Library. Fine Arts and Special Collections Department. John G. White Collection of Folklore, Orientalia and Chess

Address: Cleveland Public Library. Fine Arts and Special Collections Department, 325 Superior Avenue, Cleveland, OH 44114-1271.
Tel.: (216) 623-2818
Fax: (216) 623-7050
E-mail: white1@library.cpl.org.
Internet address: http://www.cpl.org.
Networks, consortia: OCLC, RLIN, OHIONET, MARCIVE, CAMLS, NEOMARL, CLEVNET.
Public transit access: Cleveland RTA Rapid (train) system, Red, Green and Blue Lines from: Airport through downtown to Windemere (Red); downtown to Green Rd., Shaker Heights (Green); downtown to Van Aken (Blue). Cleveland Public Library is at the downtown RTA stop. In addition, many Cleveland RTA buses go through downtown.
Founded: 1869 (Cleveland Public Library); 1899 (John G. White Collection).
Major resources: The John G. White Collection of Folklore, Orientalia and Chess.
Areas of specialization: Holdings represent three primary special collections in the broadly defined subject areas of Folklore, Orientalia and Chess and Checkers. Each of these major subject areas includes special collections of unique strengths and unusually complete representation of subject matter.

Archives/manuscripts: Archival files include the May Augusta Klipple African Folktales Manuscript Archives—a topological and geographical classification of folktales, collections of folktales and unpublished translations of folktales (19 linear ft.). Also available is the Newbell Niles Puckett Memorial Gift (126 linear ft.), which consists of original manuscripts, notes and field research collections of Newbell Puckett (1897-1967) on popular beliefs and superstitions of Ohio, black names in America, miscellaneous folklore papers, religious life of southern blacks, Canadian lumberjack songs, Maine folklore, etc., collected from 1930 until 1960. The black American materials were mainly collected in Mississippi, Georgia and other southern states. Notes and an editorial card file on Puckett's "Popular Beliefs and Superstitions of Ohio" corpus were prepared by Wayland D. Hand (1907-1986).

Holdings (books and journals): Folklore Collection: 47,630 v.; Orientalia Collection: 66,161 vols.; auxiliary subjects, linguistics, chess, etc.: 58,561 v.

Visual/audio resources: The Newbell Niles Puckett Memorial Gift includes 457 original slides, about 1,400 photographs, 147 reel-to-reel tapes of field recordings and 92 microfilm reels of Puckett archival materials.

Access: Open to scholars, students and general readers. Closed stacks. Materials are available on request for use in the Special Collections reading room only, or on interlibrary loan with "use in library only" restrictions.

References: Francis Hall, *Japan through American Eyes: The Journal of Francis Hall, Kanagawa and Yokohama, 1859-1866* (Princeton, N.J.: 1992)—edited by F.G. Notehelfer from the Hall manuscript in the John G. White Collection of Orientalia; Alice N. Loranth, "The European Ethnic Folklore Resources of the White Collection," *Journal of the Ohio Folklore Society*, n.s., vol. 1, no. 1 (Dec. 1972), p. 25-37; Newbell Niles Puckett, *Black Names in America: Origins and Usage*, edited by Murray Heller (Boston: 1975); Newbell Niles Puckett, *Popular Beliefs and Superstitions: A Compendium of American Folklore: From the Ohio Collection of Newbell Niles Puckett*, edited by Wayland D. Hand, Anna Casettam and Sondra B. Thiederman (Boston: 1981), 3 v.; Motoko B. Yatabe Reece, "John Griswold White, Trustee, and the White Collection in the Cleveland Public Library," Ph.D. dissertation, University of Michigan, 1979.

Guides/catalogs: Cleveland Public Library. John G. White Department, *Catalog of Folklife, Folklore and Folk Songs*, introduction by Alice N. Loranth (2nd ed., Boston: 1978), 3 v. The prefaces of the White Collection folklore and chess catalogs give the background of acquisitions in these areas. Several articles on the chess collection have been published in a variety of chess periodicals.

Artifacts of anthropological significance: The collection of chess sets and chessmen of the White Collection is described in Alice N. Loranth, *Enchanted Chessmen: A World of Fantasy* (Cleveland: 1996).

Artifacts from archaeological sites: There are about 55 objects from the archaeological excavations at Beth Shemesh (Palestine), conducted by Elihu Grant, 1928-1933. The Haverford College Archaeological Expedition was partially described by Grant in his *Beth Shemesh (Palestine): Progress of the Haverford Archaeological Expedition* (Haverford, Pa.: [1929]) (= *Biblical and Kindred Studies*, [no. 2]).

Description

The John G. White Collection of Folklore, Orientalia and Chess is a privately endowed research and reference library, named after its founder and principal donor, John Griswold White (1845-1928)—a Cleveland lawyer, bibliophile and long-term trustee and president of the Cleveland Public Library Board. The White Collection's holdings date back to 1899, when White gave Richard Burton's edition of *Arabian Nights* to the library. During the next nine decades a continuous series of planned acquisitions developed a great variety of subject collections in the three broadly defined subject areas of Folklore, Orientalia and Chess and Checkers. Careful selection of materials on a title-by-title basis has built complex research collections in the humanities and social sciences, and several nationally recognized special collections that, through their number, research potential and interrelatedness, take on additional research value and importance. In support of the library's general collections, White intended to furnish scholars, students and the general public with original sources and specialized scholarly materials of permanent value. In his will, dated February 9, 1928, he set forth the book selection policies that continue to serve as a collection development plan.

All materials were selected personally by Mr. White until his death in 1928. Subsequently, the successive department heads of the White Collection continued the development of the collections on the basis of White's quite elaborate book selection policies. Gordon W. Thayer continued the selection of materials until 1955. Subsequent department heads were Walter F. Vella; George J. Masciuszko; and Alice N. Loranth, to date.

The White Collection was administered as an independent subject department of the Main Library until 1982, when the Fine Arts and Special Collections Department was established, and the White Collection became part of Special Collections. The Department is located in ornate Italianate Renaissance premises on the third floor of the Main Library.

The Folklore Collection is very extensive in scope and international in coverage. Included are works pertaining to indigenous, peasant and folk cultures, within geographic restrictions. In English and American areas, the White Collection acquires research materials only, since the Library's basic collections of American and English folk culture are developed by other subject departments of the Main Library.

The wide range of materials and the depth and richness of holdings reflect White's all-inclusive interpretation of the term "folklore," for he defined it as a discipline "as broad as the German *Volkskunde*." To present the folk culture concept as an expression of cultural patterns and values, in the perspective of total folk experience, he included ethnology and ethnography, those branches of anthropology that study the origins, character and history of the various races and nations of the world.

Holdings include analyses of social structure, patterns of everyday life and traditions of occupations and human activities; descriptions of manners, customs, rituals, ceremonies and festivals; ancient, indigenous and classic Oriental music; studies of folk beliefs, magic, witchcraft, astrology and alchemy. The most extensively developed areas include all oral forms of traditional folk expression, such as folktales, fables, romances, riddles, anecdotes, proverbs, songs, ballads, rhymes and folk drama; and legends of saints and famous characters of historical, local or mythical significance.

The collection of 761 volumes on the Arabian Nights contains many versions, complete or partial, in 57 languages. The collection of Ballads and Folksongs (2,170 v.) is strongest in Romance language and Russian holdings, although the rarest items are in English. Included are 200 titles purchased from the Joliet Library of Dijon in 1922, and numerous political broadsides of the late eighteenth- and early nineteenth-centuries. A Spanish ballad card index and extensive indices for French Provençal and Italian songs provide additional access.

The Chapbook Collection (ca. 2,834 titles) is one of the largest in the United States. It is especially strong in French, Italian, German and Portuguese items and contains unique Russian holdings. Germanic Folklore (more than 4,140 v.) is strongest in nineteenth-century holdings. The Gypsy collection (766 v.) includes most titles listed in George Fraser Black's bibliographies (published in 1909 and 1914) and is rich in scarce periodical runs. The collection of Saga Literature and Icelandic and Old Norse Philological Studies (1,158 v.) is supplemented by a collection of 225 editions of Esaias Tegner's *Frithjof's Saga*, which is famous for the number of legends included. Medieval Romance Literature of Europe and the Orient (3,205 v.) focuses on related cycles and their versions in various languages. The Proverb Collection (2,930 v.) is one of the most outstanding in the U.S.

In Occult Sciences (2,735 v.) and Witchcraft (1,810 v.) the emphasis is on historical treatises, folkloric aspects and classic treatments of apparitions, ghosts, oracles, magic and sorcery. Lynn Thorndike's manuscript entitled "The History of Magic" is among the unique holdings. The collection of Sex Customs, Erotica and Prostitution (about 600 v.) includes such class rarities as Friedrich Solomon Krauss's *Kryptadia: recueil de documents pour servir à l'étude des traditions populaires* (Heilbronn: 1883-1911), 12 v., and related series; and also many early eighteenth-century French titles on the subject of prostitution.

The Orientalia Collection includes materials on Asia, the Near and Middle East, Africa, Australia and Oceania. Single copies of reference and research materials are acquired in both Western and vernacular languages. Emphasis is on the humanistic and social science aspects of traditional cultures prior to the expansion of European influence. In the words of John G. White, the scope of the collection is wide to provide "first hand information as to the thoughts, religious faith, manners and customs, literature, antiquities, and languages of the people of the East." Philology, philosophy, religion, ancient and medieval history and law are the main areas of acquisition. Original language versions and scholarly translations of classic Oriental texts are collected to allow for comparison and textual criticism. Source material and reference works on archaeology and the ancient and classical periods of art, architecture, music, astronomy and medicine are also included.

Special collections of interest to the anthropologist include Egyptology (5,555 v.). Through the 1940s the collection is one of the best representations of the subject, strong in French, British and German scholarly series; excavation reports; and museum catalogs. The Near and Middle Eastern Archaeology (7,725 v.) and Central Asian (3,165 v.) materials include rare reports and surveys published by official expeditions and academic institutions of Czarist Russia. Early Travels, Descriptions and Voyages (7,718 v.) includes 6,560 White Collection volumes on Oriental countries and 1,153 Special Collections Rare Books volumes on Europe and the Americas. An unusual special collection of more than 500 volumes is devoted to the island of Madagascar. The Language and Philology collection (15,490 v.) includes important classic dictionaries and grammars, with emphasis on philology, supplemented by a departmental Language Index that identifies and provides access to samples of more than 7,000 languages and dialects housed in the White Collection.

White Collection periodical holdings date back to the nineteenth-century.

Manuscript holdings include the East India Company collection of documents, correspondence and records relating to British affairs in India and Central Asia, 1741-1859, (201 v.). The core collection—96 percent of the East India Company manuscripts—was purchased in 1940.

White Collection holdings also include manuscripts in Oriental languages (210 titles), many lavishly illuminated, chiefly in Persian, Arabic, Pali and Burmese, but some in Batak, Ethiopian, Hebrew, Sanskrit, Syriac, Chinese and Tibetan. The collection includes classic literary, historical and religious texts and early scientific treatises, manuscript facsimiles and printed library catalogs for Oriental and other manuscripts (730 titles).

Alice N. Loranth

Oklahoma—Norman

University of Oklahoma. Libraries. Western History Collections

Address: Western History Collections, University of Oklahoma Libraries, Room 452, Monnet Hall, Norman, OK 73019.
Tel.: (405) 325-3641
Fax: (405) 325-2943
Internet address: http://www-lib.ou.edu/depts/west.
Networks, consortia: RLIN.
Founded: 1927 (Western History Collections).
Major resources: Documentation on Indians of North America.
Areas of specialization: University of Oklahoma Doris Duke American Indian Oral History collection, Robert E. Bell collection, Ralph E. Cooley collection, Alice Lee Marriott collection, Marriott-Rachlin collection, John Moore collection, Carol K. Rachlin collection, Karl and Ava Schmitt collection, Gene Weltfish collection, Indian music collections.
Archives/manuscripts: 2,000 linear ft.
Fieldnotes, etc.: Alice L. Marriott (1910-1989): Oklahoma fieldnotes for 1935-1936; Karl Schmitt (1915-1952): Oklahoma fieldnotes for 1947-1951; Carol K. Rachlin (1919-   ): Oklahoma fieldnotes for 1954; Gene Weltfish (1902-1980): Oklahoma fieldnotes for 1935.
Holdings (books and journals): 13,000 v.
Visual/audio resources: Holdings include numerous collections of photographs dating from the 1880s to the 1920s, and many collections of sound recordings from the late 1930s to the 1970s—all relating to the Indians of North America and to Indian music.
Access: Available to all researchers; all materials must be used on-site.
References: Duane K. Hale (editor), *Cooley's Traditional Stories of the Delaware* (Anadarko, Okla.: 1984); Bradford Koplowitz, "The Doris Duke Indian Oral History Projects," *Popular Culture in Libraries*, vol. 1 (1993), p. 23-38.

Guides/catalogs: Donald L. DeWitt (editor), *American Indian Resource Materials in the Western History Collections, University of Oklahoma* (Norman, Okla.: 1990); John R. Lovett and Donald L. DeWitt, *Guide to Photographs, Motion Pictures, and Sound Recordings, Western History Collections, University of Oklahoma* (Norman, Okla.: 1993); Kristina L. Southwell, *Cherokee Nation Papers: Inventory and Index* (Norman, Okla.: 1996).

Description

More than fifty Indian tribes live in Oklahoma; it is therefore not surprising that the Western History Collections has notable strength in Indian-related holdings. Among its 2,500 collections are 265 manuscript collections, 94 photograph collections and 22 sound recording collections specifically related to Indian cultures. Several of these would be of interest to anthropologists. Three collections of fieldnotes and two collections of sound recordings are examples.

The most extensive collection of fieldnotes—nearly four linear feet—is that of Karl and Ava Schmitt. The Schmitts compiled notes on several tribes between 1947 and 1951, but they concentrated on the Wichita in the Anadarko, Oklahoma, area. Also represented, however, are notes on tribes culturally related to the Wichita, such as the Caddo, Arikara and Pawnee. The Caddo notes are nearly as extensive as those on the Wichita. Supplementing the Schmitts' textual materials are sound recordings of Wichita and Caddo songs and a small photograph collection, mostly of Caddo Indians.

A second resource is the Alice Lee Marriott Collection. Marriott had only a B.A. degree in anthropology from the University of Oklahoma, but spent her entire life researching and writing about various aspects of Plains and Southwestern Indian culture. Her collection of papers includes 21 linear feet of personal and professional correspondence, printed materials, manuscripts of her books and articles, photographs, fieldnotes and research notes, all dating from 1926 to the 1970s. Marriott focused much of her research on the Kiowa, and it was in 1935 and 1936 that she compiled the fieldnotes that served as the basis of her Kiowa-related books. These notes are all typewritten and are well organized as to subject and content. They include many anecdotes by informants. Several of Marriott's informants were a pre-reservation generation of the Kiowas; thus the information in these notes has a perspective unobtainable today. A photo collection containing images of Indians, archaeological work sites and Indian basketry supplements Marriott's papers.

Another set of fieldnotes in the Western History Collections is that compiled by Gene Weltfish (1902-1980) on the Pawnee. Weltfish began her study of the Pawnee language in 1928, while she was a research associate at Columbia University. She traveled to Pawnee, Oklahoma, where she befriended several elderly Pawnee Indians who spoke only Pawnee and who had been born prior to 1875, when the Pawnees moved to Oklahoma. She worked very closely with Mark Evarts, from whom she learned much about the language. Weltfish compiled her notes during the summer of 1935. Her study focuses on the life in a Pawnee village during the year 1867, a time when her informants were in their late teens and early twenties. The more than 1,200 pages of notes are detailed, typed and contain illustrations of villages, interiors of houses, kinship family charts and other concepts or things that Weltfish believed should be illustrated. The notes are in English, but contain many names, words and phrases written in the Pawnee language. Weltfish claims that her notes have the distinction of being the only research originally compiled directly in the Pawnee language.

Three other collections in the Western History Collections, while not textual records, are of special interest. The Ralph Cooley collection consists of 155 sound recordings relating to the Delaware Indian language. Cooley was a professor in the Communication Department at the University of Oklahoma from the 1970s until his death in 1982. He was trained in linguistics and had an ongoing research interest in explaining why languages remain viable in some minority groups and not in others. In the course of his research with Delaware Indians in the area of Anadarko, Oklahoma, he found none who spoke Delaware only, and just six who were English speakers, but also fluent in Delaware. It was with these six that he recorded the 155 tapes during the period 1977-1979. While all can be related to language study, the tapes cover a variety of topics, including Delaware foods and cooking, word meanings and verb conjugations, myth and folk stories, prayers, kinship terms, the Anadarko, Oklahoma, area and weather forecasting. Some of the stories and prayers have been published posthumously under the title *Cooley's Traditional Stories of the Delaware*, edited by Duane K. Hale. The value of these recordings to researchers lies in the timing of their compilation. Since Cooley made the recordings, at least three of the informants have died. Consequently, the Cooley tapes may represent one of the last recordings of the Delaware language by fluent native speakers.

Complementing the Cooley tapes is a collection of music known as "The Indians for Indians Hour." The collection is composed of 69 recordings from a radio program broadcast from station WNAD in Norman, Oklahoma, from 1943 to 1964. The program was public service-oriented in that it gave news and announcements about the Indian community in Oklahoma and featured live performances of Indian music as entertainment. The program's host, Don Whistler, a Sac and Fox Indian, invited groups from different tribes to the show each week. Apache, Arapaho, Caddo, Cheyenne, Comanche, Creek, Crow, Hopi, Iowa, Kiowa, Oto, Pawnee, Ponca, Pueblo, Sac and Fox, Seminole, Shawnee, Sioux and Wichita music is included on the recordings. Researchers who have used this collection frequently comment on the spontaneity and authenticity of the performances. The authentic nature of the music perhaps stems from the composition of the program's audience. The performers knew that they were being heard by other Indians, not primarily by a white audience. As a result, the music has an authentic quality that is sometimes lacking in recordings made in other, more formal, settings.

Another collection of interest to anthropologists is the university's Doris Duke American Indian Oral History Collection. The University of Oklahoma was one of seven U.S. universities to receive, in 1967, a grant from tobacco heiress Doris Duke. The purpose of the grant was to record, by means of direct interviews, the Indians' perspectives on their own history and culture and also to document the changes in Indian cultures during the twentieth-century. The University of Oklahoma Doris Duke Project continued from 1967 until 1972. The Oklahoma Doris Duke Indian Oral History Collection contains 695 sound tapes that record interviews with members of all tribes represented in Oklahoma, as well as interviews with non-Indians, proceedings of tribal meetings and pow-wow activities. There are also several interview typescripts for which there is no corresponding tape.

Access to the Oklahoma Duke Collection is excellent. Working copies of all of the recordings are available on cassette tape, and all interviews have been transcribed and microfilmed. The collection is available commercially in a microfiche set from Kraus Microforms. While not indexed topically, cards 308-310 of the fiche set include a final report of the project, a list of the tapes with each entry (including the informant's name and tribal affiliation and the interviewer's name), a list of typescripts for which there are no tapes, a list of the tribes represented in the interviews and an alphabetical list of informants and field workers.

There is also a card catalog of the Duke Collection. Johnson Associates did not film this catalog for the microfiche publication, but did reproduce it in a bound three-volume set. This catalog is largely a tribal and name index. The tribal index, however, has the added advantage of some subject indexing under each tribal name.

Unpublished finding aids to all of the specific collections mentioned above are available. Researchers may obtain a photocopy of any of these by mail for copying costs. For a description of other Indian-related collections in the Western History Collections, researchers may consult *American Indian Resource Materials in the Western History Collections*, cited above.

Donald L. DeWitt

Oklahoma—Oklahoma City

Oklahoma Historical Society (OHS)

Address: Oklahoma Historical Society, Historical Building, 2100 North Lincoln Boulevard, Oklahoma City, OK 73105.
Tel.: (405) 522-5209 (Archives Division); (405) 522-5225 (Research Library).
Fax: (405) 521-2492
Internet address: http://www.ok-history.mus.ok.us.
Internet address (Native American Records): http://www.ok-history.mus.ok.us/archives/indianrc/indfront.html.
Public transit access: City bus system.
Founded: 1893 (Oklahoma Historical Society); 1934 (Indian Archives).
Major resources: Archives Division; Research Library.
Areas of specialization: Oklahoma history; the history of the 67 Indian tribes of Oklahoma, including the "Five Civilized Tribes"—the Cherokee, Chickasaw, Choctaw, Creek (Muskogee) and Seminole.
Holdings (Archives Division): 3,500,000 documents on Indian tribes; 2,500 cubic ft. of manuscripts. Resources in the Archives Division include federal Indian Agency records (Oklahoma Region); WPA interviews, 1936-1938, with members of the "Five Civilized Tribes" and with surviving Oklahoma settlers.
Holdings (Research Library): 50,000 v. (primarily on Oklahoma and Native American history).
Visual/audio resources: 650,000 photographs that document the history of Oklahoma. Among these are many archival photographs that depict the "Five Civilized Tribes." Early photos in the collection are in glass-plate, ambrotype, cardstock and other formats. OHS

photographers are continuing to record images of present-day Native American life in the region.

Access: The Archives Division and the Research Library are open to the public. There are restrictions on access to some archival materials.

References: Angie Debo, "Major Indian Record Collections in Oklahoma," in Jane F. Smith and Robert M. Kvasnicka (editors), *Indian-White Relations: A Persistent Paradox* (Washington, D.C.: 1981) (= *National Archives Conferences*, vol. 10), p. 112-118.

Guides/catalogs: William D. Welge (editor) with Mary Lee Boyle and Sharron Ashton, *Guide to the Cherokee Indian Records Microfilm Collection* (Oklahoma City, Okla.: 1996). Guides to OHS microfilm collections on the other four "Civilized Tribes" are forthcoming.

Artifacts: Extensive collections of Native American-related artifacts are curated.

Description

The Indian Archives was formally established by Act of Congress on March 4, 1934. At that time, the OHS was granted custody of some 3.5 million documents and more than 6,000 volumes relating to the Indian tribes residing in Oklahoma. Prominent among the Indian Archives materials are the records of the Cherokee, Chickasaw, Choctaw, Creek (Muskogee) and Seminole—collectively described as the "Five Civilized Tribes." The Archives also contains documents pertaining to the Cheyenne and Arapaho, Kiowa, Comanche and Apache, Pawnee, Ponca, Oto and Missouri, Tonkawa, Iowa, Sac and Fox, Absentee Shawnee, Potawatomi, Peoria, Ottawa, Wyandot (Huron), Seneca, Caddo, Wea, Tawakoni and Delaware. Other smaller tribes are also represented.

Of the more than 1,000 volumes and 500,000 pages of material on the "Five Civilized Tribes," about 1 percent is written in the respective Indian languages. The largest quantity of Indian-language material is in Choctaw. There are no examples of material in Chickasaw.

Noteworthy among the Indian-related manuscript collections are the papers of Lee Harkins (Choctaw-Chickasaw), Murial Wright (Choctaw), John T. Adair (Cherokee), Eula Doonkeen Narcomey (Seminole), Francis LeVier (Potawatomi) and a host of others.

The Oral History Collection contains approximately 6,000 interviews with individuals in all walks of life. More than half of the 25,000 WPA interviews, compiled in 1937-1938, relate to Indian tribes, cultures, languages and history. The interviews are in audio as well as video format; less than 1 percent of these have been transcribed on paper.

William D. Welge

Oklahoma—Tulsa

Gilcrease Museum

Address: Gilcrease Museum, 1400 Gilcrease Museum Road, Tulsa, OK 74127-2100.
Tel.: (918) 596-2700
Fax: (918) 592-2770

Internet address: http://www.lawnchaps.com/collection.htm.
Founded: 1949.
Major resources: Library, Archive.
Areas of specialization: American and American Indian documentation.
Archives/manuscripts: 40,000 items.
Holdings (books and journals): 40,000 v.
Visual/audio resources: 1,000 maps, 10,000 photographs.
Access: Open to scholars and general readers by appointment.
Artifacts: Native American artifacts.

Information provided by S. Erwin.

Pennsylvania—Philadelphia

American Philosophical Society (APS)

Address: American Philosophical Society, 105 South Fifth St., Philadelphia, PA 19106-3386.
Tel.: (215) 440-3400 (Reference); (215) 440-3409 (Manuscripts Department).
Fax: (215) 440-3423
Internet address: http://www.amphilsoc.org.
Networks, consortia: RLIN, PACSCL.
Public transit access: Take the Market/Frankford "El" to 5th and Market Streets. The Society is a short walk from this stop. Or, by train from 30th St. Station, exit at Market East. The Society is about five blocks from this stop.
Founded: 1743 (founding of the Society).
Major resources: The professional papers of Franz Boas, many other manuscripts and documents pertaining to anthropology and linguistics.
Areas of specialization: All aspects of the history of science; anthropology, archaeology, linguistics, folklore and Native Americans—especially Native American linguistics.
Archives/manuscripts: 6.25 million manuscripts in the Manuscripts Department. Phillips Fund grants have added many manuscripts in anthropology to the library, especially those concerning Native Americans. Manuscript holdings include the Franz Boas papers, the Alfred I. Hallowell papers and many others.
Holdings (books and journals): 190,000 v. in the Printed Materials Department.
Visual/audio resources: About 1,500 original audio tapes in many languages are held. Most were recorded in the course of anthropological and related field research that was supported by APS Phillips Fund grants. There is a language card file index to the audio recordings. Some 80 percent of sound recordings have been reformatted to RDAT (Rotary Digital Audio Tape). All APS wax cylinder recordings were transferred to the Library of Congress in the 1960s for retention and preservation. Many original photographs of ethnological or related interest are in the Manuscripts Department, although there is no general subject guide to these resources.

Access: A non-circulating research library. Closed stacks. Available for research use by appointment. The library is open to any serious scholar with proper identification or introduction. Library hours are Monday through Friday, 9:00 a.m. to 5:00 p.m., except holidays. Please call the Manuscripts Department in advance of any visit.

References: Edward C. Carter II, *"One Grand Pursuit": A Brief History of the American Philosophical Society's First 250 Years, 1743-1993* (Philadelphia, Pa.: 1993); Roy Goodman and Pierre Swiggers, "John Vaughan (1756-1841) and the Linguistic Collection in the Library of the American Philosophical Society," *Proceedings of the American Philosophical Society*, vol. 138, no. 2 (June 1994), p. 251-272; Martin L. Levitt, "Lingusitics as History: Preserving Linguistic Oral Records," *International Journal of American Linguistics,* vol. 55 (1989), p. 417-423; P. Voorhoeve, "H H Bartlett's Batak Manuscripts Collection," *Indonesia Circle*, no. 22 (June 1980), p. 70-72.

Guides/catalogs: J. Stephen Catlett (editor), *A New Guide to the Collections of the Library of the American Philosophical Society* (Philadelphia, Pa.: 1987) (= *Memoirs of the American Philosophical Society*, vol. 66s); David K. Van Keuren, *"The Proper Study of Mankind": An Annotated Bibliography of Manuscript Sources on Anthropology & Archaeology in the Library of the American Philosophical Society* (Philadelphia, Pa.: 1986) (= *Publication Library / American Philosophical Society*, no. 10).

Guides/catalogs (more specialized): Beth Carroll-Horrocks, "Manuscript Sources at the APS for the Study of Black History and Culture,"—1988, unpublished; Beth Carroll-Horrocks, "Sources for the History of Folklore in the Manuscripts Department of the American Philosophical Society Library,"—1989, unpublished; John F. Freeman, *A Guide to Manuscripts Relating to the American Indian in the Library of the American Philosophical Society* (Philadelphia, Pa.: 1980) (= *Memoirs of the American Philosophical Society*, vol. 65); Daythal Kendall, *A Supplement to a Guide to Manuscripts Relating to the American Indian in the Library of the American Philosophical Society* (Philadelphia, Pa.: 1982) (= *Memoirs of the American Philosophical Society*, vol. 65s); *Guide to the Microfilm Collection of the Professional Papers of Franz Boas* (Wilmington, Del.: 1972), 2 v.

Artifacts: Only a small number of artifact items are held.

Description

The American Philosophical Society, founded in 1743 by Benjamin Franklin, is the oldest society in the United States. The Society has a long tradition of maintaining scholarly materials. Important collections in the related areas of Native American linguistics, anthropology, ethnohistory, archaeology and folklore are held in the Society's library and constitute a significant part of the library's holdings. This collection area developed from an interest expressed by members of the Society as early as the eighteenth-century, and through continuous acquisition has resulted in an international center for anthropological scholarship. Among Society members whose early contributions to the library both established this concentration of anthropological resources, and the Society's commitment to it, are Benjamin Smith Barton, Peter S. DuPonceau, Albert Gallatin and Thomas Jefferson.

Building upon collection strengths in the library (which were further developed in the nineteenth-century), later members of the Society—including the father of American anthropology, Franz Boas—contributed their own papers. The library is the repository for Boas's personal and professional papers and the Franz Boas Collection of Materials for American Linguistics. Consequently, many of Boas's most notable students followed suit with the contribution of their own personal papers or collections, including Melville J. Herskovits, Alfred L. Kroeber, Robert H. Lowie, Elsie Clews Parsons, Paul Radin, Edward Sapir and Frank G. Speck. The Society continues to solicit and accession the papers or other contributions of distinguished anthropologists, linguists and ethnohistorians, such as Ella Deloria, William N. Fenton, Alfred I. Hallowell, John Alden Mason, Anthony Wallace and William S. Willis, Jr. In addition, since the 1940s the Society's Phillips Fund has regularly made grants to anthropologists and others for the purposes of underwriting field research in Native American linguistics, ethnohistory and culture. Copies of the grant recipients' fieldnotes and recordings, as well as the resulting unpublished or published scholarship, are collected by the library.

These well-established twin streams of collection development—solicited papers and Phillips Fund supported research—are augmented by the ongoing acquisition of an associated collection of rare printed materials. Together, manuscripts and printed materials constitute a dynamic, rich and unique resource for research in Native American anthropology. The American Philosophical Society Library is committed to the continued development and improvement of its holdings in anthropology and related areas.

It should be noted that many of the Society's manuscript collections in anthropology have been microfilmed. Students, researchers and libraries may buy copies of most microfilm, which are offered at especially low prices. Documents not already available on microfilm may be photocopied or microfilmed at the discretion of the archivists.

Also of note are the large audio and photographic collections. Audio collections are largely field recordings of language types, lexicons, stories and legends, ceremonies, oral histories and interviews. An in-house catalog by tribe/language type is available. Some photographic collections are unprocessed, but reflect the work of such anthropologists as Frank G. Speck and Alfred I. Hallowell. Permission for the duplication of audio and photographic materials is sometimes granted. Additional information on obtaining microfilms, photocopies, audio tape dubs or photographs may be obtained by calling the Manuscripts Department.

Martin L. Levitt

Balch Institute for Ethnic Studies

Address: Balch Institute for Ethnic Studies, 18 S. Seventh St., Philadelphia, PA 19106.
Tel.: (215) 925-8090, ext. 217 (Balch Institute Research Library); (215) 925-8090, ext. 228 and 229 (Philadelphia Jewish Archives Center).
Fax: (215) 925-8195 (Balch Library and Philadelphia Jewish Archives Center).
E-mail (Balch Library): balchlib@hslc.org.
Internet address: http://libertynet.org./~balch.
Networks, consortia: OCLC, Access Pennsylvania.

Public transit access: Take the Market/Frankford "El" to 8th and Market Streets. Or, by train from 30th St. Station, exit at Market East.

Parking: A commercial parking garage is near the Institute on 7th Street.

Founded: 1971 (date of incorporation); the building was first opened to the public in 1976.

Major resources: Documentation, archival and museum collections on the role of ethnicity and immigration in American life.

Areas of specialization: Ethnic studies; American immigration studies; Philadelphia Jewish Archives Center (PJAC); Scotch Irish Foundation collection; Delaware Valley Regional Ethnic Archives Project (1990-1992); others. Some eighty ethnic groups are represented in library and archival collections.

Archives/manuscripts: 2,700 linear ft. of manuscripts in the Balch archives; 2,300 linear ft. of manuscripts and records in the Philadelphia Jewish Archives Center.

Holdings (books and journals): More than 60,000 book volumes and 6,000 serial titles in the Research Library; 6,000 reels of microfilm.

Visual/audio resources: 12,000 photographic images and about 2,000 sound recordings (Balch Institute Library); about 3,000 photographs in the PJAC Archives.

Access: Open to the public 10:00 a.m. to 4:00 p.m., Tue.-Sat. There is a small fee for admission to the building. On-site use of library materials. Interlibrary loan services are also available.

Guides/catalogs: Monique Bourque and R. Joseph Anderson (editors and compilers), *A Guide to Manuscripts and Microfilm Collections of the Research Library of the Balch Institute for Ethnic Studies* (Philadelphia, Pa.: 1992).

Catalogs of artifacts: Gail F. Stern and Nancy L. Wygant (editors), *The Balch Institute for Ethnic Studies: Selections from the Museums Collections* (Philadelphia, Pa.: 1992).

Exhibit catalogs: Shalom D. Staub (editor), *Craft & Community: Traditional Arts in Contemporary Society* (Philadelphia, Pa.: [1988]); others.

Description

The Balch Institute for Ethnic Studies Museum carries out educational and research programs related to ethnicity and immigration studies, with special emphasis on the many U.S. immigrant and ethnic groups. Educational programs on ethnicity and American immigration history are provided, and museum, gallery, library and archival programs are offered at the Balch facility in Center City Philadelphia. The Museum is a focus of ongoing educational programs. On display here are immigrant documents, clothing, household goods and other artifacts that reflect the American immigrant experience.

Balch Institute Research Library and Archives

The Balch Institute Research Library collections are used by students, scholars, genealogists and others interested in their ethnic heritage or in the history of their neighborhood. The library contains books, pamphlets, newspapers, posters and microfilm of ethnographic or related interest. Book holdings are mainly in English, although titles in Norwegian, Swedish, Lithuanian, Yiddish, Ukrainian, Greek and other languages of U.S.

immigrants are also available. Many of the library's archival holdings are listed in *A Guide to Manuscripts and Microfilm Collections of the Research Library of the Balch Institute for Ethnic Studies* (Philadelphia, Pa.: 1992).

Philadelphia Jewish Archives Center

The Philadelphia Jewish Archives Center (PJAC)—an archive established in 1972 by the Jewish Federation of Greater Philadelphia—is maintained at the Museum. The PJAC includes records and documents of diverse Philadelphia-area Jewish organizations and associations, including orphanages, charities, schools, volunteer and sports associations. The PJAC archival records date from the mid-nineteenth-century. The ca. 3,000 nineteenth- and twentieth-century photographs (mainly black-and-white) in the PJAC archive depict the history of the Philadelphia Jewish community.

Scotch-Irish Society Library and Archives

Also on deposit at the Institute is the library and archives of the Scotch-Irish Foundation—a substantial collection that is maintained and supported by the Scotch-Irish Society.

Information provided by Gail E. Farr and Lily G. Schwartz.

National Archives—Mid Atlantic Region (Center City Philadelphia)

Address: National Archives—Mid Atlantic Region, 9th and Market Streets, Room 1350, Philadelphia, PA 19107.
Tel.: (215) 597-3000
Fax: (215) 597-2303
E-mail: archives@philarch.nara.gov.
Internet address: http://www.nara.gov/regional/philacc.html.
Public transit access: Take the Market/Frankford "El" to Market East. Or, from New Jersey, take the New Jersey PATCO to the 8th Street stop.
Founded: 1969.
Major resources: Records retired from federal agencies in Delaware, Maryland, Pennsylvania, Virginia and West Virginia. The Mid Atlantic Region also holds microfilm copies of some other National Archives records.
Areas of specialization: Holdings include some series of records of the U.S. Office of Immigration (RG 85).
Archives/manuscripts: More than 45,000 cubic ft. of federal records from the Mid Atlantic Region—only a small portion of these would likely be of anthropological interest.
Holdings (microfilm): 30,000 reels—only a small portion of these would likely be of anthropological interest.
Visual/audio resources: No audio recordings and very few photographs are held.

Access: A majority of holdings are open for public research. Restrictions on access to some federal records may be applied in accord with exemptions in the Freedom of Information Act. It is strongly recommended that readers call a few days in advance of a planned visit to arrange for the availability of needed materials.

Information provided by Kellee Blake.

Presbyterian Historical Society (PHS)

Address: Presbyterian Historical Society, 425 Lombard Street, Philadelphia, PA 19147.
Tel.: (215) 627-1852
Fax: (215) 627-0509
Internet address: http://philadelphia.libertynet.org81/~pacscl/phs/index.html.
Networks, consortia: OCLC, Palinet; also, until 1993, RLIN.
Public transit access: The PHS may be reached by bus, Amtrak or El. Call the Society for directions.
Founded: 1852.
Major resources: Church and missionary archives and records, including archives of the Presbyterian Church (U.S.A.).
Areas of specialization: Board of Foreign Missions (BFM) manuscripts, the American Indian Missionary Correspondence Collection and other Native American-related papers. The Sheldon Jackson collection is in the Board of National Missions, Alaska Records, 1882-1983. Manuscript holdings include missionary letters and correspondence from Presbyterian missionaries who served in numerous mission fields—e.g., Alaska, Africa, India, Thailand and the Philippines.
Holdings: 170,000 book titles; 11,000 cubic ft. of archives and papers—only a limited portion of which may be of potential anthropological interest. Many archival files have been microfilmed; other archival materials are in original format only.
Visual/audio resources: Several archival files include photographic collections of ethnographic, cultural or historical interest. The records of the Board of Foreign Missions (RG 224) contain BFM photographs, ca.1860-1970.
Access: The reading room is open to the public. Some records are restricted. Information on access to particular records should be requested from the Society's Archivist.
References: Kristin L. Gleeson, Frederick J. Heuser, Jr. and William B. Bynum, "From String-Wrapped Bundles to Cubic Feet: The Development of the Archives in the Presbyterian Historical Society," *American Presbyterians*, vol. 70, no. 1 (Spring 1992), p. 43-55.
Guides/catalogs: Robert Benedetto, *Guide to the Manuscript Collections of the Presbyterian Church, U.S.A.* (New York: 1990) (= *Bibliographies and Indexes in Religious Studies*, no. 17); Gerald W. Gillette, "Native American Research Materials in the Presbyterian Historical Society," *American Presbyterians*, vol. 65, no. 3 (Fall 1987), p. [233]-238; Frederick J. Heuser, Jr., *A Guide to Foreign Missionary Manuscripts in the Presbyterian Historical Society* (New York: 1988) (= *Bibliographies and Indexes in World History*, no. 11); Aloha

South, *Guide to Non-Federal Archives and Manuscripts in the United States Relating to Africa* (London: 1989), vol. 2, p. 933-947.

Description

The Presbyterian Historical Society is located on Lombard Street in historic Center City Philadelphia—only a few blocks from Independence Hall. The archives of the Presbyterian Church (U.S.A.) and other church and mission records are well-organized and maintained by the Society. More than 400 finding aids are available to assist in the use of the processed archival collections. Some finding aids, such as Frederick Heuser's *A Guide to Foreign Missionary Manuscripts in the Presbyterian Historical Society*, have been published, while others are unpublished. A local on-line database, "Archives Database" (in Inmagic), provides access to the archives collections and is searchable by subject.

The Society's "Biographical Files" contain records of more than 40,000 Presbyterian missionaries who served in mission fields throughout the world. The index to these files is not yet on-line, but researchers may eventually locate biographical files by means of an in-house database. The extensive overseas missionary records of the Presbyterian Church (U.S.A.) have been described in Frederick Heuser's guide, which is annotated, arranged geographically by mission field, and indexed by missionary name and place of residence.

The archival resources of the Society concerning Native Americans have been briefly described in an article by Gerald W. Gillette (1987). Of special interest with regard to Native peoples of Alaska are the papers, correspondence, journals, notebooks and photographs of Sheldon Jackson (1834-1909). After his initial missionary service in the American West, Jackson made 26 missionary trips to Alaska, beginning in 1877. The Sheldon Jackson papers, which span the years from 1855 to 1909, consist of 24 cubic feet of archival materials. Jackson's photographs of tribal villages and Alaskan scenes are also part of this archive.

The National Council files of the Division of Overseas Ministries, Southern Asia Office, contain files on India. Missionary letters from Thailand begin in the 1840s with William P. Buell's letters to mission headquarters in the United States. The missionary records pertaining to Thailand include papers of Charles R. Callendar, Edwin Charles Cort, Mabel Gilson Cort, Samuel Reynolds House and Samuel Gamble McFarland. Archives of Presbyterian missionaries who served in China are especially numerous. Included are the papers of Nathaniel Bercovitz, Nell Burgess Boone, Homer Vernon Bradshaw, William Hervie Dobson and many others.

Lee S. Dutton
Information provided by Kristin L. Gleeson.

University of Pennsylvania. Museum of Archaeology and Anthropology. Archives

Address: Archives, Museum of Archaeology and Anthropology, 33rd and Spruce Streets, Philadelphia, PA 19104-6324.

Tel.: (215) 898-8304 (Main [Elkins]); (215) 898-6720 (Photographic Archives).
Fax: (215) 898-0657
Internet address: http://www.upenn.edu/museum/Collections/archives.html.
Internet address (Museum): http://www.upenn.edu/museum.
Public transit access: Septa: take the Market/Frankford "El" to 34th and Market Streets; bus #40—exit at Convention Ave.; bus # 42—exit at 34th and Spruce Streets; bus #21—exit at 34th and Walnut Streets; by train—to 30th St. Station.
Founded: 1887 (the Museum), 1964 (Museum Archives).
Major resources: The main organizational divisions of the Archives are: Museum Administrative Records (organized by administrative unit); Archaeological and Anthropological Research Records (organized by curatorial section and then by project); and Special Collections (organized by format or subject, such as published maps or the Notable Photographers Collection, etc.).
Areas of specialization: Archaeology, ethnography, cultural and physical anthropology, linguistics and folklore. Museum curatorial sections are constituted by geographical areas and culture groupings as follows: Americas (North, Central, South); Near East (Mesopotamia, Persia, Syro-Palestine and Islamic); Cuneiform Tablets; Egypt; Mediterranean (Greco-Roman civilization); Asia; Africa (sub-Saharan); Oceania; Europe (other than Greco-Roman); and Physical Anthropology. These research interests are strongly represented in the archival holdings.
Archives/manuscripts: More than 2,000 linear ft. of textual records.
Fieldnotes, etc.: The University of Pennsylvania Museum has sponsored or participated in more than 300 projects of archaeological/anthropological significance. Many of these generated fieldnotes and records of various types. Detailed information on these documents is too voluminous for inclusion here. The general *Guide* (listed below under "References") provides concise descriptions of many of these projects and of the records that are available in the Archives. More detailed finding aids, by project, are available upon request at a nominal photocopying charge.
Holdings (books and journals): More than 250 hardbound volumes and 24 linear ft. of paperbound volumes of books published by or about the University of Pennsylvania Museum and its research during the course of its history. Also 25 linear ft. of paperbound volumes for journals and exhibition catalogs published by or about the University of Pennsylvania Museum and its research.
Holdings (other): More than 225 bound volumes (i.e., Board minutes, letter books, accession ledgers, financial records, etc.); unspecified numbers of the following: maps, museum building and archaeological site plans, art on paper, news clippings, posters, postcards and graphics, certificates, recorded sound media, oil paintings and sculpture related to the museum's history.
Visual/audio resources: More than 300,000 photographic items, including 150,000 glass and film negatives; 20,000 lantern slides; 1,000 motion picture films; unspecified numbers of color transparencies, videotapes, stereograph cards and vintage prints, including the Notable Photographers Collection. The photographic collections were generated primarily in three ways: as field documentation for archaeological/anthropological projects; in the museum's photography studio as documentation of artifacts, events and personalities, etc.; or purchased from professional photographers as research aids (especially the Notable

Photographers Collection). Recorded sound collections consist of phonograph records, reel-to-reel tapes and cassette tapes (primarily of museum lectures and events), commercial recordings used for educational purposes, radio program recordings and oral histories.

Access: Archival collections are accessible to serious researchers by prior appointment after completion of a researcher application. Research hours are Tuesday through Friday, 9:30 a.m. to 4:00 p.m. Some materials are restricted due to donor restrictions, copyright considerations or publication plans. In general, materials are not restricted.

References: University of Pennsylvania. University Museum. Archives, *A Guide to The University Museum Archives of the University of Pennsylvania* (Philadelphia, Pa.: 1984); entry by photographer in Andrew H. Eskind and Greg Drake (editors), *Index to American Photographic Collections* (2nd ed., Boston: 1990); University of Pennsylvania. Museum, *Publications of The University Museum* (Philadelphia, Pa.: 1973). Also, University of Pennsylvania. Museum, *A Complete Catalog of Publications* (Philadelphia, Pa.: 1993); Percy C. Madeira, Jr., *Men in Search of Man, The First Seventy-five Years of the University Museum of the University of Pennsylvania* (Philadelphia, Pa.: 1964); Dilys Pegler Winegrad, *Through Time, Across Continents: A Hundred Years of Archaeology and Anthropology at The University Museum* (Philadelphia. Pa.: 1993).

Artifact resources: The museum holds ca. 1.5 million archaeological and ethnographic artifacts in its collections from the curatorial sections described above. The museum collections are strongly focused on ancient civilizations to the fall of the Roman Empire, and on traditional cultures worldwide throughout history.

Archaeological sites represented in artifact collections: Sites at which the museum's artifact collections originated correspond roughly to those for which it holds archival materials. The publications cited above at "References" provide the best references to these sites. The museum's artifact and archival collections are distinguished by the fact that so many of the artifacts were recovered by the museum's own field projects (from 1887 to the present) and that the archives document the recovery. This makes the collection a valuable resource for serious researchers.

Published catalogs of artifact resources: Only a partial published catalog exists focusing on the collection highlights. It is Lee Horne (editor), *Introduction to the Collections of The University Museum* (Philadelphia: 1985). Other museum publications provide information about specific collections, such as exhibition catalogs, journals and monographs, etc.

Description

The Archives of the University of Pennsylvania Museum of Archaeology and Anthropology was established in 1964, when records formerly managed by various administrative departments and curatorial sections, or stored in inaccessible areas of the museum buildings, began to be brought together in a separate room under the charge of the first Museum Archivist, Geraldine Bruckner, who was the museum's first Registrar as well. As these resources were gathered together, an awareness developed that the museum's archives were not only its institutional memory, but also a cultural resource of international significance.

In order to accommodate qualified researchers with an accessible facility, an historic renovation of the museum's former Elkins Library (1898) was begun in 1978. The Archives was able to open to outside researchers in 1981. At that time, the museum's photographic collections were joined with the textual records in the Archives. In 1986 the first academically trained archivist, Douglas M. Haller, became the fourth Museum Archivist. Shortly thereafter the Museum Archivist and Photographic Archivist were joined by a Reference Archivist, and the museum's moving image collections were added to the Archives.

The organization of the Archives follows from the administrative and research history of the museum. In 1887 University of Pennsylvania provost William Pepper, Jr., envisioned a museum that would house artifacts evidencing the development and history of humanity. Two years later, this Museum of Archaeology and Paleontology opened to the public in a campus building simultaneously with the launching of the museum's first major field project—an archaeological expedition to uncover the remains of the ancient Sumerian city of Nippur in Mesopotamia. In the early 1890s the museum established its quintessential pattern of worldwide curatorial sections supplemented by finds from field projects, a library, a publications program and public educational events.

By 1899 the museum was able to construct its own building in West Philadelphia, the Free Museum of Science and Art, that served as a kind of bridge between the city and its parent institution, the University of Pennsylvania. An elaborate scheme by architect Wilson Eyre, Jr., for the expansion of the museum included three central rotunda devoted to the ancient civilizations of Greece and Rome; Egypt; and Mesopotamia, flanked by five and a half courtyards devoted to the traditional cultures of the Americas, Asia, Africa and Oceania. One rotunda and two courtyards had been constructed when, in 1929, the Great Depression ended the University Museum's building activity. These disparate sections of the original uncompleted plan were united with an Academic Wing in 1971—a change that reflected the increasing importance of the university's Anthropology Department and Library in the museum, as well as the enhanced role of the museum's public education efforts. In 1994 the institution's fifth name was officially adopted as the University of Pennsylvania Museum of Archaeology and Anthropology.

Although the museum did not fully realize its original building plan, it did achieve the goal of amassing 1.5 million artifacts from around the world through participation in hundreds of field projects over the course of a century. The story of the personalities and expeditions behind the acquisition of the museum's artifacts is a fascinating one that is told eloquently by the museum's archives. Following are highlights from some of these stories.

In North America, the Tlingit Louis Shotridge collected Alaskan materials; in Central America, Tatiana Proskouriakoff made breakthroughs that led to the decipherment of Maya hieroglyphics; while Max Uhle's creation of a chronology for Andean cultures made him the "Father of South American Archaeology." The museum's 1889 expedition to Nippur (Iraq) was the first American excavation in the Near East, and spectacular finds were made by C. Leonard Woolley at Ur in the 1920s. The museum also uncovered the palace of the Pharaoh Merenptah at Memphis. This is displayed in the galleries, along with one of the largest sphinxes outside of Egypt. One of the early pioneers of Minoan archaeology, the museum remains active in the Mediterranean world as it continues work at Gordion, site of the excavation of the so-called "Tomb of King Midas." Collections of Chinese, Japanese and

FIGURE 8. Jenichiro Oyabe with two Ainu leaders on Hokkaido Island, 1901. Courtesy of the Univeristy Museum of Archaeology and Anthropology, University of Pennsylvania (negative #S4-141810).

Indian objects include significant holdings of Buddhist materials begun by Maxwell Sommerville in the nineteenth-century. The museum was in the vanguard of American museums in recognizing the importance of African ethnographic collections and in sending collectors to Pacific islands such as Borneo. Technological innovation has been a hallmark of the museum's achievements—from aerial photography of sites in the 1930s and the development of trend-setting archaeological testing techniques in the 1950s, to underwater archaeology in the 1960s. Anthropologists of the caliber of Frank G. Speck, Carleton Coon and Loren C. Eiseley held curatorial positions in the museum and contributed significantly to the development of the Department of Anthropology at the University of Pennsylvania.

Douglas M. Haller

University of Pennsylvania. University Museum of Archaeology and Anthropology. Library

Address: Library, Museum of Archaeology and Anthropology, 33rd and Spruce Streets, Philadelphia, PA 19104-6324.
Location: Third floor, Kress (academic) Wing.
Tel.: (215) 898-4021
Fax: (215) 573-2008
Internet address: http://www.library.upenn.edu/museum/museum.html.
Internet address (Van Pelt Library Department of Special Collections): http://www.library.upenn.edu/special/collections.html.
Networks, consortia: RLIN.
Public transit access: Septa: Take the Market/Frankford "El" to 34th and Market Streets; bus #40—exit at Convention Ave.; bus #42—exit at 34th and Spruce Streets; bus #21—exit at 34th and Walnut Streets; by train—to 30th St. Station.
Founded: 1887. Formerly named the Elkins Library.
Major resources: A major collection of books and journals in the fields of archaeology, anthropology and museology. Manuscripts pertaining to anthropology are in various locations on campus—chiefly in Museum Archives (administratively separate from the Museum Library); and also the Department of Special Collections, Van Pelt Library.
Areas of specialization: Egyptology, Mesoamerica, Northwest Coast. Library resources include the Daniel Garrison Brinton Collection on Native American linguistics and also the Egyptian Collection.
Archives/manuscripts: In Museum Archives [see the entry, above] and also in Van Pelt Library, Department of Special Collections. Some papers of former University of Pennsylvania anthropologists are in the University of Pennsylvania Archives and others are at the American Philosophical Society—e.g., the papers of Frank G. Speck and Alfred I. Hallowell.
Holdings (books and journals): 120,000 cataloged vols.; 900 current journal and serial titles.
Visual/audio resources: Most original photographs are in the Museum of Archaeology and Anthropology Archives, not in the Library.

Access: Anyone with a need to know may use Museum Library materials during the times the museum is open. Only current University of Pennsylvania students and employees may borrow materials directly from the library. Interlibrary loan services are available in many instances.

References: Regna Darnell, *Daniel Garrison Brinton: The "Fearless Critic" of Philadelphia* (Philadelphia, Pa.: 1988) (= *University of Pennsylvania Publications in Anthropology*, no. 3); Percy C. Madeira, Jr., *Men in Search of Man: The First Seventy-Five Years of the University Museum of the University of Pennsylvania* (Philadelphia, Pa.: 1964).

Guides/catalogs: Daniel Garrison Brinton, "Catalogue of the Berendt Linguistic Collection," *Bulletin of the Free Museum of Science and Art of the University of Pennsylvania*, vol. 2, no. 4 (May 1900), p. [202]-234—this catalog lists the Mayan-language materials purchased by Brinton from Carl Hermann Berendt (1817-1878). The Berendt materials—now part of the Brinton Collection—are in the Department of Special Collections at Van Pelt Library.

Description

The University of Pennsylvania Museum Library came into being in its present form in 1971, when materials from the Elkins Library (an early Museum library), from the Egyptology Section of the Museum, and from various museum storage areas were brought together in the then newly constructed academic (Kress) wing of the museum. The Museum Library has extensive book and journal holdings in anthropology and related fields. Original manuscripts, archives and photographs of anthropological, archaeological and related interest are mainly housed either in Museum Archives, in the Van Pelt Library Department of Special Collections, or in other campus locations. Museum Library resources are supplemented by other library collections on campus, such the South Asia Collection in Van Pelt Library.

Prominent among Museum Library resources is the Daniel Garrison Brinton (1837-1899) Collection of materials on Mesoamerican linguistics—a substantial resource that was presented to the museum in 1900. The Brinton Collection books and journals (ca. 1,000 v.) are separately housed in the Museum Library. The manuscripts received with the Brinton Collection are in the Special Collections department at Van Pelt Library.

Like the Brinton Collection, the substantial Egyptology Collection of books, journals and documents is maintained as a separate collection within the Museum Library.

Lee S. Dutton
Information provided by Jean S. Adelman.

Pennsylvania—Valley Forge

American Baptist Historical Society (ABHS), **American Baptist Churches, USA American Baptist Archives Center**

Address: American Baptist Historical Society, P.O. Box 851, Valley Forge, PA 19482-0851.

Contact: Beverly Carlson, Administrator/Archivist.
Tel.: (610) 768-2378
Fax: (610) 768-2275
Founded: 1853.
Major resources: Non-current records of the Board of International Ministries, 1814- .
Areas of specialization: Archival sources: missionary correspondence, diaries, field reports, research papers, collections of personal papers. Fields of activity: Burma, Assam, South India, China, Japan, Congo Free State (Belgian Congo), the Philippine Islands and Europe. Also, historical and biographical materials concerning Adoniram Judson.
Archives/manuscripts: Ca. 325 linear ft. (all topics).
Visual/audio resources: Assorted photographs, lantern slides, photograph albums.
Restrictions: Materials are closed to the public. The Archives Center is open for research by appointment only. No interlibrary loan.
Guides/catalogs: Finding aids for many archival resources are at the Archives Center.

Description

Missionaries, like anthropologists and ethnographers, traveled to foreign places, did their work, interacted with other cultures and often returned home to share their experiences. Through their official correspondence and reports, they recorded their observations in the same way that anthropologists engage in participant observation. Many times these written narratives record the first Western contacts with indigenous peoples around the world.

In 1814 the Baptists of the United States formed the Triennial Convention, to provide for the financial support of missionaries Adoniram and Ann Judson in Burma and to raise funds to send out other missionaries. The Convention was to become a "mission society" that continues today through the American Baptist Board of International Ministries.

The American Baptist Board of International Ministries has been known as: General Missionary Convention of the Baptist Denomination in the United States for Foreign Missions (1814-1845); American Baptist Missionary Union (1845-1910); American Baptist Foreign Mission Society (1910-1972); and Board of International Ministries (1973-).

The Women's American Baptist Foreign Mission Society was founded in 1871. In 1955 it was integrated with the American Baptist Foreign Mission Society.

Tracing American Baptist missions through the eyes of missionaries allows the researcher today to see the mission task more clearly and to gain fresh insight into the cultures and peoples with whom the missionaries worked. American Baptist missionaries carried out ministries in evangelism, education and healing, and for the most part strongly worked for indigenous churches and self-supported centers of activity.

Archives Center Records

The Archives Center at Valley Forge is the official depository for the records of the National Boards of American Baptist Churches, USA. In 1984 the official ABHS records, previously stored in various locations, were brought together at the newly established Archives Center.

The International Mission archives at Valley Forge mainly pertain to those fields where American Baptist missions were historically most active: Burma, Assam, South India, China, Japan, Congo Free State (Belgian Congo/Zaire), the Philippine Islands and Europe. Diaries, letters, manuscripts and records in these files may be of potential ethnographic as well as historical interest. Also of related interest are the archives of American Baptist missions to Native Americans. These are also preserved at Valley Forge, within both National and International files. Mission work among Native Americans began in 1825—before the founding of the Home Mission Society. It continued under the auspices of the Foreign Mission Society until 1865.

Original records in the International Ministries Central Files include Biographical Files, Property Files, Historical Files and Geographical Files. All Central Files up to 1900 are arranged by geographic field of activity and are subdivided by locality or region. In contrast, Central Files records and correspondence since 1900 are organized by missionary name. The names of almost all American Baptist missionaries—active, inactive or retired, the country of their mission, date of birth and dates of appointment are contained in the Biographical Files. The Archives Center has forty vertical file drawers with missionary biographical information alone.

Especially prominent among American Baptist mission endeavors is the Burma mission work of Rev. Adoniram Judson and his wife Ann. Many Judson family belongings are preserved at the archive. Two entire Biographical File drawers of documentary material on Adoniram Judson are held. These include pictures, letters, memos and an index to his letters. A collection of books by and about the Judsons is also part of the "Judson Collection."

Within the International Ministries Central Files are thirty boxes of archival materials on Southeast Asia, produced by U.S. Baptist missionaries to Burma and other parts of Southeast Asia. The boxes are arranged by date, missionary name and the country in which the missionary worked.

The Mission Library holds a special collection of Baptist Mission Press publications in several languages of Asia—including Chinese, Burmese, Sgaw Karen, Pwo Karen, Chin and Kachin. Materials include translations into these languages of stories of the life of Christ, Judson's first Burmese-language translations of the Bible and *Pilgrim's Progress*. There are six shelves of translated works in Burmese, as well as one shelf of similar works in Thai and Filipino.

The special Mission Library is well stocked with the publications of the Mission—including books by and about missionaries. Also held are mission periodicals (usually complete sets) published in Burma, in other mission fields or the United States. Among periodical holdings are *Burma News*, published in Rangoon by the American Baptists there; the Woman's Baptist Foreign Missionary Society (East) *Annual Reports*, with holdings from 1881 to 1914; the Woman's Baptist Foreign Missionary Society (West) *Annual Reports* from 1871 to 1914; and the *Baptist Missionary Review*, 1895-1957.

Original photographs, lantern slides and related items may be found in a number of collections at the Archives Center. Photographs of cultural, ethnographic or related interest may be found in the Central Files, in some Biographical Files, in Historical Files and also in collections of donated missionary personal papers and albums. Burma and the Belgian Congo are among several mission fields depicted in photo sets and albums.

The Arthur and Laura Carson photo album contains many images of scenes of the Chin Hills and other Burma locations. Two missionary albums donated to the archive by Joseph Clark (together with his mission papers) contain snapshots and photos of mission work and village life in the Belgian Congo. The Harry S. Myers collection of sixty color slides (ca. 1920s) also depicts scenes of the Congo.

In addition to resources at the Valley Forge Archives Center, the American Baptist Historical Society maintains the extensive American Baptist-Samuel Colgate Historical Library in Rochester, New York.

Information provided by Beverly Carlson and Betty J. Layton

Rhode Island—Providence

John Carter Brown Library

Address (mailing): John Carter Brown Library, Box 1894, Providence, RI 02912.
Location: Corner of Brown and George Streets, Providence, RI.
Tel.: (401) 863-2725
Fax: (401) 863-3477
Internet address: http://www.brown.edu/Facilities/University_Library.
Internet access to on-line catalog ("Josiah"): library.brown.edu. Approximately 20 percent of John Carter Brown Library holdings are on-line.
Networks, consortia: RLIN.
Public transit access: Access to the library by public transit is very indirect and on-site parking is not immediately available. Additional travel/directional information may be obtained by contacting the library.
Founded: 1846.
Major resources: Holdings are not divided into separate units, but represent an integrated and unified collection of primary sources focused on the discovery, exploration, colonization and settlement of the entire Western Hemisphere during the colonial period, ca. 1493-1830.
Areas of specialization: Ethnohistory, Amerindian linguistics, Native-colonial relations, pre-Columbian archaeology.
Archives/manuscripts: Anthropologists' fieldnotes are not collected, although the library does have the papers of John Russell Bartlett relating to his term of service as the United States' Commissioner for the drawing of the boundary between Mexico and the United States. Between 1850 and 1853 he traveled across Texas, New Mexico, Arizona, northern Mexico and California. The collection consists of the following: (1.) Correspondence, May 1850 to August 1877; (2.) Official Despatches, 1850-1853; (3.) Official Journal, 1849-1852; (4.) Personal Journal, August 1850-December 1852; (5.) Newspaper Clippings, June 1850-August 1852. This collection is available on microfilm from the library. Also among library holdings are 200 watercolors and drawings that were produced during the boundary survey.
Holdings (books and journals): 45,000 books printed before 1830; 15,000 reference works; 150 journals; numerous codices, including fifty in Amerindian languages, usually related to early missionary efforts.

Visual/audio resources: Many of the printed books concerned with the exploration and colonization of the New World contain illustrations of Native people and locales that are significant as "evidence," as well as for a record of the European image of America and its inhabitants.

Access: Materials are available for use by scholars for research, although not by general readers. All items are paged for researchers and must be used in the reading room. Some items are consulted only under the supervision of a librarian.

Guides/catalogs: John Alden and Dennis C. Landis (editors), *European Americana: A Chronological Guide to Works Printed in Europe Relating to the Americans, 1493-1776* (New York: 1980-   ), 6 v. [The following volumes are currently available: vol. 1: 1493-1600, vol. 2: 1601-1650, vol. 3: 1651-1675, vol. 5: 1701-1725, vol. 6: 1726-1750]; *Bibliotheca Americana: Catalogue of the John Carter Brown Library. Third Catalogue.* (Providence, R.I.: 1919-1931) [reprinted, 1961], 3 v. [vol. 1: *Twelfth-Century to 1599*, vol. 2: *1600-1658*, vol. 3: *1659-1674*]; Susan Danforth, *Encountering the New World, 1493-1800: Catalogue of an Exhibition* (Providence, R.I.: 1991); Julie Greer Johnson, *The Book in the Americas: The Role of Books and Printing in the Development of Culture and Society in Colonial Latin America: Catalogue of an Exhibition* (Providence, R.I.: 1988); Cipriano Muñoz y Manzano, conde de la Viñaza, *Bibliografía española de lenguas indígenas de América* (Madrid: 1892)—lists 211 printed works issued before 1800 known in actual copies. Of this group, the Brown Library owns 143, or 68 percent, in addition to related works not included in this bibliography.

Description

Located on the Main Green of Brown University in Providence, Rhode Island, the John Carter Brown Library is one of the premier libraries for the study of the colonial period in the Americas. Although situated in the heart of New England, the focus of the collection extends well beyond the Pilgrims and Founding Fathers to include 50,000 primary historical sources related to the entire Western Hemisphere before 1830.

The scholarly value of the library is extraordinary, partly because its origins go back to a time when systematic book collecting around a historical theme was quite unusual. Although the Brown family had been acquiring books since the early eighteenth-century, the present collection was begun in earnest in the mid-nineteenth-century, when John Carter Brown (1797-1874) began his passionate pursuit of Americana. His son, John Nicholas Brown (1861-1900), actively continued the acquisition of materials. Before his death, the latter conceived the idea of transforming the collection into a research library as a memorial to his father. In his will, funds were assigned for construction of the building and for an endowment to support the library's mission. The original Beaux Arts building was dedicated in 1904. In 1991 a 15,000 square foot addition—designed in the same classical style—was completed.

An independent center for advanced research, as well as a repository of rare books, the library houses an internationally renowned and continually growing collection of rare books and manuscripts. Perhaps most well-known for its extensive holdings in the literature of European exploration and colonization in the Americas, the John Carter Brown Library also has significant sources documenting both the impression the New World made on European culture, as well as sources illustrating the interaction of Europeans and Americans. In addition to works published in Europe, the library's extensive holdings of early Latin American and North American imprints make it possible for researchers to study colonial events from different perspectives and in various contextual frameworks.

Although traditionally used primarily by historians, these sources are being investigated by scholars from many other disciplines, including anthropologists. Practitioners of subfields such as Amerindian linguistics, ethnohistory, the study of Native-colonial relations and pre-Columbian archaeology will find valuable documentary information published in the colonial period. In the area of Native American linguistics, for instance, the library owns approximately 500 works. These include dictionaries, grammars, catechisms, doctrinals and books containing individual passages and sections in Indian languages. The holdings of Nahuatl imprints are particularly strong, as are those for Quechua, but many other lesser-known languages are also represented.

Although many of the works are Latin American in origin, North American languages are also represented, as in such pioneering works as Roger Williams's *A Key into the Language of America* and the 1663 "Eliot Indian Bible,"—the first edition of the first Bible printed in the New World and the first example in history of the translation and printing of the entire Bible in a non-European language (Massachuset) as a means of evangelism. This Bible is named for its Puritan missionary translator, John Eliot (1604-1690).

The source materials in ethnohistory and Native-colonial relations are also quite rich. Histories of exploration and colonization, travel accounts and religious writings are just a few of the types of resources that can be utilized. Although the identification, excavation and reconstruction of pre-Columbian sites do not depend (completely) upon written sources, these have often been useful adjuncts to fieldwork. The existence of such sites was noted as early as the conquest period, and throughout the sixteenth- and seventeenth-centuries references to them appeared in accounts written by explorers and travelers.

For more than a century the library has served scholars from the United States and abroad. In order to facilitate and encourage use of the collection, the library offers fellowships, sponsors lectures and conferences, mounts exhibitions for the public and publishes catalogs, bibliographies and other works that represent and interpret its holdings. This tradition of publicizing the holdings of the library began with the appearance between 1865 and 1871 of *Bibliotheca Americana*, a printed catalog of the Brown family's collection at that time. The library is currently engaged in the compilation and publication of a six-volume guide to European Americana—works concerning the Americas published in Europe between 1493 and 1750. The bibliography includes works in the John Carter Brown Library, as well as works located elsewhere in the Americas and Europe. Five of the volumes have been published to date. These bibliographies, as well as exhibition catalogs and other guides to the resources of the library, allow researchers not on-site to have access to information concerning the collection. For further information regarding library holdings, publications or programs, interested scholars should write to the library.

Daniel J. Slive

South Dakota—Vermillion

University of South Dakota. Institute of American Indian Studies (IAIS)

Address: Institute of American Indian Studies, Room 12, Dakota Hall, University of South Dakota, Vermillion, SD 57069.
Tel.: (605) 677-5209
Fax: (605) 677-6525
E-mail: iais@charlie.usd.edu.
Internet address: http://www.usd.edu/iais.
Internet address (South Dakota Oral History Center): http://www.usd.edu/iais/ohc.htm.
Founded: 1955 (Institute of American Indian Studies); 1966 (Doris Duke American Indian Oral History Project—University of South Dakota).
Major resources: The South Dakota Oral History Center holds the archives of the university's Doris Duke American Indian Oral History Project and also the archives of the South Dakota State Oral History Project.
Areas of specialization: Oral histories by Dakota, Lakota and Nakota peoples (in the Doris Duke Project archives) and by non-Indians of the northern Plains region (in the South Dakota Oral History Project archives).
Archives/manuscripts: The University of South Dakota Doris Duke American Indian Oral History Project was one of six oral history projects funded by the Doris Duke Foundation.The Doris Duke Project recordings consist of nearly 5,000 recorded interviews—many with Indians of the northern Plains. The associated transcripts are also held.
Visual/audio resources: The University of South Dakota Doris Duke Project oral history recordings. A small number of photos of northern Plains Indians are also held.
Access: Open to the public.
References: Joseph H. Cash and Herbert T. Hoover (editors), *To Be an Indian: An Oral History* (New York: 1971)—this publication was based on the Doris Duke Project archives at the University of South Dakota; C. Gregory Crampton, "The Archives of the Duke Projects in American Indian Oral History," in Jane F. Smith and Robert M. Kvasnicka (editors), *Indian-White Relations: A Persistent Paradox* (Washington, D.C.: 1981) (= *National Archives Conferences*, vol. 10), p. 119-128; Bradford Koplowitz, "The Doris Duke Indian Oral History Projects," *Popular Culture in Libraries*, vol. 1 (1993), p. 23-38.
Guides/catalogs: American Indian Research Project, *Oyate Iyechinka Woglakapi: An Oral History Collection, Volumes I - IV* (Vermillion, S.D.: 1970), 4 v. in 1; *Index to the American Indian Research Project* (Pierre, S.D.: 1979).
Artifacts of anthropological interest: In the collections of the university's W.H. Over Museum.

Meg Quintal

University of Tennessee. Frank H. McClung Museum

Address: Frank H. McClung Museum, University of Tennessee, 1327 Circle Park Drive, Knoxville, TN 37996-3200.
Tel.: (615) 974-2144
Fax: (615) 974-3827
Internet address: http://mcclungmuseum.utk.edu.
Founded: 1963.
Major resources: The Lewis-Kneberg Collections. Other collections have no formal name designations.
Areas of specialization: Tennessee archaeology/prehistory.
Archives/manuscripts: 254 linear ft.
Fieldnotes and related materials: The museum contains thousands of pages of fieldnotes, forms, drawings, etc., pertaining to archaeological excavations conducted by University of Tennessee archaeologists since 1934. In addition, in the correspondence of Thomas M.N. Lewis and Madeline Kneberg are lengthy exchanges with the leading American anthropologists of the period 1934-1960.
Holdings (books and journals): Ca. 6,000 volumes.
Visual/audio resources: The museum has approximately 32,000 black-and-white negatives and 22,000 color slides related to archaeological investigations in Tennessee from 1934 to the present.
Access: Accessible to scholars by appointment.
References: Jefferson Chapman, *The Archaeological Collections at the Frank H. McClung Museum* (Knoxville: 1988) (= *University of Tennessee, Knoxville. Frank H. McClung Museum. Occasional Paper*, no. 7).
Artifacts of anthropological significance: The museum curates enormous archaeological collections, including more than 5,600 prehistoric Native American remains. The collections include lithic and ceramic artifacts, faunal remains, archaeobotanical material and freshwater mollusks. The vast majority of the specimens were recovered in scientific excavations by the university and comprise a world-class research collection.
Archaeological sites represented in artifact collections: The museum curates collections from excavations on more than 230 archaeological sites in Tennessee. Cultural affiliations of these sites range from Paleo-Indian to historic Cherokee. Excavations were conducted primarily between 1934 and 1985 and involved sites to be inundated by reservoir projects on the Tennessee River and its tributaries. There are, in addition, several private collections from sites in Tennessee that have been donated to the university.

Description

On January 8, 1934, archaeological work began in the valley of the Clinch River in eastern Tennessee—soon to be inundated by the Norris Reservoir. Thus began a program of archaeological research by the University of Tennessee, in close cooperation with the

Tennessee Valley Authority, the National Park Service and other federal and state agencies, that would span the state. Between 1934 and 1942, ten reservoirs were constructed on the Tennessee River and its tributaries, and archaeological work was conducted at nine of these locations. Hundreds of sites were recorded, and the excavations exposed more than 1,578,000 square feet.

The results of these investigations were impressive: a chronology of cultures was established that would, with the advent of radiocarbon dating in the 1950s, push back the span of human occupation 12,000 years. The generation of archaeologists trained during that period became leaders in the discipline throughout the Southeast and, under the leadership of Thomas M.N. Lewis and Madeline Kneberg, the University of Tennessee played a pivotal role in the scientific coming of age of Southeastern archaeology. In addition, the collections recovered and housed at the McClung Museum are of exceptional value for research in Southeastern archaeology.

A new era in the archaeology of Tennessee began with the passage of the National Historic Preservation Act of 1966. This legislation, and subsequent laws and directives, stimulated an enormous volume of work in the state that continues to this day. In particular, the TVA Tellico, Normandy and Columbia reservoir projects generated millions of dollars in contracts for the university and the Department of Anthropology and involved hundreds of students and staff. Building on the techniques and database of the WPA era, University of Tennessee, Knoxville, archaeologists fostered and improved new field techniques, such as using machinery to open large areas of sites, using backhoes to find sites deeply buried on the river bottoms, water-sluicing excavated soil through small screens to recover more objects and separating charred plant material from the soil by flotation. With better dating methods, they refined chronology and broadened our understanding of the history of human life across the state. Researchers explored the aboriginal location and use of lithic, animal and plant resources. Finally, they began to look at the archaeological remains to develop theories about settlement and man/land relationships.

The results of the WPA work, and much of the subsequent archaeological investigations, are housed at McClung Museum. In addition to the artifacts, the museum is the repository for the associated fieldnotes, forms, analysis sheets, drawings, photographs and correspondence. These non-artifact anthropological resources are invaluable to any research with the artifacts, but can be used alone to address certain research topics. Inherent in these records is the history of the last sixty years of Southeastern archaeology—its field methods and procedures, interpretation, personalities and research priorities.

It should be added, as a final note, that the Department of Anthropology is also a repository of archaeological material and documents generated since the late 1960s. Specifically, the Normandy and Columbia reservoir material and the artifacts and records from a large number of contract projects (e.g., highway right-of-way, industrial sites, sewer and transmission lines, etc.) are housed in the Department of Anthropology.

Jefferson Chapman

University of Texas at Austin. Institute of Latin American Studies. Latin American Network Information Center (UT-LANIC)

Address: UT-LANIC, Institute of Latin American Studies, 1.310 Sid Richardson Hall, University of Texas at Austin, Austin, TX 78713.
E-mail: info@lanic.utexas.edu.
Internet address: http://lanic.utexas.edu. The UT-LANIC website is a gateway for access to many library and other websites throughout Latin America.

University of Texas at Austin. Nettie Lee Benson Latin American Collection

Address: Nettie Lee Benson Latin American Collection, 1.108 Sid Richardson Hall, University of Texas at Austin, Austin, TX 78713.
Tel.: (512) 471-4520
Fax: (512) 495-4520
Internet address: http://www.lib.utexas.edu/Libs/Benson/benson.html.
Networks, consortia: LAMP, SALAM.
Founded: 1921.
Major resources: Library and archives.
Areas of specialization: Documentation on all regions of Latin America, with some emphasis on Mexico and Argentina; a large Mexican American collection.
Archives/manuscripts: Mexican American Archives; Guatemala Project papers (fieldnotes and other anthropological documentation); Mexican Archives collections; other archives.
Visual/audio resources: Photograph collection.

Summer Institute of Linguistics (SIL)

Address: Summer Institute of Linguistics, 7500 West Camp Wisdom Road, Dallas, TX 75326.
Tel.: (972) 708-7400
Fax: (972) 708-7433
Internet address: http://www.sil.org.
Internet address (IMC): http://www.sil.org/imc.
Internet access to on-line catalog: The SIL International Publications Catalog is available at http://sil.org/acppub/catalog/catalog.htm. The Library catalog will eventually be accessible via the Internet.
Founded: 1942 (Summer Institute of Linguistics); 1972 (International Linguistics Center).
Major resources: The Dallas SIL Library; the SIL Language and Culture Archive.

Areas of specialization: Extensive linguistic research in Africa, the Americas, Asia and the South Pacific, as well as some ethnographic research of the same areas.

Holdings (SIL Language and Culture Archives): 26,000 published titles; 6,000 additional (unpublished) titles.

Fieldnotes: Nearly 6,000 published and unpublished fieldnotes of varied quality, dealing with minority languages and cultures from around the world, are stored in microfiche archives. Most are available to the public. These fieldnotes are currently archived only by country and include many from Bolivia, Cameroon, Colombia, Peru, the Philippines and Vietnam. Initial steps have been taken to convert to a Document Imaging System.

Holdings (books and journals—SIL Library): 22,000 titles.

Visual/audio resources: Plans are being made to develop an archive of ethnomusicology field recordings.

Access: Most library materials are available for on-site use. The library participates in interlibrary loan.

Artifacts of anthropological interest: The International Museum of Cultures (IMC), a subsidiary of SIL, includes contemporary artifacts of cultural groups, especially minorities. Permanent exhibits feature Papua New Guinea, Ecuador and Peru.

Description

The Summer Institute of Linguistics is an international educational and research organization specializing in the study of languages spoken by the world's smaller linguistic groups. Serving in more than fifty countries, with nearly 1,500 language groups, SIL partners with governments, NGOs (non-government organizations), universities, churches, and the local people themselves, to promote linguistic research, language development, literacy and other projects of practical, social and spiritual value.

A distinctive feature of the Institute is its focus on unwritten languages. The fact that a language is unwritten is a near-certain indicator of an underprivileged status for those who speak that language—especially in the areas of literacy and education. Those speaking unwritten languages frequently survive on the fringes of national life, enduring geographic, social and economic isolation. Thus SIL's focus on unwritten languages coincides with service to some of the most disadvantaged people living today.

Studies of these languages are done for their local practical value, but they also make a broader contribution. For example, studies in any particular language may shed light on the theory of language (linguistics). The same is true in the areas of literacy, education and anthropology. For this purpose, the studies are published, as appropriate, for the use of libraries, universities and government agencies.

SIL's work was begun nearly sixty years ago by a handful of people in Guatemala and Mexico. The work has spread to all parts of the world, and members now include more than 6,000 people from more than forty countries. Renowned linguist Kenneth L. Pike has been a major force within SIL since its earliest days. [Adapted from the SIL *International Report,* 1966.]

The Dallas SIL Library

The Dallas SIL Library, housed in the Kenneth L. Pike Building on the campus of the International Linguistic Center, is the home of about 30,000 items that reflect the character of SIL and its concerns. Special topic areas include linguistics, minority languages, anthropology, sociolinguistics, literacy materials and Biblical studies. Included in the anthropology collection are intercultural studies, ethnologies and ethnomusicology. Nearly 1,500 unique titles in minority language materials are included—especially grammars and dictionaries. The Kenneth L. Pike collection, which includes his writings, as well as materials he donated, is a special part of the library's holdings; his personal papers are currently being processed for inclusion.

The Language and Culture Archives

More than 32,000 titles of linguistic and ethnographic work by SIL workers from around the world make up the SIL Language and Culture Archives. This includes the 26,000 titles of the SIL *Bibliography*, as well as an additional 6,000 titles of unpublished materials. The *Bibliography* lists 1,300 technical monographs, 144 published doctoral dissertations, 165 published master's theses and more than 5,000 article-length publications. Technical subjects include linguistics, anthropology and literacy. Vernacular materials include literacy and scripture. Also included are grammars, dictionaries, theses, dissertations, various series, journals and reprints, together totaling more than 6,000 local-language books and booklets. The materials are stored in both book and microfiche form. Electronic cataloging is nearly completed and an electronic database of these materials is in the early stages of development.

International Museum of Cultures

The International Museum of Cultures (IMC), a subsidiary of SIL, seeks to inform and educate the general public about the immense variety of human cultures in the world today, so that visitors might gain a fuller appreciation of this diversity. The IMC will soon be expanding its exhibits to represent contemporary cultural groups from at least twelve major culture areas of the world. The exhibits utilize, among other things, mannequins in life-size dioramas employing everyday artifacts to represent significant aspects of the lives of the people portrayed. The artifacts used in these exhibits are therefore contemporary.

Publications

SIL publications include the following:

● Published monographs and papers of SIL members are available in the series *Summer Institute of Linguistics and the University of Texas at the University of Texas at Arlington Publications in Linguistics*, with more than 120 titles listed; in the series *International Museum of Cultures Publications in Anthropology,* with more than thirty titles; and in the standard linguistic and anthropological journals.

- The *SIL International Publications Catalog* can be accessed at http://www.sil.org/acpub/catalog.
- The *Bibliography of the Summer Institute of Linguistics* contains references to more than 26,000 titles of published academic works produced by SIL, both academic and vernacular. The academic entries can be found on-line at http://www.sil.org/htbin/silbiblio.
- The *Ethnologue* is a catalog of the world's languages, including information on alternate names, numbers of speakers, location, dialects, linguistic affiliations and other sociolinguistic and demographic information. The URL is http://www.sil.org/ethnologue.
- *Notes on Anthropology and Intercultural Community Work* and *Notes on Linguistics*, prepared particularly for in-house use, are published quarterly.
- The *SIL Electronic Working Papers*, a new series, can be accessed at http://www.sil.org/silewp.
- *LinguaLinks™*, an electronic productivity support system for language workers, can be examined at http://www.sil.org/lingualinks.

Training Programs

The SIL training programs offer basic courses and select advanced courses in phonological, morphological and syntactic analysis; semantics; field methods; and anthropology at nine North American locations and six additional locations worldwide. The courses are accredited and integrated with major university programs. Further information on U.S. and U.K. schools is available at http://sil.org/schools.

Barbara J. Moore

Texas—Fort Worth

National Archives—Southwest Region (Fort Worth)

Address: National Archives—Southwest Region, 501 West Felix St., P.O. Box 6216, Fort Worth, TX 76115-0216.
Tel.: (817) 334-5525
Fax: (817) 334-5621
E-mail: archives@ftworth.nara.gov.
Internet address: http://www.nara.gov/regional/ftworth.html.
Parking: On-site parking is available.
Founded: 1969.
Major resources: The Southwest Region holds federal records retired from government agencies in Arkansas, Louisiana, Oklahoma and Texas; also microfilm copies of many other National Archives records.
Areas of specialization: Bureau of Indian Affairs (BIA) records for the Southwest Region.
Archives/manuscripts: Among holdings are ca. 15,251 cubic ft. of Bureau of Indian Affairs records.
Visual/audio resources: Some photographs of Native Americans are held.

Access: The great majority of holdings are open for public research. Restrictions on access to some federal records may be applied in accord with exemptions in the Freedom of Information Act.

Information provided by Meg Hacker.

Utah—Salt Lake City

University of Utah. Marriott Library

Address: Marriott Library, University of Utah, 295 S. 1500 E, Salt Lake City, UT 84112-0860.
Tel.: (801) 581-8864 (Ethnic Oral History Collection).
Fax: (801) 585-3464
Internet address: http://www.lib.utah.edu.
Networks, consortia: OCLC.
Founded: 1892 (University of Utah).
Major resources: Special Collections Department; Ethnic Oral History Collection; Photograph Archives.
Areas of specialization: Native Americans.
Archives/manuscripts: The University of Utah Doris Duke American Indian Oral History Project collection.
Visual/audio resources: An index to photographs in the Photograph Archives is available at http://www.lib.utah.edu/spc/photo/subject.html. Subjects of anthropological interest in the Photo Index include Archaeology and Paleontology; Ethnic Collections; Expeditions and Surveys; and Native Americans. Oral history recordings—including the University of Utah Doris Duke American Indian Oral History Project recordings—are in the library's Ethnic Oral History Collection.
Access: Open to the public. Call in advance to arrange use of Special Collections materials.
References: C. Gregory Crampton, "The Archives of the Duke Projects in American Indian Oral History," in Jane F. Smith and Robert M. Kvasnicka, *Indian-White Relations: A Persistent Paradox* (Washington, D.C.: 1981) (= *National Archives Conferences*, vol. 10), p. 119-128; Bradford Koplowitz, "The Doris Duke Indian Oral History Projects," *Popular Culture in Libraries*, vol. 1, no. 3 (1993), p. 23-38.

Information provided by Walter Jones.

Virginia—Charlottesville

University of Virginia. Library. Department of Special Collections

Address: Department of Special Collections, Alderman Library, University of Virginia, Charlottesville, VA 22903-2498.

Tel.: (804) 924-3025
Fax: (804) 924-3143
Internet address: http://www.lib.virginia.edu/speccol.
Internet address (Kevin Barry Perdue Archive of Traditional Culture):
http://www.minerva.acc.virginia.edu/~tradcult.
Networks, consortia: OCLC.
Founded: 1819 (University of Virginia); 1938 (Special Collections Department).
Major resources: Virginia Writers' Project Folklore Collection (WPA); Kevin Barry Perdue Archive of Traditional Music (in room 303, Brooks Hall).
Areas of specialization: Virginia folklore and folk music.
Archives/manuscripts: The Virginia Writers' Project Folklore Collection (33 archival boxes); the Kevin Barry Perdue Archive of Traditional Music (ca. 500 items).
Visual/audio resources: The Kevin Barry Perdue Archive of Traditional Music.
Access: Available for research use and for general readers. There are no special restrictions on access.
Guides/catalogs: Charles L. Perdue, Jr., Thomas E. Barden and Robert K. Phillips (compilers and editors), *An Annotated Listing of Folklore Collected by Workers of the Virginia Writers' Project, Work Projects Administration Held in the Manuscripts Department at Alderman Library of the University of Virginia*—available on microfilm at the Alderman Library; Bruce A. Rosenberg, *The Folksongs of Virginia: A Checklist of the WPA Holdings, Alderman Library, University of Virginia* (Charlottesville: 1969).

Description

The WPA Virginia Writers' Project Folklore Collection has been described in the guide by compiled Charles Perdue, Jr., and others. This guide has been microfilmed along with the material itself (as M1508-1512) and is available on interlibrary loan from the Department of Special Collections, Alderman Library.

The Kevin Barry Perdue Archive of Traditional Music is housed and maintained in Brooks Hall. This archive consists of records, tapes, texts and scores. Included are the Ruth McNeil collection of song and ballad texts and tunes; records of early "hillbilly" and "race" music; records of Anglo and African American traditional music; and tapes of field-recorded African American musical and narrative material.

Ann L.S. Southwell

Virginia—Hampton

Hampton University. University Archives

Address: University Archives, Hampton, University Museum, Hampton, VA 23668.
Location: University Archives is in the Hampton Museum.
Tel.: (757) 727-5374

Fax: (757) 727-5170

Internet address: http://www.hamptonu.edu (on University Archives and Hampton University Museum collections).

Founded: 1868 (Hampton Institute); 1972 (organization of the University Archives).

Major resources: The American Indian Education Program archives (ca. 1878-1924); other Hampton University archival collections.

Areas of specialization: Historical and archival documentation and photographs on Native Americans and African Americans.

Archives/manuscripts: Archives of the American Indian Educational Program; other archival collections.

Visual/audio resources: 50,000 photographs documenting the history of Hampton University.

Access: Researchers should contact the Archives in advance of a proposed research visit.

Guides/catalogs: Holdings of American Indian Educational Program materials are described in Fritz J. Malval (compiler), *A Guide to the Archives of Hampton Institute* (Westport, Conn.: 1985) (= *Bibliographies and Indexes in Afro-American and African Studies*, no. 5), p. 89-116.

Artifacts of anthropological interest: African, Native American, African American, Asian and Pacific collections (in the Museum).

Information provided by Jeanne Zeidler.

Washington—Bellingham

Western Washington University. Wilson Library. Mongolian Studies Collection

Address: Mongolian Studies Collection, Wilson Library, Western Washington University, Bellingham, WA 98225-9103.

Tel.: (360) 650-3050

Fax: (360) 650-3044

Internet address (Wilson Library): http://lis001.lis.wwu.edu.

Networks, consortia: RLIN (through Aug. 1996); OCLC (Sept. 1996-   ).

Founded: 1975 (Mongolian Studies Collection).

Major Resources: Books, journals and other materials published in, or about, Mongolia.

Areas of specialization: Mongolian studies.

Holdings (books and periodicals): More than 4,000 book and periodical titles in Mongolian and other languages. About eighty periodical titles, including many in Mongolian.

Visual/audio resources: Some videotapes and a few audio tapes pertaining to Mongolia.

Access: Open to scholars and general readers. Most of the collection is accessible through interlibrary loan. A few items (in Rare Books, Reference, etc.) must be used in the library.

Guides/catalogs: Henry G. Schwarz (compiler), *Mongolia and the Mongols: Holdings at Western Washington University* (Bellingham, Wash.: 1992) (= *East Asian Research Aids and Translations*, vol. 4).

Description

Between 1924, when the Mongolian People's Republic was established, and the late 1980s, research and travel in Mongolia were largely restricted to scholars and visitors from the socialist world. During that time, few institutions in the United States had programs of study relating to Mongolia, and few U.S. libraries collected currently published Mongolian books or journals. Those very few U.S. institutions that did maintain holdings of Mongolian manuscripts did not systematically acquire current books or other publications from any of the Mongolian areas.

A small number of U.S. libraries with important Slavic collections also acquired materials in Russian and other East European languages about the Mongols, especially the Buriat and Kalmyk Mongols within the borders of the Soviet Union. In the early 1960s Indiana University established a Uralic and Altaic Studies Center that included Mongolia within its area of interest. The libraries of the Research Institute for Inner Asian Studies and the Mongolia Society—both at Bloomington—and the Indiana University Library gradually developed largely complementary collections of books and periodicals about Mongolia.

In 1975 Western Washington University initiated its Mongolia Program, and the Wilson Library began collecting materials in support of this program. During the following decades the collection has grown rapidly as a result of acquisitions made by Henry G. Schwarz during visits to Mongolia and China, and also by means of donations by Nicholas Poppe, Paul Serruys and others. The Mongolian Studies Collection in the Wilson Library is now the largest collection of Mongolian-language publications in North America. This collection also includes books and materials in Chinese, Japanese, Russian and other European languages. Among these publications are many rare and local publications in Chinese. While most of the European-language publications are often available in other U.S. libraries, the Mongolian publications and many of the Chinese imprints are not.

The Mongolian Studies Collection currently holds more than 4,000 titles (including monographs and periodicals in all languages), chiefly in the humanities and social sciences. In the fields of archaeology and prehistory, local history, biography and genealogy, social life and customs, music, religions, medicine and general ethnography there are between fifty and 100 volumes each, while in areas of pastoral economy, traditional law, sports and games, dance and theatre, architecture and other arts, about twenty to fifty volumes are held. For anthropological research, the strongest collections are in epic and folk literature and folklore, with more than 200 volumes, and in linguistics, with nearly 600 volumes on the Mongolian languages of Mongolia, China, Russia and Afghanistan.

In addition to its monograph resources, the Mongolian Studies Collection has excellent holdings of journals devoted to Mongolian studies, including many Mongolian-language journals from Mongolia, Inner Mongolia and Xinjiang. Of particular interest are its holdings of the journals *Aman zokhiol sudlal (Studia folclorica), Arkheologijn sudlal (Studia archaeologica)* and *Etnografijn sudlal (Studia ethnographica)*. More than 100 volumes of bibliographies and museum, library and publishers' catalogs—many published in Mongolia—provide access to information on collections around the world.

Wilson Library also has several hundred volumes of related materials on neighboring ethnic groups in China, Russia and Central Asia. For example, about 300 volumes of Tibetan materials—many of which are important for the study of the cultural relations between

Mongolia and Tibet—and several hundred volumes in Uighur and other Turkic languages from Xinjiang are held.

Because of the relatively recent formation of the Mongolian Studies Collection, the bulk of imprints date from the last thirty years. Earlier materials are also included, and are continually added as they become available, but a number of nineteenth- and early twentieth-century scholarly works and first-person accounts of pre-socialist Mongolian society are not held. Nor does the collection include any manuscripts of ethnological interest, such as those found in a number of German, Scandinavian and Russian libraries.

The collection does include a few xylographs and a number of manuscript reproductions in both Mongolian and Chinese that were reprinted by the Inner Mongolia Institute of Social Sciences. In spite of these limitations, Western Washington University has the largest and finest Mongolian Collection in North America, and is the only North American library location for many modern Mongolian publications.

David Bade and Wayne V. Richter.

Washington—Seattle

National Archives—Pacific Alaska Region (Seattle)

Address: National Archives—Pacific Alaska Region, 6125 Sand Point Way NE, Seattle, WA 98115-7999.
Tel.: (206) 526-6507
Fax: (206) 526-4344
E-mail: archives@seattle.nara.gov.
Internet address: http://www.nara.gov/regional/seattle.html.
Founded: 1969.
Major resources: The Pacific Alaska Region (Seattle) holds records retired from federal agencies in Idaho, Oregon and Washington. Records pertaining to Alaska, previously kept at the Seattle Region, were transferred to Anchorage in 1990.
Areas of specialization: Archival records pertaining to Native Americans; Bureau of Indian Affairs records; correspondence of the Makah Tribal Council, 1935-1969 (part of RG 200, the National Archives Gift Collections); other records concerning Native people of the Pacific Northwest.
Archives/manuscripts: More than 30,000 cubic ft. of archival records from federal agencies in Idaho, Oregon and Washington.
Holdings (microfilm): 60,000 reels of microfilm (all subject areas). Microfilm holdings relating to Native Americans are listed in "A Current List of National Archives—Pacific Northwest Region Microfilm Publications Relating to Native Americans,"—an unpublished checklist. Microfilm holdings include *Letters Received by the Office of Indian Affairs*, 1824-1881, 964 reels; *Census of Skokomish and Nisqually Indian Reservations, Puyallup Agency*, 1861-1886, 1 reel; many others.

Access: The great majority of holdings are open for public research. Restrictions on access to some federal records may be applied in accord with exemptions in the Freedom of Information Act.

Guides/catalogs: "A Current List of National Archives—Pacific Northwest Region Microfilm Publications Relating to Native Americans,"—an unpublished list; Edward E. Hill, *Guide to Records in the National Archives of the United States of America Relating to American Indians* (Washington, D.C.: 1981).

Information provided by National Archives—Pacific Alaska Region (Seattle).

University of Washington. Thomas Burke Memorial Washington State Museum

Address: Thomas Burke Memorial Washington State Museum, University of Washington, Box 353010, Seattle, WA 98195.

Location: The Burke Museum is on the campus of the University of Washington at 17th Avenue, N.E., and N.E. 45th St.

Tel.: (206) 543-7907 (Burke Museum); (206) 685-3039 (Anthropology Division).

Fax: (206) 685-3039

Internet address (Burke Museum. Anthropology Division): http://weber.u.washington.edu/ ~burkemus/anthro.html.

Public transit access: Bus route information is available from Metro Transit at (206) 553-3000, or from Riderlink at http://transit.metrokc.gov.

Founded: 1885; designated as the Washington State Museum in 1899.

Major resources: Archives, Photo Archives, a small library.

Areas of specialization: Culture and natural history of Washington State, the Pacific Northwest and the Pacific Rim. Anthropological collections cover North, Central and South America, Asia and the Pacific.

Visual/audio resources: In Photo Archives. A videodisk system provides images of more than 14,000 Pacific Northwest objects, based on slide collections developed by Bill Holm and Robin Wright (Native American art—Northwest Coast and Plateau).

Guides/catalogs: *Pacific Northwest Native American Art in Museums and Private Collections* (Seattle: 1995)—a videodisk of images from ca. 200 museum and other collections. A printed catalog of the Holm and Wright collection is available.

Artifacts of anthropological or related interest: Extensive collections of Pacific Northwest and Pacific Rim artifact collections.

University of Washington. University Libraries

Address: Allen Library, University of Washington, Seattle, WA 98195.

Tel.: (206) 543-1760 (Allen Library); (206) 543-1879 (Manuscripts and University Archives); (206) 543-1929 (Special Collections, including the Pacific Northwest Collection).

Fax: (206) 685-8049

Internet address: http://www.lib.washington.edu.

Internet access to on-line catalog: Telnet to uwin.u.washington.edu.

Networks, consortia: OCLC.

Public transit access: Bus route information is available from Metro Transit, tel. (206) 553-3000, or from Riderlink at http://transit.metrokc.gov.

Founded: 1862 (Library); 1905 (Pacific Northwest Collection).

Major resources: Manuscripts and University Archives; Pacific Northwest Collection (a part of Special Collections). The Pacific Northwest Collection is a "print only" collection, although it also curates photographs.

Areas of specialization: The Puget Sound region, the Pacific Northwest, Native Americans, travel and exploration. The Special Collections department has extensive holdings of printed explorers' journals.

Archives/manuscripts: Manuscripts of anthropological interest are in the library's Manuscripts and University Archives Department. Manuscript holdings include the Melville Jacobs collection (on Northwest Coast Indian languages and oral traditions); the Ralph L. Roys papers (on Mayan culture); and the Erna Gunther papers. Gunther, a U.W. anthropologist, was director of the Burke Museum for many years. Her research focused on Northwest Coast Indian arts.

Holdings (Pacific Northwest Collection): The Pacific Northwest Collection, with more than 89,000 volumes, is the largest collection in the library's Special Collections department. Print holdings related to anthropology are also in other units of the library.

Visual/audio resources: The Historical Photography Collection (part of Special Collections); maps of the Pacific Northwest (only printed maps are in Special Collections; manuscript maps are in Manuscripts and University Archives). The library has reproduced more than 4,000 photographs of Northwest Coast Native people on microfiche. There is an image-by-image index to photographs in this set titled *Native Americans of the Pacific Northwest: A Photographic Record: Prints from the Collections of the Historical Photography Collection* (Seattle: 1982).

Access: Open for research use with some limitations. It is recommended that researchers call in advance to request access to material in Manuscripts and University Archives. Access to materials in the Melville Jacobs collection is restricted.

References: Victor Golla, "The Records of American Indian Linguistics," in Sydel Silverman and Nancy J. Parezo (editors), *Preserving the Anthropological Record* (2nd ed., New York: 1995), p. 143-157.

Guides/catalogs: Bob Bjoring and Susan Cunningham, *Explorers' and Travelers' Journals Documenting Early Contacts with Native Americans in the Pacific Northwest, 1741-1900* (Seattle: 1982) (= *University of Washington Libraries. Bibliography Series*, no. 3); *Comprehensive Guide to the Manuscripts Collection and to the Personal Papers in the University Archives* (Seattle: 1980); William R. Seaburg, *Guide to Pacific Northwest Native American Materials in the Melville Jacobs Collection and in Other Archival Collections in the University of Washington Libraries* (Seattle: 1982) (= *University of Washington Libraries. Communications in Librarianship*, no. 2).

Artifacts of anthropological significance: Extensive collections of Northwest Coast archaeological and cultural objects are in the Thomas Burke Memorial Washington State Museum.

Information provided by Carla Rickerson.

West Virginia—Charles Town

National Park Service. Harpers Ferry Center. National Park Service Historic Photographic Collection (NPSHPC)

Address (mailing): National Park Service Historic Photographic Collection, Harpers Ferry Center, National Park Service, Harpers Ferry, WV 25425.
Location: Charles Town, West Virginia.
For research assistance contact: Thomas A. DuRant, Photo Archivist.
Tel.: (304) 535-6707
Fax: (304) 535-6712
E-mail: tom_durant@nps.gov.
Internet address (NPS webpage—general information only): http://www.hfc.nps.gov.
Parking: On-site parking is available.
Founded: The National Park Service photographic collection was begun in 1929 at the National Park Service director's office in Washington, D.C.
Major resources: An extensive National Park Service reference photograph collection that includes the National Park Service Historic Photographic Collection.
Areas of specialization: The George Alexander Grant collection of National Park Service photographs (1920s-1950s); many Alaska Survey images from the 1960s; numerous photographic prints pertaining to individual parks—acquired from museum or library sources or received as donations from individuals. Also, non-official photo images related to many of the more than 400 U.S. National Parks and Sites. Albums, color slides, videos, films and historic lantern slides pertaining to many locations in the National Park system are also held.
Archives/manuscripts: Archival, manuscript and library materials are kept at the National Park Service Harpers Ferry Center Library and Archives, at Harpers Ferry, West Virginia [see the following entry].
Visual/audio resources: Ca. 1,000,000 photographic images.
Access: The collections primarily serve the research needs of the National Park Service. If time and work levels permit, the collections are available for on-site research at Harpers Ferry Center, by appointment only. Please contact Tom DuRant by phone (304 535-6707) for further information.
References: Selected images from the NPSHPC have been published in various books and journals—e.g., Robert Hill Lister and Florence Cline Lister, *Those Who Came Before: Southwestern Archaeology in the National Park System: Featuring Photographs from the George A. Grant Collection and a Portfolio by David Muench* (2nd ed., Albuquerque, N.M. and Tucson, Ariz.: 1993).

Description

The National Park Service Historic Photographic Collection, located at Charles Town, West Virginia, holds a large collection of National Park Service (NPS) photographic images in several formats. This photo archive includes historic as well as contemporary images that document the National Parks and related NPS programs and activities. Many of the photographs are of potential anthropological interest.

The NPSHPC was established in 1929 in Washington D.C. as part of the NPS public affairs function and continued in that use until 1980, when it was transferred to Harpers Ferry Center management, first in Springfield, Virginia, and now in Charles Town, West Virginia. It is now the major nationwide photographic repository on the history of the National Park Service.

The Historic Photographic Collection preserves the visual history of the National Park system. This collection consists of black-and-white as well as color photos in many formats; also albums, slides, films and videos. NPSHPC images include prints reproduced from negatives held at many of the individual U.S. National Parks.

Highlights of the collection include the George Alexander Grant collection of National Park images (1920s to the 1950s); the E.B. Thompson collection; more than 5,000 negatives dating from the 1900s to the 1940s; the Henry Peabody lantern slide collection; the Wright-Dixon collection of natural history images from the 1920s and 1930s; the Alaska Survey images from the 1960s; and many others.

The arrangement of interpretative photos is primarily according to individual National Park location—such as Mesa Verde National Park, Grand Teton National Park and Casa Grande Ruins National Monument. Artificial photo collections on topics such as "Native Americans" (subdivided by tribe), "archaeology," "artifacts," "ruins," etc., are also maintained.

Of special interest are the historic photos reproduced from negatives preserved at other NPS archival sites. The most comprehensive collections of historic photographs that document the National Parks are often those at the individual Parks (such as Mesa Verde), or at one of the NPS regional centers (such as the Western Archaeological and Conservation Center, in Tucson, Arizona).

The NPSHPC also includes artifacts of the photographic arts: old still and movie cameras and equipment formerly used in the National Parks.

Donations to the NPS Historic Photographic Collection are tax deductible. Please note that the NPSHPC is not permitted to provide appraisals of donated photographic materials.

Thomas A. DuRant

West Virginia—Harpers Ferry

National Park Service. Harpers Ferry Center (HFC). **Library**

Address: National Park Service, Harpers Ferry Center, Library, Harpers Ferry, WV 25425-0050.
For research assistance contact: David Nathanson.
Tel.: (304) 535-6261
Fax: (304) 535-6492
E-mail: david_nathanson@nps.gov.
Internet address (NPS webpage—general information only): http://www.nps.gov.
Networks, consortia: OCLC; West Virginia Library Commission Union Catalog; FEDLINK (Federal Library Network).
Parking: On-site parking is available.
Founded: 1970.
Major resources: The Library at Harpers Ferry Center houses the National Park Service History Collection; the National Park Service Research Reports Collection; the Rare Books Collection; and the National Park Service Oral History Collection. The Conservation Satellite Library and the National Park Service Historic Photographic Collection are located nearby, in Charles Town, West Virginia.
Areas of specialization: The HFC Library does not focus specifically on the field of anthropology, although library holdings include book and archival materials on Native American antiquities and archaeology. Note that some archaeological site information may be restricted under the Archaeological Resources Protection Act.
Archives/manuscripts: The Jesse L. Nusbaum papers, 1946-1958 (RG 5), is a small collection of correspondence produced while Nusbaum was a consulting archaeologist at the National Park Service Region III office in Santa Fe, New Mexico. The Ronald F. Lee papers, 1944-1972 (RG 1), document the work of a Chief Historian of the NPS, who was also a regional director and one of the founders of the National Trust for Historic Preservation. Lee was not specifically involved in anthropology, although he was heavily involved in the preservation of historic areas and also wrote a history of the Antiquities Act.
Holdings (books and journals): 22,000 v. (main collection). Satellite collections: 2,000 v. (Graphics Research Center); 1,500 v. (Conservation Library); 2,000 v. (Historic Furnishings Collection); 2,300 v. (National Park Service History Collection); 500 v. (Design Library); 2,000 v. (Rare Book Collection).
Visual/audio resources: The NPS Historic Photographic Collection includes numerous images of archaeological sites, artifacts and Native Americans [see the preceding entry]. Note that any images that are considered sensitive under Native American religious freedom legislation are restricted.
Access: The library serves the staff of the Harpers Ferry Center and of other National Park Service offices and areas. The library provides public on-site use of the collections as resources permit. In addition, the library accepts and processes interlibrary loan requests from across the country and participates in the West Virginia Library Commission Union Catalog, as well as the Federal Library Network (FEDLINK) and the OCLC cataloging and interlibrary loan network.

Archaeological sites represented in artifact collections: None. Researchers would need to visit the individual National Parks for information on archaeological artifacts. Many such artifacts are stored at particular parks and others are conserved for individual parks by colleges and universities or at central NPS repositories such as the Western Archaeological and Conservation Center in Tucson, Arizona.

References: *National Park Service Oral History Survey* (Harpers Ferry, W. Va.: 1981).

Description

The National Park Service Harpers Ferry Center is located on the former campus of Storer College, high on a hill overlooking the Shenandoah River and the Harpers Ferry water gap, at a place steeped in history and filled with natural beauty. In 1970 a variety of NPS curatorial and other activities were consolidated at the Harpers Ferry Center. At the same time, several NPS office collections were brought together to form the new Harpers Ferry Center Library. The primary focus of this library is natural history and also American social history and material culture of all eras. The HFC Library now contains perhaps the best general collection in the U.S. on the National Park Service and the National Park System.

The main function of the library is to provide research and reference assistance to staff of the Harpers Ferry Center. Collections and services of the library are also extended to the other offices and areas of the National Park Service. Access to library collections is provided to the public as resources allow. The Harpers Ferry Center Library and the NPS History Collection make up the Office of Library and Archival Services of the Harpers Ferry Center. The Historic Photographic Collection is in the Office of Support Services.

National Park Service Reports

HFC Library holdings of National Park Service Reports include some 12,000 volumes (estimate) of reports on paper (among these are 5,000 reports of the Cultural Resources Bibliography, formerly shelved in the NPS Washington, D.C., Office) and also some 40,000 (estimate) NPS Reports on microfiche. Many of these contain archaeological site reports or other documentation of archaeological/anthropological or cultural interest. Some of these are restricted by the Archaeological Resources Protection Act.

National Park Service History Collection

The goal of the National Park Service History Collection is to seek out and preserve the many kinds of materials that illustrate and document the history and culture of the National Park Service and to maintain these materials for research purposes.

Several themes are reflected in this collection, which consists of manuscripts, documents, museum objects and books. These themes include the history of the National Park Service; the development of the National Park idea; a history of interpretation; women in the National Park Service; early tourism in America—especially in National Parks, monuments and historic sites; historic preservation; personal papers and memorabilia (Ronald F. Lee, Harold L. Peterson); and others.

The NPS Oral History Collection—a part of the History Collection—contains more than 800 interviews that record the experiences and opinions of past National Park Service employees.

A particular goal of the NPS History Collection is to become a depository for information about significant collections of documents and artifacts at other locations relating to National Park Service history and culture. Information about such collections is invited.

Rare Book Collection

The Library's Rare Book Collection holds many nineteenth-century published journals and accounts of discovery and exploration in the American West. Among these is the first edition of James Otto Lewis's *The Aboriginal Port-folio: A Collection of Portraits of the Most Celebrated Chiefs of the North American Indians* (Philadelphia: 1835), with hand-colored plates. Also available are Henry R. Schoolcraft's *Historical and Statistical Information Respecting the History, Condition and Prospects of the Indian Tribes of the United States* (Philadelphia: 1851-1857) and Carl I. Wheat's *Mapping the Transmississippi West, 1540-1861* (San Francisco: 1957-1963).

Donations to the NPS History Collection are tax deductible. Please note that the NPSHC is not permitted to provide appraisals of donated materials.

David Nathanson

Wisconsin—Madison

State Historical Society of Wisconsin (SHSW)

Address: State Historical Society of Wisconsin, 816 State St., Madison, WI 53706-1488.
Location: The SHSW Archives Division, the SHSW Library, the SHSW Visual and Sound Archives and the Office of the State Archaeologist are located in the State Historical Society Headquarters Building at 816 State Street in Madison. The Society's Historical Museum is at 30 North Carroll Street in Madison.
Tel.: (608) 264-6460 (SHSW Archives); (608) 264-6535 (Reference, SHSW Library); (608) 264-6470 (Visual and Sound Archives); (608) 264-6495 (State Archaeologist); (608) 264-6572 (Information Desk, SHSW Historical Museum).
Fax: (608) 264-6486 (SHSW Archives); (608) 264-6520 (SHSW Library); (608) 264-6575 (SHSW Historical Museum).
Internet address (Archives Division): http://www.wisc.edu/shs-archives.
Internet address (Library Divison): http://www.wisc.edu/shs-library.
Networks, consortia: OCLC, RLIN.
Founded: 1849.
Major resources: Archives Division; Library; Visual and Sound Archives; Office of the State Archaeologist; Historical Museum.

Areas of specialization: Among Archives Division resources of anthropological interest are the Charles E. Brown papers and the Lyman Copeland Draper manuscripts. Extensive holdings of books and journals on North American Indians are in the SHSW Library. The Office of the State Archaeologist maintains the *Archaeological Site Inventory* (ASI), with records of archaeological sites within the state of Wisconsin (access is limited).

Visual/audio resources: Photographs and sound recordings are in the Visual and Sound Archives. This department holds many archaeological photographs.

Access: The Library Disision and the Archives Division are open to the public for reference use.

References: Clifford L. Lord and Carl Ubbelohde, *Clio's Servant: The State Historical Society of Wisconsin, 1846-1954* (Madison: 1967).

Guides/catalogs: James P. Danky, *Index to Wisconsin Native American Periodicals, 1897-1981* (Westport, Conn.: 1983) [microfiche edition]; Maureen E. Hady (compiler), *Native American Periodicals and Newspapers, 1828-1982. Bibliography, Publishing Record, and Holdings* (Westport, Conn.: 1984); Wisconsin. Office of the State Archaeologist, *Bibliography of Archaeological Reports* (Madison: annual).

Artifacts of anthropological significance: Extensive object collections are curated by the Society. The major emphasis of the collections is on the history, archaeology and material culture of Wisconsin.

Description

SHSW Library

Since its beginning in 1849 the State Historical Society has maintained documentary and material culture collections in North American history and prehistory. The primary area of specialization of the Society's library is the history and prehistory of Wisconsin and, more broadly, of North America north of the Rio Grande. The library holds extensive book and journal holdings in these areas, as well as on the Indians of North America, ethnic minorities, women and women's groups and the history of immigration to the United States.

Library resources include the collection of Native American periodicals and newspapers that formed the core of the published union catalog, *Native American Periodicals and Newspapers, 1828-1982* (Westport, Conn.: 1984). This catalog lists some 1,164 periodical and newspaper titles held at libraries in the United States and Canada. Most of the listed periodicals were published during the 1960s and 1970s—although some date from the nineteenth-century. The library has produced, in microform format, the *Index to Wisconsin Native American Periodicals, 1897-1981*. This source cites more than 44,000 articles from 31 Native American periodicals published in Wisconsin.

SHSW Archives Division

Original manuscripts and archives are in the Society's Archives Division. Manuscripts of anthropological interest include the papers of Charles E. Brown (1872-1946), the first full-time director of the Historical Society of Wisconsin Museum. The Brown papers consist of manuscript materials, site surveys, drawings and other records bearing on prehistoric and historic Indian habitation in Wisconsin.

Office of the State Archaeologist

The Office of the State Archaeologist maintains the *Archaeological Site Inventory* (ASI) of current and retrospective records on nearly 30,000 archaeological sites, mainly located within Wisconsin state borders. The Office of the State Archaeologist also publishes the *Bibliography of Archaeological Reports* (Madison: annual). This is a listing of unpublished reports relating to Wisconsin-area archaeology. Access to information in the *Archaeological Site Inventory* (ASI) and the *Bibliography of Archaeological Reports* is limited.

Information provided by Harold Miller and James P. Danky.

Wisconsin—Milwaukee

Milwaukee Public Museum (MPM)

Address: Milwaukee Public Museum, 800 West Wells St., Milwaukee, WI 53233.
Location: In downtown Milwaukee.
Tel.: (414) 278-2736 (Library and Archives); (414) 278-2743 (Photograph Collection).
Fax: (414) 278-6100
E-mail (Photograph Collection): otto@mpm1.mpm.edu.
Internet address: http://www.mpm.edu.
Networks, consortia: OCLC, WILS.
Founded: 1883.
Major resources: Archives, Museum Reference Library, Photograph Collection.
Areas of specialization: Human and natural history, including anthropology, ethnology, archaeology, Indians of Wisconsin.
Archives/manuscripts: Records of the museum; others.
Holdings (Reference Library): Approximately 100,000 volumes in all subject areas.
Visual/audio resources: The Photo Collection contains ca. 500,000 prints and negatives—primarily in the areas of human and natural history. Archival photos are on glass, nitrate and safety film. Photographic holdings of anthropological interest include the Wisconsin Indian Photographs Collection.
Access: Open to the Public. Call in advance to visit the Photo Collection or Archives.
References: Nancy Oestreich Lurie, *A Special Style: The Milwaukee Public Museum, 1882-1982* (Milwaukee: 1983).
Guides/catalogs: Susan Otto, *Catalog of the Milwaukee Public Museum's Wisconsin Indian Photographs* (Milwaukee: 1994) (= *Milwaukee Public Museum. Contributions in Anthropology and History Series*, no. 5).

Information provided by Judith C. Turner.

Central America

Panama

Panama—Panama City

Smithsonian Institution. Smithsonian Tropical Research Institute. Branch Library
(STRI Library)

Address: Smithsonian Tropical Research Institute Library, Building 401, Roosevelt Avenue, Ancon, Balboa, Panama City, Panama.
Alternate mailing address: STRI Library, Unit 0948, APO AA 34002-0948.
Tel.: (507) 27-6023
Fax: (507) 62-3134
E-mail (all Smithsonian Institution Libraries): libmail@sil.si.edu.
Internet address (STRI Library): http://www.sil.si.edu.
Internet access to on-line catalog: http://www.siris.si.edu or telnet://siris.si.edu.
Founded: 1946.
Areas of specialization: Latin American archaeology, anthropology, various biological sciences.
Access: Open to the public by appointment only.

Description

[See the related entry in this guide on the **Smithsonian Institution. Libraries** under the heading **United States—District of Columbia**.]

South America

Bolivia

Bolivia—La Paz

Museo Nacional de Etnografía y Folklore (MUSEF)
(National Museum of Ethnography and Folklore)

Address: Museo Nacional de Etnografía y Folklore, Calle Ingavi no. 916, La Paz, Bolivia.
Tel.: 591-2-358559
Fax: 591-2-356989
Founded: 1962.
Major resources: Library and Anthropological Archives; anthropological artifacts collections.
Areas of specialization: Anthropology, ethnology, folklore and ethnohistory of the indigenous peoples of Bolivia and the Andean and Amazonian regions.
Holdings (books and journals): 20,000 books and 1,500 serial and periodical titles.
Archival/manuscript resources: 15 meters. Papers of Indian organizations' national meetings; National Union of Indigenous Farmers of Bolivia (Confederación Sindical Unica de Trabajadores Campesinos de Bolivia); and personal papers of researchers and Indian politicians.
Fieldnotes, papers, etc.: Papers of Hugo D. Ruiz (1926-   ), ethnographer, written during 1961-1985 and 1994, relating to his fieldwork in the lowlands, with the Indian populations of El Chaco (Mataco Noctene, Tapiete, Chiriguano), Chuquisaca (Nor y Sud Cini), Amazonia (Araona, Chácobo) and in the highlands (Chipaya); a few papers of American anthropologists are on deposit (written 1985-1988), relating to their fieldwork in the highlands of Bolivia (Lipez, Potosí and the intersalar region of Oruro). Also papers of Roberto Fernández, Shigenori Minoda, Luis Oporto Ordoñez, Ignacio Ballesteros (MUSEF's ethnographers), relating to their fieldwork in the lowlands (Chácobo, Tapiete, Yungas) and highlands of Bolivia (Macha, north of Potosí; Ulla-Ulla; La Paz). Papers relating to traditional rituals, such as the Fiesta de Alasitas, Fiesta de San Pedro, Fiesta de San Juan, Fiesta de Todos los Santos, etc., from 1982 to the present. Also available are papers of fieldwork by university students, between 1986 and 1993, related to traditional rituals of the highlands of Bolivia. The extensive collections of personal papers include those of professors Wálter Solón Romero, Jesús Chávez Taborga, Carlos Salazar Mostajo, Julia Elena Fortún, as well as the personal papers of the most important union leader of the 1960s, Federico Escóbar Zapata (1924-1966), and also those of artists and educators who have worked with indigenous communities, or who have studied popular culture traditions. Unpublished catalogs of these papers are available in the library.
Visual/audio resources: Photographs, slides and video recordings are available in the MUSEF Archives pertaining to the main folkloric and ritual traditions throughout the country, collected from 1934 to the present. These include 15,000 slides, 20,000 images (photographs and negatives—includes the complete photo archives of Damián Ayma Zepita,

a rural photographer), 250 hours of ethnographic video recordings, 10,000 hours of sound recordings—includes 100 oral history interviews with Indian leaders.

Access: Open to scholars for research and to general readers. Materials must be used in the library. The services of the National Museum are free of charge to scholars and researchers worldwide during scheduled hours, except on Sundays and holidays.

References: *Fuentes Etnológicas. Boletín Bio-bibliográfico de la Biblioteca y Archivos del Museo Nacional de Etnografía y Folklore* [edited by the Library] (La Paz); *Etnología, Boletín del Museo Nacional de Etnografía y Folklore* [co-edited by the Museum's General Director and the Library] (La Paz); *Revista del Museo Nacional de Etnografía y Folklore* [edited by the MUSEF] (La Paz); *Anales de la Reunión Anual de Etnología* [edited by the MUSEF] (La Paz).

Guides/catalogs: Published guides and catalogs include: Rosario Guerra, Lola Paredes and Luis Oporto Ordoñez, *Bibliografía sobre pueblos y naciones originarias de las tierras bajas de Bolivia* (La Paz: 1995); Vivian León, "Video etnográfico sobre Bolivia: un archivo alternativo en el Museo Nacional de Etnografía y Folklore," *Fuentes Etnológicas*, vol. 5, no. 3 (1995), p. 1-2.; Luis Oporto Ordoñes and Miriam Cuevas, *Bibliografía sobre pueblos de tradición oral* (La Paz: 1981); Luis Oporto Ordoñes, "Bio-bibliografía de Fausto Reinaga, Rúpaj Katari," *Revista Cultural* (La Paz, 1994), p. 6-7, and also in *Amauta, Revista de la Fundación Cultural "Fausto Reinaga"* (La Paz, 1995); Luis Oporto Ordoñez, *Catálogo: materiales del Instituto Linguístico de Verano sobre grupos etnicos de Bolivia: 1955-1980* (La Paz: 1981); Luis Oporto Ordoñez, "Fotografía rural y acumulación histórica: el caso de Damián Ayma Zepita," *Linterna Diurna* (La Paz: 1993), p. 5-6; Luis Oporto Ordoñez, "Las fuentes primarias etnológicas en la investigación social: recursos complementarios o alternativos?," *Revista del MUSEF*, vol. 4, no. 4 (1991), p. 183-190; Luis Oporto Ordoñez, "La mina de "siglo xx" (Potosí) en la historia reciente: Federico Escóbar Zapata, 1924-1966," *Revista del MUSEF*, vol. 5, no. 5 (1995), p. 25-36; Luis Oporto Ordoñez, "Notas sobre la obra etnológica de Jürgen Riester," *Etnología*, vol. 15, no. 20 (1991), p. 77-96; Luis Oporto Ordoñez, "Recursos bibliográficos y documentales (históricos y etnográficos) sobre la mujer boliviana, existentes en la Biblioteca del MUSEF," in *Actas del Seminario Sobre la Mujer* (La Paz: 1991); Luis Oporto Ordoñez, Hugo D. Ruiz and Alvaro Diez Astete, *Una puerta abierta a la cultura boliviana. 25 años de servicio a la nación: Museo Nacional de Etnografía y Folklore* (La Paz: 1987); Jorge Ortiz Surco and Luis Oporto Ordoñez, "El Archivo Oral Etnológico del MUSEF: resumen de la memoria colectiva," *Fuentes Etnológicas*, vol. 5, no. 3 (1995), p. 3-5.

Guides/catalogs (unpublished): Luis Oporto Ordoñez and Bertha Lecoña, "Catálogo de la Biblioteca del MUSEF," 5 v.; Luis Oporto Ordoñez, "Catálogo de la Sección de Documentos Etnológicos," 2 v.; Luis Oporto Ordoñez and Bertha Lecoña, "Catálogo de la Biblioteca 'Julia Elena Fortún' existente en la Biblioteca del MUSEF"; Bertha Lecoña, *"Catálogo de publicaciones periódicas y seriadas de la Biblioteca del MUSEF"*; Rosario Guerra, "Catálogo de documentos microfilmados"; Luis Oporto Ordoñez, Miriam Cuevas and Jorge Ortiz, "Catálogo del Archivo Oral Etnológico," 10 v.; Vivian León and Luis Oporto Ordoñez, "Catálogo del Archivo Fotográfico." All of the preceding unpublished catalogs are available in the MUSEF Library.

Artifacts of anthropological significance: The MUSEF has collected ethnological artifacts and textiles from throughout Bolivia since 1961. The main collections are from the Ayoreo (a forest people) and Chipaya (an isolated highland population). Extensive collections of ethnological artifacts include those collected from thirty different Indian peoples of the highlands and lowlands, including the Araona, Tacana, Chácobo, Yamináwa, Ese Ejja, Moseten (north and northwest Amazonian region), Chiquitano, Ayoreode (south, southeast region), Tapiete, Chiriguano, Mataco Noctene (south), Quechua, Aymara, Chipaya (highland Andean region), Collahuaya, Potolo (valleys region) and a large collection of handicrafts from La Paz, Oruro, Cochabamba, Potosí and Sucre and Tarija.

Description

The National Museum of Ethnology and Folklore (MUSEF) was founded in 1962 by the President of the Republic, Dr. Víctor Paz Estenssoro (1907-   ), who donated to the new museum an important collection of ethnographic textiles assembled during his first presidential term, 1952-1956, and also during his second and fourth presidential terms, 1960-1964, and 1985-1989.

Bolivia's ethnographic museums increased in importance as a result of the "Nationalist Revolution" of 1952 that introduced important social changes in the nation. Before that time, most of the population of Bolivia consisted of indigenous peoples, belonging to some 33 ethnic groups, who were not recognized as citizens of the nation. Until 1952, the Indian populations remained locked in local communities and haciendas, in the context of a social structure that was semi-feudal in character.

After 1952 the government began to introduce educational programs for the Indian communities and also to stimulate the organization of folklore museums such as the People's Museum of Folklore and Handicrafts, which, in 1974, became the National Museum of Ethnography and Folklore. The Museum is located in La Paz, the political capital of the Republic. Its home is an eighteenth-century colonial palace. The first director of the museum was Manuel de Lucca, a rural sociologist. He was followed as director by the ethnographer Luis Zeballos Miranda—famous because he joined Thor Heyerdahl's Aymara Indian builders of the *RA II*, which crossed the Atlantic. The third and current director is the ethnographer Hugo D. Ruiz, who studied museology in Mexico and Germany.

In 1962 the National Museum organized a task force that has now collected important and representative ethnological artifacts from throughout the nation. The task force members—an anthropologist, an ethnomusicologist, a linguist and an historian—are working in five regions of Bolivia's highlands on a major museographic project about Quechua culture in the areas of La Paz, Potosí and Oruro.

In 1974 the National Museum was transferred from the Education Secretary to the Central Bank of Bolivia, in order to secure the financial resources needed for the administration of the museum. A law was passed by the Bolivian Congress that ordered the Central Bank to create a foundation to support the National Museum of Ethnography and Folklore and also the National Archives and Library, the Casa Nacional de Moneda (the colonial banking house) and the Independence and Freedom House—all of these are considered important cultural treasures of Bolivia.

The Anthropological Archives and Library

The Library, created in 1962, collects bibliographic resources related to Bolivia within the scope of the mission of the Museum. It seeks to identify, acquire and preserve significant information, in various media and formats, that documents the history of Bolivia's indigenous population. In 1982 the museum opened its private library to the public and developed a program to make its information available for purposes of scholarship, exhibitions, publication, applied research and education.

The library holds collections on anthropology as a science, and concerning the history of the indigenous population of Bolivia and, more broadly, of the populations of the Andean and Amazonian regions. The principal sections of the library are the monographs (national and international authors); serials (national and international journals); and a reference center with an important collection of dictionaries and vocabularies in native languages. The library also collects important cartographic materials. In 1994 the library received the remains of the private library of the first Bolivian anthropologist, Julia Elena Fortún. This acquisition consisted of more than 3,500 monographs and 100 periodical titles in the fields of ethnomusicology, folklore and anthropology. Also, the library purchased the complete works, 1964-1992, of the Indian politician, Fausto Reinaga, who died in August 1994. These important collections are now available for public use.

The Anthropological Archives was organized in 1982 as a repository for the museum's ethnographic papers, and to manage documentary materials that supplement the museum's artifact collections and research programs. The archives also holds papers of national and regional Indian organizations, such as the Confederación Sindical Unica de Trabajadores Campesinos de Bolivia (the Indian farmers' union) and the Central de Cabildos Mojeños (one of the Indian organizations). The principal archives are papers, photographs, videos, sound recordings and microforms. The visual and sound archives are the largest in Bolivia. The museum's task force collected information during 150 surveys of rescue anthropology among endangered Indian populations all around the country.

The video archives are available only to scholars for research use. This collection is related to the indigenous peoples of the highlands—especially Macha, Llallagua (north of Potosí), Calcha (central Potosí), Ulla Ulla (La Paz)—and also the lowlands: Tapiete (Chaco region), Entre Rios (Tarija, south of Bolivia), Chácobo and the forest peoples (Amazonian region). There are also some collections related to the Valley region, such as Cochabamba and the Yungas of La Paz. Important traditional festivities have been documented—such as the Carnaval, Todos los Santos, Alasitas, San Juan, etc.

The sound archives (collected since 1961) includes the oral records of the Indian national organizations and unions, as well as traditional and folkloric music and ethnomusicology. It also includes oral history of almost 100 Indian and indigenous leaders of Bolivia.

Special Surveys

In 1985, with the aid of a grant from the French government, the library's director studied the Bolivian ethnological artifacts and the bibliographic and manuscript collections at the Musée de l'Homme, in Paris.

The Japan International Cooperation Agency (JICA) provided a grant to the library's director to study the Chácobo people in the Amazonian region, together with Japanese anthropologist Shigenori Minoda, who also studied the Quechua culture of Macha, to the north of Potosí, Bolivia. In 1995 the Japanese government provided a large donation of video equipment for use in the development of a public video diffusion program at the museum.

In the 1990s, with a grant from the Swedish government, the General Director of the museum studied, at the Göteborg Ethnographic Museum, the ethnographic artifacts collected by Count Erland Nordenskiöld between 1900-1906. Freddy Taboada, a curator, also spent three months at the Smithsonian Institution, supported by a grant from the Getty Institution. In 1995 the library's director studied resources relating to Bolivia in the Smithsonian Institution Libraries and the National Anthropological Archives in Washington, D.C., with a grant from the American Library Association.

MUSEF has increased its collections through anonymous donations and also with the cooperation of the Bolivian Museums Friendship Association and international institutions such as USAID (a survey of the traditional use of coca leaf); UNESCO (microfilm program); and the Organization of American States (textile retrieval program). The National Museum also has agreements with universities and research centers in Bolivia and overseas.

Each year more than 7,000 scholars and researchers turn to the Library and Archives and the collections of anthropological artifacts in the MUSEF to study the ancient and original Indian cultures, their present situation and also the popular cultural expressions in the larger cities and rural towns of Bolivia.

Luis Oporto Ordoñez

Europe

Austria

Austria—Vienna

Universität Wien. Fachbibliothek für Ethnologie, Kultur-und Sozialanthropologie
(University of Vienna. Special Library for Social and Cultural Anthropology)

Address: Fachbibliothek für Ethnologie, Kultur-und Sozialanthropologie, Universität Wien, Neues Institutsgebäude (NIG), Universitätsstrasse 7, A-1010 Vienna, Austria.
Tel.: +43 1 4277-16860
Fax: +43 1 4277-9485
Internet address: http://www.univie.ac.at/UB-Wien/fbvoelk.htm.
Founded: 1928.
Major resources: Books, journals and manuscripts in the fields of social and cultural anthropology, with emphasis in the areas of bibliography, biography, peoples of the developing nations, society, manners and customs, religion, Islam, technology, material culture and economy.
Areas of specialization: West Asia; East Indies/Indonesia; North, East, Central, West and South Africa; North, Central and South America; Polynesia; Micronesia; Melanesia; New Guinea; the Caribbean.
Archives/manuscripts: Ca. 1,350 m.
Holdings (books and journals): Ca. 67,000 v. The journal section consists of 1,810 journal and series titles.
Access: Materials are available for use by students and by scholars for research.
Visual/audio resources: None.

Description

On August 11, 1986, the Library of the Institute for Social and Cultural Anthropology was designated by the Federal Ministry for Science and Research as the Special Library for Social and Cultural Anthropology (Fachbibliothek für Ethnologie, Kultur-und Sozialanthropologie) of the University of Vienna. Thus, the former Institute library became a section of the University of Vienna Library. The origins of this special library, as well as the building of its collections, went hand-in-hand with the development of the Institute for Social and Cultural Anthropology.

Both scientific branches of the Institute—Physical Anthropology and Ethnology—were represented by the Anthropology-Ethnology Teaching Office through professor Rudolf Pöch and later professor Reche. In 1927 anthropology professor Josef Weninger was entrusted with a special Teaching Office for Physical Anthropology. The following year the Teaching Office for Ethnology was transferred to Wilhelm Koppers, and in 1929 the Institute for Ethnology of the University of Vienna was founded. Professor

Koppers, the first director of the new Institute, also laid the cornerstone for the Institute's library. A small collection of books from the library of the Anthropology-Ethnology Institute of the Imperial University of Vienna must have come to the newly founded Institute for Social and Cultural Anthropology. There are no lists at all, nor any sort of written records about this, but old stamps in a few books indicate their origin.

During the library's early years emphasis was put on the acquisition of works on methodology, the history of social and cultural anthropology, and material in related disciplines. Atlases and reference works on regional ethnology were also purchased. In addition, a foundation was laid in the subject areas of sociology, religion, mythology, psychology, art, technology, crafts, etc. During the difficult war years, the collections were preserved through the selfless efforts of Anna Hohenwart-Gerlachstein and Annemarie Hefel.

In 1945 Wilhelm Koppers returned to Austria and was reestablished as director of the Institute. Under his leadership, teaching and research activities were rebuilt, exchange activities with foreign countries that had been brought to a standstill in 1938 were resumed, and the library was enlarged through new acquisitions. The early postwar years were marked by great privations and difficulties, but Professors Koppers, Heine-Geldern and later Josef Haekel struggled to rebuild the Institute library. Until 1953 the Institute for Social and Cultural Anthropology and its library were housed in the Museum for Ethnology, in Westflügel der Neuen Hofburg (Corps de Logis).

The early book collections included the most significant research achievements of the first leaders of the Institute: Robert Heine-Geldern worked on the ethnology, archaeology and art history of pre-Columbian America and the cultural relationships between the old and new worlds. Josef Haekel's interests related predominately to fundamental questions of methods; to the study of North, Middle and South America and the ethnology of India. Professors Koppers and Heine-Geldern also increased the library collections on the anthropology of India and South Asia. Even today these regional sections, together with Africa, are still the most impressive in the library. During the war years, the regional section on Africa was built by Professor Hermann Baumann, and later by the Africanist and founder of ethnohistory in Vienna, Walter Hirschberg.

In 1962 the Institute, along with its library, were relocated to the New Institute Building (Neue Institutsgebäude, NIG) of the University of Vienna, at Universitätsstrasse 7, where it remains to the present time.

Since the 1970s a new research era has dawned, and this has been clearly reflected in the library. In 1975 the Viennese ethnologist Walter Dostal took over the Teaching Office I of the Institute. He worked to establish the previously neglected field of social anthropology. This change was accompanied by corresponding new library acquisitions. He initiated a new teaching program on the developing countries that was furthered by Gabriele Rasuly-Paleczek. The current literature in this research area—textbooks, scientific research reports, reference works and bibliographies—was purchased, and library holdings in this area were expanded. Gabriele Rasuly-Paleczek, a Central Asia specialist, is actively involved in building the Central Asia section of the collection.

Walter Dostal and Andre Gingrich, both West Asian specialists, together have built an eminent collection of works on Islam and the Near East, and have greatly enlarged holdings of theoretical works in anthropology. They also expanded the sections on West

Africa and Islam. The Islamic section was also expanded through the efforts of Thomas Fillitz, who dealt especially with Islam in West Africa.

In 1962 Viennese Africanist Walter Hirscberg took over the Teaching Office II of the Institute and made ethnohistory the area of special emphasis in Vienna. This research movement continues to be developed at the Institute. Professor Hirschberg's successor, Karl Rudolf Wernhart, continues to collect materials on theoretical and methodological questions of ethnohistory and cultural history. Also, as an Oceanic specialist (together with his colleagues, Caribbean specialist Manfred Kremser and Werner Zips) he built the library sections on Polynesia, Micronesia, Melanesia, New Guinea and New Zealand. Australia—a small collection in the library—was also given attention. He also expanded the African section and initiated orders in relatively new research areas: the Caribbean and Afro-America.

In recent years the library has acquired much more literature on the Indian subcontinent. Aspects of Indian dance research have been of special interest. The newest literature presents works on the environment and questions of global communication.

The Institute and the present-day Special Library for Social and Cultural Anthropology were built from the beginning as a single unit, even though the Special Library is now administratively affiliated with the University of Vienna Library. From its beginning, the Special Library has directed its collecting activity in support of the anthropological research and teaching of the Institute. It has worked consistently to purchase the documentation needed for the education of future anthropologists, as well as the current scientific works needed to support the ongoing projects of the professors, lecturers and students.

Erika Neuber
[Translation from German: Tom Mann]

Belgium

Belgium—Tervuren

Koninklijk Museum voor Midden-Afrika
Musée royal de l'Afrique centrale
(Royal Museum of Central Africa)

Address: Koninklijk Museum voor Midden-Afrika, Steenweg op Leuven 13, B-3080 Tervuren, Belgium.
Tel.: +32 2 769 52 11
Fax: +32 2 767 02 42
Internet address: http://www.africamuseum.be/NI/index.html.
Founded: 1897.
Major resources: Archives, manuscripts, fieldnotes, books, journals, photographs and sound recordings housed in various divisions and sections of the museum.

Areas of specialization: Central Africa.

Archives/manuscripts:

● In the Ethnographic Section: unpublished manuscripts and archives (only accessible to scholars by permission).

● In the History of the Belgian Presence Overseas Section: 3 km of archives, including archives of private origin (250 fonds); archives received from businesses or Christian missions; and documents from the territorial administration. These archives are mainly related to Central Africa, but they also include documents on Belgian activity in China. Access to some archives of private origin is subject to restrictions.

● In the Prehistory and Archaeology Section: ca. 3 meters of archives.

Fieldnotes:

● In the Ethnographic Section: fieldnotes from A. Hutereau, O. Boone, F.L. Michel, A. Maesen, D. Biebuyck and others. Many of these are related to artifact collections and are kept in the files documenting those artifacts.

● In the History of the Belgian Presence Overseas Section library: fieldnotes of H.M. Stanley, etc.

● In the Linguistic Section library: many original fieldnote files, manuscripts and card-indexes, as well as other rich collections, especially from African and private sources.

● In the Prehistory and Archaeology Section: Joseph Charles Bequaert's mission fieldnotes, Zaire (1950s).

Holdings (libraries):

● In the Central Library: more than 100,000 volumes and 7,000 periodicals.

● In the Ethnosociology and Ethnohistory Section library: ca. 2,000 books and periodicals; more than 500,000 cards (150,000 titles) related to all aspects of the social sciences in sub-Saharan Africa.

● In the Ethnographic Section library: ca. 10,000 books and periodicals.

● In the History of the Belgian Presence Overseas Section library: ca. 7,000 books and periodicals.

● In the Linguistic Section library: ca. 6,000 books.

● In the Ethnomusicological Research Section library: ca. 2,000 books and periodicals

● In the Prehistory and Archaeology Section library: ca. 7,000 books and 228 periodicals.

Visual/audio resources:

● In the Ethnographic Section: an iconographic collection of some 60,000 items (includes 43,000 glass-plate negatives; other black-and-white negatives and slides; 29 16mm films).

● In the History of the Belgian Presence Overseas Section: a rich collection of audio-documentation of many African languages and oral literature, especially from Zaire, Rwanda and Burundi.

● In the Ethnomusicological Research Section: 5,000 hours of musical recordings on a variety of tapes; 6,000 slides; 15 video films; 10,000 pictures of dancers, musicians, masks, etc.

● In the Prehistory and Archaeology Section: photographs and slides made in Zaire, Libya, Nigeria, Rwanda, Burundi, Cameroon; or illustrating objects from the collections.

Access: Materials, with some exceptions, are available for on-site use by scholars and general readers.

Guides/catalogs: *Bibliographie ethnographique de l'Afrique sud-saharienne* (1925-   ) —card catalog, annual publication and database on computer, in ASE; M. Luwel, "Les archives historiques au Musée royal du Congo belge à Tervuren," *Institut royal colonial belge. Bulletin des séances*, t. 25, fasc. 2 (1954), p. 799-821; Musée royal de l'Afrique centrale, *Inventaire des documents provenant de la mission Frantz Cornet au Congo (1948-49) et conservés au Musée royal de l'Afrique centrale à Tervuren* ([Bruxelles]: 1960) (= *Académie royal des Sciences d'Outre-Mer. Classe des sciences morales et politiques. Mémoires. Nouv. série*, t. 24, fasc. 1); Musée royal de l'Afrique centrale, *Inventaire des films conservés à la Section d'Histoire de la Présence belge à l'Étranger* ([1979]) (= *Collection Inforcongo*).

References: Musée royal de l'Afrique centrale, *Catalogue des éditions du Musée royal de l'Afrique centrale = Catalogus der uitgaven van het Koninklijk Museum voor Midden-Afrika* ([Tervuren]: 1978); Francis Ramirez, *Histoire du cinéma colonial au Zaïre, au Rwanda et au Burundi* (Tervuren: 1985) (= *Annales. Sciences Historiques*, no. 7).

Artifacts of anthropological significance:

• In the Ethnographic Section: a collection of about 250,000 objects representing the cultures of Africa (90 percent of the object collection); the Americas (5 percent); and Oceania (5 percent).

• In the History of the Belgian Presence Overseas Section: more than 10,000 objects related to colonization and colonial life.

• In the Ethnomusicological Research Section: more than 8,000 musical instruments collected mainly in Central Africa.

• In the Prehistory and Archaeology Section: archeological collections of earth- and stoneware, wood, iron and other metal items.

Archaeological sites represented in the collections: Libya: Jebel Uweinat (1968); Rwanda: Nyarunazi (1942, 1947, 1957, 1960); Zaire: Dinga (1952), Gombe ex-Kalina (1932, 1947-50, 1952), Kanga di Zambi (1951), Katongo (1957), Kibanza (1951), Kinduz (1951), Kongo-dia-Vanga (1951), Mantsetsi (1951), Mukila (1952), Sanga (1957), Sumbi (1951), Sunde Lutete (1951), Tshimpangu Fuati (1951), Tumba (1951). The following collections, which remain the property of the respective governments, are on provisional deposit at the museum: Cameroon: Obobogo (1980, 1981, 1983), Shum Laka (1992, 1994); Guinée équatoriale: Carbonera (Bioko) (1987); Nigeria: Koroofa (1968, 1970); Rwanda: Kabuye (1968); Zaire: Dimba (1973), Gombe, ex-Kalina (1970, 1971), Kaoma (1970, 1971), Mashita Banza (1984), Matupi (1974), Sakusi (1984), Sanga (1974, 1975, 1976).

Description

The Royal Museum of Central Africa is located on a beautiful site on the outskirts of Brussels. The museum was founded in 1897 by King Leopold II, who was also King of the Congo Free State, later to become a Belgian colony before recovering its independence in 1960. The main museum building (which is open to the general public) was inaugurated by King Albert I in 1910. King Leopold II wanted the museum to be both a window on the colony, opened to the general public, as well as a scientific institution. The museum has successfully fulfilled both of these functions to the present time, and is widely known for its valuable scientific collections and the quality of its scientific publications. The fields investigated by the scientific staff are related to all aspects of African environment and life, natural and cultural. The geographic areas of scientific research have progressively widened to include all of Africa, as well as some other parts of the world.

The museum, which is one of the most important centers for the scientific study of Africa, comprises four departments which are supported by general services, including a Central Library of more than 100,000 book volumes and 7,000 periodicals. Two of the departments, both divided into sections and services, are devoted to the study of the humanities.

- *History of the Belgian Presence Overseas Section*

The History of the Belgian Presence Overseas Section (H) focuses mainly on the circumstances leading to colonization and on the colonial period itself. Although the activities of Europeans form the basis of the research, attention is also paid to the consequences of their presence for traditional African societies. The department has a rich archive related to the early journeys of exploration, the expansion politics of Leopold II, the independent Congo Free State and Belgian Africa. There is also an extensive photo and film collection.

- *Ethnographic Section*

The Ethnographic Section (E) collects all objects that throw some light on the material and spiritual culture of traditional societies in Africa and, secondarily, objects from Oceania and the Americas. Special attention is given to the plastic arts of Africa. This section houses an exceptionally important collection of some 250,000 objects. The object collection plays an important role in the life of the institution and is made available to the general public by means of annual (or more frequent) exhibitions.

- *Ethnosociology and Ethnohistory Section*

The Ethnosociology and Ethnohistory Section (previously Anthropologie sociale et Ethnohistoire, hence ASE) applies the methods and techniques of social anthropology to the study of history and recent changes in African societies. Intensive fieldwork, in combination with written documents, serve to enhance historical knowledge. The section has a tradition in the study of Rwanda and the interlacustrine area. A part of its work is devoted to the Documentation Service in the Human Sciences on Africa South of the Sahara (Service de Documentation en Sciences humaines sur l'Afrique au Sud du Sahara), which has published a bibliographic series since 1932. Recent data, now stored on computer, is available to visitors or by mail order.

- *Linguistic Section*

The Linguistic Section and the Centre for African languages (L) do research into the languages and oral traditions of the African continent. In so doing, they not only promote these languages, but also, in collaboration with African linguists, foster their adaptation for use in the modern world. The section has a rich collection of audio-documentation on many African languages and oral literature.

- *Ethnomusicological Research Section*

The Ethnomusicological Research Section (M) includes the traditional music of Central Africa and the interlacustrine region and the Caribbean. During fieldwork, songs, instrumental soloists and groups are recorded and later transcribed, studied and analyzed. Special attention is given to the role of music in the social and ritual life in Africa south of the Sahara. The Musicology Centre houses an important collection of musical instruments, musical recordings, slides and photographs.

- *Prehistory and Archaeology Section*

The Prehistory and Archaeology Section (P) studies the origin and evolution of anthropoid cultures on the African continent. The paleo-geographic surroundings, as well as the paleo-climatological conditions and changes in the landscape, become increasingly important in the investigations.

- *Agricultural and Forestry Economics Section*

Less closely related to social and cultural anthropology, but certainly of use in the field of applied anthropology and where the identification of wood is needed, the Agricultural and Forestry Economics Section must be mentioned. It houses a collection of wood samples that is among the most important in the world. The Centre for Informatics Applied to Development and Tropical Agriculture has a computerized data service on tropical agriculture covering all tropical areas; it also keeps a climatological data bank.

Danielle de Lame
Compiled with the participation of V. Baeke, E. Cornelissen, Cl. Grégoire, J. Gansemans, Ph. Maréchal, J. Moyersons.

France

Paris is the locale of an array of archives, museums, libraries and research centers of importance for anthropological research. Most of these are located within walking distance of one of the transit stations in the (area-wide) Paris Métro system. Of special importance for anthropological research are the Archives and Library of the Musée de l'Homme (Museum of Mankind) and the vast library collections of the Bibliothèque nationale de France (National Library of France). The Musée de l'Homme (a division of the National Museum of Natural History) and its major anthropological library and archives are located in the Palais de Chaillot (16th Arrondissement), within walking distance of the Eiffel Tower. The accumulated historical archives of most of the French anthropological societies are among the many manuscript collections stored at the Musée de l'Homme. Access to these society archives is limited.

The National Library of France (rue Richelieu and Tolbiac locations—2nd and 13th Arrondissements, respectively) maintains a wealth of research collections of anthropological importance, including the library and archives of the Société de Géographie de Paris (Geographic Society of Paris)—which, since 1942, has been a part of the National Library's Department of Maps and Plans.

The UNESCO World Heritage Centre is administered from UNESCO Headquarters in Paris, although on-line access to the Centre's important World Heritage List, and an abundance of other World Heritage documentation, is available via the World Heritage Centre website. Of related interest, the Documentation Centre of the International Council on Monuments and Sites (ICOMOS) maintains the original documentation files for all sites that have been proposed for inclusion in the World Heritage List.

The important libraries of the École française d'Extrême-Orient (French Institute of Oriental Studies), and of ten other French scholarly societies concerned with research on regions of Asia, have become available for research use at the Maison de l'Asie (Asia House). Nearby in the 16th Arrondissement is the Musée national des Arts asiatiques—Guimet (National Museum of Asian Arts—Guimet), which maintains library and photograph collections on the ancient arts and religions of Asia, in support of its unique collections of Asian arts.

Information on many collections of Islamic manuscripts preserved at repositories throughout France has been presented in a survey by Annie Berthier and Francis Richard, published in Geoffrey Roper (general editor), *World Survey of Islamic Manuscripts* (London: 1992-1994), vol. 1, p. [249]-308.

Only some of the more important French museums, archives and libraries of anthropological interest are described in the following entries. A Government of France Ministry of Culture and Communications website provides directory and index information on many French research locations, some of which are of anthropological significance. See the Ministry of Culture's "Muséofile: Répertoire des Musées français" (a directory of 645 museums in France); and also the directory of French archives and libraries titled "Les Centres de Ressources documentaires." The pertinent Ministry of Culture URL is http://www.culture.fr.

France—Aix-en-Provence

Archives nationales. Centre des Archives d'Outre-Mer (CAOM)
(National Archives. Overseas Archives Center)

Address: Centre des Archives d'Outre-Mer, Archives nationales, 29 chemin du Moulin Detesta 13090, Aix-en-Provence, France.
Tel.: +(33) (0)4 42 93 38 50
Fax: +(33) (0)4 42 93 38 89
Internet address: http://www.culture.fr/culture/sedocum/caom.htm.
Founded: 1966. The archives of the Ministry of Colonies were transferred to CAOM at Aix-en-Province in 1987.
Major resources: Official archives of the Ministry of Colonies (Ministère des Colonies), including records pertaining to Indochina and other former areas of French colonial administration. The Indochina records extend from the conquest of Cochinchina up to 1945. Official records of Indochina for the years 1945-1954 are also held. CAOM also has important collections of private papers, a Map Archive (Cartothèque) and a valuable specialized Library collection (Bibliothèque).
Areas of specialization: The geographic focus of the collections is on the former areas of French colonial administration—especially Indochina. Holdings include the Indochina Collection, the India Collection, the Fonds Dupuis, newspapers of Indochina, other official and private papers and records. Archival documentation pertaining to Madagascar, India, Somalia, Algeria and other areas is also held.
Archives/manuscripts: About 42 km. of archival materials. In addition to official French colonial records, there are important collections of private papers. These include the papers of Francis Garnier (1854-1874)—explorer of Tonkin; August Jean Marie Pavie (1847-1925)—leader of the Mission Pavie in Indochina; Paul Dislere (1876-1935)—director of the Colonial Institute in Paris; Albert Sarrault—Governor-General of Indochina, 1911-1914, and 1917-1919; and many others. The Fonds Gastaldy, 1923-1930, includes photographs and ethnographic and archaeological papers concerning Siam, Burma, Cambodia and Cochinchina. See the article by Sylvie Clair and the guide by Marie-Claude Bartoli for some additional information on available manuscripts.
Holdings (library): Ca. 100,000 book and journal volumes. Library holdings include the former libraries of the Ministry of Colonies and the Colonial Institute (École coloniale).
Visual/audio resources: Many archival photographs, prints and posters concerning Indochina and other former French colonial areas (nineteenth- and twentieth-centuries); the Gastaldy photographs; and others. The Cartothèque curates more than 50,000 printed or manuscript maps, charts and related items.
Access: Open to the public by appointment. A temporary or annual pass is issued upon the presentation of appropriate identification.
References: Sylvie Clair, "Archives française de la Péninsule indochinoise: le Centre des Archives d'Outre-Mer," *IIAS Newsletter* [International Institute of Asian Studies], no. 3 (Autumn 1994), p. 40.
Guides/catalogs: Marie-Claude Bartoli, "Dépôt des Archives d'Outre-Mer à Aix-en-Provence," in *Sources de l'histoire de l'Asie et de l'Océanie dans les archives et les*

bibliothèques française (Munich: 1981) (= *Guide des Sources de l'Histoire des Nations*, 3ème série), vol. 1, p. 233-271.

France—Paris

A guide to public transit lines in the Paris region (Métro, RER [Réseau express régional] and the Paris bus system) is available at http://www.paris.org/Metro.

Bibliothèque interuniversitaire des Langues orientales (BILO)
(Interuniversity Library of Oriental Languages)

Address: Bibliothèque interuniversitaire des Langues orientales, 4, rue de Lille, 75007 Paris, France.
Location: Left Bank, 5th Arrondissement.
Tel.: +(33) 1 44 77 87 20
Fax: +(33) 1 44 77 87 30
Public transit access: Métro: St. Germain des Prés; bus: 39, 48, 95.
Major resources: Books, journals and manuscripts in many Asian, African and Native American languages.
Areas of specialization: Oriental languages, cultures and civilizations.
Holdings (books and journals): Ca. 500,000 v.
Access: Open to the public for on-site use of materials.

Bibliothèque nationale de France (BnF)
(National Library of France)

Address (Richelieu): Bibliothèque nationale de France, 58, rue Richelieu, 75084 Paris Cedex 02, France.
Address (Tolbiac): Bibliothèque nationale de France, 63, quai de la Gare, 75013 Paris, France.
Location: Right Bank, 2nd Arrondissement (rue Richelieu location); Left Bank, 13th Arrondissement (Tolbiac location).
Tel.: +(33) 1 47 03 81 26 (Richelieu); +(33) 1 47 03 83 23 (Richelieu—Manuscripts Department, Oriental Section); +(33) 1 44 23 03 70 (Tolbiac).
Fax: +(33) 1 42 96 84 47
E-mail: opalmaster@bnf.fr.
Internet address: http://www.bnf.fr.
Public transit access: (Richelieu) Métro: Bourse or Quatre Septembre; bus: 20, 29, 39, 48, 74, 85; (Tolbiac) Métro: Quai de la Gare.
Founded: 1537—the beginning of the book deposit ordinance; 1570—the Royal Library was installed in Paris; 1692—the library was opened to the public. The Bibliothèque nationale de France now consists of two major library facilities: the old rue Richelieu library building and the monumental building at Tolbiac which first opened to the public in 1996.

Major resources: Very large collections of books, serials, manuscripts, archives, maps, photographs and other documentation in many languages and formats.

Areas of specialization: In addition to French- and other Western-language holdings, major book collections in Turkish, Persian, Chinese, Vietnamese and many other non-Western languages are held. The Paul Pelliot (1878-1945) Sinological library consists of some 30,000 volumes in languages of China and Central Asia. A published inventory of books in the George Coedès (1886-1969) collection (Khmer- and Thai-language works) is available. The extensive library of the Société de Géographie de Paris (SGP) has been in the care of the National Library's Département des Cartes et Plans since 1942. This resource includes many early and valuable works of travel and exploration. Among parts of the SGP collection is the Fonds Gallieni (composed in large part of the Gallieni donation) and the book collection of Prince Roland Bonaparte (1858-1924). The Prince Bonaparte book collection (ca. 30,000 volumes) also includes an important collection of atlases.

Archives/manuscripts: The first inventory of Oriental manuscripts in the Royal Library was published in 1739. For information on contemporary holdings of Islamic manuscripts in the National Library, see the survey by Annie Berthier and Francis Richard. BnF Oriental Section manuscript holdings include the extensive Paul Pelliot manuscript collection in Chinese, Tibetan, Sanskrit and other Asian languages; the Antoine d'Abbadie collection of Ethiopian manuscripts; the Marcel Griaule collection of 366 manuscripts bought in Gondar by the Dakar-Djbouti Expedition; the Asselin de Cherville collection of Arabic manuscripts; and many others. The Goupil-Aubin collection of 385 Mexican manuscripts was received as a bequest in 1898. BnF also holds collections of rubbings made during major French archaeological expeditions to Egypt, China, Cambodia and Nepal.

Holdings: Ca. 12 million v.

Visual/audio resources: Sound archive, films and videos. The archives of the Société de Géographie include very large photo collections. More than one million maps and charts are in the National Library's Départment des Cartes et Plans.

Access: Open to the public. Enquire regarding admission fees. Some departments may have special collection use requirements. Rare or fragile manuscripts in the "Réserve" of the Department of Manuscripts, for example, may be consulted only on Wednesdays or Fridays.

References: Simone Balayé, *La Bibliothèque nationale, des origines à 1800* (Genève: 1988) (= *Histoire des idées et critique littéraire*, 262); Alfred Fierro, "La bibliothèque et les archives de la Société de Géographie," *Acta Geographica*, no. 52-53 (1983), p. 40-44; Nguyen Ti Xuan Suong, "The Vietnamese Collections of the Bibliothèque Nationale," *South-East Asia Library Group Newsletter*, 36-38 (July 1993), p. 31-37; Monique Pelletier, "Les collections de cartes, leur passé et leur avenir," in *Introducció general a la història de la cartografia* (Barcelona: 1990), p. 57-88; Stephan Roman, *The Development of Islamic Library Collections in Western Europe and North America* (London: 1990) (= *Libraries and Librarianship in the Muslim World*), p. 80-98.

Guides/catalogs (selected): Annie Berthier and Francis Richard, "Bibliothèque nationale," in Geoffrey Roper (general editor), *World Survey of Islamic Manuscripts* (London: 1992-1994) (= *Al-Furqān Islamic Heritage Foundation. Publication,* no. 5), vol. 1, p. 275-290; Bibliothèque nationale (France), *Inventaire des livres imprimés khmers et thaï du fonds George Coedès* (Paris: 1991); Bibliothèque nationale (France), *Inventaire des manuscrits de la Société de Géographie* (Paris: 1984); Bibliothèque nationale (France), *Inventaire des* *photographies sur papier de la Société de Géographie* (Paris: 1986); Bibliothèque nationale (France), *Litteratures africaines à la Bibliothèque nationale: catalogue des ouvrages d'écrivains africains et de la littérature critique s'y rapportant entrés à la Bibliothèque nationale, 1920-1972* (Paris: 1991); Bibliothèque nationale (France). Départment des Livres imprimés, *Catalogue du fonds vietnamien: 1890-1921* (Paris: 1987); Bibliothèque nationale (France). Département des Manuscrits, *Catalogue des manuscrits singhalais* (Paris: 1983); Commission française du Guide des Sources de l'Histoire des Nations, *Sources de l'histoire de l'Asie et de l'Océanie dans les archives et les bibliothèques françaises,* II. *Bibliothèque nationale.* (München: 1981) (= *Guide des sources de l'histoire des nations,* 3ème série, vol. 2); Commission française du Guide des Sources de l'Histoire des Nations, *Sources de l'histoire du Proche-Orient et de l'Afrique dans les archives et les bibliothèques françaises,* II. *Bibliothèque nationale* (München: 1984) (= *Guide des sources de l'histoire des nations,* 3ème série, vol. 5).

Lee S. Dutton
Information provided by Francis Richard and others.

Conseil international des Monuments et des Sites (ICOMOS)
International Council on Monuments and Sites (ICOMOS)

Address: International Council on Monuments and Sites, 49-51, rue de la Fédération, 75015 Paris, France.
Location: Left Bank, 15th Arrondissement.
Tel.: +(33) 1 45 67 67 70
Fax: +(33) 1 45 66 06 22
E-mail: icomos@cicrp.jussieu.fr.
Internet address: http://www.icomos.org.
Public transit access: Métro: Dupleix or La Motte-Piquet.
Founded: 1965.
Major resources: UNESCO/ICOMOS Documentation Centre (Centre de Documentation UNESCO/ICOMOS).
Areas of specialization: Documentation on the conservation and restoration of monuments and sites throughout the world; historic preservation; archaeology.
Archives/manuscripts: Archival records include the original documentation files on all sites and monuments proposed for inclusion on the UNESCO World Heritage List.
Holdings (books, journals): Several thousand volumes on heritage conservation, historic preservation and archaeology.
Visual/audio resources: Video and slide libraries.
Access: The Documentation Centre is open for use by researchers, whether members of ICOMOS or not. No advance appointment is needed to use the Documentation Centre. Hours are Monday through Thursday, 2:00 to 5:00 p.m.
References: International Council on Monuments and Sites, *ICOMOS* (Paris: 1988).

Description

ICOMOS is an international non-governmental organization that seeks to advance the goals of the "International Charter on the Conservation and Restoration of Monuments and Sites"—also known as the Venice Charter. The organization carries out research and educational programs to further these objectives; it advises UNESCO on cultural properties proposed for inclusion on the World Heritage List and promotes the conservation of Heritage Sites throughout the world. The ICOMOS Documentation Centre is maintained at ICOMOS Headquarters in Paris.

[For information on the World Heritage List, the List of World Heritage in Danger, the Organization of World Heritage Cities, and related subjects, see the entry in this guide on the UNESCO World Heritage Centre (also located in Paris).]

Information provided by Suzanne d'Abzac.

École française d'Extrême-Orient (EFEO)
(French Institute for Oriental Studies)

Address: École française d'Extrême-Orient, Maison de l'Asie, 22, avenue du Président Wilson, F-75116 Paris, France.
Location: Right Bank, 16th Arrondissement.
Tel.: +(33) 1 53 70 18 20
Fax: +(33) 1 53 70 87 60
Public transit access: Métro: Iéna.
Founded: 1898 (in Saigon, as the Mission archéologique d'Indochine). Renamed in 1901 as the École française d'Extrême-Orient and relocated to Hanoi. At present, the EFEO maintains research programs and facilities in Paris, as well as smaller branch research centers, libraries or other facilities in India, Thailand, Malaysia, Indonesia, Cambodia, Laos, Vietnam, Taiwan, Japan and Korea.
Major resources: The main EFEO library and archive are in Paris. In 1995 the EFEO library collection was combined with the library collections of ten other Asia-related French scholarly institutes or societies to form the Maison de l'Asie (Asia House) Library. EFEO branch libraries are maintained in selected Asian cities. The larger of these are in Pondichery (ca. 27,000 titles); Kyoto (ca. 15,000 v.); Jakarta (ca. 3,000 titles); and Chiang Mai (ca. 6,000 titles).
Areas of specialization: The geographic region of Asia extending from India to Indonesia and including Japan. EFEO archival and library holdings are especially extensive for former French Indochina (Vietnam, Laos and Cambodia). Holdings on Korea are few in number, while Mongolia and most of Oceania are not within scope of the EFEO library collections.
Archives/manuscripts: EFEO manuscript holdings at Asia House include some 2,000 items of research value, in various Asian and other languages. Some of the EFEO branch libraries in Asia are also beginning to acquire manuscript materials in various (mainly Asian) languages. The important institutional archives of the EFEO have been preserved. These include the original archaeological and conservation field data from many Asian

378

archaeological sites, including Angkor Wat. Most of these records have not yet been inventoried, and research access to this material is limited. In support of conservation work at Angkor, carried out in cooperation with UNESCO, work to reorganize the archaeological records from Angkor (accumulated continuously from 1909 to 1955) was initiated in 1990. The historical background and content of the Angkor archives have been described in an article by Bruno Brugier (1992).

Holdings (books and journals): EFEO holdings in Paris consist of more than 60,000 book volumes and 1,000 periodical titles—now part of the Asia House Library collections.

Visual/audio resources: About 160,000 photographic images—many pertaining to Cambodia and other parts of former French Indochina. The Institute's photo archive in Paris includes portions of photo collections previously at Hanoi and Siem Reap. The photo archive holds thousands of archaeological and ethnological images on glass-plates as well as on film negatives and prints. Cambodian archaeology is very well represented in the photo archive—see Bruno Bruguier's article for brief information on the archaeological site photographs from the Angkor Conservancy.

Access: Library materials are generally available for on-site research use at the Asia House library.

References: "A Traditional Institute: École française d'Extrême-Orient," *IIAS Newsletter* [International Institute for Asian Studies], no. 2 (Spring 1994), p. 9; Bruno Bruguier, "Angkor. Conservation et diffusion du fonds documentaire de l'EFEO," *Bulletin de l'École française d'Extrême-Orient*, vol. 79, no. 1 (1992), p. 256-265; *Catalogue général des presses de l'École française d'Extrême-Orient* (Paris: 1996); *École française d'Extrême-Orient* (Paris: 1994).

Guides/catalogs: Printed catalogs of some EFEO Library holdings (including holdings on Indonesia, Vietnam, Thailand and Cambodia) have been published.

Description

In the summer of 1995, the library of the École française d'Extrême-Orient was reopened in new facilities at 22, avenue du Président Wilson, as a part of the new Maison de l'Asie Library and Research Center. The EFEO library is the largest of eleven specialized Asia-related library collections that have been consolidated in Paris at Asia House. Each of the eleven libraries was established by, and is affiliated with, a French scholarly research center, institute or society. Geographic areas of specialization of the Asia House centers and their libraries include Korea, India and South Asia, China, Island Southeast Asia, Indochina and Japan. Other areas of research specialization include Taoism and the religions of Tibet.

The library has recently arranged to receive archival materials from the Association des Amis du Vieux Hué (Association of the Friends of Old Hue)—a new avatar of the association that, from 1914 until about 1940, published the *Bulletin des Amis du Vieux Hué*. The Association has recently agreed to deposit its substantial collection of materials (letters, manuscripts, prints, watercolors)—many of which are of potential anthropological, cultural or related interest—at the EFEO library. As of 1997 only a portion of the archives of the Association had arrived at the library; researchers may contact the library for more current information on this or other resources.

Information provided by Jean-Louis Taffarelli.

Institute du Monde Arabe (IMA). **Bibliothèque**
(Institute of the Arab World. Library)

Address: Bibliothèque, Institute du Monde Arabe, 23, quai Saint-Bernard, 75005 Paris, France.
Location: Left Bank, 5th Arrondissement. The library is on the third floor of the IMA building.
Tel.: +(33) 1 40 51 38 05
Fax: +(33) 1 43 54 76 45
Internet address: http://ima.imarabe.org/perm/biblio_id.html.
Public transit access: Métro: Cardinal Lemoine.
Founded: 1982; open to the public since 1987.
Major resources: Library materials in all disciplines concerning the cultures and civilization of the Arab World. Holdings are primarily in French or Arabic, although books and journals in English, German, Dutch, Spanish or Italian are also held.
Areas of specialization: Special collections include the Sayyid Collection (fonds Sayyid)—classic and contemporary works on Arab culture, in Arabic; also the Ninard Collection (fonds Ninard)—2,500 titles concerning Morocco.
Holdings (books and journals): 55,000 v.
Archives/manuscripts: Not held.
Visual/audio resources: Housed in the Audiovisual Service (Service Audiovisuel)—on the eighth floor of the IMA building.
Access: Open to the public.
Guides/catalogs: Various bibliographies are available, including *Cent ans de cinéma: cinéma arabe; bibliographie d'ouvrages et d'articles disponibles à la bibliothèque de l'IMA. Repertoire des festivals arabes de cinéma* (Paris: 1995); *Le Maghreb en 2000 titres: écrits et lectures sur le Maghreb* (Casablanca and Paris: 1991); *Mille et un livres sur le monde arabe: catalogue d'ouvrages de recherche et de documentation édité en France* (2e éd., Paris: 1989).

Information provided by Sahali Nacéra.

Musée national des Arts asiatiques—Guimet
(National Museum of Asian Arts—Guimet)

Address: Musée national des Arts asiatiques—Guimet, 6, place d'Iéna, 75116 Paris, France.
Location: Right Bank, 16th Arrondissement.
Tel.: +(33) 01 45 05 00 98 (Library; Photo Archives).
Fax: +(33) 01 45 05 02 66
Internet address (library): http://www.culture.fr/culture/sedocum/guimet-b.htm.
Internet address (Photo Archives): http://www.culture.fr/culture/sedocum/mnaa-ph.htm.

Networks, consortia: CCN periodical union catalog (library).

Public transit access: Métro: Iéna.

Founded: Both the museum and the library were established in Paris in 1889 by Émile Guimet; the Photo Archives was created in 1920 by Victor Goloubew.

Major resources: Library; Photo Archives (Photothèque); Music Section.

Areas of specialization (library): The art and archaeology of Asia from ancient Iran to Japan; also holdings on the religions of Asia. About 6,000 Japanese-language book titles are held. The Alexandra David-Neel bequest to the library consists of ca. 450 Tibetan works. The personal library of Émile Guimet was part of the donation that established the museum.

Holdings (books and journals): Ca. 120,000 books; 1,400 current and retrospective periodical titles.

Archives/manuscripts: The papers of Auguste Barthes, Paul Pelliot, Édouard Chavannes, Roman Ghirshman, others.

Visual/audio resources: The organization of the Photo Archives parallels that of the museum itself. The Photo Archives has between 250,000 and 300,000 photographic items; images in the photo collections date from 1858 to the present. Photo resources include black-and-white as well as color negatives and prints on paper; color slides and glass-plate negatives. Holdings include the photo collections of Paul Pelliot, Victor Segalen, Auguste François, Georges Groslier; also some photographic prints from the archives of the École française d'Extrême-Orient.

Access: The museum is now closed for major building renovations scheduled to be completed in the latter part of 1999. During the renovations, the Library and Photo Archives have been moved to 45, rue Boissière, 75116 Paris. Until renovations are completed, reservations are required to visit the Library or the Photo Archives (Library: M. Marie-Paul Alland; Photo Archives: Mme. Dominique Fayolle or M. Jérôme Ghesquière).

References: [Henri Cordier], "Nécrologie. Émile Guimet," *T'oung Pao*, vol. 18 (1917), p. 380-382.

Guides/catalogs: No published catalogs of Library or Photo Archives holdings are available.

Artifacts of anthropological significance: The museum curates major collections of Japanese, Chinese and Khmer sculpture and paintings, as well as many other Asian art objects. Several collection guides and catalogs have been published. Among these are *L'art khmer au Musée Guimet Paris* (Zurich: 1966); Albert Le Bonheur, *La sculpture indonésienne au Musée Guimet: catalogue et étude iconographique* (Paris: 1971) (= *Publications du Musée Guimet. Étude des collections du Musée*, t. 1); Odette Monod, *Le Musée Guimet* (Paris: 1966) (= *Collection des guides du visiteur*); *Rarities of the Musée Guimet* (New York [?]: 1974 [?]).

Description

The Musée Guimet (Guimet Museum) brings together in one location a collection of more than 36,000 Asian art objects. The art and archaeology collections extend geographically from Afghanistan to Japan, and chronologically from the second-century, B.C., to the nineteenth-century. Since its creation in Paris in 1889, the museum—today known as the Musée national des Arts asiatiques (National Museum of Asian Arts)—has undergone profound changes to make room for the expanding collections. Émile Guimet (1836-1918), a research chemist and inventor by profession, wished to present his collections of objects illustrating the history of the Oriental religions. The museum soon saw its Asian vocation affirmed, however, when it began to receive—either directly or by means of deposits from the Louvre—the rich harvest of the French archaeological expeditions. In 1928 the museum became a national institution, inheriting from that time onward remarkable collections, such as those of the Afghan sites of Hadda or Bégram, which reflected the progress of archaeological research in Asia.

In 1945 Georges Salles, Director of the Museums of France, organized a redistribution of the national museum collections. At that time the great collections of Asian arts of the Louvre were transferred to the Musée Guimet, with the result that the Guimet became one of the greatest museums of Asian art in the world. Since 1945 the curators have followed a consistent acquisitions policy, while also benefiting from an exceptional series of donations—among which have been the Rousset collection of Chinese terra-cottas, the Calmann collection of Chinese and Korean ceramics, the Fournier collection of Himalayan art, the Jacques Polain collection of Chinese art and the Krishna Riboud collection of Asian textiles.

The Guimet offers what is probably the most comprehensive panorama of Asian arts under one roof. Cambodia, Champa, former South Vietnam, Burma, Laos, Thailand, Indonesia (Bali, Java and Sumatra), Nepal, Tibet, India, Pakistan, Afghanistan, China (furniture, lacquer, ceramics, antique bronzes and jades, mural paintings), North Vietnam, Korea and Japan are all represented in the collections.

The Conservation Departments

Southeast Asia

By the 1930s the museum had inherited two distinct collections: the former collection of the museum opened by Émile Guimet in the city of Lyon in 1878, following his study trip to China, Japan and the East Indies, together with materials gathered by Étienne Aymonier; and the collection of the Musée indochinois de Trocadéro, of which Louis Delaporte was the initiator and curator. The section devoted to the arts of Southeast Asia is particularly rich with regard to the arts of Cambodia and indianized Vietnam, but likewise includes works that offer a panoramic view of the arts of Thailand, Indonesia, Vietnam, Burma and Laos.

The group of Khmer sculptures, which illustrate the great periods of Cambodian art, from the beginnings to the present, is without equal in the West. These reflect the French scholarly contribution to the knowledge of Khmer civilization. The Harihara of the Mahâ Rosei ashram (seventh-century), the Fronton of Banteay Srei (ca. 967 A.D.) or the Head of Javayarman VII (end of the twelfth-beginning of the thirteenth-centuries) are among the masterpieces of world sculpture.

A rare group of sculptures from Champa represent the main phases of the evolution of that ancient kingdom of Annam, strongly indianized, with some sculptures going back to the seventh-century and others up to the thirteenth-century. Among the latter may be mentioned the great Śiva of the Tour d'Argent (eleventh-twelfth-centuries).

India

The Indian Section of the museum consists, in part, of sculptures (terra-cotta, stone, bronze and wood) extending from the third-century, B.C., up to the eighteenth-century, A.D., and also of moveable paintings or miniatures of the fifteenth- to nineteenth-centuries. Excavated objects, derived mainly from southern India, illustrate the connections of India and the Roman Empire during the first centuries of our era; sculptures representing the Buddha and various episodes from the Buddhist legend, as well as effigies of the main divinities of the Brahman pantheon, illustrate the varied aesthetic currents that spread on Indian soil and influenced the arts of the surrounding countries—especially Southeast Asia.

Nepal-Tibet

The Himalayan Section is composed of a group of about 1,600 objects. The Nepalese collections consist of a series of moveable paintings of which the finest examples date from the time of ancient Malla (1200-1482) and derive from a 1989 donation to the museum by Lionel Fournier. To this are added several painted book covers (twelfth- to fourteenth-centuries), some metal sculptures that extend chronologically from the eleventh to the nineteenth centuries, as well as images in wood (sixteenth- to eighteenth-centuries) and various liturgical objects.

The Tibetan collections have a very wide iconographic range, illustrated, in particular, throughout the group of more than 400 paintings. In addition, the assemblage formed by the *thang-ka* and bronzes of the earlier periods is enriched thanks to the Fournier donation, consisting of some 100 objects, as well as by the museum acquisitions of the last ten years. Tibetan liturgical objects and jewelry complete this group.

China

The museum's Chinese Section consists of some 20,000 objects representing 7,000 years of Chinese art—from the beginnings to the eighteenth-century. The archaeological domain begins in the Neolithic period with some jades and ceramics, continues with the bronzes of the Shang and Zhou periods—major works to which may be added some important collections with trappings, bronze mirrors and clasps, as well as coins and laquerware. In the field of sculpture—apart from the great works of sculpture from Buddhist China and Central Asia—several donations (the Calmann, Rousset, Jacob and Polain donations) have brought into being a collection of Han and Tang *minqui* that is exceptional in the variety of styles represented. The field of decorative arts offers a full array of Chinese ceramics, consisting of some 10,000 items—stoneware, celadons and porcelains—the most important kilns, the great technical innovations and the varied aspects of taste that governed production—whether for export or in response to Imperial commands. Furniture is represented by important pieces of lacquerware and rosewood. 1,000 works of painting extend from the Tang to the Qing dynasties.

Japan

The collections of the Japanese Section, consisting of about 11,000 works, offer a rich and diverse panorama of Japanese art—from its beginnings some three thousand years B.C., until the beginning of the Meiji era (1868). They illustrate, in particular, the ancient periods of Jomon (terracotta vases and figurines), Yayoi and Kofun (*haniwa* obtained by an exchange with the National Museum in Tokyo), followed by the major phases in the development of Buddhist art in the archipelago. A group of sculptures and paintings on silk—exceptional in design and quality—allows an understanding of the stylistic and iconographic development of these art forms of the eighth- and ninth-centuries.

A Center of Research

The museum is also a great center of research and scholarship, centered upon the library, which holds some 120,000 book volumes and a very important collection of periodicals. The Photographic Archives, with a collection of about 250,000 unique images, and the Music Section, which conserves some of the rarest examples of music scholarship on India and East Asia, also contribute to making the Guimet a great center of knowledge on Asia. The important role of the museum in the field of research is expressed through its collaboration with the universities and the National Center for Scientific Research. Curators, CNRS researchers, educators and museum staff all work together in the various programs that have brought honor to French Oriental studies and the results of which appear regularly in *Arts asiatique*—the museum annals, published in collaboration with the École française d'Extrême-Orient.

The Library

The Library, organized since the opening of the museum in 1889, today specializes in the ancient arts and archaeology of Central and Eastern Asia. Its collection consists of some 120,000 books and 1,500 periodicals in European, Asian and other languages. In addition to the early European books (seventeenth- and eighteenth-centuries), there are special collections such as a group of Japanese illustrated books of the Edo period (700 titles), some Tibetan works (more than 2,000 titles, including the library of Alexandra David-Neel), Chinese maps from the Qing period (the Arnold Vissière collection), Urdu texts (from Garcin de Tassy), some fragments of Uighur manuscripts, as well as the papers of various Orientalists (Auguste Barthes, Édouard Chavannes, Roman Ghirshman, Paul Pelliot and others). Due to the early museum focus on the history of Oriental religions, the library also conserves from its past an important collection of books and journals on Oriental religions—especially Buddhism.

Other Museums

Two additional museums are maintained under the responsibility of the National Museum of Asian Arts. Both are concerned with the arts of China and Japan: the Panthéon bouddhique de la Chine et du Japon (Buddhist Pantheon of China and Japan), located at 19, avenue d'Iéna, 75116 Paris (tel. 01 40 73 88 08); and the Musée d'Ennery (Ennery Museum).

Juliette Barbet
Information on the Photo Archives provided by Dominique Fayolle.
[Translation from French: Lee S. Dutton.]

Musée national des Arts d'Afrique et d'Océanie. Bibliothèque
(National Museum of the Arts of Africa and Oceania. Library)

Address: Bibliothèque, Musée national des Arts d'Afrique et d'Océanie, 293 avenue Daumesnil, 75012 Paris, France.
Location: Right Bank, 12th Arrondissement.
Tel.: +(33) 1 44 74 84 96
Fax: +(33) 1 43 43 27 53
Internet address: http://www.culture.fr/culture/sedocum/mnaao-b.htm.
Public transit access: Port Dorée.
Founded: 1931. Formerly a collection of the library of the Musée des Colonies (Museum of the Colonies). In 1935 named the library of the Musée de la France d'Outre-Mer (Museum of Overseas France); transferred to the Central Library of the Louvre in 1960-1961.
Major resources: Documentary collections.
Areas of specialization: History of art; arts and civilization of black Africa, Oceania and Madagascar; Islamic arts and civilization. The "fonds ancien" consists of eighteenth- and nineteenth-century printed voyages and travels.
Archives/manuscripts: Papers of Georges-Marie Haardt (head of the Citroën Expedition).
Holdings: More than 6,000 books and other cataloged items (other than those in the "Fonds ancien"). Also periodicals and a few maps.
Access: Open to the public for on-site use of materials. There is no annual closure at the library.
Guides/catalogs: The manual card catalogs are arranged by country and subject.
Artifacts of anthropological significance: The museum holds extensive collections of African, Islamic and Oceanic arts.

Musée national des Arts et Traditions populaires (M.N.A.T.P.) and Centre d'Ethnolgie française (CEF)
(National Museum of Folk Arts and Traditions and Center for French Ethnology)

Address: Musée national des Arts et Traditions populaires, Ministère de la Culture, 6, avenue du Mahatma Gandhi, 75116 Paris, France.
Location: Right Bank, 16th Arrondissement.
Tel.: +(33) 01 44 17 60 72 (Library); +(33) 01 44 17 60 68 (Photo Archives and Archives)
Fax: +(33) 01 44 17 60 60
Internet address: http://www.culture.fr/culture/atp/mnatp/francais/cprov.htm.

Internet address (Library): http://www.culture.fr/culture/sedocum/atp-b.htm.
Internet address (Photo Archives and Archives): http://www.culture.fr/culture/sedocum/atp-m-ph.htm.
Public transit access: Métro: les Sablons.
Founded: 1937 (both the museum and library). The library was moved to its present location in 1969.
Major resources: Library (Bibliothèque); Photo Archives and Archives (Photothèque et Archives); Picture Department (Iconothèque); Music Department (Phonothèque).
Areas of specialization: Ethnography of France, French folk arts, traditions, folklore, agriculture and rural life, various related subjects.
Archives/manuscripts: In the Archives and Photothèque.
Holdings (library): Ca. 85,000 v., 2,000 periodicals, 800 almanacs, 10,000 songs (seventeenth- to twentieth-century). Special collections include the former personal libraries of Jean Charles-Brun (regionalism), Arnold van Gennep (folklore), Paul Delarue (folk tales), René Lucien Dauven (the circus and the music hall) and Marcel Maget (ethnology).
Visual/audio resources: Many photographs, negatives, prints, drawings, paintings, etc., related to the folk arts and traditions of France.
Access: The library (located on the eighth floor) is open to researchers and others interested in the collections, Mon.-Fri., from 1:30-5:00 p.m. Closed annually, July 15-Aug. 31. During the annual closure, limited access is available for visiting researchers (from outside Paris) who call in advance to request an appointment.
Guides/catalogs: A guide to the library is forthcoming. Available published guides include Prince Roland Bonaparte, *Kaliña, des Amérindiens à Paris* (Paris: 1992)—photographs of Carib Indians, made in Paris in 1892; Musée national des Arts et Traditions populaires (France). Bibliothèque, *Catalogue des ouvrages en occitan du XVIIe siècle à 1945 conservés à la Bibliothèque du Musée national des Arts et Traditions populaires* (Béziers: 1990) (= *Publications du Centre international de documentation occitane. Série bibliographique*, 9).
Artifacts: Numerous French folk art objects, costumes, agricultural implements, also traditional medical formulas, posters, etc.
Catalogs of artifacts: *Amulettes et talismans. La collection Lionel Bonnemère* (Paris: 1991) (= *Notes et documents des musées de France*, no. 23); Musée national des Arts et Traditions populaires (France), *La vannerie française* (Paris: 1990); Jean-René Trochet, *Catalogue des collections agricoles araires et autres instruments aratoires attelés symétriques: M.N.A.T.P.* (Paris: 1987). For a listing of other museum publications, see "Brochures et ouvrages sur les collections du M.N.A.T.P."

Information provided by A. Thill.

Museum national d'Histoire naturelle. Musée de l'Homme
(National Museum of Natural History. Museum of Mankind)

Address: Musée de l'Homme, Palais de Chaillot, place du Trocadéro, 75116 Paris, France.
Location: Right Bank, 16th Arrondissement.

Tel.: +(33) 1 44 05 72 01 or 72 02 (Bibliothèque); +(33) 1 44 05 72 28 (Photothèque); +(33) 1 44 05 73 34 (Départment d'Ethnomusicologie).

Fax: +(33) 1 44 05 72 12 (Bibliothèque); +(33) 1 44 05 72 93 (Photothèque).

Internet address (Museum national d'Histoire naturelle): http://www.mnhn.fr/mnhn/pmh.

Internet address (Photothèque): http://www.mnhn.fr/mnhn/ph.

Networks, consortia: OCLC (catalog records of the museum's book holdings are included, but not of manuscripts or pamphlets); CCN periodical union catalog.

Public transit access: Métro: Trocadéro; bus: 22, 30, 32, 63, 72, 82.

Founded: 1877 (establishment of the Musée d'Ethnographie du Trocadéro—see Nélia Dias's history of the Musée d'Ethnographie du Trocadéro). In 1928 that museum was combined with the Muséum national d'Histoire naturelle (National Museum of Natural History). In 1937 the Museum and Library were moved to the present site at the Palais de Chaillot.

Major resources: Bibliothèque (Library); Photothèque (Photo Archive); Départment d'Ethnomusicologie (Department of Ethnomusicology).

Areas of specialization: Prehistory, physical anthropology, cultural and social anthropology, ethnology, archaeology, linguistics; Africa, Latin America, Asia, Oceania, Arctic regions.

Archives/manuscripts: The library conserves its own archives, as well as some private archives (the "fonds privés") and a portion of the institutional archives of the Musée de l'Homme. Among archives in the fonds privés are the papers of Nöel Ballif (1922-1993)—ethnologist, Pygmy specialist, 2 boxes containing papers, lecture notes, fieldnotes; Constantin Brailoiu (1893-1958)—a Romanian ethnomusicologist, 20 boxes; Abbé Henri Breuil (1877-1961)—South African prehistory, 8 boxes; A.C. Eugène Caillot—an Oceanist, 4 boxes; Gaëtan Gatian de Clérambault (1872-1934), 8 boxes; Jeanne Cuisinier (1885-1964)—ethnologist and Indonesianist, 30 boxes (includes papers, notes, photographs and film); Maurice Delafosse (1870-1926)—ethnologist and African linguist, 10 boxes; Henri Frey (1847-1933), correspondence—Southeast Asia, China and Africa, 15 boxes; Christian Merlo—ethnologist and Africanist linguist, 6 boxes, including materials on fetishism in Dahomey; Jacques Millot (1897-1980)—director of the Musée de l'Homme, 1961-1968, 20 boxes; Édouard Piette (1827-1906)—prehistorian, 2 boxes; Paul Rivet (1876-1958)—director (in 1928) of the Musée d'Ethnographie du Trocadéro, subsequently director of the Musée de l'Homme (between 1938-1940 and 1944-1958), physician, anthropologist, South America specialist, linguist, 140 boxes (including some 15,000 items of correspondence, unpublished writings, etc.); Georges-Henri Rivière (1897-1985)—established the Musée des Arts et Traditions populaires, 20 boxes; Paul-Émile Victor (1907-1995)—fieldnotes on his stay with the Inuit in Greenland, 1933 to 1937, 20 boxes, including ethnographic sketches, 70 drawings and 2,000 photographs. The library of the museum holds some 129 boxes of archives of the museum itself.

Holdings (books and journals): 250,000 book and journal volumes are in the library. Also at this location are the scholarly libraries of several French learned societies: the Société des Américanistes; the Société des Océanistes; the Société des Africanistes; the Société préhistorique française; the Société des Études sino-asiatiques; and the Société française d'Anthropologie. The important *archives* of these societies remain with the respective societies—not the museum library.

Visual/audio resources: The Photothèque has ca. 400,000 black-and-white photographs and color slides, including the noteworthy Roland Bonaparte (1858-1924) photograph collection, the Désiré Charnay (1828-1915) photographs, the Jacques Dournes photographs, the Miot photo collection and many others. An exhibit catalog of photographs in the Bonaparte collection has been published.

Access: Open to the public for on-site use of materials. Closed in August.

References: *Objets et Mondes* (Paris: 1961-1989)—a journal of the museum that is no longer published; Christine Barthe, "La photothèque du Musée de l'Homme," *Bulletin des Bibliothèques de France*, vol. 39, no. 2 (1994), p. 56-57; Martin Blumenson, *The Vildé Affair: Beginnings of the French Resistance* (Boston: 1977)—Blumenson's account of the role of Musée de l'Homme staff in the World War II-era French resistance, also available in a French-language translation: *Le réseau du Musée de l'Homme: les débuts de la résistance en France* (Paris: 1979); Nélia Dias, *Le Musée d'Ethnographie du Trocadéro, 1878-1908: anthropologie et muséologie en France* (Paris: 1991).

Guides/catalogs: Anne MacKaye Chapman, et al., *Cap Horn, 1882-1883: Rencontre avec les Indiens Yahgan: Collection de la Photothèque du Musée de l'Homme* (Paris: 1995); *Collection Musée de l'Homme (Paris): Catalogue établi par la Commission internationale des Arts and Traditions populaires (C.I.A.P.)* (Paris: 1952) (= *Archives de la musique enregistrée. Série C. Music ethnographique et folklorique,* vol. 2); *"Peaux-Rouges": Autour de la collection anthropologique du Prince Roland Bonaparte* (Thonon-les-Bains: 1992).

Artifacts of anthropological significance: Very extensive collections of ethnological and archaeological artifacts are preserved in the museum.

Catalogs of artifacts: Many exhibition catalogs have been published, including *Ancien Pérou: vie, pouvoir et mort* (Paris: 1987) (= *Museum national d'Histoire naturelle. Musée de l'Homme. Exposition du cinquantenaire*); Christine Hemmet, *Montagnards des pays d'Indochine dans les collections du Musée de l'Homme* (Boulogne-Billancourt: 1995); Francine Ndiaye, Bruno Martinelli and Geneviève Calame-Griaule, *L'art du pays dogon dans les collections du Musée de l'Homme* (Zurich: 1995); Francine Ndiaye, *Secrets d'initiés: masques d'Afrique noire dans les collections du Musée de l'Homme* (Paris: 1994).

Information provided by Jacqueline Dubois and Dominique Morelon.

Société asiatique de Paris. Bibliothèque
(Asiatic Society of Paris. Library)

Address: Bibliothèque, Société asiatique, 52, rue du Cardinal Lemoine, Paris, France.
Location: Left Bank, 5th Arrondissement.
Tel.: +(33) 1 44 41 43 14
Fax: +(33) 1 44 41 43 14
Networks, consortia: None.
Public transit access: Métro: Cardinal Lemoine.
Founded: 1822.
Major resources: The Society's library consists of books, journals, manuscripts, maps and drawings from or concerning Asia, in Western and many Asian languages. Among library

holdings are the former personal libraries of several Society members who were noted scholars of Asia.

Areas of specialization: Asia; there are significant retrospective holdings on Asian languages and history. Among the book collections are the former personal libraries of Henri Maspero (1883-1945), Édouard Chavannes (1865-1918), Alfred Charles Auguste Foucher (1865-1952), Paul Demiéville (1894-1979) and Émile Charles Marie Senart (1847-1928).

Archives/manuscripts: The archives of the society; other manuscript materials in various languages.

Holdings (books, journals, etc.): Ca. 100,000 v.

Visual/audio resources: A few photogaphs.

Access: Materials may be borrowed by members of the Society. Visitors who are non-members may request on-site reference use of library materials.

UNESCO. World Heritage Centre (WHC)
UNESCO. Centre du Patrimoine mondial (CPm)

Address: World Heritage Centre, UNESCO, 7, place de Fontenoy, 75352 Paris 07 SP France.

Location: Left Bank, 7th Arrondissement.

Tel.: +(33) 1 45 68 15 71

Fax: +(33) 1 45 68 55 70

E-mail: wh-info@unesco.org.

Internet address: http://www.unesco.org/whc.

Internet address (World Heritage List): http://www.unesco.org/whc/heritage.html.

Internet address (List of World Heritage in Danger): http://www.unesco.org/whc/danglist.htm.

Internet address (World Heritage Information Network): http://www.unesco.org/whin.

Public transit access: Métro: Ségur.

Founded: 1992.

Major resources: The Centre maintains the World Heritage List, the List of World Heritage in Danger and the World Heritage Information Network. All WHC publications and reports of meetings since 1979 are now available on its website.

Areas of specialization: Natural or cultural properties or sites of universal interest, located throughout the world.

Guides/catalogs: *Guiá del Patrimonio Mundial* (Madrid: 1987).

Description

The World Heritage Centre and the World Heritage List

The World Heritage List (WHL) is maintained on the basis of the 1972 UNESCO "Convention Concerning the Protection of the World Cultural and Natural Heritage." Sites are nominated by States Parties, based on the criteria defined in the UNESCO World

Heritage Convention and the Operational Guidelines for the Implementation of the World Heritage Convention. More than 506 sites and properties had been selected for inclusion on the World Heritage List as of late 1997. The cultural properties (as distinguished from natural sites) on the List consist of:

- "Monuments: architectural works, works of monumental sculpture and painting, elements or structures of an archaeological nature, inscriptions, cave dwellings and combinations of features, which are of outstanding universal value from the point of view of history, art or science."
- "Groups of buildings: groups of separate or connected buildings which, because of their architecture, their homogeneity or their place in the landscape, are of outstanding universal value from the point of view of history, art or science."
- "Sites: works of man or the combined works of nature and man, and areas including archaeological sites which are of outstanding universal value from the historical, aesthetic, ethnological or anthropological points of view."

Among the cultural and/or archaeological sites on the World Heritage List are the ruins of the Buddhist Vihara at Paharpur (Bangladesh); Mount Taishan (China); Jelling Mounds, Runic Stones and Church (Denmark); the Maya site of Copán (Honduras); and the Sun Temple at Konarak (India). The full World Heitage List, with digital color photos of many sites, and links to associated websites, is available on the Web.

Related Organizations

The work of the World Heritage Centre is carried out in cooperation with three advisory bodies: the International Centre for the Study of the Preservation and Restoration of Cultural Property (ICCROM); the International Council on Monuments and Sites (ICOMOS); and the World Conservation Union (IUCN); these bodies advise the World Heritage Committee on technical matters.

A related organization is the Organization of World Heritage Cities (OWHC), established to develop a cooperative relationship between the more than 100 World Heritage Cities to date inscribed on the World Heritage List.

The URLs of these related organizations are:

ICCROM: http://www.iccrom.org.
ICOMOS: http://www.icomos.org.
IUCN: http://www.iucn.org.
OWHC: http://www.ovpm.org.

Information provided by Vesna Vujicic and Julie Hage.

Germany

Germany—Frankfurt am Main

Frobenius-Institut. Völkerkundliche Bibliothek
(Frobenius Institute. Ethnological Library)

Address: Völkerkundliche Bibliothek, Frobenius-Institut, Liebigstrasse 47, 60323 Frankfurt am Main, Germany.
Tel.: (069) 719 199-34; (069) 798-23687
Fax: (069) 719 199-11 (Frobenius Institute)
Internet address: http://www.rz.uni-frankfurt.de:80/FB/fb08/IHE/ihe4.htm.
Networks, consortia: OCLC.
Founded: 1898 (founding of the Institute and the Library).
Major resources: See below.
Areas of specialization: The ethnology of Africa and the Americas; general ethnology; cultural philosophy; non-European prehistory.
Archives/manuscripts: The Africa Archive; the archives of the Research Institute for Cultural Morphology.
Holdings (books and journals): Ca. 95,000 v.
Visual/audio resources: The Frobenius Institute's extensive photographic collection is separate from the Ethnological Library, although images in the photo collection are accessible to interested researchers, by appointment. The photo collection includes many prints and more than 74,000 negatives. Among the latter are: Africa—more than 31,000 negatives; Asia—more than 1,600 negatives; Oceania—more than 17,000 negatives; the Americas—more than 14,500 negatives; Europe—more than 3,800 negatives. Photo holdings for Ethopia, South Africa, New Guinea, Australia, Bolivia and Venezuela are particularly numerous.
Access: Open to scholars and general readers. Access for readers located outside the Frankfurt am Main area is by interlibrary loan request only.
References: László Vajda, "Frobenius, Leo," in Christopher Winters (general editor), *International Dictionary of Anthropologists* (New York: 1991) (= *Garland Reference Library of the Social Sciences*, vol. 638), p. 220-221.

Description

Although the official foundation of the Ethnological Library (as it is known today) was, like that of the Frobenius Institute, in 1898, its origins date back to 1893-1894, when the young Africa researcher, Leo Frobcnius (1873-1938), started assembling his vast Afrika-Archiv (Africa Archive) in Berlin—a collection of extracts from literature on Africa, ethnographic pictorial materials and questionnaires relating to ethnographic studies in Africa—which he continued to supplement with newly acquired ethnographic writings about African peoples.

The library, which is the largest ethnographic library in the Federal Republic of Germany, was renamed on October 24, 1968, when the libraries of the Frankfurter Museum für Völkerkunde (Frankfurt Museum of Ethnology), the Frobenius Institute and the Institute of Historical Ethnology (formerly the Seminar of Ethnology) of the Johann Wolfgang Goethe University in Frankfurt am Main, and of the Frobenius Society (the former German Society of Cultural Morphology) were combined. Their respective inventories had already been brought together after the end of World War II, and displayed on the premises of the Frobenius Institute, which manages the library today. In addition, some 5,000 volumes are kept in a reference library at the Museum of Ethnology in Frankfurt.

After World War I Frobenius relocated his Africa Archive (including the library), and also the German Research Expedition to Central Africa (another research institute founded by him in 1904), to Munich. In 1920 these different branches were united in the Forschungsinstitut für Kulturmorphologie (Research Institute for Cultural Morphology), which in the same year was relocated to Frankfurt am Main and affiliated with the local university. In 1946, almost eight years after the founding father's death, the institute was given his name.

By the first decade of the twentieth-century, the developing scientific tasks of the Research Institute, and Frobenius's new fields of interest, led to the acquisition of new comparative materials pertaining to non-African cultures. This resulted in a broadening of the collections, which came to include scientific material relating to all continents, general ethnology, cultural philosophy and extra-European prehistory. The library collections were further increased in 1935, when Frobenius was appointed director of the Museum of Ethnology, and the libraries of the Africa Archive and the Research Institute for Cultural Morphology were united with the museum library (the latter had been founded in 1908).

From 1938 onward, the book collection was enlarged and supplemented by the addition of the library of the newly established German Society of Cultural Morphology (now named the Frobenius Society—a promotional society of the institute), which in turn had been acquired from the former Frankfurt Society of Anthropology, Ethnology and Prehistory (founded in 1900). Frobenius's private library was added after his death. The most recent addition is the library of the Institute of Historical Ethnology, founded in 1958.

The concentration of the several Frankfurt ethnological libraries at one location is a major advantage for visitors and library users alike; it offers a centralization of the archives and also allows the library to pursue a coordinated acquisitions policy. The collections in the general department of ethnology and extra-European ethnology have been steadily increased by means of acquisitions, donations and ongoing exchanges of publications with more than 200 cognate institutions in more than fifty countries. Remaining gaps have thus been filled, although the library has wisely refrained from adding collections on ancient civilizations or in European ethnology—areas within scope of other Frankfurt scientific libraries. The acquisition of the private libraries of Theodor Koch-Grünberg (1949) and Walter Krickeberg (1962)—both with very important collections of historical materials—were particularly valuable additions for the department of American Ethnology. The department of Oceania was expanded in 1966 by the acquisition of Carl-August Schmitz's separata collection.

Siegfried Seyfarth

Germany—Göttingen

Institut für den Wissenschaftlichen Film (IWF)
(Scientific Film Institute)

Address: Institut für den Wissenschaftlichen Film, Nonnenstieg 72, 37075 Göttingen, Germany.
Tel.: +49 551 5024-0
Fax: +49 551 5024-400
Internet address: http://www.iwf.gwdg.de/iwfeng.html.
Founded: 1956.
Major resources: A very extensive film library in ethnology and related fields.

Italy

Italy—Florence

Università degli Studi di Firenze. Biblioteca di Antropologia
(University of Florence. Library of Anthropology)

Address: Biblioteca di Antropologia, Palazzo Nonfinito, Università degli Studi di Firenze, via del Proconsolo 12, 50122 Florence, Italy.
Tel.: +(39) 55-217482
Fax: +(39) 55-283358
E-mail: biantr@cesit1.unifi.it.
Founded: 1977 (see below).
Areas of specialization: Ethnography, physical anthropology, physiognomy.
Holdings (books and journals): 10,000 book vols. (many published prior to 1900); 170 journals (80 of which are current).
Access: Open to all for consultation. Loans of materials are only to students, scholars and researchers of Italian universities. The library offers on-line bibliographic searching and photocopying. By the end of 1998 the on-line library catalogue will be fully functional.
References: Charles Darwin, *The Expression of the Emotions in Man and Animals* (London: 1872); Paolo Mantegazza, *Atlante della espressione del dolore: fotografie prese dal vero e da molte opere d'arte che illustrano gli studi sperimentali sull'espressione del dolore* (Firenze: 1876); Paolo Mantegazza, *Fisonomia e minica: con più che cento disegni originali di Ettore Edmondo Ximenes* (Milano: 1881) (= *Biblioteca scientifica internazionale*, vol. 28).

Description

The Library of Palazzo Nonfinito may be regarded as one of the most important in Italy in the field of anthropological sciences. It originated between 1869 and 1871 with the foundation of the Museum (1869) and the Società Italiana di Antropologia (Italian Anthropological and Ethnological Society) by Paolo Mantegazza—who recorded in two distinct lists the publications that were purchased and those received as gifts or by exchange. Only in 1909 was an official inventory established by the Regio Istituto di Studi Superiori, Pratici e di Perfezionamento (Royal Institute for Superior, Practical and Specialization Courses), and at that point the Museum and the Society began two distinct lives.

In 1924 the Regio Istituto di Studi Superiori, Practici e di Perfezionamento, now called University, moved to the Palazzo Nonfinito, which is still the official site of the Anthropological Institute. Here in 1977 the library was founded. Its history is deeply linked with the history of the Società Italiana di Antropologia. In the old inventories of the Society one can find, close to the list of acquired publications, many donations from people who belonged to the scientific world and who brought prestige not only to the Institute, but to science in general—scholars such as Paolo Mantegazza (1831-1910), Aldobrandino Mochi (1874-1931), Lidio Cipriani (1894-1962) and Lamberto Loria (1855-1913).

The unique value of the library lies in the ethnographic monographs and the complete collection of journals (e.g., *Antropologie*) and bulletins. There are also fifty old volumes (32 of these from the sixteenth-century), a part of which came from the partition of the library of the Biblioteca dell'Imperial Regio Museo di Fisica e Storia Naturale (Imperial-Royal Museum of Physics and Natural Science). Forty of these bear the impression of the Medicean stamp of the Biblioteca Palatina. There are also books on physiognomy that date from the sixteenth- and seventeenth-centuries. Also among the early imprints are Captain James Cook's voyages (1787). From 1986 the library holds the volumes of the Società Italiana di Ecologia Umana (Italian Society of Human Ecology).

Anna Lisa Bebi

Netherlands

The era of Dutch East India Company (Verenigde Oost-Indische Compagnie, or VOC) trading voyages to the Indian Ocean and the East Indies, beginning in the seventeenth-century, was succeeded by a period of Dutch colonial involvement in insular Southeast Asia that ended only in 1949. The extensive historical archives of the VOC are now preserved at The Hague, in the General State Archives (Algemeen Rijksarchief). Leiden and Amsterdam are also important centers for scholarly research on Indonesia and insular Southeast Asia. The library of the University of Leiden, and the nearby Royal Institute for Linguistics and Anthropology (Koninklijk Instituut voor Taal-, Land- en Volkenkunde, or KITLV), jointly maintain exceptional library and manuscript collections on Indonesia and the former Netherlands East Indies. Included in University of Leiden and KITLV collections are printed and manuscript materials in Dutch and other Western languages, as well as in Malay, Indonesian, Javanese, Balinese and many other languages and scripts of the insular Southeast Asian region. In Amsterdam, the Royal Tropical Institute (Koninklijk Instituut voor de Tropen) preserves fine colonial-era collections of books, journals, maps, prints, drawings, photographs, wax cylinder recordings and other documentation from the former Netherlands East Indies. Several other Dutch museums also curate and display outstanding collections of Indonesian artifacts, traditional arts and handicrafts (including textiles, musical instruments and woodcarvings). The Japanese (Siebold) and Indonesian object collections of the National Museum of Ethnology (Rijksmuseum voor Volkenkunde) in Leiden are of particularly fine quality.

A detailed list of the many Asia-related research centers and repositories in Holland has been published in the International Institute for Asian Studies' *Guide to Asian Studies in Europe* (Richmond, Surrey: 1998), p. 271-295. Also see "Asia Collections in the Netherlands" on the Web at http://iias.leidenuniv.nl/bib/collections.html.

Netherlands—Amsterdam

Koninklijk Instituut voor de Tropen (KIT)
(Royal Tropical Institute)

Address: Royal Tropical Institute, Linnaeusstraat 2, 1092 AD Amsterdam, Netherlands.
Tel.: +31 (20) 5688200
Fax: +31 (20) 5688331
E-mail: IBD@support.nl.
Internet address: http://www.kit.nl.
Internet address (Map Room): http://www.kit.nl/IBD/Map_Room/maphomep.asp
Public transit access: Take tram no. 9 to Mauritskade.
Founded: The Colonial Museum, established at Haarlem in 1871, was incorporated into the Association of the Colonial Institute (VKI) when the latter was founded in Amsterdam in 1910. The Institute moved into an imposing new building at Mauritskade in 1926. The VKI was renamed as the Indies Institute in 1945 and was again renamed as the Royal Tropical

Institute in 1950. The landmark building at Mauritskade in Amsterdam has remained the Institute's headquarters since 1926.

Major resources: Tropical Museum (Tropenmuseum); Central Library (Centrale Bibliotheek); Photo Archives.

Areas of specialization (library): Prior to World War II, library collections focused largely on the Netherlands East Indies and other areas of historic Dutch colonial activity. More recent library acquisitions give emphasis to economic development, social conditions, agriculture and culture in Asia and the Third World. Library holdings include the personal library of J.E. van Lohuizen-deLeeuw (known as the BAKA collection) on South and Southeast Asian culture, history, philosophy and religion. The library has important pre-World War II book and journal holdings in the languages of Indonesia, but has not acquired Indonesian-language imprints since 1950.

Archives/manuscripts: Manuscripts that were previously in the Colonial Museum; other archival materials.

Holdings (library): Ca. 180,000 vols. of books, journals, manuscripts, pamphlets, maps and atlases—many from or concerning the former Netherlands East Indies (now Indonesia), Surinam and the Netherlands Antilles.

Visual/audio resources: The extensive photo archives includes colonial-era photographic prints, negatives, glass-plate images and albums from the Netherlands East Indies. The museum's very fine collection of nineteenth-century prints of Indonesia has been described in a guide compiled by John Bastin and Bea Brommer (1979). A list of the original wax cylinder recordings preserved at the museum is available—see the inventory by Felix van Lamsweerde (1994). The Map Room curates some 25,000 mostly retrospective maps, including many pre-1950 city maps from Indonesia.

Access: Open to the public.

References: Sarah Cummings, "The Library of the Royal Tropical Institute," *IIAS Newsletter* [International Institute for Asian Studies], no. 7 (Winter 1996), p. 14; Roger Tol, "Orientalist Library Resources in the Netherlands: An Introduction to the South and Southeast Asian Collections," *IIAS Newsletter* [International Institute for Asian Studies], no. 4 (Spring 1995), Supplement, p. 19-22.

Guides/catalogs: John Bastin and Bea Brommer, *Nineteenth Century Prints and Illustrated Books of Indonesia, With Particular Reference to the Print Collection of the Tropenmuseum, Amsterdam: A Descriptive Bibliography* (Utrecht: 1979); Felix van Lamsweerde (editor), "Inventory of the Wax Cylinder Collection of the Tropenmuseum," in Jaap Kunst, *Indonesian Music and Dance: Traditional Music and Its Interaction with the West* (Amsterdam: 1994), p. 247-273; J. Woudsma, *The Royal Tropical Institute: An Amsterdam Landmark* (Amsterdam: 1990). The Institute has produced a series of indexes of Netherlands East Indies journals, based on KIT's extensive pre-1940 journal holdings. Some seven volumes in the *Klein Repertorium* series have been published. Indexed journals include the *Tijdschrift voor Nederlandsch Indië* (1838-1902); journals of the Indisch Genootschap (1854-1940); others.

Artifacts of anthropological significance: The Tropenmuseum curates extensive material culture collections from the Netherlands East Indies (Indonesia) and other areas of historic Dutch colonial activity. See, for example, van Brakel's guide to the Georg Tillmann collection of Indonesian textiles, carvings and other objects (1996).

Catalogs of artifacts of anthropological significance: J.H. van Brakel, David van Duuren and Itie C. van Hout, *A Passion for Indonesian Art: The Georg Tillmann (1882-1941) Collection at the Tropenmuseum Amsterdam* (Amsterdam: 1996); Elisabeth den Otter, *Pre-Columbian Musical Instruments: Silenced Sounds in the Tropenmuseum Collection* (Amsterdam: 1994) (= *Koninklijk Instituut voor de Tropen. Bulletin*, 335).

Netherlands—The Hague

Algemeen Rijksarchief (A.R.)
(General State Archive)

Address: Algemeen Rijksarchief, Prins Willem Alexanderhof 20, 2595 BE The Hague, Netherlands.
Location: Near the Central Station in The Hague.
Tel.: +31 (070) 3315400
Fax: +31 (070) 3805885
Public transit access: Take a train, bus or tram to the Central Station in The Hague.
Founded: 1802.
Archives/manuscripts: The archives of the Dutch East India Company; official Dutch government archives pertaining to the Netherlands East Indies/Indonesia; many other archival records and documents.
Access: Open to the public.
Guides/catalogs: M.A.P. Meilink-Roelofsz, *De Archieven van de Verenigde Oostindische Compagnie = The Archives of the Dutch East India Company (1602-1795)* ('s-Gravenhage: 1992); Netherlands State Archives Service, *Sources of the History of Asia and Oceania in The Netherlands* (München: 1982-1983) (= *International Council on Archives. Guides to the Sources for the History of Nations*, 3rd series, vol. 4, pt. 1-2).

Koninklijke Bibliotheek (KB)
(Royal Library)

Address: The Royal Library, Prins Willem-Alexanderhof 5, Postbus 90407, 2509LK The Hague, Netherlands.
Location: Near the Central Station in The Hague.
Tel.: +31 (071) 3140911
Fax: +31 (070) 3549851
Internet address: http://www.konbib.nl/home-en.html.
Public transit access: Take a train, bus or tram to the Central Station in The Hague.
Founded: 1798 (as the National Library).
Areas of specialization: Humanities; South and Southeast Asia, Dutch East Indies, Dutch colonial newspapers, others.
Archives/manuscripts: Many historical archives and manuscripts are in the adjacent General State Archives (Algemeen Rijksarchief). Most of the many Islamic manuscripts once

held by the Royal Library were transfered (in the nineteenth-century) to the University of Leiden Library. These are now part of the Leiden University Library Oriental manuscripts collections.

Access: Open to the public.

References: Roger Tol, "Orientalist Library Resources in the Netherlands: An Introduction to the South and Southeast Asian Collections," *IIAS Newsletter* [International Institute for Asian Studies], no. 4 (Spring 1995), Supplement, p. 19-22.

Netherlands—Leiden

Koninklijk Instituut voor Taal-, Land- en Volkenkunde (KITLV)
(Royal Institute of Linguistics and Anthropology)

Address: Royal Institute of Linguistics and Anthropology, Reuvensplaats 2, Postbus 9515, 2300 RA Leiden, Netherlands.

Tel.: +31 (71) 5272295

Fax: +31 (71) 5272638

Internet address: http://iias.leidenuniv.nl/institutes/kitlv/index.html.

Internet address (Department of Historical Documentation): http://iias.leidenuniv.nl/institutes/kitlv/hisdoc.html.

Networks, consortia: PICA (Project for Integrated Catalogue Information).

Public transit access: The Institute is a fifteen-minute walk from Leiden Station. Or bus line no. 43 from Leiden Station stops in front of the University Library.

Founded: In 1851 at the University of Delft—as a center and library for students and faculty in the field of Indology.

Major resources: KITLV Library; Department of Historical Documentation (Western and Oriental manuscripts and archives, photographs, drawings, maps and microforms).

Areas of specialization: Indonesia, including Austronesian languages and literatures. A Malaysian Resources Centre was opened in 1998; also, library holdings for the Caribbean area.

Archives/manuscripts: 80 meters of archival materials, including 1,200 items of Western-language material are in the Department of Historical Documentation. A majority of Historical Documentation archives relate to the Dutch East Indies/Indonesia.

Holdings (books and journals): Ca. 500,000 book and journal volumes (including major book and journal collections for Indonesia/the Dutch East Indies); also holdings for other Southeast Asian countries, Austronesian culture areas and the Caribbean.

Visual/audio resources: 100,000 photographs and 2,500 drawings (in Historical Documentation); also ca. 10,000 maps and atlases. Holdings also include prints, drawings, paintings and (recently) some audio-visual materials. The major emphasis of photographic holdings is on Indonesia, Surinam, Netherlands Antilles and Aruba. Steven Wachlin's *Woodbury & Page—Photographers Java* (Leiden: 1994) is based on images in the KITLV photo archives.

Access: Access is for members of the Institute. Other scholars (and students) can be introduced. Books older than 100 years and non-library materials will not be lent out.

References: Roger Tol, "Orientalist Library Resources in the Netherlands: An Introduction to the South and Southeast Asian Collections," *IIAS Newsletter* [International Institute for Asian Studies], no. 4 (Spring 1995), Supplement, p. 19-22.

Guides/catalogs: Herman C. Kemp, *Annotated Bibliography of Indonesian Bibliographies* (Leiden: 1990); Koentjaraningrat, *Anthropology in Indonesia: A Bibliographical Review* ('s-Gravenhage: 1975) (= *Koninklijk Instituut voor Taal- Land- en Volkenkunde. Bibliographical series*, 8); J.H. Maronier, *Pictures of the Tropics: A Catalogue of Drawings, Water-Colours, Paintings, and Sculptures in the Collection of the Royal Institute of Linguistics and Anthropology in Leiden* ('s-Gravenhage: 1967); many other published guides and catalogs concerning Indonesia.

Information provided by F.G.P. Jaquet.

Rijksmuseum voor Volkenkunde
(National Museum of Ethnology)

Address: Rijksmuseum voor Volkenkunde, Steenstraat 1, NL-2300 AE Leiden, Netherlands.
Tel.: +31 (71) 5168800
Fax: +31 (71) 5128437
Internet address: No website is available.
Public transit access: The Rijksmuseum is just a few minutes walk from Leiden Station.
Founded: 1837.
Major resources: Media Center (photographs, slides); Library (books, journals and other library materials).
Areas of specialization: Traditional cultures of Africa, the Americas, Asia and Oceania. Areas of exceptional collection strength include the ethnology of Japan and Indonesia.
Archives/manuscripts: The institutional archives and records of the Rijksmuseum voor Volkenkunde.
Visual/audio resources: About 300,000 ethnographic and related photographs, color slides, videos, etc. Holdings include photographs by Hendrik F. Tillema, the Anton W. Nieuwenhuis collection and others.
Access: The Library is open to the public. The Media Center may be used only by appointment. Due to an extensive rebuilding program underway at the museum (scheduled for completion in 2000), the artifact and media collections may not always be accessible to researchers.
References: Willem van Gulik, "Von Siebold and His Japanese Collection in Leiden," in Willem Otterspeer (editor), *Leiden Oriental Connections, 1850-1940* (Leiden: 1989) (= *Studies in the History of Leiden University*, vol. 5), p. 378-391; *Overzicht van de Geschiedenis van het Rijksmuseum voor Volkenkunde, 1837-1937* (Leiden: [1937]).
Guides/catalogs: Some of the museum's photo holdings are illustrated in Hendrik F. Tillema, *A Journey Among the Peoples of Central Borneo in Word and Picture* (Singapore: 1989).
Artifacts of anthropological significance: The Siebold Japanese Collection (some 5,000 items); the J.F. Royer bequest; many others.

Published catalogs of artifact resources: Paul L.F. van Dongen, Matthi Forrer and Willem van Gulik (editors), *Topstukken uit het Rijksmuseum voor Volkenkunde = Masterpieces from the National Museum of Ethnology* (Leiden: 1987); Hendrik Herman Juynboll (and others), *Catalogus van 's Rijks Ethnographisch Museum* (Leiden: 1910-1932), 22 v.—on the insular Southeast Asian artifact collections, particularly those from Indonesia; various other exhibit catalogs.

Description

The National Museum of Ethnology originated in 1837 with the name Rijks Japansch Museum von Siebold (National Japanese Museum von Siebold). The museum's early holdings consisted of a major collection of ethnographic and scientific materials gathered in Japan (under very adverse conditions) by Philipp Franz von Siebold (1796-1866). The Siebold Collection is still among the most significant of the museum's many cultural and ethnological holdings. All of Siebold's Japanese collections are still preserved at the museum, with the exception of the natural history materials—these are nearby in Leiden at the Museum of Natural History. Siebold's very systematic collection techniques have been described in an article by Willem van Gulik (1989). The current museum name (Rijksmuseum voor Volkenkunde) dates from 1937.

The Museum's Library and Media Center include books, journals and a large accumulation of archival photographs—many of Southeast Asian cultural or ethnological interest. Numerous archival photographs depict peoples and scenes of the former Dutch East Indies. Borneo photographs by Hendrik F. Tillema (1870-1952) have been published in *A Journey Among the Peoples of Central Borneo in Word and Picture* (1989).

Lee S. Dutton
Information provided by David Stuart-Fox.

Rijksuniversiteit te Leiden. Universiteitsbibliotheek
(University of Leiden. University Library)

Address: University Library, University of Leiden, Witte Singel 27, 2300 RA Leiden, Netherlands.
Tel.: +31 (71) 5272832
Fax: +31 (71) 5272836
Internet address: http://www.leidenuniv.nl/ub.
Internet address (Oriental Department): http://www.leidenuniv.nl/ub/olg.htm.
Networks, consortia: PICA (Project for Integrated Catalogue Information).
Public transit access: The University Library is a fifteen-minute walk from Leiden Station. Bus 43 from Leiden Station stops in front of the Library.
Founded: 1575 (the university); 1587 (the library).
Major resources: The Legatum Warnerianum (Oriental Department) has extensive holdings of Islamic manuscripts in Arabic and many other languages, as well as a very large collection

of manuscripts from the Dutch East Indies/Indonesia. The Leiden University Library also has substantial book and journal holdings on the cultures, ethnography, languages and history of insular Southeast Asia and other areas of historic Dutch colonial activity. Additional book and journal holdings on insular Southeast Asia are nearby (across the street) at the library of the Royal Institute of Linguistics and Anthropology (Koninklijk Instituut voor Taal-, Land- en Volkenkunde).

Areas of specialization: The library's large collection of Islamic manuscripts includes some manuscripts transferred to Leiden in the nineteenth-century from the Royal Library (Koninklijke Bibliotheek) in The Hague. Many manuscripts in Malay, Javanese, Balinese and other languages of insular Southeast Asia are held.

Manuscripts/archives: Ca. 23,000 Oriental manuscripts. The Oriental manuscript collections are still being expanded.

Holdings (books and journals): 2,700,000 v., including about 50,000 volumes on the Dutch East Indies/Indonesia and other parts of Southeast Asia; 11,500 periodicals.

Visual/audio resources: The library's Hotz collection contains photographs by Albertus Paulus Hermanus Hotz (1855-1930), taken in Persia and the Caucasus, 1890-1891; other photographic collections and holdings.

Access: A reader's permit is needed to borrow circulating books.

References: *Levinus Warner and His Legacy: Three Centuries Legatum Warnerianum in the Leiden University Library* (Leiden: 1970); Stephan Roman, *The Development of Islamic Library Collections in Western Europe and North America* (London: 1990) (= *Libraries and Librarianship in the Muslim World*), p. 170-184; Roger Tol, "Catalogues of the Manuscripts in Indonesian Languages Kept in the Library of the University of Leiden, the Netherlands," *South-East Asia Library Group Newsletter*, no. 32 (March 1988), p. 10-14; Roger Tol, "Orientalist Library Resources in the Netherlands: An Introduction to the South and Southeast Asian Collections," *IIAS Newsletter* [International Institute for Asian Studies], no. 4 (Spring 1995), Supplement, p. 19-22; Jan Just Witkam, "Bibliographical Resources for the Study of Islamic Manuscripts in Collections in the Netherlands," *IIAS Newsletter* [International Institute for Asian Studies], no. 4 (Spring 1995), Supplement, p. 23-25.

Guides/catalogs: The earliest printed catalogs of Leiden University Library holdings were produced in the seventeenth-century. Most of the library's subsequent catalogs included references to holdings of Islamic manuscripts. Only the library catalogs produced since the beginning of the nineteenth-century remain in current use, however. Catalogs of Islamic manuscripts include Petrus Voorhoeve, *Handlist of Arabic Manuscripts in the Library of the University of Leiden and Other Collections in the Netherlands* (Leiden: reprinted, 1980) (= *Bibliotheca Universitatis Leidensis. Codices manuscripti*, 7); and many others—see the annotated list of catalogs of Islamic manuscripts in the University Library, compiled by Jan Just Witkam, in Geoffrey Roper (general editor), *World Survey of Islamic Manuscripts* (London: 1992-1994) (= *Al-Furqān Islamic Heritage Foundation. Publication*, no. 5), vol. 2, p. 367-376. Among the Southeast Asian manuscript catalogs of the library are Hedy I.R. Hinzler, *Catalogue of Balinese Manuscripts in the Library of the University of Leiden and Other Collections in The Netherlands* (Leiden: 1986-1987) (= *Bibliotheca Universitatis Leidensis. Codices manuscripti*, 22-23), 2 v.; Theodore G. Th. Pigeaud, *Literature of Java. Catalogue Raisonné of Javanese Manuscripts in the Library of the University of Leiden and Other Public Collections in the Netherlands* (Leiden: 1967-1980) (= *Bibliotheca*

Universitatis Leidensis. Codices manuscripti, 9-11, 20), 4 v.; Petrus Voorhoeve (compiler, with T. Iskandar; translated and edited by Mark Durie), *Catalogue of Acehnese Manuscripts in the Library of Leiden University and Other Collections Outside Aceh* (Leiden: 1994) (= *Bibliotheca Universitatis Leidensis. Codices manuscripti*, 24); many others.

Information provided by Jan Just Witkam.

Van Vollenhoven Instituut voor Recht en Bestuur in niet-Westerse Landen. Bibliotheek
(Van Vollenhoven Institute for Law and Administration in Non-Western Countries. Library)

Address: Library, Van Vollenhoven Institute for Law and Administration in Non-Western Countries, Rapenburg 33, 2311 GG Leiden, Netherlands.
Tel.: +31 (71) 5277261
Fax: +31 (71) 5277670
E-mail: Jfvviad@Ruljur.LeidenUniv.nl; Jfvvicw@Ruljur.LeidenUniv.nl.
Internet address: http://ruljis.leidenuniv.nl/group/jfvvi/www/homepage.htm.
Networks, consortia: PICA (Project for Integrated Catalogue Information) contains catalog records of library holdings from 1963 to the present.
Public transit access: The Institute and Library are a ten-minute walk from Leiden Station.
Founded: 1978. In 1989 the Institute was renamed in honor of Cornelis van Vollenhoven.
Major resources: Books and other documentation on Indonesian and other non-Western law and administration; materials on Islamic law. Documentation on the law and public administration of developing countries in general is also acquired.
Areas of specialization: Library holdings include the personal library of Cornelius van Vollenhoven on the *adat* law of Indonesia. Other countries substantially represented in library holdings are Aruba, Egypt, Indonesia, Mexico, Morocco, Netherlands Antilles and Surinam.
Archives/manuscripts: Van Vollenhoven's personal papers have been transferred to the General State Archives in The Hague, where they are available for research use. Manuscript resources at the Van Vollenhoven Institute Library include, among others, the J.F. Holleman papers on Philippine customary law.
Holdings (books and periodicals): More than 18,000 books, periodicals, offprints and other items; 8,000 microfiche.
Access: By appointment. Books published before 1945 are available for on-site use only.
References: Henriëtte L.T. de Beaufort, *Cornelis van Vollenhoven, 1874-1933* (Haarlem: 1954); *Cornelis van Vollenhoven, 1874-1933* (The Hague: 1992); J.F. Holleman (editor), *Van Vollenhoven on Indonesian Adat Law: Selections from Het Adatrecht van Nederlandsch-Indië* (The Hague: 1981) (= *Koninklijk Instituut voor Taal-, Land- en Volkenkunde. Translation Series*, 20); *Indonesian Law, 1949-1989, A Bibliography of Foreign-Language Materials With Brief Commentaries on the Law* (Dordrecht: 1992); J.M. Otto and S. Pompe, "The Legal Oriental Connection," in William Otterspeer (editor), *Leiden Oriental Connections, 1850-1940* (Leiden: 1989) (= *Studies in the History of Leiden University*, vol. 5), p. 230-249; Brian Z Tamanaha, *Bibliography on Law and Developing Countries* (London: 1995); Roger Tol, "Orientalist Library Resources in the Netherlands: An

Introduction to the South and Southeast Asian Collections," *IIAS Newsletter* [International Institute for Asian Studies], no. 4 (Spring 1995), Supplement, p. 19-22; "Van Vollenhoven Institute for Law and Administration in Non-Western Countries, Leiden University"—a pamphlet, Leiden, 1997[?]; Laila Al-Zwaini and Rudolph Peters, *A Bibliography of Islamic Law, 1980-1993* (Leiden: 1994) (= *Handbuch der Orientalistik. Erste Abeilung de Nahe und Mittlere Osten*, 19 Bd. = *Handbook of Oriental Studies. Near and Middle East*, 0169-9423). The Van Vollenhoven Institute publishes (since 1995) the twice-yearly *Indonesian Law and Administration Review*. This journal presents studies of Indonesian law and administration from an analytical, historical, political and comparative perspective.

Description

The Van Vollenhoven Institute and Library are located in a picturesque old row house alongside the Rapenburg canal in an historic area of Leiden. The library maintains a unique collection of documentation on Indonesian traditional law (adat) as well as modern Indonesian state law. Also here are printed materials on the constitutional law of the Netherlands East Indies, on Islamic law and on law and administration in the non-Western world. Library holdings also include books and journals on the legal systems of Surinam and the Dutch Antilles and other areas of historic or contemporary Dutch scholarly interest.

From its beginnings the Institute was known as the Netherlands Research Centre for Law in Southeast Asia and the Caribbean (Nederlands Onderzoek Centrum voor het Recht in Zuidoost Azië en het Caraïbisch Gebied, or NORZOAC). In 1989 the Institute was renamed as the Van Vollenhoven Institute for Law and Administration in Non-Western Countries, to more fully reflect the geographic scope of research programs and collections. In that year, North Africa (Egypt and Morocco) and Latin America (in particular, Mexico) were included among areas of research interest. In 1995 China and South Africa were added to the geographic areas of specialization.

Major resources include the former personal library of Cornelis van Vollenhoven (1874-1933), who was "Professor of the Constitutional and Administrative Law of the Dutch Overseas Territories and of the Adat Law of the Netherlands East Indies" at Leiden University from 1901 until his death. About 65 percent of current Institute library holdings pertain to the law of the Netherlands East Indies/Indonesia.

The library holds retrospective books and journals on non-Western law published between 1800 and 1945, as well as more recent books and other documentation. Holdings are in several languages, including Dutch, English, Spanish and Indonesian.

Library acquisitions are now coordinated with those of the nearby Library of the Royal Institute for Linguistics and Anthropology (Koninklijk Instituut voor Taal-, Land- en Volkenkunde). The library also cooperates with the Law Documentation Center (Pusat Dokumentasi Hukum) of the University of Indonesia to provide research access to both colonial-era journals on Indonesian law and modern (post-Independence) Indonesian legal journals.

Lee S. Dutton
Information provided by Cora W.H. de Waaij-Vosters and Albert J. Dekker.

Netherlands—Rotterdam

Museum voor Volkenkunde
(Museum of Ethnology)

Address: Museum voor Volkenkunde, Willemskade 25, 3016 DM Rotterdam, Netherlands.
Tel.: +(31) 10-4551311
Fax: +(31) 10-455 67 01
Public transit access: Metro to Leuvehaven or tram no. 5 to Willemsplein.
Founded: 1885.
Major resources: Important photograph collections. The Museum holds artifact collections from Indonesia and New Guinea assembled by the Dutch Missionary Society during the mid-nineteenth-century.
Areas of specialization: Oceania, insular Southeast Asia—especially the Dutch East Indies/Indonesia; also (more broadly) the Third World.
Visual/audio resources: The photo archive contains some 20,000 photographs. Most of these date from the late nineteenth-century.
Guides/catalogs: Paul Faber, et al. (editors) and Anneke Groeneveld, et al. (text), *Toekang Potret: 100 Jaar Fotografie in Nederlands Indië 1839-1939 = 100 Years of Photography in the Dutch East Indies 1839-1939* (Amsterdam: 1989) (= *Fotografie uit de Collectie van het Museum voor Volkenkunde,* dl. 3/4); *Fotografie in Suriname, 1839-1939 = Photography in Surinam, 1839-1939* (Amsterdam: [1991?]) (= *Fotografie uit de Collectie van het Museum voor Volkenkunde,* dl. 5); Anneke Groeneveld, Paul Faber and Hardwicke Knight (text), *Burton Brothers: Fotografen in Nieuw-Zeeland, 1866-1898 = Burton Brothers: Photographers in New Zealand, 1866-1898* (Amsterdam: 1987).
Catalogs of artifacts: Paul Faber, Liane van der Linden and René Wassing (editors), *Schatten van het Museum voor Volkenkunde Rotterdam* (Amsterdam: 1987).

United Kingdom

S ome emphasis has been given, in the following United Kingdom entries, to major library, museum or archival repositories located in London or its vicinity. For some additional information on selected U.K. library collections, researchers may consult B.C. Bloomfield's detailed *A Directory of Rare Book and Special Collections in the United Kingdom and the Republic of Ireland* (2nd ed., London: 1997), as well as available websites. Among various repositories not represented in the following entries are those that focus primarily on U.K. or European archaeology or folklore. For directory information on collections of Islamic manuscripts in the U.K., see the survey by Geoffrey J. Roper and C.H. Bleaney in Geoffrey J. Roper (general editor), *World Survey of Islamic Manuscripts* (London: 1992-1994) (= *Al-Furqān Islamic Heritage Foundation. Publication*, no. 10), vol. 3, p. [429]-533.

United Kingdom—Cambridge

University of Cambridge. Cambridge University Library

Address: Cambridge University Library, West Road, Cambridge CB3 9DR, United Kingdom.
Tel.: +44 (1223) 333000 [Within the U.K.: (01223) 333000].
Fax: +44 (1223) 333160 [Within the U.K.: (01223) 333160].
Internet address: http://www.lib.cam.ac.uk.
Networks, consortia: CURL (Consortium of University Research Libraries).
Founded: Mid-fourteenth-century or earlier.
Major resources: A legal deposit library; one of the largest British collections of ethnographers' papers; the library of the Royal Commonwealth Society.
Archives/manuscripts: Alfred Cort Haddon papers, W.H.R. Rivers papers and others—see below. The library and archives of the Royal Commonwealth Society were transferred from London to the Cambridge University Library in 1993.
Visual/audio resources: The Royal Commonwealth Society collection includes 70,000 historical photographs related to former British overseas colonies.
Access: The library is open to members of Cambridge University. Other persons over the age of 21, and engaged in private study or research, may obtain Reader's Tickets by producing evidence of academic standing, need and fitness for admission.
References: B.C. Bloomfield (editor), *A Directory of Rare Book and Special Collections in the United Kingdom and the Republic of Ireland* (2nd ed., London: 1997), p. 25-29; Stephan Roman, *The Development of Islamic Library Collections in Western Europe and North America* (London: 1990) (= *Libraries and Librarianship in the Muslim World*), p. 34-38.
Guides/catalogs: Peter Fox (editor), *Cambridge University Library: The Great Collections* (Cambridge, U.K.: 1998); Ian Proudfoot, *Early Malay Printed Books: A Provisional Account of Materials Published in the Singapore-Malaysia Area Up to 1920, Noting Holdings in Major Public Collections* ([Kuala Lumpur]: 1993), p. 854-856; M.C. Ricklefs and P.

Voorhoeve, *Indonesian Manuscripts in Great Britain: A Catalogue of Manuscripts in Indonesian Languages in British Public Collections* (Oxford: 1977) (= *London Oriental Bibliographies*, vol. 5), [various pages].

Description

The library was founded in the mid-fourteenth-century or earlier, to serve the needs of the university. It is also a legal deposit library and is entitled to receive all United Kingdom publications. It therefore covers all fields of knowledge, including anthropology, but it is not possible to estimate the number of books and journals in any one field.

The library is a member of CURL (Consortium of University Research Libraries). There is an on-line catalog of books published from 1978 onwards, to which details of earlier publications are being added retrospectively. It can be accessed through the Internet, although the on-line catalog does not include manuscripts.

Within the library, the Manuscripts Department holds a wide variety of materials, including the papers of the following anthropologists, which are described below: Alfred Cort Haddon, Meyer Fortes, G.K. Roth, J.C. Trevor. In addition, the University Archives has records relating to the teaching of anthropology within the university. The Manuscripts Department also holds all Cambridge Ph.D. dissertations from 1922 to the present day. Preliminary enquiries may be made in writing to the Keeper of Manuscripts.

The library does not hold artifacts of anthropological significance. For material of this sort within the University, and a more specialized library collection, there is the Department of Archaeology and Anthropology, Downing Street, Cambridge CB2 3DZ, which contains the Haddon Library and the Museum of Archaeology and Anthropology.

Manuscript Department

- A.C. Haddon papers (reference: Haddon).

Alfred Cort Haddon (1855-1940) studied natural sciences at Cambridge University, graduating in 1878. In 1880 he became Professor of Zoology at the Royal College of Sciences and Assistant Naturalist to the Science and Art Museum in Dublin, where he developed an interest in ethnology. In 1888-1889 he made his first visit to the Torres Straits to study marine biology and to record the life of the people. On his return, he accepted a part-time lectureship in physical anthropology at Cambridge University, and in 1898-1899 Haddon led the Cambridge Anthropological Expedition to the Torres Straits. In 1900 he was appointed University Lecturer in Ethnology in Cambridge. His *Reports of the Cambridge Anthropological Expedition to Torres Strait*s was published at Cambridge, 1901-1912, with the final (seventh) volume appearing in 1935. Haddon's papers (139 boxes) were transferred from the Museum of Archaeology and Anthropology to the University Library in 1968 and 1975. There is a typescript list of the papers, which are housed in envelopes or files that are numbered serially and arranged in the following broad categories:

Early material, diaries, personal correspondence: nos. 1-31.

Torres Straits expeditions: correspondence, journals, fieldnotes and sketches:
Torres Straits: nos. 1001-1055.
New Guinea: nos. 2000-2073.
Publications: notes and correspondence: nos. 3000-3079.
Offprints belonging to Haddon, but not by him: nos. 5000-5431.

The Haddon collection also includes papers of several anthropologists who had dealings with A.C. Haddon, as follows:

• James Hornell (1865-1949) worked as marine biologist to the Government of Ceylon, 1902-1906, and Director of the Fisheries Department for the Government of Madras. After retirement in 1924, he accompanied the St. George Expedition to the Pacific as ethnographer. He collaborated with Haddon in writing *Canoes of Oceania* (Honolulu: 1936) (= *Bernice Pauahi Bishop Museum, Honolulu. Special Publication*, 27-29), 3 v.

Journals, correspondence, fieldnotes: nos. 10001-10085.

• Northcote Whitridge Thomas (1868-1936) graduated from Trinity College, Cambridge in 1890, published anthropological studies relating to Orkney, Australia, Nigeria and Sierra Leone.

Fieldnotes, drawings, typescripts for books, relating to Edo-speaking peoples, Bantu languages and Igbo language: nos. 11001-11071.

• William Halse Rivers (1864-1922) qualified as a doctor in 1888. In 1893 W.H.R. Rivers went to Cambridge to lecture on psychology, and in 1898 took part in the Cambridge Anthropological Expedition to the Torres Straits. In 1908 he made an expedition to Melanesia, followed by a second visit in 1914.

Notes, correspondence, publications: nos. 12000-12086.

• Arthur Bernard Deacon (1903-1927) studied Natural Sciences at Cambridge and came under the influence of Haddon, who encouraged him to take up anthropology. He did extensive work on Malekula in 1926 and died there of blackwater fever. His notes were edited and published posthumously in 1934.

Notes, correspondence: nos. 16000-16015.

It may be noted that a good deal of the Haddon collection has been microfilmed by the Australian Joint Copying Project—that is, material relating to Australia, New Guinea, Torres Straits, Oceania, etc. Microfilms are available for consultation at the National Library of Australia and at some other major libraries in Australia.

• G.K. Roth papers (reference: Add. MS 8780).

George Kingsley Roth (1903-1960) was an anthropologist and administrator in Fiji in the 1920s and 1930s. He was Secretary for Fijian Affairs, 1954-1957, and wrote *Fijian Way of Life* (Melbourne: 1953). The papers (11 boxes, 1928-1957) consist of notes, correspondence and photographs on Fijian affairs, culture, history, sociology and administration. They include papers of Adolf B. Brewster (1854-1937), a member of the Fijian Colonial Service and author of *The Hill Tribes of Fiji: A Record of Forty Years' Intimate Connection With the Tribes* (Philadelphia: 1922), on the history of Fiji and other Pacific Islands, ca. 1870-1930. These papers have also been microfilmed for the Australian Joint Copying Project.

- Meyer Fortes papers (reference: Add. MS 8405).

Meyer Fortes (1906-1983), born in South Africa, held various academic posts in the Universities of London, Oxford and Birmingham, including two years as Head of the Sociological Department, West African Institute, Accra, Gold Coast (Ghana), 1944-1946. He did field research in the Gold Coast, Nigeria and Bechuanaland. He was Professor of Social Anthropology in the University of Cambridge, 1950-1973. His working papers, fieldnotes, correspondence, etc. (31 boxes and ca. 150 notebooks) are being sorted at present and access to them is restricted.

- J.C. Trevor papers (reference: Trevor).

Jack Carrick Trevor (1907-1967) was educated at Oxford University and was Assistant Inspector of Police, Dar es Salaam, Tanzania, 1929-1931. He then pursued an academic career and was University Lecturer in Archaeology and Anthropology in the University of Cambridge from 1938 until his death, with a break for war service in East Africa. His papers (24 boxes) are in rough order only and not listed. They include research material in British prehistory and on the West Indies, especially the Virgin Islands.

University Archives:

Records of the General Board: subsection, records of Boards of Studies, Faculties etc.:

- Anthropology: registry file, 1903-1927 (ref. CUR.130); minutes of Board of Anthropological Studies, 1915-1926 (ref. Min.V.92).

- Archaeology and Anthropology: reports of the Board, 1910-1924 (ref.: CUR.63.1); minutes of Faculty Board and associated committees from 1926 (ref.: Min.V.92a-101), restricted access to later material.

Kathleen Cann

University of Cambridge. Centre of African Studies. Library

Address: African Studies Centre Library, University of Cambridge, Free School Lane, Cambridge CB2 3RQ, United Kingdom.
Tel.: +44 (1223) 334396 [Within the U.K.: (01223) 334396].
Fax: +44 (1223) 334396 [Within the U.K.: (01223) 334396].
Internet address: http://www-library.african.cam.ac.uk.

University of Cambridge. Centre of South Asian Studies. Library

Address: Library, Centre of South Asian Studies, University of Cambridge, Laundress Lane, Cambridge CB2 1SD, United Kingdom.
Tel.: +44 (01223) 338094
Fax: +44 (01223) 316913
Internet address: http://www.s-asian.cam.ac.uk/s_asian/web2.htm.
Founded: 1966 (beginning of the Cambridge South Asian Archive).
Major resources: Cambridge South Asian Archive.
Areas of specialization: South Asia (British period).
Archival/manuscript resources: Extensive manuscript holdings.
Visual/audio resources: Photographs, films, maps.

University of Cambridge. Museum of Archaeology and Anthropology

Address: Museum of Archaeology and Anthropology, University of Cambridge, Downing Street, Cambridge CB2 3DZ, United Kingdom.
Tel.: +44 (1223) 333516 [Within the U.K.: (01223) 333516] (Museum).
Tel.: +44 (01223) 333505 (Haddon Library)
Fax: +44 (1223) 333503 [Within the U.K.: (01223) 333503] (Museum).
Fax: +44 (01223) 333503 (Haddon Library)
Founded: 1884 (Museum); 1936 (Haddon Library).
Major resources: Museum collections and associated documentation relating to prehistoric archaeology and anthropology of all parts of the world; Haddon Library.
Areas of specialization (Haddon Library): Books and library materials received as gifts or bequests from Alfred Court Haddon, Sir James George Frazer and others.
Archives/manuscripts: Papers of Alfred Court Haddon and other scholars and specialists in anthropology are housed in the Cambridge University Library [see the entry on the Haddon and other papers in the Cambridge University Library by Kathleen Cann].
Reference: J.D. Pickles, "The Haddon Library, Cambridge," *Library History*, vol. 8, no. 1 (1988), p. 1-9.—provides an account of the accumulation of library materials in anthropology at the University of Cambridge prior to 1936.
Access: Exhibition galleries are open daily. Access to research collections is by prior written appointment.

University of Cambridge. Scott Polar Research Institute (SPRI). **Library and Archives**

Address: Library and Archives, Scott Polar Research Institute, University of Cambridge, Lensfield Road., Cambridge CB2 1ER, United Kingdom.
Tel.: +44 (1223) 336540. [Within the U.K.: (01223) 336540.]
Fax: +44 (1223) 336549. [Within the U.K.: (01223) 336549.]
E-mail (library): wjm13@cam.ac.uk.
Internet address: http://www.spri.cam.ac.uk/lib/libhome.htm.
Internet access to on-line catalog: No Internet access to the catalog is available. The on-line catalog is SPRILIB; since 1985 all library catalog records have been entered into SPRILIB, an in-house library database. The Museum and Archives have manual catalog systems.
Founded: 1920.
Major resources: Library and Archives collections on the polar regions.
Areas of specialization: Arctic and Antarctic regions.
Archives/manuscripts: 200 meters.
Holdings (books and journals): Ca. 30,000 v.; also a large pamphlet collection.
Visual/audio resources: The Institute's museum has a collection of prints, drawings, photographs, lantern slides and daguerreotypes of both polar regions. Early Sami and Inuit visual materials are of ethnographic interest.
Access: Readers, including scholars from overseas, are welcome to visit the Library and the Archives. For a brief visit to the Library, simply write to the Librarian, advising of your planned arrival date and intended length of stay. Scholars wishing to make use of the Archives should first make an appointment with the Archivist. Archival material is not made available for use outside the Institute.
References: Alan Cooke and Clive Holland, *The Exploration of Northern Canada, 500 to 1920: A Chronology* (Toronto: 1978); Clive Holland, *Arctic Exploration and Development, c. 500 B.C. to 1915: An Encyclopedia* (New York: 1994) (= *Garland Reference Library in the Humanities*, vol. 930).
Guides/catalogs: Clive Holland, *Manuscripts in the Scott Polar Research Institute, Cambridge, England* (London: 1982). Supplementary indices are available for manuscript materials received subsequently. Catalog records of holdings at the Scott Polar Research Institute Library are included in the *Arctic and Antarctic Regions* CD-ROM.
Artifacts of anthropological importance: Sami and Inuit artifacts.
Catalog of artifact resources: The museum catalog is not published, but is available to visitors by appointment.

Information provided by Scott Polar Research Institute Library and Archives.

United Kingdom—Durham

University of Durham. Library. Sudan Archive

Address: Sudan Archive, University Library, University of Durham, Stockton Road, Durham DH1 3LY, United Kingdom.

Tel.: +44 (091) 3743018
Fax: +44 (091) 3747481
Founded: 1957.
Major resources: Official and personal papers, maps, photographs and artifacts.
Areas of specialization: Sudan
Visual/audio resources: Photographs from the Sudan taken between 1899 and 1955.
References: Lesley E. Forbes, "African Photographic Resources in the Sudan Archive of the University of Durham," in Andrew Roberts (editor), *Photographs as Sources for African History* (London: 1988), p. 87-95.
Guides/catalogs: M.W. Daly and Lesley E. Forbes, *The Sudan: Photographs from the Sudan Archive, Durham University Library* (Reading: 1994) (= *Caught in Time*); Gillian Grant, *Middle Eastern Photographic Collections in the United Kingdom* (Durham: 1989) (= *Middle East Libraries Committee. Research Guides*, vol. 3), p. 53-58.

United Kingdom—Hull

University of Hull. Brynmor Jones Library. South-East Asia Collection

Address: South-East Asia Collection, Brynmor Jones Library, University of Hull, Hull HU6 7RX, United Kingdom.
Tel.: +44 (1482) 465269
Fax: +44 (1482) 466205
Networks, consortia: Member of JANET (Joint Academic Network).
Internet address: http://www.hull.ac.uk/lib.
Internet access to on-line catalog: http://library.hull.ac.uk. Web access is available to virtually all catalog records and to HUMAD (Hull University Manuscripts and Archives Database), an on-line guide to the archive collections.
Founded: 1928 (the University Library).
Major resources: South-East Asia Collection; University Archives.
Areas of specialization: Material on Southeast Asia, predominantly in the social sciences and humanities.
Manuscripts, papers, etc. (in Archives): 16 meters.
Fieldnotes: M.A. Jaspan (1926-1975): Indonesia, 1955-1966 (notably on the Rejang of southwest Sumatra), 1961-1964, Cambodia, 1966-1969 (mostly on the Cham) and the Igorot of northern Luzon, Philippines, 1974; R.A. Bruton (1936-1993): Sarawak, 1973-1976.
Holdings (books and journals): 36,000 v.
Visual/audio resources: Audio tapes and photographs on Sumatra and Cambodia (Edê, Cham), pre-1970, are in the Jaspan collection, Centre for South-East Asian Studies; photographs of Sumatra, Malaya, Singapore, Cambodia (Cham) and the Philippines (Igorot) in the Brynmor Jones Library.
Access: Open to scholars by appointment. The library is also open to all members of British universities during vacations. The Archives Section is open to general readers by appointment.

411

Guides/catalogs: Geoffrey Marrison, *A Catalogue of the Collections of Dr. Roy Bruton on Sarawak, Malaysia and on the Sociology of Education* (Hull: 1995) (= *University of Hull. Centre for South-East Asian Studies. Bibliography and Literature Series. Paper*, no. 13); Geoffrey Marrison, *A Catalogue of the Collections of the Rev. Dr. Harry Parkin on Asian Religions and Batak Studies in the Brynmor Jones Library* (Hull: 1993) (= *University of Hull. Centre for South-East Asian Studies. Bibliography and Literature Series. Paper*, no. 11); Geoffrey Marrison, *A Catalogue of the South-East Asian Collections of Professor M.A. Jaspan in the Brynmor Jones Library, University of Hull* (Hull: 1989) (= *University of Hull. Centre for South-East Asian Studies. Bibliography and Literature Series. Paper*, no. 6); Geoffrey Marrison, *A Catalogue of the South-East Asian History Collection of Dr. D.K. Bassett in the Brynmor Jones Library in the University of Hull* (Hull: 1992) (= *University of Hull. Centre for South-East Asian Studies. Bibliography and Literature Series. Paper*, no. 9); University of Hull. Brynmor Jones Library, *South-East Asian Studies* (new ed., Hull: 1997).

Artifacts: In the University of Hull Collection of South-East Asian Art and Traditional Craftsmanship are some 3,000 items of ethnographic interest from Southeast Asia, largely collected since 1968, and used mainly for teaching. Strengths are in textiles, costumes, basketry and souvenirs, but there is a broad coverage of all aspects of culture. Also held are slides and photographs, postage stamps and currency. Important ethnographic collections: Robert Cooper (Hmong and other hill peoples of northern Thailand, 1975—costume and domestic artifacts); M.A. Jaspan (Southeast Asia, 1955-1974—general); Philla Davis (Indonesia, 1970s-1980s—basketry and weaving); Ifor Ball Powell (Philippines, 1928-1929—general); Dartington Hall (Java and Bali, 1930s-1970s—textiles, costumes and woodcarvings).

Guides to the artifact collections: Lewis Hill, *Guide to the University of Hull Collection of South-East Asian Art and Traditional Craftsmanship* (Hull: 1997); Michael Hitchcock's *Indonesian Textiles* (London: 1992) has illustrations of many of the textiles from maritime Southeast Asia; Fiona Kerlogue, *Scattered Flowers: Textiles from Jambi, Sumatra* (Hull: 1996).

Description

The University of Hull has had a special interest in Southeast Asia since 1962, when a Centre for South-East Asian Studies was set up following the recommendations of the Hayter Report—the report of a Subcommittee on Oriental, Slavonic, East European and African Studies of the University Grants Committee (the body responsible at that time for the funding of British universities) that advocated the setting up of centers for area studies to specialize in modern studies such as anthropology, economics, history and politics. The extent of the area studied at Hull has an ethnographic basis, covering peoples of Southeast Asian origin from Assam to the Philippines and from southern China to Indonesia.

Research materials in the university can be divided into three categories: library materials in the Brynmor Jones Library; archival materials in the University Archives (also housed in the Brynmor Jones Library); and artifacts in the Collection of South-East Asian Art and Traditional Craftsmanship (housed in the Centre for South-East Asian Studies).

The library collection originates in the foundation of the Centre in 1962. The Librarian, the late Philip Larkin, was involved in the project from its earliest stages, and the library began to purchase material with the dual aim of supporting the teaching and research needs of the Centre and building up a sound general collection on Southeast Asia. Much of the early work was done by Brenda Moon, Chief Cataloguer and later Deputy Librarian, who also compiled a number of reference works important for Southeast Asian librarianship in Britain, and played a leading part in the foundation of the South-East Asia Library Group in 1968. To publicize the resources of the library, she initiated in 1968 the compilation of a list of *Recent Accessions in the Field of South-East Asian Studies* which continues to be distributed to interested institutions and scholars throughout the world.

A great impetus in the growth of the collection came with the arrival of Mervyn A. Jaspan in 1968 as Director of the Centre and Professor of South-East Asian Sociology. Jaspan took a keen interest in the library and embarked on a vigorous acquisition policy, donating many books and a number of manuscripts and obtaining others during visits to Southeast Asia. When the library moved into a new building in 1969, Southeast Asian material—hitherto scattered throughout the library—was collected and relocated in a South-East Asia Collection, and in 1972 Helen Cordell was appointed the first in a succession of South-East Asia Librarians. Some impetus was lost after the death of M.A. Jaspan in 1975, but further encouragement came from a new government report, *Speaking for the Future: A Review of the Requirements of Diplomacy and Commerce for Asian and African Languages and Area Studies*, compiled by Sir Peter Parker in 1986. V.T. King was appointed to a new chair of South-East Asian Studies, and additional library funding was made available for the growth of the collection. The library now possesses the best consolidated collection on Southeast Asian studies in Britain outside London.

The Brynmor Jones Library uses the Library of Congress classification. All material in the South-East Asia Collection is classified by this scheme, but has superimposed on it a primary classification by area, creating shelving sequences for reference and general material and for individual countries and regions.

Holdings on Malaysia and Indonesia are particularly strong, while the already substantial collection on Thailand is likely to grow considerably in the near future owing to increased study and research in this area. As a major aim of the collection has been to satisfy the needs of undergraduates, the bulk of acquisitions are of English-language material, but there are also large holdings in Dutch, French, German, Indonesian, Malay and other European and Asian languages. Types of material extend from expedition reports, mostly of the nineteenth- and twentieth-centuries, but including volumes of the German edition of *India Orientalis* (1597-1600) and Jacob Jansz de Roy's *Hachelijke reys-togt na Borneo en Atchin* (1706) and collections of documents such as the VOC *Dagh-register 1624-1682* (1887-1931), to current statistical and census information. There are also strengths in a variety of topics such as peripheral and minority peoples, tourism, environmental problems, Krakatau and Indonesian novels. About 220 periodicals are received currently, including *Journal of the Malaysian Branch of the Royal Asiatic Society*, *Brunei Museum Journal* and *Sarawak Museum Journal*. There are back runs of these and many others.

Fine collections were bequeathed to the library by M.A. Jaspan and David Bassett, successive directors of the Centre for South-East Asian Studies. The British Association of Malaysia and Singapore presented a collection of books on permanent loan in 1971 and offered most of the rest of its library to Hull when it ceased to exist in 1973. The library has also received materials from the library of the Indian High Commission in London, from the Foreign and Commonwealth Office, from the British Institute in South-East Asia and from the collections of Christiaan Hooykaas, Alfred Wynne of the Malaya Drainage and Irrigation Department, Ronald Stead, former *Christian Science Monitor* reporter in Southeast Asia and Rev. Harry Parkin, former Director of Religious Studies at Trinity Theological College, Singapore.

The growth of the collection of printed materials in the library has been accompanied by the receipt of a number of important deposits in the University Archives. The Jaspan (Indonesia, Cambodia, Philippines), Bassett (East India Company), Parkin (Sumatra) and Bruton (Sarawak) papers all have printed catalogs [see above]. There is also a small collection of original manuscripts that includes Batak bark books and Rejang Ka-Ga-Nga texts from Sumatra, Indonesia; bamboo texts from Palawan Island, Philippines; and Burmese palm leaf texts. Major manuscript deposits with significant sections relating to Southeast Asia include papers of F.W. Dalley (Malaya, Singapore), Commander E.P. Young (Indonesia), the National Council for Civil Liberties (Malaya, Sarawak, Singapore) and the Union of Democratic Control (Malaya, Indonesia, Philippines).

Margaret Nicholson and Lewis Hill

United Kingdom—London (Greater)

British Library (BL)

Address: British Library, 96 Euston Road, St. Pancras, London, NW1 2DB, United Kingdom.
Tel.: +44 (0171) 4127677 (British Library); +44 (0171) 4127516 (Department of Western Manuscripts); +44 (0171) 4127288 (Science Reference and Information Service); +44 (0171) 412 7873 (Oriental and India Office Collections); +44 (0171) 412 7427 (International Music Collection).
Fax: +44 (0171) 4127736 (British Library); +44 (0171) 4127745 (Department of Western Manuscripts); +44 (0171) 412 7217 (Science Reference and Information Service); +44 (0171) 4127858 (Oriental and India Office Collections); +44 (0171) 4127416 (International Music Collection).
Internet address: http://portico.bl.uk.
Networks, consortia: RLIN.
Public transit access: Underground (to St. Pancras): King's Cross; (to Great Russell Street area): Tottenham Court Road, Russell Square or Holborn. Buses (to St. Pancras): 10, 73, C12, etc.; (to Great Russell St. area): 7, 8, 10, 19, 24, 25, 29, 38, 55, 68, 73, 91, 98, 134 and 188.
Founded: 1753 (British Museum Library); 1759 (opened to the public); 1973 (British Library).
Major resources: Material of importance to anthropology is diffused through the general printed collections and the Manuscripts Department. Among units of the library of

significance for anthropology are Humanities and Social Sciences (St. Pancras); Western Manuscripts; Oriental Manuscripts; Science Reference and Information Service; International Music Collection (St. Pancras); and Document Supply Centre (at Boston Spa in Yorkshire).

Archives/manuscripts: Among manuscript collections are letters to Sir Edward B. Tylor (1832-1917) and also notebooks of Sir James G. Frazer (1854-1941).

Fieldnotes: Not held.

Holdings (books and periodicals): It is not possible to quantify holdings pertaining to anthropology. British Library holdings as a whole are estimated to consist of some 150 million separate items that are in every format from papyrus to CD-ROM, in every known written language.

Visual/audio resources: [See the following entry for the British Library National Sound Archive (NSA). The BL Oriental and India Office Collections holds several important collections of early drawings and prints from Indonesia, India and other Asian regions—see the entry on the BL Oriental and India Office Collections, below.]

Access: The collections are open to all those not able to find what they require elsewhere.

References: B.C. Bloomfield (editor), *A Directory of Rare Book and Special Collections in the United Kingdom and the Republic of Ireland* (2nd ed., London: 1997), p. 132-179; P.R. Harris, *A History of the British Museum Library, 1753-1973* (London: 1998).

Guides/catalogs: *The British Library General Catalogue of Printed Books to 1975* (London: 1979-1992), 366 v. This catalog is also available in machine-readable form on CD-ROM, published by Chadwyck-Healey; *Subject Index of the Modern Books Added to the Library of the British Museum in the years 1881-1900* [-1985] (London: 1902-[1986]), 60 v.; *The British Museum Catalogue of Printed Maps, Charts, and Plans ... to 1964* (London: 1967); also the ten year supplement, 1965-1974 (London: 1977).

"Department of Western Manuscripts," in J.D. Pearson (compiler), *A Guide to Manuscripts and Documents in the British Isles Relating to South and South-East Asia* (London: 1989), vol. 1, p. 72-106. For information on BL manuscript and archival materials concerning East Africa, see Anne Thurston, *Guide to Archives and Manuscripts Relating to Kenya and East Africa in the United Kingdom*, vol. 2: *Non-Official Archives and Manuscripts* (London: 1991), p. 625-643.

Description

The British Library was founded in 1973 by bringing together a number of older institutions. The most important of these from the point of view of anthropology were perhaps the former library departments of the British Museum. Also of importance are the Document Supply Centre, located at Boston Spa in Yorkshire, with its very large collections, especially of periodicals, used for lending to other libraries from all over the world and for photocopies; and the former India Office Library, now part of the Oriental and India Office Collections.

The British Museum was founded following the holding of a lottery in 1753. The occasion of this was that the collections, both of books and objects in the collections of Sir Hans Sloane (1660-1753), had been offered on his death for purchase by the nation. Sir

Hans's collections were universal in scope. He was a physician and had spent time in Jamaica and elsewhere, and some of his collection were the first nucleus of the ethnographic collections of the British Museum. Similarly, some of his books began the anthropological collections of the library departments that later became part of the British Library. But his books form a relatively small part of the library as a whole that now contains perhaps eleven million volumes, with very large collections on all subjects and in most languages that have been committed to writing. Since Sloane's time the library has absorbed numerous other libraries, including two royal libraries, both the old Royal Library of the Kings of England and the library built up by George III. A collection of particular anthropological interest is the library of Sir Joseph Banks (1743-1820). But these already formed collections are, as it were, swallowed up by 240 years of books received by the legal deposit privilege and purchased from all over the world. It is not possible to single out particular collections and items in the general collections of anthropological interest, but they contain rich stores of anthropological information in the form of books and periodicals making contributions to anthropology and also in the many other types of material, for example, accounts of travels or official publications of colonies, providing evidence about cultures throughout the world.

Sources on Anthropology in the Western Manuscripts Collections

This department does not hold rich collections on the modern discipline of anthropology, though it does contain much material of broad relevance to the field as a whole. The resources of the department can be summarized as follows:

Sources on the "pre-history" of modern anthropology are to be found in our large holdings of the papers of Sir Joseph Banks, Bart., President of the Royal Society; the papers of the circumnavigator Captain James Cook; and in the many political and family archives of British nationals who spent all or part of their careers governing India in the nineteenth-century.

Among holdings of late nineteenth- and early twentieth-century papers are the archives of intellectuals whose circles included many academic anthropologists. Thus papers of the naturalists John Lubbock, 1st Baron Avebury (1834-1913); Alfred Russell Wallace (1823-1913); the sociologist Havelock Ellis (1859-1939); and the birth control pioneer Marie Stopes (1880-1958) contain very small sequences of correspondence with, among others, Sir James Frazer, Ernest Westermarck, Lorimer Fison (1832-1907) and Bronislaw Malinowski (1884-1942). The most substantial holdings of anthropologists' papers include a volume of letters written between 1861 and 1906 to Sir Edward B. Tylor, Professor of Anthropology at the University of Oxford (Add. MS. 50254); notebooks of Sir James George Frazer, described in the catalogue as "anthropological extracts and notes, mainly from printed sources" (Add MSS. 45442-45496); and correspondence of the publishers Macmillan & Co. with anthropological authors. The latter are Sir James George Frazer (Add. MSS. 55134-55155); Ernest Westermarck (Add. MS. 55156); Charles Hose (Add. MS. 55157); Sir Baldwin Spencer and Alfred Court Haddon (Add. MS. 55158).

The principal finding aids through which modern historical materials in the Western Manuscripts collections can be located are the *Catalogues of Additions to the Manuscripts in the British Library* (formerly British Museum), published quinquennially, in which collections are listed by incorporation number and indexed by place, personal or institutional name, as appropriate. Subject indexing—somewhat restricted in scope in the published indexes—is being extended with the creation of a machine-readable database on which all post-1956 acquisitions are now being cataloged.

Some Other British Library Collections of Anthropological Significance.

The library's reference collections on physical anthropology are housed in the Aldwych Reading Room of the Science Reference and Information Service, located at 9 Kean Street, London, WC2B 4AT. [Tel.: +44 (0171) 4127288; fax: +44 (0171) 4127217; Underground: Chancery Lane; buses: 8, 17, 22b, 25, 45, 46, 171a, 221, 243, 259, 501, 521.] [Information on the manuscript and other resources of the Oriental and India Office Collections and also the International Music Collection (National Sound Archive) is provided separately, below.]

St. Pancras

The British Library is in process of moving to its new headquarters building near the St. Pancras Rail Station. The St. Pancras building first opened in 1997. When this move has been completed, the OPAC will be linked to an automated requesting system and a mechanical bookhandling system that will allow 90 percent of reader requests to be delivered within thirty minutes.

The British Museum

The British Museum, from which the British Library is now administratively distinct, has large anthropological collections currently housed at the Museum of Mankind [described separately, below].

David Jervis (Humanities and Social Sciences) and Anne Summers (Western Manuscripts Collections).

British Library. National Sound Archive (NSA). **International Music Collection** (IMC)

Address: International Music Collection, British Library National Sound Archive, 96 Euston Road, St. Pancras, London, NW1 2DB, United Kingdom.
Tel.: +44 (0171) 4127440 (General); +44 (0171) 4127427 (International Music Collection).
Fax: +44 (0171) 4127441
E-mail (IMC): Janet.Topp-Fargion@bl.uk; Marie-Laure.Manigand@bl.uk.
E-mail (NSA): NSA@bl.uk.
Internet address: http://portico.bl.uk/nsa/imc.html.
Public transit access: Underground: King's Cross. Buses: 10, 73, C12, etc.
Founded: 1955 (as the British Institute of Recorded Sound); became the National Sound Archive on joining the British Library in 1983.

Areas of specialization: Ethnomusicology. Strong holdings in African music, in particular from West Africa, and in South Asian music.

Holdings (books and periodicals): Approximately 750 books, including classic works in ethnomusicology and contemporary writings about traditional and popular musical styles. About sixty different journals are held—e.g., *African Music*, *British Journal of Ethnomusicology*, *English Dance and Song*, *Ethnomusicology*, *Folk Roots*, *Latin American Music Review*, *The World of Music*, *Yearbook for Traditional Music*.

Visual/audio resources: The IMC collection consists mainly of audio and (some) video recordings (in total about 100,000 items) of traditional or traditionally-based music from around the world.

Access: All materials may be consulted on the premises (without charge) by members of the public. Provision of audio material for other use is subject to copyright clearance and the payment of a transcription fee.

Description

While sound recording came into existence more than a century ago, it was only in 1955 that a national collection of recordings, the British Institute of Recorded Sound (BIRS), was established in the United Kingdom. In 1983 it became a nationally-funded department of the British Library under its current name, the National Sound Archive (NSA)—now considered one of the largest and most diverse sound archives in the world.

From the early days of the BIRS, its founder, Patrick Saul, showed a strong interest in collecting material of ethnomusicological importance and sought advice from some of the most respected ethnomusicologists of the time about the best way to pursue this project. His initial efforts were continued and greatly developed when he appointed the ethnomusicologists Alistair Dick and Lucy Durán, who successively ran the department of ethnomusicology, the first specialist area to be established at the NSA. It was under Lucy Durán's appointment, which lasted more than fifteen years, that the department assumed its present form and name, the International Music Collection (IMC). Having traveled extensively to West Africa and having studied the music of that region, Lucy Durán greatly developed this part of the collection and, to a large extent, introduced this music to the British public.

The department is presently staffed by the curator, Janet Topp Fargion, whose primary research areas include South Africa and the Swahili coast in East Africa (particularly Zanzibar) and by the assistant-curator, Marie-Laure Manigand.

Scope of the IMC Collection

The IMC is the Archive's special collection of recordings of music variously described as traditional, ethnic, folk or, more recently, "world music". It encompasses most musical traditions worldwide, from the infancy of recording technology (the collection includes the earliest British field recordings made on cylinders in the Torres Straits in 1898) to the present day. It covers thousands of different styles and genres: art music traditions, music of most of the world's major religions, work songs, wedding and funeral music, unaccompanied songs and instrumental music, as well as popular styles based on folk traditions. Its holdings consist of approximately 100,000 items—most of them kept in their original formats.

The aim of the IMC is to collect, preserve and make accessible for research and for pleasure a comprehensive cross-section of musics which it may not otherwise be possible to hear in the United Kingdom and, in some cases, anywhere in the world. Its richness in terms of variety, quantity and rarity makes it a unique research source and the largest public access collection of this kind in Western Europe. It is an essential reference collection for students and scholars of ethnomusicology and anthropology, for the media, for musicians of all backgrounds, or for anyone interested in listening to and learning about the wealth of folk music from around the world.

IMC Activities

The IMC's activities are divided between three main areas: acquisition of sound recordings and related printed material; processing and preservation of the recordings; and "promotion" of the collection.

Acquisition of Sound Recordings

The IMC receives by donation most of the output from British companies and purchases much of its European and U.S.-produced material through British distributors. A great emphasis is put on acquiring complete series published on specialist labels (such as Smithsonian-Folkways, Library of Congress, International Library of African Music, Topic, Ocora, etc.). The IMC also purchases small representative collections from overseas —including rare cassettes only published in the country of origin. It also relies greatly on donations from private collectors.

In addition, a large part of its acquisition effort is centered around the acquisition of original field recordings (i.e., unpublished recordings made privately by individuals, usually in the context of some ethnomusicological or anthropological work). A deposit system has been devised to that effect, enabling the rights over the recordings to be protected. This policy, and emphasis on unpublished recordings, has facilitated the acquisition of some of the most important collections in the field of ethnomusicology—e.g., Klaus Wachsmann (Uganda), Brian Moser and Donald Taylor (Columbia), Ewan MacColl and Peggy Seeger (U.K./Ireland), Albert Lloyd (Eastern Europe), Jean Jenkins (Africa and Muslim communities). These currently add up to more than 200 collections. The IMC particularly encourages deposits of original material, by giving support to individuals recording in the field in the form of equipment and tape loans.

In the United Kingdom, the IMC is also in constant contact with concert and festival organizers, who frequently allow us to make our own recordings of performances given by visiting musicians.

Processing and Preservation

This area of work ranges from accessioning and cataloging each recorded item in the collection, to conservation tasks requiring skilled technical work. Because of the degree of expertise required, cataloging is almost entirely carried out by the department, with an occasional input by the NSA's small unit of qualified catalogers. In some cases, external help is sought from experts in specific areas of ethnomusicology. In the past, catalogs dealing with ethnomusicological material were compiled on diverse formats—e.g., index cards, various data systems. Since 1995 IMC has started to catalog its new acquisitions and part of its previous holdings onto a new automated and unified system (CADENSA). The first fully cataloged materials made accessible to the public on this system were our collections of early ethnographic recordings on wax cylinders (some 3,200 products).

The recordings collected by the IMC come under a great variety of formats: cylinders, discs, wires, tapes and videos. Whenever possible, the original carriers are kept, and their life prolonged by storing them in an adequate environment. However, many collections need to be copied onto a more reliable support. This work is mainly carried out by the technical staff, and the IMC's involvement is limited to the identification of material in need of attention.

Promotion of the IMC Collection

The IMC has always been committed to making its material accessible to a wide public. A first level of access is provided on the premises, where the collection is available for listening. The NSA operates a reference library and listening service free of charge or membership constraint. In addition, the IMC is extensively involved in researching and providing musical samples for public use by external bodies, usually of a commercial or educational nature. The collection is often used as a source for film and theater productions, for museums in need of a musical background to their displays, for schools where non-Western music is part of their National Curriculum and, finally, for the researcher in ethnomusicology and anthropology.

A last level of promotional activity is provided by the IMC's own initiative to "publicize" the collection. This involves using the already existing channels to increase public awareness of its material. In particular, the IMC has been involved in a number of audio publications—e.g., two publications in collaboration with Rogue Records: *BA Togoma—Manding Music from Mali*, featuring kora master Sidiki Diabaté and his ensemble; *Music of the Tukano and Cuna People of Columbia*, consisting of field recordings made by Brian Moser and Donald Taylor in 1961. Both publications are still available for purchase from the NSA. Broadcasting on a national (BBC radio) and local (London Jazz FM) scale has also been an important medium for promoting the collection in recent years. The IMC also publishes a free quarterly newsletter (*International Music Connection*), available by postal mailing or on the IMC Web page.

Marie-Laure Manigand

British Library. Oriental and India Office Collections (OIOC)

Address: Oriental and India Office Collections, British Library, Orbit House, 197 Blackfriars Road, London SE1 8NG, United Kingdom.
Tel.: +44 (0171) 4127873
Fax: +44 (0171) 4127641
E-mail: oioc-enquiries@bl.uk.
Internet address: http://www.bl.uk.
Public transit access: Underground: Waterloo or Blackfriars; buses: 45, 59, 63, 149 172 and P11.
Founded: 1753 (British Museum); 1801 (India Office Library). The Oriental and India Office Collections were formed in 1991, incorporating materials from the former British Museum Department of Oriental Manuscripts and Printed Books (established in 1892) and the India Office Library and Records.
Major resources: Books and manuscripts in Oriental and Western languages, private papers, serials, newspapers, prints, drawings, maps, photographs, official publications.
Areas of specialization: Asia and the Middle-East, including India, Pakistan, Burma (Myanmar), Bangladesh, Iran and the Gulf States, North Africa, Malaysia, Singapore, China and Japan.
Archives/manuscripts: Ca. 45,000 Asian and Middle-Eastern manuscripts; the Archives of the East India Company (1600-1858); the India Office records. Holdings also include extensive collections of private papers—e.g., Colonel Colin Mackenzie (1753[?]-1821) manuscripts, Sir Thomas Stamford Raffles (1781-1826) papers, many others.
Holdings (books): Ca. 650,000 printed books in Asian, Middle-Eastern or Western languages—many published in Asia or North Africa.
Visual/audio resources: Numerous Islamic, Hebrew and Arabic illuminated manuscripts and texts; more than 250,000 photographs; many maps and drawings. Information on some printed guides to prints, drawings and photographs is available on the Web: ("Prints, Drawings and Photographs Section: Catalogues of and Guides to the Collections") at http://portico.bl.uk/oioc/prints/pdcats.html. Early prints of Indonesian and Malayan scenes are illustrated in John Bastin and Pauline Rohatgi's *Prints of Southeast Asia in the India Office Library: The East India Company in Malaysia and Indonesia, 1786-1824* (London: 1979). Information on the Archaeological Survey of India Photographs collection ("Prints, Drawings and Photographs Section: Archaeological Survey of India Photographs") is available at http://portico.bl.uk.oioc/prints/asipho.html. The Oral Archives collection includes, among others, recordings and transcripts of interviews of British residents of India during the first half of the twentieth-century.
Access: Open to the public. The Oriental and India Office Collections will be moved from Orbit House to the British Library St. Pancras building, 96 Euston Road, London NW1 2DB, beginning in 1998. Information on the relocation is available at http://portico.bl.uk/st-pancras/ news/moves/oioc.html.
References: B.C. Bloomfield (editor), *A Directory of Rare Book and Special Collections in the United Kingdom and the Republic of Ireland* (2nd ed., London: 1997), p. 170-177; Stephan Roman, *The Development of Islamic Library Collections in Western Europe and North America* (London: 1990) (= *Libraries and Librarianship in the Muslim World*), p. 7-

23; Geoffrey Roper (general editor), *World Survey of Islamic Manuscripts* (London: 1992-1994) (= *Al-Furqān Islamic Heritage Foundation. Publication*, no. 10), vol. 3, p. 471-490.
Guides/catalogs: Some printed OIOC pamphlets are available. Among published OIOC guides and lists are Mildred Archer, *British Drawings in the India Office Library* (London: 1969), 2 v., and a supplement by Patricia Kattenhorn (London: 1994); British Library, *Guide to the Department of Oriental Manuscripts and Printed Books* (London: 1976); Thaung Blackmore, *Catalogue of the Burney Parabaiks in the India Office Library* (London: 1985) (= *Oriental Documents*, vol. 7); Annabel Teh Gallop, *Early Views of Indonesia: Drawings from the British Library = Pemandangan Indonesia di Masa Lampau: Seni Gambar dari British Library* (Honolulu: 1995); Andrew Griffin, *A Brief Guide to Sources for the Study of Burma in the India Office Records* (London: 1979); Martin I. Moir, *A General Guide to the India Office Records* (London: 1988); Timothy N. Thomas, *Indians Overseas: A Guide to Source Materials in the India Office Records for the Study of Indian Emigration, 1830-1950* (London: 1985); various other published or unpublished guides and catalogs.

British Museum. Department of Ethnography. Library
(Museum of Mankind)

Address: Library, Department of Ethnography, British Museum, Museum of Mankind, 6 Burlington Gardens, London W1X 2EX, United Kingdom.
Tel.: +44 (0171) 3238031
Fax: +44 (0171) 3238013
Internet access to on-line catalog: No Internet access. The library is in process of change from BOOKSHELF.
Public transit access: Underground: Green Park or Piccadilly Circus. Buses: 3, 6, 9, 12, 13, 14, 15, 19, 22, 23, 38, 53, 88, 94, 139 and 159.
Founded: No precise date.
Major resources: Department of Ethnography Library.
Areas of specialization: All aspects of anthropology. Particular strengths are in Latin American and Eastern European archaeology and ethnography.
Archives/manuscripts: There are three different archival holdings within the museum: (1.) In the Ethnography Library is a small (about 15 meters) collection of manuscripts and typescripts including theses. (2.) The British Museum Central Archives includes administrative records of all gifts to the museum and of major purchases from 1756 onwards. (3.) Ethnography Department document holdings number about 1,400 items.
Holdings (books and journals): More than 110,000 volumes of books and about 1,000 current periodical titles.
Visual/audio resources: The photograph collection of the Department of Ethnography at present is not available for public reference.
Access: The library is available to ticket holders only. These are given to scholars and postgraduate students, with special privileges accorded to Fellows of the Royal Anthropological Institute. The British Museum Central Archives are available to the public on application. Department of Ethnography documents are available to the public only with permission of the Keeper of the Department. Note: at the end of 1997 the Museum of

Mankind was scheduled for closure in preparation for the relocation of the Department of Ethnography to the British Museum site in Bloomsbury.

References: B.C. Bloomfield (editor), *A Directory of Rare Book and Special Collections in the United Kingdom and the Republic of Ireland* (2nd ed., London: 1997), p. 182-183; Audrey Gregson, "The Ethnography Library," *British Museum Magazine*, no. 10 (Summer 1992), p. 22-23; Lucy Mair, "The R[oyal] A[nthropological] I[nstitute] Library," *Times Literary Supplement*, no. 3722 (July 6, 1973), p. 788; Janet Wallace, "The Central Archives of the British Museum," *Archives: The Journal of the British Records Association*, vol. 19, no. 84 (Oct. 1990), p. 213-223.

Guides/catalogs: British Museum. Department of Ethnography, *Guide to the Library* (London: 1995); British Museum. Museum of Mankind Library, *Museum of Mankind Library Catalogues* (Bath, U.K.: 1989), [763 microfiche].

Description

The British Museum Department of Ethnography Library is a major anthropological collection with its roots in the nineteenth-century. The library developed to support the museum's ethnic art collections and features many nineteenth-century travel books and exhibition and sales catalogues. When the department moved away from the main museum building (with its easy access to the British Library's collections) to its present location (the Museum of Mankind) in 1970, the growth of the library accelerated. In 1976 the important library of the Royal Anthropological Institute (RAI) was donated to the Museum Library, and the RAI continues to support the library with donations of books and periodicals.

The RAI Library began by combining the collections of the Ethnological Society (founded in 1843) and the Anthropological Society of London (founded in 1871). This became a rich resource, with gifts from the Society's Fellows and Members that included books and many offprints of articles. Unlike the Museum collection, physical anthropology was an important focus of RAI Library holdings. The RAI Library is particularly strong in its collection of periodicals—many acquired by exchange agreement—with a wide coverage of Eastern Europe.

The origins and historical background of the RAI Library have been described in some detail in an article by Lucy Mair, published in 1973 in the *Times Literary Supplement*.

Department of Ethnography Library holdings now consist of books (including many rare or uncommon imprints), pamphlets, periodicals, congress reports, newsletters, maps and microforms. The collection covers every aspect of anthropology: cultural anthropology (notably material culture and the arts), archaeology, some biological anthropology and linguistics, together with such related fields as history, sociology, description and travel. Geographically the collection's scope is world-wide, although it is particularly strong on the British Commonwealth, Eastern Europe and the Americas. Mesoamerica is well represented and the library holds the Sir John Eric Thompson (1898-1975) collection.

The archival resources are dispersed. The Central Archives of the British Museum holds the administrative reports (some with associated correspondence) of all gifts to, and purchases of, the Museum from its founding in 1756. These are public records—available to researchers by appointment. The Department of Ethnography has a Documents

Section—associated with its artifact collections—consisting of lists, notes, correspondence and sometimes photographs (the provenance notes are often by the donor of the items). These are available to researchers by permission of the Keeper of the Department.

The Royal Anthropological Institute retains its own archival and manuscript collections [see the separate entry for the Institute].

Since 1988 all current cataloging has been computerized and the catalogers are developing a subject thesaurus (including the names of ethnic groups) based on Library of Congress subject headings.

The old card catalog has subject access based on a modified form of the Bliss Classification. Entries from this catalog, as well as the pre-1976 card catalog of the Department of Ethnography Library, are in process of being entered and sometimes recataloged onto the computer catalog.

The bulk of the library is in stacks closed to readers. Access to the stock is through the catalogs in the Reading Room—which is small, holding a maximum of about twelve visitors. The Reading Room reference stock includes encyclopedias, bibliographies, newsletters, dictionaries and journal indexes. The *Anthropological Index*—compiled by the RAI from the journal holdings in the library—has its author card catalog in the Reading Room. This covers the years from 1963 to 1992, when this catalog was closed due to computerization.

The Library offers a photocopying service and has access to the Photography Department of the British Museum.

Anne Alexander

Horniman Museum

Address: Horniman Museum, 100 London Road, Forest Hill, London SE23 3PQ, United Kingdom.
Tel.: +44 (0181) 6991872
Fax: +44 (0181) 2915506
E-mail: enquiry@horniman.demon.co.uk.
Internet address: http://www.horniman.demon.co.uk.
Public transit access: Rail: Forest Hill (from London Bridge). Buses: 352, 122, 63, 176, 312, 185, P4, P13.
Founded: 1901. The museum was founded by London tea merchant Frederick John Horniman (1835-1906). Horniman's personal collection of anthropological objects and "curiosities" was first opened to the public at his home at Forest Hill, South London, in 1890. A Horniman Museum building was opened in 1897, and in 1901 the museum and collections were presented to the London County Council.
Major resources: The library holds about 35,000 vols. of books and journals in the fields of ethnography, natural history and related subjects.
Areas of specialization: Anthropology, ethnography, natural history, ethnomusicology.
Visual/audio resources: The Beryl de Zoete/Walter Spies photo archive (Bali, 1930s).
Access: The library is open to the public, without appointment, for reference use.

References: No detailed history of the museum has been published, although extracts from selected printed sources on Horniman family history and the origins of the museum are available from the library. Some additional information on the museum and library is in B.C. Bloomfield (editor), *A Directory of Rare Book and Special Collections in the United Kingdom and the Republic of Ireland* (2nd ed., London: 1997), p. 237. On the Beryl de Zoet/Walter Spies photo collection, see Michael Hitchcock and Lucy Norris, *Bali, the Imaginary Museum: The Photographs of Walter Spies and Beryl de Zoete* (Kuala Lumpur: 1995).

Information provided by the Horniman Museum.

Imperial War Museum (IWM)

Address: Imperial War Museum, Lambeth Road, London SE1 6HZ, United Kingdom.
Tel.: +44 (0171) 4165344 (Department of Printed Books); +44 (0171) 4165221 (Department of Documents); +44 (0171) 4165333 (Photograph Archive).
Fax: +44 (0171) 4165374 (Museum); +44 (0171) 4165379 (Photograph Archive).
Internet address: http://chide.bournemouth.ac.uk/information.office/imperial.war. museum.html
Public transit access: Underground: Lambeth North or Elephant and Castle. British Rail to Waterloo or Elephant and Castle. Buses: 3, 109, 159, 196, 344 and C10.
Founded: 1917 (founding of the Museum). The IWM has been located in the former Bethlem Royal Hospital since 1936.
Major resources: Department of Printed Books; Department of Documents; Department of Art; Sound Archive; Film and Video Archive; Photograph Archive.
Areas of specialization: The collections include historical documentation and photographs of armed conflict during World Wars I and II, with special emphasis on the geographic areas of the Commonwealth.
Archives/manuscripts: British private papers, foreign records.
Holdings (books and pamphlets): More than 100,000 book volumes; 25,000 pamphlets.
Visual/audio resources: The extensive IWM collection of photographs and films is in the Photograph Archive and the Film and Video Archive, both located near the museum at All Saints' Annexe.
Access: Open for research use by appointment only. The All Saints' Annexe building is located very near the IWM, at Austral Street, London SE11.
Guides/catalogs: Gillian Grant, *Middle Eastern Photographic Collections in the United Kingdom* (Durham: 1989) (= *Middle East Libraries Committee. Research Guides*, vol. 3), p. 103-106.

Description

The Imperial War Museum occupies the landmark building that for many years was the Bethlem Royal Hospital (commonly known as "Bedlam"). Documentation of possible anthropological interest may be found scattered among some of the IWM Library and Archives collections of books, documents and manuscripts on military and related subjects. The very extensive IWM photograph and film collections are potential sources for images of cultural, historical and anthropological interest.

Department of Printed Books

The museum's Department of Printed Books is a national reference library that holds books, pamphlets, periodicals and maps—primarily concerning the history of World Wars I and II and related military topics. Monographs acquired since 1984 (and many of the pre-1984 books) may now be accessed on the library's local on-line catalog.

Department of Documents

The most extensive groups of materials in the Department of Documents are the collections of British private papers and also the foreign records of warfare in the twentieth-century.

Photograph Archive

Nearly five million photographs are in the museum's Photograph Archives—located in the nearby All Saints' Annexe. About four million of these are official war photographs, and one million other images are donated war or related photographs. In addition, about eight million feet of film on wars and military topics are preserved in the Film and Video Archive. Access to individual photographs is by means of detailed index card files.

Information provided by the Imperial War Museum.

Natural History Museum (NHM)

Address: Natural History Museum, Cromwell Road, London SW7 5BD, United Kingdom.
Tel.: +44 (0171) 9389207 (Earth Sciences Library enquiries).
 +44 (0171) 9388979 (Earth Sciences Librarian).
 +44 (0171) 9389238 (Museum Archivist).
Fax: +44 (0171) 9389290 (Department of Library and Information Services).
E-mail: earthscilib@nhm.ac.uk (Earth Sciences Library).
 A.Lum@nhm.ac.uk (Earth Sciences Librarian).
 J.Thackray@nhm.ac.uk (Museum Archivist).
Internet address: http://www.nhm.ac.uk.
Public transit access: Underground: South Kensington (Piccadilly, District and Circle lines). Buses: 14, 45a, 49, 70, 74 and C1.
Founded: In 1753 as part of the British Museum at Bloomsbury. The Natural History collections moved to South Kensington in 1881. For a history of the museum to 1980, see

William T. Stearn, *The Natural History Museum at South Kensington*: *A History of the British Museum (Natural History), 1753-1980* (London: 1981).

Major anthropological resources in the museum: The Earth Sciences Library (Anthropology Library Collection); Museum Archives.

Areas of specialization: Palaeoanthropology, physical and biological anthropology, palaeopathology, history of anthropology.

Relevant holdings in anthropology: Books and journals: 3,500 monographic titles, 300 serial titles; manuscripts: ca. 20 collections. Collections also include prints, drawings and photographs; archives: 4 collections.

Access: The collections in the Library and Archives are available to all readers for consultation. Appointments made in advance are necessary. A Reader's Ticket can be obtained on proof of identity. Reading facilities and reprographic services (including self-service photocopying) are available.

References: Catalogs and guides to the Anthropology Library Manuscript and Drawings Collections are in preparation.

Description

Manuscripts in the Anthropology Library Collections:

(Shelf length: 10 meters.) Manuscript collections include:

• George Busk (1807-1887). 38 unpublished lithographic plates, representing types of human crania.
• William Henry Flower (1836-1899). Manuscript notes on racial types. 2 boxes.
• Kenneth Page Oakley (1911-1981). Scientific correspondence, 1969-1981.
• Joseph Sydney Weiner. Metrical data sheets: Swanscombe skull report. 1964. 2 boxes of charts and letters.
• Joseph Sydney Weiner. Piltdown papers. 10 boxes of letters, reprints and notes.
• George Williamson. Catalog of human crania formerly in the Army Medical Department. 5 v.
• Arthur Smith Woodward (1864-1944). Autobiographical notes (and including Lady Woodward's). 1 box.

Original Drawings in the Anthropology Library:

• Maurice Wilson (1914-1987). A collection of watercolor drawings of fossil hominids, ca. 1950-1987. These drawings were mostly commissioned by the museum for exhibition or for publication. A large number were published in Peter Andrews and Chris Stringer, *Human Evolution: An Illustrated Guide* (London, 1989).

Photographic Collection in the Anthropology Section, Department of Palaeontology.

The historical collection on Human Geographical Variation, 1860-1930. Contains more than 2,000 images.

Anthropological Papers in the Museum Archives:

1. Piltdown Man, 1912-1983. This class contains correspondence, papers, drawings, photographs and news clippings relating to the discovery and controversy over the Piltdown skull. Parts of a human skull, mandible and a canine tooth were discovered in Pliocene gravels near Piltdown Common in Sussex by Charles Dawson (1864-1916), an amateur fossil collector. The specimens, together with associated fossils and implements, were presented to the British Museum (Natural History) the following year and were the subject of intense research by, among others, Arthur Smith Woodward (1864-1944), who was Keeper of Geology from 1901 to 1924. In 1949 Kenneth Page Oakley (1911-1981) used chemical tests to show that the skull was not as ancient as the associated fossils, and in 1953 it was demonstrated that the skull, mandible and tooth were fakes. In spite of research and speculation, the identity of the forger has not been proved.

The class is an artificial one, containing papers drawn from the departmental correspondence, the Keeper's miscellaneous files and the Anthropology correspondence files.

Many of the items include detailed lists of contents. Additional materials relating to the Piltdown affair are held in the papers of J.S. Weiner, in the Palaeontology Manuscripts.

References: Frank Spencer, *Piltdown: A Scientific Forgery* (London: 1990) (= *Natural History Museum Publication*); Frank Spencer, *The Piltdown Papers, 1908-1955*: *The Correspondence and Other Documents Relating to the Piltdown Forgery* (London: 1990).

(Dates of transfer: ca. 1985; number of items: 54; shelf length: 0.6 m.; microfiche: entire; code: DF116.)

2. Anthropology Sub-Department: Correspondence, 1913-1985. This class contains the correspondence of members of the Sub-Department of Anthropology and its predecessors. Letters in the collection deal with the donation, purchase, exchange and disposal of human remains and artifacts, anthropological enquiries from members of the public and research correspondence with fellow anthropologists.

Anthropology was first studied within the Osteology Section of the Zoology Department, and items 1-4 date from that period. William Plane Pycraft (1868-1942) was Head of the Section from 1907 until his retirement in 1932, when he was succeeded by Francis Charles Fraser (1903-1978). In 1949 it was decided to appoint an anthropologist to take charge of both the recent and fossil collections. No suitable external candidate was found, and in 1953 Kenneth Page Oakley (1911-1981), a member of the Department of Geology, with responsibility for fossil man and some invertebrate groups, was given the post. The new Anthropology Section spanned the departments of Zoology and Geology, though Oakley himself remained in Geology. In 1959 the Section was given the status of a

Sub-Department, and in 1960 it was placed within the Department of Palaeontology, and the collection of recent anthropological specimens was transferred accordingly.

(Dates of transfer: 1992; number of items: 15; shelf length: 1 m.; microfiche: none; code: DF140.)

3. Anthropology Sub-Department: Subject Files, 1935-1968. This class contains the remnants of a long series of slender subject files held in the Sub-Department of Anthropology. They relate mainly to accessions to the collection and to research correspondence on particular topics and with particular individuals.

Items 1-27, 118 and 129, with the 'GL' references, were kept by Francis Charles Fraser, Head of the Osteology Section in the Zoology Department. The remainder contain the correspondence and papers of Kenneth Page Oakley and Rosemary Powers of the Anthropology Section, later the Anthropology Sub-Department. These all bear an 'AL' (Anthropology Letters) reference code. Files 28 and 29 contain papers of K.P. Oakley before his appointment to the Section.

The arrangement of the class is generally chronological, except that items 57-136 have been listed in the order in which they were housed in the Section's subject boxes.

(Dates of transfer: 1992; number of items: 138; shelf length: 0.7 m.; microfiche: none; code: DF141.)

4. Anthropology Sub-Department: Visitors Books, 1954-1971. This class contains the two books that were used to record the names of visitors to the Anthropology Section, later the Sub-Department. The section was first located in the southwest basement corridor of the Zoology Department.

Artifacts: Specimen Collections of Anthropological Significance: The Fossil Hominid Collection in the Department of Palaeontology.

Reference: Kenneth Page Oakley; Bernard Grant Campbell and Theya Ivitsky Molleson (editors), *Catalogue of Fossil Hominids* (London: 1967-1975) (= *British Museum (Natural History). Publication*, no. 661), 3 v., [pt. 1: *Africa*; pt. 2: *Europe*; pt. 3: *Americas, Asia, Australasia;* pt. 1 revised, 1977].

Ann Lum and John Thackray

Public Record Office (PRO)

Address: Public Record Office, Ruskin Avenue, Kew, Richmond, Surrey, TW9 3DU, United Kingdom.
Tel.: +44 (0181) 8763444
Fax: +44 (0181) 8788905
Internet address: http://www.pro.gov.uk.

Founded: 1838.
Major resources: The national archives of the United Kingdom, 1086-1992.
Areas of specialization: Original records and documents of the United Kingdom.
Archives/manuscripts: Extensive.
Visual/audio resources: Large holdings of maps and photographs.
Access: Open to the public.
Guides/catalogs: *The Current Guide to the Contents of the Public Record Office, 1994* (Richmond, Surrey: 1994)—available on microfiche from the Public Record Office; Anne Thurston, *Guide to Archives and Manuscripts Relating to Kenya and East Africa in the United Kingdom*, vol. 1, *Official Records* (London: 1991), p. 2-539. A list of Cherokee-related manuscripts held in the PRO is in William L. Anderson and James A. Lewis, *A Guide to Cherokee Documents in Foreign Archives* (Metuchen, N.J.: 1983) (= *Native American Bibliography Series*, no. 4), p. 79-505.

Information provided by Miss A. Crawford.

Royal Anthropological Institute of Great Britain and Ireland (RAI)

Address: Royal Anthropological Institute of Great Britain and Ireland, 50 Fitzroy Street, London W1P 5HS, United Kingdom.
Tel.: +44 (0171) 3870455
Fax: +44 (0171) 3834235
E-mail: rai@cix.compulink.co.uk.
Internet address: http://lucy.ukc.ac.uk/rai.
Internet address (Anthropological Index On-line): http://lucy.ukc.ac.uk/AIO.html.
Public transit access: Underground: Warren Street. Buses: 14, 18, 24, 27, 29, 30, 73.
Founded: 1871. The RAI traces its origins to the establishment of the Ethnological Society of London in 1843. The Anthropological Institute of Great Britain and Ireland was established in 1871, as a result of the merger of the Ethnological Society of London and the Anthropological Society of London. In 1976 the RAI library was merged with the Library of the Museum of Mankind.
Major resources: RAI archives and manuscripts (located at the Museum of Mankind Library); RAI library (now merged with the Museum of Mankind Library); RAI Photo Library (at Fitzroy Street); RAI Film Library (at Ipswich, U.K.); RAI International Video Cassette Sales (at Fitzroy Street). [See the separate entry in this guide under "British Museum. Department of Ethnography. Library," for information on the books and other materials donated by the RAI to the Museum of Mankind Library.]
Areas of specialization: The RAI House Archives and the RAI Manuscript Collection, both conserved at the Museum of Mankind Library (London). The latter includes many British ethnographers' papers.
Archives/manuscripts: RAI manuscript materials include papers of Robert Sutherland Rattray, M.W. Hilton-Simpson, Mary Edith Durham, Everard im Thurn, Marian Wesley Smith, William Crooke, A.B. Deacon, Mary Edith Durham, N.G. Munro, Henry B.T. Somerville and many others. An index to the RAI House Archives is available.

Visual/audio resources: The RAI Photo Library (at Fitzroy Street) holds more than 40,000 photographic prints, plates, slides and negatives. Most of these images derive from the period 1860-1960. Many of these are of exceptional importance in the field of anthropology. Approximately one-half of the Photo Library images have been cataloged. Anthropological photographs by Charles A. Woolley, J.W. Lindt, Edward Horace Man, Everard im Thurn, Henry B.T. Somerville, Charles Hose, W.L. Hildburgh, Charles Gabriel Seligman, Emil Torday, M.W. Hilton-Simpson and others are held. Photo collections include the Hilton-Simpson collection (photos of Algeria); the H.M. Gluckman collection (photos of Barotseland); and the W.B. Fagg collection (photos of African art).

Access: Visitors by appointment. RAI Fellows and Junior Fellows in the U.K. enjoy special borrowing and access rights to RAI books housed in the Museum of Mankind Library.

Guides/catalogs: Roslyn Poignant, *Observers of Man: Photographs from the Royal Anthropological Institute* (London: 1980); Roslyn Poignant, "Surveying the Field of View: The Making of the RAI Photographic Collection," in Elizabeth Edwards (editor), *Anthropology and Photography, 1860-1920* (London: 1992), p. 42-73; *Royal Anthropological Institute Teachers' Resource Guide* (4th ed., London: 1990); James Woodburn (editor), *The Royal Anthropological Institute Film Library Catalogue* (London: 1982-1990), 2 v.

Description

The former Royal Anthropological Institute Library was merged with the Museum of Mankind Library in 1976. Fellows of the Royal Anthropological Institute retain special access and borrowing privileges for use of books donated by the Institute. [Information on anthropological library resources of the Museum of Mankind Ethnography Library (British Museum) is provided in a separate entry of this guide.]

The principal commitment of the RAI is the publication of the quarterly *Journal of the Royal Anthropological Institute* (incorporating *Man*) and the bimonthly *Anthropology Today*. The RAI's quarterly *Anthropological Index* is a standard reference source for subject and author access to journal articles in the field. From 1997 it is being made available on the Internet (*Anthropological Index On-line*) as a public service to the discipline—see the AIO Internet address, above.

The RAI encourages the use of its photographic resources for educational purposes. The *National Inventory of Documentary Sources* contains, in microfiche form, copies of all RAI Photo Library index cards.

Since 1971 the Institute has operated the RAI Film Lending Library, which lends films and video cassettes from its collections for educational use (within the U.K. only). In addition, Film Prizes are regularly awarded by the RAI Film Committee at the biennial International Festival of Ethnographic Film. With the obsolescence of 16mm film, the Institute has a growing department which markets VHS video cassettes internationally for educational use at reasonable prices.

Jonathan Benthall

Royal Asiatic Society of Great Britain in Ireland (RAS)

Address: Library, Royal Asiatic Society of Great Britain in Ireland, 60 Queen's Gardens, London W2 3AF, United Kingdom.
Tel.: +44 (1171) 7244741
Fax: +44 (1171) 7064008
Catalog: The Library's card catalog is arranged by author. A printed catalog (see below) lists library book accessions up to about 1932.
Public transit access: Underground: Central line, Lancaster Gate station. The Society is within walking distance of this station.
Founded: 1823 (founding of the Society).
Major resources: Library; Archives; Prints and Drawings.
Areas of specialization: Asia and the Middle East until 1949. Sections of the library include the Art Room (books on Asian art), the Reading Room (books on India), the Lecture Room (books on India), the Council Room (journals) and the Treasurer's Room (books on Japan, China and Southeast Asia). Special resources are the Richard Burton collection, the Maxwell collection and many Oriental manuscript collections.
Archives/manuscripts: The archives of the Society. Also more than 1,000 Asian and Oriental manuscripts—including about 350 manuscripts in Persian, 70 in Arabic, 40 in Turkish, 14 in Hindustani, 250 in Javanese and Malay. Also, palm-leaf manuscripts from South Asia.
Holdings (books and journals): The library has about 100,000 books, journals and other materials concerning all regions of Asia.
Visual/audio resources: Ca. 2,500 prints, drawings and watercolors—most of these are by Asian artists. Also, photo albums, a few thousand glass-plate photographs and color slides. The photo collections are well cataloged.
Access: Open to Fellows of the Society. Visitors may contact the Librarian to request an appointment.
References: B.C. Bloomfield (editor), *A Directory of Rare Book and Special Collections in the United Kingdom and the Republic of Ireland* (2nd ed., London: 1997), p. 324; Michael Pollock, "Southeast Asian Materials in the Library of the Royal Asiatic Society," South-East Asia Library Group, *Newsletter*, no. 39 (Dec. 1994), p. 28-36; Geoffrey Roper (general editor), *World Survey of Islamic Manuscripts* (London: 1992-1994) (= *Al-Furqān Islamic Heritage Foundation. Publication,* no. 10), vol. 3, p. 497-500; C.E.J. Whitting, "The Burton Collection at the Royal Asiatic Society," in Stuart Simmonds and Simon Digby (editors), *The Royal Asiatic Society: Its History and Treasures* (Leiden: 1979), p. 145-154.
Guides/catalogs: *Catalogue of Printed Books Published Before 1932 in the Library of the Royal Asiatic Society* (London: 1940). For information on the Society's holdings of paintings, etc., see Raymond Head, *Catalogue of Paintings, Drawings, Engravings and Busts in the Collection of the Royal Asiatic Society* (London: 1991).
Artifacts of anthropological significance: A museum was maintained by the Society until 1869. Objects from that museum were donated to the India Office and may perhaps now be in collections of one or more London-area museums.

Royal Commission on Historical Manuscripts/National Register of Archives

Address: Royal Commission on Historical Manuscripts/National Register of Archives, Quality House, Quality Court, Chancery Lane, London WC2A 1HP, United Kingdom.
Tel.: +(44) (0171) 2421198
Fax: +(44) (0171) 8313550
Internet address: http://www.hmc.gov.uk.

Description

The National Register of Archives may be able to provide information on archival materials at selected U.K. repositories. The National Register provides access to archival documents by organization name or by author.

Royal Geographical Society (RGS) with the Institute of British Geographers (IBG)

Address: Royal Geographical Society, 1 Kensington Gore, London SW7 2AR, United Kingdom.
Tel.: +44 (0171) 5895466 (the Society); +44 (0171) 5844381 (Picture Library).
Fax: +44 (0171) 5844447 (the Society); +44 (0171) 5844381 (Picture Library).
E-mail: info@rgs.org.
Public transit access: Underground: Circle or District lines—High Street Kensington station. Buses 9, 9a, 10 or 52 pass and stop near the RGS House.
Founded: 1830 (founding of the Society). The Royal Geographical Society combined with the Institute of British Geographers in 1995.
Major resources: RGS Archives, Map Room, Library, Picture Library.
Areas of specialization: Geography, cartography, exploration and travel.
Archives/manuscripts: Records of the Society, as well as manuscripts and papers donated by RGS members, are preserved in the Archives.
Holdings (books, periodicals, maps): The Map Room has more than 850,000 sheet maps and charts, 2,500 atlases and 700 gazetteers. The Library holds about 150,000 book and journal volumes on travel and exploration, geography, or related topics. Some 800 current periodical titles are received.
Visual/audio resources: More than a half-million historic and contemporary photographs and other images are in the Picture Library.
Access: The Map Room collection is open to the public (10:00 a.m. to 5:00 p.m. on weekdays). U.K. residents are normally expected to apply for Fellowship if they wish to use the Archives or the Library, as these services are supported by the subscriptions of the Fellows and Members of the Society and are principally for their use. Written application for admission to the Library should be made to the Librarian, and written application for use of the Archives should be made to the Archivist. Bona fide scholars from overseas are normally admitted for short visits, upon written application to the Archivist or the Librarian, stating the nature of their research and their institutional affiliation. Admission is by appointment,

and first appointments to see the Archives are usually available on Tuesdays only. The Society's House is closed to visitors for one month each year during June/July for stocktaking.

References: B.C. Bloomfield (editor), *A Directory of Rare Book and Special Collections in the United Kingdom and the Republic of Ireland* (2nd ed., London: 1997), p. 335-337; Ian Cameron, *To the Farthest Ends of the Earth: The History of the Royal Geographical Society, 1830-1980* (London: 1980); Gillian Grant, *Middle Eastern Photographic Collections in the United Kingdom* (Durham: 1989) (= *Middle East Libraries Committee. Research Guides*, 3), p. 131-136.

Guides/catalogs: Christine Kelly (compiler), *The RGS Archives: A Handlist* (London: 1977)—reprinted from parts published in the *Geographical Journal*, vol. 141-143 (1975-1977); Christine Kelly, "The RGS Archives: Supplementary Material,"—reprinted from the *Geographical Journal*, vol. 154, pt. 2 (July 1988), p. 251-257; "Royal Geographical Society. Archives," in *National Inventory of Documentary Sources in the United Kingdom and Ireland* (London: 1984 [and subsequent editions])—on microfiche.

Artifacts of anthropological significance: The Society has selected artifacts and "relics"—especially objects associated with noted RGS member explorers and travelers. Relics include, among others, Charles Darwin's sextant and David Livingstone's hat.

Description

The main units of the Royal Geographical Society of potential interest for anthropological research are the Map Room, the Library, the Archives and also the Picture Library. Staffing of these units is limited, and (except for the Map Room, which is open to the public) research visits should be arranged in advance by written application.

The Map Room

The Map Room collection of more than 850,000 sheet maps and charts has been described as the "largest private map collection in the world." The wealth of maps and other cartographic items available here will be of interest to researchers in many disciplines.

The Library

The Society's library of about 150,000 volumes holds books, journals, pamphlets and other materials concerning geography, cartography, travel, exploration and related topics. Special library collections include the F.J. Rennell collection (books on Asia, the Middle East and Africa), the Robert Brown collection (travel in Morocco), the Albertus Paulus Hermanus Hotz collection (Persia and neighboring areas), others.

The Archives

The Archives holds the Society's manuscript collections. Individual manuscript collections are rarely comprehensive, but they often complement those held in other U.K.

archives. There are few papers in the Archives dated prior to the Society's foundation in 1830. A somewhat detailed listing of the archival resources—organized by author within geographic regions—has been published in Christine Kelly (compiler), *RGS Archives: A Handlist* (London: 1977). A supplement (1988) to the handlist is available. Archival holdings include papers and correspondence of many prominent explorers and also original expedition reports. Holdings include papers of David Livingstone, Henry Morton Stanley, Ney Elias, J.B. Thurston, George Younghusband and others.

With the exception of a few items in the Special Collections series, the Archives are not cataloged in great detail. There are as yet no computerized finding aids, so an electronic search is not possible. Only the researcher can find specific information, by consulting such papers as seem appropriate after using the *Handlist* or the card index to the Archives. The available finding aids for access to the archives are author and geographical region-based.

The RGS Archives card index catalogs were filmed in 1992 and are included (in microfiche format) in the *National Inventory of Documentary Sources in the United Kingdom and Ireland* (London: 1984-   ).

The location of the papers of a particular person or organization can often be found by inquiry at the National Register of Archives, Quality House, Quality Court, Chancery Lane, London WC2A 1HP; phone (0171) 2421198.

With a few exceptions, the Archives does not hold pictures or maps—these are in the Society's Picture Library or in the Map Room, respectively. Museum pieces are in the care of the assistant to the Keeper of the Collections.

The Picture Library

More than a half-million photographic images (from 1830 to the present) are preserved in the Picture Library. In addition to photographic images, the Picture Library holds sketches, watercolors, pastel and oil paintings and portraits. Many Picture Library photo images were donated by explorers or travelers who were Society members. Special collections in the Picture Library include paintings, drawings or other picture images by Thomas Baines, Samuel White Baker and others. The Picture Library is currently in the early stages of electronic cataloging of photographs and other images. The Picture Library is a commercial enterprise and fees are charged accordingly.

For information on the various RGS collections, please contact the Map Curator, the Archivist, the Librarian, the Picture Library Manager or the Keeper's Assistant, as appropriate.

Information provided by Paula Lucas, Archivist.

University of London. School of Economics and Political Science. British Library of Political and Economic Science (BLPES)

Address: British Library of Political and Economic Science, School of Economics and Political Science, University of London, 10 Portugal Street, London WC2A 2HD, United Kingdom.

Tel.: +44 (0171) 4057686
Fax: +44 (0171) 9557454
E-mail: Library@lse.ac.uk.
Internet address: http://www.lse.ac.uk.blpes.
Public transit access: Underground: Holborn or Temple. See the Library website for bus information and a transit map.
Major resources: Papers of British anthropologists.
Areas of specialization: The social sciences—including social anthropology.
Archives/manuscripts: Manuscript resources include the papers of Bronislaw Malinowski, Siegfried Nadel, Margaret Read, Charles Gabriel Seligman, Brenda Z. Seligman, Phyllis Kaberry, Isaac Schapera and others; holdings also include the extensive archives of the International African Institute.
Holdings (books and journals): Ca. 1 million v. and 28,000 journals.
Visual/audio resources: The library has no separate photograph collection. The Malinowski and Nadel collections include significant numbers of field photographs.
Access: The archives are open to the public for research. Non-academic readers are charged a fee for use of the library, but not for use of the archives.
Guides/catalogs: A separate guide to BLPES collections is not available. It is anticipated that a database of library holdings will be mounted on the Web in 1998.

Description

Major holdings of papers and manuscripts in the field of anthropology include the following:

- Virginia Adam—field work relating to the Ihanzu and Isanzu of Tanzania, 1961-1963.
- Edith Clarke (fl. 1930-1960), anthropologist—fieldnotes and working files, 1948-1949, collected by Clarke and others in a survey of marriage and parentage in Jamaica; published as *My Mother Who Fathered Me: A Study of the Family in Three Selected Communities in Jamaica* (London: 1957). The collection is closed because individuals surveyed are identified.
- Peter, Prince Peter of Greece and Denmark—records of fieldwork in India and Ladakh, 1935-1963, with particular reference to Tibet and to polyandry.
- Raymond William Firth (1901-   ), professor of anthropology—records of fieldwork in Tikopia and Malaya/Malaysia, 1930s-1990s.
- Ernest Andre Gellner (1925-1995), professor of social anthropology—fieldnotes and papers relating to Morocco, 1950s-1995.
- International African Institute (1920s-1980s)—the archives of this institute for the scholarly study of African society and languages.
- Phyllis Kaberry (1910-1977), anthropologist—fieldwork notes, correspondence, photographs and papers relating to the Abelam of Papua New Guinea and the peoples of the Bamenda province, Cameroon—with additional materials by Mrs. E.M. Chilver.

- Siegfried Nadel (1903-1956), anthropologist—field notebooks and diaries, research papers, texts of his lectures and photographs relating to the Nupe of Nigeria and the Nuba of Kordofan and to his fieldwork and government service in Eritrea and Ethopia.
- Margaret Read (1889-1992), professor of anthropology—fieldnotes relating to her work among the Ngoni of Malawi, 1935-1939.
- Audrey Isabel Richards (1889-1984), anthropologist—papers relating to the Bemba of Tanzania and to the kingdom of Buganda in Uganda.
- Isaac Schapera (1905-   ), professor of anthropology—fieldwork records, 1929-1960s, relating to thc Bakgatla and Ngwato of Botswana.
- Brenda Z. Seligman and Charles Gabriel Seligman (1873-1940), professor of ethnology—fieldwork notes of expeditions to Borneo and the Torres Straits, Papua New Guinea, Sri Lanka and the Sudan.

Angela Raspin

University of London. School of Oriental and African Studies (SOAS). Library

Address: Library, School of Oriental and African Studies, Thornhaugh Street, Russell Square, London WC1H OXG, United Kingdom.
Tel.: +44 (0171) 6372388
Fax: +44 (0171) 4363844
Networks, consortia: LIBERTAS.
Internet address: http://www.soas.ac.uk/Library.
Internet access to on-line catalog: Use the website or telnet to lib.soas.ac.uk. About 50 percent of the library's catalog records are available on the LIBERTAS system.
Public transit access: Underground: Russell Square. Buses: 7, 8, 10, 14, 14a, 19, 22b, 24, 25, 29, 38, 55, 73, 98, 134 and 176.
Founded: 1916.
Major resources: School of Oriental and African Studies Library.
Areas of specialization: Social and cultural anthropology; ethnography; linguistics and archaeology with reference to Asia and Africa and the islands of the Pacific.
Archives/manuscripts: 6,500 boxes and volumes of Missionary Society archives and 18,000 photographs. About 130 boxes of papers of individuals contain anthropological source material.
Holdings (books and periodicals): More than 750,000 volumes (total book stock). About 5,000 periodicals are received currently.
Visual/audio resources: The collection includes slides, photographs, commercially produced sound recordings and ethnographic maps. There are special collections of slides relating to the Braj area of India and the Hunza. The Library also houses the Williams-Hunt collection which contains some 5,000 ethnographic and archaeological aerial photographs of Southeast Asia, taken by the Royal Air Force between 1944 and 1952. The ethnographic photographs are of the Malayan peninsula during the Emergency of 1952, and the archaeological photographs are mainly of Thailand and Burma between 1944 and 1947. Sound recordings include cassette tapes and transcripts from the BBC series "Plain Tales

from the Raj," as well as 77 recorded interviews from the "British in India" oral archive project.

Access: Open to scholars and general readers. There are some restrictions on access.

References: The Library, *Calendar, 1994-1995* (London: 1994), p. 76-83; The Library, *Library Guide* (London: 1993); The Library, *Library Catalogue* (Boston: 1963-1979); *Library Catalogue*: Supplement, 1978-1989, [on microfiche]; The Library, *Guide to Archives and Manuscript Collections* (London: 1994); Ian Proudfoot, "Major Library Holdings of Early Malay Books," *Kekal Abadi*, jil. 8, bil. 1 (Mac 1989), p. 10-11; Barbara Turfan, "The Hardyman Madagascar Collection at SOAS Library," *IIAS Newsletter* [International Institute for Asian Studies], no. 4 (Spring 1995), p. 34.

Description

The School of Oriental and African Studies was founded by royal charter on 5 June, 1916, as a constituent college of the University of London. The original aim was to concentrate the teaching of modern Asian and African languages in London in a single institution, but from its foundation the School's teaching also embraced the history, geography, manners, customs, law and literature of the peoples of Asia and Africa. It was also intended that the School should house a major library dealing with these topics.

The nucleus of the library was formed at that time by the collection of Oriental books owned by the London Institution. The University Library and the libraries of University and King's College transferred to the School their Oriental books (other than Hebrew and Syriac) in exchange for Western books from the London Institution Library. Foremost among these collections were the printed books and manuscripts, containing many rare editions and unique items, presented to King's Colleges in 1835 by the Orientalist and numismatist, William Marsden (1754-1836).

The present library accommodation was opened in 1973, and has space for one million volumes and seats for 600 readers. The primary purpose of the library is the support of the teaching, study and research activities of the School, but it also functions as a national resource for Asian and African studies in the fields of the humanities and social sciences. The material collected is in both Western languages and those of Asia and Africa.

For the most part, the collections are arranged by region, country or language, on open access. The classification scheme that is currently used for books employs an initial letter or combination of letters, usually followed by a Dewey Decimal classification number. Periodicals are shelved separately, and archives, manuscripts, rare books and special collections are kept in closed accommodation.

Archives and Manuscript Collections Containing Anthropological Source Materials.

Archives of Societies and Organizations:

- The China Inland Mission (Overseas Missionary Fellowship).

Minutes, 1872 to 1951, of the London Council of the China Inland Mission and of its Finance Committee; minutes, 1866-1947 and 1951, of the Mission's China Council; registers of missionaries, some correspondence, private papers and various publications, including the *Chinese Missionary Gleaner*, 1853-1859; and *China's Millions*, 1875-1964. In addition, there is a large photographic collection. In a separate section are the substantial papers of the mission's founder, James Hudson Taylor (1832-1905), that include some records, ca. 1850-1860, of the Chinese Evangelization Society. Also, six boxes relating to the Chefoo Schools, founded by Hudson Taylor, including registers of pupils. (Deposited 1991-1994. 161 boxes, 394 volumes. Handlists in two volumes are available. Part 1 lists written materials and Part 2 lists photographs.)

• The Council for World Mission (incorporating the London Missionary Society (LMS) and the Commonwealth Missionary Society).

Archives, dated 1795-1970, concerning LMS work in the South Seas, China and Madagascar, South and Southeast Asia, southern and central Africa and, to a lesser extent, in North America and the West Indies. Minutes, correspondence, reports, personal papers, as well as ca. 11,000 photographs. Among the private collections are papers of James Chalmers, James Legge, David Livingstone, Robert Moffat, Robert Morrison, J.E. Newell, John Philip and John Williams. Also, records of the Commonwealth Missionary Society (formerly the Colonial Missionary Society) that worked in Australia, North America, New Zealand, South Africa and the West Indies. (Deposited 1973-1994. 2,358 boxes.) See *The Archives of the Council for World Mission (Incorporating the London Missionary Society): An Outline Guide* (London: 1973). A new guide is in preparation. Bound handlists. Also the Council for World Mission Library of ca. 13,000 books and pamphlets, including LMS serials. A card index is available.

• The Melanesian Mission.

The Mission was founded in 1840 to evangelize the Melanesian islands of the South Pacific—i.e., the Solomon, Santa Cruz and northern New Hebrides islands. Correspondence, photographs dated ca. 1872-1963, and *Southern Cross Logs,* 1895-1970. Includes papers of R.H. Codrington and Bishop Patterson. The surviving records date from ca. 1848-1969. (Deposited in 1990. 44 boxes.) A handlist is available.

• The Methodist Church Overseas Division (Methodist Missionary Society).

The archives, dated from 1798 to 1955, document the work of the Wesleyan Methodist Missionary Society, the United Methodist Missionary Society and the Primitive Methodist Missionary Society in Europe, North America, the West Indies, Africa, India, Burma, Sri Lanka and Australia. The societies united in 1933 to form the Methodist Missionary Society. Biographical collections include papers of Thomas Birch Freeman, David Hill, Samuel Pollard and Edwin Smith. (Deposited, 1978-1994. 1,760 boxes.) See Elizabeth Bennett, *Guide to the Archives of the Methodist Missionary Society* (Zug: 1979).

Handlists are available. Also, a library of approximately 6,500 books and pamphlets. Card index. A handlist of serial publications is available.

- Presbyterian Church of England, Foreign Missions Committee and Women's Missionary Association.

The society was founded in 1847, although, unfortunately, little survives from before 1900. English Presbyterian Missionaries worked chiefly in mainland China and Formosa, but also in Malaysia and in what is now Bangladesh. Correspondence, reports, photographs and published material. (Deposited in 1982, 1988 and 1992. 247 boxes.) A handlist is available.

Papers of Individuals:

- Arkell, Anthony John (MS 210522).

Reports, articles and notes, dated ca. 1919-1947, of Anthony John Arkell (1898-1980). Arkell served in the Sudan Political Service, 1920-1948. He was Archaeological Adviser to the Sudan Government, 1948-1953, and subsequently became Reader in Egyptian Archaeology at the University of London. On retirement he became a vicar in Oxfordshire. The collection chiefly concerns archaeology, history and ethnology of the Sudan, together with some administrative papers. (17 boxes.) A handlist is available.

- Aylward, Gladys (MS 291571).

Letters and relics of Gladys Aylward, missionary to China. Aylward worked chiefly in Shansi Province, from 1931 to 1951. For a life of Gladys Aylward, see Alan Burgess, *The Small Woman* (New York: 1957). (1 box.)

- Baké, Arnold A. (PP MS 21).

Indian music and folklore—songs in various Indian (South Asian) languages, with related material and translations, by Arnold A. Baké. (7 boxes.) A handlist is available.

- Banks Photograph Collection (MS 380389).

Photographs (dated ca. 1897-1917), chiefly taken in North East India, of A.L. Banks, missionary of the Regions Beyond Missionary Union. The photographs show groups of missionaries, Indian Christians, Hindus and Muslims, local festivals, buildings and views. (11 albums.) A handlist is available.

- Boyd, Jean (PP MS 36).

Material collected by Jean Boyd on the Nigerian woman poet, Nana Asma'u (1793-1865), works by her father, Shehu dan Fodio (1754-1817), and works by female members of her family. Includes manuscript copies of poems by Asma'u in Fulfuede, Hausa and Arabic, together with translations. Also, papers relating to women's organizations in northern Nigeria. (13 boxes.) A detailed catalog is available.

- Carpenter, John Baker (MS 201813).

Letters, papers, photographs, dated 1899-1926, of John Baker Carpenter. He served with the Church Missionary Society in Fukien, China, 1899-1921, and taught at Union Theological College, 1915-1920. He was Examining Chaplain to the Bishop of Fukien, 1917-1920. (1 box, 2 files.) A handlist is available.

- Cousins, (Ethel) Constance (MS 380325).

Letters and papers concerning the life of Constance Cousins (1882-1944). She worked with the Church of Scotland's medical mission at Kalimpong and Almora, 1911-1944; went to Bhutan in 1911 to help combat a cholera epidemic there. The collection also includes letters, dated 1893-1900, from her father, the Rev. W.C. Cousins, missionary in Madagascar from 1862 to 1899. (4 boxes.) A handlist is available.

- Earthy, Emily Dora (MS 380515).

Field work and language material of Emily Dora Earthy, missionary in Mozambique, 1917-1930. The collection contains her manuscript notes on Valenge (Chopi) women that were published under the title *Valenge Women: The Social and Economic Life of the Valenge Women of Portuguese East Africa: An Ethnographic Study* (London: 1933). (3 boxes.) A handlist is available.

- Francis, David Lloyd (MS 380565).

Diaries, correspondence and papers, dated 1933-1989, of the Rev. David Lloyd Francis, who worked for sixteen years with the Melanesian Mission in the New Hebrides, the Solomon Islands and New Guinea. (1 box.) A handlist is available.

- Fürer-Haimendorf, Christoph von (PP MS 19).

Diaries (mostly in German), anthropological fieldnotes, published and unpublished papers (in English) relating to peoples of India, of professor Christoph von Fürer-Haimendorf (1909-1995), who was Special Officer Subansiri, External Affairs Department, Government of India, 1944-1945; Adviser to HEH the Nizam's Government and Professor of Anthropology in the Osmania University, 1945-1949; Professor of Anthropology at the School of Oriental and African Studies, 1951 until 1976. (8 boxes. Accruing.) A draft handlist is available.

- Hake, Andrew (PP MS 46).

Correspondence and papers of Andrew Augustus Gordon Hake (1925-   ). Hake worked as an industrial missionary in Kenya, 1957-1969, under the auspices of the national Christian Council for Kenya. The papers detail his work in seeking to establish fair working conditions in Kenya's industrial sector, while also presenting the case of the unemployed and bringing the plight of the homeless and refugees to the consciousness of government officials. (95 boxes.) A handlist is available.

- Higgins, John Comyn (MS 95022).

Notes and narratives, dated ca. 1910-1946, of political and social significance regarding Manipuri State, India, by John Comyn Higgins (1882-1952). Higgins entered the Indian Civil Service in 1906, was Political Agent, Manipur State, from 1917 until 1933, and Chairman, Assam Public Service Commission, from 1944 to 1945. (2 boxes.) A handlist is available.

- Huntingford, George Wynn Brereton (PP MS 17).

Correspondence, seminar papers and reports relating to the history, languages and culture of the peoples of East Africa, collected by George Wynn Brereton Huntingford, Lecturer in East African Languages and Cultures, School of Oriental and African Studies, 1950 to 1966. Papers dated 1920s-1974. (13 boxes.) A handlist is available.

- Lorimer, Lt.-Col. David Lockhart Robertson (MS 181247).

Papers of Lieutenant-Colonel David Robertson Lorimer (1876-1962), Indian Political Service, 1903-1924, Political Agent, Gilgit, 1920-1924. The collection chiefly relates to his work on the Burushaski, Khowar, Shina and Bakhtiari languages. Also photographs and film of a field trip to the Hunza Valley in the mid-1930s. (62 boxes, 1 trunk.) A handlist is available.

- Mackenzie, Melville Douglas (MS 380483).

Copies of papers and photographs of Melville Douglas Mackenzie as Special Commissioner, League of Nations Mission to the Kru peoples of Liberia, 1931-1932. (3 boxes.) A handlist is available.

- Millman, William (PP MS 34).

Correspondence, educational and language (Lokele) material, dated 1890-1957, concerning missionary work in Yakusu, Belgian Congo, of William Millman (1872-1956) and of his wife's first husband, Walter Stapleton, a pioneer missionary at Yakusu. (13 boxes.) A handlist is available.

- Moore, Reginald John Beagaric (MS 380399).

Correspondence and papers, dated 1926-1945, concerning the missionary work of Reginald John Beagarie [Mike] Moore (1909-1943). Moore served with the London Missionary Society's Central African Mission and the United Missions in the Copperbelt. A copy of his anthropological study, "The Witchdoctor's Prescription" is included. (2 boxes.) A handlist is available.

- Perlman, Melvin Lee (PP MS 38).

A collection of research data gathered by Melvin Lee Perlman (1933-1988), American anthropologist, during 1959-1962, for a study on Toro marriages in Uganda. Also data gathered by Perlman for research on tea estate workers in Uganda and articles and transcripts of lectures. (42 boxes.) A handlist is available.

- Powell, I.B.—Collection on the Philippines. (PP MS 26).

Correspondence and Philippine reference material, dated 1926-1986, collected by Ifor Ball Powell (1902-1985), historian and Philippine specialist. Includes photographs taken during his field trips in the 1920s. (164 boxes.) A handlist is available.

- Ray, Sidney Herbert (PP MS 3).

Papers, dated ca. 1900-1939, of Sidney Herbert Ray (1858-1939). Ray was a schoolmaster and scholar of Oceanic languages, chiefly relating to the languages and ethnology of the Pacific Islands. (18 boxes.) A handlist is available.

- Shembe, Prophet Isaiah (MS 380453).

Photocopies of three manuscript notebooks containing chronicles of the Nazareth Baptist Church founded by Isaiah Shembe in Natal in 1910. The text is in Zulu, written ca. 1932, and covers material ranging from accounts of miraculous events, to the day-to-day life of the Church in Inanda, letters to dissident priests and accounts of church finances. (3 v.)

- Stencl, Abraham Nahum (PP MS 44).

Writings in verse and prose of the Yiddish poet of Whitechapel, Abraham Nahum Stencl (1897-1983). He came to Britain in the mid-1930s; was editor of the Yiddish literary journal *Loshn and Lebn*. The collection contains photographs and is rich in correspondence with Stencl's extensive network of friends and acquaintances. (18 boxes.) A detailed catalog is in preparation.

- Thomson, John Boden (MS 380311).

Letters, documents, press cuttings, dated 1866-1880, of and about John Boden Thomson (1841-1878). He worked for Matabeleland Mission of the London Missionary Society, 1869-1877; leader of the Central African Mission to Ujiji, Central Africa, 1877-1878. (2 boxes.) A handlist is available.

Subject Collection:

- Kaduna Housing Survey. (PP MS 41).

Completed questionnaires on households, by district, in Kaduna Province, Nigeria. The survey was undertaken by the Centre for Social and Economic Research, at Ahmadu Bello University, and the Division for Urban and Rural Planning, at Kaduna Polytechnic, in 1978. (12 boxes.) A handlist is available.

Angela Sabin and Rosemary Seton

Wellcome Institute for the History of Medicine. Library

Address: Wellcome Institute Library, Wellcome Institute for the History of Medicine, 183 Euston Road, London NW1 2BE, United Kingdom.
Tel.: +44 (0171) 6118582
Fax: +44 (0171) 6118703
E-mail: library@wellcome.ac.uk.
Internet addresss (Wellcome Institute): http://www.wellcome.ac.uk.
Internet access to on-line catalog: The library's on-line catalog can be accessed at telnet://wihm.ucl.ac.uk.
Networks, consortia: OCLC.
Public transit access: Underground: Euston Square, Euston Station or Warren Street. Buses: 10, 18, 24, 27, 29, 30, 73, 74, 134, 135.
Founded: About 1895; first opened to the public in 1949.
Major resources: Anthropological resources are scattered throughout the library collections. Many such resources are in the library's Oriental Collections.
Areas of specialization: History of medicine and related areas.
Holdings (books and serials): It is not possible to estimate the size of holdings of anthropological importance.
Visual/audio resources: Visual resources include paintings, drawings, prints and photographs (including moving-image films). Available are visual resources concerning Africa—e.g., seventeenth- to nineteenth-century engravings, photographs by Duggan Cronin; North America (Edward S. Curtis); South America (prints by Gallo Gallina, etc.); Nubia, etc.; moving film of circumcision and urethral incision (Western Australia).
Access: Materials are accessible to scholars as well as to general readers. There are no restrictions on access to most collections.

References: Nigel Allan, "The Library of the Wellcome Institute for the History of Medicine and Its Oriental Collections, with a Note on the Malay Collection of Manuscripts," *Kekal Abadi*, vol. 3, no. 4 (Dis. 1984), p. 1-8; Nigel Allan, *The Oriental Collections of the Wellcome Institute for the History of Medicine* (London: 1984); B.C. Bloomfield (editor), *A Directory of Rare Book and Special Collections in the United Kingdom and the Republic of Ireland* (2nd ed., London: 1997), p. 417-421; R.F. Ellen, M.B. Hooker and A.C. Milner, "The Hervey Malay Collection in the Wellcome Institute," *Journal of the Malaysian Branch of the Royal Asiatic Society*, vol. 54, no. 1 (1981), p. 82-91; Robert Rhodes James, *Henry Wellcome* (London: 1994)—the official biography of Sir Henry Wellcome; Robin Price, *The American Collections of the Wellcome Institute for the History of Medicine* (London: 1986); Stephan Roman, *The Development of Islamic Library Collections in Western Europe and North America* (London: 1990) (= *Libraries and Librarianship in the Muslim World*), p. 25-27; William Schupbach, *The Iconographic Collections of the Wellcome Institute for the History of Medicine* (London: 1989); John Symons, *Wellcome Institute for the History of Medicine: A Short History* (London: 1993); Dominik Wujastyk, *The South Asian Collections of the Wellcome Institute for the History of Medicine* (2nd ed., London: 1988).

Guides/catalogs: *The Wellcome Institute for the History of Medicine: A Brief Description* (London: 1993). The Wellcome Institute folder (1994) and the Wellcome Library video (1995) provide details of resources and access to them. The main catalogs of the larger manuscript collections that have been published and that contain material of anthropological interest are: Peter Friedlander, *A Catalogue of Hindi Manuscripts in the Library of the Wellcome Institute for the History of Medicine* (London: 1996); Fateme Keshavarz, *A Descriptive and Analytical Catalogue of Persian Manuscripts in the Library of the Wellcome Institute for the History of Medicine* (London: 1986); K. Somadasa, *A Catalogue of Sinhalese Manuscripts in the Library of the Wellcome Institute for the History of Medicine* (London: 1996); Hartmut Walravens, *A Catalogue of Chinese Books and Manuscripts in the Library of the Wellcome Institute for the History of Medicine* (London: 1994); Marianne Winder, *A Catalogue of the Tibetan Manuscripts and Xylographs, and Catalogue of Thankas, Banners and Other Paintings and Drawings in the Library of the Wellcome Institute for the History of Medicine* (London: 1989).

Description

The anthropological/ethnographic content of the Wellcome Institute Library derives from the wide-ranging interests of Sir Henry (Solomon) Wellcome (1853-1936), creator and sole owner (after the death of his partner Silas Burroughs, in 1895) of what later became the Wellcome Foundation, Ltd.—then the largest pharmaceutical company in the world (now merged to form Glaxo-Wellcome, PLC). Not formally educated, Wellcome perceived the connection between all forms of knowledge and, about 1895, began collecting books, first as an aid to the promotion of his products, and soon—as his understanding widened—on all aspects of the growth and history of medicine at all times and in all places. As the description below indicates, he turned his attention to the Near and Middle East, as also to the Far East. He organized and financed archaeological excavations, collected some 30,000 ethnographic artifacts from a wide range of cultures (now dispersed to major national collections) and employed the multi-linguist Dr. Paira Mall to collect materials on medicine, religion and philosophy within the Indian subcontinent.

Wellcome's ethnographic interests are thus also represented throughout the printed book collections of the library, not least in the field of Americana, where his personal interest in the Amerindians predominated. Such interests are further reflected in the many travel books relating to most parts of the world—both among the early printed books to 1850 and thereafter. These often yield useful first-hand descriptions of exotic medical customs seen through the lively if untrained eyes of the intelligent traveler.

The printed holdings in ethnography are for that reason somewhat sporadic and descriptive, rather than interpretive. The library has continued to collect in Amerindian medicine and rather less systematically in other cultures where curing practices are specific to the account.

Given the main trajectory of the library, therefore, there is no original anthropological/ethnographic material in the shape of fieldnotes, etc., but much material is dispersed throughout the primary and secondary sources and in manuscript form, mostly from the East, as described below.

The Oriental Collections

The Wellcome Institute's distinguished collections of Oriental manuscripts and printed books have few peers in the sphere of medical history and the many subjects that impinge upon it. They are also in the first rank of Oriental collections in the West, with almost every area of human endeavor represented among the 11,000 manuscripts and 3,000 books printed in Oriental types. Some 43 different languages are represented, illustrating the history of mankind in relation to the development of the healing art, and the cultures in which this development has occurred, from as early as an Egyptian papyrus of the thirteenth-century, B.C., to the present day. In a collection of such diversity and breadth, there is much to offer the anthropologist.

Sir Henry Wellcome was keenly interested in anthropology—an interest that is reflected in the Oriental Collections. Out of concern for the poverty of the people of Sudan, Wellcome established his celebrated Tropical Research Laboratories on the Nile. Following this, in 1910, he was approached by Lord Kitchener for further assistance to the people of Sudan. Wellcome's response was a program of excavation at a site known as Jebel Moya, situated between the Blue and White Nile. The discoveries, dating from 1,000 to 400, B.C., made a significant contribution to the historical knowledge of the area and of the peoples that inhabited it. The results were published between 1949 and 1951 in three volumes. Another important excavation in 1932 investigated the Amorite city of Lachish, some 25 miles south of Jerusalem. Here also Wellcome's interest and financial support were significant for the success of the dig. It was important not only for anthropologists, but also for biblical scholars, as here the famous Lachish letters relating to the Old Testament prophet Jeremiah were discovered. The results were published between 1938 and 1958 in three volumes.

Areas of particular interest to the anthropologist may be found in the collection of Ethiopian magical scrolls, largely relating to ethnomedicine. The Institute's Batak collection (from Sumatra) is possibly the largest of its kind in the United Kingdom, and is rich in anthropological interest. Buddhist texts are held in profusion, and Pali manuscripts may be found in the Burmese, Sinhalese and Thai manuscript collections. The culture and religion of Tibet is well represented in xylograph and manuscript. The strongest of all the Oriental collections comes from India, with more than 6,000 Sanskrit manuscripts dating from as early as a palmleaf manuscript of the eleventh-century A.D., containing the Buddhist text *Astasāhasrikāprajñāpāramitāsūtra*. The Hindi collection is the largest collection of manuscripts in the language outside the subcontinent. The Persian collection includes a number of important Sufi texts, as well as several other aspects of Islam, in both the Arabic and Persian collections. Six Egyptian papyri give an insight to the world of ancient and Ptolemaic Egypt, while Judaism is represented by Hebrew material, Christianity by Armenian, Coptic, Syriac and Georgian manuscripts.

Robin Price and Nigel Allan

United Kingdom—Oxford

University of Oxford. Bodleian Library

Address: Bodleian Library, University of Oxford, Broad Street, Oxford OX1 3BG, United Kingdom.
Tel.: +44 (01865) 277000; +44 (01865) 277164 (Department of Western Manuscripts).
Fax: +44 (01865) 277182; +44 (01865) 277187 (Department of Western Manuscripts).
Internet address: http://www.bodley.ox.ac.uk.
Internet address (Indian Institute Library): http://www.rsl.ox.ac.uk/boris/guides/ind/ind01.html.
Internet address (Rhodes House Library): http://www.bodley.ox.ac.uk/boris/guides/rhl/chl01.html.
Founded: 1598.
Major resources: The Bodleian is a university as well as a copyright library.
Areas of specialization: Department of Western Manuscripts; Department of Oriental Books; Indian Institute Library; Rhodes House Library.
Visual/audio resources: J.J. Fahie photo collection, John Johnson photo collection, others.
Access: A reader's ticket is required.
References: B.C. Bloomfield (editor), *A Directory of Rare Book and Special Collections in the United Kingdom and the Republic of Ireland* (2nd ed., London: 1997), p. 493-520; Edmund Craster, *History of the Bodleian Library, 1845-1945* (Oxford: 1952); Patricia M. Pugh, "The Oxford Colonial Records Project and the Oxford Development Records Project," *Journal of the Society of Archivists*, vol. 6, no. 2 (Oct. 1978), p. 76-86; Stephan Roman, *The Development of Islamic Library Collections in Western Europe and North America* (London: 1990) (= *Libraries and Librarianship in the Muslim World*), p. 29-34.

University of Oxford. Institute of Social and Cultural Anthropology. Haddon Project

Address: Haddon Project, c/o Institute of Social and Cultural Anthropology, University of Oxford, 51 Banbury Road, Oxford OX2 6PE United Kingdom.
Internet address: http://www.rsl.ox.ac.uk/isca/haddon/HADD_home.html.
Founded: 1994.
Major resources: The Haddon Project on-line catalogue of ethnographic film footage, 1895-1945. The project website also provides links to related Internet sites throughout the world. The Project was named for British anthropologist and zoologist, Alfred Court Haddon (1855-1940).

University of Oxford. Pitt-Rivers Museum (PRM)

Address: Pitt-Rivers Museum, University of Oxford, South Parks Road, Oxford OX1 3PP, United Kingdom.
Locations: The Balfour Library adjoins the main Museum site on South Parks Road. The Archive Collections are in the Pitt-Rivers Museum Research Centre—more than a mile from Balfour Library.
Tel.: +44 (01865) 270939 (V. Lawrence, Librarian); +44 (01865) 270927 (Elizabeth Edwards, Assistant Curator, Archive Collections).
Fax: +44 (01865) 270943
E-mail (Library): veronica.lawrence@prm.ox.ac.uk.
E-mail (Archives): elizabeth.edwards@prm.ox.ac.uk.
Internet address (Library): http://www.lib.ox.ac.uk/guides/bal.htm.
Internet address (Museum): http://info.ox.ac.uk/departments/anthropology.
Internet access to on-line catalog: OLIS (Oxford Library Information System) can be accessed via the Internet at Library@ox.ac.uk.
Networks, consortia: The library is a member of CURL (Consortium of University Research Libraries).
Public transit access: Accessible by town bus service.
Founded: 1884 (founding of the museum).
Major resources: Balfour Library; Archive Collections—in the Pitt-Rivers Museum Research Centre.
Areas of specialization: Visual anthropology, ethnology, material culture, ethnographic art, archaeology, museology, ethnomusicology.
Archival/manuscript resources: Archive Collections comprise about 56 manuscript collections of varying sizes and about 125,000 photographs.
Fieldnotes, papers, etc.: Major collections are those of Baldwin Spencer (Australia)—field letters and other correspondence, ca. 1890-1929; and Beatrice Blackwood (North America) 1925-1927, (Papua New Guinea and Melanesia) 1930s. An unpublished handlist is available. Also available are area guides for the Americas and Oceania.
Holdings (books and journals): 15,000 books and 15,000 periodical volumes.
Visual/audio resources: The library has about 100 films of anthropological interest that are used for teaching purposes. These may be viewed on the premises. The Photographs

Collection in the Archives Department holds material dating from the 1850s and later and is of international significance.

Access: Admission to the Library for reference purposes is at the discretion of the Librarian. Admission to Archives for bona fide researchers is by written application to Mrs. Elizabeth Edwards, Assistant Curator, Archives, and is by appointment on Thursday and Friday only. Note: Archives form a separate curatorial department and are *not* part of Library services. They are governed by the same regulations as access to all reserve collections in the museum. **References:** William Ryan Chapman, "Arranging Ethnology: A.H.L.F. Pitt-Rivers and the Typological Tradition," in George W. Stocking, Jr. (editor), *Objects and Others: Essays on Museums and Material Culture* (Madison: 1985) (= *History of Anthropology*, vol. 3), p. 15-48; Julia Cousins, *The Pitt-Rivers Museum* (Oxford: 1993); Paul Morgan (editor), *Oxford Libraries Outside the Bodleian: A Guide* (Oxford: 1973).

Guides/catalogs: Elizabeth Edwards, "African Photographs in the Archives of Pitt-Rivers Museum, University of Oxford," in Andrew Roberts (editor), *Photographs as Sources for African History* ([London]: 1988), p. 101-104; Elizabeth Edwards, "Photography in Ethnographic Museums: A Reflection," *Journal of Museum Ethnography*, vol. 7 (1995), p. 131-139; Elizabeth Edwards and Lynne Williamson, *World on a Glass Plate: Early Anthropological Photographs from the Pitt-Rivers Museum, Oxford* (Oxford: 1981).

Artifacts of anthropological significance: A worldwide collection of approximately one million artifacts.

Archaeological sites represented by artifact collections: Collections are from various archaeological sites worldwide—mainly excavated in the late nineteenth- and early twentieth-centuries.

Catalogs of artifact collections: An unpublished catalog of all artifacts is maintained. A published catalog of North American collections is available: Linda Mowat (editor), *Catalogue of the Native American Collection* (Oxford: 1993).

Description

Balfour Library

The Balfour Library was built to illustrate and explain the subjects of the Pitt-Rivers Museum. The Museum was founded when General A.H.L.F. Pitt-Rivers (1827-1900) presented his ethnological and archaeological collections to the University of Oxford. He also stipulated that someone be appointed to lecture on the subject of the collection—the first full-time position in anthropology in any British university, a position filled by Edward B. Tylor in 1883 (Cousins, p. 9). Thus, from its earliest days the museum was involved in both teaching and research. This dual function is reflected in the library collection.

The library is named after Henry Balfour (1863-1939), Curator of the museum from 1891 until his death. Balfour's own books and pamphlets—numbering about 10,000 volumes—form the backbone of the library (Morgan, p. 182). Frequently one finds letters in the books from the work's author to Henry Balfour. If the book was actually authored by Balfour himself, and in his possession, one often finds his notes and drawings interleaved with the text—much as one can still find labels attached to some of the artifacts in the museum that were hand-written by Balfour (Cousins, p. 23). Balfour wrote on a variety of subjects, including the origins of decorative art, the natural history of the musical bow, primitive currency, fish hooks, West African brass casting and stone technology (Cousins, p. 15).

The subjects represented by the library are similarly wide-ranging. As the museum's research collection, it tends to be fairly materially-based. Although the library does contain a significant number of general works on the subject of anthropology (mainly for teaching purposes), it specializes in the material culture and technology of small-scale societies. Areas of current library expansion include ethnographic art, ethnomusicology, visual anthropology, museology and archaeology.

The library owns very few of the books possessed by General Pitt-Rivers. Recently, however, the library received a donation of eighteen books that were owned by General Pitt-Rivers.

Quite a number of the books owned by the library have an interesting provenance. They include two books by Henry Schliemann, given by the author to Edward B. Tylor, another major benefactor of the library.

The main part of the library's collection adjoins the main museum site on South Parks Road. A small collection of Quaternary research materials, as well as some of the music collection, are based at a second site, at 60 Banbury Road.

In contrast to the museum—which is arranged largely by subject—the library is primarily arranged on a geographic basis. Originally, books were organized into geographic areas or broad subject areas such as "Anthropology" or "Art," and then arranged alphabetically by author. This was considered a suitable arrangement for a small research collection, but, as the collection grew, problems arose with this system of organization, which provided no subject index to the collection. The reader wishing to examine the library's holdings on "kinship" in "Southeast Asia" would have to browse through shelf upon shelf of books on Southeast Asia, as there was no form of organization by subject within each geographical area. This situation was not deemed very satisfactory, and a solution was sought in the adoption of the Bliss classification scheme for the library. Progress in reclassifying the library into Bliss has been slow and piecemeal. Although the Bliss classification scheme has provided the flexibility to overcome the difficulties raised by the old classification system, it has proved difficult for library users to accustom themselves to its complexities. In addition, readers have to contend with the fact that half of the library is classified in Bliss and half is still in the old classification scheme.

The number of library users has expanded significantly over time. This has corresponded to the expansion in the museum's teaching responsibilities. The museum has had taught postgraduates attached to it for much of this century (see, in Cousins, p. 28, the photograph of the first diploma students with Henry Balfour in 1908). The museum continues to teach those studying for the degree of Master of Studies in Anthropology and Museum Ethnography, as well as to supervise postgraduate doctoral students. Although undergraduates have been using the library in the form of University of Oxford Geographers and Human Scientists taking an Ethnography option, 1992 saw the first undergraduate intake for the Honours' Degree in Anthropology and Archaeology. The Balfour Library is the first port of call for the Anthropology and Archaeology undergraduates. The Balfour Library is thus rapidly becoming a busy undergraduate lending library, as well as being an important research collection for the study of material culture.

Archive Collections

The Archive Collections has developed out of an active collecting policy within the museum since its foundation in 1884. The Department developed with a dual function: to extend the documentation of objects in the collections and to "collect" the intellectual framework in which the museum's collections developed. The collections were administered alternately over the years by the museum itself and by the library until, in 1981, the Archive Collections were given formal "object" status within the institution. This allows the collection to be curated as an integrated research resource within the museum, from whose history it is inseparable.

Although the Archives hold some internationally important manuscript collections, such as those of Sir Edward B. Tylor (1832-1917) and Sir Baldwin Spencer (1860-1929), its strength is in its photographic collections. The Archives holds about 125,000 photographic images. In addition to nineteenth-century "ethnographic" images, the holdings include some important field collections. Notable are those of Sir E.E. Evans-Pritchard (Nuer and Azande), Beatrice Blackwood (Melanesia), Robert Sutherland Rattray (Asante, Ghana), Sir Charles Bell and F. Spencer Chapman (Tibet), Diamond Jenness (Papua New Guinea), J.H. Hutton & J. Mills (Naga Hills, Assam) and Sir Wilfred Thesiger (Middle East).

The collection is curated as a research resource—not as a picture library. Photographs are curated as material culture objects in their own right, and a special effort is made to maintain the history of the use of the image as part of its historical meaning. There is a substantial database catalog which, although far from complete, grows almost daily. There are also manual handlists for the collection. Finding aids and collections management follow the patterns established for the object collections.

The use of the collections is largely by academic researchers at an advanced level and reflects the double agenda of modern visual anthropology—the image as historical document and the image as representation. The Archives are actively involved in teaching visual anthropology at post-graduate level, mounting photography exhibitions in the museum and working with contemporary photographers and visual artists.

Veronica Lawrence and Elizabeth Edwards

Middle East

Israel

Israel—Jerusalem

Beit ha-Sefarim ha-Le'umi veha-Universita'i
(Jewish National and University Library)

Address: Jewish National and University Library, P.O.B. 34165, Givat Ram, Jerusalem, Israel.
Tel.: (972) 2-660351
Fax: (972) 2-511771
Internet address: http://sites.huji.ac.il/jnul.
Founded: 1892.
Major resources of anthropological interest: The Manuscripts and Archives Department; the Institute of Microfilmed Hebrew Manuscripts; and the National Sound Archives (NSA).
Areas of specialization: Manuscripts relating to folklore, sociology and prayer customs of Jews throughout the world; also, sound recordings relating to prayer customs and folklore of Jews throughout the world.
Holdings: 3,000,000 v. (library holdings in all fields). Quantative Information on holdings of anthropological interest is not available.
Visual/audio resources: The National Sound Archives has sound recordings of traditional prayers of the various Jewish communities, their folksongs and folktales, in the various languages and dialects of Jews throughout the world.
Guides/catalogs: About the Manuscripts and Archives Department: Some 20 percent of the catalog cards of Institute of Microfilmed Hebrew Manuscripts holdings are now on the ALEPH computer system. Work is underway to convert the remaining cards; Makhon le-tatslume kitve-ha-yad ha-'Ivriyim (Jerusalem), *The Collective Catalogue of Hebrew Manuscripts from the Institute of Microfilmed Hebrew Manuscripts and the Department of Manuscripts of the Jewish National and University Library, Jerusalem: User's Guide* (France: 1989) [with a set of 830 microfiche]; *Finding Aids to Manuscript and Archives Collections* (Zug, Switzerland: 1983), [with 183 microfiche]; Arie Morgenstern, "Documents from the Archives of the Pekidim and Ammarkalim of Amsterdam," *Books & People* [Jerusalem], no. 4 (Nov. 1992), p. 3-5; Rivka Plesser, "Professor Nehemia Allony Manuscript Collection," *Books & People*, no. 5 (Feb. 1993), p. 5-6; Rivka Plesser, "Rabbi Samuel Salant Rents a House for 375 Years," *Books & People*, no. 7 (Oct. 1993), p. 18-19.

About the National Sound Archives: Yaakov Gelman and Yaakov Mazor, "The National Sound Archives," *Books & People*, no. 2 (Jan. 1992), p. 2-4; Makhon le-tatslume kitve-ha-yad ha-'Ivriyim (Jerusalem), *Masorot musikah be-Yisra' el me-otsrot ha-fonotekah ha-le'umit = Musical Traditions in Israel: Treasures of the National Sound Archives* (Jerusalem: 1992), [1 sound cassette]; Yaakov Mazor, "Impressions from Daghestan," *Books & People*, no. 5, (Feb. 1993), p. 8-10; Yaakov Mazor, "Some NSA [National Sound Archives] Recording Projects," *Books & People*, no. 2 (Jan. 1992), p. 12-14.

Access: Materials are accessible to all.

Artifacts of anthropological significance: The Manuscripts and Archives Department has amulets, marriage contracts, wedding invitations, bills of divorce, last wills and testaments, cookbooks, communal records and prayer customs in the various languages and dialects of Jews throughout the world.

Libby Kahane
Information provided by Nira Ilsar.

Africa

A number of available reference guides or directories provide information on selected African libraries, archives or museums. Among these is John McIlwaine, *Writings on African Archives* (London: 1996), published for the Standing Conference on Library Materials on Africa (SCOLMA). For survey information on Islamic manuscripts in African locales, see the pertinent sections in Geoffrey Roper (general editor), *World Survey of Islamic Manuscripts* (London: 1992-1994), 5 v. Also available is International African Institute (editor), Philip Baker (compiler), *International Directory of African Studies Research = Répertoire international des études africaines* (3rd rev. and expanded ed., London: 1994).

Congo

République démocratique du Congo—Bamanya (near Mbandaka)
(Democratic Republic of Congo—Bamanya (near Mbandaka))

Centre Aequatoria. Archives et Bibliothèque
(Aequatoria Center. Archives and Library)

Address: Centre Aequatoria, B.P. 276, Mbandaka, République démocratique du Congo.
Contact (in Belgium): Aequatoria, Te Boelaerlei 11, B-2140 Borgerhout, Belgium.
Tel.: +(32) 3-321-37-39 (in Belgium).
Fax: +(32) 3-321-01-11 (in Belgium).
Internet access to on-line catalog: Not available.
Founded: 1937.
Major resources: Aequatoria Library (Bibliothèque Aequatoria); Aequatoria Archives (Archives Aequatoria).
Areas of specialization: Schoolbooks in African languages, Lomongo dialects documentation, maps of Zaire/Congo, colonial documentation.
Archival/manuscript resources: 36 meters of archival materials, including papers of Edmond Boelaert, Mgr. Edward van Goethem, Louis Vertenten and the Trappist missionaries who were in the Congo between 1895 and 1925. Personal papers of Fr. Gustaaf Hulstaert, including extensive linguistic archives documenting his research during a period of sixty years.
Holdings (books and journals): 10,000 v., including 6,000 books in European languages and 500 items in 35 African languages.
Visual/audio resources: Not held.
Access: Open to the public. No special restrictions. Microfiche copies of the Aequatoria archives are available in the CAMP (Cooperative Africana Microfilm Project) collection at the Center for Research Libraries, Chicago; at the Memorial Library, University of Wisconsin, Madison; and the IPrA Research Center, University of Antwerp, Belgium.
Guides/catalogs: *Catalogue des Archives Aequatoria* (Bamanya, Zaire: 1995)—available on diskette (in Microsoft Word, 6.0 version) from the Center.

Artifact resources: A small ethnological museum related to Mongo material culture is maintained—see Honoré Vinck, "Les débuts d'un musée de la culture mongo," in *West African Museums Project*, vol. 1, no. 1 (1990), p. 17.

Description

The origin of the Aequatoria Archives and Library at Bamanya, République démocratique du Congo (formerly Zaire), goes back to 1937, when Edmond Boelaert (1899-1966) and Gustaaf Hulstaert (1900-1990) launched a new periodical, *Aequatoria*. The objective of Boelaert and Hulstaert was to promote the exchange of ideas and experiences between like-minded people working in Équateur province and confronted with similar colonial problems. Both were Catholic missionaries, although their concepts and strivings were broader and were integrated in a global concept of civilization in a colonial context. A large audience (expressed by means of correspondence, publishing, participation in meetings and associations) was brought together around *Aequatoria*. At the same time, a select group of collaborators, consisting of missionaries (Joseph van Wing, Leo Bittremieux, Raf van Caeneghem, Basiel Thange, Placide Tempels, Alexis Kagame), lawyers (Emiel Possoz, Antoine Sohier, Antoine Rubbens) and civil servants (Georges Brausch, Maurits De Ryck, Maurice Mamet, Charles Lodewijckx and Georges van der Kerken) was particularly active in this scholarly mission setting.

Situated as they were in the region occupied by the cluster of Mongo peoples, the full attention of Boelaert and Hulstaert was dedicated to the defense and promotion of the Lomongo language and of Mongo cultural values. The socio-economic situation of the population under colonial rule was lucidly analyzed at that time by Boelaert. After a series of conflicts with the highest Catholic authorities in the colony, resulting from their critique of colonial methods, Fr. Hulstaert oriented the journal in a less engaging way. *Aequatoria* was focussed, from 1946, on the linguistics and ethnic history of the Équateur region. In 1954 Boelaert left the Congo and in 1962 Hulstaert, for practical reasons, ceased publication of *Aequatoria*, which had been published at Bamanya from 1937 until 1962. Publication of the journal was later continued, beginning in 1980, as the *Annales Aequatoria*.

Aequatoria Center

The archives and documentation that are now the core of Aequatoria Center activities were formed in this context. Books were received for review in *Aequatoria*, serials arrived through journal exchange relationships, a few purchases were made, and the careful accumulation of pamphlets, circulars and similar ephemera built up a unique documentary resource that, since 1980, has been organized in a library and archive.

The Aequatoria Center is located ten kilometers from Mbandaka, the capital of Équateur province, at Bamanya, the rustic site of the oldest mission station in the region. The Bamanya mission station was founded in 1895. A new building was constructed at the Center in 1987, with a guest house for the use of national and foreign scholars. More than forty Western scholars and thousands of local students and scholars have used the Aequatoria research facilities since then.

References: Sam Nelson, "The Archives of the Missionnaires du Sacré Coeur (M.S.C.) at Bamanya (Zaire)," *History in Africa*, vol. 11 (1984), p. 391-394; Honoré Vinck, "Le Centre Aequatoria de Bamanya, 50 ans de recherches africanistes," *Zaire-Afrique*, no. 212 (1987), p. 79-102; Honoré Vinck, "Les conditions de recherches en sciences sociales: le Centre Aequatoria de Bamanya, Mbandaka-Zaire," *Canadian Association of African Studies Newsletter* (Spring 1992), p. 77-82. On Edmond Boelaert and Gustaaf Hulstaert, see Christopher Winters (general editor), *International Dictionary of Anthropologists* (New York: 1991) (= *Garland Reference Library of the Social Sciences,* vol. 638), p. 69-70, 313-314.

The Library

The research library of the Aequatoria Center focusses on Bantu linguistics, colonial history and Central African zoology. Publications related to the Belgian colony, such as *Le mouvement géographique*; *Notre Congo*; *La Belgique coloniale*; *Congo*; *Kongo Overzee*; and *Zaïre,* as well as the current publications of the area academic institutions, the complete collection of publications of the Musée royale d'Afrique centrale (Tervuren) and of the Académie royale des Sciences d'Outre-Mer (Brussels) are available, together with a selection of more than fifty current Africa-related periodicals. An author catalog and subject catalogs of books and periodical articles are maintained at the library. A complete collection of local newspapers and periodicals in the Lomongo language (published by the Catholic church between 1936 and 1960), and also some other local newspapers, are available. These constitute an invaluable resource for insight into daily life in this area during the colonial period. The newspapers, special monographs and brochures in the library have recently been microfilmed.

The Aequatoria Archives

The manuscripts and documents that constitute the Aequatoria Archives have been brought together from many sources. The largest contribution comes from Father Hulstaert himself; he bequeathed his entire scholarly correspondence, his Lomongo dialect manuscripts, his collection of clippings on colonial themes (1940-1960) and his botanical and zoological notes. Fr. Hulstaert's legacy also included the notes from Boelaert on Mongo history, a few manuscripts with linguistic and ethnological information by the Trappist Fathers, a collection of oral literature compiled by Edward van Goethem (the first Bishop of Coquilhatville) and papers of Regnier van Egeren, a civil administrator. Later, photocopies of documents in the diocesan archive and of the provincial ethnographic holdings were added. In the same period, the Archives acquired records and documents related to the schools of the mission stations of Boteka, Bamanya, Wafanya and Boende. Since 1980 the Aequatoria Center has collected all available documents of historical value, within the scope of its collections.

Since 1993 the whole archive has been microfilmed with grant support of the Social Science Research Council/American Council of Learned Societies. A catalog of archival holdings on microfiche is available (free, on diskette) from the Centre Aequatoria. In this way, more than 180,000 pages of archival materials have been made accessible to scholars.

Individual microfiche may be purchased for research use, or the full Archives Aequatoria collection of 2,458 microfiche may be purchased.

References: Honoré Vinck, "Le microfilmage des Archives Aequatoria," *History in Africa*, vol. 20 (1993), p. 423-427; also *Annales Aequatoria*, vol. 16 (1995), p. 600-602.

Material in the Archives Aequatoria

- Lomongo Dialects and Literature.

The Lomongo language (C61 in Guthrie's classification) has been the object of intense research and publication, based on the collection of comparative vocabularies (about 1,000 pages) and on classical language inventories, using the forms elaborated by the International African Institute (London) and by Hulstaert himself. Between 1930 and 1980, more than 300 Lomongo dialects were recorded in this way. Findings on only 47 dialects have been published. More than 4,000 cards and several notes constitute a comprehensive record of ethnonyms, toponyms and hydronyms of the Mongo region. Only 60 percent of the collection of Lomongo oral literature materials has been published. The entire Lomongo dialects and literature documentation at the Center consists of about 25,000 pages.

References: Gustaaf Hulstaert, "Onomastique mongo," *Annales Aequatoria,* vol. 12 (1991), p. 161-275; Gustaaf Hulstaert, "Témoignages pour la dialectologie mongo," *Bulletin des séances de l' Académie royale des Sciences d'Outre-Mer*, (1978), p. 357-371; A. De Rop, *Bibliographie over de Mongo* (Brussels: 1956); Honoré Vinck, "Dialectologie mongo: evolution depuis 1984," *Annales Aequatoria,* vol. 15 (1994), p. 425-437.

- The School System and Education.

The colonial school system of the Congo was exclusively in the hands of the Christian missions. The Aequatoria Archives has a systematic collection of documentation related to the school system in the region, dated between 1926 and 1972. This resource consists of circulars, statistics and instructions emanating from the central diocesan school administration. Some reports of school inspections are also available. The history of the schools of Bamanya, Boteka, Wafanya and Boende is abundantly documented from the beginnings until 1972 and more sparsely for subsequent years. Since the diocesan school office at Mbandaka was plundered and burned down in 1992, the Aequatoria Archives is the only remaining important source for study of the history of the school system and education in this region. The school records and documentation consist of 12,000 pages. Also held are more than 600 school and religious textbooks in 35 languages of the Congo region. The earliest of these was published in 1897. More than half of the textbooks are in non-Lomongo languages of the region.

References: Gustaaf Hulstaert, "Terminologie Chrétienne dans les langues bantoues," *Neue Zeitschrift für Missionswissenschaft*, 8 (1952), p. 49-66; Ndolo Obwong Muwoko, "Terminologie grammaticale du Lingala," *Annales Aequatoria*, vol. 11 (1990), p. 263-279; Honoré Vinck, "The Influence of Colonial Ideology on Schoolbooks in the Belgian Congo," *Paedagogica Historica* (Gent), vol. 31, no. 2 (1995), p. 355-405; Honoré Vinck, "Terminologie scolaire du Lomongo," *Annales Aequatoria*, vol. 11 (1990), p. 281-325.

- Special Colonial Questions.

Hulstaert was a member of the Commission for the Protection of the Indigenous, 1953-1960, and Boelaert was a member of the Council of the Équateur province and of the governmental linguistic commission. Both thus had access to important information and documentation. In addition, both were members of the Académie royale des Sciences d'Outre-Mer.

The dramatic decline of the birth rate in the region and the search for understanding of, and solutions to, this problem generated special documentation in the form of demographic statistics, field studies (Charles Lodewijckx), correspondence and commission reports, as well as notes on dowry, polygamy and marriage.

References: Edmond Boelaert, "La situation démographique des Nkundo-Móngo," *Cepsi* [Elisabethville] (1946), [55 pp.]; Honoré Vinck, "Charles Lodewijckx [bio-bibliographie]," *Annales Aequatoria,* vol. 15 (1994), p. 461-477.

The land tenure disputes, as a consequence of recent colonial reforms (extension of the city of Mbandaka; *Paysannat Indigène*) provoked studies on the family and on traditional authority structures. Several private cases, generated during legal disputes in the 1950s, were documented by court sessions, correspondence with judicial authorities and occasional publications.

References: Edmond Boelaert, "La question des terres indigènes. Pourquoi les indigènes sont-ils mécontents?," *Zaïre*, vol. 9 (1955), p. 969-972.

The control of the indigenous courts was one of the functions of the colonial civil servants. Reignier van Egeren (1912-1972) left to the Archives documentation related to his function in the region of Mbandaka, Ingende, Basankoso and Bikoro. These records contain summaries of court cases, proverb collections, notes on judicial terminology in Lomongo and Lingala.

References: Lonkama Ekono, "Archivalia [le Fonds van Egeren dans les Archives Aequatoria]," *Annales Aequatoria*, vol. 10 (1989), p. 321-328.

Labor legislation, as applied in the region and by the Catholic missions (illustrated by several specific disputes), is documented for the period from 1944 to 1990.

The annual reports of the "Commission de Protection" of the indigenous city of Mbandaka (from 1951 to 1959) and the reports of the "Commission pour la Protection des Indigénes" (from 1953 to 1960) are an exceptional witness of the colonial policy in the 1950s.

- The History of the Équateur Region.

Edmond Boelaert systematically collected all available information about the pre-colonial and early colonial history of the Équateur region. He (as well as Hulstaert) took notes in the archives of the colonial administration. He also launched, in 1954, an inquiry about the recollections of the first arrival of whites in the region. In the 1950s, in collaboration with Maurits De Ryck, he collected additional documents on the history of the Équateur region.

References: Honoré Vinck, "Les papiers De Ryck: documents pour l'étude de l'époque coloniale au Zaire," *History in Africa,* vol. 21 (1994), p. 441-446. The full text of the inquiry of 1954 was published in *Annales Aequatoria*, vol. 16 (1995), p. 13-134, and in vol. 17 (1996), p. 7-415.

- Ethnological Inquiries of the Colonial Administration.

Between 1920 and 1960 the colonial authorities of the Congo tried to base their policies for the administrative organization of the country on previous ethnological research. The Aequatoria Archives has about 500 documents (in original, copy, summary or photocopy versions) representing ethnological studies with reference to the geographic region between Mbandaka, Ikela, Inongo and Lisala.

References: Honoré Vinck, "Les enquêtes ethnologiques dans les Archives Aequatoria," *Annales Aequatoria*, vol. 14 (1993), p. 595-617.

- Mission History.

Missionary activities in the region are documented by hundreds of papers, circulars, reports, letters to superiors, mission accounts, etc. The Archives has this kind of documentation from the mission stations of Bamanya, Boende, Wafanya and Boteka (including, for a limited period, the medical and economic activities). The parish registers of the mission of Bamanya are the oldest of the diocese and have annotations as early as 1898.

References: Honoré Vinck, "Inventaire des registres de la mission catholique de Bokuma," *Annales Aequatoria*, vol. 9 (1988), p. 279-286; Honoré Vinck, "Parish Registers of Bakusu (Mbandaka)," *Annales Aequatoria*, vol. 1, no. II (1980), p. 124-127; Honoré Vinck, "Parish Registers of Bamanya," *Annales Aequatoria*, vol. 1, no. II (1980), p. 119-123.

- Correspondence of Gustaaf Hulstaert.

The personal scholarly correspondence of Gustaaf Hulstaert, exchanged with more than 200 persons, is held at the Archives. This correspondence includes the letters (in typewritten carbon copy) to and from Tempels, Kagame, Sohier, Possoz, Boelaert, Meeussen, Carrington, De Boeck and others.

References: Fr. Bontinck, "Aux origines de la philosophie bantoue. La correspondance Tempels-Hulstaert (1944-1948)," Faculté de Théologie, Kinshasa 1985; Fr. Bontinck, "Tempelsiana II," *Revue africaine de théologie* (1987), p. 237-244; Gustaaf Hulstaert, "Tempels et Possoz," *Revue africaine de théologie*, vol. 7 (1983), p. 215-221; Honoré Vinck, "Correspondance," *Annales Aequatoria*, vol. 11 (1990), p. 24-50; Honoré Vinck, "Correspondance, G. Hulstaert-E. De Boeck," *Annales Aequatoria*, vol. 15 (1994), p. 505-575; Honoré Vinck, "Correspondence Kagame-Hulstaert," *Annales Aequatoria*, vol. 16 (1995), p. 467-588; Honoré Vinck, "La correspondence scientifique de Gustaaf

Hulstaert," *Annales Aequatoria*, vol. 9 (1988), p. 269-276; Honoré Vinck, "John Carrington," *Annales Aequatoria*, vol. 14 (1993), p. 565-583.

- History of the Aequatoria Center.

The Aequatoria Center has had a troubled history. Its pro-Indigenous attitude caused continuing friction with the Catholic church hierarchy between 1940 and 1945. This situation disturbed the normal evolution of the Center and affected the orientation of its publications. Archival records on the ideological orientation of the local Catholic church authorities document this aspect of the Center's history.

- The Map Collection.

The map collection consists of more than 600 items and is the result of some sixty years of work. Included are cartographic sketches, annotated maps, drafts of the *Carte linguistique du Congo*, copies of old administrative maps and copies of the plans of the cadastre and plans of the mission buildings from 1950 to 1975.
References: Honoré Vinck, "Cartographie historique de Mbandaka," *Annales Aequatoria*, vol. 4 (1983), p. 151-157.

- National Conference of Zaire.

The secretary of the Aequatoria Center was a delegate to the National Conference of Zaire. He collected for the Archives the complete set of documents issued by the National Conference, from April 6 to November 29, 1992.

- Emile Possoz Papers.

A former lawyer, Emile Possoz (1885-1969), was one of the early collaborators of Aequatoria. The Center acquired a typewritten copy of a part of Possoz's unpublished essays on African philosophy and ethnology.
References: Honoré Vinck, "Emile Possoz, bio-bibliographie et inventaire des papiers Possoz à Sint Truiden (B)," *Annales Aequatoria,* vol. 10 (1989), p. 297-320.

- Isidore Bakanja Papers.

Isidore Bakanja (1885-1909) is one of two Zairians who have been recognized by the Catholic church as Saints (1993). The Bakanja papers include documentation collected in the course of historical research on Bakanja's life and during the proceedings of the ecclesiastical process. These records have been acquired by the Aequatoria Archives.
References: A. Claessens, "Isidore Bakanja, martyr? Étude critique des conflits entre la mission des Trappistes et la Société anonyme belge du Haut Congo," [Paris: 1978], unpublished, 2 v.

- Bible Translations.

Between 1935 and 1984, Hulstaert and his collaborators translated either portions of the Bible, or the entire text, into Bantu languages. Reports of Translation Board meetings, drafts, correspondence with editors and printers, with sponsors and ecclesiastical authorities constitute an important source of information in this special translation field.

References: Gustaaf Hulstaert, "Problèmes de traduction en langue bantoue," *Bulletin des séances de l'Académie royale des Sciences d'Outre-Mer* (1977), p. 331-371.

Honoré Vinck

Southeast Asia

Information on Southeast Asian documentary resources of anthropological interest is gradually becoming more accessible on the Internet. Websites of several Southeast Asian national or university libraries, archives or museums are now available. The URL of the Centre for Malay Manuscripts (administered by the National Library of Malaysia) is http://www.pnm.my/database/col-man.htm. The Dewan Bahasa dan Pustaka in Kuala Lumpur, Malaysia, maintains the Malaysian Documentation Centre (Pusat Dokumentasi Melayu). The Centre's URL is http://www.dbp.gov.my/pdm.htm. In Manila, the Cultural Center of the Philippines (CCP) administers national collections in Philippine culture and arts. The Center administers the Museum of Philippine Culture (Museo ng Kalinangang Pilipino), the CCP Library and also an archival collection of "Masterworks of Philippine Cinema." The URL of the Cultural Center of the Philippines is http://www3.admu.edu.ph/ccp.

Numerous scholarly or research-oriented websites related to Southeast Asia are also maintained in Australia, the United States, the Netherlands, France or elsewhere. Texts from Ian Proudfoot's Malay Concordance Project, for example, are available at http://online.anu.edu.au/asianstudies/ahcen/proudfoot/MCP.

Philippines

Philippines—Misamis Oriental—Cagayan de Oro City

Xavier University (XU). Museum and Archives

Address: Museum and Archives, Xavier University, Cagayan de Oro City, 9000 Philippines.
Tel.: (63-8822) 72-38-18 (office); (63-8822) 72-60-69 (residence).
Fax: (63-8822) 72-6355.
Internet address: http://www.cc.xu.edu.ph.
Founded: 1967.
Major resources: Recorded epics of Mindanao tribes: Bukidnon, Manobo and Subanun; the Elio collection; the Charles Cameron collection of documents on Mindanao and the Philippine South—especially the Moro tribes; the Collection of Philippine Folk Beliefs and Customs.
Areas of specialization: Philippine folk beliefs and customs; local historical sources of northern Mindanao—especially of Cagayan de Oro, Camiguin and Misamis Oriental; Mindanao epics, folktales and narratives.
Archival/manuscript resources: The Elio collection (31 m.) contains 100 manuscripts. The Charles Cameron collection (21 m.) contains 74 manuscripts. Only manuscript materials that have been photocopied are available for research use. This is due to the fragile condition of the manuscripts. With additional resources the Archives plans to photocopy all of the manuscripts that are in delicate condition.
Fieldnotes, etc.:

- Fieldnotes containing data on the ethnobotanical study of indigenous Philippine forest plants—collected by Irene S. Llesis, Marelino C. Panis, Jr., and Luis E. Ortique. This data was gathered from the Talaandig tribe of Lantapan, Bukidnon, and also from the Manobo tribe of San Fernando, Bukidnon.
- Fieldnotes on traditional songs and music: folk narratives and rituals and riddles—collected by Irene S. Llesis.
- Fieldnotes on epics (on 13 tapes)—collected by Victorino Saway.
- Fieldnotes on nine epics (on 29 tapes)—collected by Irene S. Llesis.
- 26 riddles—written in the researcher's fieldnotes.
- Proverbs and wise sayings—collected by Irene S. Llesis—places (towns) collected are Songco, Lantapan, Bukidnon, Tinaytayan and Talacag.
- Fieldnotes on Talaandig methods of food preparation. Places (towns) collected are Songco, Lantapan, Bukidnon.

Holdings (books and journals): 7,824 book vols.; 861 periodical vols.

Visual/audio resources: Watercolor paintings on illustration boards or murals of local myths, legends and folktales.

Audio resources (sound recordings and related documentation): Many tape recordings of traditional songs, epics and folk narratives of Mindanao:
- Nine epics (on 42 audio tapes). Dates of collection extend from 1981. The epics were collected at Tinaytayan, Talacag, Bukidnon; Sitio Salimbubunug, Capinonan, Cabalanglasan and other locations.
- Traditional songs and music (on 27 audio tapes) collected by Irene S. Llesis. Places (towns) collected are Lantapan, Talakag and Cabalanglasan—all in Bukidnon.
- Traditional songs—written in the researcher's fieldnotes. Researcher: Irene S. Llesis. Places (towns) collected are Tulugan, Songco and Lantapan—all in Bukidnon.
- Folk narratives (legends, stories of origin, folktales, riddles, proverbs, etc.), rituals, etc. (recorded on 33 audio tapes). Researcher: Irene S. Llesis. Places (towns) collected are Lantapan, Bukidnon; Manolo Fortich.

Access: Manuscripts are restricted to use only within the Archives. Books in the departmental library are available even for visitors, who may use them for a fee. Rare and valuable books are kept in the curator's office. These may be used by scholars in the library and a listing of these is available.

References: Francisco R. Demetrio, S.J., *Encyclopedia of Philippine Folk Beliefs and Customs* (Cagayan de Oro City: 1991), 2 v.; Francisco R. Demetrio, S.J. (editor), *The Local Historical Sources of Northern Mindanao* (Cagayan de Oro City: 1995); Francisco R. Demetrio, S.J., "The Xavier Folklife Museum & Archives: A Report," *Mindanao Journal*, vol. 6, no. 2-4 (Oct. 1979-June 1980), p. 203-227; Vicente Elio y Sanchez, "The History of Camiguin," *Philippine Studies*, vol. 20, no. 1 (1st quarter 1972), p. 106-146 [The Elio Collection is described in this article, p. 106-108]; Mardonio M. Lao, *History of Cagayan de Oro, 1622-1901* (Cagayan de Oro City: 1980); Francis C. Madigan, "The Early History of Cagayan de Oro," *Philippine Studies*, vol. 11, no. 1 (Jan. 1963), p. 76-130; Delia S. Magana, "Cagayanon Folklore: An Exploratory Study of Its Historical Elements," M.A. thesis, Xavier University, Cagayan de Oro City, 1980.

Guides/catalogs: Guidebooks to Xavier University Museum Exhibit Rooms One, Two and Three—compiled by Francisco R. Demetrio, S.J., Marelino C. Panis, Jr., and Albert S.J. Vamenta—have been published by the Museum.

Artifact resources in museum collections: These include a collection of saints statues (*santos*)—wooden and a few ivories; church equipment and paraphernalia; boat coffins of wood, recovered from caves in the vicinity of Cagayan de Oro City; also twelve bronze *versos* or compact gunpowder-filled cannons to explode on days of religious and civic celebrations; a good collection of amulets and talismans used by the various native religious sects in Mindanao is also available.

Archaeological sites represented by the artifact collections: The museum has artifacts and archaeological collections from the Huluga Caves and from the Huluga Open Site Excavation, Macasandig and Balulang, Cagayan de Oro City. The museum also has the reports by the National Museum personnel who helped with the excavations at the Huluga Caves and the Huluga Open Sites in 1970, 1981, 1988 and 1991:

- Angel Bautista, "Field Report on the Investigation of an Archeological Site in Cagayan de Oro, Misamis Oriental," Manila: 1991—typescript MS.
- Linda Burton, "Progress Report no. 1. Exploration of Huluga Sites, Tagwanao Region, Cagayan de Oro, Misamis Oriental," Manila: 1975—typescript MS.
- Israel Cabanilla, "Xavier University—National Museum Archeological Research Cooperation," 1970—typescript MS.
- Francisco R. Demetrio, S.J., "The Huluga Caves and the Prehistory of Cagayan de Oro," in *Cagayan* (Cagayan de Oro: 1971) (= *Museum and Archives Publication*, no. 3), p. 9-14.

Description

Xavier University Folkloric Museum and Archives

The Museum

During the past three decades, the Museo de Oro has tried to illustrate by watercolor and enamel and color painting—either on half illustration boards or large *katcha* (cloth) or wood—our local legends, myths and epics. Two Museum artists, Albert Vamenta and Pennsencio Estarte, have produced 500 illustrations. Estarte painted 360 pieces (three large murals) and Vamenta 140 pictures depicting our epics, legends and myths.

The Archives

- The Elio Collection.

The Xavier University Archives received a major donation in May 1969 of the Elio Collection—named after the late Don Vicente Elio y Sanchez—a circuit judge of Camiguin and a civic, political and religious leader. He was the local correspondent of Manila and

Cebu newspapers at the end of the nineteenth century and early in the twentieth. He was also an avid collector of curiosities and often wrote on political, civic and religious matters.

His father, Don Joaquin, besides being head of Tabacalera, was a painter in watercolor, even before settling in Mambajao. The collection has ten watercolors by Don Joaquin on religious themes and also three paintings of Spanish ships. Priceless are Don Joaquin's thirteen watercolors of the Camiguin volcano when it erupted in 1871. He was an eyewitness —painting from a launch on the Bohol Sea. For almost a year he drew the volcano, which started out as a hillock and eventually grew into a good-sized mountain.

Don Vicente (1884-1927) was not a painter, but he drew portraits, buildings and landscapes, using charcoal as a medium. The collection also includes Rizaliana materials. In 1911 Don Vicente authored a short biography of Jose Rizal. He collected literary compositions in Spanish and also local historical accounts—including clippings from Manila and Cebu newspapers published at the turn-of-the-century and during the first decades of the twentieth. The newspaper accounts of Don Vicente give a good slice of life in Manbajao, Camiguin, Cagayan de Oro and Misamis Oriental at that time.

Citizens of Cagayan de Oro will greatly enjoy reading Elio's 1892 description of the first hanging bridge in Cagayan. It was longer by eighteen meters than the Claveria Bridge in Manila (now Quezon Bridge) and also was 78 meters longer than the only other hanging bridge in Mindanao—which spanned the Agus river in Iligan.

Elio does not mention the fact that, when the bridge was inaugurated, it collapsed. At the blessing, the people from Carmen side and Cagayan side were stopped from crossing. When the banquet began, people started crossing from both sides. The posts supporting the bridge on each side then buckled, and the whole structure slowly, but surely, landed in the river. An uncle, then a teenager, was eyewitness to the event, and he remarked how the Spanish señoras and señoritas twittered away as their pretty ankles got a sudden dowsing. One death was reported, a Spanish gentleman, Don Herbard del Castilbe (married to the Borromeos in Mambajao) was pinned down by a falling joist. We get these details from the Bautista manuscript.

● The Philippine Folk Beliefs and Customs Collection Project.

The project, which began in 1967, resulted in the publication in 1970 of the *Dictionary of Philippine Folk Beliefs and Customs*. The four small volumes of this first edition contained fewer than 3,000 entries. After discovering the imperfection in our work, it was decided to make the dictionary more pan-Philippine and to update its content. So, for twenty years, from 1970 to 1990, we excerpted folk beliefs from books, articles and masters and doctoral dissertations for inclusion. With the help of the Toyota Foundation and Adam Schall von Bell, a revised and enlarged edition titled *Encyclopedia of Philippine Folk Beliefs and Customs*, in two large volumes, was published in 1991. This publication contains more than 8,000 entries from throughout the Philippines, as well as many cross references. We plan to publish a supplement to the *Encyclopedia* every ten years, including references to all materials that have appeared since 1991.

In the original collection project, a consistent format for recording each entry of a folk belief or custom was followed. Four 6 x 4″ cards were used for each entry. The original is typed on a card cartolina, and three copies are on ordinary bond paper. As new folk beliefs and customs are gathered in the field, or excerpted from publications, the cards are added to filing cabinets, in accord with the format of the collection.

Francisco R. Demetrio, S.J.

Philippines—Quezon City

University of the Philippines (U.P.) University Library

Address: University Library, University of the Philippines, Diliman, Quezon City, Philippines.
Tel.: (63) 982-471; local 6284.
Fax: (63) 98-67-80
Founded: 1922.
Major resources: The Whitfield Harnish Collection of Philippine photographs is an accumulation of photos that provide visual documentation of late nineteenth-century Philippine life, including views pertinent to the anthropology, history, sociology, description and travel, social life and customs, costumes, art and architecture of the Philippines. The Harnish photographs were produced between 1898 and 1907.
Areas of specialization: The Harnish Collection is especially valuable for its visual documentation of the turn-of-the-century Philippines—including views of the Moros and of Mindanao.
Holdings: The Harnish Collection consists of more than 500 glass negatives, slide plates, film negatives and prints.
Access: The library is open to the University of the Philippines community and to other researchers. Harnish Collection resources must be used in the library.
Guides/catalogs: There is a checklist of the Harnish Collection photos, consisting of three catalogs: a catalog of plate negatives; a catalog of small film negatives; and a catalog of slide plate negatives.

Description

In 1965 the California Historical Society, through its Librarian, James de T. Abajan, offered the Whitfield Harnish Collection to "...any institution of learning or a qualified repository of documents in the Philippines." But it was only on June 30, 1966, that this valuable photographic collection was formally given to the University of the Philippines Library. Acceptance of the collection was made for the University by U.P. History Professor Serafin D. Quiason—who learned of the availability of the collection during a survey he undertook with a Ford Foundation grant for the development of the University Library collection. Marina Dayrit, the University Librarian, has a program to develop the library's Philippine materials collection.

The Harnish Collection photographs received from the California Historical Society were actually a portion of the photo collection previously at that society. The Society donated the Philippine portion of the collection to the U.P., while other Harnish photographs dealing with Mexico and California were retained at the Society's library in San Francisco.

The Harnish Collection consists of more than 500 glass negatives, slide plates, film negatives and prints depicting scenery, peoples and edifices from northern Luzon to Zamboanga (in southwestern Mindanao) at the close of the nineteenth-century and in the early 1900s. The photographs were taken between 1898 and 1907. Their value derives in part from the fact that the Harnishes took sequences of images that depict significant aspects of Philippine economic and social life. Pictures of American camp life and personalities are also part of the collection, since the Harnishes also took photographic portraits.

The Harnish photographs were taken by Harry Whitfield Harnish, a Private of Company D, 14th U.S. Infantry, who served in the American campaign against the Moros in 1898. After his discharge from service in the same year, Harnish and his wife, Josephine Peas Barnes, ran a photograph gallery: the Mrs. H. W. Harnish Gallery, in Zamboanga. They took "Filipino and Moro" views, many of which were sold in the United States and Europe as postcards with excellent and quite detailed images.

The Harnish Collection is a useful iconographic collection for researches in the history, sociology and anthropology of Filipinos and the local architecture at the turn-of-the-century. Researchers may consult the prints made from the Harnish negatives at the Filipiniana Section of the University of the Philippines Main Library.

Belen B. Angeles

Thailand

Thailand—Bangkok

Sayām Samākhom
(Siam Society)

Address: Library, Siam Society, 131 Soi 21 (Asoke 21), Sukhumvit Road, Bangkok 10110 Thailand.
Tel.: (66) 2-258-3491 or (66) 2-258-3494.
Fax: (66) 2-258-3491
Networks, consortia: CDS/ISIS.
Founded: 1904.
Major resources: The Society's library contains rare books, manuscripts, old maps, photographs and other documentation on the history, culture and natural history of Thailand and neighboring countries.
Areas of specialization: Printed and manuscript materials in the humanities, social sciences and natural sciences on Thailand and neighboring countries. The library holds many Thai- and English-language books and manuscripts; palm-leaf manuscripts in Thai script; Thai-language theses and research data funded by the James H.W. Thompson Foundation; materials donated by Chao Phaya Bhaskarawongse; and other special collections.

Holdings: 25,000 book volumes in Thai and other languages; 94 Thai-language periodical titles; 437 periodical titles in English and other Western languages; microfilms.

Access: The library is open Tue.-Sat., 9:00 a.m. to 5:00 p.m. Books are circulated to Siam Society members only.

Visual/audio resources: Photographs, color slides, old maps, paintings and drawings, video cassettes and sound recordings on cassette tape.

References: Bonnie Davis, *The Siam Society Under Five Reigns* (Bangkok: 1989); Sonia Krug, *The Kamthieng House: Its History and Collections: A Classic Example of Northern Thai Residential Architecture of the Nineteenth-Century* (Bangkok: 1982); *Prawat Sayām Samākhom* [History of the Siam Society] (Bangkok: 1976); Subhadradis Diskul, "Denmark and the Siam Society," in Pensak C. Horowitz (editor), *Thai-Danish Relations: 30 Cycles of Friendship* (Copenhagen: 1980), p. 334-337.

Guides/catalogs: Oskar V. Hinüben, "The Pāli Manuscripts Kept at the Siam Society, Bangkok, A Short Catalogue," *Journal of the Siam Society*, vol. 75 (1987), p. 9-74; Siam Society, *Index: The Journal of the Siam Society, 1904-1993 and the Siam Society Newsletter, 1985-1989* ([Bangkok]: 1996[?]).

Artifacts of anthropological significance: The Kamthieng House, a traditional Northern Thai dwelling that was relocated from northern Thailand to Soi Asoke in Bangkok, is an attraction for visitors to the Society's headquarters. Material culture objects curated by the Society also include hill tribe costumes collected in the field in the 1930s, with assistance of the Department of the Interior; other cultural objects.

Description

The Siam Society Under Royal Patronage is a learned society that has been active in the cultural and scholarly life of Thailand for more than ninety years. To fully understand the origins of the Society's library, it is necessary to know something of the history and goals of the Society itself. From its beginnings in 1904, the Society was aided by generous donations from Thai, Danish and American institutions and individuals. In the early years, the greatest support came from the royal families of Thailand and also from foreign learned societies. His Royal Highness Crown Prince Vajiravudh (later King Rama VI) (1881-1925) was the first Patron of the society. Prince Damrong Rajanubhab (1862-1943) was the first Vice Patron and Chao Phaya Bhaskarawongse was named as an Honorary Member in recognition of his distinguished literary work and his generosity in placing his valuable collection in the society's library. Early support for the society was received from the Royal Asiatic Society (London), the Batavian Association of Arts and Science (Batavia), the Società Asiatica Italiana (Florence) and other foreign learned bodies.

The Siam Society was created with the objective of "promoting and encouraging the arts and sciences in Siam and in the neighboring countries," (*Prawat Sayām Samākhom*, 1976, p. 11). Five study areas were established to aid in the realization of these goals. These were technology and fine arts; sociology; physical anthropology and archaeology; history, literature and comparative philology; and agriculture, transport and travel (*Prawat Sayām Samākhom*, 1976, p. 11). To report on the activities of the Society, and to disseminate articles and notices by the members, the *Journal of the Siam Society* (JSS) was created in 1905. The *Natural History Bulletin* of the Society has also been published for many decades.

By 1921 the Society and its library were located on the first floor of the Falck Beidek Building in Bangkok. Members were encouraged to donate printed materials, manuscripts, old photographs and relics to expand and enhance the collections. The donated materials received as a result of these appeals have occasionally been listed in the JSS. Scholarly journals received on exchange from foreign learned associations also formed a part of the growing library collections.

During the 1920s an expanding membership, increased activities and the growing usage of the library caused the Falck Beidek Building to become increasingly overcrowded. On the Society's 25th anniversary, in 1929, the decision was made to build a new headquarters building. The building at Soi Asoke was opened in 1933, and continues in use today as the main site of the Society. In 1954, on the Society's 50th anniversary, the Council established a research fund to support selected research projects. Part of the fund was used to construct a separate building for the library at Soi Asoke. The library building was officially opened by His Majesty the King, Her Majesty the Queen, Her Majesty Queen Rambai Barni and their Majesties King Frederick IX and Queen Ingrid of Denmark, on January 13, 1962.

In 1980 increased library usage, and the need to provide better services to members, led to the establishment of an interlibrary loan program in cooperation with the libraries of Chulalongkorn and Thammasat Universities and the Thai National Documentation Center.

The library collection has continued to grow as a result of member donations, exchanges with other libraries and, very importantly, as a result of funds made available for the purchase of library materials. The Edwin F. Stanton Fund provided for the acquisition of books on Buddhism, a complete set of King Chulalongkorn's diaries and copies of the Pāli Text Society's series on Buddhism. The Jim Thompson Foundation donated a collection of Thai theses and also research works in Thai.

As the collections have expanded, measures for the conservation of library materials have become increasingly necessary. As a first step, air conditioning was installed in the library for humidity control. In 1987 the fumigation of rare books was begun with the assistance of the National Archives. Selected rare and fragile books and materials have also been microfilmed. In 1996 a new building was constructed at Soi Asoke to house the Society's library, an exhibit area and offices.

The Society's collections of books, palm-leaf manuscripts, old maps, historical photographs and films are very precious and, in some cases, unique. The Siam Society Library is thus an increasingly important resource for research and study on many aspects of Thai life and culture.

Chalermsee Olson

Wat Bovornives Vihara

Address: Wat Bovornives Vihara, Phra Sumen Road, Bangkok 10200 Thailand.
Location: In the Pho. Bo. Ro. Building, Wat Bovornives Vihara.

Tel.: (66) 2-282-8715

Founded: 1972.

Major resources: A large Thai cremation volume collection.

Areas of specialization: Thai biographical studies, religion and religious texts, history, Thai cultural and folk knowledge (including herbal medicine, literature, folk tales and others).

Holdings: More than 25,000 Thai cremation volumes.

Visual/audio resources: Not held.

Access: Open to scholars and general readers by appointment. Materials must be used in the library.

References: Chun Prabhavi-vadhana, "Special Publications for Free Distribution," *Journal of the Siam Society*, vol. 61, no. 1 (1973), p. 227-260; Grant A. Olson, "Thai Cremation Volumes: A Brief History of a Unique Genre of Literature," *Asian Folklore Studies,* vol. 51, no. 2 (1992), p. 279-294; Sanguan Ankhong, *Sing ræk nai müang Thai* ["Firsts" in Thailand] (Bangkok: 1960 [2503]), vol. 3; Suphat Songsængchan, "Kānsüksā praphēt khong nangsü anuson nai ngānchāpanakitsop thī khatlok rüang čhāk tonchabap Hosamut hæng Chāt læ rüang thī dai čhāk læng ün-ün rawāng pī Pho. So. 2501-2510" [A Study of the Tradition of Cremation Volumes Created from Manuscripts Held at the National Library and Other Places Between 1958-1967], Master's thesis, Thammasat University, 1969 [2512]; "Thailand's Funeral Books," *Asiaweek*, vol. 12, no. 23 (June 8, 1986), p. 57-58; [various authors], *Nangsü anuson ngānsop: Hongsamut Wat Bowonniwǣwihān* [Cremation Volumes: The Wat Bovornives Library] (Bangkok: 1972 [2515]).

Guides/catalogs: Grant Olson has translated the list of subject headings in this collection, but it has yet to be published. The subject headings are in the Dewey Decimal classification system.

Artifacts of anthropological significance: A Buddha-image collection of some significance is also housed in this building.

Description

A royal temple in Bangkok houses a collection of literature unique to Thailand, the Cremation Volume Collection. Wat Bovornives Vihara, a temple of first-class ranking, built by royalty about 1828, is one of Thailand's most famous temples. It has been the dwelling place of many members of the royal family during their temporary stay in the Buddhist monkhood. The Thai cremation volume collection is housed in a relatively new building in the temple complex, which bears the initials of the current king, Bhumibol Adulyadej (Pho. Bo. Ro.). King Bhumibol dedicated the building in February 1971, when it was set aside as library and museum space. The Pho. Bo. Ro. building is accessible from the northern temple gates via Phra Sumen Road. The current cremation volume collection came about due to the auspicious coincidence of the establishment of the Pho. Bo. Ro. building, the interest of journalist Nares Naropakorn in establishing a cremation volume collection and the willingness of Wat Bovornives to house such a collection.

For years people who have done scholarly work on Thailand have depended on a genre of literature unique to Thai culture, the cremation volume or *nangsü anuson ngānsop*. These volumes, published and distributed as gifts to mourners on the occasion of cremation ceremonies, are a rich source of biographical, religious, historical, cultural and literary information; they also constitute a unique cultural artifact of Thai society.

The origin of cremation volume literature can be traced to Western Christian missionary influence and to the influx of the printing technology these missionaries brought to Thailand to publish their own religious literature. The free distribution of cremation volumes in Thai society grew out of a strong cultural value of gift-giving (*thān*; Pali, *dāna*), already present and associated with Buddhism and merit-making in Thailand. More specifically, the free distribution of cremation volumes is an extension of a cultural practice of giving gifts to people to celebrate a special, meritorious occasion (*nai ngān kuson*). This practice also shows a concern for reading and the preservation of literature in a country noted for its high literacy rate.

With the rise of printing technology and increasing access to printing presses, the practice of creating books for certain auspicious occasions (*nai wan mongkhon*) and celebrations, including funerals, began to spread. The earliest volume found at the National Library (in Bangkok) that was freely given out for an auspicious occasion can be dated to 1876 [2419]. Some people have claimed that some of the first Thai cremation or funeral volumes may be traced back to about 1807—to works that were handwritten on *khoi* paper. The bark of a tree or shrub, *Streblus asper*, was used for making this paper. This claim, however, is dubious and the history of these early volumes remains sketchy.

The role of *kuson* volumes in building library collections in Thailand is an important one: commemorative books and cremation volumes became a key factor in building book collections at the early royal libraries. Through an agreement with the Ho Phrasamut Wachirayan—which later (in 1905) became the National Library—those wishing to create volumes for auspicious occasions were permitted to reprint library manuscripts. Some of these volumes were handed out on the stipulated occasion and others were sold to benefit library acquisitions.

Thai cremation volumes can usually be identified by their white, black or silver gray covers, although the combination of fuchsia and black recently enjoyed some popularity. The earliest volumes did not always contain a biography of the deceased; this practice began around 1895 (Sanguan, 1960 [2503], p. 469). Almost all recent samples of cremation volumes, however, are comprised of a short biography of the deceased, eulogies from friends and relatives (called *kham wai-ālai*) and selected essays or pieces of prose and literature. Often, the "look" of these volumes—their length, size and quality of appearance—can be an indicator of status.

The volumes often contain works that had been personal favorites of the deceased or the family. By republishing long-out-of-print material, many reprints were intended as a contribution to the preservation of Thai literature. The first wave of cremation volumes usually dealt with (the Buddhist) religion. Most cremation volumes included Pali passages and chants, often printed to assist those present at rituals to understand what the monks were chanting. Damrong Rajanubhab wrote that "In 1904 [2447] Somdet Phra Phutthachao-luang (King Chulalongkorn, Rama V) proclaimed that these volumes that contained all this deep Buddhist philosophy were not very enjoyable for most people to read. He requested that people begin to publish fables, Jataka Tales (moral "birth stories" of the previous lives of the Buddha), and fiction" (*Nangsü anuson*, 1972 [2515], p. 6). The King claimed that enough 'heavy' (*nak samong*) and 'dry' (*hæng-læng*) works had been published and that it was time to let this genre of literature evolve in a new direction (Sanguan, 1960 [2503], p. 471-472). However, it was not until the 1950s and 1960s that the subject matter of cremation volumes spread very far beyond the realms of religion, history and archeology (*Nangsü anuson*, 1972 [2515], p. 7-8).

The distribution of cremation volumes has always been rather haphazard, a matter of being in the right place at the right time. Realizing the value of these relatively ephemeral works, some Southeast Asian collections in Western libraries have made a conscious effort to bolster their collections with Thai cremation volumes.

It was not until the early 1970s, after Nares Naropakorn became interested in finding a home for cremation volumes, that a special collection was established. In 1971 Nares Naropakorn, a writer for the popular Bangkok newspaper *Siam Rath*, invited people to submit samples and gifts of cremation volumes in order to establish a special library of these books. The response was overwhelming and left him with a big storage problem until Wat Bovornives came to the rescue. In the early days of the collection, a librarian from Ramkhamhæng University, Ranjuan Intharakamhæng, started the process of planning and cataloging the collection. Ranjuan left the project to be ordained a Buddhist nun at the famous temple in southern Thailand, Suan Mokkh (Garden of Liberation), where she has become a renowned religious teacher. Later, Tongyot Pratoomvongs, a librarian at Thammasat University, led a volunteer team that continues to catalog donations to the collection and keeps the library available for public access, by appointment.

An early organizational decision was to adapt the Dewey Decimal classification system "to fit Thai society." By giving priority to cataloging the volumes according to the name and occupation of the deceased, rather than according to the subject of the literature and essays contained in each volume (as the U.S. Library of Congress does), the catalog of the collection has increasingly become a reflection of Thai social structure—an interesting model in itself.

Note: Dates in brackets, are according to the Buddhist Era—which begins with the passing of Lord Buddha and, in Thailand, is held to be 543 years before the beginning of our Christian calendar.

Grant A. Olson

East Asia

Japan

Japan—Ōsaka

Kokuritsu Minzokugaku Hakubutsukan. Toshokan
(National Museum of Ethnology. Library)

Address: Library, National Museum of Ethnology, 10-1 Senri Expo Park, Suita, Ōsaka, 565 Japan.
Tel.: 81 (06) 876-2151
Fax: 81 (06) 875-0401
Networks, consortia: NACSIS.
Local on-line catalog: JAIRS.
Founded: 1974.
Major resources: Books, journals.
Areas of specialization: The Reichel-Dolmatoff collection, the Makino collection.
Holdings (books and journals): 393,000 book vols., 11,300 journal vols.

Description

The 7,081 volumes of the Reichel-Dolmatoff collection originally were in the private library of cultural anthropologist Gerardo Reichel-Dolmatoff. The collection contains books on the ethnological, archaeological or sociological study of Central and South America, and also some books on basic approaches in ethnology and related fields of study.

The Makino collection, accumulated by the late professor of sociology, Tatsumi Makino, contains 19,898 volumes in several subject areas such as sociology, history, and ethnology. Among the books on China, 13,302 volumes of Chinese classics (a legacy of the Makino family) are the most important and valuable.

Information Service Division, National Museum of Ethnology.

Ōsaka Gaikokugo Daigaku. Toshokan
(Ōsaka University of Foreign Studies. Library)

Address: Library, Ōsaka University of Foreign Studies, 8-1-1 Aomatani-higashi, Minoo-shi, Ōsaka-562, Japan.
Tel.: 81 (0727) 28-3111, ext. 232.
Fax: 81 (0727) 28-8590
Networks, consortia: NACSIS.
Founded: 1922 (founding of the library).
Major resources: The Juntarō Ishihama Collection.
Areas of specialization: Archaeology, cultural anthropology, Asian studies, cultural history of Ōsaka.

Holdings (books and journals): 42,295 v. (Ishihama Collection).
Visual/audio resources: Not held.
Access: Available for research use and for general readers.

Description

Of special prominence among resources of anthropological interest at the Library of Ōsaka University of Foreign Studies is the former personal library of the late Juntarō Ishihama (1888-1968). Ishihama was born in Ōsaka in 1888 and graduated in 1910 from the Imperial University of Tokyo in the field of Chinese Literature. He devoted himself to scholarship throughout his life, despite the fact that he inherited the family pharmacy business in Ōsaka after his graduation. Although initially educated in the field of Chinese studies, he became increasingly interested in the languages and cultures of the neighboring regions, trying to explore these new fields of study. These interests, for example, took the form of studying Mongolian for two years as an auditor at the Ōsaka School of Foreign Studies (the forerunner of Ōsaka University of Foreign Studies), when it was established in 1921.

He also became a pupil of Torajirō Naitō, at that time professor in Oriental history at the Imperial University of Kyoto. Through this relationship he became acquainted with the scholars of the so-called Kyoto Circle. This group was then devoted to the study of documents found in the stone caves in Tun-huang; he soon took a serious part in this work, becoming a leading figure in Tun-huang studies. In subsequent years his field of study kept expanding from Chinese studies to linguistics and history, and his area of specialization also expanded geographically from China to Central Asia and India. His works are renowned for precision in historical investigation and for the broad scope of his scholarship.

Following the tradition of scholars of the Ōsaka merchant class, Ishihama took pride in being a scholar outside the proverbial ivory tower. His love of books was second to none in academia, and he expended great efforts in collecting books for more than half a century. These are the books that are now the Ishihama Collection at the Ōsaka University of Foreign Studies Library.

The Ishihama Collection

The Ishihama Collection consists of the entirety of the library that once belonged to Ishihama. Part of the collection was purchased in March 1970 by the Ōsaka University of Foreign Studies Library, and the other part was received as a gift from Ishihama's family after his death in 1968. The collection comprises 20,262 volumes in Chinese, 9,021 volumes in Japanese, 3,269 volumes in Western languages and 9,743 issues of periodicals.

The most prominent feature of the collection is that it contains works in Tangut, Mongolian and various other languages, including rare materials. It also contains a large number of documents in Mongolian, Manchu, Tangut, Uighur, Tibetan, etc.—areas in which Ishihama's scholarship was particularly profound.

The collection is also very rich in Chinese classics, reflecting his original interest in that field. Its coverage is extensive in materials on Confucianism, history, scholarly works and prose and poetry, and also the works of modern Chinese scholars in philosophy, history, languages and literature, with particular emphasis on Luo Zhen-yu and Wang Guo-wei, by whom Ishihama was strongly influenced. The collection is particularly strong in materials on writing, epigraphy, phonology and philology, and almost exhaustive in materials on *Yin-hsü* or the Ruins of Yin (Shang Dynasty) and in Tun-huang studies, reflecting his interest in these developing areas.

Another distinctive feature of the collection is that it includes so-called *zoku-sho* or popular books, which universities at that time were reluctant to purchase. These add to the value of the collection.

The holdings in Western languages are splendid, especially in the fields of linguistics and history. There is a story (which seems to have been true) that he bought almost all the Western books on Oriental studies imported and sold by Maruzen Co., Ltd., between 1918 and 1939. The area of focus ranges from East Asia to Central and Southwest Asia, and the collection is almost complete in the reports of Central Asian expeditions in the early twentieth-century, made by such persons as Mark Aurel Stein, Paul Pelliot and Sven Anders Hedin. Ishihama was also known for his familiarity with Oriental studies in Russia, and his collection of these materials is without equal elsewhere. In addition to published books, the collection holds numerous offprints sent to Ishihama by Western Orientalists, many of which are very rare.

The holdings in Japanese include materials on Oriental studies, linguistics and Buddhist studies, published throughout the Meiji, Taishō and Shōwa periods, until his death in 1968. The collection also contains a large number of back volumes of journals published in Japan, China and Western countries—these include most of the main journal publications and many old issues in these fields. It should also be noted that the collection is very rich in materials on the cultural history of modern-era Ōsaka—a collection that has no equal elsewhere, in either quality or quantity.

Sho Kuwajima
[Translation from Japanese: Hisami Suzuki]

Australia and New Zealand

Australia

The Australian Museums On Line (AMOL) National Directory is available on the Web at http://amol.phm.gov.au/directory. This resource provides directory and other concise information on Australian museums and their collections. Also available on the Web is the Directory of Archives in Australia. The Web address of the latter is http://www.asap.unimelb.edu.edu.au/ asa/directory. Another electronic resource, the Register of Australian Archives and Manuscripts (RAAM), is available at http://www2/nla.gov.au/raam. The Coombs Computing Unit, part of the Research School of Social Sciences and the Research School of Pacific and Asian Studies, Australian National University, provides on-line access to a wealth of social science documentation on Asia and the Pacific. The URL is http://coombs.anu.edu.au.

Australia—Acton

Australian Institute of Aboriginal and Torres Strait Islander Studies (AIATSIS). **Library**

Address: The Library, Acton House, Marcus Clarke St., Acton ACT Australia.
Address (mailing): The Library, AIATSIS, GPO Box 553, Canberra ACT 2601, Australia.
Tel.: +(61) 262461182
Fax: +(61) 262497310
Internet address: http://www.aiatsis.gov.au/lib_abt.htm.
Internet address (Aboriginal Studies Electronic Data Archive): http://coombs.anu.edu.au/ SpecialProj/ASEDA/ASEDA.html.
Internet address (AIATSIS): http://www.aiatsis.gov.au.
Founded: An interim Council was established in 1961.
Major resources: Books, manuscripts, photos, films, audio recordings and other library materials in the field of Aboriginal and Torres Strait Islander studies.
Areas of specialization: Aboriginal and Torres Strait Islander collections. Library holdings include an Australian language collection.
Visual/audio resources: Photos, slides, films, audio recordings.
Access: On-site use of materials. There may be limitations on access to some materials.
Guides/catalogs: The AIATSIS *Annual Bibliography* (first published in 1965) is no longer available in print form, although the latest *Annual Bibliography* is available on the Web at http://www.aiatsis.gov.au/annbib96/rannbib.htm.

Australia—Canberra

Australian Archives (AA)

Address: Australian Archives, National Archives Building, East Victoria Terrace, Parkes, Canberra, 2600 Australia.
Address (mailing): Australian Archives, P.O. Box 7425, Canberra Mail Centre, Canberra, ACT 2610 Australia.
Tel.: +(61) 262093411
Fax: +(61) 262093447
E-mail: ref@aa.gov.au.
Internet address: http://www.aa.gov.au/AA_WWW/AA_Home_Page.html.
Public transit access: Buses to East Victoria Terrace leave the Civic Interchange at regular intervals.
Founded: The Archives was initially established in 1944, renamed as the Australian Archives in 1974, and given its statutory basis under the *Archives Act 1983*.
Major resources: The Australian Archives is the national archives of Australia. The Archives selects, preserves, makes available for research and promotes the use of the archives of the Commonwealth government. These archives constitute a vast and rich resource for the study of Australian history, Australian society and the Australian people.
Holdings: The collection spans almost 200 years of Australian history. The main focus of the collection is material that documents federal government activities since federation in 1901. There are also significant holdings of nineteenth-century records that relate to functions transferred by the colonies to the Commonwealth government at the time of federation and subsequently.
Visual/audio resources: All record formats are included in the holdings of the Archives.
Access: Australian Archives provides public access to Commonwealth records more than thirty years of age, in accordance with the *Archives Act 1983*. The Archives has offices in all State capitals, as well as Canberra and Darwin. Physical access is available only at the Archives office which holds the records; however, Australian Archives offers a photocopying service for distance researchers. General reference assistance is available, with referral to paid researchers.
References: *Australian Archives Annual Reports*, Australian Government Publishing Service. Published yearly since 1983.
Guides/catalogs: Australian Archives has two major finding aids: ANGAM II, an item-level database, and RINSE, a descriptive database of Commonwealth agencies and persons, record series and functions. Both ANGAM II and RINSE are on-line databases available for public use at any office of the Archives. The Archives also produces fact sheets and other reference guides relating to particular themes and topics. Examples include Australian Archives (compiler), *'My Heart is Breaking': A Joint Guide to Records About Aboriginal People in the Public Record Office of Victoria and the Australian Archives, Victoria Regional Office* (Canberra: 1993); Ros Fraser (compiler), *Aboriginal and Torres Strait Islander People in Commonwealth Records: A Guide to Records in the Australian Archives ACT Regional Office* (Canberra: 1993); Rowena MacDonald, *Between Two Worlds: The Commonwealth Government and the Removal of Aboriginal Children of Part Descent in the Northern Territory* (Alice Springs: 1995); Peter Nagle and Richard Summerrell (compilers),

Aboriginal Deaths in Custody: The Royal Commission and Its Records, 1987-1991 (Canberra: 1996). These guides are available for sale through Australian Archives offices.

Description

Commonwealth records include a wealth of information of potential relevance to anthropological studies. Some of it is about policy, some relates to day-to-day administration, some describes particular events or people. Much of the information is not separately serialized, but is contained within general correspondence file series. A portion of the record series of interest to researchers have been entered at item-level onto the ANGAM II database. This database is searchable by keyword, and provides an excellent starting point for research. However, an exhaustive search of the holdings entails searching indexes or inventory lists that are kept at the Archives office that has custody of the particular record series.

Records of relevance to anthropological research will be found in the record series of Commonwealth Government departments that were involved in the government, administration and development of external territories, particularly Papua and New Guinea, and in the administration of the Northern Territory. Records relating to the administration of the Northern Territory are the main source for issues relating to Aboriginal and Torres Strait Islander people.

The principal departments involved are the Department of Foreign Affairs and Trade; the Territories Branch of the Department of Transport and Regional Development; the Department of Defence; and the Department of the Prime Minister and Cabinet. These departments have either created relevant records themselves, or control the records that were created by now defunct government agencies.

The following list of record series is intended as an example of the holdings and is in no way an exhaustive list of relevant material.

Correspondence Files, Multiple Number Series With Alphabetical Prefix (A518).

The series dates from 1928 to 1956, and is now controlled by the Department of Foreign Affairs and Trade. It is concerned principally with the administration of external territories, but includes records about the administration of the Northern Territory. Examples of files from this series are:

- P213/3/2: Native Labour—Papua and New Guinea—Employment of Native Women. 1908-1953.
- BB841/1: Attacks by Natives—Papua and New Guinea—Attack on Tolhurst patrol traveling Tapini to Ononge. 1952-1953.
- T840/1/4: Papua and New Guinea Natives—Village Council at Vunakalkalulu.
- AJ800/1/2: Nauru Administration. Council of Chiefs. Minutes of Meeting. 1949-1951.
- FK16/2/1: Defence. Torres Strait Islanders (Evacuees). 1942-1945.
- LY112/1: Territories. Miscellaneous. Thursday Island—General. 1945-1947.
- B241/6/19: Public Works NT. Native Settlement, Jay Creek. 1948-1956.

Papua and New Guinea Patrol Reports. (A7034).

This series dates from 1922 to 1955. It is now controlled by the Department of Foreign Affairs and Trade. The series consists mainly of reports of specific patrols in Papua and the Territory of New Guinea. It also includes a small number of more general reports, such as district monthly reports, anthropological reports, etc. Some reports contain detailed maps and occasional photographs. The majority of the patrol reports are very detailed—including a brief memorandum to the District Officer giving subject, duration, object of patrol, personnel accompanying the patrol and, at the end, a résumé of such subjects as geological features, native customs and physical appearance, differing dialects and vocabulary, health and sanitation, investigations of unrest or murders, and general observations on such matters as initiation ceremonies, methods of cooking, housing, vegetable gardens and cannibalism.

Other record series relating to external territories include:

- Specific bundles, files of correspondence, station journals, patrols, patrol reports from out-stations. (G91). Dates range from 1922 to 1941.
- Microfilm copies of Papua and New Guinea Patrol Reports Collected by Ivan F. Champion, 1 Jan. 1928-26 Nov. 1955. (A7357).
- Photographs Taken on the Tari-Strickland Patrol, Papua. March-June 1954. (A6514).

Record series that contain records of interest to Aboriginal and Torres Strait Islander peoples include:

- Correspondence Files, Annual Single Number Series. (A1).

The series dates from 1903 to 1938. It was started by the Department of External Affairs and then became the principal general file series of the successive departments that administered the Northern Territory. Examples of files within the series include:

- 1904/1329: Trepang Fishing. 1903-1904.
- 1908/1748: Allegations of Ill-Treatment of Aborigines in Western Australia. 1907-1908.
- 1911/14164: Chief Protector of Aborigines—Proposed Visit to Alice Springs. 1911.
- 1925/23976: Australian Aborigines. Status of. 1925.
- 1929/1639: Removal of Natives from Alice Springs to Hermannsburg. 1928-1929.
- 1934/8108: Tribal Murder at Alligator River. 1934.
- 1938/33269: D.F.Thomson—Anthropological Investigations—Arnhem Land—Northern Territory. 1936-1939.

Correspondence Files, Annual Single Number Series With Northern Territory Prefix. (A3).

This series dates from 1912 to 1925 and is a major source of information about the establishment and early years of Commonwealth administration in the Northern Territory.

Album of Anthropological Photographs in Connection With the Aboriginal Enquiry, Central and North Australia, 1928. (A263)

Correspondence Files, Annual Single Number Series. (A432) 1929-

This is the main general correspondence series of the Attorney-General's Department. The department's involvement with Aboriginal and Torres Strait Islander matters includes the responsibility for advising other Commonwealth agencies on legal and constitutional matters, drafting and interpreting legislation, administering court registries and the judiciary in the Northern Territory.

Correspondence Files, Single Number Series With A (Administration) Prefix. (A884). 1951-1974.

Correspondence Files, Single Number Series With B (Child Endowment) Prefix. (A885).1951-1974; and

Correspondence Files, Single Number Series With C (Pensions) Prefix. (A886). 1951-1974.

These are record series of the Department of Social Security. Many of the files have been destroyed, but those remaining may contain information about missions, pastoral stations and towns in all States and the Northern Territory.

Exhibits Tendered Before the Commission, Alpha-Numeric Series. (A6455), 1952-1967, and

Original Agency Records Transferred to the Commission, R Series. (A6456). 1946-1985.

These are two of the series of the Royal Commission into British Nuclear Tests in Australia during the 1950s and 1960s. They include statements by Aboriginal people, submissions by Counsel acting on behalf of Aboriginal organizations and individuals, submissions by anthropologists, statements by others mentioning Aborigines, or matters relevant to them, and government and other records of various kinds from before, during and after the tests. Listings of files exist, and most are available for public access despite the fact that some records are less than thirty years of age.

Records of the Royal Commission Into Aboriginal Deaths in Custody, 1987-1991.

The Royal Commission investigated and reported on the causes of deaths of Aboriginal people while held in State and Territory jails. It also assessed the social, cultural and legal factors which appeared to have a bearing on these deaths. The Royal Commission produced reports on each death, on the underlying issues and on regional matters. It also produced an Interim Report and a final National Report. The text of many of these reports is available at http://www.austlii.edu.au/car_rc_deaths.html. Information about the access status of the Commission's records is provided in Peter Nagle and Richard Summerrell (compilers), *Aboriginal Deaths in Custody: The Royal Commission and Its Records, 1987-1991.*

Richard Summerrell
Additional information provided by Anne-Marie Schwirtlich.

Australian National University. Library

Address: Library, Australian National University, Menzies Building, Canberra ACT 0200 Australia.
Tel.: +(61-6) 2492005
Fax: +(61-6) 2490734
Internet address: http://info.anu.edu.au/elisa.html.
Internet address (Pacific Manuscripts Bureau): http://sunsite.anu.edu.au/spin/RSRC/PMB
Networks, consortia: ABN.
Founded: 1947.
Areas of specialization: Australian Aborigines, Asia and the Pacific.
Archives/manuscripts: Pacific Manuscripts Bureau microfilms: 1,600 reels [see below]; papers in the William Edward Hanley Stanner collection [see below].
Holdings (books and journals): A substantial collection of general texts in the above fields for teaching and research purposes at a large university.
Visual/audio resources: A small number of commercially available videos on people and society in Australia, Asia and the Pacific.
Access: Available to members of the ANU community. To the public on application (possible charge).
Guides/catalogs: See the Pacific Manuscripts Bureau website (the URL is above).
Artifact resources: Not held.

Description

The Pacific Manuscripts Bureau

The Pacific Manuscripts Bureau (PMB) is a non-profit organization established in 1968 to promote the preservation of unpublished or semi-published materials relating to the Pacific Islands. The PMB was the inspiration of H.E. Maude, supported by the ANU. Robert Langdon (author of *The Lost Caravel*) was the Executive Officer between 1968 and 1985 and the driving force of its collecting activities. It is sponsored by a group of six major Australian and overseas libraries specializing in Pacific research. The sponsors are: (Australia)—the Library, Australian National University, Canberra; the National Library of Australia, Canberra; the State Library of New South Wales (Mitchell Library), Sydney; (New Zealand)—the National Library of New Zealand (Alexander Turnbull Library), Wellington; (United States)—the Library, University of Hawai'i at Mānoa, Honolulu; the Library, University of California, San Diego (Melanesian Studies Resource Center), La Jolla, California.

The specific aim of the PMB is to locate manuscripts and other unpublished or semi-published material that may be of value, either now or in the future, to research workers engaged in any branch of Pacific studies, whether historical, literary or scientific. Of particular concern to the Bureau are those documents at risk either from adverse climatic conditions, insect infestation, civil unrest, lack of knowledge of their value or simply deterioration through age or poor storage facilities.

Materials of all kinds are copied and sought: correspondence, notebooks and diaries; missionary, trading and shipping records; accounts and journals; grammars, dictionaries and vocabularies; genealogies; and any other manuscripts written by Islanders in their own languages—nothing is unimportant, however brief, that may help in the study and understanding of life in the islands.

The material is copied by microfilming and then returned to the owner or deposited in a library or archive at the owner's direction. The Bureau does not purchase or retain possession of any of the material copied.

Access: The Bureau has two series of microforms: Manuscript series; and Printed Document series. With the exception of one title on microfiche and one on 16mm microfilm, all the material is available on 35mm silver halide microfilm (or vesicular microfilm, if appropriate). Some of the titles are restricted, but these restrictions are noted in the catalogue entries. Unless restricted, the microfilms are available on interlibrary loan, either from one of the sponsoring libraries or any other institution that may hold copies. Published catalogues for the two series are available. These catalogues are also available on-line via ELISA.

Publications: The Bureau's newsletter *Pambu* is available at the PMB website. The Bureau has published several indexes to materials copied as special projects—e.g., the New England Microfilming Project. A list of current publications is available on request.

The Bureau welcomes information from anyone who has, or has knowledge of, any Pacific Island documents similar to those mentioned above. It is also interested in collating listings of Pacific manuscript material held in institutions, but which is not easily accessible to researchers. The Bureau can be contacted at the following address: Executive Officer, Pacific Manuscripts Bureau, Research School of Pacific and Asian Studies, Australian National University, Canberra, ACT, 0200; telephone: (612) 62492521; fax: (612) 62490198; e-mail: pambu@coombs.anu.edu.au.

The Papers of William Edward Hanley Stanner

The collection consists of the following material of the former professor of anthropology at ANU:

- Papers on Fiji and the Pacific Islands, 1933-1947 (3 boxes).
- Papers on Africa, 1938-1954 (5 boxes plus maps).
- Miscellaneous papers, including photographs of Birhors and Oraons of West Bengal (1 box).
- Papers on Papua-New Guinea, 1946-1966 (1 box).
- Papers on the South Pacific Commission, 1947-1955 (7 boxes).

Other papers on general issues relating to underdevelopment are included in the collection. The boxes of papers are held in the manuscript collection and are arranged by subject according to Library of Congress classification.

George Miller

Australian National University. Research School of Pacific and Asian Studies. Department of Anthropology. Library

Address: Library, Department of Anthropology, Research School of Pacific and Asian Studies, Australian National University, Canberra, ACT 2100, Australia.
Tel.: +(61) 62492162
Fax: +(61) 62494896
Internet address: http://online.anu.edu.au/nadel/index.html.
Founded: 1960.
Major resources: The J.S. Furnival collection; fieldnotes and off-prints of various scholars associated with the department.
Areas of specialization: Southeast Asia and the Pacific region.
Archives/manuscripts:
- The J.S. Furnival collection (four boxes).
- Fieldnotes (in files and boxes).
- Off-prints (30 box files).

Visual/audio resources: A collection of video tapes on Aborigines and on Javanese religious practices is available.
Access: Open to scholars. Material must be used in the library.
References: Frank N. Trager (compiler and editor), *Furnival of Burma: An Annotated Bibliography of the Works of John S. Furnivall* (New Haven, Conn.: 1963) (= *Yale University. Southeast Asia Studies. Bibliography Series*, no. 8).

Description

The J.S. Furnivall collection.

John Sydenham Furnivall (1878-1960) was a noted British civil servant with a strong interest in the economic and administrative history of British and Dutch colonies in Southeast Asia. He wrote several books and had gathered material for a book on Burmese economic history. The Furnivall collection contains notes, abstracts from various Burmese government publications and statistical material gathered by Furnivall.

M.R. Fernando

National Library of Australia

Address: National Library of Australia, Canberra ACT 2600 Australia.
Tel.: +(61) 062621614
Fax: +(61) 062571703
Internet address: http://www.nla.gov.au.
Networks, consortia: Aussinet.
Founded: 1961.
Major resources: Library resources on Australia, the Pacific, Asia.
Areas of specialization: Australia, the Pacific, Southeast Asia.

Archival/manuscript resources: Southeast Asia-related manuscript holdings include the H. Otley Beyer papers—more than 160 bound volumes of Philippine ethnological materials and 98 boxes of loose manuscripts. The Beyer collection has been reproduced on microfiche. Philippine-related holdings also include the Goldenberg and Villanueva collections. The George Coedès collection relates to Thailand and Cambodia. Among Indonesian manuscript holdings are the Kern collection and a collection of Sundanese manuscripts. Manuscript materials for Burma include the Gordon Luce collection. See the National Library's website for additional information and collection guides.

References: "Burma: Manuscripts in the Luce Collection," *National Library of Australia: Current Awareness Bulletin*, IE 171 (July 1982); "A Description of the Collection of Professor George Coedès in the National Library of Australia," *National Library of Australia: Area Studies, July 1980;* Andrew Gosling, "National Library of Australia Thai Collection," *CORMOSEA Bulletin,* vol. 23, no. 1 (June 1994), p. 5-6. A computer print-out (untitled), dated 10/20/92, lists the contents of the George Coedès collection.

Australia—Darwin

Northern Territory University. University Library

Address: Research Services, Northern Territory University Library, P.O. Box 41246, Casuarina NT 0811 Australia.
Tel.: +(61) 08 89466992
Fax: +(61) 08 89451317
Internet address: http://www.ntu.edu.au/library.
Internet address (INTAN MAS database): http://www.ntu.edu.au/library/intanmas.html. The INTAN MAS database contains references on eastern Indonesia, Australian-Indonesian relations, ASEAN and related topics;
Internet address (Djorra' Djagamirri Collection): http://www.ntu.edu.au/library/djorradj.html.
Internet address (East Timor Collection): http://www.ntu.edu.au/library/eastimor.html.
Areas of specialization: East Timor Collection; Dorra' Djagamirri Collection (on northern Australia and contiguous areas).

Australia—Sydney

State Library of New South Wales (Mitchell Library). Australian Research Collections

Address: Australian Research Collections, State Library of New South Wales, Macquarie St., Sydney, NSW, 2000, Australia.
Tel.: +(61) (02) 92731466
Fax: +(61) (02) 92731245
E-mail: mitchell@ilanet.slnsw.gov.au.
Internet address (Mitchell and Dixson Libraries—Australian Research Collections): http://www.slnsw.gov.au/ml/mitchell.htm.
Networks, consortia: ABN (Australian Bibliographic Network).

Internet access to on-line catalog: GOPHER to Dixson.SL NSW.GOV.AU PORT 70.
Public transit access: Via underground train to Martin Place railway station.
Founded: 1910.
Archives/manuscripts: Ca. 500 m.
Holdings (books and journals): Ca. 25,000 v. (Australian Research Collections).
Access: A Reader's Ticket is required for access to original material. Specific restrictions apply to some collections.

Description

The Australian Research Collections of the State Library of New South Wales consist of the Mitchell Library, the Dixson Library and the Dixson Galleries. These contain materials in all formats relating to Australia and the adjacent regions, including all places as far north as the Philippines and Hawai'i, as far south as the Antarctic, as far east as Easter Island and as far west as Sumatra.

The Mitchell Library is based on the collection of David Scott Mitchell (1836-1907), Australia's first and greatest collector of Australian historical materials. It opened in 1910 as part of the then Public Library of New South Wales, now the State Library of New South Wales. It is a continually growing collection in all formats—printed, manuscript, pictorial, microform and electronic.

The Dixson Library was the private collection of Sir William Dixson (1870-1952). The collection, which is not being added to, includes books, manuscripts, maps, pictures, coins, medals and stamps. The Dixson Galleries collection of pictures consists of those given by Sir William during this lifetime, or bought from endowment funds since his death.

Printed Materials

The collections are especially strong on anthropology and native peoples of the area. Material on Australian Aboriginal peoples, their cultures and languages has been collected comprehensively and intensively. In relation to the other peoples of the area, especially the Māori people, the collections are strong in materials printed up to the end of the 1970s. A change in collection policy at that time has limited the intensity of collection since then to the peoples, Aboriginal and otherwise, of Australia.

Manuscript Collections Concerning Anthropology

Anthropology-related manuscript holdings in the Mitchell Library, State Library of New South Wales, date from the late eighteenth-century. Valuable early insights into the customs and traditions of the indigenous inhabitants of the Southwest Pacific region were recorded in both the journals kept by Captain James Cook and his associates during his voyages of exploration to the South Seas. The Sir Joseph Banks papers are now available through the library's website at http://www.slnsw.gov.au/Banks. This URL includes the journal (Aug. 1768-July 1771) of *H.M. Bark Endeavour*. The official records of the various churches which commenced missionary activity in the region early in the nineteenth-century also provide quite detailed observations of many societies, and information about the attitudes and policies of churches and governments. These extensive holdings cover the period from 1839 to the present.

From the time of European settlement of Australia in 1788, many aspects of the lives of Australian Aborigines—including their languages, music, ceremonies, folklore and art—have been observed and described by both government officials and private individuals. Strongly represented in the Mitchell Library, these accounts include, for example, the papers of George Augustus Robinson, Protector of Aborigines for the Port Phillip District from 1838-1849, as well as those of settlers, pastoralists, inland explorers, medical practitioners and clergymen.

A number of early anthropologists, notably Sir Walter Baldwin Spencer and Herbert Basedow, are also represented. Although in most cases their papers do not include documentation of systematic, long term studies of particular societies, they nevertheless represent a useful addition to the body of anthropological information.

While the papers of many twentieth-century Australian anthropologists have remained with the institutions to which they were appointed, the Mitchell collection does include the papers of Frederick David McCarthy, archaeologist and ethnologist, for the period 1932-1989. Some earlier papers of the late Frederick Rose, who carried out significant field work relating to the Groote Eylandt Aborigines between 1938 and 1948, are also held. Although Rose lived and worked in Europe from 1956 until his death in 1991, he revisited Australia periodically in connection with his study of the social, economic and political changes affecting Aborigines. His remaining papers were received by the library from Germany in 1995.

Included in the later twentieth-century material relating to Australian Aborigines is the George Gibbs Memorial Collection, which to date comprises the records of the Northern Territory Council for Aboriginal Rights, 1961-1965; and the papers of professor Frank Stevens, for the period 1930-1975, relating to his research into Aboriginal working conditions, health and housing in the Northern Territory and Queensland. Also significant for their documentation of particular aspects of Australian Aboriginal life in the late twentieth-century are the records of the Federal Council for the Advancement of Aborigines and Torres Strait Islanders, 1957-1973; these deal particularly with Aboriginal health and land rights issues; and the papers of lawyer Neil Richard MacLaurin Mackerras concerning his work with the Aboriginal Legal Service during the 1970s. Restrictions apply to some manuscript collections.

Anthropological and Ethnographic Pictorial Collections

The Mitchell Library Pictures Collection is rich in nineteenth-century anthropological and ethnographic material. While the Pictures Collection has not specifically concentrated on this kind of material, its generalist collection areas, until the 1970s, included the South Pacific as well as Australia. Because it was one of the earlier institutions to begin collecting historical and documentary material in Australia, the Mitchell Library's collections cover much of the country, but a change of emphasis in the 1970s means it now collects only New South Wales (NSW) material.

The collections of the Pictures Section are closely linked to those of the Manuscripts Collections—the one illuminating the other—and should be used and searched in conjunction. The library has always collected material that could be described as historic or documentary, rather than ethnographic or anthropological. The latter has tended to go to museums. The library's collections are nevertheless a valuable resource because of their breadth.

The library has a number of artworks associated with the early exploration of Australia and the Pacific. It holds a good collection of pictorial and manuscript material relating to Captain James Cook and Sir Joseph Banks's material, including a small number of William Hodge (artist with Cook's second voyage) South Sea island portraits; and some John Webber third voyage drawings of Tahiti and Alaska. These include portraits, landscapes and studies on material culture and ceremonies.

A number of drawings by Jacques Arago, who was the expedition artist for Louis Freycinet's world cruise of 1817-1820 on the *Uraine*, are also held by the library. These include Australian and South Pacific portrait drawings.

Drawings made by Sir Oswald Brierly while on *HMS Rattlesnake*'s voyage through Torres Strait, New Guinea and the Louisiade Archipelago, from 1848 to 1850, concentrate in precise detail on local boat construction.

The library has a good collection of the papers of nineteenth-century missionaries that are often accompanied by pictorial material. Missionaries of the second half of the nineteenth-century often put together large photographic collections of the communities in which they worked—thus, for instance, the library holds several thousand photographs put together by the Reverend George Brown, who worked in Samoa and Fiji for the Methodist Missionary Society.

The collections are particularly strong in images of Australian Aborigines. Nineteenth-century descriptions of Australia invariably discussed the situation of Aboriginal peoples, their customs and future. While much of this material was not created specifically for anthropological or ethnographic purposes, it nevertheless provides valuable documentation on changing Aboriginal circumstances.

Portraits of Aborigines and descriptions of their material culture were painted from the earliest days of settlement. The largest collection of pre-1800 images—the Watling collection—is owned by the Museum of Natural History (London). But the Mitchell Library holds an extensive collection of post-1800 images. Artists found a ready market for images of Aboriginal people. For example, Richard Browne, an ex-convict working in the 1810s, worked up a series of about ten portraits of Sydney Aborigines which he would duplicate for sale. In 1834 Charles Rodius published a series of six crayon portraits of Aborigines, while in 1836 William Fernyhough issued a series of twelve profile portraits. This kind of material, while not traditionally considered anthropological, does contain important information which is as much about European attitudes as it is about Aboriginal people.

The collections also contain an excellent range of ephemeral images, published by local publishing houses. These images, which cover the entire century, reflect the wide span of attitudes of Europeans to Aborigines.

A considerable amount of information can also be found in the sketchbooks of travelers and the journals of residents. The library has a large collection of such sketchbooks and journals, and some of these contain relevant material. William Anderson Cawthorne, for instance, a South Australian schoolmaster, illustrated his 1840s and 1850s journals, in which he documented Aboriginal manners and customs with detailed watercolors. An unknown artist, "T.W.," drew some thirty pencil portrait sketches of Melbourne Aborigines in the early 1830s.

Most sketchbooks do not concentrate exclusively on Aboriginal people, but the information they contain can still be valuable.

The collection also contains sketches by Aborigines that date from the 1850s to the 1900s. Artists such as Tommy McRae, Black Johnny and Mickey of Ulladulla were given sketchbooks and pens and asked to fill them. Initially viewed as curiosities by the Europeans who collected them, these volumes are now seen as providing illuminating insights into Aboriginal perceptions of European culture.

Not surprisingly, the collection contains large numbers of photographs of Aboriginal people. Most of these were taken for commercial purposes and are thus posed studio shots (see the work of commercial photographers Henry King and John William Lindt), but some amateur photographs have survived. In the Macarthur-Onslow albums there are a number of close-up portraits of Aborigines taken at King George Sound, Western Australia, which are dated 1858. The album, compiled by William Macarthur, contains similar images of Queensland Aborigines and Pacific islands people.

The Mitchell pictorial collections are complex, diverse and rich. This brief description is intended to highlight the kinds of material the library holds, rather than be a comprehensive record of them. The images can be located through the library's card and computer pictures catalogues.

Alan Ventress

New Zealand

In addition to the following entries, see the website of the National Archives of New Zealand (Te Whare Tohu Tuhituhingo o Aotearoa) at http://www.archives.gov.nz.

New Zealand—Auckland

University of Auckland. Library. New Zealand and Pacific Collection

Address: New Zealand and Pacific Collection, Library, University of Auckland, Private Bag 92019, Auckland, New Zealand.
Tel.: (649) 3737599
Fax: (649) 3737565
Internet address: http://www.auckland.ac.nz/lbr/nzp/nzphome.htm.
Networks, consortia: NZBN (New Zealand Bibliographical Network).
Founded: 1883.
Major resources: New Zealand and Pacific Collection.
Areas of specialization: A comprehensive collection of published material relating to Polynesia, Melanesia, Micronesia and New Zealand.
Holdings: 80,000 book volumes, including non-anthropological resources; 400 linear metres of manuscripts, including non-anthropological resources.
Access: Open for use by scholars, but to borrow materials non-students/staff must register as approved borrowers and pay an annual fee. Some published materials and all manuscripts are closed access. Restrictions on access apply to some manuscript collections.
Archives/manuscripts: Elizabeth Bott (1923-   ), research notes, 1958-1960. This collection consists of fieldnotes and papers gathered in Tonga, as well as records of interviews with

Queen Salote Tupou III—an invaluable record of Tongan history and culture. Access restrictions apply and an inventory is available.

Guides/catalogs: University of Auckland Library, *A List of Manuscripts and Archives Held in Auckland University Library* (Auckland: 1981); University of Auckland Library, *Manuscripts and Archives Accessioned in the New Zealand and Pacific Collection, September 1980-* (Auckland: 1990-   ), loose-leaf.

Stephen Innes

New Zealand—Wellington

Museum of New Zealand [previously the Dominion Museum].
Te Papa Tongarewa

Address: Museum of New Zealand, Buckle St., POB 467, Wellington, New Zealand.
Tel.: +(64) 04 3869609
Fax: +(64) 04 3857157
Internet address: http://www.hmu.auckland.ac.nz:8001/monz.
Founded: 1992 (incorporates the National Art Gallery and the National Museum).
Major resources: Important Māori collections.

National Library of New Zealand. Alexander Turnbull Library
Te Puna Mātauranga o Aotearoa. Alexander Turnbull Library

Address: Alexander Turnbull Library, 58-78 Molesworth Street, P.O. Box 12-349, Wellington, New Zealand.
Tel.: +(64) 04 4743000
Fax: +(64) 04 4743063
Internet address (National Library of New Zealand): http://www.natlib.govt.nz. This website includes a "Timeframes" service that provides access to Alexander Turnbull Library images from all parts of the collections. The URL is http://timeframes.natlib.govt.nz.
Networks, consortia: NZBN (New Zealand Bibliographic Network).
Local on-line catalog: Dynix Integrated Library System (ILS) for published items. AWAIRS for TAPUHI database for unpublished Heritage materials (manuscripts and archives and pictorial materials). The ILS catalogue can be accessed via the National Library's homepage, under telnet://ils.natlib.govt.nz. It is expected that the TAPUHI database will be available on the Internet by 1998.
Founded: 1919.
Major resources: Māori and selected Pacific peoples.
Areas of specialization: National Heritage Collection of New Zealand resources, Māori culture and language, Island languages collections.
Archives/manuscripts: Collections of the Polynesian Society, the New Zealand Māori Purposes Fund Board, Arthur Maurice Hocart (1883-1939), Reo Fortune (1903-1979), William Colenso (1811-1899), William Leonard Williams (1829-1916), Sir Walter Lawry Buller (1838-1906), Alexander Francis McDonnell (1866-1938), Sir Donald McLean (1820-

1877), Hetaraka Tautahi (fl. 1897), Elsdon Best (1856-1931), Horatio Emmons Hale (1817-1896), Stephenson Percy Smith (1840-1922), John White (1826-1891), George Leslie Adkin (1888-1964), John Houston (1891-1962), Henry Matthew Stowell (Here Hongi) (1859-1944).

Fieldnotes: Arthur Maurice Hocart (1883-1939) was in Fiji, Rotuma and Tonga from ca. 1900-1914. The library holds his field notebooks for the Solomon Islands, Fiji, Rotuma, Uvea and Samoa, Tonga, Futuna, Ceylon and Egypt. Part of the collection has been microfilmed and a place-level inventory is available. The library also holds collections of other researchers containing notes made in the field and written up later.

Visual/audio resources: The only collection of anthropological photographs by an anthropologist are those of Arthur Maurice Hocart—ca. 420 of his original captioned photographic prints, mainly from Fiji and Rotuma, but including some taken in Tonga, the Solomon Islands and Samoa. Hocart's negatives are held in the Pitt-Rivers Museum in Oxford. The library also holds photographs collected by Stephenson Percy Smith (ethnologist), Elsdon Best (ethnographer), and G.L. Adkin (who photographed some archaeological sites). There is a range of photographs of Māori and Pacific Islanders—particularly Samoans, Fijians and Tongans.

The Drawings & Prints Collection includes several thousand paintings, drawings and prints of Māori and Pacific subjects, including portraits, depictions of daily life, artifacts and settlements, principally in the nineteenth-century. The work of G.F. Angas, J.J. Merrett and H.G. Robley in the anthropological field is particularly numerous, and there is a full collection of the prints published to illustrate the writings of the early Pacific explorers, especially Cook and the French voyagers, between 1769 and 1840. From Cook's third voyage the drawings of William Ellis are significant.

The Oral History Centre holds copies of forty interviews with Cook Islanders in the Cook Islands languages, by Kauraka Kauraka, received under the Manihiki Oral Tradition Project and the Kōrero Mangaia Project. The recordings include songs, legends, life and customs. A sample printout is available. A further oral history collection, also by Kauraka Kauraka, is the Atuikōrero Project. This consists of the recordings of a 1993 workshop held in Raratonga to share information between Māori and Cook Islanders relating to the five canoes, looking at the connections between Māori and Cook Islanders through common ancestors.

Access: Open to scholars and general researchers who need to use the unique collections (the materials themselves are kept in closed stacks). Material which has been microfilmed is available on inter-library loan.

Guides/catalogs: Sally Edridge (compiler), *Solomon Islands Bibliography to 1980* (Suva: 1985); *Hawaiian Language Publications in the Alexander Turnbull Library* (Wellington: 1992)—a copy of the Alexander Turnbull Library shelf-list of the Hawai'ian-Language Collection; *Samoan Language Publications in the Alexander Turnbull Library* (Wellington: 1992)—a copy of the Alexander Turnbull Library shelf-list of the Samoan-Language Collection; J.E. Traue, "Māori Resources in the Alexander Turnbull Library," *Turnbull Library Record*, vol. 13, no. 1, (May 1990), p. 6-12.

Artifact resources: In 1913 (prior to his death in 1918), Alexander Turnbull's collection of Māori and Pacific artifacts—some 500 items, including greenstone adzes and *hei tiki*, carvings and clothing—was donated anonymously to the Dominion Museum, Wellington (now the Museum of New Zealand, Te Papa Tongarewa).

Description

The Alexander Turnbull Library is a specialist research library within the National Library of New Zealand. It holds the national non-government collection of New Zealand and Pacific resources that includes published items (books, serials and newspapers) and original materials (manuscripts and archives, sound archives, photographs, paintings, drawings, prints, maps and plans). In recent years the library has given particular attention to increasing its holdings (both contemporary and historical) about the Pacific and its peoples. Some of the more important collections that include materials of anthropological interest are listed below. Additional details for these collections are in print-outs generated from the Manuscripts and Archives database, TAPUHI. Researchers can request photocopies of any inventory, if one has been compiled for a particular collection. The library welcomes queries from researchers about any of its collections.

- The Polynesian Society was established in 1892 "to promote the study of anthropology, ethnology, philology, history and antiquities of the Polynesian race." A recent history of the Society is M.P.K. Sorrenson's *Manifest Duty: The Polynesian Society Over 100 Years* (Auckland, 1992). The Alexander Turnbull Library holds on behalf of the Society its collection of books, serials (with many unique titles), manuscripts and archives. The books, manuscripts and archives are kept as separate collections within the stacks, and the serials are incorporated with the Alexander Turnbull Library's serials collection. Some of the books are listed in *List of Books in the Polynesian Society Library, 1 April 1965* (Wellington, 1965). A partial inventory is available of the manuscript papers, 1845-1940. Some manuscripts have been microfilmed. In 1992 the National Library of New Zealand mounted an exhibition based on the collection, curated by David Colquhoun, Curator of Manuscripts and Archives, Alexander Turnbull Library, for which an exhibition catalogue was published: *The Polynesianists: Early Anthropology in Aotearoa* (Wellington: 1992).
- The New Zealand Māori Purposes Fund Board papers, ca. 1867-1953, have substantial material, including research notes collected by Sir Apirana Ngata (1874-1950), dealing with his work for the publication of Māori songs, *Nga Moteatea*. Some material has been microfilmed and a detailed inventory of the collection is available.
- Arthur Maurice Hocart (1883-1939), also listed above. Arthur Hocart's collection of field notebooks, working papers, genealogical charts, manuscripts and photographs was given to the Alexander Turnbull Library in 1948. Some of the papers have been microfilmed and a place-level inventory is available. The Photographic Archive holds ca. 420 of Hocart's original photographs, predominantly from Fiji and Rotuma, with his captions. In 1993 the National Library of New Zealand mounted an exhibition of Hocart's photographs, entitled *Heart of Fiji: Photographs by Arthur Hocart, 1909-1914*. It was the first time they had been exhibited. The exhibition was curated by Jonathan Dennis and Sharon Dell, former Assistant Chief Librarian, Alexander Turnbull Library.
- Reo Fortune (1903-1979) was a noted anthropologist, particularly for his work in New Guinea. The library holds his collection, including manuscripts and research notes for New Guinea, 1907-1978. A preliminary inventory is available. Some personal photographs are held, mainly of Dr. Fortune, and including some of Margaret Mead.

The Manuscripts and Archives Section also holds many other collections (not of anthropologists) which give early eyewitness accounts, such as:

Missionaries:

- William Colenso (1811-1899). Some items have been microfilmed and an inventory is available.
- William Leonard Williams (1829-1916).

People Involved with Māori and Māori Land Issues:

- Sir Walter Lawry Buller (1838-1906). An inventory is available.
- Alexander Francis McDonnell (1866-1938).
- Sir Donald McLean (1820-1877). Papers partly microfilmed and an inventory is available.
- Hetaraka Tautahi (fl. 1897) (of Nga Rauru tribe).

Ethnographers and Ethnologists:

- Elsdon Best (1856-1931). Papers, 1869-1930. An inventory is available.
- Horatio Emmons Hale (1817-1896). Some items have been microfilmed.
- Stephenson Percy Smith (1840-1922).
- John White (1826-1891), scholar and linguist. Papers, 1869-1930. Some Items have been microfilmed and an inventory is available.

People of Other Professions Who Also Wrote books and Articles:

- George Leslie Adkin (1888-1964).
- John Houston (1891-1962). An inventory is available.
- Henry Matthew Stowell (Here Hongi) (1859-1944). Papers, 1892-1943. An inventory is available.

Compiled by Janet Horncy in consultation with the following staff of the Alexander Turnbull Library: David Retter, Sharon Dell, David Colquhoun, John Sullivan, Marian Minson, Anita Carlisle, Linda Evans.

APPENDICES

Index of Personal Names

Bateson, Gregory, 136, 137
Baumann, Hermann, 367
Bautista, Angel, 464, 465
Beals, Ralph L., 163
Beaman, E.O., 219
Beaugrand-Champagne, Claire, 43
Beebe, William Sully, 117
Beecher family, 118
Beeler, Madison Scott, 92, 94
Belknap, Robert Jackson, 263
Bell, Charles, 451
Bell, James Ford, 239, 240
Bell, Robert, 33
Bell, Robert E., 316
Bell, Thomas, 252
Bell, William, 42, 220
Bellegarde, Dantès, 133
Belo, Jane, 294
Benedict, Ruth Fulton, 136, 304-306
Benedict, Stanley, 306
Bennett, Elizabeth, 439
Bennett, Paul J., 198
Bennett, Wendell C., 124, 282
Benson, Nettie Lee, 342
Bent, George, 122
Bequaert, Joseph Charles, 369
Bercovitz, Nathaniel, 327
Berendt, Carl Hermann, 333
Berger, Kenneth W., 198
Bergmann, W., 79
Bernhiemer, Charles L., 97
Berthier, Annie, 373
Best, Elsdon, 490, 492
Beyer, H. Otley, 233, 484
Beynon, William, 281
Bhaskarawongse, Chao Phaya, 467, 468
Bhumibol Adulyadej, King of Thailand, 470
Bickmore, Albert C., 277
Biebuyck, D., 369
Billings, John S., 142, 143
Bingham, Hiram (1789-1869), 118
Bingham, Hiram (1831-1908), 118
Bingham, Hiram (1875-1956), 116, 118, 124, 139
Bingham, Millicent Todd, 118

Bingham family, 118
Bird, Junius B., 282
Birket-Smith, Kaj, 76
Bishop, Bernice Pauahi, 174, 175, 281
Bishop, Carl Whiting, 146
Bittremieux, Leo, 455
Black, George Fraser, 315
Black, Glenn A., 217
Black Johnny, 488
Blacklidge, C.F., 142
Blackmore, William, 163
Blackwood, Beatrice, 448, 451
Blanding, Sarah Gibson, 306
Bleaney, C.H., 405
Bliss, Mildred, 130
Bliss, Robert Woods, 130
Blodgett, Peter J., 92
Blom, Frans F., 225
Bloomfield, B.C., 405
Bloomfield, Leonard, 118, 163
Blu, Karen I., 269
Blue, Charles A., 264
Bluestone, Rose Whipple, 242
Boas, Franz, 67, 136, 151, 158, 161, 162, 181, 183, 214, 274, 276, 278, 280, 282, 283, 297, 305, 306, 321-323
Bodmer, Karl, 122
Boelaert, Edmond, 454-456, 458, 459
Bolitho, Hector, 239
Bolles, Laurens C., 256
Bolodimas, James, 187
Bolton, Reginald Pelham, 265, 270
Bonaparte, Louis-Lucien, 189, 190
Bonaparte, Roland, 376, 386, 388
Bonk, Jon, 133
Bonnemère, Lionel, 386
Boone, Nell Burgess, 327
Boone, O., 369
Boorne, W. Hanson, 42
Booy, Theodoor de, 302
Bopp, Franz, 264
Borome, Joseph Alfred, 265
Borromeo family, 465
Bott, Elizabeth, 488
Boudinot, Elias, 121

Dalley, F.W., 414
Damon, Albert, 227
Damrong Rajanubhab, 468, 471
Darwin, Charles, 28, 75, 227, 393
Dauven, René Lucien, 386
David-Neel, Alexandra, 381, 384
Davie, Maurice Rea, 118
Davies, Nina, 284
Davies, Norman deGaris, 284
Davis, Edward H., 165, 265, 302
Davis, Griffith, 133
Davis, Mary B., 266, 267, 269, 272, 303
Davis, Philla, 412
Dawson, Charles, 428
Dawson, G.M., 33
Day, Caroline Bond, 227
Dayrit, Marina, 466
Deacon, Arthur Bernard, 407, 430
Deagan, Kathleen A., 169
De Boeck, E., 459
Dehn, Mura, 293
Dehuff, Elizabeth, 256
Delafosse, Maurice, 387
De Laguna, Frederica, 128
Delaporte, Louis, 382
Delarue, Paul, 386
Dell, Sharon, 491
Deloria, Ella, 323
Demetrio, Francisco R., 463, 464, 466
Demiéville, Paul, 389
Dennis, Jonathan, 491
Densmore, Frances, 83, 84, 128, 162, 270
De Ryck, Maurits, 455, 459
Dewdney, Alexander, 25
Dewey, John, 305
De Zoete, Beryl, 294, 424, 425
Diabaté, Sidiki, 420
Dias, Nélia, 387
Dick, Alistair, 418
Dion, Joseph F., 2, 3
Dislere, Paul, 374
Dixson, William, 485
Djagamirri, Dorra', 484
Dobson, William Hervie, 327
Dodd, Edward H., 286

Dorman, Peter, 284
Dorsey, George A., 181, 182, 184, 274
Dorsey, J. Owen, 162
Dorson, Richard, 215
Dostal, Walter, 367
Dournes, Jacques, 388
Douwes Dekker, Niels A., 263
Doyon-Ferland, Madeleine, 45, 46
Dozier, Edward P., 63
Draper, Lyman Copeland, 358
Drewal, Henry John, 153, 155
Drewal, Margaret Thompson, 153, 155
Drucker, Philip, 162
DuBois, Constance, 266
DuBois, Cora Alice, 196, 227, 230, 294
Duggan, Mary, 266
Duke, Doris, 61, 62, 64, 170, 171, 204, 205, 252-254, 316, 318, 339, 346
Duncan, William, 55, 56, 163, 182
Dunning, R.W., 28
DuPonceau, Peter S., 322
Dupuis (fonds), 374
Durán, Lucy, 418
Durham, Mary Edith, 430
Dusenberry, Verne, 2, 3
Dutton, Lee S., 198, 200
Duvall, D.C., 280
Dwight, Timothy, 118
Dwight family, 118
Dye, Daniel Sheets, 113

Eagle, William H., 65
Earthy, Emily Dora, 441
Easterday, Robert, 103
Eber, Dorothy, 40, 41
Echols, John M., 150, 261-263
Eckhardt, George B., 65
Edel, May Mandelbaum, 296, 297
Edenshaw, Charlie, 8
Egeren, Regnier van, 456, 458
Eggan, Fred, 193, 194, 196
Ehrich, Robert W., 226
Eichelberger, Marie, 305
Eiseley, Loren C., 332
Ekholm, Gordon F., 282

Hall, James, 151
Hall, Joseph T., 215
Haller, Douglas M., 330, 332
Hallowell, Alfred I., 270, 321, 323, 332
Halpern, Joel M., 163, 264
Hamelin, Jean, 46
Hamilton, Alexander, 302
Hammond, William A., 198, 200
Hand, Wayland D., 313
Hanfmann, George M.A., 230
Hanks, Jane Richardson, 189
Hanna, Forman, 64
Harkins, Lee, 320
Harley, George, 226
Harmand, François-Jules, 263
Harn, Alan, 204
Harnish, Harry Whitfield, 466, 467
Harnish, Mrs. H.W., 467
Harrington, John P., 83, 92-94, 128, 160, 162, 163
Harrington, Mark R., 83, 225, 270, 271, 302
Harris, Bob, 185
Harris, Elizabeth Merwin Page, 119, 120
Harris, R. King, 163
Hart, Donn V., 198, 200
Hartmann, Paul, 264
Harvey, Byron, 61
Harvey, Fred, 256, 270
Hastings, Warren, 239
Hatcher, Harlan, 233
Haury, Emil W., 63
Havemeyer, Loomis, 119
Hayden, Ferdinand V., 163
Hayden (survey), 219
Hayes, Alden, 251
Hayes, William C., 283, 284
Hazen, Hervey Crosby, 265
Heard, John, 263
Hearst, Phoebe Apperson, 67, 72
Hedin, Sven Anders, 475
Hefel, Annemarie, 367
Heider, Karl, 158
Heine-Geldern, Robert, 367
Heizer, Robert Fleming, 67-69, 92, 163
Hemenway, Mary, 225

Hemenway (expedition), 266
Hemmings, E. Thomas, 168, 169
Hencken, Hugh O'Neill, 226
Hendee, Russell W., 186, 187
Henderson, Alexander, 41
Henderson, Junius, 97
Hendricks, H.W., 271
Henry, Joseph, 142, 165
Henry, Matthew Stowell, 490, 492
Henry, Thomas, 270
Henshaw, Henry W., 164
Herskovits, Frances S., 202, 296-298
Herskovits, Jean, 202, 298
Herskovits, Melville J., 69, 159, 200-202, 296, 298, 323
Herzfeld, Ernest, 146
Herzog, George, 213, 214
Heuser, Frederick, 327
Hewett, Edgar, 251
Hewitt, J.N.B., 162, 164
Heye, Carl Friederich Gustav, 300
Heye, George G., 125, 268, 270, 298-303
Heye, Marie Antoinette Lawrence, 300
Heyerdahl, Thor, 363
Hickey, Gerald C., 198, 200
Higgins, John Comyn, 442
Hildburgh, W.L., 431
Hilger, M. Inez, 163
Hill, David, 439
Hill, Edward, 138
Hill, Kenneth E., 81
Hill, Polly, 202
Hillers, John K., 123, 190, 219
Hilton-Simpson, M.W., 430, 431
Hime, Humphrey Lloyd, 42
Hirschberg, Walter, 367, 368
Hocart, Arthur Maruice, 489-491
Hockings, Paul, 158
Hodge, Frederick, W., 83, 84, 91, 148, 265, 266, 268, 270, 271, 302
Hodge, William, 487
Hoefler, Paul L., 103
Hohenwart-Gerlachstein, Anna, 367
Holleman, J.F., 402
Holm, Bill, 351

Keyword Index of Selected Ethnic Group Names

514